PUBLICATIONS OF THE NEWTON INSTITUTE

On-line Learning in Neural Networks

T0297146

Publications of the Newton Institute

Edited by H.K. Moffatt
Director, Isaac Newton Institute for Mathematical Sciences

The Isaac Newton Institute of Mathematical Sciences of the University of Cambridge exists to stimulate research in all branches of the mathematical sciences, including pure mathematics, statistics, applied mathematics, theoretical physics, theoretical computer science, mathematical biology and economics. The four six-month long research programmes it runs each year bring together leading mathematical scientists from all over the world to exchange ideas through seminars, teaching and informal interaction.

ON-LINE LEARNING IN NEURAL NETWORKS

edited by

David Saad

Aston University

CAMBRIDGE
UNIVERSITY PRESS

CAMBRIDGE UNIVERSITY PRESS
Cambridge, New York, Melbourne, Madrid, Cape Town, Singapore, São Paulo, Delhi

Cambridge University Press
The Edinburgh Building, Cambridge CB2 8RU, UK

Published in the United States of America by Cambridge University Press, New York

www.cambridge.org
Information on this title: www.cambridge.org/9780521117913

First published 1998
This digitally printed version 2009

A catalogue record for this publication is available from the British Library

ISBN 978-0-521-65263-6 hardback
ISBN 978-0-521-11791-3 paperback

CONTENTS

ACKNOWLEDGEMENTS

I would like to thank Chris Bishop for his help in setting up the workshop on on-line learning, to Renato Vicente for helping me with preparing the manuscript for publication, to Magnus Rattray for his helpful comments and to the participants of the workshop for their contribution to this book.

Finally, I would like to thank Christiane and Jonathan for their considerable patience.

CONTRIBUTORS

Luís B. Almeida, INESC, R. Alves Redol, 9. 1000 Lisboa, Portugal.

José D. Amaral, INESC, R. Alves Redol, 9. 1000 Lisboa, Portugal.

Shun-ichi Amari, Brain Science Institute, RIKEN, Wako-shi, Saitama 351-0198, Japan.

David Barber, Department of Medical Biophysics, University of Nijmegen. 6525 EZ Nijmegen, The Netherlands.

Michael Biehl, Institut für Theoretische Physik, Universität Würzburg, Am Hubland. D-97074 Würzburg, Germany.

Siegfried Bös, Brain Science Institute, RIKEN, Wako-shi, Saitama 351-0198, Japan.

Léon Bottou, AT&T Labs–Research Red Bank, NJ07701, USA.

Nestor Caticha, Instituto de Física, Universidade de São Paulo Caixa Postal 66318, 05389-970 São Paulo, SP, Brazil.

Anthony C.C. Coolen, Department of Mathematics, King's College, University of London, Strand, London WC2R 2LS, U.K.

Mauro Copelli, Limburgs Universitair Centrum, B-3590 Diepenbeek, Belgium.

Ansgar Freking, Institut für Theoretische Physik, Universität Würzburg, Am Hubland. D-97074 Würzburg, Germany.

Tom Heskes, Real World Computing Partnership, Theoretical Foundation, Dutch Foundation for Neural Networks, Department of Medical Physics and Biophysics, University of Nijmegen, Geert Grooteplein 21, 6525 EZ Nijmegen, The Netherlands.

Matthias Hölzer, Institut für Theoretische Physik, Universität Würzburg, Am Hubland. D-97074 Würzburg, Germany.

Yoshiyuki Kabashima, Dept. of Comp. Intelligence and Systems Science, Graduate School of Science and Engineering, Tokyo Institute of Technology, Yokohama 226, Japan.

Thibault Langlois, INESC, R. Alves Redol, 9. 1000 Lisboa, Portugal.

Todd K. Leen, Dept. of Computer Science and Engineering and Dept. of Electrical and Computer Engineering, Oregon Graduate Institute of Science & Technology. P.O. Box 91000, Portland, Oregon, USA.

Klaus-Robert Müller, GMD-First, Rudower Chaussee 5. D-12489 Berlin, Germany.

Noboru Murata, Lab. for Information Synthesis, RIKEN Brain Science Institute, Wako, Saitama 351-0198, Japan.

Manfred Opper, Neural Computing Research Group, Aston University, Birmingham B4 7ET, UK.

Alexander Plakhov, INESC, R. Alves Redol, 9. 1000 Lisboa, Portugal.

Magnus Rattray, Neural Computing Research Group, Aston University, Birmingham B4 7ET, UK.

Georg Reents, Institut für Theoretische Physik Universität Würzburg, Am Hubland. D–97074 Würzburg, Germany.

David Saad, Neural Computing Research Group, Aston University, Birmingham B4 7ET, UK.

Enno Schlösser, Institut für Theoretische Physik, Universität Würzburg, Am Hubland. D–97074 Würzburg, Germany.

Shigeru Shinomoto, Dept. of Physics, Kyoto University, Sakyo-ku, Kyoto, 606-8502, Japan.

Sara A. Solla, Physics and Astronomy, Northwestern University, Evanston, IL 60208, USA and Physiology, Northwestern University Medical School, Chicago, IL 60611, USA.

Peter Sollich, Department of Physics, University of Edinburgh, Edinburgh EH9 3JZ, U.K.

Wim Wiegerinck, Real World Computing Partnership, Theoretical Foundation, Dutch Foundation for Neural Networks, Department of Medical Physics and Biophysics, University of Nijmegen, Geert Grooteplein 21, 6525 EZ Nijmegen, The Netherlands.

Ole Winther, The Niels Bohr Institute, 2100 Copenhagen Ø, Denmark and Theoretical Physics II, Lund University, S-223 62 Lund, Sweden.

Andreas Ziehe, GMD-First, Rudower Chaussee 5. D-12489 Berlin, Germany.

Introduction

David Saad

Neural Computing Research Group, Aston University
Birmingham B4 7ET, UK.
saadd@aston.ac.uk

Artificial neural networks (ANN) is a field of research aimed at using complex systems, made of simple identical non-linear parallel elements, for performing different types of tasks; for review see (Hertz et al 1990),(Bishop 1995) and (Ripley 1996). During the years neural networks have been successfully applied to perform regression, classification, control and prediction tasks in a variety of scenarios and architectures. The most popular and useful of ANN architectures is that of layered feed-forward neural networks, in which the non-linear elements (neurons) are arranged in successive layers, and the information flows unidirectionally; this is in contrast to the other main generic architecture of recurrent networks where feed-back connections are also permitted. Layered networks with an arbitrary number of hidden units have been shown to be universal approximators (Cybenko 1989; Hornik et al 1989) for continuous maps and can therefore be used to implement any function defined in these terms.

Learning in layered neural networks refers to the modification of internal network parameters, so as to bring the map implemented by the network as close as possible to a desired map. Learning may be viewed as an optimization of the parameter set with respect to a set of training examples instancing the underlying rule. Two main training paradigms have emerged: batch learning, in which optimization is carried out with respect to the entire training set simultaneously, and on-line learning, where network parameters are updated after the presentation of each training example (which may be sampled with or without repetition). Although batch learning is probably faster for small and medium training sets and networks, it seems to be more prone to local minima and is very inefficient in the case of training large networks and for large training sets. On-line learning is also the more natural approach for learning non-stationary tasks, whereas batch learning would require retraining on continuously changing data sets.

On-line learning of continuous functions, mostly via gradient based methods on a differentiable error measure is one of the most powerful and commonly used approaches to training large layered networks in general, e.g., (LeCun et al 1989), and for nonstationary tasks in particular; it is also arguably the most efficient technique in these cases. However, on-line training suffers from several drawbacks:

- The main difficulty with on-line training is the sensitivity of most training methods to the choice of training parameters. This dependence may not only slow down training, but may also have bearing on its ability to converge successfully to a desired stable fixed point.

- Most advanced optimization methods (e.g., conjugate gradient, variable metric, simulated annealing etc) rely on a fixed error surface whereas on-line learning produces an inherently stochastic error surface.

- The Bayesian approach provides an efficient way of training and has been applied quite naturally and successfully within the framework of batch learning. Extensions to the on-line case, where explicit information on past examples is not stored, have been limited so far.

These shortcomings of current on-line training methods and the quest for more insight into the training process itself motivate the analytical study of these methods presented in this book. This collection is based on presentations given during the workshop on 'On-line learning in neural networks' as part of the Newton Institute program on Neural Networks and Machine Learning in November 1997.

The second chapter of the book opens with a thorough overview of traditional on-line training methods starting from the early days of neural networks These include Rosenblatt's perceptron, Widrow's Adaline, the K-means algorithm, LVQ2, quasi-Newton methods, Kalman algoritms and more. A unified framework encompasing most of these methods which can be analyzed using the tools of stochastic approximation, is presented and utilized to obtain convergence criteria under rather weak conditions.

Chapter 3 provides a different point of view for describing the parameter training dynamics based on the master equation, which monitors the evolution of their probability distribution. This chapter examines two different scenarios: In the first case, one derives exact dynamical equations for a general architecture when the learning rule is based on using only the sign of the error gradient. The analysis is carried out by monitoring the evolution of all surviving moments of the parameter probability distribution, providing an exact solution of the moments evolution. In the second case, one employs a perturbation approach based on monitoring the evolution of leading moments of the parameter probability distribution in the asymptotic regime. This is carried out for both constant and decaying learning rate and enables one to obtain the typical generalization error decay and convergence criteria for different polynomial annealing schedules which become exact asymptotically.

A statistical based description of on-line training techniques, with emphasis on more advanced training methods, is presented in chapter 4. A rigorous comparison between the asymptotic performance of batch and on-line training methods is carried out for both variable and fixed learning rates, showing that on-line learning is as effective as batch learning asymptotically. The chapter also introduces a practical modification of an established method (Barkai et al 1996) for learning rate adaptation and its analysis. The new method is based on gradient flow information and can be applied to learning continuous functions and distributions even in the absence of an explicit loss function. The method is first analyzed and then successfully applied in the subsequent chapter to handle the real-world problems of blind source separation and learning in non-stationary environments, demonstrating the method's potential.

One of the main difficulties with using on-line learning methods for practical applications is sensitivity to the choice of training parameters such as teh learning rate. These parameters often have to be varied continuously to ensure optimal performance. Chapter 6 offers a practical method for varying the parameters continuously and automatically and examines the performance of the suggested algorithm on some benchmark problems.

Statistical mechanics offers an alternative description of on-line learning which enables us to examine all stages of the training process. This description, which may formally be derived from the master equation description of the stochastic training process (Mace and Coolen 1998), is based on monitoring the evolution of a set of macroscopic variables, sometimes termed order parameters, which are sufficient to capture the main features of the training process. This framework usually relies on a teacher-student scenario, where the model (student) parameters are modified in response to examples generated by the underlying rule (teacher) simulated by a parallel network which generates the training examples. The first in a series of chapters which make use of statistical mechanics techniques focuses on the analytical derivation of globally optimal learning parameters and learning rules for two layer architectures, known as soft committee machines (Biehl and Schwarze 1995; Saad and Solla 1995), these are two layer networks with unit hidden to output weights. Variational methods are applied to the order parameter dynamics in order to determine optimal learning rate schedules under different learning scenarios. Locally optimal methods are shown to be inadequate for complicated network architectures.

Similar techniques are employed in chapter 8 for studying the effect of noise on locally optimal training methods in tree committee machines with a general number of hidden nodes. This architecture, of two layer networks of binary elements with no overlapping receptive fields and unit hidden to output weights, realizes a discrete mapping in contrast to the continuous one realized by the soft committee machine considered in the previous chapter. The asymptotic properties of the optimal training rule and the robustness of the process to multiplicative output noise are studied within the statistical mechanics framework.

Next, in chapter 9, the statistical mechanics description is employed to examine the efficacy of several second order training methods aimed at speeding up training, for instance Newton's method, matrix momentum (Orr and Leen

1997) and natural gradient descent (Amari 1998). This study quantifies the advantage gained by using second order methods in general, and natural gradient descent in particular, in non-asymptotic regimes. A practical cheaper alternative to the latter, based on insights gained form information geometry, is presented in the subsequent chapter and analyzed using similar theoretical tools for various training scenarios, showing a significant improvement in training times.

Most chapters so far have concentrated on supervised learning. However, in chapter 11 the statistical mechanics framework is extended to the analysis of unsupervised learning scenarios and their dynamics. More specifically, this chapter examines the dynamics of on-line methods aimed at extracting prototypes and principle components from data. The authors consider on-line competitive learning (Winner Takes All and K-means) and Sanger's rule for on-line PCA. A similar set of equations to those used for supervised learning is constructed once the macroscopic variables have been identified, facillitating the study of their dependence on the choice of training parameters.

One of the main defficiencies of the current statistical mechanics framework is that training examples are presumed to be uncorrelated. This restriction exists in most analyses except in certain specific scenarios and limits considerably the usefulness of the theoretical analysis for practical cases where correlations typically emerge either due to the limited training data (which forces sampling with repitition) or due to correlations which exist within the data naturally.

Chapters 12, 13 and 14 tackle training scenarios where correlations within the data exist. In chapter 12, the effect of temporal correlations within the data is handled using the approaches of both stochastic approximation and statistical mechanics for small and large networks respectively. The small network analysis concentrates on a small learning rate expansion where the effect of correlations may be handled straightforwardly. Correlations in the large networks analysis are handled by assuming the distribution for the local fields to be Gaussian, rendering the analysis tractable. Special emphasis is given to the effect of correlations on plateaus in the evolution of the generalization error, which are often characteristic of on-line learning in complex non-linear systems.

The main difficulty of training with fixed example sets is the emerging correlations between parameter updates due to re-sampling, which generally give rise to non-Gaussian local field distributions. The method presented in chapter 13 extends the framework of (Saad and Solla 1995) in both linear and non-linear networks by projecting the evolving macroscopic parameters onto the most significant eigenspaces, obtaining an exact result in the linear case and an approximation in the general non-linear one. The performance of on-line methods is then compared to that of off-line methods in the case of biased and unbiased input distributions and for different types of noise. A different approach, presented in chapter 14, makes use of the dynamical replica method for closing the equations of motion for a new set of order parameters. This enables one to monitor the evolving non-Gaussian distributions explicitly. The new order parameters include the old set, derived from the infinite training data analysis, as a subset in addition to a new continuous parameter which results from the emerging correlations between updates. The accuracy of results obtained by the method is demonstrated for simple training scenarios.

One method of speeding up training in both on-line and batch training scenarios is by learning with queries, in which case the input distibution is continuously modified to select the most informative examples. These modifications will depend on the current mapping realized by the system, and thus on the current set of parameters, and will improve the network's performance considerably. Chapter 15 deals with the estimation of decision boundaries from stochastic examples with and without queries, investigating the convergence rate in both cases and comparing them to the results obtained in batch learning. Results are also obtained for the fastest feasible convergence rates with and without queries.

An important extension of the Bayesian approach to on-line training is presented in chapter 16, based on approximating the evolving posterior by a multivariate Gaussian distribution. Updating the parameters of this distribution is carried out by on-line methods in response to the sequential presentation of training examples. This elegant and principled approach complements the Bayesian framework of batch learning and may hold a significant practical potential. The analysis shows a similar asymptotic behavior to that obtained by the somewhat less practical variational methods. This approach is investigated further in chapter 17 where it is employed for studying generic feed-forward architectures. The approximation used in the case of continuous weights is shown to have a similar computational complexity to that of Bayesian off-line methods while a different approach, based on a Hebbian approximation, was found to outperform several other on-line approaches, especially in the case of binary weights.

This book is aimed at provideing a fairly comprehensive overview on recent developments in theoretical analysis of online learning methods in neural networks. The chapters were designed to contain sufficient detailed material to enable the non-specialist reader to follow most of it with minimal background reading.

References

Amari, S. (1998). Natural gradient works efficiently in learning. *Neural Computation*, 10, 251–276.

Biehl, M. and Schwarze , H. (1995). Learning by online gradient descent. *J. Phys. A*, 28, 643–656.

Bishop, C. M. (1995). *Neural networks for pattern recognition*, Oxford university Press, Oxford, UK.

Cybenko, G. (1989). Approximation by superpositions of a sigmoidal function, *Math. Control Signals and Systems*, 2, 304–314.

Hertz, J., Krogh, A. and Palmer, R.G. (1991). *Introduction to the Theory of Neural Computation*, Addison Wesley , Redwood City, CA.

Hornik, K. Stinchcombe, M. and White, H. (1989). Multilayer feedforward networks are universal approximators, *Neural Networks*, 2, 359–366.

LeCun, Y., Boser, B., Denker, J.S., Henderson, D., Howard, R.E., Hubbard, W. and Jackel, L.D. (1989). Backpropagation applied to handwritten zip code recognition. *Neural Computation*, 1, 541–551.

Mace, C.W.H. and Coolen , A.C.C (1998a). Statistical mechanical analysis of the dynamics of learning in perceptrons. *Statistics and Computing*, 8, 55–88.

Orr, G.B. and Leen, T.K. (1997). Using Curvature Information for Fast Stochastic Search. *Advances in Neural Information Processing Systems 9*, edited by Mozer, Jordan and Petsche (Cambridge, MA: MIT Press) p 606–p 612.

Ripley, B.D. (1996). *Pattern Recognition and Neural Networks*, Cambridge University Press, Cambridge, UK.

Saad, D. and Solla, S.A. (1995). Exact solution for online learning in multilayer neural networks. *Phys. Rev. Lett.*, 74, 4337–4340 and Online learning in soft committee machines. *Phys. Rev. E*, 52, 4225–4243.

Sompolinsky, H., Barkai, N., Seung, H.S. (1995), On-line learning of dichotomies: algorithms and learning curves. J-H. Oh, C. Kwon, S. Cho (eds.), *Neural Networks: The Statistical Mechanics Perspective*, 105–130 (Singapore: World Scientific) and Barkai, N., Seung, H.S. Sompolinsky, H. (1995). Local and global convergence of online learning. *Phys. Rev. Lett.*, 75, 1415–1418.

Online Learning and Stochastic Approximations

Léon Bottou

AT&T Labs–Research Red Bank, NJ07701, USA.
leonb@research.att.com

Abstract

The convergence of online learning algorithms is analyzed using the tools of the stochastic approximation theory, and proved under very weak conditions. A general framework for online learning algorithms is first presented. This framework encompasses the most common online learning algorithms in use today, as illustrated by several examples. The stochastic approximation theory then provides general results describing the convergence of all these learning algorithms at once.

1   Introduction

Almost all of the early work on *Learning Systems* focused on online algorithms (Hebb, 1949; Rosenblatt, 1957; Widrow and Hoff, 1960; Amari, 1967; Kohonen, 1982). In these early days, the algorithmic simplicity of online algorithms was a requirement. This is still the case when it comes to handling large, real-life training sets (LeCun et al., 1989; Müller, Gunzinger and Guggenbühl, 1995).

The early *Recursive Adaptive Algorithms* were introduced during the same years (Robbins and Monro, 1951) and very often by the same people (Widrow and Stearns, 1985). First developed in the engineering world, recursive adaptation algorithms have turned into a mathematical discipline, namely *Stochastic Approximations* (Kushner and Clark, 1978; Ljung and Söderström, 1983; Benveniste, Metivier and Priouret, 1990).

Although both domains have enjoyed the spotlights of scientific fashion at different times and for different reasons, they essentially describe the same elementary ideas. Many authors of course have stressed this less-than-fortuitous similarity between learning algorithms and recursive adaptation algorithms (Mendel and Fu, 1970; Tsypkin, 1971).

The present work builds upon this similarity. Online learning algorithms are analyzed using the stochastic approximation tools. Convergence is characterized under very weak conditions: the expected risk must be reasonably well behaved and the learning rates must decrease appropriately.

9

The main discussion describes a general framework for online learning algorithms, presents a number of examples, and analyzes their dynamical properties. Several comment sections illustrate how these ideas can be generalized and how they relate to other aspects of learning theory. In other words, the main discussion gives answers, while the comments raise questions. Casual readers may skip these comment sections.

2   A Framework for Online Learning Systems

The starting point of a mathematical study of online learning must be a mathematical statement for our subjective understanding of what a learning system is. It is difficult to agree on such a statement, because we are learning systems ourselves and often resent this mathematical reduction of an essential personal experience.

This contribution borrows the framework introduced by the Russian school (Tsypkin, 1971; Vapnik, 1982). This formulation can be used for understanding a significant number of online learning algorithms, as demonstrated by the examples presented in section 3.

2.1   Expected Risk Function

In (Tsypkin, 1971; Tsypkin, 1973), the goal of a learning system consists of finding the minimum of a function $J(w)$ named the *expected risk function*. This function is decomposed as follows:

$$J(w) \triangleq \mathbf{E}_z \, Q(z, w) \triangleq \int Q(z, w) \, dP(z) \qquad (2.1)$$

The minimization variable w is meant to represent the part of the learning system which must be adapted as a response to observing events z occurring in the real world. The *loss function* $Q(z, w)$ measures the performance of the learning system with parameter w under the circumstances described by event z. Common mathematical practice suggests to represent both w and z by elements of adequately chosen spaces $\mathcal{W}$ and $\mathcal{Z}$.

The occurrence of the events z is modeled as random independent observations drawn from an unknown probability distribution $dP(z)$ named the *grand truth distribution*. The risk function $J(w)$ is simply the expectation of the loss function $Q(z, w)$ for a fixed value of the parameter w. This risk function $J(w)$ is poorly defined because the grand truth distribution $dP(z)$ is unknown by hypothesis.

Consider for instance a neural network system for optical ZIP code recognition, as described in (LeCun et al., 1989). An observation z is a pair (x, y) composed of a ZIP code image x and its intended interpretation y. Parameters w are the adaptable weights of the neural network. The loss function

$Q(z, w)$ measures the economical cost (in hard currency units) of delivering a letter marked with ZIP code z given the answer produced by the network on image x. This cost is minimal when the network gives the right answer. Otherwise the loss function measures the higher cost of detecting the error and re-routing the letter.

Comments

Probabilities are used in this framework for representing the unknown truth underlying the occurrences of observable events. Using successive observations z_t, the learning system will uncover a part of this truth in the form of parameter values w_t that hopefully decrease the risk functional $J(w_t)$. This use of probabilities is very different from the Bayesian practice, where a probability distribution represents the increasing knowledge of the learning system. Both approaches however can be re-conciliated by defining the parameter space $\mathcal{W}$ as a another space of probability distributions. The analysis then must carefully handle two different probability distributions with very different meanings.

In this framework, every known fact about the real world should be removed from distribution $dP(z)$ by properly redefining the observation space $\mathcal{Z}$ and of the loss function $Q(z, w)$. Consider for instance that a known fraction of the ZIP code images are spoiled by the image capture system. An observation z can be factored as a triple (κ, x, y) composed of an envelope x, its intended ZIP code y, and a binary variable κ indicating whether the ZIP code image is spoiled. The loss function can be redefined as follows:

$$
\begin{aligned}
J(w) &= \int Q(z, w)\, dP(\kappa, x, y) \\
&= \int \left(\int Q(z, w)\, dP(\kappa|x, y) \right)\, dP(x, y)
\end{aligned}
$$

The inner integral in this decomposition is a new loss function $Q'(x, y, w)$ which measures the system performance on redefined observations (x, y). This new loss function accounts for the known deficiencies of the image capture system. This factorization technique reveals a new probability distribution $dP(x, y)$ which is no longer representative of this a priori knowledge.

This technique does not apply to knowledge involving the learning system itself. When we say for instance that an unknown function is smooth, we mean that it pays to bias the learning algorithm towards finding smoother functions. This statement does not describe a property of the grand truth distribution. Its meaning is attached to a particular learning system. It does not suggests a redefinition of the problem. It merely suggests a modification of the learning system, like the introduction of a regularization parameter.

2.2   Gradient Based Learning

The expected risk function (2.1) cannot be minimized directly because the grand truth distribution is unknown. It is however possible to compute an

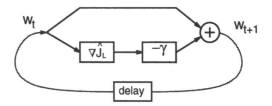

Figure 1: Batch Gradient Descent. The parameters of the learning system are updated using the gradient of the empirical risk $\hat{J}_L$ defined on the training set.

approximation of $J(w)$ by simply using a finite *training set* of independent observations $z_1, \ldots, z_L$.

$$J(w) \approx \hat{J}_L(w) \triangleq \frac{1}{L} \sum_{n=1}^{L} Q(z_n, w) \qquad (2.2)$$

General theorems (Vapnik, 1982) show that minimizing the *empirical risk* $\hat{J}_L(w)$ can provide a good estimate of the minimum of the expected risk $J(w)$ when the training set is large enough. This line of work has provided a way to understand the *generalization* phenomenon, i.e. the ability of a system to learn from a finite training set and yet provide results that are valid in general.

2.2.1   Batch Gradient Descent

Minimizing the empirical risk $\hat{J}_L(w)$ can be achieved using a *batch gradient descent* algorithm. Successive estimates w_t of the optimal parameter are computed using the following formula (figure 1) where the learning rate γ_t is a positive number.

$$w_{t+1} = w_t - \gamma_t \nabla_w \hat{J}_L(w_t) = w_t - \gamma_t \frac{1}{L} \sum_{i=1}^{L} \nabla_w Q(z_n, w_t) \qquad (2.3)$$

The properties of this optimization algorithm are well known (section 4.2). When the learning rate γ_t are small enough, the algorithm converges towards a local minimum of the empirical risk $\hat{J}_L(w)$. Considerable convergence speedups can be achieved by replacing the learning rate γ_t by a suitable definite positive matrix (Dennis and Schnabel, 1983).

Each iteration of the batch gradient descent algorithm (figure 1) however involves a burdening computation of the average of the gradients of the loss function $\nabla_w Q(z_n, w)$ over the entire training set. Significant computer resources must be allocated in order to store a large enough training set and compute this average.

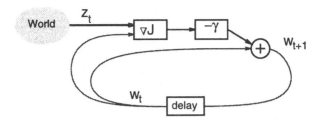

Figure 2: Online Gradient Descent. The parameters of the learning system are updated using information extracted from real world observations.

2.2.2 Online Gradient Descent

The elementary *online gradient descent* algorithm is obtained by dropping the averaging operation in the batch gradient descent algorithm (2.3). Instead of averaging the gradient of the loss over the complete training set, each iteration of the online gradient descent consists of choosing an example z_t at random, and updating the parameter w_t according to the following formula.

$$w_{t+1} = w_t - \gamma_t \nabla_w Q(z_t, w_t) \qquad (2.4)$$

Averaging this update over all possible choices of the training example z_t would restore the batch gradient descent algorithm. The online gradient descent simplification relies on the hope that the random noise introduced by this procedure will not perturbate the average behavior of the algorithm. Significant empirical evidence substantiate this hope.

Online gradient descent can also be described without reference to a training set. Instead of drawing examples from a training set, we can directly use the events z_t observed in the real world, as shown in figure 2. This formulation is particularly adequate for describing *adaptive algorithms* that simultaneously process an observation and learn to perform better. Such adaptive algorithms are very useful for tracking a phenomenon that evolves in time. An airplane autopilot, for instance, may continuously learn how commands affect the route of the airplane. Such a system would compensate for changes in the weather or in petrol weight.

Comments

Formulating online gradient descent without reference to a training set presents a theoretical interest. Each iteration of the algorithm uses an example z_t drawn from the grand truth distribution instead of a finite training set. The average update therefore is a gradient descent algorithm which directly optimizes the expected risk.

This direct optimization shortcuts the usual discussion about differences between optimizing the empirical risk and the expected risk (Vapnik, 1982; Vapnik, 1995) . Proving the convergence of an online algorithm towards the minimum of the expected risk provides an alternative to the Vapnik proofs of the consistency of learning algorithms. Discussing the convergence speed of such an online algorithm provides an alternative to the Vapnik-Chervonenkis bounds.

This alternative comes with severe restrictions. The convergence proofs proposed here (section 5) only address the convergence of the algorithm towards a local minimum. We can safely conjecture that a general study of the convergence of an online algorithm towards a global minimum should handle the central concepts of the necessary and sufficient conditions for the consistency of a learning algorithm (Vapnik, 1995) .

2.3   General Online Gradient Algorithm

The rest of this contribution addresses a single *general online gradient algorithm* algorithm for minimizing the following cost function $C(w)$.

$$C(w) \triangleq \mathbf{E}_z Q(z, w) \triangleq \int Q(z, w) \, dP(z) \qquad (2.5)$$

Each iteration of this algorithm consists of drawing an event $\mathbf{z}_t$ from distribution $dP(z)$ and applying the following update formula.

$$w_{t+1} = w_t - \gamma_t H(\mathbf{z}_t, w_t) \qquad (2.6)$$

The learning rates γ_t are either positive numbers or definite positive matrices. The update term $H(\mathbf{z}, w)$ fulfills the following condition.

$$\mathbf{E}_\mathbf{z} H(\mathbf{z}, w) = \nabla_w C(w) \qquad (2.7)$$

The distribution function $dP(z)$ can be understood as the grand truth distribution. The cost function $C(w)$ minimized by this algorithm is then equal to the expected risk $J(w)$. This setup addresses the adaptive version of the online gradient descent, without reference to a training set.

All results however remain valid if we consider a discrete distribution function defined on a particular training set $\{z_1, \ldots, z_L\}$. The cost function $C(w)$ minimized by this algorithm is then equal to the empirical risk $\hat{J}_L$. This second setup addresses the use of online gradient descent for optimizing the training error defined on a finite training set.

Comments

Typography conscious readers will notice the subtle difference between the observable events z used in the cost function (2.5) and the events $\mathbf{z}$ drawn before each iteration of the algorithm (2.6). In the simplest case indeed, these two variables represent similar objects: a single example is drawn before each iteration of the online gradient descent algorithm. The framework described above also applies to more complex cases like *mini-batch* or *noisy* gradient descent. Mini-batch gradient descent uses several examples for each iteration, collectively referred to as z_t. Noisy gradient descent uses a noisy update term $\nabla_w C(w_t) + \xi_t$. The analysis presented in this contribution holds as long as the update term fulfills condition (2.7).

Finally the examples z_t are assumed to be independently drawn from a single probability distribution function $dP(z)$. In practice however, examples are often chosen sequentially in a training set. There are tools indeed for dealing with examples z_t drawn using a Markovian process (Benveniste, Metivier and Priouret, 1990).

3 Examples

This section presents a number of examples illustrating the diversity of learning algorithms that can be expressed as particular cases of the general online gradient descent algorithm (section 2.3). More classical algorithms can be found in (Tsypkin, 1971).

Some algorithms were designed with a well defined cost function, like the adaline (section 3.1.1) or the multi-layer perceptron (section 3.1.2). Other algorithms did not initially refer to a particular cost function, but can be reformulated as online gradient descent procedures, like K-Means (section 3.2.2) or LVQ2 (section 3.2.3). The cost function then provides a useful characterization of the algorithm. Finally, certain algorithms, like Kohonen's topological maps (Kohonen, 1982), are poorly represented as the minimization of a cost function. Yet some authors have found useful to coerce these algorithms into an online gradient descent anyway (Schumann and Retzko, 1995) .

3.1 Online Least Mean Squares

3.1.1 Widrow's Adaline

The *adaline* (Widrow and Hoff, 1960) is one of the few learning systems designed at the very beginning of the computer age. Online gradient descent was then a very attractive proposition requiring little hardware. The adaline could fit in a refrigerator sized cabinet containing a forest of potentiometers and electrical motors.

The adaline (figure 3) learning algorithm adapts the parameters of a single *threshold element*. Input patterns x are recognized as class $y = +1$ or $y = -1$ according to the sign of $w'x + \beta$. It is practical to consider an *augmented input* pattern x containing an extra constant coefficient equal to 1. The bias β then is represented as an extra coefficient in the parameter vector w. With

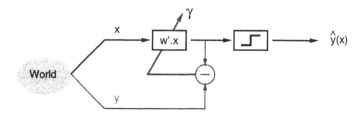

Figure 3: Widrow's Adaline. The adaline computes a binary indicator by thresholding a linear combination of its input. Learning is achieved using the *delta rule*.

this convention, the output of the threshold element can be written as

$$\hat{y}_w(x) \triangleq \text{sign}(w'x) = \text{sign} \sum_i w_i x_i \qquad (3.1)$$

During training, the adaline is provided with pairs $z = (x, y)$ representing input patterns and desired output for the adaline. The parameter w is adjusted after using the *delta rule* (the "prime" denotes transposed vectors):

$$w_{t+1} = w_t - \gamma_t (y_t - w_t' x_t)' x_t \qquad (3.2)$$

This delta rule is nothing more than an iteration of the online gradient descent algorithm (2.4) with the following loss function:

$$Q_{\text{adaline}}(z, w) \triangleq (y - w'x)^2 \qquad (3.3)$$

This loss function does not take the discontinuity of the threshold element (3.1) into account. This linear approximation is a real breakthrough over the apparently more natural loss function $(y - \hat{y}_w(x))^2$. This discontinuous loss function is difficult to minimize because its gradient is zero almost everywhere. Furthermore, all solutions achieving the same misclassification rate would have the same cost $C(w)$, regardless of the margins separating the examples from the decision boundary implemented by the threshold element.

3.1.2   Multi-Layer Networks

Multi-layer networks were initially designed to overcome the computational limitation of the threshold elements (Minsky and Papert, 1969). Arbitrary binary mappings can be implemented by stacking several layers of threshold elements, each layer using the outputs of the previous layers elements as inputs. The adaline linear approximation could not be used in this framework, because ignoring the discontinuities would make the entire system linear regardless of the number of layers. The key of a learning algorithm for multi-layer networks (Rumelhart, Hinton and Williams, 1986) consisted of noticing that the discontinuity of the threshold element could be represented by a smooth non-linear approximation.

$$\text{sign}(w'x) \approx \tanh(w'x) \tag{3.4}$$

Using such *sigmoidal elements* does not reduce the computational capabilities of a multi-layer network, because the approximation of a step function by a sigmoid can be made arbitrarily good by scaling the coefficients of the parameter vector w.

A multi-layer network of sigmoidal elements implements a differentiable function $f(x, w)$ of the input pattern x and the parameters w. Given an input pattern x and the desired network output y, the *back-propagation* algorithm, (Rumelhart, Hinton and Williams, 1986) provides an efficient way to compute the gradients of the mean square loss function.

$$Q_{\text{mse}}(z, w) = \frac{1}{2} (y - f(x, w))^2 \tag{3.5}$$

Both the batch gradient descent (2.3) and the online gradient descent (2.4) have been used with considerable success. On large, redundant data sets, the online version converges much faster then the batch version, sometimes by orders of magnitude (Müller, Gunzinger and Guggenbühl, 1995). An intuitive explanation can be found in the following extreme example. Consider a training set composed of two copies of the same subset. The batch algorithm (2.3) averages the gradient of the loss function over the whole training set, causing redundant computations. On the other hand, running online gradient descent (2.4) on all examples of the training set would amount to performing two complete learning iterations over the duplicated subset.

3.2 Non Differentiable Loss Functions

Many interesting examples involve a loss function $Q(z, w)$ which is not differentiable on a subset of points with probability zero. Intuition suggests that this is a minor problems because the iterations of the online gradient descent have zero probability to reach one of these points. Even if we reach one of these points, we can just draw another example z.

This intuition can be formalized using the general online gradient descent algorithm (2.6). The general algorithm can use any update term $H(\mathbf{z}, w)$ which fulfills condition (2.7). We assume here that the cost function $C(w)$ is made differentiable when the loss function $Q(z, w)$ is integrated with the probability distribution $dP(z)$.

The following update term amounts to drawing another example whenever

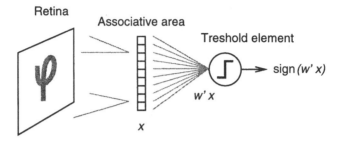

Figure 4: Rosenblatt's Perceptron is composed of a fixed preprocessing and of a trainable threshold element.

we reach a non differentiable point of the loss function.

$$H(z,w) = \begin{cases} \nabla_w Q(z,w) & \text{when differentiable} \\ 0 & \text{otherwise} \end{cases} \quad (3.6)$$

For each parameter value w reached by the algorithm, we assume that the loss
function $Q(z,w)$ is differentiable everywhere except on a subset of examples
z with probability zero. Condition (2.7) then can be rewritten using (3.6) and
explicit integration operators.

$$\int H(z,w)\,dP(z) = \int \nabla_w Q(z,w)\,dP(z) \stackrel{?}{=} \nabla_w \int Q(z,w)\,dP(z) \quad (3.7)$$

The Lebesgue integration theory provides a sufficient condition for swapping
the integration ($\int$) and differentiation (∇_w) operators. For each parameter
value w reached by the online algorithm, it is sufficient to find an integrable
function $\Phi(z,w)$ and a neighborhood $\vartheta(w)$ of w such that:

$$\forall z,\ \forall v \in \vartheta(w),\ |Q(z,v) - Q(z,w)| \leq |w - v|\,\Phi(z,w) \quad (3.8)$$

This condition (3.8) tests that the maximal slope of the loss function $Q(z,w)$
is conveniently bounded. This is obviously true when the loss function $Q(z,w)$
is differentiable and has an integrable gradient. This is obviously false when
the loss function is not continuous. Given our previous assumption concerning the zero probability of the non differentiable points, condition (3.8) is a
sufficient condition for safely ignoring a few non differentiable points.

3.2.1   Rosenblatt's Perceptron

During the early days of the computer age, the *perceptron* (Rosenblatt, 1957)
generated considerable interest as a possible architecture for general purpose computers. This interest faded after the disclosure of its computational

limitations (Minsky and Papert, 1969). Figure 4 represents the perceptron architecture. An *associative area* produces a feature vector x by applying predefined transformations to the *retina* input. The feature vector is then processed by a *threshold element* (section 3.1.1).

The perceptron learning algorithm adapts the parameters w of the threshold element. Whenever a misclassification occurs, the parameters are updated according to the *perceptron rule*.

$$w_{t+1} = w_t + 2\gamma_t y_t\, w_t' x_t \qquad (3.9)$$

This learning rule can be derived as an online gradient descent applied to the following loss function:

$$Q_{\text{perceptron}}(z, w) = (\text{sign}(w'x) - y)\, w'x \qquad (3.10)$$

Although this loss function is non differentiable when $w'x$ is null, is meets condition (3.8) as soon as the expectation $\mathbf{E}(x)$ is defined. We can therefore ignore the non differentiability and apply the online gradient descent algorithm:

$$w_{t+1} = w_t - \gamma_t(\text{sign}(w_t' x_t) - y_t)\, x_t \qquad (3.11)$$

Since the desired class is either $+1$ or -1, the weights are not modified when the pattern x is correctly classified. Therefore this parameter update (3.11) is equivalent to the perceptron rule (3.9).

The perceptron loss function (3.10) is zero when the pattern x is correctly recognized as a member of class $y = \pm 1$. Otherwise its value is positive and proportional to the dot product $w'x$. The corresponding cost function reaches its minimal value zero when all examples are properly recognized or when the weight vector w is null. If the training set is linearly separable (i.e. a threshold element can achieve zero misclassification) the perceptron algorithm finds a linear separation with probability one. Otherwise, the weights w_t quickly tend towards zero.

3.2.2 *K*-Means

The K-Means algorithm (MacQueen, 1967) is a popular clustering method which dispatches K centroids $w_{(k)}$ in order to find clusters in a set of points $x_1, \ldots, x_L$. This algorithm can be derived by performing the online gradient descent with the following loss function.

$$Q_{\text{kmeans}}(x, w) \overset{\triangle}{=} \min_{k=1}^{K} (x - w_{(k)})^2 \qquad (3.12)$$

This loss function measures the quantification error, that is to say the error on the position of point x when we replace it by the closest centroid. The corresponding cost function measures the average quantification error.

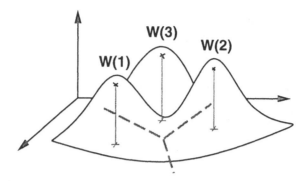

Figure 5: K-Means dispatches a predefined number of cluster centroids in a way that minimizes the quantification error.

This loss function is not differentiable on points located on the Voronoï boundaries of the set of centroids, but meets condition (3.8) as soon as the expectations $\mathbf{E}(x)$ and $\mathbf{E}(x^2)$ are defined. On the remaining points, the derivative of the loss is the derivative of the distance to the nearest centroid w^-. We can therefore ignore the non-differentiable points and apply the online gradient descent algorithm.

$$w_{t+1}^- = w_t^- + \gamma_t(x_t - w_t^-) \qquad (3.13)$$

This formula describes an elementary iteration of the K-Means algorithm. A very efficient choice of learning rates γ_t will be suggested in section 3.3.2.

3.2.3   Learning Vector Quantization II

Kohonen's LVQ2 rule (Kohonen, Barna and Chrisley, 1988) is a powerful pattern recognition algorithm. Like K-Means, it uses a fixed set of reference points $w(k)$. A class $y(k)$ is associated with each reference point. An unknown pattern x is then recognized as a member of the class associated with the nearest reference point.

Given a training pattern x, let us denote w^- the nearest reference point and denote w^+ the nearest reference point among those associated with the correct class y. Adaptation only occurs when the closest reference point w^- is associated with an incorrect class while the closest correct reference point w^+ is not too far away:

$$\text{if } \begin{cases} x \text{ is misclassified } (w^- \neq w^+) \\ \text{and } (x - w^+)^2 < (1 + \delta)(x - w^-)^2 \end{cases}$$

$$\text{then } \begin{cases} w_{t+1}^- = w_t^- - \varepsilon_t(x - w_t^-) \\ w_{t+1}^+ = w_t^+ + \varepsilon_t(x - w_t^+) \end{cases} \qquad (3.14)$$

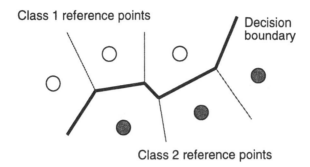

Figure 6: Kohonen's LVQ2 pattern recognition scheme outputs the class associated with the closest reference point to the input pattern.

Reference points are only updated when the pattern x is misclassified. Furthermore, the distance to the closest correct reference point w^+ must not exceed the distance to the closest (incorrect) reference point w^- by more than a percentage defined by parameter δ. When both conditions are met, the algorithm pushes the closest (incorrect) reference point w^- away from the pattern x, and pulls the closest correct reference point w^+ towards the pattern x.

This intuitive algorithm can be derived by performing an online gradient descent with the following loss function:

$$Q_{\text{lvq2}}(z, w) \triangleq \begin{cases} 0 & \text{if } x \text{ is well classified } (w^+ = w^-) \\ 1 & \text{if } (x - w^+)^2 \geq (1 + \delta)(x - w^-)^2 \\ \frac{(x-w^+)^2 - (x-w^-)^2}{\delta(x-w^-)^2} & \text{otherwise} \end{cases} \quad (3.15)$$

This function is a continuous approximation to a binary variable indicating whether pattern x is misclassified. The corresponding cost function therefore is a continuous approximation of the system misclassification rate (Bottou, 1991). This analysis helps understanding how the LVQ2 algorithm works.

Although the above loss function is not differentiable for some values of w, it meets condition (3.8) as soon as the expectations $\mathbf{E}(x)$ and $\mathbf{E}(x^2)$ are defined. We can therefore ignore the non-differentiable points and apply the online gradient descent algorithm:

$$\text{if} \begin{cases} x \text{ is misclassified } (w^- \neq w^+) \\ \text{and } (x - w^+)^2 < (1 + \delta)(x - w^-)^2 \end{cases} \quad (3.16)$$

$$\text{then} \begin{cases} w^-_{t+1} = w^-_t - \gamma_t k_1 (x - w^-_t) \\ w^+_{t+1} = w^+_t + \gamma_t k_2 (x - w^+_t) \end{cases}$$

$$\text{with } k_1 = \frac{1}{\delta(X - w^-)^2} \quad \text{and} \quad k_2 = k_1 \frac{(X - w^+)^2}{(X - w^-)^2} \quad (3.17)$$

This online gradient descent algorithm (3.16) is equivalent to the usual LVQ2 learning algorithm (3.14). The two scalar coefficients k_1 and k_2 merely modify the proper schedule for the decreasing learning rates γ_t.

3.3 Quasi-Newton Online Algorithms

Both theoretical and empirical evidences demonstrate that batch gradient descent algorithms converge much faster when the scalar learning rates γ_t are replaced by definite positive symmetric matrices that approximate the inverse of the Hessian of the cost function. The so-called *super-linear* algorithms achieve very high terminal convergence speed: the number of correct figures in the numerical representation of the solution increases exponentially (Dennis and Schnabel, 1983).

The same techniques are also effective for speeding up online gradient algorithms. The results however are much less impressive than those achieved with batch algorithms. No online gradient descent algorithm can achieve super-linear convergence (cf. comments to section 4). The terminal convergence of an online gradient algorithm is limited by the size of the learning rates. As will be shown in sections 4 and 5, decreasing the learning rates too quickly can prevent convergence.

The accuracy of a super-linear algorithm however is largely irrelevant to a learning system. Severe approximations, such as using a finite training set, would spoil the benefits of such an algorithm. Practitioners prefer techniques blessed with robust convergence properties, such as the Levenberg-Marquardt algorithm (Dennis and Schnabel, 1983). Furthermore, storing and processing a full learning rate matrix quickly becomes expensive when the dimension of the parameter vector w increases. Less efficient approximations have been designed (Becker and LeCun, 1989) and have proven effective enough for large size applications (LeCun et al., 1989).

3.3.1 Kalman Algorithms

The Kalman filter theory has introduced an efficient way to compute an approximation of the inverse of the Hessian of certain cost functions. This idea is easily demonstrated in the case of linear algorithms such as the adaline (section 3.1.1). Consider online gradient descent applied to the minimization of the following mean square cost function:

$$C(w) = \int Q(z,w)\,dP(z) \quad \text{with} \quad Q(z,w) \stackrel{\triangle}{=} (y - w'x)^2 \quad (3.18)$$

Each iteration of this algorithm consists of drawing a new pair $z_t = (x_t, y_t)$ from the distribution $dP(z)$ and applying the following update formula:

$$w_{t+1} = w_t - H_t^{-1} \nabla_w Q(z_t, w_t) = w_t - H_t^{-1}(y_t - w_t'x_t)'x_t \quad (3.19)$$

where H_t denotes the Hessian of the *online empirical cost* function. The online empirical cost function is simply an empirical estimate of the cost function $C(w)$ based on the examples $z_1, \ldots, z_t$ observed so far.

$$C_t(w) \stackrel{\triangle}{=} \frac{1}{2}\sum_{i=1}^{t} Q(z_i, w) = \frac{1}{2}\sum_{i=1}^{t}(y_i - w'x_i)^2 \tag{3.20}$$

$$H_t \stackrel{\triangle}{=} \nabla_w^2 C_t(w) = \sum_{i=1}^{t} x_i x_i' \tag{3.21}$$

Directly computing the matrix H_t^{-1} at each iteration would be very expensive. We can take advantage however of the recursion $H_t = H_{t-1} + x_t x_t'$ using the well known matrix equality:

$$(A + BB')^{-1} = A^{-1} - (A^{-1}B)\,(I + B'A^{-1}B)^{-1}\,(A^{-1}B)' \tag{3.22}$$

Algorithm (3.19) then can be rewritten recursively using the *Kalman matrix* $K_t = H_{t-1}^{-1}$. The resulting algorithm (3.23) converges much faster than the delta rule (3.2) and yet remains quite easy to implement:

$$\left[\begin{array}{rcl} K_{t+1} & = & K_t - \dfrac{(K_t x_t)(K_t x_t)'}{1 + x_t' K_t x_t} \\[2mm] w_{t+1} & = & w_t - K_{t+1}\,(y_t - w_t' x_t)' x_t \end{array} \right. \tag{3.23}$$

Comments

This linear algorithm has an interesting optimality property (Tsypkin, 1973). Because the cost function (3.20) is exactly quadratic, it is easy to prove by induction that (3.23) minimizes the online empirical cost $C_t(w)$ at each iteration. Assuming that w_t is the minimum of $C_{t-1}(w)$, the following derivation shows that w_{t+1} is the minimum of $C_t(w)$.

$$\begin{aligned} \nabla_w C_t(w_{t+1}) & = \nabla_w C_t(w_t) - H_t\,(w_{t+1} - w_t) \\ & = \nabla_w C_{t-1}(w_t) + \nabla_w Q(z_t, w_t) - H_t\,H_t^{-1}\nabla_w Q(z_t, w_t) \\ & = 0 \end{aligned}$$

Although this property illustrates the rapid convergence of algorithm (3.23), it only describes how the algorithm tracks an empirical approximation (3.20) of the cost function. This approximation may not provide very good generalization properties (Vapnik, 1995).

Non linear least mean square algorithms, such as the multi-layer networks (section 3.1.2) can also benefit from non-scalar learning rates. The idea consists of using an approximation of the Hessian matrix. The second derivatives of the loss function (3.5) can be written as:

$$\begin{aligned} \frac{1}{2}\nabla_w^2\,(y - f(x, w))^2 & = \nabla_w f(x, w)\,\nabla_w' f(x, w) - (y - f(x, w))\nabla_w^2 f(x, w) \\ & \approx \nabla_w f(x, w)\,\nabla_w' f(x, w) \end{aligned} \tag{3.24}$$

Approximation (3.24), known as the Gauss Newton approximation, neglects the impact of the non linear function f on the curvature of the cost function. With this approximation, the Hessian of the empirical online cost takes a very simple form.

$$H_t(w) \approx \sum_{i=1}^{t} \nabla_w f(x_i, w) \, \nabla'_w f(x_i, w) \qquad (3.25)$$

Although the real Hessian can be negative, this approximated Hessian is always positive, a useful property for convergence. Its expression (3.25) is reminiscent of the linear case (3.21). Its inverse can be computed using similar recursive equations.

3.3.2   Optimal Learning Rate for K-Means

Second derivative information can also be used to determine very efficient learning rates for the K-Means algorithm (section 3.2.2). A simple analysis of the loss function (3.12) shows that the Hessian of the cost function is a diagonal matrix (Bottou and Bengio, 1995) whose coefficients $\lambda_{(k)}$ are equal to the probabilities that an example x is associated with the corresponding centroid $w_{(k)}$.

These probabilities can be estimated by simply counting how many examples $n_{(k)}$ have been associated with each centroid $w_{(k)}$. Each iteration of the corresponding online algorithm consists in drawing a random example x_t, finding the closest centroid $w_{(k)}$, and updating both the count and the centroid with the following equations:

$$\left[\begin{array}{rcl} n_{t+1}(k) & = & n_t(k) + 1 \\ w_{t+1}(k) & = & w_t(k) + \frac{1}{n_{t+1}(k)}(x_t - w_t(k)) \end{array} \right. \qquad (3.26)$$

Algorithm (3.26) very quickly locates the relative position of clusters in the data. Terminal convergence however is slowed down by the noise implied by the random choice of the examples. Experimental evidence (Bottou and Bengio, 1995) suggest that the best convergence speed is obtained by first using the online algorithm (3.26) and then switching to a batch super-linear version of K-means.

4   Convex Online Optimization

The next two sections illustrate how nicely the convergence of online learning algorithm is analyzed by the modern mathematical tools designed for stochastic approximations. This particular section addresses a simple convex case, while focusing on the mathematical tools and on their relation with the classical analysis of batch algorithms. This presentation owes much to a remarkable lecture by Michel Metivier (Metivier, 1981).

4.1   General Convexity

The analysis presented in this section addresses the convergence of the general online gradient algorithm (section 2.3) applied to the optimization of a differentiable cost function $C(w)$ with the following properties:

- The cost function $C(w)$ has a single minimum w^*.

- The cost function $C(w)$ satisfies the following condition:

$$\forall \varepsilon > 0, \quad \inf_{(w-w^*)^2 > \varepsilon} (w - w^*)\, \nabla_w C(w) > 0 \qquad (4.1)$$

Condition (4.1) simply states that the opposite of the gradient $-\nabla_w C(w)$ always points towards the minimum w^*. This particular formulation also rejects cost functions which have plateaus on which the gradient vanishes without making us closer to the minimum.

This condition is weaker than the usual notion of convexity. It is indeed easy to think of a non convex cost function which has a single minimum and satisfies condition (4.1). On the other hand, proving that all differentiable strictly convex functions satisfy this condition is neither obvious nor useful.

4.2   Batch Convergence Revisited

The convergence proof for the general online learning algorithm follow exactly the same three steps than the convergence proofs for batch learning algorithms. These steps consist of (a) defining a *Lyapunov* criterion of convergence, (b) proving that this criterion converges, and (c) proving that this convergence implies the convergence of the algorithm. These steps are now illustrated in the cases of the continuous gradient descent and the batch gradient descent.

4.2.1   Continuous Gradient Descent

The *continuous gradient descent* is a mathematical description of the ideal convergence of a gradient descent algorithm. A differential equation defines the parameter trajectory $w(t)$ as a continuous function of the time.

$$\frac{\mathrm{d}w}{\mathrm{d}t} = -\nabla_w C(w) \qquad (4.2)$$

Step a.   The convergence proof begins with the definition of a *Lyapunov function*, i.e. a positive function which indicates how far we are from the target.

$$h(t) \stackrel{\triangle}{=} (w(t) - w^*)^2 \qquad (4.3)$$

Step b. Computing the derivative of $h(t)$ shows that the Lyapunov function $h(t)$ is a monotonically decreasing function.

$$\frac{\mathrm{d}h}{\mathrm{d}t} = 2(w - w^*)\frac{\mathrm{d}w}{\mathrm{d}t} = -2(w - w^*)\nabla_w C(w) \leq 0 \qquad (4.4)$$

Since $h(t)$ is a positive decreasing function, it has a limit when $t \to \infty$.

Step c. Since the monotonic function $h(t)$ converges when t grows, its gradient tends towards zero.

$$\frac{\mathrm{d}h}{\mathrm{d}t} = -2(w - w^*)\nabla_w C(w) \xrightarrow[t\to\infty]{} 0 \qquad (4.5)$$

Let us assume that the Lyapunov function $h(t)$ converges to a value greater than zero. After a certain time, the distance $h(t) = (w(t) - w^*)^2$ would remain greater than some positive value ε. This result is incompatible with condition (4.1) and result (4.5). The Lyapunov function $h(t)$ therefore converges to zero. This result proves the convergence of the continuous gradient descent (4.2).

$$w(t) \xrightarrow[t\to\infty]{} w^* \qquad (4.6)$$

4.2.2   Discrete Gradient Descent

The batch gradient descent algorithm has been introduced in section 2.2.1 in the context of learning algorithms. The cost function $C(w)$ is minimized by iteratively applying the following parameter update:

$$w_{t+1} = w_t - \gamma_t \nabla_w C(w) \qquad (4.7)$$

Equation (4.7) is a discrete version of the continuous gradient descent (4.2). Although the discrete dynamics brings new convergence issues, the analysis of the convergence follows the same three elementary steps.

Step a. The convergence proof begins with the definition of a *Lyapunov sequence*, i.e. a sequence of positive numbers whose value measure how far we are from our target.

$$h_t \stackrel{\triangle}{=} (w_t - w^*)^2 \qquad (4.8)$$

Lemma. It is useful at this point to introduce a sufficient criterion for the convergence of a positive sequence (u_t). Intuitively, a sequence (u_t) converges when it is bounded and when its oscillations are damped. The oscillations can be monitored by summing the variations $u_t - u_{t-1}$ whenever $u_t > u_{t-1}$. These positive variations are represented with thick lines in figure 7. When the infinite sum of the positive variations converges, we are certain that the oscillations are damped. If all terms of the sequence are positive, this condition also ensures that the sequence if bounded.

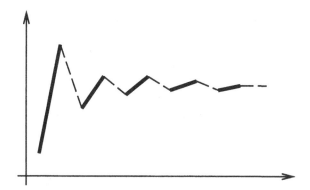

Figure 7: The convergence of the infinite sum of the positive increases (thick lines) is a sufficient (although not necessary) condition for the convergence of a positive sequence h_t. This condition ensures *(i)* that the sequence is bounded, and *(ii)* that the oscillations are damped.

This intuition is easily formalized by decomposing a term u_t of a sequence using the sum S_t^+ of the *positive variations*:

$$S_t^+ \overset{\triangle}{=} \sum_{i=1}^{t-1} (u_{i+1} - u_i)_+ \quad \text{with} \quad (x)_+ \overset{\triangle}{=} \begin{cases} x & \text{if } x > 0 \\ 0 & \text{otherwise} \end{cases} \quad (4.9)$$

and the sum S_t^- of the *negative variations*:

$$S_t^- \overset{\triangle}{=} \sum_{i=1}^{t-1} (u_{i+1} - u_i)_- \quad \text{with} \quad (x)_- \overset{\triangle}{=} \begin{cases} 0 & \text{if } x > 0 \\ x & \text{otherwise} \end{cases} \quad (4.10)$$

If the sum of the positive variations converges to S_∞^+, this decomposition provides an upper bound for the positive sequence u_t.

$$0 \le u_t = u_1 + S_t^+ + S_t^- \le u_1 + S_\infty^+ + S_t^- < u_0 + S_\infty^+ \quad (4.11)$$

Furthermore, since $u_t \ge 0$, the same decompositions also provides a lower bound for the sum of the negative variations S_t^-.

$$0 - u_1 - S_\infty^+ \le S_t^- \le 0 \quad (4.12)$$

Since S_t^- is a bounded monotonically decreasing sequence, it converges to a limit S_∞^-. Since both sequences S_t^+ and S_t^- converge, the sequence u_t converges to $u_\infty = u_1 + S_\infty^+ + S_\infty^-$.

$$\left. \begin{array}{c} \forall t, \ u_t \ge 0 \\ \sum_{t=1}^{\infty} (u_{t+1} - u_t)_+ < \infty \end{array} \right\} \implies u_t \underset{t \to \infty}{\longrightarrow} u_\infty \ge 0 \quad (4.13)$$

The convergence of the infinite sum of the positive variations is therefore a sufficient condition for the convergence of the sequence. Since the positive variations are positive, it is sufficient to prove that they are bounded by the summand of a convergent infinite sum.

Step b. The second step consists in proving that the Lyapunov sequence (h_t) converges. Using the the definition (4.8) and from the gradient descent algorithm (4.7), we can write an expression for the variations of the Lyapunov criterion.

$$h_{t+1} - h_t = -2\gamma_t (w_t - w^*)\nabla_w C(w_t) + \gamma_t^2 (\nabla_w C(w_t))^2 \qquad (4.14)$$

The convexity criterion (4.1) ensures that the first term of this expression is always negative. Unlike the continuous variations (4.4), this expression contains a positive second term which reflects the discrete dynamics of the algorithm.

Additional conditions must be introduced in order to contain the effects of this second term. The first condition (4.15) states that the learning rates γ_t decrease fast enough. This is expressed by the convergence of the infinite sum of the squared learning rates.

$$\sum_{i=1}^{\infty} \gamma_t^2 < \infty \qquad (4.15)$$

The second condition (4.16) ensures that the size of gradients do not grow too fast when we move away from the minimum. This linear condition is met as soon as the eigenvalues of the Hessian matrix are bounded.

$$(\nabla_w C(w))^2 \leq A + B(w - w^*)^2 \quad A, B \geq 0 \qquad (4.16)$$

Such a condition is required because the polynomial decrease of the learning rates would be too easily canceled by exponentially growing gradients. We can now transform equation (4.14) using the bound on the size of the gradients (4.16).

$$h_{t+1} - (1 - \gamma_t^2 B)h_t \leq -2\gamma_t (w_t - w^*)\nabla_w C(w_t) + \gamma_t^2 A \leq \gamma_t^2 A \qquad (4.17)$$

We now define two auxiliary sequences μ_t and h_t':

$$\mu_t \overset{\Delta}{=} \prod_{i=1}^{t} \frac{1}{1 - \gamma_i^2 B} \xrightarrow[t\to\infty]{} \mu_\infty \quad \text{and} \quad h_t' \overset{\Delta}{=} \mu_t h_t \qquad (4.18)$$

The convergence of μ_t is easily verified by writing $\log \mu_t$ and using condition (4.15). Multiplying both the left-hand-side and the right hand side of (4.17) by μ_t, we obtain:

$$(h_{t+1}' - h_t') \leq \gamma_t^2 \mu_t A \qquad (4.19)$$

Since the right hand side of (4.19) is positive, the positive variations of h'_t are at most equal to $\gamma_t^2 \mu_t A$, which is the summand of a convergent infinite sum. According to lemma (4.13), the sequence h'_t converges. Since μ_t converges, this convergence implies the convergence of the Lyapunov sequence h_t.

Step c. We now prove that the convergence of the Lyapunov sequence implies the convergence of the discrete gradient descent algorithm. Since the sequence h_t converges, equation (4.17) implies the convergence of the following sum:

$$\sum_{i=1}^{\infty} \gamma_i (w_i - w^*) \nabla_w C(w_i) < \infty \qquad (4.20)$$

We must introduce an additional condition on the learning rates γ_i. This condition limits the rate of decrease of the learning rates. Such a condition is required, because decreasing the learning rates too quickly could stop the progression of the algorithm towards the minimum. This condition is expressed by the divergence of the infinite sum of the learning rates:

$$\sum_{i=1}^{\infty} \gamma_i = \infty \qquad (4.21)$$

Condition (4.21) is intuitively natural if we imagine that the current parameter is far away from the minimum in an area where the gradient is approximately constant. Successive updates $\gamma_t \nabla_w C(w_t)$ should be allowed to move the parameter to arbitrary distances.

Since we are dealing with positive quantities only, conditions (4.20) and (4.21) imply that:

$$(w_t - w^*) \nabla_w C(w_t) \xrightarrow[t \to \infty]{} 0 \qquad (4.22)$$

This result is similar to (4.5) and leads to the same conclusion about the convergence of the gradient descent algorithm.

$$w_t \xrightarrow[t \to \infty]{} w^* \qquad (4.23)$$

Besides the existence of a single minimum w^* and the general convexity criterion (4.1), we had to introduce three additional conditions to obtain this convergence. Two conditions (4.15) and (4.21) directly address the learning rate schedule. The last condition (4.16) states that the growth of the gradients is limited.

Comments

Condition (4.16) states that the gradient should not increase more than linearly when we move away from the minimum. Bounding the eigenvalues of the Hessian is an easy way to make sure that this condition holds. More general theorems however only require a polynomial bound on the size of the gradient (Benveniste, Metivier and Priouret, 1990).

The proof presented in this section addresses the case of *decreasing learning rates*. A different approach to step (b) leads to convergence results for the case of *constant learning rates*. Instead of bounding the second term of the variations (4.14) we can compare the sizes of both terms. Assuming condition (4.16) with $A = 0$, it appears that choosing a constant learning rate smaller than $\sqrt{2/B}$ makes the variations (4.14) negative. This result is consistent with the usual criterion since the minimal value of B is the square of the highest eigenvalue of the Hessian matrix.

This analysis also provides convergence speed results: bounding the right hand side of (4.14) gives a measure of how quickly the Lyapunov sequence decreases. As expected, the best bounds are obtained when $(w_t - w^*)$ and $\gamma_t \nabla_w C(w_t)$ are aligned. This can be achieved by choosing a learning rate matrix γ_t which approximates the inverse of the Hessian. Such a non scalar learning rates only introduces minor changes in the proofs. The learning rate matrix must be symmetric and definite positive. Conditions (4.15) and (4.21) then must refer to the highest and lowest eigenvalues of the learning rate matrix.

4.3   Lyapunov Process

Convergence proofs for the general online gradient algorithm (section 2.3) can be established using the same approach. It is obvious however that any online learning algorithm can be mislead by a consistent choice of very improbable examples. There is therefore no hope to prove that this algorithm always converges. The best possible result then is the *almost sure convergence*, that is to say that the algorithm converges towards the solution with probability 1.

Each iteration of the general gradient descent algorithm consists of drawing an event $\mathbf{z}_t$ from distribution $dP(z)$ and applying the update formula

$$w_{t+1} = w_t - \gamma_t H(\mathbf{z}_t, w_t) \tag{4.24}$$

where the update term $H(\mathbf{z}_t, w_t)$ fulfills the condition

$$\mathbf{E}_{\mathbf{z}} H(\mathbf{z}, w_t) = \nabla_w C(w_t) \tag{4.25}$$

and where the learning rates γ_t are positive numbers or definite positive matrices. The main discussion in this section addresses scalar learning rates. Using a learning rate matrix introduces only minor changes discussed in the comments.

Step a.   The first step in the proof consists in defining a *Lyapunov process* which measures how far we are from the solution.

$$h_t \overset{\triangle}{=} (w_t - w^*)^2. \tag{4.26}$$

Although definition (4.26) looks similar to the discrete batch gradient case (4.8), the notation h_t in (4.26) denotes a random variable that depends on all the previous choices of example events $\mathbf{z}_t$.

Step b. As in the batch gradient case, an expression for the variations of h_t can be derived using equations (4.24) and (4.26).

$$h_{t+1} - h_t = -2\gamma_t(w_t - w^*)H(\mathbf{z}_t, w_t) + \gamma_t^2(H(\mathbf{z}_t, w_t))^2 \qquad (4.27)$$

The convergence proof for the discrete gradient descent (section 4.2.2) relies on lemma (4.13) to establish the convergence of the Lyapunov criterion. The lemma defines a sufficient condition based on the variations of the criterion. Expression (4.27) however explicitly refers to the random example $\mathbf{z}_t$. Using lemma (4.13) here would be an attempt to prove that the algorithm converges for all imaginable choice of the examples, including the most improbable, such as continuously drawing the same example.

The correct approach consists in removing this dependency by taking the conditional expectation of the variations (4.27) given all the information $\mathcal{P}_t$ that was available just before iteration t.

$$\mathcal{P}_t \overset{\triangle}{=} \mathbf{z}_o, \dots, \mathbf{z}_{t-1}, \; w_0, \dots, w_t, \; \gamma_0, \dots, \gamma_t \qquad (4.28)$$

This conditional expectation of the variations gives sufficient information to apply the *quasi-martingale convergence theorem*.

4.4 Quasi-Martingales

The quasi-martingale convergence theorem is in fact very similar to the lemma (4.13) presented in section 4.2.2. The following discussion only presents the theorem without proof and exposes its analogy with this lemma. Proofs can be found in (Metivier, 1983) or (Fisk, 1965).

Given all the past information $\mathcal{P}_t$, we wish to define a deterministic criterion for distinguishing the "positive variations" from the "negative variations" of a process u_t. The sign of the variation $u_{t+1} - u_t$ is not an acceptable choice because it depends on u_{t+1} which is not fully determined given $\mathcal{P}_t$. This problem can be solved by considering the conditional expectation of the variations.

$$\delta_t \overset{\triangle}{=} \begin{cases} 1 & \text{if } \mathbf{E}\left(u_{t+1} - u_t \mid \mathcal{P}_t\right) > 0 \\ 0 & \text{otherwise} \end{cases} \qquad (4.29)$$

The variable δ defined in (4.29) defines which variations are considered positive. The convergence of the infinite sum of the positive expected variations is a sufficient condition for the *almost sure convergence* of a positive process u_t.

$$\left. \begin{array}{l} \forall t, \; u_t \geq 0 \\ \sum_{t=1}^{\infty} \mathbf{E}(\delta_t(u_{t+1} - u_t)) < \infty \end{array} \right\} \implies u_t \xrightarrow[t \to \infty]{a.s.} u_\infty \geq 0 \qquad (4.30)$$

This result is a particular case of theorem 9.4 and proposition 9.5 in (Metivier, 1983). The name *quasi-martingale convergence theorem* comes from the fact that condition (4.30) also implies that the process u_t is a quasi-martingale (Fisk, 1965). Comparing theorem (4.30) and lemma (4.13) explains easily why quasi-martingales are so useful for studying the convergence of online algorithms. This fact has been known since (Gladyshev, 1965).

4.5   Convergence of Online Algorithms (Convex Case)

This convergence result allow us to proceed with step (b) of our proof.

Step b (continued). The following expression is obtained by taking the conditional expectation of (4.27) and factoring the constant multipliers.

$$\begin{aligned}
\mathbf{E}\left(h_{t+1} - h_t \mid \mathcal{P}_t\right) = \ & - 2\,\gamma_t(w_t - w^*)\,\mathbf{E}\left(H(\mathbf{z}_t, w_t) \mid \mathcal{P}_t\right) \\
& + \gamma_t^2\,\mathbf{E}\left(H(\mathbf{z}_t, w_t)^2 \mid \mathcal{P}_t\right)
\end{aligned} \tag{4.31}$$

This expression can be further simplified using condition (4.25).

$$\begin{aligned}
\mathbf{E}&\left(h_{t+1} - h_t \mid \mathcal{P}_t\right) \\
&= \ - 2\,\gamma_t(w_t - w^*)\,\mathbf{E}_{\mathbf{z}}(H(\mathbf{z}, w_t)) + \gamma_t^2\,\mathbf{E}_{\mathbf{z}}(H(\mathbf{z}_t, w_t)^2) \\
&= \ - 2\,\gamma_t(w_t - w^*)\nabla_w C(w_t) + \gamma_t^2\,\mathbf{E}_{\mathbf{z}}(H(\mathbf{z}_t, w_t)^2)
\end{aligned} \tag{4.32}$$

The first term of this upper bound is negative according to condition 4.1. As in section 4.2.2, two additional conditions are required to address the discrete dynamics of the algorithm. The first condition (4.33), similar to (4.15), states that the learning rates are decreasing fast enough.

$$\sum_{i=1}^{\infty} \gamma_t^2 < \infty \tag{4.33}$$

The second condition (4.34) serves the same purpose than condition (4.16). This term bounds the growth of the second moment of the update $H(\mathbf{z}, w)$.

$$\mathbf{E}_{\mathbf{z}}(H(\mathbf{z}, w)^2) \leq A + B(w - w^*)^2 \quad A, B \geq 0 \tag{4.34}$$

We can now transform equation (4.32) using this condition.

$$\mathbf{E}\left(h_{t+1} - (1 - \gamma_t^2 B)h_t \mid \mathcal{P}_t\right) \leq -2\gamma_t\,(w_t - w^*)\nabla_w C(w_t) + \gamma_t^2 A \tag{4.35}$$

We now define two auxiliary sequences μ_t and h_t' as in (4.18). Multiplying both the left-hand-side and the right hand side of (4.32) by μ_t, we obtain:

$$\mathbf{E}\left(h_{t+1}' - h_t' \mid \mathcal{P}_t\right) \leq \gamma_t^2 \mu_t A \tag{4.36}$$

A simple transformation then gives a bound for the positive expected variations of h'_t.

$$\mathbf{E}(\delta_t\,(h'_{t+1} - h'_t)) = \mathbf{E}(\delta_t\,\mathbf{E}\left(h'_{t+1} - h'_t \mid \mathcal{P}_t\right)) \leq \gamma_t^2 \mu_t A \qquad (4.37)$$

Since this bound is the summand of a convergent infinite sum, theorem (4.30) implies that h'_t converges almost surely. Since the sequence μ_t converges, the Lyapunov process h_t also converges almost surely.

Step c. We now prove that the convergence of the Lyapunov process implies the convergence of the discrete gradient descent algorithm. Since h_t converges, equation (4.35) implies the convergence of the following sum:

$$\sum_{i=1}^{\infty} \gamma_i(w_i - w^*)\nabla_w C(w_i) < \infty \quad \text{a.s.} \qquad (4.38)$$

We must introduce an additional condition on the learning rates γ_i which limits the rate of decrease of the learning rates. This condition is similar to condition (4.21).

$$\sum_{i=1}^{\infty} \gamma_i = \infty \qquad (4.39)$$

Since we are dealing with positive quantities only, conditions (4.38) and (4.39) imply that:

$$(w_t - w^*)\nabla_w C(w_t) \xrightarrow[t \to \infty]{a.s.} 0 \qquad (4.40)$$

This result is similar to (4.5) or (4.22) and leads to the same conclusion about the convergence of the gradient descent algorithm.

$$w_t \xrightarrow[t \to \infty]{a.s.} w^* \qquad (4.41)$$

Besides the general convexity criterion (4.1), we had to introduce three additional conditions to obtain this convergence. Two conditions (4.33) and (4.39) directly address the learning rate schedule as in the batch gradient case. The last condition (4.34) is similar to condition (4.16) but contains an additional variance term which reflects the stochastic dynamics of the online gradient descent.

Comments

Equations (4.14) and (4.32) look very similar. The second term of the right hand side of (4.32) however refers to the second moment of the updates instead of the norm of the gradients. This term can be decomposed as follows:

$$\gamma_t^2 \mathbf{E}_z(H(z, w))^2 = \gamma_t^2(\nabla_w C(w))^2 + \gamma_t^2 \text{var}_z H(z, w) \qquad (4.42)$$

The second term of this decomposition depends on the noise implied by the stochastic nature of the algorithm. This variance remains strictly positive in general, even at the solution w^*. This fact is the main explanation for the dynamical differences between batch gradient descent and online gradient descent.

Let us assume that the algorithm converges. The first term of the right hand side of (4.32) tends towards zero, as well as the first term of (4.42). We can therefore write an asymptotic equivalent to the expected variation the Lyapunov criterion:

$$\mathbf{E}\left(h_{t+1} - h_t \mid \mathcal{P}_t\right) \underset{t \to \infty}{\asymp} \gamma_t\left(\gamma_t \mathbf{var_z} H(\mathbf{z}, w^*) - (w_t - w)\nabla_w C(w)\right) \qquad (4.43)$$

This result means that the quantities $\gamma_t \mathbf{var_z} H(\mathbf{z}, w^*)$ and $(w_t - w)\nabla_w C(w)$ keep the same order of magnitude during the convergence. Since the latter quantity is related to the distance to the optimum (cf. comments to section 4.2.2) the convergence speed depends on how fast the learning rates γ_t decrease. This decrease rate is in turn limited by condition (4.39).

This analysis can be repeated with non scalar learning rates approximating the inverse of the Hessian. This algorithm converges faster than using a scalar learning rate equal to the inverse of the largest eigenvalue of the Hessian. This result of course assume that these learning rates still fulfill criterions (4.33) and (4.39), as in the batch gradient descent case (cf. comments to section 4.2.2).

The final comment expands section 3.2 discussing online gradient descent with non differentiable functions. The proof presented in this section never uses the fact that $\nabla_w C(w)$ is actually the gradient of the cost $C(w)$. All references to this gradient can be eliminated by merging conditions (4.1) and (4.25):

$$\forall \varepsilon > 0, \quad \inf_{(w-w^*)^2 > \varepsilon} (w - w^*)\, \mathbf{E}_z H(z, w) > 0 \qquad (4.44)$$

This condition (4.44), together with the usual conditions (4.33), (4.39) and (4.34), is sufficient to ensure the convergence of algorithm (4.24). This result makes no reference to a differentiable cost function.

5 General Online Optimization

This section analyzes the convergence of the general online gradient algorithm (section 2.3) without convexity hypothesis. In other words, the cost function $C(w)$ can now have several local minima.

There are two ways to handle this analysis. The first method consists of partitioning the parameter space into several attraction basins, discussing the conditions under which the algorithm confines the parameters w_t in a single attraction basin, defining suitable Lyapunov criterions (Krasovskii, 1963), and proceeding as in the convex case. Since the online gradient descent algorithm never completely confines the parameter into a single attraction basin, we must also study how the algorithm hops from one attraction basin to another.

A much simpler method quickly gives a subtly different result. Instead of proving that the parameter w_t converges, we prove the cost function $C(w_t)$ and its gradient $\nabla_w C(w_t)$ converge. The discussion presented below is an expanded version of the proof given in (Bottou, 1991).

5.1 Assumptions

The convergence results rely on the following assumptions:

i) The cost function $C(w)$ is three times differentiable with continuous derivatives. It is bounded from below, i.e. $C(w) \geq C_{\min}$. We can assume, without loss of generality, that $C(w) \geq 0$.

ii) The usual conditions on the learning rates are fulfilled.

$$\sum_{i=1}^{\infty} \gamma_t^2 < \infty, \quad \sum_{i=1}^{\infty} \gamma_t = \infty \qquad (5.1)$$

iii) The second moment of the update term should not grow more than linearly with the size of the parameters. This condition is similar to (4.34).

$$\mathbf{E}_z (H(\mathbf{z}, w))^2 \leq A + Bw^2 \qquad (5.2)$$

iv) When the norm of the parameter w is larger than a certain horizon D, the opposite of the gradient $-\nabla_w C(w)$ points towards the origin.

$$\inf_{w^2 > D} w \nabla_w C(w) > 0 \qquad (5.3)$$

v) When the norm of the parameter w is smaller than a second horizon E greater than D, the norm of the update term $H(\mathbf{z}, w)$ is bounded regardless of $\mathbf{z}$. This is usually a mild requirement.

$$\forall \mathbf{z}, \quad \sup_{w^2 < E} \|H(\mathbf{z}, w)\| \leq K_0 \qquad (5.4)$$

Hypothesis (5.3) prevents the possibility of plateaus on which the parameter vector can grow indefinitely without ever escaping. Beyond a certain horizon, the update terms always moves w_t closer to the origin on average.

This condition is easy to verify in the case of the K-Means algorithm (section 3.2.2) for instance. The cost function is never reduced by moving centroids beyond the envelope of the data points. Multi-layer networks (section 3.1.2) however do not always fulfill this condition because the sigmoid has flat asymptotes. In practice however, it is common to choose desired values that are smaller than the sigmoid asymptotes, and to add a small linear term to the sigmoid which makes sure that rounding errors will not make the sigmoid gradient negative. These well known tricks in fact ensure that condition (5.3) is fulfilled. A similar discussion applies to the LVQ2 algorithm (section 3.2.3).

5.2   Global Confinement

The first part of the analysis consists in taking advantage of hypothesis (5.3) and proving that the parameter vector w_t is almost surely confined into a bounded region. The proof again relies on the same three steps.

Step a. We define a suitable criterion:

$$f_t \overset{\triangle}{=} \max(E, w_t^2) \tag{5.5}$$

Step b. The definition of f_t implies that the variations of f_t are bounded by the variations of w_t^2.

$$f_{t+1} - f_t \le -2\gamma_t w_t H(\mathbf{z}_t, w_t) + \gamma_t^2 (H(\mathbf{z}_t, w_t))^2 \tag{5.6}$$

Inequality (5.6) is actually an equality when both w_{t+1}^2 and w_t^2 are greater than E. We can the write a bound for the expected variations:

$$\mathbf{E}\left(f_{t+1} - f_t \mid \mathcal{P}_t\right) \le -2\gamma_t w_t \nabla_w C(w_t) + \gamma_t^2 \mathbf{E}_{\mathbf{z}}(H(\mathbf{z}, w_t))^2 \tag{5.7}$$

We can eliminate the first term of this bound by considering several cases:

- When both w_{t+1}^2 and w_t^2 are smaller than E, the variations $f_{t+1} - f_t$ are zero. The expected variations are therefore bounded by the second term of (5.7) which is positive.

- When w_t^2 is greater than E, hypothesis (5.3) ensures that the second term of the bound (5.7) is negative. We can safely remove this term.

- The remaining case has $w_t^2 < E$ and $w_{t+1}^2 \ge E$. The difference between w_{t+1} and w_t is $\gamma_t H(\mathbf{z}_t, w_t)$. Since hypothesis (5.4) ensures that $H(\mathbf{z}_t, w_t)$ is bounded, we can conclude that w_t is greater than D as soon as the decreasing learning rates become small enough. Invoking hypothesis (5.3) gives the final argument.

The following bound therefore is valid when t is large enough:

$$\mathbf{E}\left(f_{t+1} - f_t \mid \mathcal{P}_t\right) \le \gamma_t^2 \mathbf{E}_{\mathbf{z}}(H(\mathbf{z}, w_t))^2 \le \gamma_t^2(A + Bf_t) \tag{5.8}$$

We now proceed along the well known lines. We first transform the bound on the expected variations as in (4.35). We define two auxiliary quantities μ_t and f_t' as in (4.18). The expected variations of f_t' are bounded as shown in equation (4.36). We can then bound the positive expected variations of f_t'.

$$\mathbf{E}(\delta_t(f_{t+1}' - f_t')) \le \mathbf{E}(\delta_t \mathbf{E}\left(f_{t+1}' - f_t' \mid \mathcal{P}_t\right)) \le \gamma_t^2 \mu_t A \tag{5.9}$$

Theorem (4.30) then implies that f'_t converges almost surely. This convergence implies that f_t converges almost surely.

Step c. Let us assume that f_t converge to a value f_∞ greater than E. When t is large enough, this convergence implies that both w_t^2 and w_{t+1}^2 are greater than E. Bound (5.6) is then an equality. This equality implies that the following infinite sum converges almost surely:

$$\sum_{i=1}^{\infty} \gamma_t w_t \nabla_w C(w_t) < \infty \quad \text{a.s.} \tag{5.10}$$

Since $\sum \gamma_t = \infty$ this result is not compatible with hypothesis (5.3). We must therefore conclude that f_t converges to the smallest possible value E.

Global confinement. The convergence of f_t means that the norm w_t^2 of the parameter vector w_t is bounded. In other words, hypothesis (5.3) guarantees that the parameters will be confined in a bounded region containing the origin.

This confinement property means that all continuous functions of w_t are bounded (we assume of course that the parameter space has finite dimension). This include w_t^2, $\mathbf{E_z}(H(\mathbf{z}, w))^2$ and all the derivatives of the cost function $C(w_t)$. In the rest of this section, positive constants K_1, K_2, etc... are introduced whenever such a bound is used.

5.3   Convergence of Online Algorithms (General Case)

We now proceed with the analysis of the general online gradient algorithm.
Step a. We define the following criterion:

$$h_t \overset{\triangle}{=} C(w_t) \geq 0 \tag{5.11}$$

Step b. We can then bound the variations of the criterion h_t using a first order Taylor expansion and bounding the second derivatives with K_1.

$$|h_{t+1} - h_t + 2\gamma_t H(\mathbf{z}, w_t)\nabla_w C(w_t)| \leq \gamma_t^2 H(\mathbf{z}, w_t)^2 K_1 \quad \text{a.s.} \tag{5.12}$$

This inequality can be rewritten as:

$$h_{t+1} - h_t \leq -2\gamma_t H(\mathbf{z}, w_t)\nabla_w C(w_t) + \gamma_t^2 H(\mathbf{z}, w_t)^2 K_1 \quad \text{a.s.} \tag{5.13}$$

We now take the conditional expectation using (2.7):

$$\mathbf{E}\left(h_{t+1} - h_t \mid \mathcal{P}_t\right) \leq -2\gamma_t (\nabla_w C(w_t))^2 + \gamma_t^2 \mathbf{E_z}(H(\mathbf{z}, w_t))K_1 \tag{5.14}$$

This result leads to the following bound:

$$\mathbf{E}\left(h_{t+1} - h_t \mid \mathcal{P}_t\right) \leq \gamma_t^2 K_2 K_1 \tag{5.15}$$

The positive expected variations of h_t are then bounded by

$$\mathbf{E}(\delta_t\,(h_{t+1}-h_t)) = \mathbf{E}(\delta_t\,\mathbf{E}\,(h_{t+1}-h_t\,|\,\mathcal{P}_t)) \leq \gamma_t^2 K_2 K_1 \qquad (5.16)$$

Since this bound is the summand of a convergent infinite sum, theorem (4.30) implies that $h_t = C(w_t)$ converges almost surely.

$$C(w_t) \xrightarrow[t\to\infty]{a.s} C_\infty \qquad (5.17)$$

Step c. The last step of the proof departs from the convex case. Proving that $C(w_t)$ converges to zero would be a very strong result, equivalent to proving the convergence to the global minimum. We can however prove that the gradient $\nabla_w C(w_t)$ converges to zero almost surely.

By taking the expectation of (5.14) and summing on $t = 1\ldots\infty$, we see that the convergence of $C(w_t)$ implies the convergence of the following infinite sum:

$$\sum_{t=1}^{\infty} \gamma_t (\nabla_w C(w_t))^2 < \infty \quad \text{a.s} \qquad (5.18)$$

This convergence does not imply yet that the squared gradient $\nabla_w C(w_t)$ converges. We now define a second criterion:

$$g_t \overset{\triangle}{=} (\nabla_w C(w_t))^2 \qquad (5.19)$$

The variations of g_t are easily bounded using the Taylor expansion procedure demonstrated for the variations of h_t.

$$g_{t+1} - g_t \leq -2\gamma_t H(\mathbf{z}, w) \nabla_w^2 C(w_t) \nabla_w C(w_t) + \gamma_t^2 (H(\mathbf{z}, w)^2 K_3 \quad \text{a.s.} \qquad (5.20)$$

Taking the conditional expectation and bounding the second derivatives by K_4:

$$\mathbf{E}\,(g_{t+1} - g_t\,|\,\mathcal{P}_t) \leq 2\gamma_t (\nabla_w C(w_t))^2 K_4 + \gamma_t^2 K_2 K_3 \qquad (5.21)$$

We can then bound the positive expected variations of g_t:

$$\mathbf{E}(\delta_t(g_{t+1}-g_t)) = \mathbf{E}(\delta_t \mathbf{E}\,(g_{t+1}-g_t\,|\,\mathcal{P}_t))$$
$$\leq \gamma_t (\nabla_w C(w_t))^2 K_4 + \gamma_t^2 K_2 K_3 \qquad (5.22)$$

The two terms on the right hand side are the summands of convergent infinite sums (5.18) and (5.1). Theorem (4.30) then implies that g_t converges almost surely. Result (5.18) implies that this limit must be zero.

$$g_t \xrightarrow[t\to\infty]{a.s} 0 \quad \text{and} \quad \nabla_w C(w_t) \xrightarrow[t\to\infty]{a.s} 0 \qquad (5.23)$$

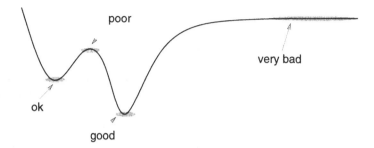

Figure 8: Extremal points include global and local minima. They also include poor solutions like saddle points and asymptotic plateaus. Every user of multi-layer network training algorithms is well aware of these possibilities.

5.4 Convergence to the Extremal Points

Let us summarize the convergence results obtained for the general gradient descent algorithm (section 2.3). These results are based on the five hypotheses presented in section 5.1.

i) The parameter vectors w_t are *confined* with probability 1 in a bounded region of the parameter space. This result essentially is consequence of hypothesis (5.3).

ii) The cost function $C(w_t)$ converges almost surely.

$$C(w_t) \xrightarrow[t \to \infty]{a.s.} C_\infty$$

iii) The gradient $\nabla_w C(w_t)$ converges almost surely to 0.

$$\nabla_w C(w_t) \xrightarrow[t \to \infty]{a.s.} 0$$

The convergence of the gradient is the most informative result. Figure 8 shows several regions in which the gradient goes to zero. These regions include local minima, saddle points, local maxima and plateaus.

The confinement result prevents the parameter vector w_t to diverge on an asymptotic plateau. Experience shows that hypothesis (5.3) is very significant. It is well known indeed that such a divergence occurs easily when the desired outputs of a multi-layer network are equal to the asymptotes of the sigmoid.

Saddle points and local maxima are usually unstable solutions. A small isotropic noise in the algorithm convergence can move the parameter vector away. We cannot however discard these solutions because it is easy to construct cases where the stochastic noise introduced by the online gradient descent procedure is not sufficient because it is not isotropic.

This *convergence to the extremal points* concludes our discussion.

6   Conclusion

The online learning framework presented in this document addresses a significant subset of the online learning algorithms, including, but not limited to, adaline, perceptron, multi-layer networks, k-means, learning vector quantization, and Kalman style algorithms. This formalism provides a clear statement of the goal of the learning procedure. It includes provisions for handling non-differentiable cost functions and quasi-Newton algorithms.

General convergence results are based on the theory of stochastic approximations. The main results address the convergence to the minimum of a convex cost function, and the convergence to the extremal points of a general cost function. The final convergence speed of online learning algorithm is amenable to a theoretical analysis using the same tools. The possibility of analyzing long range convergence speed, as achieved in restricted cases (Saad and Solla, 1996), remains an open question.

Acknowledgements
I am very grateful to both Vladimir Vapnik and Yoshua Bengio. Their comments and suggestions resulted in many improvements to this document.

References

Amari, S. (1967). A theory of adaptive pattern classifiers. *IEEE Trans.*, EC-16, 299–307.

Becker, S. and LeCun, Y.(1989). Improving the Convergence of Back-Propagation Learning with Second-Order Methods. In Touretzky, D., Hinton, G., and Sejnowski, T., editors, *Proceedings of the 1988 Connectionist Models Summer School*, pages 29–37, San Mateo. Morgan Kaufman.

Benveniste, A., Metivier, M., and Priouret, P.(1990). *Adaptive Algorithms and Stochastic Approximations*. Springer Verlag, Berlin, New York.

Bottou, L. (1991). *Une Approche théorique de l'Apprentissage Connexionniste: Applications à la Reconnaissance de la Parole*. PhD thesis, Université de Paris XI, Orsay, France.

Bottou, L. and Bengio, Y. (1995). Convergence Properties of the KMeans Algorithm. In *Advances in Neural Information Processing Systems*, volume 7, Denver. MIT Press.

Dennis, J. and Schnabel, R. B. (1983). *Numerical Methods For Unconstrained Optimization and Nonlinear Equations*. Prentice-Hall, Inc., Englewood Cliffs, New Jersey.

Fisk, D. (1965). Quasi-martingales. *Transactions of the American Mathematical Society*, (120), 359–388.

Gladyshev, E.(1965). On stochastic approximations. *Theory of Probability and its Applications*, 10, 275–278.

Hebb, D. O.(1949). *The Organization of Behavior*. Wiley, New York.

Kohonen, T. (1982). Self-Organized Formation of Topologically Correct Feature Maps. *Biological Cybernetics*, 43, 59–69.

Kohonen, T., Barna, G., and Chrisley, R. (1988). Statistical pattern recognition with neural network: Benchmarking studies. In *Proceedings of the IEEE Second International Conference on Neural Networks*, volume 1, pages 61–68, San Diego.

Krasovskii, A. A. (1963). *Dynamic of continuous self-organizing systems*. Fizmatgiz, Moscow. (in russian).

Kushner, H. J. and Clark, D. S. (1978). Stochastic Approximation for Constrained and Unconstrained Systems. *Applied Math. Sci.* 26. Springer Verlag, Berlin, New York.

LeCun, Y., Boser, B., Denker, J. S., Henderson, D., Howard, R. E., Hubbard, W., and Jackel, L. D. (1989). Backpropagation Applied to Handwritten Zip Code Recognition. *Neural Computation*, 1, 541–551.

Ljung, L. and Söderström, T.(1983). *Theory and Practice of recursive identification*. MIT Press, Cambridge, MA.

MacQueen, J. (1967). Some Methods for Classification and Analysis of Multivariate Observations. In LeCam, L. M. and Neyman, J., editors, *Proceedings of the Fifth Berkeley Symposium on Mathematics, Statistics, and Probabilities*, volume 1, pages 281–297, Berkeley and Los Angeles, (Calif). University of California Press.

Mendel, J. M. and Fu, K. S. (1970). *Adaptive, Learning, and Pattern Recognition Systems: Theory and Applications*. Academic Press, New York.

Metivier, M. (1981). Martingale et convergence p.s. d'algorithmes stochastiques. In *Outils et modèles mathématiques pour l'automatique et le traitement du signal*, volume 1, pages 529–552. Editions du CNRS, Paris, France.

Metivier, M. (1983). *Semi-Martingales*. Walter de Gruyter, Berlin.

Minsky, M. and Papert, S. (1969). *Perceptrons*. MIT Press, Cambridge, MA.

Müller, U., Gunzinger, A., and Guggenbühl, W. (1995). Fast neural net simulation with a DSP processor array. *IEEE Trans.*, NN-6, 203–213.

Robbins, H. and Monro, S.(1951). A Stochastic Approximation Model. *Ann. Math. Stat.*, 22, 400–407.

Rosenblatt, F.(1957). The Perceptron: A perceiving and recognizing automaton. *Technical Report* 85-460-1, Project PARA, Cornell Aeronautical Lab.

Rumelhart, D. E., Hinton, G. E., and Williams, R. J. (1986). Learning internal representations by error propagation. In *Parallel distributed processing: Explorations in the microstructure of cognition*, volume I, pages 318–362. Bradford Books, Cambridge, MA.

Saad, D. and Solla, S. A. (1996). Dynamics of On-Line Gradient Descent Learning for Multilayer Neural Networks. In Touretzky, D. S., Mozer, M. C., and Hasselmo, M. E., editors, *Advances in Neural Information Processing Systems*, volume 8, pages 302–308, Cambridge, MA. MIT Press.

Schumann, M. and Retzko, R. (1995). Self Organizing Maps for Vehicle Routing Problems - minimizing an explicit cost function. In Fogelman-Soulié, F. and Gallinari, P., editors, *Proc. ICANN'95, Int. Conf. on Artificial Neural Networks*, volume II, pages 401–406, Nanterre, France. EC2.

Tsypkin, Y. (1971). *Adaptation and Learning in automatic systems*. Academic Press, New York.

Tsypkin, Y. (1973). *Foundations of the theory of learning systems*. Academic Press, New York.

Vapnik, V. N. (1982). *Estimation of dependences based on empirical data*. Springer Series in Statistics. Springer Verlag, Berlin, New York.

Vapnik, V. N. (1995). *The Nature of Statistical Learning Theory*. Springer Verlag, Berlin, New York.

Widrow, B. and Hoff, M. E. (1960). Adaptive switching circuits. In *IRE WESCON Conv. Record, Part 4.*, pages 96–104.

Widrow, B. and Stearns, S. D. (1985). *Adaptive Signal Processing*. Prentice-Hall.

Exact and Perturbation Solutions for the Ensemble Dynamics

Todd K. Leen

Dept. of Computer Science and Engineering and
Dept. of Electrical and Computer Engineering
Oregon Graduate Institute of Science & Technology P.O. Box 91000
Portland, Oregon, USA.
tleen@cse.ogi.edu

Abstract

This paper presents two approaches to characterize the dynamics of weight space probability density starting from a master equation. In the first, we provide a class of algorithms for which an exact evaluation of the integrals in the master equation is possible. This enables the time evolution of the density to be calculated at each time step *without approximation*. In the second, we expand earlier work on the small noise expansion to a complete perturbation framework. As an example application, we give a perturbative solution for the equilibrium density for the LMS algorithm. Finally, we use the perturbation framework to review annealed learning with schedules of the form $\mu(t) = \mu_0/t^p$.

1 Introduction

Several of the contributions to this volume apply order parameter techniques to describe the dynamics of on-line learning. In these approaches, the description assumes the form of a set of ordinary differential equations that describe the motion of macroscopic quantities, the order parameters, from which observables such as generalization error can be computed directly, without intermediate averaging. The (typically non-linear) differential equations are usually solved numerically to provide the dynamics throughout the training. Recently, this author and colleagues have obtained analytic results from the order parameter equations applied to the late time (asymptotic) convergence of annealed learning (Leen, Schottky and Saad, 1998). However, most of the application of these techniques has involved numerical integration. Indeed, the ability to track the ensemble dynamics at all times by solution of ordinary differential equations establishes an attractive analysis tool.

In contrast, this paper examines analytic approaches to the master equation that describes the dynamics of the weight space probability density in time. These dynamics are expressed as partial differential equations, of infinite order, that do not ordinarily admit simple numerical solution. Instead, one identifies useful approximations and uses the equations in the applicable domain. These approaches have proved most valuable to describe learning with very small learning rates and for asymptotic phenomena such as equilibrium distributions (Heskes and Kappen, 1991; Heskes, 1993) and the late-time behavior of annealed learning (Leen and Orr, 1994), though there has been some application to describe transients as well (Radons, Schuster and Werner, 1990; Heskes, Slijpen and Kappen, 1992; Orr and Leen, 1993).

Here we develop this approach in two ways. First, we identify a class of algorithms, and a particular case of interest, for which the integrals appearing in the master equation can be solved in closed form. This provides an *exact*, closed form expression for the operator that generates the time displacements of the system. This does not imply that the density is available analytically at each time step, but rather that it can be calculated (numerically perhaps) *without approximation* by simple matrix multiplication. The solution for the density as a function of time does not rely on numerical integration of any kind, and is given without approximation.

Secondly, we develop a perturbation expansion for solutions of the master equation. Here the weight space density is expressed directly as a power series in the learning rate. At each power (order of perturbation theory), one solves a set of partial differential equations to obtain the density to that order. This framework includes, as a special case, earlier work that treated only the lowest order contribution without consideration of how they fit into a perturbation scheme. We also adopt the perturbation scheme to treat annealed learning with rates of the form μ_0/t^p, $0 < p \leq 1$. Retaining the leading terms, we recover the classic asymptotic normality results on $1/t$ annealing, and analogous, though markedly different, results $p \neq 1$.

2   Ensemble Dynamics

Our starting point is learning rules of the form

$$w(n+1) \;=\; w(n) \;+\; \mu(n)\, Q(w(n), x(n)) \tag{2.1}$$

where $w(n)$ and $\mu(n)$ are the weight estimate and learning rate (gain) at time n, $x(n)$ is the datum input to the algorithm at time n, and $Q(w, x)$ is the parameter update function. We assume that the input, which may be an input/target pair in the case of supervised learning, is drawn i.i.d from the distribution $p(x)$[1]

---

[1]The interesting case of correlated inputs is discussed in (Wiegerrinckand and Heskes, 1994).

In stochastic *gradient descent* algorithms, the update function $Q(w(n), x)$ is minus the gradient of the instantaneous cost $E(w, x)$. The ensemble average of the instantaneous cost is the *true* cost $E(w)$. The latter drives the corresponding deterministic, or batch-mode, gradient descent algorithm.

The learning rate μ may be independent of time, or it may follow a specified time-dependence, or may change in time in response to the progress of the learning (Venter, 1967; Darken and Moody, 1992; Murata et al., 1997). Constant learning rates are commonly employed during the initial phases (and sometimes through all phases) of stochastic learning algorithms. Constant μ allows the system to converge on local optima at rates comparable to the equivalent batch algorithm (e.g. exponential convergence in quadratic minima). However, most problems require that the learning rate be annealed at late times in order to obtain convergence (in mean square, or with probability one) to a local optima. The learning rate may be either scalar, or matrix. Though the former is simpler and far more commonly implemented, optimal convergence rates require consideration of *matrix* learning rates as for example in (Leen and Orr, 1994; Orr and Leen, 1997; Yang and Amari, 1998).

Our goal is to describe the describe the ensemble dynamics of w in terms of an evolving probability distribution $P(w, n)$ on the weights. Towards this end, we develop a master equation for $P(w, n)$ from the learning rule (2.1). The first step is to recognize the that single-step transition probability, conditioned on the datum x is a Dirac delta function whose arguments satisfy the learning rule (2.1)

$$T(w|w', x, n) = \delta(w - w' - \mu(n) Q(w', x)) \ . \tag{2.2}$$

We recover the net transition probability by integrating the conditional transition probability over the measure on the input data[2] x

$$\begin{aligned} T(w|w', n) &= \int \rho(x) T(w|w', x, n) \, dx \\ &\equiv \langle \delta (w - w' - \mu(n)Q(w', x)) \rangle_x \ . \end{aligned} \tag{2.3}$$

Finally, the transition probability provides a *Master equation* that describes the dynamics of the density on w

$$\begin{aligned} P(w, n+1) &= \int dw' \ T(w|w', n) \, P(w', n) \\ &= \int dw' \, dx \, \rho(x) \, \delta(w - w' - \mu(n)Q(w', x)) \, P(w', n) \end{aligned} \tag{2.4}$$

This provides a complete description of the ensemble dynamics of the learning rule (2.1) including: generalization, equilibrium distributions, convergence with annealed learning $\mu(n)$, and escape from local optima. Unfortunately, for

---

[2]We assume that the data x are sampled i.i.d. from the density $\rho(x)$. Experimentally, this corresponds to random sampling *with replacement* from a training dataset.

most learning rules of interest, we cannot evaluate the integral on the right
hand side in closed form. Thus approximation schemes are usually required.

We proceed in two ways. First we will give a family of algorithms, and
a particular example of interest, for which the integral can be complete in
closed form, and hence the time evolution specified exactly. Since the integral
moves the probability density forward one step in time, it can be regarded
as the operator that generates time displacements. Hence we refer to this
as an exact integration of the time evolution operator. Following the exact
solution, we will discuss approximations to the integral in (2.4) coupled with
perturbation solutions for $P(w, n)$ that give approximate analytic solutions.

3   Exact Integration of the Time Evolution Operator

A class of algorithms for which the transition probability (2.3) assumes a
simple, closed form can be constructed with reasonable constraints. Although
the constraints may seem unnatural at first, a bit later we will give a concrete
example that was suggested independently in a very natural way.

Suppose that the learning rate μ is constant in time. Further, suppose that
the update function $Q(w', x)$ is such that for any w', $Q(w', x)$ is *piecewise
constant in x*, and can only assume a *finite number* of possible values. We
denote the values that Q assumes by q_i, $i = 1 \ldots m$ and the sets on which Q
attains these values by $S_i(w')$

$$S_i(w') \;=\; \{\, x \,|\, Q(w', x) = q_i \,\} \;\;. \tag{3.1}$$

We denote the data measure associated with each of these sets by f_i

$$f_i(w') \;\equiv\; \int_{S_i(w')} \rho(x)\, dx \;\;. \tag{3.2}$$

With this construction, the transition probability (2.3) reduces to a weighted
sum of delta functions

$$T(w \,|\, w') \;=\; \sum_{i=1}^{m} f_i(w')\, \delta(w - w' - \mu\, q_i) \tag{3.3}$$

and the right-hand side of the master equation (2.4) integrates simply to

$$P(w, n+1) \;=\; \sum_{i=1}^{m} P(w - \mu\, q_i, n)\, f_i(w - \mu\, q_i) \;\;. \tag{3.4}$$

Equation (3.4) generates the dynamics of the $P(w, n)$ without approximation. It provides, for example, a means to numerically compute the evolution

of the density *exactly*, provided numerical values of the measures f_i are available. The expression tells us to compute the density at w at time step $n + 1$ by locating the points $w - \mu\, q_i$ that can jump to the point w in one time step, and accumulate the densities at those points, each weighted by the f_i. The latter is just the probability that one chooses an x that generates the required jump q_i.

3.1 An Example: Sign-of-the-Gradient Descent

Most commonly used algorithms are some variant of stochastic gradient descent; for which the update $Q(w, x)$ is minus the gradient of an instantaneous cost function

$$Q(w, x) = -\nabla_w E(w, x) \ .$$

If instead, we base the update on the *sign* of the gradient, we retrieve a simple algorithm that is a member of our class of algorithms with integrable time-evolution operator. There are two variants, one of which we briefly describe here. A more thorough development is in (Leen and Moody, 1997).

The algorithm proceeds as follows. At each time step, select a single weight at random (with equal probability of selecting any weight) and update it according to the sign of the instantaneous gradient

$$Q_j(w, x) = -\xi_j \operatorname{sign}\left[\frac{\partial E(w, x)}{\partial w_j}\right] \tag{3.5}$$

where $\xi_j \in \{0, 1\}$ are indicator variables that denote which weight is chosen for updating.

For this system, $q_i = 0, \pm 1$. For a system of N weights, one finds

$$
\begin{aligned}
P(w, n+1) - P(w, n) &= -\frac{1}{2N} \sum_{j=1}^{N} \left[D_j^{(1)}(w + \mu_j)\, P(w + \mu_j, n) \right. \\
&\qquad\qquad \left. - D_j^{(1)}(w - \mu_j)\, P(w - \mu_j, n) \right] \\
&\quad + \frac{1}{2N} \sum_{j=1}^{N} \left[D_{jj}^{(2)}(w + \mu_j)\, P(w + u_j, n) \right. \\
&\qquad\qquad - 2 D_{jj}^{(2)}(w)\, P(w, n) \\
&\qquad\qquad \left. + D_{jj}^{(2)}(w - \mu_j)\, P(w - \mu_j, n) \right] \tag{3.6}
\end{aligned}
$$

Here we have rewritten the terms in f_i in terms of the drift vector

$$D_j^{(1)}(w) = N \left\langle \xi_j\, Q_j(w, x) \right\rangle_{x, \xi}$$

and diagonal terms of the diffusion matrix

$$D_{jk}^{(2)}(w) = N \left\langle \xi_j \xi_k\, Q_j(w, x)\, Q_k(w, x) \right\rangle_{x, \xi}$$

whose relation to the f_i for this problem are given in (Leen and Moody, 1997), and can be easily derived from (3.5). The quantity μ_j in (3.6) is a displacement of length μ along the jth weight coordinate.

The system (3.6) is of the form of a finite difference approximation to a Fokker-Planck equation. However, the equation describes the dynamics to all orders, without approximation. There are several interesting features. With proper initialization, the dynamics can be developed by simple matrix multiplication. Suppose that the initial density $P(w, 0)$ is non-zero *only* at weight values corresponding to integer multiples of μ_j, $w = (i_1 \mu_1, i_2 \mu_2, \ldots)^T$. Then, since at each iteration weights only change by $\pm\mu_j$ or zero, the density $P(w, n)$ at any time step n will have support only at weight values that are integer multiples of μ_j. Thus, the density is confined to a *rectangular grid* with spacings μ_j along the w_j axis. The dynamics is generated simply by matrix multiplication. One forms a vector $P(n)$ whose entries consist of the densities $P(w, n)$ at the grid points, and a matrix A whose entries contain the coefficients of the density in equation (3.6). The evolution of the ensemble density is then given by

$$P(n+1) = (1 + A)\,P(n) = (1+A)^{n+1}\,P(0) \ .$$

The evolution matrix $1 + A$ is sparse, since the learning rule only connects nearest neighbor points on the weight grid. For a one-dimensional configuration space, the evolution matrix $1 + A$ is tri-diagonal, and the computation is particularly easy to set up and execute. Equilibrium distributions correspond to the null space of A, and first passage time calculations reduce to the solution of a linear system.

Also of interest are problems with trapping states; values of w for which $Q(w_*, x) = \nabla_w E(w_*, x) = 0$ for *all possible* x. One example is regression problems with noiseless targets generated by a function that can be exactly fit by the network. In general, there are several such states that we denote by $w_*^{[i]}, i = 1, \ldots, p$. It is straightforward to verify that the master equation (2.4) has equilibria consisting of Dirac delta functions at the $w_*^{[i]}$

$$P_{eq}(w) = \sum_{i=1}^{p} a_i \delta(w - w_*^{[i]})$$

where the occupation probabilities a_i for each solution weight are determined by the initial distribution $P(w, 0)$.

Under standard stochastic gradient descent, the system will converge into the set of optima $w_*^{[i]}$. For learning driven by the sign of the gradient, these solutions are only accessible if they all fall on the weight grid with spacings μ_j, and if all the initial density also lies on this grid. If this is *not* the case, then instead of convergence to these solution weights, the density will, at late times, execute oscillations between the grid states neighboring the $w_*^{[i]}$.

Finally, we point out that in most problems, such trapping states are *not* present. In order to achieve convergence of the weights in the usual stochastic gradient descent, one must anneal the learning rate. In sign of the gradient learning, annealing corresponds to shrinking the grid size.

4 Perturbation Approach

In physics, it is common to approach a problem for which a closed solution cannot be found by treating it as a perturbation of a similar problem that one *can* solve in closed form. The attempt to analytically describe the ensemble dynamics of on-line learning algorithms fits this paradigm well.

Gardiner (Gardiner, 1990) describes a small noise perturbation approach for diffusion (Fokker-Planck) systems. Our development here is similar in form, but appropriately modified for the master equation we encounter in stochastic learning. The material here extends the basic small-noise expansion introduced by Heskes (Heskes, 1993) in two ways. First, we emphasize that the combination of Heskes' small noise expansion with a perturbation expansion for $P(w, n)$ is a natural structure that incorporates the now-familiar Gaussian solutions as the lowest-order term in a series expansion. This series is closely related to the Edgeworth and Gram-Charlier expansions of classical statistics (Kendall and Stuart, 1977). Secondly, we extend the treatment in a minor way to accommodate fixed-schedule learning rate annealing.

Our starting point is the continuous time Kramers-Moyal (Gardiner, 1990, for example) expansion of the master equation (2.4). This is obtained by expanding the transition probability (2.3) in a Taylor series in the learning rate μ. We also change from integer to continuous time, but gloss over the intricacies of the transition, referring the interested reader to (Heskes, 1993)) Furthermore, as appropriate to most annealed learning algorithms, we restrict the form of $\mu(t)$ to a simple power law $\mu(t) = \mu_0/t^p$. One finds (in one dimension for notational simplicity)

$$\partial_t P(w, t) = \sum_{k=1}^{\infty} \frac{(-1)^k}{k!} \left(\frac{\mu_0}{t^p}\right)^k \partial_w^k \left(\left\langle Q^k(w, x)\right\rangle_x P(w, n)\right) , \quad (4.1)$$

where ∂_t denotes the partial derivative with respect to time, and ∂_w^k denotes the kth partial derivatives with respect to w. Next we decompose the trajectory $w(t)$ into a deterministic piece and a stochastic piece

$$w \equiv \phi(t) + \mu_0^\gamma f(t) \xi \quad \text{or} \quad \xi = \left(\frac{1}{\mu_0^\gamma f(t)}\right) (w - \phi(t)) \quad (4.2)$$

where $\phi(t)$ is the deterministic trajectory and ξ are the fluctuations. Apart from the factor $\mu_0^\gamma f(t)$ that scales the fluctuations, this is identical to Heskes' formulation for constant learning in (Heskes, 1993). We will obtain the proper value for the unspecified exponent γ, and the form of the function $f(t)$ from homogeneity requirements.

Next, the dependence of the jump moments $\langle Q^i(w,x)\rangle_x$ on μ_0 is explicated
by a Taylor series expansion about the deterministic path ϕ. The coefficients
in this series expansion are denoted

$$\alpha_i^{(j)} \equiv \left.\frac{\partial^j \langle Q^i(w,x)\rangle_x}{\partial w^j}\right|_{w=\phi} \;.$$

For convenience, we define a new time variable

$$s = t$$

and transform the differential operators and densities in (4.1) as dictated by
(4.2)

$$\partial_t = \partial_s - \frac{1}{\mu_0^\gamma f(s)}\frac{d\phi(s)}{ds}\partial_\xi - \left(\frac{f'}{f}\right)\xi\partial_\xi$$

$$\partial_w = \frac{1}{\mu_0^\gamma f(s)}\partial_\xi$$

$$P(w,t) = (\mu_0^\gamma f(s))^{-1}\,\Pi(\xi,s)\;, \tag{4.3}$$

where $\Pi(\xi,s)$ is the density of the fluctuations.

Finally, we rewrite (4.1) in terms of ϕ and ξ and the expansion of the
jump moments, using the transformations (4.3), and suitably resumming the
series. These transformations leave equations of motion for the deterministic
trajectory $\phi(s)$ and the density of the fluctuations

$$\frac{d\phi}{ds} = \left(\frac{\mu_0}{s^p}\right)\alpha_1^{(0)}(\phi) = \left(\frac{\mu_0}{s^p}\right)\langle Q(\phi,x)\rangle_x \tag{4.4}$$

$$\partial_s\Pi = \left(\frac{f'}{f}\right)\partial_\xi(\xi\Pi)$$
$$+ \sum_{m=2}^\infty\sum_{i=1}^m \frac{(-1)^i}{i!(m-i)!}\alpha_i^{(m-i)}\frac{\mu_0^{i(1-2\gamma)+m\gamma}}{s^{ip}}\,f(s)^{m-2i}\,\partial_\xi^i(\xi^{(m-i)}\Pi)\;. \tag{4.5}$$

This last is the basic form that we use in developing the perturbation expansion.

We are going to use the system (4.4) and (4.5) to describe the late-time
evolution of learning systems with either small, constant learning rate, or with
annealed learning rate. In either case, we will concentrate on the behavior near
asymptotically stable fixed points w_* of the vector field $\langle Q(w,x)\rangle_x$. Thus we
are assuming that the system has evolved long enough so that $\phi \to w_*$ and
we can evaluate the $\alpha_i^{(j)}$ at the local optimum. We assume that we have
$\alpha_1^{(1)} < 0$ in a neighborhood of w_*, i.e. that the linearization is non-zero[3]. For

---

[3]In the multi-dimensional case, all of the eigenvalues of the matrix $\alpha_1^{(1)}$ should have
negative real part.

a gradient descent algorithm, this corresponds to a *quadratic minimum* w_*, with positive-definite cost function curvature

$$H = -\nabla_w \nabla_w E(w_*) = -\alpha_1^{(1)}(w_*) \ .$$

With this structure assumed for the vector field in the vicinity of the fixed point w_*, we can proceed to specify the constant γ and the form of $f(s)$. To insure that for each m, the terms in the sum over i in (4.5) are homogeneous in powers of μ_0, we take

$$\gamma = 1/2 \ . \tag{4.6}$$

Similarly, to insure that for each value of m, the terms in the sum over i are homogeneous in time, we take

$$f(s) = \frac{1}{s^{p/2}} \ . \tag{4.7}$$

4.1 Perturbation Expansion for Constant Learning Rate

For constant learning rate, $p = 0$, we rescale time as $\mu_0 s \equiv t$ and rewrite the equation of motion for the fluctuations as

$$\partial_t \Pi = \left(L_0 + \mu_0^{1/2} L_1 + \mu_0^1 L_2 + \ldots \right) \Pi(\xi, t) = \sum_{i=0}^{\infty} \mu^{i/2} L_i \Pi(\xi, t) \tag{4.8}$$

where the action of the operators L_i are defined by the expansion (4.5) with the choice for γ (4.6 and $f(s)$ (4.7), and the time re-scaling above. The action of the first several operators are

$$L_0 F(\xi) \equiv -\partial_\xi(\alpha_1^{(1)} \xi F) + \frac{1}{2}\alpha_2^{(0)}\partial_\xi^2 F \tag{4.9}$$

$$L_1 F(\xi) \equiv -\frac{1}{2}\alpha_1^{(2)} \partial_\xi(\xi^2 F) + \frac{1}{2}\alpha_2^{(1)}\partial_\xi^2(\xi F) - \frac{1}{3!}\alpha_3^{(0)}\partial_\xi^3 F \tag{4.10}$$

$$\vdots$$

In the limit $\mu_0 \to 0$ only the L_0 term of (4.8) contributes. By evaluating the drift $\alpha_1^{(1)}$ and diffusion $\alpha_2^{(0)}$ at a local optimum w_*, (4.8) describes the time evolution of the fluctuation density about the local optimum, in the limit of small learning rate. Solving this lowest order piece for the equilibrium density gives the now-familiar Gaussian approximation to the asymptotic density. However, this is only a piece of the picture.

The lowest-order solution can be augmented by a perturbation expansion for the density. We write

$$\Pi(\xi, t) \equiv \Pi^{(0)} + \mu^{1/2}\Pi^{(1)} + \mu^1\Pi^{(2)} + \mu^{3/2}\Pi^{(3)} + \ldots \tag{4.11}$$

where the $\Pi^{(i)}$ are functions to be solved for. Next, we substitute this expansion of Π into the equation of motion (4.8) and equate the coefficients of like powers of μ on the left and right-hand sides. This leaves the set of perturbation equations

$$\partial_t \Pi^{(0)} = L_0 \Pi^{(0)} \tag{4.12}$$
$$\partial_t \Pi^{(1)} = L_0 \Pi^{(1)} + L_1 \Pi^{(0)} \tag{4.13}$$
$$\partial_t \Pi^{(2)} = L_0 \Pi^{(2)} + L_1 \Pi^{(1)} + L_2 \Pi^{(0)} \tag{4.14}$$

$$\vdots$$

The solution strategy is to solve (4.12) for $\Pi^{(0)}$, use this solution in (4.13) and solve the latter for $\Pi^{(1)}$, then use these two solutions to solve (4.14) for $\Pi^{(2)}$ etc. Thus, we solve the equations order-by-order in perturbation, obtaining approximations to Π in powers of $\mu^{1/2}$. Below we briefly describe how this is accomplished.

4.1.1   Solving the Perturbation Equations

Solution of the system (4.12), (4.13), etc relies on obtaining a complete set of eigenfunctions of the operator L_0

$$L_0 f_n = \lambda_n f_n$$

and its conjugate

$$L_0^\dagger g_n = \lambda_n g_n \ .$$

These functions form a bi-orthogonal set

$$\int g_k(\xi) f_j(\xi) \, d\xi \equiv = (g_k, f_j) = \delta_{ij} \ . \tag{4.15}$$

The operator L_0 corresponds to an Ornstein-Uhlenbeck process and has well-known eigenfunctions (Gardiner, 1990) (recall our constraint $\alpha_1^{(1)} < 0$)

$$f_n(\xi) = \sqrt{\frac{|\alpha_1^{(1)}|}{\pi \alpha_2^{(0)}}} \exp\left(-\frac{|\alpha_1^{(1)}|}{\alpha_2^{(0)}} \xi^2\right) g_n(\xi)$$

$$g_n(\xi) = \frac{1}{\sqrt{2^n n!}} H_n\left(\sqrt{\frac{|\alpha_1^{(1)}|}{\alpha_2^{(0)}}} \xi\right)$$

$$\lambda_n = n|\alpha_1^{(1)}|, \quad n = 0, 1, 2, \ldots \tag{4.16}$$

with H_n the nth order Hermite polynomials

It is trivial to verify that the solution of the lowest order equation (4.12) is

$$\Pi^{(0)}(\xi, t) = \sum_{n=0}^{\infty} a_n \exp(-\lambda_n t) f_n(\xi) \ ,$$

where the coefficients a_n are determined by the initial distribution. Hence as $t \to \infty$, $\Pi^{(0)}$ converges to $f_0(\xi)$ which is a zero mean Gaussian equilibrium distribution with variance $\sigma_\xi^2 = \alpha_2^{(0)}/(2|\alpha_1^{(1)}|)$. Hence the lowest order approximation to the equilibrium distribution on w is a Gaussian peaked up about the local optimum w_* with variance $\sigma_w^2 = \mu \alpha_2^{(0)}/(2|\alpha_1^{(1)}|)$.

The higher order corrections to the equilibrium density can be calculated using (4.13), (4.14) etc. with the left-hand sides set to zero. We expand each perturbation correction $\Pi^{(i)}$ in the basis of eigenfunctions f_n

$$\Pi^{(i)}(\xi) \equiv \sum_{j=0}^{\infty} \gamma_j^{(i)} f_j(\xi) \ .$$

Thus, the perturbation expansion develops each $\Pi^{(i)}$, and thus the total solution Π, as a series of Hermite polynomials times Gaussians (the eigenfunctions f_n). In this respect, our perturbation expansion recalls the classical Edgeworth and Gram-Charlier expansions for density functions (Kendall and Stuart, 1977).

The coefficients $\gamma_j^{(i)}$ are obtained by substituting this assumed form of the solution into the appropriate equation of motion for the $\Pi^{(i)}$, and using the bi-orthogonality relation (4.15). For example, the first-order correction satisfies

$$L_0 \Pi^{(1)} = L_0 \sum_{i=1}^{\infty} \gamma_j^{(1)} f_j = -L_1 \Pi^{(0)} \ ,$$

or

$$\sum_{i=1}^{\infty} \gamma_j^{(1)} \lambda_j f_j = -L_1 \Pi^{(0)} \ .$$

Taking the inner product with g_k, we obtain

$$\gamma_k^{(1)} = -\frac{1}{\lambda_k} \left(g_k, L_1 \Pi^{(0)} \right), \quad k \neq 0 \ . \tag{4.17}$$

So the first order perturbation correction for the equilibrium density is

$$\Pi^{(1)} = \sum_{k=1}^{\infty} \frac{-1}{\lambda_k} \left(g_k, L_1 \Pi^{(0)} \right) f_k(\xi) \ . \tag{4.18}$$

Using this solution along with the equation for the second order correction (4.14), we obtain

$$\begin{aligned}
\Pi^{(2)} &= \sum_{i=1}^{\infty} \frac{-1}{\lambda_i} \left[(g_i, L_1 \Pi^{(1)}) + (g_i, L_2 \Pi^{(0)}) \right] f_i(\xi) \\
&= \sum_{i,j=1}^{\infty} \frac{(g_i, L_1 f_j)(g_j, L_1 \Pi^{(0)})}{\lambda_i \lambda_j} f_i(\xi) - \sum_{i=1}^{\infty} \frac{(g_i, L_2 \Pi^{(0)})}{\lambda_i} f_i(\xi)
\end{aligned} \tag{4.19}$$

Clearly, one can calculate the corrections to arbitrary order provided one can evaluate the appropriate matrix elements $(g_i, L_j f_k)$ of the perturbation operators. Given the corrections, the density is re-assembled according to (4.11).

4.1.2 LMS Equilibrium Density

To illustrate, we give examples of perturbation solutions for the equilibrium density $P_e(w)$ of a single weight, linear neuron trained by the LMS algorithm (stochastic gradient descent on the mean squared error). The target signals are generated by a linear teacher neuron with weight w_* and zero mean Gaussian noise with variance σ_{noise}^2 added to the output. The inputs were zero mean Gaussian with variance σ_x^2. The details of the calculations, and the results were originally presented in (Orr, 1996). The equilibrium density is given in terms of the weight error $v \equiv w - w_*$. One finds for the first few perturbative solutions

$$P_e^{(0)}(v) = \frac{1}{\sqrt{\pi\mu\sigma_{noise}^2}} \exp(-v^2/\mu\sigma_{noise}^2)$$

$$P_e^{(1)}(v) = \frac{3}{4}\sigma_x^2 \left(-1 + \frac{2v^2}{\mu\sigma_{noise}^2}\right) P_e^{(0)}(v)$$

$$P_e^{(2)}(v) = \frac{9}{32}\sigma_x^4 \left(-1 - \frac{4v^2}{\mu\sigma_{noise}^2} + \frac{4v^4}{\mu^2\sigma_{noise}^4}\right) P^{(0)} \ . \quad (4.20)$$

For comparison, we also include the equilibrium density obtained from the nonlinear Fokker-Planck equation obtained by truncating the Kramers-Moyal expansion (4.1) at second order in μ. This Fokker-Planck equation has a closed form equilibrium solution (Leen and Moody, 1993)

$$P_e^{FP}(v) = \frac{1}{B\left(1/2, 1/2 + 1/(3\mu\sigma_x^2)\right)} \left(1 + \frac{3\sigma_x^2}{\sigma_{noise}^2} v^2\right)^{-(1+\frac{1}{3\mu\sigma_x^2})} \quad (4.21)$$

where $B(\cdot, \cdot)$ is the Riemann beta function.

The solid curves in Figures 1 and 2 show the perturbation solution for the equilibrium densities obtained with input variance $\sigma_x^2 = 4$ and noise variance $\sigma_{noise}^2 = 1$ for learning rates $\mu = 0.05$ and $\mu = 0.1$ respectively. Also shown are empirical estimates of the densities obtained from Monte Carlo simulations (dashed curves). The density predicted by the Fokker-Planck equation (dotted curve from equation (4.21)) is more peaked than the empirical density.

For the smaller of the two learning rates depicted in figure 1, the first order perturbation solution (Fig. 1 b) fits the empirical density quite well, and offers a substantial improvement relative to the zero order (Gaussian) approximation (Fig. 1 a). At higher learning rate, as in figure 2, the first order perturbation solution fits less well, and adding the next non-zero order term $\Pi^{(4)}$ further degrades the fit. The reader should note that $\mu = 0.1$ is already quite high as, for this input variance level, the equilibrium density has finite covariance only for $\mu < 0.1666$. The failure of the perturbation expansion at relatively high learning rates is not unexpected; perturbation expansions in physics are often asymptotic rather than convergent, and this is likely to be the case here. Finally, we note that another approach to specifying the LMS equilibrium density is given by (Bershad and Qu, 1989).

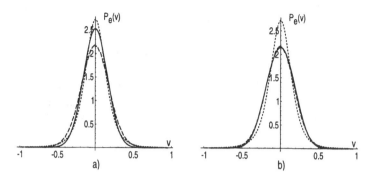

Figure 1: Comparision of equilibrium densities for 1-D LMS with $\mu = .05$, $\sigma_{noise} = 1$, $\sigma_x^2 = 4$. The dashed curves are the density estimated from an ensemble of simulations. The dotted curves are the density predicted from the Fokker-Planck equation obtained by truncating the Kramer-Moyal expansion (4.1). The solid curves are those obtained from the perturbation expansion. a) Using the 0th order approximation $\Pi^{(0)}$. b) Using terms through the 1st order correction.

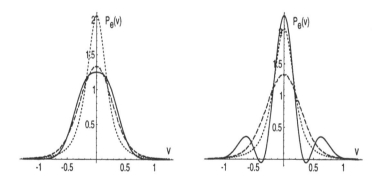

Figure 2: Same as figure 1, but with $\mu = 0.1$. a) Using terms through the first order correction $\Pi^{(1)}$. b) Using terms through the fourth order correction $\Pi^{(4)}$.

The perturbation technique, while discussed above for a one-dimensional problem, applies in principle to problems of arbitrary dimension. To carry out the program, one needs to be able to find eigenfunctions of the multidimensional operator L_0

$$L_0\, f(\xi) \;=\; \nabla_\xi \cdot \left(-\alpha_1^{(1)}\, \xi\, f(\xi) \right) \;+\; \frac{1}{2} \nabla_\xi \cdot \left(\alpha_2^{(0)}\, \nabla_\xi\, f(\xi) \right) \;=\; \lambda\, f(\xi) \;\; .$$

This will pose a technical difficulty unless one can find coordinates in which this partial differential equation is separable. Since the drift $\alpha_1^{(1)}$ and diffusion

$\alpha_2^{(0)}$ matrices may not be diagonalized by the same transformation – this may indeed be difficult.

There is, however, a class of problems for which these two matrices are simultaneously diagonalized by the same coordinate transformation. Fluctuations about the global optimum in supervised learning problems where the network is capable of representing the true regression function (so-called "realizable" problems) are treatable. In this case, using the negative log-likelihood of the data as a cost function, one finds that the drift and diffusion matrices are scalar multiples of one-another. In this case, the eigenfunction equations separate in coordinates that diagonalize the curvature matrix H.

4.2   Annealed Learning

As discussed earlier, most practical applications of on-line learning employ some form of learning rate annealing. Power-law decay of the learning rate can be analyzed in the present framework in a straightforward manner. We recall our earlier assumption that the learning rate behaves as

$$\mu(s) \;=\; \frac{\mu_0}{s^p}$$

with $0 < p \leq 1$. We re-write the equations of motion for the fluctuations (4.5), using the chosen form of γ (4.6) and the form of $f(s)$ in (4.7), and writing now, the general n-dimensional form

$$\partial_s \Pi(\xi) \;=\; \nabla_\xi \cdot \left[\left(-\frac{\mu_0}{s^p} \alpha_1^{(1)} - \frac{p}{2s} \right) \xi \, \Pi \right]$$
$$+ \frac{\mu_0}{2s^p} \nabla_\xi \cdot \left(\alpha_2^{(0)} \nabla_\xi \Pi \right)$$
$$+ \mathcal{O} \left(\frac{\mu_0}{s^p} \right)^{3/2} \tag{4.22}$$

where $\alpha_1^{(1)}$ is the *negative definite* drift matrix, and $\alpha_2^{(0)}$ is the positive definite diffusion matrix.

Since $0 < p \leq 1$, at late times the right-hand side of (4.22) is dominated by the terms explicitly written explicitly. Since we are primarily concerned with the asymptotic dynamics, it is adequate to retain only the given terms. Precisely which terms dominate depends on the value of p, i.e. on the rate at which the learning rate is annealed. We will briefly review the results for classical annealing ($p = 1$) and for slower rates. These results are compared with an order parameter approach in (Leen, Schottky and Saad, 1998).

Classical Annealing

For $p = 1$, the explicit terms on the right-hand side of (4.22) all decay as $1/s$. Relative to the constant learning rate case, the substantive change in the fluctuation dynamics is the modification of the drift by the term $-1/2s$ to form an *effective drift*. We confine attention to gradient descent algorithms for which $-\alpha_1^{(1)} = H$ is the cost function curvature. We assume that this is positive definite in a neighborhood of a local optimum w_* where we carry out the analysis[4]. Then the effective drift is

$$d_{eff} = \left(\frac{\mu_0}{s} H - \frac{1}{2s} \right) \xi \equiv \frac{1}{s} A \xi$$

In order to get a stable system, and hence a normalizable equilibrium density, the matrix A must be positive definite. This clearly requires that

$$\mu_0 > \frac{1}{2 \lambda_{min}} \tag{4.23}$$

where λ_{min} is the smallest eigenvalue of the curvature H.

We next transform (4.22) to the new time coordinate $b = \ln s$ and recover the equation of motion valid at large times

$$\partial_b \Pi(\xi,t) = \nabla_\xi \cdot (A \xi \, \Pi) + \frac{\mu_0}{2} \nabla_\xi \cdot \left(\alpha_2^{(0)} \nabla_\xi \Pi \right) . \tag{4.24}$$

Assuming that the criticality condition (4.23) is met, this gives rise to a zero-mean Gaussian equilibrium density for the fluctuations ξ, or using (4.2) with $\phi(t) = w_*$, a Gaussian equilibrium density for $\sqrt{s}\,(w - w_*)$. Thus we recover the classical result (Fabian, 1968; White, 1989) ; provided the criticality condition (4.23) is met, the random variable $\sqrt{s}\,v \equiv \sqrt{s}\,(w - w_*)$ is *asymptotically normal*.

This asymptotic normality implies a convergence rate for the algorithm. Given a finite covariance Σ_ξ for the fluctuations, the covariance of the weight error $v \equiv w - w_*$, denoted Σ_v, is inversely proportional to time

$$\Sigma_v = \frac{\mu_0}{s} \Sigma_\xi .$$

and consequently the expected squared weight error drops off inversely with time

$$E\left[|v|^2 \right] = \text{Trace } (\Sigma_v) = \frac{\mu_0}{s} \text{Trace} (\Sigma_\xi)$$

provided the criticality condition (4.23) is satisfied. This appears to be the optimal convergence rate that can be sustained over an extended period of time (Goldstein, 1987).

If the criticality condition is *not* met, the convergence will be *slower* than $1/s$. One can derive the asymptotic convergence rate by developing from

---

[4]We are assuming as before that the system has evolved until the deterministic piece of the trajectory $\phi(s)$ is arbitrarily close to a local optimum.

(4.24) equations of motion for the second moments $R_\xi \equiv E[\xi_i \xi_j]$. Then using their solution, compute

$$E[|v|^2] = \text{Trace}(E[vv^T]) = \frac{\mu_0}{s}\text{Trace}(R_\xi) \ .$$

The solution (derived by another approach in (Leen and Orr, 1994)) is

$$
\begin{aligned}
E[|v|^2] &= \sum_{k=1} n\tilde{C}_{kk}(s_0)\left(\frac{s_0}{s}\right)^{2\mu_0\lambda_k} \\
&+ \frac{\mu_0^2\, \widetilde{\alpha^{(0)}}_{2\,kk}}{(2\mu_0\lambda_k - 1)}\left[\frac{1}{s} - \frac{1}{s_0}\left(\frac{s_0}{s}\right)^{2\mu_0\lambda_k}\right]
\end{aligned}
\tag{4.25}
$$

where λ_k are the eigenvalues of the curvature H (at the local optimum w_*), and $\tilde{C}_{kk}$ and $\widetilde{\alpha^{(0)}}_{2\,kk}$ are the diagonal elements of the weight error covariance, and the diffusion matrix, in coordinates for which H is *diagonal*.

Equation (4.25) shows that when the criticality condition is met, one has $1/s$ decay of the expected squared weight error, but when the criticality condition is *not* met, the convergence is as $(1/s)^{2\mu_0\lambda_{min}}$, i.e. *slower* than $1/s$.

Since the criticality condition (4.23) relates the minimal required μ_0 to the *unknown* cost function curvature, one is not guaranteed to achieve the optimal convergence rate for an arbitrarily chosen μ_0. Since the actual convergence rate given in (4.25) can be *much* slower than optimal, this situation has led many researchers (Venter, 1967; Darken and Moody, 1992; Leen and Orr, 1994; Orr and Leen, 1997; Murata et al., 1997) to devise algorithms that attempt to adaptively set μ_0.

Alternative Annealing Schedules

The situation is rather different for $p < 1$. Referring to (4.22), at late times the right-hand side is dominated by the terms in $1/s^p$, and the $1/s$ and $\mathcal{O}(1/s^p)^{3/2}$ terms can be neglected. Then there is *no* criticality condition, and the fluctuations are asymptotically normal regardless of μ_0. By arguments similar to those in the last section, this implies that the expected squared weight error drops off asymptotically as

$$E[|v|^2] \propto \frac{1}{s^p} \tag{4.26}$$

This is, since $p < 1$, *slower* than the optimal rate achievable for $1/s$ annealing. However, there is *no* critical value of μ_0 to reach the $1/s^p$ rate[5].

---

[5]This may seem rather paradoxical, as one could take p arbitrarily close to 1 and thereby achieve convergence rate arbitrarily close to $1/s$ regardless of μ_0. However, the analysis here only describes what happens when one reaches the asymptotic equilibrium distribution on ξ. The time to relax to that equilibrium distribution is *not* addressed by this analysis

5 Summary

We discussed the dynamics of on-line learning from the perspective of the master equation for the probability density on the weights. We found a class of algorithms, a member of which proceeds by updating the weight according to the *sign* of the gradient (sometimes called Manhattan learning), for which the time-evolution can be expressed in closed form. For such algorithms, the analysis proceeds without approximation, and without the need to integrate a set of differential equations. The existence of an exactly integrable model, even for a rather severely restricted set of algorithms, provides a potentially useful analysis tool.

We also developed a perturbation approach, to analyze the density of fluctuations about a deterministic trajectory. This approach is most useful to characterize learning in the vicinity of a local optimum. Our application to equilibrium distributions for constant learning, showed both the efficacy, and the limits of the technique. The perturbation equations are also applicable to annealed learning. The discussion here concentrated only on the asymptotic behavior, which requires retaining only the lowest order non-trivial terms. However it seems likely that some information on the late-time transient behavior can be obtained by retaining further orders in perturbation.

Finally, we note that all the examples discussed within the perturbation framework assumed that the curvature matrix $-\alpha_1^{(1)}$ at the local optimum is positive definite. If in some direction the curvature is zero, then the minimum is quartic (or of higher order) along that direction. One can address quartic minima in one dimension in a straightforward way, by suitable choice of the scaling exponent γ. More interesting, and yet to be addressed, is the case of singular curvature in multiple dimensions where some directions are quadratic, and some quartic or higher order. Such cases presumably require theoretical development analogous to center manifold theory in bifurcating deterministic dynamical systems.

Acknowledgements

The author would like to thank the Newton Institute and the International Human Frontier Science Program for travel support, and the NSF for continued research support under grant ECS-9704094.

References

Bershad, N.J. and Qu, L.Z. (1989). On the probability density function of the lms adaptive filter weights. *IEEE Transactions on Acoustics, Speech, and Signal Processing*, 37, 43–56.

Darken, C. and Moody, J.(1992). Towards faster stochastic gradient search. In J.E. Moody, S.J. Hanson, and R.P. Lipmann, editors, *Advances in Neural Information Processing Systems 4*. Morgan Kaufmann Publishers, San Mateo, CA.

Fabian, V. (1968). On asymptotic normality in stochastic approximation. *Ann. Math. Statist.*, 39, 1327–1332.

Gardiner, C.W. (1990). *Handbook of Stochastic Methods, 2nd Ed.* Springer-Verlag, Berlin.

Goldstein, L. (1987) Mean square optimality in the continuous time Robbins Monro procedure. *Technical Report* DRB-306, Dept. of Mathematics, University of Southern California, LA.

Heskes, T.M. (1993). *Learning Processes in Neural Networks*. PhD thesis, Department of Medical Physics and Biophysics, University of Nijmegen, The Netherlands.

Heskes, T.M. and Kappen, B. (1991). Learning processes in neural networks. *Phys. Rev. A*, 44, 2718–2726.

Heskes, T.M., Slijpen, E.T.P. and Kappen, B. (1992). Learning in neural networks with local minima. *Phys. Rev. A*, 46, 5221–5231.

Kendall, M. and Stuart, A. (1977). *The Advanced Theory of Statistics, Volume 1 Distribution Theory*. MacMillan Publishing Co., New York, fourth edition.

Leen, T.K. and Moody, J.E. (1993). Weight space probability densities in stochastic learning: I. Dynamics and equilibria. In Giles, Hanson, and Cowan, editors, *Advances in Neural Information Processing Systems, vol. 5*, San Mateo, CA. Morgan Kaufmann.

Leen, T.K. and Moody, J.E. (1997). Stochastic manhattan learning, an exact time-evolution operator for the ensemble dynamics. *Phys. Rev. E*, 56, 1262–1265.

Leen, K.T., Schottky, B. and Saad, D. (1998). Two approaches to optimal annealing. In Jordan, M.I., Kearns, M. J. and Solla, S.A. editors, *Advances in Neural Information Processing Systems 10*. The MIT Press.

Leen, T. K. and Orr., G.B. (1994). Optimal stochastic search and adaptive momentum. In Cowan, J.D., Tesauro,G. and Alspector, J. editors, *Advances in Neural Information Processing Systems 6*, San Francisco, CA., Morgan Kaufmann Publishers.

Murata, N., Muller,K., Ziehe, A. and Amari, S. (1997). Adaptive on-line learning in changing environments. In *Advances in Neural Information Processing Systems 9*. The MIT Press.

Orr, G.B. (1996). *Dynamics and Algorithms for Stochastic Search*. PhD thesis, Oregon Graduate Institute.

Orr, G.B. and Leen, T.K. (1993). Weight space probability densities in stochastic learning: II. Transients and basin hopping times. In Giles, Hanson, and Cowan, editors, *Advances in Neural Information Processing Systems, vol. 5*, San Mateo, CA. Morgan Kaufmann.

Orr, G.B. and Leen, T.K. (1997). Using curvature information for fast stochastic search. In *Advances in Neural Information Processing Systems 9*. The MIT Press.

Radons, G., Schuster, H. G. and Werner,D. (1990). Fokker-Planck description of learning in backpropagation networks. In *International Neural Network Conference - INNC 90, Paris*, pages II 993–996. Kluwer Academic Publishers.

Venter, J.H. (1967). An extension of the robbins-monro procedure. *Ann. of Math. Statist.*, 38, 117–127.

White, H. (1989). Learning in artificial neural networks: A statistical perspective. *Neural Computation*, 1, 425–464.

Wiegerinckand, W. and Heskes, T.M. (1994). On-line learning with time-correlated patterns. *Europhys. Lett.*, 28, 451–455.

Yang, H.H. and Amari, S. (1998). The efficiency and the robustness of natural gradient descent learning rule. In Michael I. Jordan, Michael J. Kearns, and Sara A. Solla, editors, *Advances in Neural Information Processing Systems, 10*. The MIT Press.

A Statistical Study of On-line Learning

Noboru Murata

Lab. for Information Synthesis, RIKEN Brain Science Institute
Wako, Saitama 351-0198, Japan.
mura@irl.riken.go.jp

Abstract

In this paper we examine on-line learning with statistical framework. Firstly we study the cases with fixed and annealed learning rate. It can be shown that on-line learning with $1/t$ annealed learning rate minimizes the generalization error with the same rate as batch learning in the asymptotic regime, that is, on-line learning can be as effective as batch learning asymptotically. Using these analyses, we study an adaptive learning rate algorithm which is based on Sompolinsky-Barkai-Seung algorithm and which achieves $1/t$-annealing automatically.

1   Batch Learning and On-line Learning

Let us consider a learning system which is specified by a parameter vector $\boldsymbol{\theta} = (\theta^1, \dots, \theta^m)^T \in \boldsymbol{R}^m$. Let $(\boldsymbol{x}, \boldsymbol{y})$ be a input-output pair, which the system learns, where $\boldsymbol{x} = (x_1, \dots, x_r)^T \in \boldsymbol{R}^r$ and $\boldsymbol{y} = (y_1, \dots, y_s)^T \in \boldsymbol{R}^s$. For each input-output pair, we define a loss function

$$d(\boldsymbol{x}, \boldsymbol{y}; \boldsymbol{\theta}) \qquad (1.1)$$

which measures the performance of learning system $\boldsymbol{\theta}$ for given input $\boldsymbol{x}$ and desired output $\boldsymbol{y}$. In general, loss function $d(\boldsymbol{x}, \boldsymbol{y}; \boldsymbol{\theta})$ can be divided into two part, pointwise loss $l(\boldsymbol{x}, \boldsymbol{y}; \boldsymbol{\theta})$ and regularization $r(\boldsymbol{\theta})$

$$d(\boldsymbol{x}, \boldsymbol{y}; \boldsymbol{\theta}) = l(\boldsymbol{x}, \boldsymbol{y}; \boldsymbol{\theta}) + \lambda r(\boldsymbol{\theta}), \qquad (1.2)$$

where λ determines the strength of regularization. We assume that the loss $d(\boldsymbol{x}, \boldsymbol{y}; \boldsymbol{\theta})$ is differentiable up to the appropriate order and we use ∇ and $\nabla\nabla$ to indicate vector and matrix differential operators

$$\nabla = \begin{pmatrix} \dfrac{\partial}{\partial \theta^1} \\ \vdots \\ \dfrac{\partial}{\partial \theta^m} \end{pmatrix}, \quad \nabla\nabla = \begin{pmatrix} \dfrac{\partial^2}{\partial \theta^1 \partial \theta^1} & \cdots & \dfrac{\partial^2}{\partial \theta^1 \partial \theta^m} \\ \vdots & \ddots & \vdots \\ \dfrac{\partial^2}{\partial \theta^m \partial \theta^1} & \cdots & \dfrac{\partial^2}{\partial \theta^m \partial \theta^m} \end{pmatrix}.$$

A typical example of the loss function is the squared error for the three-layered perceptron with l_2 regularization, such as

$$d(\boldsymbol{x}, \boldsymbol{y}; \boldsymbol{\theta}) = \frac{1}{2} \sum_{i=1}^{s} |y_i - f_i(\boldsymbol{x}; \boldsymbol{\theta})|^2 + \lambda \sum_{j=1}^{m} |\theta^j|^2,$$

where

$$f_i(\boldsymbol{x}; \boldsymbol{\theta}) = \sum_{j=1}^{h} v_{ij} \phi \left(\sum_{k=1}^{r} w_{jk} x_k - b_j \right), \quad i = 1, \ldots, s,$$

h is the number of hidden units, $\phi(x)$ is a sigmoidal function, and $\boldsymbol{\theta}$ denotes a set of all the modifiable parameters v_{ij}, w_{jk} and b_j.

We also define a total loss function averaged over all the possible inputs and desired outputs

$$D(\boldsymbol{\theta}) = E_p\left(d(\boldsymbol{X}, \boldsymbol{Y}; \boldsymbol{\theta})\right) = \int_{\mathbf{R}^{r+s}} d(\boldsymbol{x}, \boldsymbol{y}; \boldsymbol{\theta}) p(\boldsymbol{x}, \boldsymbol{y}) d\boldsymbol{x} d\boldsymbol{y}, \qquad (1.3)$$

where E_p denotes expectation taken under distribution $p(\boldsymbol{x}, \boldsymbol{y})$. The optimal parameter is defined as a parameter which minimizes total loss function $D(\boldsymbol{\theta})$

$$\boldsymbol{\theta}_* = \operatorname*{argmin}_{\boldsymbol{\theta}} D(\boldsymbol{\theta}). \qquad (1.4)$$

The goal of learning is to obtain optimal parameter $\boldsymbol{\theta}_*$, however, in usual settings, the true input-output distribution $p(\boldsymbol{x}, \boldsymbol{y})$ is unknown and only a finite number of input-output examples $\{(\boldsymbol{x}_i, \boldsymbol{y}_i)\}_{i=1}^{n}$ are available, which are i.i.d. random variables sampled from the target system $p(\boldsymbol{x}, \boldsymbol{y})$. A plausible approach is defining the empirical total loss function by

$$\hat{D}(\boldsymbol{\theta}) = E_{\hat{p}}\left(d(\boldsymbol{X}, \boldsymbol{Y}; \boldsymbol{\theta})\right) = \int d(\boldsymbol{x}, \boldsymbol{y}; \boldsymbol{\theta}) \hat{p}(\boldsymbol{x}, \boldsymbol{y}) d\boldsymbol{x} d\boldsymbol{y} \qquad (1.5)$$

with the empirical distribution

$$\hat{p}(\boldsymbol{x}, \boldsymbol{y}) = \frac{1}{n} \sum_{i=1}^{n} \delta(\boldsymbol{x} - \boldsymbol{x}_i, \boldsymbol{y} - \boldsymbol{y}_i), \qquad (1.6)$$

and defining an estimator by

$$\hat{\boldsymbol{\theta}} = \operatorname*{argmin}_{\boldsymbol{\theta}} \hat{D}(\boldsymbol{\theta}). \qquad (1.7)$$

Note that estimator $\hat{\boldsymbol{\theta}}$ is a function of given examples $\{(\boldsymbol{x}_i, \boldsymbol{y}_i)\}_{i=1}^{n}$

$$\hat{\boldsymbol{\theta}} = \hat{\boldsymbol{\theta}}(\boldsymbol{x}_1, \boldsymbol{y}_1, \ldots, \boldsymbol{x}_n, \boldsymbol{y}_n), \qquad (1.8)$$

therefore $\hat{\theta}$ is a random variable which depends on examples.

This procedure is called batch learning or non-sequential learning. From the statistical point of view, batch learning is a sort of statistical inference, and it has close relation with estimating function method (see for examples, Godambe 1991, Kawanabe and Amari 1994). As well known in statistics, if the optimal parameter gives the strict minimum of the total loss, i.e.

$$D(\theta_*) < D(\theta), \quad |\theta - \theta_*| > 0, \tag{1.9}$$

the ensemble mean and the variance of estimator $\hat{\theta}$ are asymptotically given by the following lemma.

Lemma 1. *Let $\hat{\theta}$ be an estimator which minimizes empirical total loss function (1.5). The mean and the variance of $\hat{\theta}$ are asymptotically given by*

$$E(\hat{\theta}) = \theta_*, \tag{1.10}$$

$$V(\hat{\theta}) = \frac{1}{n} Q_*^{-1} G_* Q_*^{-1}, \tag{1.11}$$

where E and V denote the mean and the variance over all the possible sets of n i.i.d. examples $\{(x_i, y_i)\}_{i=1}^{n}$ from $p(x, y)$, and G_* and Q_* are symmetric matrices defined by

$$G_* = E_p \left(\nabla d(X, Y; \theta_*) \nabla d(X, Y; \theta_*)^T \right), \tag{1.12}$$

$$Q_* = E_p \left(\nabla \nabla d(X, Y; \theta_*) \right), \tag{1.13}$$

To find estimator $\hat{\theta}$, non-linear optimization methods are applied, such as gradient descent, Newton and quasi-Newton method. For a huge number of parameters, Newton-like methods don't have any specific advantage because of large computational complexity, hence many acceleration methods for gradient descent and approximated or abbreviated methods based on Newton method are proposed.

We have to note that in artificial neural network learning, a problem of local minima often becomes a subject of discussion. There are two main problems:

- How many local minima exist in parameter space?

- How local minima distribute around the optimal parameter?

Unfortunately nobody succeeded to give a rigorous answer yet. In this paper, we don't go into the matter of local minima deeply, but we just note that by substituting the locally optimal parameter for the optimal parameter, most lemmas and theorems hold in each basin of attraction of the local minima.

Also when the optimal parameter θ_* is not a point but a connected region in parameter space the above lemma doesn't hold. For example, in over-realizable case of teacher-student scenario, that is the case in which the student networks have bigger structure than the teacher network, experimentally it is known that distribution of estimator has a longer tail than regular cases. This is a problem of degenerated Fisher information matrices in statistics, and asymptotic distributions of estimators are unknown except for special cases (Fukumizu 1997).

Let us consider the following updating rule.

$$\hat{\boldsymbol{\theta}}_{t+1} = \hat{\boldsymbol{\theta}}_t - \eta_t C_t \nabla d(\boldsymbol{x}_{t+1}, \boldsymbol{y}_{t+1}; \hat{\boldsymbol{\theta}}_t), \qquad (1.14)$$

where $(\boldsymbol{x}_{t+1}, \boldsymbol{y}_{t+1})$ is a pair of input and desired output, η_t is a positive value and C_t is a positive definite matrix which can depend on $\hat{\boldsymbol{\theta}}_t$. This procedure is called on-line learning, sequential learning or stochastic descent method. Main difference of on-line learning from batch learning is that observing examples and modifying parameters are alternatively taken place. Namely, on-line update rule uses only information available at time t. Estimator $\hat{\boldsymbol{\theta}}_t$ is a function of previous estimator $\hat{\boldsymbol{\theta}}_{t-1}$ and a given example $(\boldsymbol{x}_t, \boldsymbol{y}_t)$, hence it can be thought as a function of initial value $\boldsymbol{\theta}_0 \equiv \hat{\boldsymbol{\theta}}_0$ and all the given examples $\{(\boldsymbol{x}_i, \boldsymbol{y}_i)\}_{i=1}^t$

$$\hat{\boldsymbol{\theta}}_t = \hat{\boldsymbol{\theta}}_t \left(\hat{\boldsymbol{\theta}}_{t-1}, \boldsymbol{x}_t, \boldsymbol{y}_t \right) = \hat{\boldsymbol{\theta}}_t \left(\boldsymbol{\theta}_0, \boldsymbol{x}_1, \boldsymbol{y}_1, \ldots, \boldsymbol{x}_t, \boldsymbol{y}_t \right),$$

and it is a random variable which depends on a sequence of examples. Unless there is any confusion, we use abbreviated form $\hat{\boldsymbol{\theta}}_t$.

Note that other update rules can be applicable to on-line learning. An example is to use a small set of examples $\{(\boldsymbol{x}_{t+1}^j, \boldsymbol{y}_{t+1}^j)\}_{j=1}^k$ at time t

$$\hat{\boldsymbol{\theta}}_{t+1} = \hat{\boldsymbol{\theta}}_t - \eta_t C_t \sum_{j=1}^k \nabla d(\boldsymbol{x}_{t+1}^j, \boldsymbol{y}_{t+1}^j; \hat{\boldsymbol{\theta}}_t).$$

Although the detailed behavior of this sort of gradient based on-line learning differs from the simple ones, still update rule (1.14) is essential. Also we can use more general update rule such as

$$\hat{\boldsymbol{\theta}}_{t+1} = \hat{\boldsymbol{\theta}}_t - \eta_t F(\boldsymbol{x}_{t+1}, \boldsymbol{y}_{t+1}; \hat{\boldsymbol{\theta}}_t),$$

however, in usual cases the above update rule can be well approximated by Equation (1.14) by utilizing the dependency of C_t on $\hat{\boldsymbol{\theta}}_t$, and in order to investigate asymptotic property, this approximation is sufficient. Therefore, in this paper we deal with the simplest update rule.

The procedure (1.14) is validated as a method that reduces total loss at each time in an average sense, i.e.

$$
\begin{aligned}
E_p(D(\hat{\boldsymbol{\theta}}_{t+1})) - D(\hat{\boldsymbol{\theta}}_t) &= E_p \left(D \left(\hat{\boldsymbol{\theta}}_t - \eta_t C_t \nabla d(\boldsymbol{X}, \boldsymbol{Y}; \hat{\boldsymbol{\theta}}_t) \right) \right) - D(\hat{\boldsymbol{\theta}}_t) \\
&= -\nabla D(\hat{\boldsymbol{\theta}}_t)^T E_p \left(\eta_t C_t \nabla d(\boldsymbol{X}, \boldsymbol{Y}; \hat{\boldsymbol{\theta}}_t) \right) + O\left(\eta_t^2\right) \\
&= -\eta_t \nabla D(\hat{\boldsymbol{\theta}}_t)^T C_t \nabla D(\hat{\boldsymbol{\theta}}_t) + O\left(\eta_t^2\right) < 0,
\end{aligned}
$$

if η_t and C_t are appropriately chosen. When C_t is fixed, from the theory of a stochastic approximation (Robbins and Monro 1951), a sufficient condition for convergence is given by

$$\sum_{t=1}^{\infty} \eta_t = \infty, \quad \sum_{t=1}^{\infty} \eta_t^2 < \infty. \tag{1.15}$$

Hence learning rate η_t plays an important role in on-line learning.

Compared with batch learning, on-line learning has several advantages. One is low computational cost because less memory is needed to store examples and experimentally on-line learning is said to be faster than batch learning in terms of computational time. Another advantage is adaptation ability to changing environment. Since in on-line learning, used examples are abandoned and never referred, newly given examples have more influence to the estimator. This forgetting effect helps to follow the gradual change of the environment. On the other hand, estimation of the parameter is thought to be less accurate because of its stochastic property.

2 Asymptotic Behavior of On-line Learning

To have a good intuition of on-line learning, we calculate the mean and the variance of estimator $\hat{\boldsymbol{\theta}}_t$

$$\boldsymbol{\theta}_t = E(\hat{\boldsymbol{\theta}}_t), \tag{2.1}$$

$$V_t = V(\hat{\boldsymbol{\theta}}_t). \tag{2.2}$$

In the following we discuss convergence property around local minima which are stable fixed points of dynamics. Except for special models such as simple perceptrons, it is difficult to discuss the whole process of on-line learning. If the estimator is in the neighborhood of the optimal parameter or the locally optimal parameter, the evolution of the mean and the variance are approximated in a simple form that is given by Amari (1967). In the case that there exist local minima, learning dynamics is conditioned within the basin of attraction of a certain local minimum and the similar statement holds in each basin.

Lemma 2 (Amari 1967). *If η_t is sufficiently small, the mean value of a smooth function $f(\boldsymbol{\theta})$ is approximated by the recursive equation*

$$
\begin{aligned}
E^{\hat{\boldsymbol{\theta}}_{t+1}}\left(f(\hat{\boldsymbol{\theta}}_{t+1})\right) = {}& E^{\hat{\boldsymbol{\theta}}_t}\left(f(\hat{\boldsymbol{\theta}}_t)\right) - \eta_t E^{\hat{\boldsymbol{\theta}}_t}\left(\nabla f(\hat{\boldsymbol{\theta}}_t)^T C_t \nabla D(\hat{\boldsymbol{\theta}}_t)\right) \\
& + \frac{\eta_t^2}{2} \operatorname{tr}\left(E^{\hat{\boldsymbol{\theta}}_t}\left(C_t G(\hat{\boldsymbol{\theta}}_t) C_t^T \nabla\nabla f(\hat{\boldsymbol{\theta}}_t)\right)\right) + O(\eta_t^3),
\end{aligned}
\tag{2.3}
$$

where $E^{\hat{\boldsymbol{\theta}}}$ denotes expectation with respect to $\hat{\boldsymbol{\theta}}$.

From the above lemma, the evolution of the mean and the variance of the estimator are given as follows in the neighborhood of the optimal parameter, where total loss function $D(\boldsymbol{\theta})$ is well approximated by quadratic form

$$D(\boldsymbol{\theta}) = D(\boldsymbol{\theta}_*) + \frac{1}{2}(\boldsymbol{\theta} - \boldsymbol{\theta}_*)^T Q_*(\boldsymbol{\theta} - \boldsymbol{\theta}_*). \tag{2.4}$$

Lemma 3. *In the neighborhood of the optimal parameter, evolution of mean and the variance are approximated by recursive equations*

$$\boldsymbol{\theta}_{t+1} = \boldsymbol{\theta}_t - \eta_t C_t Q_*(\boldsymbol{\theta}_t - \boldsymbol{\theta}_*), \tag{2.5}$$

$$V_{t+1} = V_t - \eta_t(C_t Q_* V_t + V_t Q_* C_t^T) + \eta_t^2 C_t G_* C_t^T$$
$$- \eta_t^2 C_t Q_*(\boldsymbol{\theta}_t - \boldsymbol{\theta}_*)(\boldsymbol{\theta}_t - \boldsymbol{\theta}_*)^T Q_* C_t^T. \tag{2.6}$$

In this section we investigate two specific cases:

- C_t is a constant matrix C and η_t is a constant value η,

- C_t is a constant matrix C and η_t is controlled as $O(1/t)$.

Introducing notations

$$K_* = CQ_*, \tag{2.7}$$
$$V_* = Q_*^{-1} G_* Q_*^{-1}, \tag{2.8}$$

we hereafter use simplified recursive equations

$$\boldsymbol{\theta}_{t+1} = \boldsymbol{\theta}_t - \eta_t K_*(\boldsymbol{\theta}_t - \boldsymbol{\theta}_*), \tag{2.9}$$

$$V_{t+1} = V_t - \eta_t(K_* V_t + V_t K_*^T) + \eta_t^2 K_* V_* K_*^T$$
$$- \eta_t^2 K_*(\boldsymbol{\theta}_t - \boldsymbol{\theta}_*)(\boldsymbol{\theta}_t - \boldsymbol{\theta}_*)^T K_*^T. \tag{2.10}$$

Since Q_* and C are positive definite, all the eigenvalues of matrix K_* are positive and we refer the eigenvalues of K_* by

$$\lambda_1, \ldots, \lambda_m, \quad \lambda_1 \geq \cdots \geq \lambda_m > 0. \tag{2.11}$$

Also we use two linear operators Ξ and Ω which are defined by

$$\Xi_A B = AB + (AB)^T, \tag{2.12}$$
$$\Omega_A B = ABA^T, \tag{2.13}$$

where A and B are square matrices. The eigenvalues of Ξ_A and Ω_A are given by

$$\nu_i + \nu_j, \tag{2.14}$$
$$\nu_i \nu_j, \quad i, j = 1, \ldots, m \tag{2.15}$$

respectively, where ν_i's are eigenvalues of matrix A.

2.1 Fixed Learning Rate

In the case that learning rate η_t does not vary during the training process, i.e. $\eta_t = \eta$, Equations (2.9) and (2.10) can be solved directly.

Theorem 1. *For fixed learning rate η, the mean and the variance of the estimator are given by*

$$\boldsymbol{\theta}_t = \boldsymbol{\theta}_* + (I - \eta K_*)^t (\boldsymbol{\theta}_0 - \boldsymbol{\theta}_*), \tag{2.16}$$

$$V_t = \left\{ I - (I - \Xi_{\eta K_*})^t \right\} \eta V_\infty$$
$$- \left\{ (\Omega_{I - \eta K_*})^t - (I - \Xi_{\eta K_*})^t \right\} V_0, \tag{2.17}$$

where $\boldsymbol{\theta}_0$ is the initial value and

$$V_0 = (\boldsymbol{\theta}_0 - \boldsymbol{\theta}_*)(\boldsymbol{\theta}_0 - \boldsymbol{\theta}_*)^T, \tag{2.18}$$

$$V_\infty = \Xi_{K_*}^{-1} \Omega_{K_*} V_*. \tag{2.19}$$

Proof is given in Appendix A.3. Also we can do various analysis of fixed learning rate case, such as step response and frequency response. They are given in Appendix C.

From the above theorem, we know that with an appropriate η, the mean and the variance of the estimator converge as $t \to \infty$

$$\lim_{t \to \infty} \boldsymbol{\theta}_t = \boldsymbol{\theta}_* \tag{2.20}$$

$$\lim_{t \to \infty} V_t = \eta V_\infty. \tag{2.21}$$

The mean converges to the optimal parameter, however there remains a fluctuation of order $O(\eta)$. To avoid the divergence of the variance, η must be smaller than the inverse of the maximal eigenvalue $1/\lambda_1$. On the other hand, the convergence speed of the mean and the variance is dominated by the minimal eigenvalue λ_m. As the first term of the variance represents the remaining fluctuation of the estimator around the optimal parameter, small η is preferable. On the other hand, to eliminate the dependency on the initial value in the second term as fast as possible, large η is better. Roughly speaking, if the learning rate η is large, the speed of approaching to the optimal parameter $\boldsymbol{\theta}_*$ is fast, however, large fluctuation remains even if time t becomes infinitely large. And if η is small, the fluctuation is small but it takes a long time for the convergence.

This effect can be seen from the viewpoint of generalization errors (Murata *et al.* 1991, 1993). The ensemble average of total loss function is called generalization error or predictive error, and its behavior through time is called learning curve. By using the above result and expanding the total loss around the optimal parameter, i.e.

$$E\left(D(\hat{\boldsymbol{\theta}}_t) \right)$$
$$= D(\boldsymbol{\theta}_*) + \frac{1}{2} \operatorname{tr} \left(Q_* E \left((\hat{\boldsymbol{\theta}}_t - \boldsymbol{\theta}_t)(\hat{\boldsymbol{\theta}}_t - \boldsymbol{\theta}_t)^T + (\boldsymbol{\theta}_t - \boldsymbol{\theta}_*)(\boldsymbol{\theta}_t - \boldsymbol{\theta}_*)^T \right) \right),$$

we know the asymptotic behavior of the learning curve.

Corollary 1. *In the case of fixed rate on-line learning, the learning curve is asymptotically given by*

$$E\left(D(\hat{\boldsymbol{\theta}}_t)\right) = D(\boldsymbol{\theta}_*) + \frac{1}{2}\eta\,\mathrm{tr}\,(Q_*V_\infty) + \frac{1}{2}\,\mathrm{tr}\,\left(Q_*(I - \Xi_{\eta K_*})^t(V_0 - \eta V_\infty)\right).$$
(2.22)

The first term is possible minimal loss, and the second term is additional loss caused by the fluctuation of estimation. Only the third term depends on time and it describes decreasing speed of errors. Here we emphasize that it is not possible to determine an universal optimal rate because there is a trade-off between convergence speed and accuracy of learning. However, for example, if the training time is limited up to T_{end}, we can define an optimal rate in terms of minimal expected generalization errors from Equation (2.22) by

$$\eta_{\mathrm{opt}} = \operatorname*{argmin}_{\eta} E\left(D(\hat{\boldsymbol{\theta}}_{T_{\mathrm{end}}})\right).$$
(2.23)

It is interesting to compare the stochastic descent and the true gradient descent. Suppose that we know true input-output distribution $p(\boldsymbol{x}, \boldsymbol{y})$, then we can use the following update rule to obtain the optimal parameter:

$$\boldsymbol{\theta}_{t+1} = \boldsymbol{\theta}_t - \eta C E_p\left(\nabla d(\boldsymbol{X}, \boldsymbol{Y}; \boldsymbol{\theta}_t)\right).$$
(2.24)

In this case, estimator $\boldsymbol{\theta}_t$ is not a random variable and it obeys the same recursive equation of the ensemble mean of on-line estimator $\hat{\boldsymbol{\theta}}_t$. Hence we can calculate the learning curve of this case as follows.

Corollary 2. *In the case of batch learning, the learning curve is approximated by*

$$D(\boldsymbol{\theta}_t) = D(\boldsymbol{\theta}_*) + \frac{1}{2}\,\mathrm{tr}\,\left(Q_*(\Omega_{I-\eta K_*})^t V_0\right).$$
(2.25)

The second term describes decreasing speed of errors, and it is slightly slower than the corresponding term of the on-line leaning. However, there is no fluctuation in this case, the total performance is better than the on-line learning.

2.2   Annealed Learning Rate

An effective adaptation of the learning rate is $\eta_t = O(1/t)$, because the convergence is guaranteed by conditions

$$\sum_{t=1}^{\infty} \frac{1}{t} = \infty, \quad \sum_{t=1}^{\infty} \frac{1}{t^2} < \infty$$
(2.26)

from the theory of stochastic approximation (Robbins and Monro 1951). Here we investigate how this annealing works asymptotically. Since we can not solve the equation of the variance directly, we give only the leading order of the solution.

Theorem 2. *Suppose the learning rate is $\eta_t = 1/(t+1)$, then mean and the variance of estimator $\hat{\theta}_t$ are asymptotically given by*

$$\theta_t = \theta_* + S_t(\theta_0 - \theta_*), \quad t \geq 2, \quad \theta_0 \equiv \theta_1 \tag{2.27}$$

$$V_t = \begin{cases} R_t V' & \lambda_m < \frac{1}{2} \\ \dfrac{1}{t+1}\left(\Xi_{K_*} - I\right)^{-1} K_* V_* K_*^T & otherwise, \end{cases} \tag{2.28}$$

where

$$S_t = \prod_{k=2}^{t}\left(I - \frac{1}{k}K_*\right), \tag{2.29}$$

$$R_t = \prod_{k=2}^{t} \Xi_{\frac{1}{2}I - \frac{1}{k}K_*}, \tag{2.30}$$

and V' is a positive definite matrix, which depends on the initial value and the learning process and cannot be written in a general form.

Proof is found in Appendix A.4. Note that for the simplicity of notations, in this case the learning starts at time $t = 2$ with initial value θ_1. Since the order of S_t is bounded by

$$\prod_{k=2}^{t}\left(1 - \frac{\lambda_m}{k}\right) \sim \prod_{k=2}^{t} e^{-\frac{\lambda_m}{k}} = e^{-\sum_{k=2}^{t}\frac{\lambda_m}{k}}$$

$$\sim e^{-\log\frac{\lambda_m}{t} + \text{const.}} = O(1/t^{\lambda_m}),$$

large λ_m is preferable for the fast convergence of the mean. And since the eigenvalues of the operator $(\Xi_{K_*} - I)^{-1}\Omega_{K_*}$ are represented by

$$\frac{\lambda_i\lambda_j}{\lambda_i + \lambda_j - 1}, \quad i,j = 1,\ldots,m,$$

and the minimum value is achieved when $\lambda_i = 1$, $i = 1,\ldots,m$, the smallest variance can be realized if all the eigenvalues of K_* are 1, which is realized by $C = Q_*^{-1}$ as the simplest case. If the minimum eigenvalue λ_m is larger than $1/2$, the variance has the bigger contribution to the fluctuation of the on-line learning. Therefore we know the following situation is the optimal case of the annealed rate learning.

Corollary 3. *The optimal case of $1/t$-annealed rate is achieved when all the eigenvalues of K_* are 1. Then the mean and the variance of the estimator are asymptotically given by*

$$\theta_t = \theta_* + \frac{1}{t}(\theta_0 - \theta_*), \tag{2.31}$$

$$V_t = \frac{1}{t}V_* + O\left(\frac{1}{t^2}\right). \tag{2.32}$$

When we use the batch learning with t examples, the mean and the variance of the estimator is given by Lemma 1. Expanding the total loss function around the optimal parameter, we obtain the learning curve of batch learning as

$$E\left(D(\hat{\theta}_t^B)\right)$$
$$= D(\theta_*) + \frac{1}{2}\operatorname{tr}\left(Q_*E\left((\hat{\theta}_t^B - \theta_*)(\hat{\theta}_t^B - \theta_*)^T\right)\right) + o\left(\frac{1}{t}\right)$$
$$= D(\theta_*) + \frac{1}{2t}\operatorname{tr}\left(Q_*V_*\right) + o\left(\frac{1}{t}\right),$$

where $\hat{\theta}_t^B$ denotes the estimator obtained by t-example batch learning. Similarly, we can calculate the learning curve of optimally annealed on-line learning as

$$E\left(D(\hat{\theta}_t)\right)$$
$$= D(\theta_*) + \frac{1}{2}\operatorname{tr}\left(Q_*E\left((\hat{\theta}_t - \theta_t)(\hat{\theta}_t - \theta_t)^T + (\theta_t - \theta_*)(\theta_t - \theta_*)^T\right)\right) + o\left(\frac{1}{t}\right)$$
$$= D(\theta_*) + \frac{1}{2}\operatorname{tr}\left(Q_*\left(\frac{1}{t}V_* + \frac{1}{t^2}(\theta_0 - \theta_*)(\theta_0 - \theta_*)^T\right)\right) + o\left(\frac{1}{t}\right),$$

The above relationship supports efficiency of optimally annealed on-line learning, and it is summarized as follows.

Corollary 4. *In the case of optimally annealed on-line learning, the learning curve is asymptotically given by*

$$E\left(D(\hat{\theta}_t)\right) = D(\theta_*) + \frac{1}{2t}\operatorname{tr}\left(Q_*V_*\right) + o\left(\frac{1}{t}\right). \tag{2.33}$$

This is coincide with the case of batch learning in the order of $O(1/t)$.

Therefore, optimally annealed on-line learning is as asymptotically effective as batch learning in the sense of the generalization error.

Here we give a quite simple explanation why $1/t$-annealing is feasible in a class of $1/t^{\alpha}$-annealed rate learning. For $\eta_t = 1/(1+t)^{\alpha}$ annealing, from lemma 3 we have the solution

$$\boldsymbol{\theta}_t = \boldsymbol{\theta}_* + S_t^{\alpha}(\boldsymbol{\theta}_0 - \boldsymbol{\theta}_*), \qquad (2.34)$$

where

$$S_t^{\alpha} = \prod_{k=2}^{t}(I - \frac{1}{k^{\alpha}}K_*). \qquad (2.35)$$

Obviously the convergence speed of the variance is slower than order $O(1/t^{\alpha})$. From this fact, we know that the larger α is preferable. On the other hand, if we assume $\alpha > 1$, the slowest term of Equation (2.35) can be bounded by

$$\prod_{k=2}^{t}(1 - \frac{1}{k^{\alpha}}\lambda_n) = \exp\left\{\sum_{k=2}^{t}\log(1 - \frac{1}{k^{\alpha}}\lambda_n)\right\}$$

$$\geq \exp\left\{\sum_{k=2}^{t}\frac{1}{k^{\alpha}}\lambda_n\right\}$$

$$\geq \exp\left\{-\frac{1}{\alpha-1}\left(\frac{1}{2^{\alpha-1}} - \frac{1}{t^{\alpha-1}}\right)\lambda_n\right\} > 0,$$

where we assumed that $\lambda_n/2^{\alpha}$ is less than 1. This means that if α is larger than 1, the mean of the estimator does not converge to the optimal parameter. In this sense, $1/t$-annealing is feasible.

3   Adaptive Learning Rate

¿From the results of the previous section, we have an intuitive idea about the learning rate for on-line learning. In practical applications, the learning rate might be scheduled as follows:

- When the estimator $\hat{\boldsymbol{\theta}}_t$ is far from the optimal parameter $\boldsymbol{\theta}_*$, use an appropriately large η.

- When $\hat{\boldsymbol{\theta}}_t$ is close to $\boldsymbol{\theta}_*$, use $1/t$-annealing with an appropriate C.

A simple implementation is

$$\eta_t = \begin{cases} \eta_0 & t < T, \\ \dfrac{\eta_{t-1}}{\eta_{t-1} + \eta_0}\eta_0 & t \geq T, \end{cases}$$

where T is a switching time and η_0 is a initial learning rate. However, it is difficult to give a proper switching time a priori and when the rule changes over time, an annealed learning rate cannot follow the changes fast enough since η_t is too small. Hence we need some sophisticated method to perform the above simple strategy automatically.

3.1 Sompolinsky-Barkai-Seung Algorithm

The idea of an adaptively changing η_t was called learning of learning rule (Amari 1967, Sompolinsky *et al.* 1995). The Sompolinsky-Barkai-Seung algorithm is extended to the differentiable loss function version as follows.

Definition 1.

$$\hat{\theta}_{t+1} = \hat{\theta}_t - \eta_t Q^{-1}(\hat{\theta}_t)\nabla d(x_t, y_t; \hat{\theta}_t), \tag{3.1}$$

$$\eta_{t+1} = \eta_t + \alpha\eta_t \left\{ \beta\left(d(x_t, y_t; \hat{\theta}_t) - D_*\right) - \eta_t \right\}, \tag{3.2}$$

where α and β are positive constants, D_* is the minimal loss function $D(\theta_*)$ and

$$Q(\hat{\theta}_t) = E_p\left(\nabla\nabla d(X, Y, \hat{\theta}_t)\right). \tag{3.3}$$

Intuitively speaking, the coefficient η in Equation (3.1) is controlled by the remaining error. When the error is large, the learning rate takes a relatively large value

$$\eta_t \sim \beta\left(d(x_t, y_t; \hat{\theta}_t) - D_*\right).$$

When the error is small, that is, the estimator is close to the optimal parameter, the learning rate approaches to 0 automatically as

$$\eta_{t+1} = \eta_t - \alpha\eta_t^2.$$

In order to know how the algorithm works, let us consider the averaged dynamical behavior of $(\hat{\theta}_t, \eta_t)$ asymptotically. For simplicity of the treatment, we consider a continuous version of the algorithm

$$\frac{d}{dt}\theta(t) = -\eta(t)Q(\theta(t))^{-1}E_p\left(\nabla d(X, Y; \theta(t))\right), \tag{3.4}$$

$$\frac{d}{dt}\eta(t) = \alpha\eta(t)\left\{\beta E_p\left(d(X, Y; \theta(t)) - D_*\right) - \eta(t)\right\}, \tag{3.5}$$

where $\theta(t)$ and $\eta(t)$ denote the mean of the estimator and the learning rate at continuous time t respectively. When the estimator is in the neighborhood of the optimal parameter, we can use the following relation and approximations

$$E_p\left(\nabla d(X, Y; \theta_*)\right) = 0,$$

$$E_p\left(d(X, Y; \theta(t))\right) \simeq D_* + \frac{1}{2}(\theta(t) - \theta_*)^T Q_*(\theta(t) - \theta_*),$$

$$E_p\left(\nabla d(X, Y; \theta(t))\right) \simeq Q_*\left(\theta(t) - \theta_*\right).$$

Then the equations are rewritten as

$$\frac{d}{dt}\boldsymbol{\theta}(t) = -\eta(t)\left(\boldsymbol{\theta}(t) - \boldsymbol{\theta}_*\right), \tag{3.6}$$

$$\frac{d}{dt}\eta(t) = \alpha\eta(t)\left\{\frac{\beta}{2}(\boldsymbol{\theta}(t) - \boldsymbol{\theta}_*)^T Q_*(\boldsymbol{\theta}(t) - \boldsymbol{\theta}_*) - \eta(t)\right\}. \tag{3.7}$$

Finally introducing a squared error variable

$$e(t) = \frac{1}{2}(\boldsymbol{\theta}(t) - \boldsymbol{\theta}_*)^T Q_*(\boldsymbol{\theta}(t) - \boldsymbol{\theta}_*) \tag{3.8}$$

we obtain an equation system

$$\begin{cases} \dfrac{d}{dt}e(t) = -2\eta(t)e(t), \\[2mm] \dfrac{d}{dt}\eta(t) = \alpha\beta\eta(t)e(t) - \alpha\eta(t)^2. \end{cases} \tag{3.9}$$

It is easy to check that the equation system has a solution

$$\begin{cases} e(t) = \dfrac{1}{\beta} \cdot \left(\dfrac{1}{2} - \dfrac{1}{\alpha}\right) \cdot \dfrac{1}{t}, \quad \alpha > 2, \\[2mm] \eta(t) = \dfrac{1}{2} \cdot \dfrac{1}{t}. \end{cases} \tag{3.10}$$

Therefore the learning rate is automatically annealed as $1/t$, if the estimator approaches to the optimal parameter. Thus Equations (3.6) and (3.7) give us an adaptive on-line learning algorithm in which the learning rate is annealed as $O(1/t)$. This algorithm is also expected to follow slow fluctuation or sudden change of target rule. Note that in this explanation, we omitted the effect of randomness which is a natural characteristics of on-line learning. We will discuss it in the next section.

3.2   Modified Algorithm

From the viewpoint of practical implementation, the algorithm dealt in the previous section has some problems such as

- the Hessian Q_* of the total loss must be calculated at each iteration,

- the minimal value of the loss function must be known.

Here we consider a slightly alleviated learning rule.

   Let us consider the averaged dynamics of the estimator in the neighborhood of the optimal parameter:

$$\frac{d}{dt}\boldsymbol{\theta}(t) = -\eta(t)K_*(\boldsymbol{\theta}(t) - \boldsymbol{\theta}_*), \tag{3.11}$$

where the approximation

$$E_p\left(C\nabla d(\boldsymbol{X}, \boldsymbol{Y}; \boldsymbol{\theta}(t))\right) \simeq K_*(\boldsymbol{\theta}(t) - \boldsymbol{\theta}_*) \tag{3.12}$$

is used. Suppose that we have a vector $\boldsymbol{v}$ which satisfies

$$\boldsymbol{v}^T K_* = \lambda \boldsymbol{v}^T, \tag{3.13}$$

where λ is an eigenvalue of matrix K_*. Using a new value

$$\xi(t) = E_p\left(\boldsymbol{v}^T C\nabla d(\boldsymbol{X}, \boldsymbol{Y}; \boldsymbol{\theta}(t))\right) \simeq \boldsymbol{v}^T K_*(\boldsymbol{\theta}(t) - \boldsymbol{\theta}_*), \tag{3.14}$$

we define an update rule for learning rate as

$$\frac{d}{dt}\eta(t) = \alpha\eta(t)\left(\beta|\xi(t)| - \eta(t)\right), \tag{3.15}$$

where $|\cdot|$ denotes the absolute value. Taking account of relationship between ξ and η, we obtain an equation system

$$\begin{cases} \dfrac{d}{dt}\xi(t) = -\lambda\eta(t)\xi(t), \\[2mm] \dfrac{d}{dt}\eta(t) = \alpha\eta(t)\left(\beta|\xi(t)| - \eta(t)\right), \end{cases} \tag{3.16}$$

and a solution is described as

$$\begin{cases} |\xi(t)| = \dfrac{1}{\beta}\cdot\left(\dfrac{1}{\lambda} - \dfrac{1}{\alpha}\right)\cdot\dfrac{1}{t}, \quad \alpha > \lambda \\[2mm] \eta(t) = \dfrac{1}{\lambda}\cdot\dfrac{1}{t}. \end{cases} \tag{3.17}$$

Intuitively $|\xi|$ plays a role of a distance, where the average gradient is projected to a certain direction. If we choose a clever projection, the learning rate is automatically well annealed, as the estimator approaches the optimal parameter.

It is an important problem to find a good projection direction $\boldsymbol{v}$ and here we use a knowledge of learning process shown in section 2. Usually the learning speed is dominated by the minimum eigenvalue, hence the average trajectory of the estimator is almost parallel to the eigendirection of the minimum eigenvalue after reasonably many iterations. This means that in an average sense the learning process can be seen as a one-dimensional problem along the eigendirection of minimum eigenvalue of K_*. Therefore we can use the averaged gradient of the loss function as $\boldsymbol{v}$

$$\boldsymbol{v} = \frac{E_p\left(C\nabla d(\boldsymbol{X}, \boldsymbol{Y}; \boldsymbol{\theta}(t))\right)}{|E_p\left(C\nabla d(\boldsymbol{X}, \boldsymbol{Y}; \boldsymbol{\theta}(t))\right)|} \tag{3.18}$$

to approximate the eigenvector of the minimum eigenvalue, where $|\cdot|$ denotes l_2 norm. In this case, ξ is expressed as

$$\xi(t) = |E_p\left(C\nabla d(\boldsymbol{X}, \boldsymbol{Y}; \theta(t))\right)|. \tag{3.19}$$

Based on the above consideration, we propose the following practical implementation by substituting the running average (leaky average) for the ensemble average.

Definition 2.

$$\hat{\boldsymbol{\theta}}_{t+1} = \hat{\boldsymbol{\theta}}_t - \eta_t^\dagger C\nabla d(\boldsymbol{x}_{t+1}, \boldsymbol{y}_{t+1}; \hat{\boldsymbol{\theta}}_t), \tag{3.20}$$
$$\eta_t^\dagger = \min(\eta_0, \eta_t)$$
$$\boldsymbol{r}_{t+1} = (1 - \delta)\boldsymbol{r}_t + \delta C\nabla d(\boldsymbol{x}_{t+1}, \boldsymbol{y}_{t+1}; \hat{\boldsymbol{\theta}}_t), \tag{3.21}$$
$$\eta_{t+1} = \eta_t + \alpha\eta_t\left(\beta|\boldsymbol{r}_{t+1}| - \eta_t\right), \tag{3.22}$$

where δ is a constant between 0 and 1, which controls the leakiness of the average and $\boldsymbol{r}$ is used as an auxiliary variable to calculate the running average of the gradient.

Note that due to the use of the running average, η_t doesn't converge to 0 even though $t \to \infty$. When the size of $\boldsymbol{r}_t$ is large compared with its fluctuation, the above algorithm shows automatic $1/t$-annealing as we expect. However, η_t fluctuates around the mean of $|\boldsymbol{r}_t|$ because of the fluctuation of $\boldsymbol{r}_t$, and this can be expressed as

$$\eta_t \sim \beta E(|\boldsymbol{r}_t|) + \epsilon(\alpha, \beta),$$

where ϵ is a random variable and its amplitude is controlled by α. Roughly speaking, if α is large, modification of η_t is fast and as a result η_t is highly affected by the fluctuation of $\boldsymbol{r}_t$. If α is small, the fluctuation is smoothed and ϵ is small. Also the fluctuation of $\boldsymbol{r}_t$ originates from the running average and the estimation error of $\hat{\boldsymbol{\theta}}_t$, hence $\boldsymbol{r}_t$ is approximated with a zero-mean random variable by

$$\boldsymbol{r}_t \sim \epsilon'(\delta, \eta_t).$$

The amplitude of ϵ' is reduced when δ and η_t become small. According to these mutual interaction, the size of η_t is determined.

For practical applications of this algorithm, refer to Müller *et al.* 1998.

4   Conclusion

In this paper we studied on-line learning with fixed and annealed learning rate with the framework of statistics, and asymptotic evolutions of the mean and the variance of the estimators are investigated,

In the case of fixed learning rate we have found an exponential convergence of the mean of estimators and the variance, i.e. the estimation error is proportional to the learning rate. Also we have shown that with the annealing rule $\eta = O(1/t)$, the same convergence speed as in batch learning can be achieved asymptotically. This means that on-line learning is as efficient as batch learning with optimal $1/t$-annealing.

Also we gave a theoretically motivated adaptive on-line algorithm extending the work of Sompolinsky *et al.* On-line learning is especially important under non-stationary environments, and strategies for the learning of learning rate might be applied in the case of such changing environments.

Appendices

A   Proofs of Lemmas and Theorems

In the following, we adopt Einstein summation convention, that is summation is automatically taken without the summation symbol $\sum$ for those indices which appear as a subscript and a superscript simultaneously

$$a^i b_i \equiv \sum_i a^i b_i,$$

and we use the following abbreviation

$$\partial_i \equiv \frac{\partial}{\partial \theta^i}.$$

For any vector a, $(a)^i$ denotes the i-th element of a, and for any matrix A, $(A)^{ij}$ denotes the ij element of A.

A.1   Proof of Lemma 2

Let θ and θ' be $\hat{\theta}_t$ and $\hat{\theta}_{t+1}$ which are estimators at time t and $t+1$ respectively, and let z be a pair of input-output example (x_{t+1}, y_{t+1}) which obeys probability density $p(z) = p(x, y)$ and which is used to modify the estimator from $\hat{\theta}_t$ to $\hat{\theta}_{t+1}$. We write the relationship between θ and θ' by

$$\theta'(z, \theta) = \theta + \delta\theta(z, \theta), \tag{A.1}$$

where

$$\delta\theta(z, \theta) = -\eta C \nabla d(z; \theta), \tag{A.2}$$

and η_t and C_t are simply denoted by η and C respectively. First we derive the probability density of θ' for fixed θ, that is conditioned probability density $q(\theta'|\theta)$. Let $q(\theta'|\theta)d\theta'$ be the probability that estimator θ' is in a rectangle

$$[\theta', \theta' + d\theta'] = [\theta'^1, \theta'^1 + d\theta'^1] \times \cdots \times [\theta'^m, \theta'^m + d\theta'^m] \in \mathbf{R}^m, \qquad (A.3)$$

then the following relation holds,

$$q(\theta'|\theta)d\theta' = p(z(\theta, \theta'))dz(\theta, \theta'), \qquad (A.4)$$

where $z(\theta, \theta')$ and $dz(\theta, \theta')$ define a set of examples and a volume elements respectively, such that examples $z(\theta, \theta')$ modify the estimator from θ to θ' and volume elements $dz(\theta, \theta')$ specifies region of examples which modify the estimator from θ to a point in rectangle $[\theta', \theta' + d\theta']$. Let $q(\theta)$ be the probability density of estimator θ. By averaging both sides of Equation (A.4) with respect to $q(\theta)$, we obtain the probability density of estimator θ'

$$\begin{aligned} q(\theta')d\theta' &= \left(\int_{\theta \in \mathbf{R}^m} q(\theta'|\theta)q(\theta)d\theta \right) d\theta' \\ &= \int_{\theta \in \mathbf{R}^m} p\left(z(\theta, \theta')\right) dz(\theta, \theta')q(\theta)d\theta. \end{aligned} \qquad (A.5)$$

Since the domain of integration for $z(\theta, \theta')$ is whole $\mathbf{R}^{r+s}$ when the domain of integration for θ' is $\mathbf{R}^m$ for fixed θ, then

$$\begin{aligned} E^{\theta'}\left(f(\theta')\right) &= \int_{\theta' \in \mathbf{R}^m} f(\theta')q(\theta')d\theta' \\ &= \int_{z \in \mathbf{R}^{r+s}} \int_{\theta \in \mathbf{R}^m} f(\theta'(z, \theta))p(z(\theta, \theta'))dz(\theta, \theta')q(\theta)d\theta \\ &= \int_{\theta \in \mathbf{R}^m} \left(\int_{z \in \mathbf{R}^{r+s}} f(\theta'(z, \theta))p(z)dz \right) q(\theta)d\theta \\ &= E^{\theta}\left(E^z\left(f(\theta'(z, \theta))\right)\right) \end{aligned} \qquad (A.6)$$

holds, where E^{θ}, $E^{\theta'}$ and E^z denote average over θ, θ' and z respectively. Expanding θ' around θ and knowing that the order of $\delta\theta$ is $O(\eta)$, we obtain

$$\begin{aligned} E^z\left(f(\theta')\right) &= E^z\left(f(\theta + \delta\theta)\right) \\ &= E^z\left(f(\theta) - \partial_i f(\theta)\delta\theta^i + \frac{1}{2}\partial_i\partial_j f(\theta)\delta\theta^i\delta\theta^j + O(\eta^3)\right) \\ &= f(\theta) - \eta\partial_i f(\theta)c^{ij}E^z\left(\partial_j d(z; \theta)\right) \\ &\quad + \frac{\eta^2}{2}\partial_i\partial_j f(\theta)c^{ik}c^{jh}E_z\left(\partial_k d(z; \theta)\partial_h d(z; \theta)\right) + O(\eta^3) \\ &= f(\theta) - \eta\partial_i f(\theta)c^{ij}\partial_j D(\theta) + \frac{\eta^2}{2}\partial_i\partial_j f(\theta)c^{ik}c^{jh}g_{kh}(\theta) + O(\eta^3) \\ &= f(\theta) - \eta\nabla f(\theta)^T C\nabla D(\theta) + \frac{\eta^2}{2}\operatorname{tr}\left(CG(\theta)C^T\nabla\nabla f(\theta)\right) + O(\eta^3), \end{aligned}$$
$$\qquad (A.7)$$

where c^{ij} and $g_{ij}(\boldsymbol{\theta})$ are the ij elements of C and $G(\boldsymbol{\theta})$ respectively. By taking average with respect to $q(\boldsymbol{\theta})$, the proof is completed. $\qquad\qquad\square$

A.2   Proof of Lemma 3

Recalling that $D(\boldsymbol{\theta})$ takes the minimum value at optimal parameter $\boldsymbol{\theta}_*$,

$$\nabla D(\boldsymbol{\theta}_*) = 0 \qquad\qquad (A.8)$$

holds. $D(\boldsymbol{\theta})$ is expanded at $\boldsymbol{\theta}_*$ as

$$D(\boldsymbol{\theta}) = D(\boldsymbol{\theta}_*) + \frac{1}{2}(\boldsymbol{\theta} - \boldsymbol{\theta}_*)^T Q_*(\boldsymbol{\theta} - \boldsymbol{\theta}_*) + O(|\boldsymbol{\theta} - \boldsymbol{\theta}_*|^3), \qquad (A.9)$$

where the relation

$$\nabla\nabla D(\boldsymbol{\theta}_*) \equiv Q_*, \qquad\qquad (A.10)$$

is used. Hence, gradient of $D(\boldsymbol{\theta})$ can be written

$$\nabla D(\boldsymbol{\theta}) = Q_*(\boldsymbol{\theta} - \boldsymbol{\theta}_*) + O(|\boldsymbol{\theta} - \boldsymbol{\theta}_*|^2). \qquad (A.11)$$

First, suppose that

$$f(\boldsymbol{\theta}) = \theta^i \qquad\qquad (A.12)$$

in Lemma 2, then

$$E^{\hat{\boldsymbol{\theta}}_t}\left(f(\hat{\boldsymbol{\theta}}_t)\right) = \theta^i_t, \qquad\qquad (A.13)$$

and

$$\nabla f(\boldsymbol{\theta}) = \begin{pmatrix} \delta^i_1 \\ \vdots \\ \delta^i_m \end{pmatrix}, \quad \nabla\nabla f(\boldsymbol{\theta}) = 0,$$

where δ^i_j denotes Kronecker's delta, i.e.

$$\delta^i_j = \begin{cases} 1 & \text{if } i = j, \\ 0 & \text{if } i \neq j. \end{cases} \qquad\qquad (A.14)$$

Assuming that $\epsilon_t^2 = E(|\hat{\boldsymbol{\theta}}_t - \boldsymbol{\theta}_*|^2)$ is small, we obtain

$$\theta^i_{t+1} = \theta^i_t - \eta_t \left(C_t Q_*(\boldsymbol{\theta}_t - \boldsymbol{\theta}_*)\right)^i + O(\eta_t^3) + O(\epsilon_t^2 \eta_t). \qquad (A.15)$$

By collecting the above relation for all i, we obtain Equation (2.5).

Next suppose that

$$f(\boldsymbol{\theta}) = \theta^i \theta^j, \tag{A.16}$$

then

$$E^{\hat{\boldsymbol{\theta}}_t}\left(f(\hat{\boldsymbol{\theta}}_t)\right) = V_t^{ij}, \tag{A.17}$$

where V_t^{ij} denote the ij element of V_t and

$$\nabla f(\boldsymbol{\theta}) = \begin{pmatrix} \delta_1^i \theta^j + \theta^i \delta_1^j \\ \vdots \\ \delta_m^i \theta^j + \theta^i \delta_m^j \end{pmatrix},$$

$$\nabla \nabla f(\boldsymbol{\theta}) = \begin{pmatrix} \delta_1^i \delta_1^j + \delta_1^i \delta_1^j & \cdots & \delta_1^i \delta_m^j + \delta_m^i \delta_1^j \\ \vdots & \ddots & \vdots \\ \delta_m^i \delta_1^j + \delta_1^i \delta_m^j & \cdots & \delta_m^i \delta_m^j + \delta_m^i \delta_m^j \end{pmatrix}.$$

Using the relations

$$\nabla f(\boldsymbol{\theta})^T C \nabla D(\boldsymbol{\theta})$$
$$= \left(\delta_1^i \theta^j + \theta^i \delta_1^j, \ldots, \delta_m^i \theta^j + \theta^i \delta_m^j\right) C Q_*(\boldsymbol{\theta} - \boldsymbol{\theta}_*) + O(|\boldsymbol{\theta} - \boldsymbol{\theta}_*|^2)$$
$$= \left(C Q_*(\boldsymbol{\theta} - \boldsymbol{\theta}_*)\right)^i \theta^j + \theta^i \left(C Q_*(\boldsymbol{\theta} - \boldsymbol{\theta}_*)\right)^j + O(|\boldsymbol{\theta} - \boldsymbol{\theta}_*|^2)$$
$$= \left(C Q_*(\boldsymbol{\theta} - \boldsymbol{\theta}_*)\boldsymbol{\theta}^T\right)^{ij} + \left(\boldsymbol{\theta}(\boldsymbol{\theta} - \boldsymbol{\theta}_*)^T Q_* C^T\right)^{ij} + O(|\boldsymbol{\theta} - \boldsymbol{\theta}_*|^2) \tag{A.18}$$

and

$$\mathrm{tr}\left(C G(\boldsymbol{\theta}) C^T \nabla \nabla f(\boldsymbol{\theta})\right)$$
$$= \mathrm{tr}\left(C G(\boldsymbol{\theta}) C^T \begin{pmatrix} \delta_1^i \delta_1^j + \delta_1^i \delta_1^j & \cdots & \delta_1^i \delta_m^j + \delta_m^i \delta_1^j \\ \vdots & \ddots & \vdots \\ \delta_m^i \delta_1^j + \delta_1^i \delta_m^j & \cdots & \delta_m^i \delta_m^j + \delta_m^i \delta_m^j \end{pmatrix}\right)$$
$$= \left(C G(\boldsymbol{\theta}) C^T\right)^{ij} + \left(C G(\boldsymbol{\theta}) C^T\right)^{ji}$$
$$= 2\left(C G(\boldsymbol{\theta}) C^T\right)^{ij}$$
$$= 2\left(C G_* C^T\right)^{ij} + O(|\boldsymbol{\theta} - \boldsymbol{\theta}_*|), \tag{A.19}$$

and assuming that $\epsilon_t = E(|\hat{\boldsymbol{\theta}}_t - \boldsymbol{\theta}_*|)$ is small we obtain

$$E^{\hat{\boldsymbol{\theta}}_{t+1}}\left(\hat{\boldsymbol{\theta}}_{t+1}\hat{\boldsymbol{\theta}}_{t+1}^T\right)$$
$$= E^{\hat{\boldsymbol{\theta}}_t}\left(\hat{\boldsymbol{\theta}}_t \hat{\boldsymbol{\theta}}_t^T\right) - \eta_t C_t Q_* E^{\hat{\boldsymbol{\theta}}_t}\left((\hat{\boldsymbol{\theta}}_t - \boldsymbol{\theta}_*)\hat{\boldsymbol{\theta}}_t^T\right)$$
$$\quad - \eta_t E^{\hat{\boldsymbol{\theta}}_t}\left(\hat{\boldsymbol{\theta}}_t(\hat{\boldsymbol{\theta}}_t - \boldsymbol{\theta}_*)^T\right) Q_* C_t^T + \eta_t^2 C_t G_* C_t^T + O(\eta_t^3) + O(\epsilon \eta_t^2) + O(\epsilon^2 \eta_t)$$
$$= E^{\hat{\boldsymbol{\theta}}_t}\left(\hat{\boldsymbol{\theta}}_t \hat{\boldsymbol{\theta}}_t^T\right) - \eta_t C_t Q_* E^{\hat{\boldsymbol{\theta}}_t}\left(\hat{\boldsymbol{\theta}}_t \hat{\boldsymbol{\theta}}_t^T\right) - \eta_t E^{\hat{\boldsymbol{\theta}}_t}\left(\hat{\boldsymbol{\theta}}_t \hat{\boldsymbol{\theta}}_t^T\right) Q_* C_t^T$$
$$\quad + \eta_t C_t Q_* \boldsymbol{\theta}_* \hat{\boldsymbol{\theta}}_t^T + \eta_t \boldsymbol{\theta}_t \hat{\boldsymbol{\theta}}_*^T Q_* C_t^T + \eta_t^2 C_t G_* C_t^T + O(\eta_t^3) + O(\epsilon \eta_t^2) + O(\epsilon^2 \eta_t). \tag{A.20}$$

Noting the definition

$$V_t = E^{\hat{\theta}_t}(\hat{\theta}_t \hat{\theta}_t^T) - \theta_t \theta_t^T, \tag{A.21}$$

and using the relation

$$\theta_{t+1} \theta_{t+1}^T$$
$$= \{\theta_t - \eta_t C_t Q_*(\theta_t - \theta_*)\} \{\theta_t - \eta_t C_t Q_*(\theta_t - \theta_*)\}^T + O(\eta_t^3) + O(\epsilon^2 \eta_t)$$
$$= \theta_t \theta_t^T - \eta_t C_t Q_* \theta_t \theta_t^T - \eta_t \theta_t \theta_t^T Q_* C_t^T$$
$$+ \eta_t C_t Q_* \theta_* \theta_t^T + \eta_t \theta_t \theta_*^T Q_* C_t^T + \eta_t^2 C_t Q_*(\theta_t - \theta_*)(\theta_t - \theta_*)^T Q_* C_t^T$$
$$+ O(\eta_t^3) + O(\epsilon^2 \eta_t), \tag{A.22}$$

we obtain

$$V_{t+1} = E^{\theta_{t+1}} \left(\hat{\theta}_{t+1} \hat{\theta}_{t+1}^T \right) - \theta_{t+1} \theta_{t+1}^T$$
$$= V_t - \eta_t C_t Q_* V_t - \eta_t V_t Q_* C_t^T$$
$$+ \eta_t^2 C_t G_* C_t^T - \eta_t^2 C_t Q_*(\theta_t - \theta_*)(\theta_t - \theta_*)^T Q_* C_t^T$$
$$+ O(\eta_t^3) + O(\epsilon \eta_t^2) + O(\epsilon^2 \eta_t). \tag{A.23}$$

□

A.3 Proof of Theorem 1

From Equation (2.9), the solution of the mean is trivial.

From the properties of operators Ξ and Ω,

$$\eta^2 K_*(\theta_t - \theta_*)(\theta_t - \theta_*)^T K_*^T = \Omega_{\eta K_*} \Omega_{(I-\eta K_*)^t}(\theta_0 - \theta_*)(\theta_0 - \theta_*)^T$$
$$= \Omega_{\eta K_*}(\Omega_{I-\eta K_*})^t(\theta_0 - \theta_*)(\theta_0 - \theta_*)^T$$
$$= (\Omega_{I-\eta K_*})^t \Omega_{\eta K_*}(\theta_0 - \theta_*)(\theta_0 - \theta_*)^T \tag{A.24}$$

holds. Let us define

$$v_t = V_t - \eta V_\infty, \tag{A.25}$$
$$u_t = (\Omega_{I-\eta K_*})^t \Omega_{\eta K_*}(\theta_0 - \theta_*)(\theta_0 - \theta_*)^T, \tag{A.26}$$

then the recursive equation for the variance can be written by two equations

$$v_{t+1} = (I - \Xi_{\eta K_*})v_t - u_t, \tag{A.27}$$
$$u_{t+1} = \Omega_{I-\eta K_*} u_t, \tag{A.28}$$

and they are rewritten in matrix form as

$$\begin{pmatrix} v_{t+1} \\ u_{t+1} \end{pmatrix} = \begin{pmatrix} I - \Xi_{\eta K_*} & -I \\ 0 & \Omega_{I-\eta K_*} \end{pmatrix} \begin{pmatrix} v_t \\ u_t \end{pmatrix}. \tag{A.29}$$

Noting the commutativity of operators and the relation

$$\Omega_{I-\eta K_*} = I - \Xi_{\eta K_*} + \Omega_{\eta K_*},$$

the solution of the recursive equation system is

$$\begin{pmatrix} v_t \\ u_t \end{pmatrix} = \begin{pmatrix} (I - \Xi_{\eta K_*})^t & -(\Omega_{\eta K_*})^{-1}\{(\Omega_{I-\eta K_*})^t - (I - \Xi_{\eta K_*})^t\} \\ 0 & (\Omega_{I-\eta K_*})^t \end{pmatrix} \begin{pmatrix} v_0 \\ u_0 \end{pmatrix},$$

$$\tag{A.30}$$

where the initial values are given by

$$v_0 = -(\Xi_{\eta K_*})^{-1}\Omega_{\eta K_*}V_* = -\eta(\Xi_{K_*})^{-1}\Omega_{K_*}V_* = -V_\infty \tag{A.31}$$
$$u_0 = \Omega_{\eta K_*}(\theta_0 - \theta_*)(\theta_0 - \theta_*)^T = \Omega_{\eta K_*}V_0 \tag{A.32}$$

By using the definition of v_t, V_t is obtained.   □

A.4   Proof of Theorem 2

From Equation (2.9) and the definition of S_t, the solution of the mean is trivial.

The solution of the variance is given by considering the following two cases.

Let us assume the order of V_t is slower than $O(1/t)$. Considering the contribution to the leading term, Equation (2.10) is written as

$$V_{t+1} = V_t - \frac{1}{t+1}(K_*V_t + V_tK_*^T) + \frac{1}{(t+1)^2}K_*V_*K_*^T$$
$$= \left(\frac{1}{2}I - \frac{1}{t+1}K_*\right)V_t + V_t\left(\frac{1}{2}I - \frac{1}{t+1}K_*\right)^T$$

by omitting the higher order terms. This recursive equation gives the solution, and knowing that the eigenvalue of $\Xi_{\frac{1}{2}I-\frac{1}{t+1}K_*}$ is represented by

$$1 - \frac{\lambda_i + \lambda_j}{t+1}, \quad i,j = 1,\ldots,m,$$

the order of R_t is bounded by $O(1/t^{2\lambda_m})$. Therefore, when $\lambda_m < 1/2$ holds, R_tV' is slower than $O(1/t)$.

Let us assume the order of V_t is $O(1/t)$ and write V_t with $1/tV$. By omitting the higher order terms, we have the equation for the leading order as

$$V_{t+1} = V_t - \frac{1}{t+1}(K_*V_t + V_tK_*^T) + \frac{1}{(t+1)^2}K_*V_*K_*^T$$
$$\frac{1}{t+1}V = \frac{1}{t}V - \frac{1}{t(t+1)}(K_*V + VK_*^T) + \frac{1}{(t+1)^2}K_*V_*K_*^T$$

$$\frac{1}{t(t+1)}\left(K_*V + VK_*^T - V\right) = \frac{1}{(t+1)^2}K_*V_*K_*^T$$

Then we have the solution

$$V = \frac{t}{t+1}\left(\Xi_{K_*} - I\right)^{-1}K_*V_*K_*^T. \tag{A.33}$$

□

B Asymptotic Distribution of Fixed Rate Learning

Here we calculate the evolution of the characteristic function of estimator $\hat{\boldsymbol{\theta}}_t$. Let f be

$$f(\boldsymbol{\theta}) = e^{\sqrt{-1}z_i(\theta^i - \theta_*^i)}, \tag{B.1}$$

where $\boldsymbol{z} = (z_i) \in \mathbf{R}^m$ and m is the dimension of the parameter $\boldsymbol{\theta}$. Without loss of generality, we can assume that the optimal parameter θ^* is at origin, that is, we use such a coordinate for simplicity. Then f can be written as

$$f(\boldsymbol{\theta}) = e^{\sqrt{-1}z_i\theta^i}, \tag{B.2}$$

The characteristic function of the distribution of $\hat{\boldsymbol{\theta}}_t$ is

$$E^{\cdot t}(f(\hat{\boldsymbol{\theta}}_t)) = \varphi_t(\boldsymbol{z}). \tag{B.3}$$

Knowing that $\hat{\boldsymbol{\theta}}_t \sim O(\sqrt{\eta})$ after sufficient learning steps, ∂D can be expanded around the origin up to order $O(\eta)$ as

$$\partial_i D(\hat{\boldsymbol{\theta}}_t) = q_{ij}\hat{\theta}_t^j + \frac{t_{ijk}}{2}\hat{\theta}_t^j\hat{\theta}_t^k + O(\eta^{3/2}),$$

where

$$q_{ij} = \partial_i\partial_j D(\boldsymbol{\theta}_*), \quad t_{ijk} = \partial_i\partial_j\partial_k D(\boldsymbol{\theta}_*).$$

From Lemma 2, we obtain the recursive equation

$$\varphi_{t+1}(\boldsymbol{z}) = \varphi_t(\boldsymbol{z}) - \eta E^{\cdot t}\left(c^{ij}\sqrt{-1}z_i f(\hat{\boldsymbol{\theta}}_t)\left(q_{jk}\hat{\theta}_t^k + \frac{t_{jkl}}{2}\hat{\theta}_t^k\hat{\theta}_t^l\right)\right)$$
$$- \frac{\eta^2}{2}E^{\cdot t}\left(c^{ik}c^{jl}g_{kl}z_iz_j f(\hat{\boldsymbol{\theta}}_t)\right) + O(\eta^{5/2})$$
$$= \varphi_t(\boldsymbol{z}) - \eta c^{ij}z_i E^{\cdot t}\left(q_{jk}\frac{\partial}{\partial z_k}f(\hat{\boldsymbol{\theta}}_t) - \sqrt{-1}\frac{t_{jkl}}{2}\frac{\partial^2}{\partial z_k\partial z_l}f(\hat{\boldsymbol{\theta}}_t)\right)$$
$$- \frac{\eta^2}{2}c^{ik}c^{jl}g_{kl}z_iz_j E^{\cdot t}(f(\hat{\boldsymbol{\theta}}_t)) + O(\eta^{5/2})$$
$$= \varphi_t(\boldsymbol{z}) - \eta c^{ij}z_i\left(q_{jk}\frac{\partial}{\partial z_k}\varphi_t(\boldsymbol{z}) - \sqrt{-1}\frac{t_{jkl}}{2}\frac{\partial^2}{\partial z_k\partial z_l}\varphi_t(\boldsymbol{z})\right)$$
$$- \frac{\eta^2}{2}c^{ik}c^{jl}g_{kl}z_iz_j\varphi_t(\boldsymbol{z}) + O(\eta^{5/2}), \tag{B.4}$$

where c^{ij} is the ij element of matrix C and relations

$$\partial_k f(\boldsymbol{\theta}) = \sqrt{-1} z_k f(\boldsymbol{\theta}), \ldots \quad \frac{\partial}{\partial z_k} f(\boldsymbol{\theta}) = \sqrt{-1} \theta_k f(\boldsymbol{\theta}), \ldots$$

are used.

Assuming that as $t \to \infty$, a sequence of characteristic functions $\{\varphi_t\}$ converge to a function

$$\varphi_t(\boldsymbol{z}) \to \varphi(\boldsymbol{z}),$$

we have the equation from Equation (B.4)

$$c^{ij} z_i \left(q_{jk} \frac{\partial}{\partial z_k} \varphi(\boldsymbol{z}) - \sqrt{-1} \frac{t_{jkl}}{2} \frac{\partial^2}{\partial z_k \partial z_l} \varphi(\boldsymbol{z}) \right) = -\frac{\eta}{2} c^{ik} c^{jl} g_{kl} z_i z_j \varphi(\boldsymbol{z}) + O(\eta^{3/2}) \tag{B.5}$$

for any $\boldsymbol{z}$. Using an expansion

$$\varphi(\boldsymbol{z}) = e^{h_0(\boldsymbol{z}) + \eta h_1(\boldsymbol{z}) + O(\eta^{3/2})}, \tag{B.6}$$

we obtain equations

$$c^{ij} z_i \left(q_{jk} \frac{\partial}{\partial z_k} h_0(\boldsymbol{z}) - \sqrt{-1} \frac{t_{jkl}}{2} \frac{\partial^2}{\partial z_k \partial z_l} h_0(\boldsymbol{z}) \right) = 0 \tag{B.7}$$

$$c^{ij} z_i \left(q_{jk} \frac{\partial}{\partial z_k} h_1(\boldsymbol{z}) - \sqrt{-1} \frac{t_{jkl}}{2} \frac{\partial^2}{\partial z_k \partial z_l} h_1(\boldsymbol{z}) \right) = -\frac{1}{2} c^{ik} c^{jl} g_{kl} z_i z_j. \tag{B.8}$$

Knowing that $\varphi(0) = 1$ from the property of the characteristic function, we obtain solutions

$$h_0(\boldsymbol{z}) = 0 \tag{B.9}$$

$$h_1(\boldsymbol{z}) = -\frac{1}{2} z_i z_j v^{ij} - \sqrt{-1} z_i u^i, \tag{B.10}$$

where v^{ij} is a symmetric matrix which satisfies

$$c^{ik} q_{kl} v^{lj} + c^{jk} q_{kl} v^{li} = c^{ik} c^{jl} g_{kl}$$

and $\boldsymbol{u}$ is given by

$$u^i = -q^{ij} t_{jkl} v^{kl}.$$

Therefore we have the following theorem and corollary.

Theorem 3. *The characteristic function of the estimator obtained by on-line learning with Equation (1.14) converges to*

$$\varphi(\boldsymbol{z}) = \exp \left\{ \sqrt{-1} z_i \left(\theta_*^i - \eta u^i \right) - \frac{\eta}{2} z_i z_j v^{ij} + O(\eta^{2/3}) \right\}. \tag{B.11}$$

Corollary 5. *The mean of the estimator with Equation* (1.14) *converges to*

$$\lim_{t\to\infty} E(\boldsymbol{\theta}_t) = \boldsymbol{\theta}_* - \eta\boldsymbol{u} + O(\eta^{2/3}). \tag{B.12}$$

There exists bias of order $O(\eta)$ in the mean of the estimator, but the order of standard deviation is $O(\sqrt{\eta})$, which comes from the second derivative of the characteristic function. As η goes to 0, the bias can be neglected asymptotically.

C Dynamical Property of Fixed Rate Learning

C.1 Step Response

Let us consider the situation in which the distribution of examples changes at $t = 0$

$$p(\boldsymbol{x}, \boldsymbol{y}) \to p(\boldsymbol{x}, \boldsymbol{y}) + \delta p(\boldsymbol{x}, \boldsymbol{y}), \tag{C.1}$$

and as a result, the optimal parameter changes as

$$\boldsymbol{\theta}_* + \delta\boldsymbol{\theta} = \underset{\boldsymbol{\theta}}{\operatorname{argmin}}\, E_{p+\delta p}(d(\boldsymbol{X}, \boldsymbol{Y}; \boldsymbol{\theta})). \tag{C.2}$$

For simplicity, we assume that $\delta\boldsymbol{\theta}$ is sufficiently small and the approximations

$$G(\boldsymbol{\theta}_* + \delta\boldsymbol{\theta}) \simeq G(\boldsymbol{\theta}_*) = G_*, \tag{C.3}$$
$$Q(\boldsymbol{\theta}_* + \delta\boldsymbol{\theta}) \simeq Q(\boldsymbol{\theta}_*) = Q_* \tag{C.4}$$

hold. Suppose before $t = 0$ the estimator has converged in an average sense, i.e.

$$\boldsymbol{\theta}_t = \boldsymbol{\theta}_*,$$
$$V_t = \eta V_\infty,$$

then from Equation (2.9), the mean of the estimator at t is given by

$$\boldsymbol{\theta}_t = \boldsymbol{\theta}_* + (I - (I - \eta K_*)^t)\delta\boldsymbol{\theta}. \tag{C.5}$$

Therefore, the step response of the mean is represented by operator

$$I - (I - \eta K_*)^t. \tag{C.6}$$

From Equation (2.10), the variance of the estimator is also calculated as

$$V_t = \eta V_\infty - \left\{(\Omega_{I-\eta K_*})^t - (I - \Xi_{\eta K_*})^t\right\}\delta\boldsymbol{\theta}\delta\boldsymbol{\theta}^T. \tag{C.7}$$

The second term corresponds to the transitional response. It is interesting that the variance becomes once slightly smaller than ηV_∞ while the mean is apart from the optimal parameter, and as the mean converges to the optimal parameter the variance goes back to ηV_∞.

The learning curve can be calculated by using above result. Noting

$$E\left((\hat{\theta}_t - (\theta_* + \delta\theta))(\hat{\theta}_t - (\theta_* + \delta\theta))^T\right)$$

$$= E\left((\hat{\theta}_t - \theta_t)(\hat{\theta}_t - \theta_t)^T\right) + E\left((\theta_t - (\theta_* + \delta\theta))(\theta_t - (\theta_* + \delta\theta))^T\right)$$

$$= V_t + (\Omega_{I-\eta K_*})^t \delta\theta\delta\theta^T$$

$$= \eta V_\infty + (I - \Xi_{\eta K_*})^t \delta\theta\delta\theta^T, \tag{C.8}$$

and expanding new total loss $D'(\theta_t)$ around the new optimal parameter $\theta_* + \delta\theta$, we obtain

$$E\left(D'(\theta_t)\right)$$

$$= D'(\theta_* + \delta\theta) + \frac{1}{2}\operatorname{tr}\left(Q_* E\left((\theta_t - (\theta_* + \delta\theta))(\theta_t - (\theta_* + \delta\theta))^T\right)\right)$$

$$= D'(\theta_* + \delta\theta) + \frac{1}{2}\eta\operatorname{tr}\left(Q_* V_\infty\right) + \frac{1}{2}\operatorname{tr}\left((I - \Xi_{\eta K_*})^t Q_* \delta\theta\delta\theta^T\right). \tag{C.9}$$

The third term corresponds to the step response of the learning curve.

C.2 Frequency Response

Let us consider the situation in which the optimal parameter fluctuates around parameter θ_* as

$$\theta_* + \delta\theta_t = \theta_* + \kappa_i \sin\omega_i t, \tag{C.10}$$

where κ_i is an eigenvector of matrix K_* with the i-th eigenvalue λ_i

$$K_*\kappa_i = \lambda_i\kappa_i. \tag{C.11}$$

Here we assume that $\delta\theta_t$ is sufficiently small and the approximations

$$G(\theta_* + \delta\theta_t) \simeq G(\theta_*) = G_*, \tag{C.12}$$
$$Q(\theta_* + \delta\theta_t) \simeq Q(\theta_*) = Q_*. \tag{C.13}$$

hold. From Equation (2.9), the evolution of the mean is given by

$$\theta_{t+1} = (I - \eta K_*)\theta_t + \eta K_*\theta_* + \eta\lambda_i\kappa_i \sin\omega_i t. \tag{C.14}$$

Suppose the stationary solution is written as

$$\theta_t = \theta_* + a_i\kappa_i \sin(\omega_i t - \alpha_i). \tag{C.15}$$

From the addition theorem of the trigonometric functions, the relations

$$\eta\lambda_i \cos\alpha_i = a_i\{\cos\omega_i - (1 - \eta\lambda_i)\} \tag{C.16}$$

$$\eta\lambda_i \sin\alpha_i = a_i \sin\omega_i \tag{C.17}$$

are obtained, then a_i and α_i are given by

$$a_i = \frac{\eta\lambda_i}{\sqrt{(\cos\omega_i - (1 - \eta\lambda_i))^2 + (\sin\omega_i)^2}}, \tag{C.18}$$

$$\tan\alpha_i = \frac{\sin\omega_i}{\cos\omega_i - (1 - \eta\lambda_i)}. \tag{C.19}$$

When ω_i is small, that is, the fluctuation is slow, the approximated solution is given by

$$a_i = \frac{1}{\sqrt{1 + \alpha_i^2}}, \tag{C.20}$$

$$\alpha_i = \frac{\omega_i}{\eta\lambda_i}. \tag{C.21}$$

In this case, the stationary solution is written as

$$\theta_t = \theta_* + \frac{1}{\sqrt{1 + \alpha_i^2}}\kappa_i \sin(\omega_i t - \alpha_i), \tag{C.22}$$

and the solution means that when the optimal parameter oscillates with period $2\pi/\omega_i$ along the eigendirection of eigenvalue λ_i, the estimator follows the optimal parameter with delay α_i and the amplitude is reduced as $1/\sqrt{1 + \alpha_i^2}$ times. If the direction of oscillation $\delta\theta_t$ is general, we can consider the linear combination of eigenvectors. In any cases, if α_i is sufficiently small

$$\omega_i \ll \eta\lambda_i, \quad i = 1, \ldots, m, \tag{C.23}$$

the on-line learning can follow the fluctuation of the target.

Similarly the frequency response of the variance can be discussed as follows. Here we assume that α_i is small and the difference between the estimator and the optimal parameter is approximated by

$$\theta_t - (\theta_* + \delta\theta_t) = \kappa_i \left(\frac{1}{\sqrt{1 + \alpha^2}} \sin(\omega_i t - \alpha_i) - \sin(\omega_i t) \right)$$

$$= \kappa_i \left(\alpha_i \cos(\omega_i t) + O(\alpha_i^2) \right). \tag{C.24}$$

By neglecting the higher order term of α_i, the recursive equation for the variance is given by

$$V_{t+1} = (I - \eta\Xi_{K_*})V_t + \eta^2 K_* V_* K_*^T - \eta^2\alpha_i^2 \cos^2(\omega_i t)\Omega_{K_*}\kappa_i\kappa_i^T. \tag{C.25}$$

Let us assume the stationary solution of the variance is

$$V_t = \eta V_\infty + \{b_i \cos(2\omega_i t + \phi_i) + c_i\} \kappa_i \kappa_i^T. \qquad (C.26)$$

Using the relations

$$\Xi_{K_\bullet} \kappa_i \kappa_i^T = 2\lambda_i \kappa_i \kappa_i^T, \qquad (C.27)$$

$$\Omega_{K_\bullet} \kappa_i \kappa_i^T = \lambda_i^2 \kappa_i \kappa_i^T, \qquad (C.28)$$

the magnification of the amplitude b_i and bias c_i and phase shift ϕ_i satisfy the equations

$$\frac{\eta^2 \lambda_i^2 \alpha_i^2}{2} \cos \phi_i = b_i (1 - 2\eta\lambda_i - \cos 2\omega_i), \qquad (C.29)$$

$$\frac{\eta^2 \lambda_i^2 \alpha_i^2}{2} \sin \phi_i = b_i \sin 2\omega_i, \qquad (C.30)$$

$$\frac{\eta^2 \lambda_i^2 \alpha_i^2}{2} = -2\eta\lambda_i c_i. \qquad (C.31)$$

The solutions are

$$b_i = \frac{\eta^2 \lambda_i^2 \alpha_i^2}{2\sqrt{(1 - 2\eta\lambda_i - \cos 2\omega_i)^2 + (\sin 2\omega_i)^2}}, \qquad (C.32)$$

$$c_i = -\frac{1}{4}\eta\lambda_i \alpha_i^2, \qquad (C.33)$$

$$\tan \phi_i = \frac{\sin 2\omega_i}{1 - 2\eta\lambda_i - \cos 2\omega_i}. \qquad (C.34)$$

By neglecting the higher order terms in the same way as the mean, we obtain the approximations

$$b_i = \frac{\eta\lambda_i \alpha_i^2}{4\sqrt{1 + \alpha_i^2}}, \qquad (C.35)$$

$$c_i = -\frac{\eta\lambda_i \alpha_i^2}{4}, \qquad (C.36)$$

$$\phi_i = \frac{\omega_i}{\eta\lambda_i} = \alpha_i. \qquad (C.37)$$

Therefore the stationary solution is

$$V_t = \eta V_\infty - \frac{\eta\lambda_i \alpha_i^2}{4} \left(1 - \frac{1}{\sqrt{1 + \alpha_i^2}} \cos(2\omega_i t + \alpha_i)\right) \kappa_i \kappa_i^T. \qquad (C.38)$$

Similar to the step response, V_t becomes slightly smaller than the case where the target doesn't move.

Using the relation

$$E^{\hat{\theta}_t}\left((\hat{\theta}_t - (\theta_* + \delta\theta_t))(\hat{\theta}_t - (\theta_* + \delta\theta_t))^T\right)$$

$$= E^{\hat{\theta}_t}\left((\hat{\theta}_t - \theta_t)(\hat{\theta}_t - \theta_t)^T\right) + \left((\theta_t - (\theta_* + \delta\theta_t))(\theta_t - (\theta_* + \delta\theta_t))^T\right)$$

$$= V_t + (\alpha_i \cos\omega_i t)^2 \kappa_i \kappa_i^T$$

$$= \eta V_\infty - \frac{\eta\lambda_i\alpha_i^2}{4}\left(1 - \frac{1}{\sqrt{1+\alpha_i^2}}\cos(2\omega_i t + \alpha_i)\right)\kappa_i\kappa_i^T$$

$$+ \frac{\alpha_i^2}{2}(\cos 2\omega_i t + 1)\kappa_i\kappa_i^T$$

$$\simeq \eta V_\infty + \left\{\left(\frac{1}{2} - \frac{\eta\lambda_i}{4}\right) + \left(\frac{1}{2} + \frac{\eta\lambda_i}{4\sqrt{1+\alpha_i^2}}\right)\cos 2\omega_i t\right\}\alpha_i^2\kappa_i\kappa_i^T, \qquad (C.39)$$

the frequency response of the learning curve can be also calculated in the same way as the step response,

$$E^{\hat{\theta}_t}\left(D_t(\hat{\theta}_t)\right)$$

$$= D_t(\theta_* + \delta\theta_t) + \frac{1}{2}\operatorname{tr}\left(Q_* E^{\hat{\theta}_t}\left((\theta_t - (\theta_* + \delta\theta_t))(\theta_t - (\theta_* + \delta\theta_t))^T\right)\right)$$

$$= D_t(\theta_* + \delta\theta_t) + \frac{1}{2}\eta\operatorname{tr}(Q_* V_\infty)$$

$$+ \frac{1}{2}\left\{\left(\frac{1}{2} - \frac{\eta\lambda_i}{4}\right) + \left(\frac{1}{2} + \frac{\eta\lambda_i}{4\sqrt{1+\alpha_i^2}}\right)\cos 2\omega_i t\right\}\alpha_i^2\operatorname{tr}\left(Q_*\kappa_i\kappa_i^T\right),$$

$$(C.40)$$

where D_t denotes the total loss defined by the input-output distribution at time t. Note that the third term represents the fluctuation of the learning curve and its order is

$$O(\alpha_i^2) = O\left(\frac{\omega_i^2}{(\eta\lambda_i)^2}\right). \qquad (C.41)$$

Hence, if

$$\frac{\omega_i^2}{(\eta\lambda_i)^2} \ll \eta$$

holds, the on-line learning can follow the target with negligible loss of the performance.

References

Akahira, M., and Takeuchi, K. (1981) Asymptotic Efficiency of Statistical Estimators: Concepts and Higher Order Asymptotic Efficiency, vol. 7 of *Lecture Notes in Statistics*, Springer-Verlag.

Amari, S. (1967) Theory of adaptive pattern classifiers, *IEEE Trans.* EC-16, 299–307.

Amari, S. (1985) Differential-Geometrical Methods in Statistics, vol. 28 of *Lecture Notes in Statistics*, Springer-Verlag.

Amari, S., Fujita, N., and Shinomoto, S. (1992) Four types of learning curves, *Neural Computation*, 4, 605–618.

Amari, S., and Murata, N. (1993) Statistical theory of learning curves under entropic loss criterion, *Neural Computation*, 5, 140–153.

Fukumizu, K. (1997) Special statistical properties of neural network learning, *Proceedings of 1997 International Symposium on Nonlinear Theory and Its Applications (NOLTA'97)*, 747–750.

Godambe, V.P. (ed.) (1991) *Estimating Functions* New York: Oxford University Press.

Heskes, T. M., and Kappen, B. (1991) Learning processes in neural networks, *Phys. Rev.*, A 44, 2718–2726.

Kawanabe, M. and Amari, S. (1994) Estimation of Network Parameters in Semiparametric Stochastic Perceptron, *Neural Computation*, 6, 1244–1261.

Kim, J. W., and Sompolinsky, H. (1995) On-line Gibbs learning, Submitted to *Phys. Rev.Lett.*

Levin, E., Tishby, N., and Solla, S. A. (1990) A statistical approach to learning and generalization in layered neural networks, *Proceedings of the IEEE* 78, 1568–1574.

Minsky, M., and Papert, S. (1988) *Perceptrons – An Introduction to Computational Geometry* (Expanded Edition) , MIT Press.

Murata, N., Yoshizawa, S., and Amari, S. (1991) A criterion for determining the number of parameters in an artificial neural network model, In *Artificial Neural Networks* (Holland), Kohonen, T. et al., Eds., ICANN, Elsevier Science Publishers, 9–14.

Murata, N., Yoshizawa, S., and Amari, S. (1993) Learning curves, model selection and complexity of neural networks, In *Advances in Neural Information Processing Systems 5*, Hanson, S.J., Cowan, J.D., and Giles, C.L. Eds. Morgan Kaufmann Publishers, San Mateo, CA, 607–614.

Murata, N., Yoshizawa, S., and Amari, S. (1994) Network information criterion — determining the number of hidden units for an artificial neural network model, *IEEE Trans.* NN-5, 865–872.

Müller, K.-R., Ziehe, A., Murata, N., and Amari, S. (1998) On-line Learning in Switching and Drifting Environments with Application to Blind Source Separation, *in this volume*.

Niyogi, P., and Girosi, F. (1994) On the relationship between generalization error, hypothesis complexity, and sample complexity for radial basis functions, *Technical Report A.I.* Memo No. 1467, C.B.C.L. Memo No. 88, MIT.

Opper, M., and Haussler, D. (1991) Calculation of the learning curve of Bayes optimal classification algorithm for learning a Perceptron with noise, In *Proceedings of COLT* (San Mateo, CA), Morgan Kaufmann Publishers, 75–87.

Opper, M., and Haussler, D. Bounds for predictive errors in the statistical mechanics of supervised learning, Submitted to *Phys. Rev. Lett.*

Rissanen, J. (1986) Stochastic complexity and modeling, *Ann. of Statist.* 14, 1080–1100.

Robbins, H., and Monro, S. (1951) A stochastic approximation method, *Ann. of Math. Statist.*, 22, 400–407.

Rosenblatt, F. (1961) *Principle of Neurodynamics*, Spartan.

Rumelhart, D., McClelland, J. L., and the PDP Research Group (1986) *Parallel Distributed Processing : Explorations in the Microstructure of Cognition*, The MIT Press.

Seung, H. S., Sompolinsky, H., and Tishby, N. (1992) Statistical mechanics of learning from examples, *Phys. Rev. A*, 45, 6056–6091.

Sompolinski, H., and Barkai, N. (1993) Theory of learning from examples, In *IJCNN'93-NAGOYA Tutorial Texts*, International Joint Conference on Neural Networks, 221–240.

Sompolinsky, H., Barkai, N., Seung, H.S. (1995) On-line learning of dichotomies: algorithms and learning curves, Oh,J-H, Kwon,C. Cho, S. (eds.), *Neural Networks: The Statistical Mechanics Perspective*, 105–130, Singapore: World Scientific.

White, H. (1989) Learning in artificial neural networks : A statistical perspective, *Neural Computation* 1, 425–464.

Widrow, B. (1963) *A Statistical Theory of Adaptation* , Pergamon Press.

On-line Learning in Switching and Drifting Environments with Application to Blind Source Separation

Klaus-Robert Müller and Andreas Ziehe

GMD-First
Rudower Chaussee 5
D-12489 Berlin, Germany
klaus@first.gmd.de

Noboru Murata * *and Shun-ichi Amari* ‡

Brain Science Institute, RIKEN
Wako-shi, Saitama 351-0198, Japan
*mura@irl.riken.go.jp
‡amari@brain.riken.go.jp

Abstract

An adaptive on-line algorithm extending the learning of learning idea is proposed and theoretically motivated. Relying only on gradient flow information it can be applied to learning continuous functions or distributions, even when no explicit loss function is given and the Hessian is not available. Its efficiency is demonstrated for drifting and switching non-stationary blind separation tasks of accoustic signals.

1   Introduction

Neural networks are powerful tools that can capture the structure in data by learning. Often the batch learning paradigm is assumed, where the learner is given all training examples simultaneously and allowed to use them as often as desired. In large practical applications batch learning is experienced to be rather infeasible and instead on-line learning is employed.

In the on-line learning scenario only one example is given at a time and then discarded after learning. So it is less memory consuming and at the same time it fits well into more natural learning, where the learner receives new information at every moment and should adapt to it, without having a large memory for storing old data. Appart from easier feasibility and data handling the most important advantage of on-line learning is its ability to adapt to changing environments, a quite common scenario in industrial applications

93

where the data distribution changes gradually over time (e.g. due to wear and tear of the machines). If the learning machine does not detect and follow the change it is impossible to learn the data properly and large generalization errors will result. With batch learning, changes go undetected and we obtain rather bad results since we are likely to average over several rules, whereas on-line learning – if operated properly (see below) – will track the changes and yield good approximation results.

On-line learning has been analyzed extensively within the framework of statistics (Robbins and Monro, 1951; Amari, 1967; Murata, 1992; Murata, 1998 and others) and statistical mechanics (see eg. Saad and Solla, 1995) and contributions to this volume). It was shown that on-line learning is asymptotically as effective as batch learning (cf. Robbins and Monro, 1951). However this only holds, if the appropriate learning rate η is chosen. A too small η makes learning impractically slow and is therefore not useful and a too large η spoils the convergence of learning.

In earlier work on dichotomies Sompolinsky et al.(1995) showed the effect on the rate of convergence of the generalization error of a constant, annealed (cf. Eq.(2.2)) and adaptive learning rate. In particular, although the annealed learning rate provides an optimal convergence rate in estimation error, it cannot follow rule changes. Since on-line learning aims to follow the change of the rule which generated the data, Sompolinsky et al. (1995), Darken and Moody (1991), Sutton (1992), Murata et al. (1997) proposed adaptive learning rates, which learn how to learn. They enable the learning rate to increase and decrease depending on the error and control the speed of convergence.

We will extend the reasoning of Sompolinsky et al. (1995) in several points: (1) we give an adaptive learning rule for learning continuous functions (section 3) and (2) we consider the case, where no explicit loss function is given and the Hessian cannot be accessed (section 4). This will help us to apply our idea to the problem of on-line blind separation in a changing environment (section 5). The conclusion emphasizes the general applicability of our proposed adaptive learning rule.

2   On-line Learning

Let us consider an infinite sequence of independent examples

$$(x_1, y_1), (x_2, y_2), \ldots.$$

The purpose of learning is to obtain a network with parameter $\hat{w}$ which can simulate the rule inherent to this data. To this end, the neural network modifies its parameter $\hat{w}_t$ at time t into $\hat{w}_{t+1}$ by using only the next example (x_{t+1}, y_{t+1}) given by the rule. We introduce a loss function $l(x, y; w)$ to evaluate the performance of the network with parameter w. Let

$$R(w) = \langle l(x, y; w) \rangle$$

be the expected loss or the generalization error of the network having parameter w, where $\langle \; \rangle$ denotes the average over the distribution of examples (x, y). The parameter w^* of the best machine is given by

$$w^* = \operatorname{argmin} R(w).$$

We use the following stochastic gradient descent algorithm (see Amari , 1967) and Rumelhart et al., 1986)):

$$\hat{w}_{t+1} = \hat{w}_t - \eta_t C(\hat{w}_t) \frac{\partial}{\partial w} l(x_{t+1}, y_{t+1}; \hat{w}_t), \qquad (2.1)$$

where η_t is the learning rate which may depend on t and $C(\hat{w}_t)$ is a positive-definite matrix which may depend on $\hat{w}_t$. The matrix C plays the role of the Riemannian metric tensor of the underlying parameter space $\{w\}$.
When η_t is fixed to be equal to a small constant η, $E[\hat{w}_t]$ converges to w^* and $\operatorname{Var}[\hat{w}_t]$ converges to a non-zero matrix which is proportional to η. It means that $\hat{w}_t$ fluctuates around w^* (see Amari (1967), Heskes & Kappen (1991), Murata (1992), (1998)). If

$$\eta_t = c/t \qquad \text{(annealed learning rate)} \qquad (2.2)$$

(c is a constant) $\hat{w}_t$ converges to w^* locally (Sompolinsky et al., 1995)). However when the rule changes over time, an annealed learning rate cannot follow the changes fast enough since $\eta_t = c/t$ is too small. So we need an adaptive rate η_t that can both increase when the rule changes and then decrease to converge to a better estimate of w^* (cf. Darken and Moody, 1991; Sutton, 1992; Murata et al., 1997).

3 Adaptive Learning Rate

The idea of an adaptively changing η_t was called learning of the learning rule (Sompolinsky et al., 1995). In this section we investigate an extension of this idea to differentiable loss functions. Following their algorithm, we consider

$$\hat{w}_{t+1} = \hat{w}_t - \eta_t K^{-1}(\hat{w}_t) \frac{\partial}{\partial w} l(x_{t+1}, y_{t+1}; \hat{w}_t), \qquad (3.1)$$

$$\eta_{t+1} = \eta_t + \alpha \eta_t \left(\beta \left(l(x_{t+1}, y_{t+1}; \hat{w}_t) - \hat{R} \right) - \eta_t \right), \qquad (3.2)$$

where α and β are constants, $K(\hat{w}_t)$ is a Hessian matrix of the expected loss function $\partial^2 R(\hat{w}_t)/\partial w \partial w$ and $\hat{R}$ is an estimator of $R(w^*)$. Intuitively speaking, the coefficient η in Eq.(3.2) is controlled by the remaining error. When the error is large, η takes a relatively large value. When the error is small, it means that the estimated parameter is close to the optimal parameter; η approaches to 0 automatically. However, for the above algorithm all quantities $(K, l, \hat{R})$

have to be accessible, which they are certainly not in general. Furthermore
$l(x_{t+1}, y_{t+1}; \hat{w}_t) - \hat{R}$ could take negative values. In order to understand the
learning behaviour, we use the continuous versions of (3.1) and (3.2) and
average with respect to the current input-output pair (x_t, y_t). Furthermore we
omit correlations and variances between the quantities (η_t, w_t, l), which would
complicate the equations and conceil their intuitive meaning. We obtain the
following simplified differential equations

$$\frac{d}{dt}w_t = -\eta_t K^{-1}(w_t) \left\langle \frac{\partial}{\partial w}l(x, y; w_t) \right\rangle$$

$$\text{and} \quad \frac{d}{dt}\eta_t = \alpha\eta_t \left(\beta\langle l(x, y; w_t) - \hat{R}\rangle - \eta_t\right).$$

Noting that $\langle \partial l(x, y; w^*)/\partial w \rangle = 0$, we have the asymptotic evaluations

$$\left\langle \frac{\partial}{\partial w}l(x, y; w_t) \right\rangle \simeq K^*(w_t - w^*),$$

$$\langle l(x, y; w_t) - \hat{R}\rangle \simeq R(w^*) - \hat{R} + \frac{1}{2}(w_t - w^*)^T K^*(w_t - w^*),$$

with $K^* = \partial^2 R(w^*)/\partial w \partial w$. Assuming $R(w^*) - \hat{R}$ is small and $K(w_t) \simeq K^*$
yields

$$\frac{d}{dt}w_t = -\eta_t(w_t - w^*),$$

$$\frac{d}{dt}\eta_t = \alpha\eta_t \left(\frac{\beta}{2}(w_t - w^*)^T K^*(w_t - w^*) - \eta_t\right). \tag{3.3}$$

Introducing the squared error $e_t = \frac{1}{2}(w_t - w^*)^T K^*(w_t - w^*)$, gives rise to

$$\frac{d}{dt}e_t = -2\eta_t e_t, \quad \frac{d}{dt}\eta_t = \alpha\beta\eta_t e_t - \alpha\eta_t^2. \tag{3.4}$$

The behavior of the above equation system is interesting: The origin $(0, 0)$ is
its attractor and the basin of attraction has a fractal boundary. Starting from
an adequate initial value, it has a solution of the form

$$e_t = \frac{1}{\beta}\left(\frac{1}{2} - \frac{1}{\alpha}\right) \cdot \frac{1}{t} \quad (\alpha > 2), \quad \text{and} \quad \eta_t = \frac{1}{2} \cdot \frac{1}{t}. \tag{3.5}$$

It is important to note that this $1/t$-convergence rate of the generalization
error e_t is the optimal order of any estimator $\hat{w}_t$ converging to w^*. So we find
that Eq.(3.3) gives us an on-line learning algorithm which converges with a
fast rate. This holds also if the target rule is slowly fluctuating or suddenly
changing. The technique to prove convergence was to use the scalar distance
in weight space e_t. Note also that Eq.(3.5) holds only within an appropriate
parameter range; for larger η and $w_t - w^*$ correlations the variances between
(η_t, w_t, l) can no longer be neglected.

4 Modification

From the practical point of view (1) the Hessian K^* of the expected loss or (2) the minimum value of the expected loss $\hat{R}$ are in general not known or (3) in some applications we cannot access the explicit loss function (e.g. blind separation). Let us therefore consider a generalized learning algorithm:

$$\hat{w}_{t+1} = \hat{w}_t - \eta_t f(x_{t+1}, y_{t+1}; \hat{w}_t), \qquad (4.1)$$

where f is a flow which determines the modification as an example (x_{t+1}, y_{t+1}) is given. Here we do not assume the existence of a loss function and we only assume that the averaged flow vanishes at the optimal parameter, i.e. $\langle f(x, y; w^*) \rangle = 0$. With a loss function, the flow corresponds to the gradient of the loss. We consider again the averaged continuous equation and expand it around the optimal parameter:

$$\frac{d}{dt} w_t = -\eta_t \langle f(x, y; w_t) \rangle \simeq -\eta_t K^*(w_t - w^*), \qquad (4.2)$$

where $K^* = \langle \partial f(x, y; w^*)/\partial w \rangle$. Suppose that we have an eigenvector v of the matrix K^* satisfying

$$v^T K^* = \lambda v^T$$

and let us define

$$\xi_t = \left\langle v^T f(x, y; w_t) \right\rangle \simeq v^T K^*(w_t - w^*), \qquad (4.3)$$

then the dynamics of ξ can be approximately represented as

$$\frac{d}{dt} \xi_t = -\lambda \eta_t \xi_t. \qquad (4.4)$$

By using ξ, we can define a discrete and continuous modification of the rule for η:

$$\eta_{t+1} = \eta_t + \alpha \eta_t \left(\beta |\xi_t| - \eta_t \right) \quad \text{and} \quad \frac{d}{dt} \eta_t = \alpha \eta_t \left(\beta |\xi_t| - \eta_t \right). \qquad (4.5)$$

Intuitively ξ corresponds to a 1-dimensional pseudo distance, where the average flow f is projected down to a single direction v. The idea is to choose a clever direction such that it is sufficient to observe all dynamics of the flow only along this projection. In this sense the scalar ξ is the simplest obtainable value to observe the progress of learning. Noting that ξ is always positive or negative (depending on its initial value) and that η can only be positive, these two equations (4.4) and (4.5) are equivalent to the equation system (3.4). Therefore their asymptotic solutions are

$$\xi_t = \frac{1}{\beta} \left(\frac{1}{\lambda} - \frac{1}{\alpha} \right) \cdot \frac{1}{t}, \quad \text{and} \quad \eta_t = \frac{1}{\lambda} \cdot \frac{1}{t}. \qquad (4.6)$$

Again similar to the last section we have shown that the algorithm converges properly, however this time *without* using loss or Hessian.

In this algorithm, an important problem is how to get a good projection v. Here we assume the following facts and approximate the previous algorithm: **(1)** the minimum eigenvalue of matrix K^* is sufficiently smaller than the second minimum eigenvalue and **(2)** therefore after a large number of iterations, the parameter vector $\hat{w}_t$ will approach from the direction of the minimum eigenvector of K^* (cf. Fig.1). Since under these conditions the evolution of the estimated parameter can be thought of as a one-dimensional process, any vector can be used as v except for vectors which are orthogonal to the minimum eigenvector. The most efficient vector will be the minimum eigenvector itself which can be approximated (for a large number of iterations: see Fig.1) by

$$v = \langle f \rangle / \| \langle f \rangle \|,$$

where $\| \ \|$ denotes the L^2 norm. Hence we can adopt

$$\xi = \langle v^T f \rangle = \| \langle f \rangle \|.$$

Substituting the instantaneous average of the flow by a leaky average, we arrive at

$$\hat{w}_{t+1} = \hat{w}_t - \eta_t f(x_{t+1}, y_{t+1}; \hat{w}_t), \tag{4.7}$$

$$r_{t+1} = (1 - \delta)r_t + \delta f(x_{t+1}, y_{t+1}; \hat{w}_t), \quad (0 < \delta < 1) \tag{4.8}$$

$$\eta_{t+1} = \eta_t + \alpha \eta_t \left(\beta \|r_{t+1}\| - \eta_t \right), \tag{4.9}$$

where δ controls the leak size of the average and r is used as auxiliary variable to calculate the leaky average of the flow f.

Note that this set of rules is easy to compute and straightforward to implement. We simply have to keep track of an additional vector in Eq.(4.8): the averaged flow r (or averaged gradient if we are given an explicit loss function). The norm of this vector then controls the size of the learning rate (cf. Eq.(4.9)).

In order to discuss the asymptotics of Eq.(4.7)-(4.9), let us consider the averaged Eq.(4.8) with respect to the given example:

$$r_{t+1} = (1 - \delta)r_t + \delta K^* \left\{ (\hat{w}_t - w_t) + (w_t - w^*) \right\},$$

where w_t denotes the mean of the parameter at t and the relation

$$\langle f(x, y; w_t) \rangle \simeq K^*(w_t - w_t^*)$$

is used. Intuitively speaking $\hat{w}_t - w_t$ corresponds to fluctuation caused by the on-line learning procedure, and $w_t - w^*$ shows how far the estimation is from the optimal, and the randomness of r_t is caused by them. Knowing

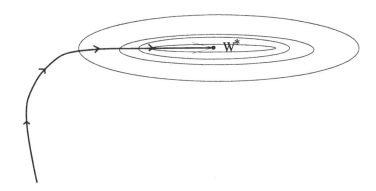

Fig.1: Convergence of the flow. During the final stage of learning
the average flow is approximately one dimensional towards w^* and
it is a good approximation of the minimum eigenvalue direction
of the Hessian.

that asymptotically the parameter $\hat{w}_t$ can be well approximated as a Gaussian
random variable (e.g. Heskes and Kappen, 1991; Murata, 1992; Murata, 1998),
the behavior of the system can be separately discussed depending on the sizes
of r_t and its fluctuation $V(r_t)$ (V denotes the variance).

When the magnitude of r_t is considerably larger than its fluctuation, by
omitting the fluctuation $\hat{w}_t - w_t$ the update rule for r_t can be approximately
written as

$$r_{t+1} = (1 - \delta)r_t - \delta K^*(w_t - w^*).$$

This case occurs when the parameter is far from the optimal parameter. Since
we adopt leaky average, r_t is different from

$$\langle f \rangle = K^*(w_t - w^*)$$

and there exists a lag of estimation, however, with appropriately small δ the
learning rate update rule works as we mentioned above (with this time lag).

When r_t is rather small compared with the fluctuation, i.e. the parameter
is close to the optimal, then the update rule for r_t is approximated by

$$r_{t+1} = (1 - \delta)r_t - \delta K^*(\hat{w}_t - w_t).$$

Since $\hat{w}_t - w_t$ is a Gaussian random variable fluctuating around 0, r_t also
fluctuates around 0. Therefore $\|r_t\|$ doesn't converge to 0 and also η_t doesn't
converge to 0. Assuming that η_t and $\|r_t\|$ converges to non-zero constants,
we can roughly estimate the size of η_t. Let us assume $\eta_t = \eta$. Under this
assumption, we can use the analysis for fixed learning rate case (Heskes and
Kappen, 1991; Murata, 1992; Murata, 1998). For fixed learning rate η, the

variance of $\hat{w}_t - w_t$ is known as order $O(\eta)$. Let ηV denote the variance of $\hat{w}_t - w_t$. The variance of r_t is calculated as

$$V(r_{t+1}) = (1 - \delta)^2 V(r_t) + \delta^2 \eta K^* V K^{*T}$$

and by imposing $V(r_{t+1}) = V(r_t)$ we know that the variance of r_t is order $O(\eta)$, i.e.

$$V(r_t) = \frac{\delta\eta}{2 - \delta} K^* V K^{*T}.$$

Hence we know $\langle \|r_t\| \rangle$ is a function of δ and η and it can be denoted as $\sqrt{\eta}c(\delta)$. From Eq. (4.9), we have a solution

$$\eta = \beta^2 c(\delta)^2.$$

Therefore if we know the size of $c(\delta)$, we can control the minimum learning rate.

In usual case, $c(\delta)$ is not known a priori, but for example, we can consider the situation in which at the beginning of learning stage, batch learning is applied and after determining initial parameters and learning parameters, on-line learning is applied. Thinking about the purpose of adaptation, this situation is not so unnatural. In the batch learning stage, we can access various statistics such as V and $c(\delta)$. Of course they differ if the target changes, but as the initial values we can utilize these knowledge. After starting on-line adaptation, we can keep watch on η and r, then the learning parameters can be tuned depending on the behavior of η and r.

This is one possibility of how to choose the parameters, but depending on the situation and the amount of prior knowledge available, other kinds of criteria can be applied to determine the parameters.

In practice, to assure the stability of the algorithm, the learning rate in Eq.(4.7) should additionally be limited to a maximum value $\eta_{\max}$ and a cut-off $\eta_{\min}$ should be imposed.

5 Numerical Experiment: an Application to Nonstationary Blind Source Separation

In blind source separation we assume that n unknown and independent sources $s = (s^1, \ldots, s^n)$, which have zero mean, are mixed by an unknown (linear) *time dependent* mixing process A_t

$$x = A_t s \qquad \text{where} \qquad x = (x^1, \ldots, x^m), \ m \geq n. \qquad (5.1)$$

Statistical independence is defined as

$$p(s^1, \ldots s^n) = \prod_{i=1}^{n} p_i(s^i). \qquad (5.2)$$

Only the mixed signals x are observed. Note that both: the mixing process A and the sources s are unknown. Techniques to achieve blind source separation therefore try to unmix the measurements x through

$$u = Wx$$

by imposing statistical independence on the result of this demixing u and in this sense by inverting the unknown mixing matrix A (up to a diagonal scaling matrix D and a permutation matrix P).

$$u = Wx = WAs = DPs.$$

For further details on blind source separation we refer to e.g. Bell and Sejnowski, 1995; Jutten and Herault, 1991; Cardoso and Laheld, 1996; Molgedey and Schuster, 1994; Decco et al., 1996; Amari et al., 1996; Hyvärinen et al., 1997 and Common (1994).

5.1 Construction of Flows

In the following we will construct the flow needed in Eqns.(4.7)-(4.9). Let u_t be the unmixed signals

$$u_t = W_t x_t = (I + T_t)^{-1} x_t, \tag{5.3}$$

where T are the off-diagonal elements of the estimated mixing matrix. The diagonal is assumed to be I for simplicity. Along the lines of Molgedey and Schuster, 1994 we can define an error function

$$L(T^{ij}) = \sum_{i \neq j} \left\{ \langle u_t^i u_t^j \rangle^2 + \langle u_t^i u_{t-\tau}^j \rangle^2 \right\},$$

which minimizes the equal time and lagged time cross correlations of the mixed channels u_t, trying to enforce independence in the time course of the signal waveform. By taking the derivative of L with respect to T^{ij}, we obtain a flow that can be used as modification rule for T_t

$$\begin{aligned}
\Delta T_t^{ij} &\propto \eta_t f\left(\langle x_t^j u_t^i \rangle, \langle u_t^i u_t^j, \rangle, \langle x_t^j u_{t-\tau}^i \rangle, \langle u_t^i u_{t-\tau}^j \rangle, \dots \right) \\
&\propto \eta_t \left(\langle x_t^j u_t^i \rangle \langle u_t^i u_t^j \rangle + \langle x_t^j u_{t-\tau}^j \rangle \langle u_t^i u_{t-\tau}^j \rangle \right),
\end{aligned} \tag{5.4}$$

where we substitute instantaneous averages with leaky averages

$$\langle x_t^j u_t^j \rangle_{\text{leaky}} = (1 - \epsilon) \langle x_{t-1}^j u_{t-1}^j \rangle_{\text{leaky}} + \epsilon x_t^j u_t^j.$$

Note that the necessary ingredients for the flow f in Eq.(4.7)-(4.8) are in this case simply the cross correlations at equal or different times; η_t is computed according to Eq.(4.9). Clearly the learning rule in Eq.(5.4) will stop if the averaged correlation matrices $\langle u_t^i u_t^j \rangle$ and their time lagged counterparts $\langle u_t^i u_{t-\tau}^j \rangle$ vanish. One critical point of the correlation based learning rule in Eq.(5.4) is the choice of the delay parameter τ. If the lagged and equal-time cross correlation matrices are too similar then the algorithm cannot get enough information for a proper estimate of the mixing matrix. We therefore extend the above algorithm by choosing a larger number of lagged cross correlation matrices yielding the on-line version of the TDSEP algorithm (Ziehe, 1998; Ziehe et al., 1998)

$$L(T_{ij}) = \sum_{i \neq j} \langle u_t^i u_t^j \rangle^2 + \sum_{\tau} \sum_{i \neq j} \langle u_t^i u_{t-\tau}^j \rangle^2$$

and

$$\Delta T_t^{ij} \propto \eta_t f = \eta_t \sum_{\tau=0}^{\kappa} \langle x_t^j u_{t-\tau}^j \rangle \langle u_t^i u_{t-\tau}^j \rangle, \qquad (5.5)$$

where κ denotes the number time lags beeing used. A larger number of lagged values gives a more stable learning behaviour (Ziehe, 1998) and is therefore used throughout the simulations.

Other possible update rules (flows) in blind separation algorithms are often based on higher order correlations, e.g.

$$\frac{dW}{dt} \sim \eta\{I - 2g(\mathbf{u})\mathbf{x}^T\}W \qquad \text{(Bell and Sejnowski, 1995))}$$

w. natural Gradient

$$\frac{dW}{dt} \sim \eta\{\mathbf{u}\mathbf{u}^T - I - h(\mathbf{u})\mathbf{u}^T + \mathbf{u}h(\mathbf{u})^T\} \quad \text{(Cardoso and Laheld, 1996)}$$

$$\frac{dW}{dt} \sim \eta h(\mathbf{u})g(\mathbf{u})^T \qquad \text{(Jutten and Herault, 1991;}$$

Common, 1994;,

Decco et al.,1996)

$$\frac{dW}{dt} \sim \eta\{I - h(\mathbf{u})\mathbf{u}^T\}\mathbf{W} \qquad \text{(Amari et al., 1996)}$$

with e.g. $h(\mathbf{u}) = 3/4\mathbf{u}^{11} + 25/4\mathbf{u}^9 - 47/4\mathbf{u}^5 + 29/4\mathbf{u}^3.$

with e.g. $g(\mathbf{u}) = \tanh(\mathbf{u}) \quad \text{or} \quad g(u) = \text{sign}(u),$ \qquad (5.6)

where e.g. $h(\mathbf{u}) = (h(u^1), h(u^2), \ldots, h(u^m))$. In the following experiments we use the on-line version of TDSEP with several delays to demonstrate the efficiency of our adaptive learning rate scheme. Using the flow proposed by Cardoso and Laheld (1996) we show that other flows from Eq.(5.6) give similar results to the TDSEP flow.

5.2   Numerical Experiments

As a first example we mix two artificial signals according to Eq.(5.1) (see Fig.2, cf. Amari et al. (1996))

$$s_t^1 = \text{sign}\left(\cos(2\pi 155 t)\right)$$

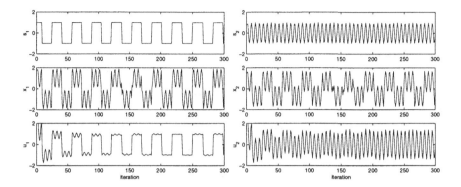

Fig.2: We use the challenging problem of on-line blind source separation as demonstration for the working of our adaptive learning rate scheme. The original, mixed and unmixed signals are shown (from top to bottom) for the first 500 iterations of the on-line algorithm. Note that after only about 200 iterations we obtain already rather good signal approximations.

$$s_t^2 = \sin(2\pi 800t), \tag{5.7}$$

that we mixed with A_t. The change in A_t starts at iteration t=4000 and ends at t=6000. The schemes include (a) a switching case, a smooth (b) sigmoidal, (c) sinusoidal and finally (d) a non-smooth linear drift (cf.Fig.3 and 4). Note that a batch algorithm would result in the averaged mixing matrix $\langle A_t \rangle$ which is obviously a wrong estimate of A_t (cf.Fig.3 and 4).

The goal of the experiments is to obtain the sources s_t by estimating A_t enforcing statistical independence (or time lagged decorrelation) of the separated signals u_t, given *only* the measured mixed signals x_t .

5.2.1 Artificial Signals

The five experiments with artificial uniquely show the following picture for the estimates of the mixing matrix T_t^{ij}: after an intitial phase of annealing, η_t reaches a constant problem dependent value (see discussion in previous section) and the estimates for T_t^{ij} have settled to the desired values. At t=4000 iterations, the mixing matrix starts to change and so does the learning rate automatically. Depending on the degree of change in A_t, we observe a stronger (switch) or more gradual increase (drifts) in η_t. During the drift phases η_t stays at almost constant level and decays only after the drift phase is over. In the switch case the estimates settle towards the proper values and then the learning rate cools down but only to leap up a second time as the rule switches again. If inspected even closer we can see that the algorithm even reflects the

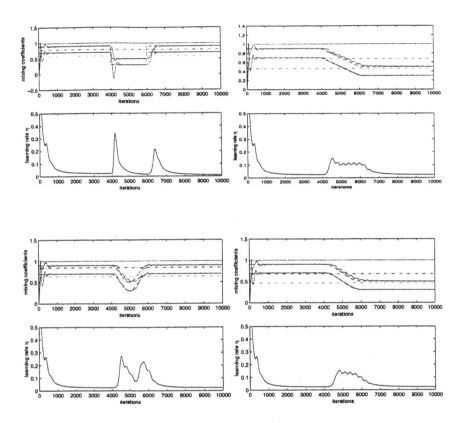

Fig.3: Using time delayed decorrelation based on TDSEP for BSS
(flow). Evolution of mixing coefficients and corresponding adaptation of learning rate in time are shown for different changing
environments. Above left: switching. Above right: linear drift. Below left: sinusodial drift. Below right: sigmoidal drift. Afer a short
delay time the estimated mixing coefficients can follow the change
(dashed lines) in the mixture quite rapidly due to a strong increase
of the learning rate. Note: Dashed-dotted lines indicate estimated
mixing matrix for batch learning. Any batch algorithm would not
be able to separate the signals and instead obtain $\langle A(t) \rangle$, because the mixture is non-stationary. Simulation parameters are
$\tau = [1, 2, 3, 4, 5], \alpha = 0.05, \beta = 1/\max \|\langle \mathbf{r} \rangle\|, \epsilon = 0.005, \delta = 0.02$,
where $\max \|\langle \mathbf{r} \rangle\|$ denotes the maximal value of the past observa-
tions.

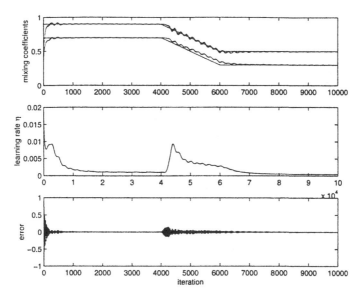

Fig. 4: Using higher order statistics for constructing the flow (EASI algorithm by Cardoso and Laheld (1996)). We perform stochastic gradient descent to minimize this function. After a few iterations the learning rate decreases to a small constant, but if the mixing changes its increased automaticaly. The resulting separation error is decreasing rapidly. Simulation parameters are $\alpha = 2, \beta = 0.02, \epsilon = \delta = 0.005$, where $\max \|\langle \mathbf{r} \rangle\|$ denotes the maximal value of the past observations.

fine detail whether the drift is smooth (sigmoidal, sinusoidal) or non-smooth as for the linear drift example. In the first case η_t decays smoothly while in the scond case the change in η_t is more abrupt.

In case (d) we also use the EASI algorithm of Cardoso et al. (1996) from Eq.(5.6) to demonstrate that the good performance of the proposed learning rate adaptation method is independent of the particular flow chosen and is also observed for flows other than the ones derived from TDSEP. In Fig.2 we show the evolution of the source signals $\mathbf{s}_t$, the mixed signals $\mathbf{x}_t$ and the on-line unmixing $\mathbf{u}_t$. Already after about 200 patterns the on-line unmixed signal shows a clear resemblance to the original signals. We also see the separation error in this case (cf. Fig.4). It first decays then stays at a constant very small value due to the fixed small learning rate (cf. previous section). The separation error increases after t=4000 to stay almost constant until t=6000 and then decays again to a small value.

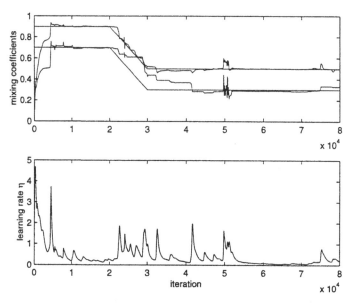

Fig.5: Estimated mixing matrix T_t and evolution of the learning rate η_t over time. The rule (mixing ratio) changes slowly to another level by a linear drift. During this period drastic changes of η_t occur. Simulation parameters are $\tau = [1, 3, 4, 5, 11, 12, 13], \alpha = 0.0025, \beta = 5/\max \|\langle \mathbf{r} \rangle \|, \epsilon = \delta = 0.01$, where $\max \|\langle \mathbf{r} \rangle \|$ denotes the maximal value of the past observations.

5.2.2 Speech and Music Signals

A change of the mixing is a scenario often encountered in blind separation tasks of accoustic signals, e.g. a speaker turns his head or moves during his utterances. Our on-line algorithm is especially suited to this non-stationary separation task, since adaptation is not limited by the above-discussed generic drawbacks of a constant learning rate. In the experiment we simulate the effect of a moving speaker by imposing a linear drift in the mixing coefficients from t=2000 to t=3000. Clearly the learning rate decays until t=2000 and then rapidly increases in the drift region (see Fig.5). For our learning rate adaptation scheme it makes sense to also increase η_t in cases where the signal variance changes strongly, e.g. near t=4200 or very prominently around t=5000 (see Fig.6). It is also interesting to observe that although the estimate lags behind particularly strong between t=2500 and t=2900, this does not necessarily result in large separation errors since the speaker pauses in this period (see Fig.6). The unmixed signal is of audibly good quality with very low crosstalk. This can also be seen from the low separation errors and

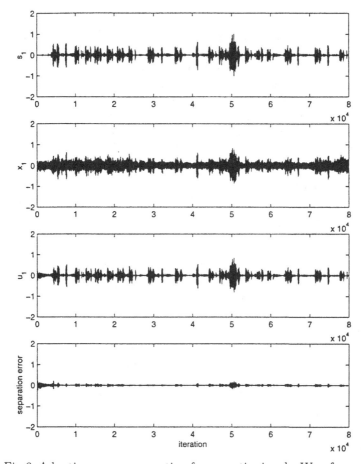

Fig.6: Adaptive source separation for acoustic signals. Waveforms of original, mixed and separated signals: s_t^1 speech signal "Fischers Fritz", the mixture signal x_t^1, the unmixed signal u_t^1 and the separation error $u_t^1 - s_t^1$ as functions of time in seconds. Note: Only the speech channel (out of speech and music) is shown, because speech signal can be better distinguished.

by comparing waveforms.

So, the simulation with real speech data shows similarly interesting results as for artificial signals. Altogether we found an excellent adaptation behavior of the proposed on-line algorithm, which was also reproduced in other nonstationary simulation examples omitted here.

6 Conclusion

We gave a theoretically motivated adaptive on-line algorithm extending the work of Sompolinsky et al. (1995). Our algorithm applies to general feed-forward networks and can be used to accelerate their learning. Furthermore it provides a learning strategy in the difficult setting where (a) continuous functions or distributions are to be learned, (b) the Hessian K is not available and (c) no explicit loss function is given. Obviously, if an explicit loss function or K is given, this additional information can be incorporated easily, e.g. we can make use of the real gradient where we otherwise would only rely on the *flow*.

Non-stationary blind separation is a typical realization of the setting (a)-(c) and we used it in this work to demonstrate the applicability of our adaptive on-line algorithm in a changing environment. Note that we can apply the learning rate adaptation scheme to most existing blind separation algorithms (see Eq.(5.6) – as exemplified for TDSEP and EASI – and thus make them feasible for a non-stationary environment. However, we would like to emphasize that blind separation is just an example for the general adaptive on-line strategy proposed and applications of our algorithm are by no means limited to this scenario or the training of multilayer neural networks. Recently, for example, Held & Buhmann (1998) applied the algorithm to the unsupervised learning of decision trees in hierarchical data analysis.

In EEG/MEG[1]-analysis (cf. Makeig et al. (1996), Vigário (1997), Ziehe et al. (1998)) blind separation techniques have proven to be useful for artifact removal. However so far the implicit assumption about the data was always stationarity of the mixing process. Clearly the mixing in EEG/MEG recordings can change quite drastically over time due to moving sources of neural activity, so a future application of on-line strategies for this scenario seems very interesting.

Acknowledgements
We thank the participants of the 1997 on-line learning workshop at the Newton Institute in Cambridge for interesting discussions. A.Z. was partly funded by DFG under contracts JA 379/51 and JA 379/71.

References

Amari, S. (1967), Theory of adaptive pattern classifiers. *IEEE Trans.* EC-16, 299-307.

Amari, S. (1997), Neural Learning in Structured Parameter Spaces — Natural Riemannian Gradient, in *Advances in Neural Information Processing*

---
[1] Electro/Magnetoencephalogram.

Systems 9, Michael C. Mozer and Michael I. Jordan and Thomas Petsche (eds.), The MIT Press, 127-133.

Amari S., Cichocki A., Yang, H. (1996), A New Learning Algorithm for Blind Signal Separation, in *Advances in Neural Information Processing Systems 8*, David S. Touretzky and Michael C. Mozer and Michael E. Hasselmo (eds.), The MIT Press, 757–763.

Bell, T., Sejnowski, T. (1995), An information-maximization approach to blind separation and blind deconvolution, *Neural Comp.* 7, 1129-1159.

Cardoso, J.F., Laheld, B. (1996), Equivariant adaptive source separation, *IEEE Trans. Signal Processing*, 44, 3017-3030.

Cichocki A., Amari S., Adachi M., Kasprzak W. (1996), Self-Adaptive Neural Networks for Blind Separation of Sources, ISCAS'96 (IEEE), Vol. 2, 157-160.

Comon, P. (1994), Independent component analysis, a new concept?, *Signal Processing* 36, 287-314.

Darken, C., Moody, J. (1991), Note on Learning Rate Schedules for Stochastic Optimization, in NIPS 3 (eds. Lippmann, Moody, and Touretzky), Morgan Kaufmann, Palo Alto.

Decco, G., Obradovic, D. (1996), *An information-theoretic approach to neural computing*, Springer.

Held, M., Buhmann, J. (1998), Unsupervised On-Line Learning of Decision Trees for Hierarchical Data Analysis, in *Advances in Neural Information Processing Systems 10*, in Press

Heskes, T.M., Kappen, B. (1991), Learning processes in neural networks. *Phys. Rev. A*, 440, 2718-2726.

Jutten, C., Herault, J. (1991), Blind separation of sources, Part I: An adaptive algorithm based on neuromimetic architecture, *Signal Processing*, 24, 1-10.

Makeig, S., Jung, T.P., Sejnowski, T. (1996), Using feedforward neural networks to monitor alertness from changes in EEG correlation and coherence, *Advances in Neural Information Processing Systems 8* (Nips'95), D.S. Touretzky, M.C. Mozer and M.E. Hasselmo (eds.), MIT Press: Cambridge, MA, 931-937.

Müller, K.-R., Murata, N., Ziehe, A., Amari, S. (1996), Verfahren und Vorrichtung zur nichtstationären Quellentrennung, *Patent application*, No.: 196 52 336.2, GMD 46.6.

Murata, N. (1992), *PhD thesis* (in Japanese), University of Tokyo.

Murata, N., Müller, K.-R., Ziehe, A., Amari, S. (1997), Adaptive on-line learning in changing environments, *Advances in Neural Information Processing Systems 9* (NIPS'96), D.S. Touretzky, M.C. Mozer and M.E. Hasselmo (eds.), MIT Press: Cambridge, MA, 599-605.

Murata, N. (1998), A statistical study on on-line learning, *in this volume*.

Molgedey, L., Schuster, H.G. (1994), Separation of a mixture of independent signals using time delayed correlations. *Phys. Rev. Lett.*, 72, 3634-3637.

Hyvärinen, A., Oja, E. (1997), A Fast Fixed-Point Algorithm for Independent Component Analysis, *Neural Computation* 9, 1483–1492.

Robbins, H., Monro, S. (1951), A stochastic approximation method, *Ann. Math. Statist.*, 22, 400-407.

Rumelhart, D., Hinton, G.E., Williams, R.J. (1986), Learning internal representation by error propagation. In Rumelhart, D., McClelland, J.L and the PDP Research Group (eds.), *Parallel Distributed Processing: Explorations in the Microstructure of Cognition 1, Foundations*, pp. 318-362. Cambridge, MA: MIT Press.

Saad D., and Solla S. (1995), *Workshop at NIPS'95*, see World–Wide–Web page: http://neural-server.aston.ac.uk/nips95/workshop.html and references therein.

Sompolinsky, H., Barkai, N., Seung, H.S. (1995), On-line learning of dichotomies: algorithms and learning curves. J-H. Oh, C. Kwon, S. Cho (eds.), , *Neural Networks: The Statistical Mechanics Perspective*, pp. 105-130. Singapore: World Scientific.

Sutton, R.S. (1992), Adapting Bias by Gradient Descent: An Incremental Version of Delta-Bar-Delta,*Proceedings of the Tenth National Conference on Artificial Intelligence*, pp. 171-176, MIT Press.

Vigário, R., N. (1997), Extraction of ocular artifacts from EEG using independent component analysis, *Electroencephalography and clinical Neurophysiology* 103, 395-404.

Ziehe, A., Müller, K.-R., Nolte, G., Mackert, B.-M., Curio, G. (1998), Artifact Removal in Biomagnetic Recordings with Several Time-delayed Second Order Correlations, in preparation for *IEEE Trans. on biomedical Eng.*

Ziehe, A. (1998), *Statistische Verfahren zur Signalquellentrennung*, Diploma thesis (in german).

Parameter Adaptation in Stochastic Optimization

Luís B. Almeida [†], Thibault Langlois, José D. Amaral and Alexander Plakhov

INESC
R. Alves Redol, 9
1000 Lisboa, Portugal[1]
† luis.almeida@inesc.pt

Abstract

Optimization is an important operation in many domains of science and technology. Local optimization techniques typically employ some form of iterative procedure, based on derivatives of the function to be optimized (objective function). These techniques normally involve parameters that must be set by the user, often by trial and error. Those parameters can have a strong influence on the convergence speed of the optimization. In several cases, a significant speed advantage could be gained if one could vary these parameters during the optimization, to reflect the local characteristics of the function being optimized. Some parameter adaptation methods have been proposed for this purpose, for deterministic optimization situations. For stochastic (also called on-line) optimization situations, there appears to be no simple and effective parameter adaptation method.

This paper proposes a new method for parameter adaptation in stochastic optimization. The method is applicable to a wide range of objective functions, as well as to a large set of local optimization techniques. We present the derivation of the method, details of its application to gradient descent and to some of its variants, and examples of its use in the gradient optimization of several functions, as well as in the training of a multilayer perceptron by on-line backpropagation.

1 Introduction

Optimization is an operation that is often used in several different domains of science and technology. It normally consists of maximizing or minimizing a given function (called *objective function*), that is chosen to represent the quality of a given system. The system may be physical, (mechanical, chemical,

---

[1]LBA and TL are also with IST. JDA is also with ISEL.

etc.), a mathematical model, a computer program, etc., or even a mixture of several of these. The system's quality, measured by the function to be optimized, may represent its performance, degree of fitness to a given set of data, error rate, etc.

Maximizing or minimizing a complex function is a hard task. Two basic classes of techniques exist. Local techniques are based on local information (usually derivatives of first or higher orders), and normally can only find local extrema. Global techniques usually involve a stochastic component, and many of them don't use derivatives. Given infinite time, some of them are guaranteed to find the global extrema of the function. However, in many situations, they are considerably slower than local techniques. Hybrid techniques also exist, which try to exploit the advantages of both classes.

In this paper we are essentially concerned with local techniques. We will use minimization as the kind of problem to be solved (all that we say can be easily changed for maximization problems, of course). Probably, the simplest local minimization technique is gradient descent, which can be stated as follows: Given a function $f(\mathbf{x})$, where $\mathbf{x}$ is a vector (vectors shall be denoted by bold lowercase letters, and matrices by bold uppercase letters), update $\mathbf{x}$ iteratively, according to

$$\mathbf{x}^{(n+1)} = \mathbf{x}^{(n)} - p\left(\nabla f|_{\mathbf{x}=\mathbf{x}^{(n)}}\right) \qquad (1.1)$$

where a superscript between parentheses, as in $\mathbf{x}^{(n)}$, denotes the iteration number, and p is a scalar *step size parameter*. Gradient descent probably is the best known local mimization method, and forms the basis of several learning algorithms, such as backpropagation, used in the field of neural networks. Other local techniques include second order methods such as the Newton method and its variants (Battiti 1992), and the various conjugate gradient techniques (Press *et al.*, 1986; Moller 1990).

Many of these methods have adjustable parameters, such as p in gradient descent. There is often no good way to choose these parameters a priori. For example, in gradient descent, choosing too small a value for p will lead to a slow optimization, whereas choosing too large a value may lead to divergence of the minimization process. Even if one knew the optimal value of p for a given problem, this value might lead to slow convergence, and the convergence speed might be improved by varying p during the minimization procedure, to reflect the changing local characteristics of f along the minimization path. This has led several authors to propose techniques for adapting p (Chan et al., 1987; Werbos, 1989 and 1992) or for adapting multiple p's, one for each coordinate (Silva and Almeida, 1990a and 1990b; Tollenaere, 1990). Other acceleration techniques have also been proposed (Becker and Le Cun, 1989; Fahlman, 1989; Silva and Almeida, 1991).

Most of these techniques were devised only for deterministic optimization (also called batch-mode learning, in the neural networks field). In many situations, however, one has to use stochastic optimization, the gradient of f being corrupted with noise,

$$\mathbf{x}^{(n+1)} = \mathbf{x}^{(n)} - p \left(\nabla f|_{\mathbf{x}=\mathbf{x}^{(n)}} + \mathbf{r}^{(n)} \right) \tag{1.2}$$

where $\mathbf{r}^{(n)}$ is a zero-mean random vector. For example, in many real-life situations we wish to follow an optimum that is changing slowly with time, and we have available a stream of values of ∇f with corrupting noise. In the neural networks field we may want to perform stochastic (real-time) training either because we have a very large, somewhat redundant training set or, again, because we are trying to model a slowly time varying system. A few methods to accelerate the convergence in stochastic optimization have been proposed (Becker and Le Cun, 1989; Sutton, 1992; Murata et al., 1997; Orr and Leen, 1997). However, none of them seems to have gained widespread application.

In this paper we derive a simple method for adapting the parameters of local stochastic optimization algorithms in order to improve their speed. The method can be applied to a relatively wide class of algorithms, including gradient descent/ascent with or without momentum. No quadratic approximation of f is needed, which makes the method applicable to a very wide range of functions. The method is a generalization of the one proposed in (Almeida et al, 1997). Its derivation bears some similarity to that of Incremental Delta-Bar-Delta (IDBD) (Sutton, 1992), although the assumptions and approximations that are made here are different, leading to a simpler adaptation equation. In comparison tests reported in this paper, the method proposed here surpassed IDBD in convergence speed.

The paper is structured as follows. In Section 2 we describe a deterministic step sizes adaptation method that has strong similarities with the stochastic one proposed in this paper. Section 3 derives the general form of the stochastic parameter adaptation method. In Section 4 we discuss how to apply the adaptation method to the case of gradient descent and several of its variants. Section 5 presents experimental results and Section 6 concludes.

2   Deterministic step size adptation

Following ideas of Kesten (1958) and Jacobs (1988) a step size adaptation method for deterministic gradient optimization was proposed in (Silva and Almeida 1990a and 1990b), see also (Almeida 1996). A similar method was independently proposed in (Tollenaere, 1990). The central idea behind these methods is that if successive updates of x_i (a component of $\mathbf{x}$), are made in the same direction, then the movement along that component should be made faster. On the other hand, if successive updates are made in opposite directions, then the movement along that component should be made slower. The method uses an independent, adaptive learning rate parameter $p_i^{(n)}$ for each component x_i. The components are thus updated according to

$$x_i^{(n+1)} = x_i^{(n)} - p_i^{(n)} \frac{\partial f^{(n)}}{\partial x_i} \tag{2.1}$$

where we use the shorthand notation

$$\frac{\partial f^{(n)}}{\partial x_i} = \left. \frac{\partial f}{\partial x_i} \right|_{x_i = x_i^{(n)}} \tag{2.2}$$

and the parameters are updated by

$$p_i^{(n+1)} = \begin{cases} p_i^{(n)} u & \text{if } \frac{\partial f^{(n)}}{\partial x_i} \frac{\partial f^{(n-1)}}{\partial x_i} > 0 \\ p_i^{(n)} d & \text{if } \frac{\partial f^{(n)}}{\partial x_i} \frac{\partial f^{(n-1)}}{\partial x_i} < 0 \end{cases} \tag{2.3}$$

where $u > 1$ and $d < 1$. Normally one uses $u \approx 1.1$ and $d \approx 0.9$.

This step size adaptation method has shown to be very effective in increasing the learning speed of multilayer perceptrons (MLPs) trained by backpropagation. Used together with momentum and an error control scheme (Almeida, 1996), it yields a very fast and robust training method for multilayer perceptrons.

The method, as defined above, is not directly applicable to stochastic gradient optimization, since the partial derivatives that appear in (2.3) are not available in such a case. Tests where the noisy derivatives available in stochastic gradient were used in (2.3), in place of the exact derivatives, have frequently failed, and had formerly convinced us that this *sign-based* stochastic adaptation method was not usable. Below, we reinterpret sign-based adaptation in the light of the new stochastic adaptation method proposed in this paper, and find that stochastic sign-based adaptation is still often usable, as long as one makes $d = 1/u$.

3   The stochastic adaptation method

To derive the new stochastic adaptation method, let us consider that we wish to minimize a function $f(\mathbf{x})$ by means of an iterative algorithm. We shall denote by $\mathbf{X}^{(n)} = \left[\mathbf{x}^{(0)}, \dots, \mathbf{x}^{(n)} \right]$ a matrix that contains the arguments that were visited during the optimization up to the n-th iteration.

We consider iterative minimization algorithms of the form

$$\mathbf{x}^{(n+1)} = \mathbf{u}\left(\mathbf{X}^{(n)}, \mathbf{p}^{(n)}, \mathbf{r}^{(n)} \right) \tag{3.1}$$

In this expression, the vector function $\mathbf{u}$ represents the update rule for $\mathbf{x}$. It is assumed to depend on $\mathbf{X}^{(n)}$ (possibly indirectly, through f and/or its derivatives), on some parameter vector $\mathbf{p}^{(n)}$ and on a random vector $\mathbf{r}^{(n)}$, to take into account the stochastic nature of the optimization. The dimensions of $\mathbf{x}$, $\mathbf{p}$ and $\mathbf{r}$ need not be the same.

We shall assume that we can obtain a noisy estimate of the gradient of the function to be minimized,

$$\mathbf{d}^{(n)} = \frac{\partial f\left(\mathbf{x}^{(n)}\right)}{\partial \mathbf{x}^{(n)}} + \mathbf{s}^{(n)} \tag{3.2}$$

where $\mathbf{s}^{(n)}$ is a random vector with zero mean. We shall see below that in some cases we can assume that $\mathbf{r}^{(n)}$ and $\mathbf{s}^{(n)}$ coincide, but this need not always be the case.

We wish to derive an adaptation rule for the parameter vector $\mathbf{p}^{(n)}$, in order to obtain a fast stochastic minimization of f. For that purpose assume that, after completing iteration n, we are at a known point $\mathbf{x}^{(n)}$, which was obtained from the point $\mathbf{x}^{(n-1)}$ through the use of (3.1).

The expected value of the function f after the next iteration will be

$$\left\langle f\left(\mathbf{x}^{(n+1)}\right)\right\rangle = \left\langle f\left[\mathbf{u}\left(\mathbf{X}^{(n)}, \mathbf{p}^{(n)}, \mathbf{r}^{(n)}\right)\right]\right\rangle \tag{3.3}$$

and a reasonable criterion for the choice of $\mathbf{p}^{(n)}$ would be to choose the one that would minimize this expected value. We shall see that we cannot directly choose that value, but we can approximate it in an indirect way. Let us differentiate both sides of (3.3) relative to a component of $\mathbf{p}^{(n)}$,

$$\frac{\partial \left\langle f\left(\mathbf{x}^{(n+1)}\right)\right\rangle}{\partial p_i^{(n)}} = \left\langle \frac{\partial f\left(\mathbf{x}^{(n+1)}\right)}{\partial \mathbf{x}^{(n+1)}} \cdot \frac{\partial \mathbf{x}^{(n+1)}}{\partial p_i^{(n)}} \right\rangle \tag{3.4}$$

$$= \left\langle \frac{\partial f\left(\mathbf{x}^{(n+1)}\right)}{\partial \mathbf{x}^{(n+1)}} \cdot \frac{\partial \mathbf{u}\left(\mathbf{X}^{(n)}, \mathbf{p}^{(n)}, \mathbf{r}^{(n)}\right)}{\partial p_i^{(n)}} \right\rangle \tag{3.5}$$

where the product of vectors, denoted by a dot, is the inner product. Using (3.2), we have

$$\frac{\partial \left\langle f\left(\mathbf{x}^{(n+1)}\right)\right\rangle}{\partial p_i^{(n)}} = \left\langle \left(\mathbf{d}^{(n+1)} - \mathbf{s}^{(n+1)}\right) \cdot \frac{\partial \mathbf{u}\left(\mathbf{X}^{(n)}, \mathbf{p}^{(n)}, \mathbf{r}^{(n)}\right)}{\partial p_i^{(n)}} \right\rangle \tag{3.6}$$

In several situations it is reasonable to assume that the random vectors $\mathbf{r}^{(n)}$ and $\mathbf{s}^{(n+1)}$ are independent from one other, since they are obtained in different iterations of the minimization procedure. For example, in stochastic backpropagation the random term obtained at each iteration depends on the pattern presented to the network at that iteration. If the patterns are drawn independently, from the training set, at every iteration, the assumption seems reasonable. If we take that assumption, then

$$\frac{\partial \left\langle f\left(\mathbf{x}^{(n+1)}\right)\right\rangle}{\partial p_i^{(n)}} = \left\langle \mathbf{d}^{(n+1)} \cdot \mathbf{u}_i'^{(n)} \right\rangle \tag{3.7}$$

where we have used the shorthand notation

$$\mathbf{u}_i^{\prime(n)} = \frac{\partial \mathbf{u}\left(\mathbf{X}^{(n)}, \mathbf{p}^{(n)}, \mathbf{r}^{(n)}\right)}{\partial p_i^{(n)}} \tag{3.8}$$

for convenience.

It would be desirable to be able to set the derivatives (3.7) to zero for all i, to obtain the optimal parameter vector $\mathbf{p}^{(n)}$. This can't be done, however, because we don't know $\mathbf{d}^{(n+1)}$ in advance, and because, in a stochastic procedure, we can't compute the expectation that appears in the right hand side of this equation. This is why we have to resort to an indirect method for optimizing the parameters. We note, however, that for the optimal parameters the expected value of the inner product in the right hand side of (3.7) is zero.

Let us then see how to indirectly make the derivatives in (3.7) approach zero. It is often the case that the optimal parameters $\mathbf{p}^{(n)}$ change slowly with n. For example, in a stochastic gradient procedure, when approaching a quadratic minimum, the optimal parameters change asymptotically with $1/n$, and thus change very slowly in the asymptotic regime. We will derive a slow adaptation procedure for $\mathbf{p}^{(n)}$. In cases where the optimal parameters change fast, this procedure will only slowly follow that variation.

Let us consider using a stochastic gradient adaptation of the parameter vector, aimed at driving the right hand side of (3.7) to zero:

$$p_i^{(n)} = p_i^{(n-1)} - K_i^{(n)} \mathbf{u}_i^{\prime(n)} \cdot \mathbf{d}^{(n+1)} \tag{3.9}$$

This expression uses $\mathbf{d}^{(n+1)}$, which is not available at the n-th iteration. But given our assumption that $\mathbf{p}^{(n)}$ changes slowly with n, we can use the values from the previous iteration,

$$p_i^{(n)} = p_i^{(n-1)} - K_i^{(n)} \mathbf{u}_i^{\prime(n-1)} \cdot \mathbf{d}^{(n)} \tag{3.10}$$

which are all available at the n-th iteration. In this equation we have allowed the step size factor of the adaptation, K_i, to vary with n, to improve the properties of the parameter adaptation, as will be discussed in the next section.

Equation (3.10) is our basic result. It expresses the way to adapt the parameters of the optimization algorithm. The exact form that this equation takes in practice will depend on the specific update rule $\mathbf{u}$ that we use. In the following section we shall discuss how to apply it in the case of gradient descent.

4   A special case: gradient descent

A case of special interest because of its numerous applications, is gradient optimization. In this section we shall see how to apply the adaptation method derived in the previous section to gradient optimization and to some of its variants. We shall also see how to set $K_i^{(n)}$ so that the procedure becomes rather insensitive to the specific function being optimized, thus making it applicable without any change to a wide range of optimization problems.

4.1 Basic gradient descent

Plain gradient descent corresponds to the update function

$$\mathbf{u} = \mathbf{x}^{(n)} - p^{(n)} \left[\nabla f|_{\mathbf{x}=\mathbf{x}^{(n)}} + \mathbf{r}^{(n)} \right] \tag{4.1}$$

where $p^{(n)}$ is a scalar step size parameter. The expression in square brackets is a noisy estimate of the gradient. We can use the same estimate that was assumed available above, given by (3.2), resulting in

$$\mathbf{u} = \mathbf{x}^{(n)} - p^{(n)} \mathbf{d}^{(n)} \tag{4.2}$$

which corresponds to making $\mathbf{r}^{(n)} = \mathbf{s}^{(n)}$, as mentioned in Section 3. Applying the adaptation rule (3.10) we obtain

$$p^{(n)} = p^{(n-1)} + K^{(n)} \sum_i d_i^{(n-1)} d_i^{(n)} \tag{4.3}$$

which is the step size adaptation method for the basic gradient algorithm. This basic algorithm is of the same degree of complexity as the multiple step sizes variant, described in the next section, but usually is much less efficient. It is preferable, in almost every case, to use the multiple step sizes variant, instead of the basic one. For this reason we shall not discuss the basic procedure further here. However, a method similar to the one described in the next section could be used to choose $K^{(n)}$ so as to make the procedure applicable to a wide range of functions without any change in parameters.

4.2 Multiple step sizes

In this and the next section we wish to use a more general gradient based optimization algorithm. We shall assume that the update equation is of the form

$$\mathbf{u} = \mathbf{x}^{(n)} - \mathbf{P}^{(n)} \mathbf{d}^{(n)} \tag{4.4}$$

where the step size parameter has been replaced by a matrix $\mathbf{P}$. The use of a matrix will allow us to use variants of the gradient procedure which move along a direction that does not necessarily coincide with that of the gradient, to accelerate the optimization. As above, we can make $\mathbf{r}^{(n)} = \mathbf{s}^{(n)}$, which corresponds to using the same noisy estimate of the gradient of f in (3.2) and in (4.1).

We will examine in this section the special case where $\mathbf{P}$ is restricted to be diagonal, which corresponds to using an independent step size parameter for each of the components of $\mathbf{x}$, as in the batch-mode adaptive step sizes procedure of Section 2. If we designate by p_i the i-th diagonal element of $\mathbf{P}$, the parameter adaptation equation (3.10) becomes

$$p_i^{(n)} = p_i^{(n-1)} + K_i^{(n)} d_i^{(n-1)} d_i^{(n)} \qquad (4.5)$$

where d_i are the components of $\mathbf{d}$, the noisy estimate of the gradient of f.

We know from our extensive experience with the batch mode adaptive step sizes procedure that it is convenient to adapt step sizes in a geometric way. This makes the adaptation method insensitive to the order of magnitude of the optimal step size parameters, and allows the adaptation to reach very large, as well as very small parameter values quickly. The geometric adaptation can be achieved by choosing $K_i^{(n)} = k p_i^{(n-1)}$, yielding the update equation

$$p_i^{(n)} = p_i^{(n-1)} \left[1 + k d_i^{(n-1)} d_i^{(n)} \right] \qquad (4.6)$$

We would like the adaptation procedure to be insensitive to the specific function that is being minimized, so that the same value of the parameter k can be used for almost any function f. However, in (4.6) the adaptation speed depends heavily on the values of the partial derivatives of f. If f is multiplied by a constant a, k should be multiplied by $1/a^2$, in order not to change the adaptation speed. To eliminate that dependency, we modify the choice of $K_i^{(n)}$ to

$$K_i^{(n)} = \frac{k p_i^{(n-1)}}{v_i^{(n)}} \qquad (4.7)$$

where $v_i^{(n)}$ is an exponential average of the square of $d_i^{(n)}$, obtained through

$$v_i^{(n)} = \gamma v_i^{(n-1)} + (1 - \gamma) \left[d_i^{(n)} \right]^2 \qquad (4.8)$$

The parameter update equation then becomes

$$p_i^{(n)} = p_i^{(n-1)} \left[1 + k \frac{d_i^{(n-1)} d_i^{(n)}}{v_i^{(n)}} \right] \qquad (4.9)$$

We shall call (4.6) the unnormalized update rule, and (4.9) the normalized one. The normalized rule is the one that was used in most of the experimental tests described in the next section. We have found the value $k = 0.01$ to be appropriate for most situations. This value yields a parameter adaptation speed of about 1% per iteration.

A relatively short average can normally be used in (4.8). We have used $\gamma = 0.9$, which seems appropriate for most situations. It is useful to set a lower bound for the step size parameters, so that they don't become zero or negative. It may also be useful to set an upper bound. In all the tests reported in this paper we have used a lower bound of 10^{-10} and no upper bound.

Variants of the adaptation method

In an earlier work (Almeida et al., 1997) we have proposed an exponential adaptation of the step size parameters

$$p_i^{(n)} = p_i^{(n-1)} e^{k \frac{d_i^{(n-1)} d_i^{(n)}}{v_i^{(n)}}} \tag{4.10}$$

This form can also be obtained from the basic equation (3.10). The derivation is given in the Appendix. Equation (4.9) can be seen as a first order approximation to the exponential in (4.10), and for small values of k the two forms will give almost identical updates. We don't see any special advantage of the exponential form in practical use, although it may be more amenable to theoretical analysis (Plakhov and Almeida, 1998).

The stochastic sign-based adaptation method mentioned in Section 2 can be obtained from the exponential adaptation (4.10) by using a drastic normalization,

$$v_i^{(n)} = \left| d_i^{(n-1)} d_i^{(n)} \right| \tag{4.11}$$

resulting in

$$p_i^{(n)} = p_i^{(n-1)} e^{k \, \text{sgn}\left(d_i^{(n-1)} d_i^{(n)} \right)} \tag{4.12}$$

Making $u = e^k$, $d = e^{-k}$ we obtain the equation of the sign-based rule (2.3). While the values of u and d didn't have to be tied to one another in the batch mode sign-based method, we have found by experience that, in the stochastic sign-based method, if d differs from $1/u$ by even an amount as small as 1%, the adaptation becomes ineffective. If $d > 1/u$, the algorithm will tend to diverge, because step size parameters become too large. If $d < 1/u$, the step sizes decrease too rapidly, and often "freeze" the optimization before the minimum is reached. In the tests reported in this paper we have used $d = 1/u$, with $u = 1 + k$, to obtain similar adaptation speeds in the normalized and sign-based adaptation methods.

If the distributions of the components of the noise vector **s** are symmetric, sign-based adaptation may be expected to perform well. However, if these distributions are skewed (still with a zero mean), we can expect sign-based adaptation to perform poorly, or even to cause divergence. In fact, in such a situation, if we are at the optimal step size value, then $\left\langle d_i^{(n-1)} d_i^{(n)} \right\rangle = 0$ and, because of the skewness, the signs of successive derivative estimates will be the equal to one other more than 50% of the time, causing the step size parameters to increase above the optimal values. This may lead to oscillation or even divergence of the minimization process.

4.3   Full matrix P

Use of independent step size parameters for the various components of $\mathbf{x}$ is appropriate to deal with ravines that are parallel to the coordinate axes, as discussed in (Silva and Almeida, 1990a and 1990b). When ravines are not parallel to the axes, this form of the gradient algorithm loses some of its efficiency. For that case, the use of the full matrix $\mathbf{P}$ (or of momentum, which we discuss in the next section) is more appropriate. Note, however, that use of a full $\mathbf{P}$ increases the complexity of the method from $O(N)$ to $O(N^2)$ per step, N representing the dimension of $\mathbf{x}$.

To see how to adapt the parameters with a full matrix $\mathbf{P}$, let us now designate the elements of $\mathbf{P}$ by p_{ij}. The unnormalized update equation is

$$p_{ij}^{(n)} = p_{ij}^{(n-1)} + K_{ij}^{(n)} d_j^{(n-1)} d_i^{(n)} \tag{4.13}$$

To make the adaptation insensitive both to the order of magnitude of the optimal parameters and to the specific function being minimized, we choose

$$K_{ij}^{(n)} = k \sqrt{\frac{p_{ii}^{(n-1)} p_{jj}^{(n-1)}}{v_i^{(n)} v_j^{(n)}}} \tag{4.14}$$

The parameter update equation becomes

$$p_{ij}^{(n)} = p_{ij}^{(n-1)} + k \sqrt{\frac{p_{ii}^{(n-1)} p_{jj}^{(n-1)}}{v_i^{(n)} v_j^{(n)}}} d_j^{(n-1)} d_i^{(n)} \tag{4.15}$$

which we call the normalized update equation. This is the equation that we have used in the experiments, reported below, which involved the full matrix $\mathbf{P}$.

A sign-based version can also be obtained in the case of a full matrix $\mathbf{P}$. We have used, in the tests presented in Section 5,

$$p_{ii}^{(n)} = p_{ii}^{(n-1)} e^{k \, \mathrm{sgn}\left(d_i^{(n-1)} d_i^{(n)} \right)} \tag{4.16}$$

for the diagonal terms, and

$$p_{ij}^{(n)} = p_{ij}^{(n-1)} - k \sqrt{p_{ii}^{(n-1)} p_{jj}^{(n-1)}} \, \mathrm{sgn}\left(d_j^{(n-1)} d_i^{(n)} \right) \tag{4.17}$$

for the non-diagonal ones.

4.4   Momentum term

Use of a momentum term is a simpler solution to deal with diagonal ravines than the use of a full matrix $\mathbf{P}$, because its complexity remains at $O(N)$

per step. Experiments reported below suggest that the use of momentum is also more effective than the use of the full $\mathbf{P}$. The update function with a momentum term (and with multiple step sizes, which we find always desirable) becomes

$$\mathbf{u} = \mathbf{x}^{(n)} - \mathbf{P}^{(n)}\mathbf{d}^{(n)} + \alpha\left(\mathbf{x}^{(n)} - \mathbf{x}^{(n-1)}\right) \tag{4.18}$$

where, again, $\mathbf{P}$ is diagonal, and its diagonal elements will be represented by p_i. The parameter update equations are the same as without momentum. The normalized update equation is

$$p_i^{(n)} = p_i^{(n-1)}\left[1 + k\frac{d_i^{(n-1)}d_i^{(n)}}{v_i^{(n)}}\right] \tag{4.19}$$

Of course, α is a new parameter, which could also be adapted using (3.10):

$$\alpha^{(n)} = \alpha^{(n-1)} - K_\alpha^{(n)}\left(\mathbf{x}^{(n-2)} - \mathbf{x}^{(n-1)}\right) \cdot \mathbf{d}^{(n)} \tag{4.20}$$

However, experimental results suggest that the use of an adaptive parameter α is less effective than simply using a fixed value, $\alpha = 0.9$, which is the option we recommend.

Once again, a sign-based version can be obtained, with the same parameter update equation as without momentum:

$$p_i^{(n)} = p_i^{(n-1)}e^{k\,\mathrm{sgn}\left(d_i^{(n-1)}d_i^{(n)}\right)} \tag{4.21}$$

5 Experimental results

This section presents a number of experimental results on the use of the parameter adaptation procedure in minimization problems, using the gradient method and its above mentioned variants. To emphasize the capability of the normalized versions of the procedure to deal with a wide variety of problems, we have used the same values for the parameters k, γ and α in all tests, except in the one described in Section 5.5, where the problem is not a simple minimization. The values that we used were

$$k = 0.01 \quad \gamma = 0.9 \quad \alpha = 0.9 \quad u = 1.01 \quad d = 1/u \tag{5.1}$$

In all cases except the multilayer perceptron one of Section 5.6, we used for each component of the noise vector $\mathbf{s}^{(n)}$, at each iteration, a double-sided exponential distribution with zero mean and variance equal to 1. This distribution was always symmetrical, except where specifically indicated. In the multilayer perceptron case of Section 5.6, the noise was provided by the random choice of the training pattern at each iteration of the real-time training procedure.

Except where otherwise noted, the stopping criterion was of the form

$$f_a^{(n)} < \theta \tag{5.2}$$

where $f_a^{(n)}$ was an exponential average of f, obtained through

$$f_a^{(n)} = \mu f_a^{(n-1)} + (1 - \mu) f\left(\mathbf{x}^{(n)}\right) \tag{5.3}$$

with $\mu = 0.95$. Except if noted otherwise, 41 tests were performed for each situation, differing from one another only in the seed of the random number generator.

In each group of tests, a maximum number of iterations was allowed. In the plots of the results, the curves that saturate at that number don't indicate convergence with that number of steps but, instead, indicate that convergence had not yet been achieved when that number of steps was reached.

5.1   One-dimensional quadratic

We used $f(x) = x^2/2$, starting the minimization at $x^{(0)} = 10$. The stopping criterion was $f_a < 0.002$. Figure 5.1 shows the medians of the number of iterations needed to reach the stopping criterion, as a function of the initial value of the step size parameters, for the basic gradient algorithm with fixed step sizes, for two variants of the adaptive algorithm (normalized and sign-based) and for IDBD.

The fixed step sizes algorithm is the one which reaches the fastest convergence, in this case, if it has the right value of the step size parameter. This is not surprising, given that for a quadratic function the optimal step size has the same value almost everywhere. However, this algorithm yields good performance only for a very narrow range of values of the step size parameter, while both the normalized and sign-based ones have a good performance for a wide range of initial step sizes. In a real-world problem, this low sensitivity to the initial step sizes is much more important than having the absolute best performance for a narrow range of the step size parameter, because this narrow range is not known a priori, and can only be found by trial and error. The time taken in such trials should be counted in the total optimization time. On the other hand, for the adaptive algorithms, it is relatively easy to find a good initial step size, since these algorithms have a wide range of acceptable values for that parameter.

In this case, IDBD also shows a low sensitivity to the initial step sizes, but with a worse performance than either the normalized or the sign-based adaptive algorithms.

In the end of Section 4.2 we guessed, from an informal reasoning, that the sign-based algorithm may use step sizes that are too large, and may even diverge, when the distribution of the noise in the derivatives is not

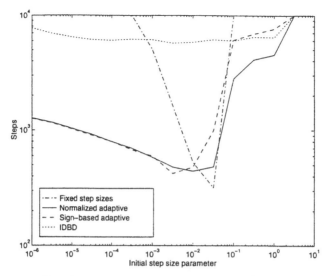

Fig. 5.1. One dimensional quadratic. Medians of the numbers of training steps for the various methods.

symmetrical. To check the correctness of that guess we made another test, where the only difference relative to the previous test was that the noise distribution was now unsymmetric. The noise distribution was still double-sided exponential (i.e. an exponential on the positive semi-axis and another one on the negative semi-axis), still with zero mean and variance equal to 1, but with two different exponentials on the two semi-axes, chosen so that $P(s > 0) = 0.9$ and $P(s < 0) = 0.1$. Figures 5.2 and 5.3 show the results obtained for the normalized and sign-based algorithms. While the behavior of the normailzed algorithm remained almost undisturbed by the change in the noise distribution, the sign-based algorithm now only converged in less than one half of the tests. We should note, however, that we also tried to use unsymmetric noise with other functions, described in the next sections, and the brittleness of the sign-based algorithm was never as apparent in those cases as with the simple one-dimensional quadratic.

5.2 Non-quadratic function

In the derivation of the adaptation method we did not need to make any quadratic approximation to the function f. Therefore, we expected the method to be applicable to functions where such an approximation is not valid. To test this we chose a function that is not quadratic in the vicinity of its minimum, $f(x) = |x|$. The initial point was $x^{(0)} = 1$ and the stopping criterion

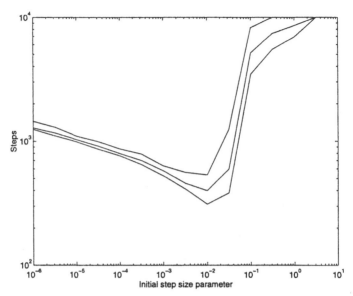

Fig. 5.2. Normalized adaptation with skewed noise: Percentiles 20, 50 and 80 of the numbers of training steps.

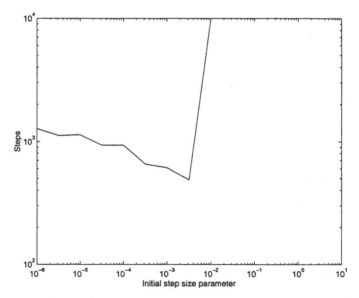

Fig. 5.3. Sign-based adaptation with skewed noise: Percentile 20 of the numbers of training steps, with skewed noise. The 50% and 80% percentiles are above the upper limit of the graph.

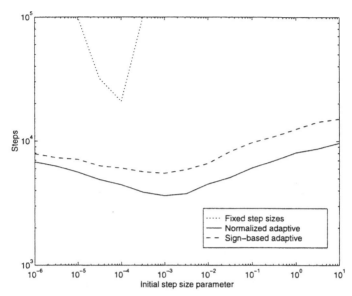

Fig. 5.4. Absolute value function. Medians of the numbers of training steps for the various methods.

was $f_a < 10^{-4}$. The noise distribution was symmetric, and all other parameters were as above. Figure 5.4 shows the results. We see that the normalized and sign-based algorithms both show a low sensitivity to the initial step size value, and both perform better than the best fixed step size.

5.3 Diagonal ravines

To test the effectiveness of the versions of the algorithm that use the full matrix $\mathbf{P}$ and of those that use momentum, we chose a quadratic function with a narrow ravine, $g(x) = x_1^2 + 1000x_2^2$, with initial point $(1, 1)$. To obtain the function f to be minimized and the actual initial point, we rotated g and the initial point $(1, 1)$ together, by a given angle ϕ around the origin. We tried several values of ϕ, to test the behavior of the various methods as a function of the angle that the valley makes with the axes.

Figure 5.5 shows the results. The methods that have one step size parameter per coordinate (diagonal $\mathbf{P}$), with no momentum, show a large sensitivity to the angle between the ravine and the axes, as expected. With a full matrix $\mathbf{P}$ this sensitivity disappears almost completely, and the same happens with diagonal $\mathbf{P}$ and momentum, the latter having a somewhat faster convergence. Since the use of the full matrix $\mathbf{P}$ is of complexity $O(N^2)$ per iteration, while the use of the diagonal $\mathbf{P}$ with momentum is only $O(N)$, we think that the

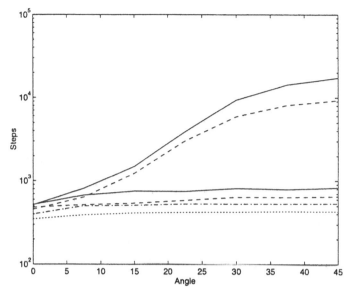

Fig. 5.5. Diagonal ravine. Medians of the numbers of training steps, as a function of the angle between the ravine and the x axis. Solid lines: Normalized (upper line - diagonal **P**; lower line - full **P**). Dashed line: Sign-based (upper line - diagonal **P**; lower line - full **P**). Dash-dot line: Normalized, diagonal **P**, momentum = 0.9. Dotted line: Sign-based, diagonal **P**, momentum = 0.9.

latter method will be almost always preferable. This conjecture still has to be validated with more extensive tests in higher-dimensional problems, however.

5.4 Rosenbrock function

The Rosenbrock function, $f(x) = 100\left(x_2 - x_1^2\right)^2 + (x_1 - 1)^2$, is a well known benchmark in the optimization domain. The function has a narrow valley along the parabola $x_2 = x_1^2$. This valley has a gently sloping bottom, with a single minimum at $(1,1)$. To create a stochastic minimization problem, we added symmetric noise, of the type described above, to both partial derivatives of f. The minimization was started at $(-1,1)$ and the stopping criterion was $f_a < 0.01$. Figure 5.6 shows the results of this test. Once again, we see the insensitivity of the adaptive algorithms within a wide range of values of the initial step size, and the large sensitivity of the fixed step sizes algorithm. Diagonal **P** with momentum again yielded the best performance.

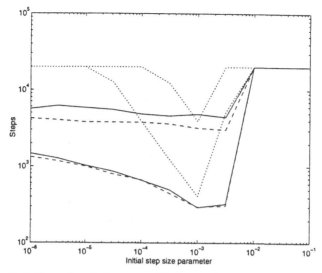

Fig. 5.6. Rosenbrock function. Medians of the numbers of training steps. Solid lines: Normalized. Dashed lines: Sign-based. Dotted lines: Fixed step sizes. In all three cases, the upper curve corresponds to no momentum and the lower curve to a momentum of 0.9.

5.5 Following a moving target

The step size adaptation method should be able to handle changing conditions during the optimization. As a test we created a situation in which the location of the function's minimum jumps abruptly every 5000 pattern presentations. We used the function

$$f(x) = \frac{(x - x_0)^2}{1 + |x - x_0|} \tag{5.4}$$

and alternated the position of the minimum x_0 between 0 and 100 every 5000 steps. We didn't use a simple quadratic function because, as already said above, the optimal step size for such a function is approximately the same almost everywhere, and thus it wouldn't allow us to put into evidence the capability of the method to adapt the step sizes to changing conditions. The function f that we used is approximately quadratic around the minimum, but is approximately linear far from the minimum, and thus the optimal step size increases with the distance from the minimum.

A higher step size adaptation speed was used in this test, with $k = 0.1$. The assumption that the optimal step size parameter varies slowly is clearly not valid here, and a larger value of k allows the step size parameter to adapt more quickly to the discontinuities of its optimal value.

128   Almeida, Langlois, Amaral and Plakhov

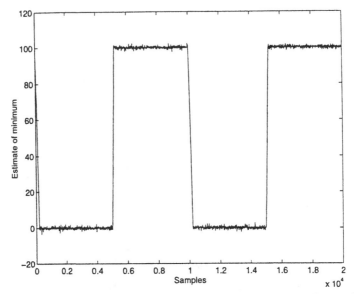

Fig. 5.7. Following a moving target. Target estimates obtained with a fixed step size parameter value of 0.5.

Figures 5.7 and 5.8 show the evolution of $x^{(n)}$ as a function of time with a fixed step size parameter. With a relatively large value of the parameter, the minimization follows the change in the location of the minimum relatively quickly, but has a large amount of noise in the steady state periods. A small value of the step size parameter yields a relatively small amount of noise in the steady state periods, but at the cost of a slow transition between the locations of the minimum.

Figures 5.9 and 5.10 show the behavior of the normalized step size adaptation algorithm. It has fast transitions between locations of the minimum, and in the steady-state regions the amount of noise decreases markedly in a short period of time after the transition. The step size parameter increases after each jump in the location of the minimum, to yield a fast transition, and then decreases, allowing the amount of noise in $x^{(n)}$ to become small in the steady state periods.

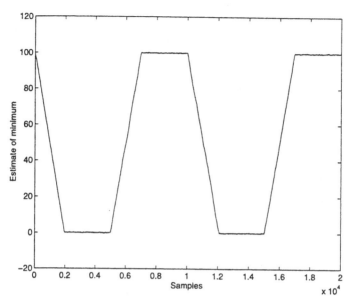

Fig. 5.8. Following a moving target. Target estimates obtained with a fixed step size parameter value of 0.05.

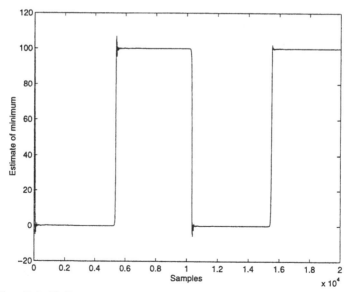

Fig. 5.9. Following a moving target. Target estimates obtained with adaptive step sizes.

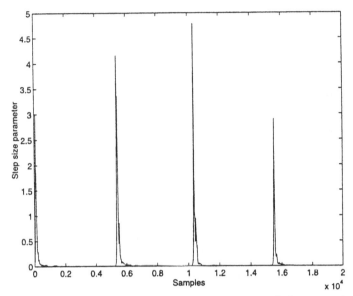

Fig. 5.10. Following a moving target. Values of the step size parameter.

5.6 Training an MLP

Finally we show an example of the application of step size adaptation to the training of an MLP using stochastic backpropagation. The MLP was trained to approximate the mapping defined by

$$g\left(x_1, x_2\right) = \frac{\sin\left(20\sqrt{x_1^2 + x_2^2}\right)}{20\sqrt{x_1^2 + x_2^2}} + \frac{1}{5}\cos\left(10\sqrt{x_1^2 + x_2^2}\right) + \frac{x_2}{2} - 0.3 \quad (5.5)$$

which has the approximate shape of a Mexican hat function on a sloping surface. The MLP had two inputs, 40 sigmoidal hidden units and one linear output unit, and was totally connected between successive layers, with no direct connections between inputs and the output unit. The sigmoids were hyperbolic tangent functions. The weights were uniformly initialized in the interval $[-1, 1]$.

The training set consisted of a uniformly spaced grid of 40×40 points, in the square $x_1 \in [-1, 1]$, $x_2 \in [-1, 1]$. At every iteration of the stochastic training, a new pattern was randomly drawn (with replacement) from this training set, independently from previous iterations. The cost function for training was the average squared error in the training set. The stopping criterion was met when this average error was below 0.05. A maximum of 32000 training steps was allowed.

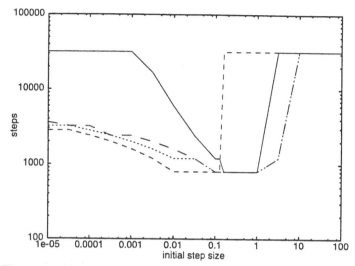

Fig. 5.11. Training a multilayer perceptron. Medians of the numbers of steps for convergence. Solid line: fixed step size parameter. Large dashes: Normalized without momentum. Small dashes: Normalized with momentum = 0.9. Dotted: Sign-based without momentum. On the right-hand side of the graph, the lines for normalized and sign-based are superimposed.

In these tests we used the same parameter values as before, given by (5.1). The derivatives were computed by backpropagation and no noise was added to them: they inherently contained noise, due to the random choice of input pattern at each iteration.

Figure 5.11 shows the results. Once more, we see the low sensitivity of the adaptive methods in a wide range of values of the initial step size parameter, while the fixed step size parameter algorithm showed a good behavior only in a much narrower range of parameter values.

6 Conclusions

We have proposed a simple parameter adaptation method for stochastic optimization algorithms, which can be applied to a wide range of algorithms and of functions to be optimized. We have shown how to apply the method to gradient descent and to some of its variants, and how to choose normalization terms so that the resulting algorithm is rather insensitive to the specific function being optimized. Experimental tests showed the good performance of the adaptive gradient algorithms. The fact that the same set of parameter values for k, α and γ was used in all problems (excluding the special case of following a moving target, Section 5.5, which was not a strict minimization problem) shows that we have succeeded in making the optimization procedure rather general, able to be used with the same set of parameters in most cases, so that trial and error is eliminated when optimizing a function in stochastic mode.

Acknowledgements

This work was partially supported by the Portuguese projects PRAXIS 2/2.1/ TIT/1585/95 and JNICT PBIC/C/TIT/2455/95, and by a NATO grant to A. Plakhov.

Appendix

To derive the exponential adaptation rule of eq. (4.10), let us define a set of auxiliary parameters q_i, related to p_i by $p_i = e^{q_i}$. Let us adapt the parameters p_i indirectly, through the adaptation of the q_i. The update rule for q_i, obtained from eq. (3.10), is

$$q_i^{(n)} = q_i^{(n-1)} + K_i'^{(n)} d_i^{(n-1)} d_i^{(n)} e^{q_i^{(n-1)}} \tag{6.1}$$

where $K_i'^{(n)}$ is the adaptation factor for q_i. In terms of the p_i, the adaptation becomes

$$p_i^{(n)} = p_i^{(n-1)} e^{K_i'^{(n)} d_i^{(n-1)} d_i^{(n)} e^{q_i^{(n-1)}}} \tag{6.2}$$

Since the factors $K_i^{(n)}$ can be chosen arbitrarily, we make $K_i^{(n)} = K_i'^{(n)} e^{q_i^{(n-1)}}$. We obtain

$$p_i^{(n)} = p_i^{(n-1)} e^{K_i^{(n)} d_i^{(n-1)} d_i^{(n)}} \tag{6.3}$$

which is the rule that we wanted to derive. Equation (4.10) corresponds to choosing

$$K_i^{(n)} = \frac{k}{v_i^{(n)}} \tag{6.4}$$

References

Almeida, L.B. (1996) Multilayer Perceptrons, section C1.2 of *Handbook of Neural Computation*, Fiesler, E. (ed.), New York, NY: Oxford University Press.

Almeida, L.B., Langlois, T., Amaral, J.D. (1997) On-Line Step Size Adaptation, *Technical Report* RT07/97, INESC, Lisbon, Portugal.

Battiti, R. (1992) First- and second-order methods for learning: Between steepest descent and Newton's method, *Neural Computation*, 4, 141-166.

Becker, S., Le Cun, Y. (1989) Improving the convergence of back-propagation learning with second order methods, *Proc. 1988 Connectionist Models Summer School*, Touretzky, D., Hinton, G., Sejnowski, T. (eds.), San Mateo, CA: Morgan Kaufmann, 29-37.

Chan, L.W., Fallside, F. (1987) An adaptive training algorithm for back propagation networks, *Computer Speech & Language*, 2, 205-218.

Darken, C., Moody, J.E. (1992) Towards faster stochastic gradient search, in *Advances in Neural Information Processing Systems 4*, Moody, J.E., Hanson, S.J., Lipmann, R.P. (eds), San Mateo, CA: Morgan Kaufmann.

Fahlman, S.E. (1989) Fast-learning variations on back-propagation: An empirical study, *Proc. 1988 Connectionist Models Summer School*, Touretzky, D., Hinton, G., Sejnowski, T. (eds.), San Mateo, CA: Morgan Kaufmann, 38-51.

Jacobs, R (1988) Increased rates of convergence trough learning rate adaptation, *Neural Networks*, 1, 295–307

Kesten, H. (1958) Accelerated stochastic approximation, *Ann. of Math. Statist.*, 29, 41-59.

Moller, M.F. (1990) A scaled conjugated gradient algorithm for fast supervised learning, *Preprint* PB-339, Computer Science Department, University of Aarhus, Aarhus, Denmark.

Murata, N., Mueller, K., Ziehe, A., Amari, S. (1997) Adaptive on-line learning in changing environments, in *Advances in Neural Information Processing Systems 9*, Mozer, M.C., Jordan, M.I., Petsche, T. (eds.), Cambridge, MA: MIT Press.

Orr, G. and Leen, T. (1997) Using curvature information for fast stochastic search, in *Advances in Neural Information Processing Systems 9*, Mozer, M.C., Jordan, M.I., Petsche, T. (eds.), Cambridge, MA: MIT Press.

Plakhov, A., Almeida, L.B. (1998) *in preparation*.

Press, W.H., Flannery, B.P., Teukolsky, S.A., Vetterling, W.T. (1986) *Numerical Recipes*, Cambridge, UK: Cambridge University Press.

Silva, F.M., Almeida, L.B. (1990a) Acceleration techniques for the backpropagation algorithm, in *Neural Networks*, Almeida, L.B., Wellekens, C.J. (eds.), Berlin: Springer, 110-119.

Silva, F.M., Almeida, L.B. (1990b) Speeding up backpropagation, in *Advanced Neural Computers*, Eckmiller, R. (ed.), Amsterdam: Elsevier, 151-160.

Silva, F.M., Almeida, L.B. (1991) 'Speeding-up backpropagation by data orthonormalization', in *Artificial Neural Networks* vol. 2, Kohonen, T., Mäkisara, K., Simula, O., Kangas, J. (eds.), Amsterdam: Elsevier, 149-156

Sutton, R.S. (1992) Adapting bias by gradient descent: An incremental version of delta-bar-delta, *Proc. Tenth Nat. Conf. Artif. Intell.*, Cambridge, MA: MIT press, 171-176.

Tollenaere, T. (1990) SuperSAB: Fast adaptive back propagation with good scaling properties, *Neural Networks*, 3, 561-574.

Werbos. P.J. (1989) Maximizing long-term gas industry profits in two minutes in Lotus using neural network methods, *IEEE Trans. Sys. Man Cybernet.*, 19, 315-333.

Werbos, P.J. (1992) Neurocontrol and Supervised learning: An overview and evaluation, in *Handbook of Intelligent Control*, White, D.A., Sofge, D.A. (eds.), New York: Ván Nostrand Reinhold, 65-89.

Optimal On-line Learning in Multilayer Neural Networks

David Saad [†] and Magnus Rattray

Neural Computing Research Group, Aston University
Birmingham B4 7ET, UK.
†saadd@aston.ac.uk
‡rattray@aston.ac.uk

Abstract

The choice of training parameters and training rules is of great significance in on-line training of neural networks. We employ a variational method for determining globally optimal learning parameters and learning rules for on-line gradient descent training of multi-layer neural networks. The approach is based on maximizing the total decrease in generalization error over a fixed time-window, using a statistical mechanics description of the learning process. The method is employed for obtaining optimal learning rates in both realizable and noise-corrupted tasks, for determining the relation between optimal learning rates of different weights and for examining the efficacy of regularizers in noisy and over-realizable training scenarios. Scaling rules for the optimal learning rates are obtained in learning generic tasks by linearizing the dynamics around transient and asymptotic fixed points. The method is further employed for determining the globally optimal on-line learning rule, which is shown to be superior to the locally optimal rule.

1 Introduction

Feed-forward neural networks have been extensively applied during the last decade for a variety of classification, regression, prediction and control tasks and are the most commonly used neural network architecture. On-line learning is arguably the most efficient way of training large feed-forward networks, especially when the task to be learnt is non-stationary, and is based on instantaneous modifications of the network parameters calculated according to only the latest in a sequence of training examples. This process is inherently stochastic because a new training example is selected at random each time the training error is determined. This is to be contrasted with batch learning, in which all the training examples are used to determine the training error, leading to a deterministic algorithm. On-line learning can be beneficial in terms of both storage and computation time for large systems. One of the main obstacles for efficient on-line training is the dependence of the training process to the choice of training parameters and rules.

In this chapter we will focus on a principled way of deriving optimal training parameters and training rules. Specifically, we will consider a learning scenario whereby a feed-forward neural network model, the 'student', emulates an unknown mapping, the 'teacher', given examples of the teacher mapping (in this case another feed-forward neural network) which may be corrupted by noise. This provides a rather general learning scenario since both student and teacher can represent a very broad class of functions (Cybenko, 1989). Student performance is typically measured by the generalization error, which is the student's expected error on an unseen example. The object of training is to minimize the generalization error by adapting the student network's parameters appropriately. Throughout the chapter we will employ a statistical mechanics framework for analysing on-line learning (Biehl and Schwarze, 1995; Saad and Solla, 1995) to determine the training parameters and rules which provide the maximum decrease in generalization error over the entire process.

First we will consider gradient descent on-line learning on a differentiable error measure, which is one of the most popular neural network training methods, and optimize it with respect to it's learning parameters. The error measure is defined to be the squared discrepancy between the teacher and student and at each learning step the student network's weights are adapted in the direction of negative gradient of this error, calculated according to the latest training example. On-line methods are often sensitive to the choice of learning parameters and for gradient descent in particular the choice of learning rate can be critical. If the learning rate is chosen too large then the learning process may diverge, but if the learning rate is too low then convergence can take an extremely long time; moreover, in either case the algorithm may get trapped at a sub-optimal fixed point. The appropriate learning rate will also vary substantially over time and may require annealing towards the end of the learning process. Existing analytical results for defining optimal learning rates, based on either the stochastic approximation (Robbins and Monro, 1951) or the order parameters approach (Leen et al., 1998) concentrate on the asymptotic regime where the system may be linearized.

We will then extend the basic framework to site-dependent learning rates, for examining relations between learning rates of different parameters and for studying the effect of regularization in both noiseless and noisy on-line learning scenarios.

A more desirable, though harder, task is to try and optimize the learning rule itself rather then the training parameters. Many modifications to the basic gradient descent algorithm have been suggested in the literature. Some of these methods may be used throughout the learning process (Amari, 1997) while others are restricted to late times (e.g., the use of on-line estimates of second order information, the Hessian of the error or its eigenvalues, to ensure asymptotically optimal performance (Orr and Leen, 1997; LeCun et al, 1993) and our other chapter in this volume). A number of heuristics also exist which attempt to improve performance during the transient phase of learning (for a review, see (Bishop, 1995)). However, these heuristics all require the careful setting of parameters which can be critical to their performance; and it would be desirable to have principled and theoretically well motivated algorithms. With this goal in mind, the method for determining globally optimal learning rates will be generalized here to determine globally optimal learning rules for both discrete and continuous machines, i.e., rules which provide the maximum reduction in generalization error over the whole learning process. This provides a natural extension to work on locally optimal learning rules (Kinouchi and Caticha, 1992; Vicente and Caticha, 1997), where only the rate of change in generalization error is optimized. In fact, for simple systems we sometimes find that the locally optimal rule is also globally optimal.

Throughout the chapter we will emphasize the differentiation between local and global optimization. A locally optimal, greedy, learning rate or learning rule can be chosen which maximizes the decrease in generalization error at each learning step. This will be far from optimal in many cases, especially in more complex systems when the dynamics is characterized by phases of different nature. We will also show how local optimization of the learning rate may even be sub-optimal at late times.

The chapter is organized as follows. In sections 2 and 3 we briefly describe a framework for modelling on-line learning in a soft committee machine (SCM) and derive the optimal time-dependent learning rate for this case using variational methods. We then study, in sections 4 and 5, the dynamics with the optimal learning rate first numerically under a number of different learning scenarios and then analytically in the neighbourhood of fixed points which dominate the dynamical trajectory. Links are made with recent numerical and analytical studies of these fixed points (West and Saad, 1997). In sections 6, 7 and 8 we show how our variational approach can be generalized in order to deal with different learning rates and for studying the efficacy of regularizers. Finally, in section 9 we derive a general result for the optimal on-line learning rule and demonstrate the differences between locally and globally optimal rules on two simple learning scenarios for which the optimal rule can be determined in closed form. In section 10 we discuss the limitations of the current approach and possible extensions to this work.

2   Learning in soft committee machines

In order to demonstrate our optimization method we first establish a framework for describing the learning process.

We consider a student mapping from an N-dimensional input space $\boldsymbol{\xi} \in \Re^N$

onto a scalar function $\sigma(\mathbf{J}, \boldsymbol{\xi}) = \sum_{i=1}^{K} g(\mathbf{J}_i \cdot \boldsymbol{\xi})$, which represents a SCM (Biehl and Schwarze, 1995), where $g(x) \equiv \mathrm{erf}(x/\sqrt{2})$ is the activation function of the hidden units, $\mathbf{J} \equiv \{\mathbf{J}_i\}_{1 \leq i \leq K}$ is the set of input-to-hidden adaptive weights for the K hidden nodes and the hidden-to-output weights are set to one. The activation of hidden node i in the student under presentation of the input pattern $\boldsymbol{\xi}^\mu$ is denoted $x_i^\mu = \mathbf{J}_i \cdot \boldsymbol{\xi}^\mu$. This general configuration represents most properties of a general multi-layer network and can easily be extended to accommodate adaptive hidden-to-output weights (briefly considered in section 6) (Riegler, 1997; Riegler and Biehl, 1995).

Training examples are of the form $(\boldsymbol{\xi}^\mu, \zeta^\mu)$ where $\mu = 1, 2, \ldots$ labels each independently drawn example in a sequence. Components of the independently drawn input vectors $\boldsymbol{\xi}^\mu$ are uncorrelated random variables with zero mean and unit variance. The corresponding output ζ^μ is given by a teacher which may be corrupted by output noise and is of a similar configuration to the student except for a possible difference in the number M of hidden units: $\zeta^\mu = \sum_{n=1}^{M} g(\mathbf{B}_n \cdot \boldsymbol{\xi}^\mu) + \rho^\mu$, where $\mathbf{B} \equiv \{\mathbf{B}_n\}_{1 \leq n \leq M}$ is the set of input-to-hidden adaptive weights for teacher hidden nodes and ρ^μ is zero mean Gaussian noise of variance σ^2. The activation of hidden node n in the teacher under presentation of the input pattern $\boldsymbol{\xi}^\mu$ is denoted $y_n^\mu = \mathbf{B}_n \cdot \boldsymbol{\xi}^\mu$. We will use indices i, j, k, l to refer to units in the student network and n, m for units in the teacher network.

The error made by the student is given by the quadratic deviation,

$$\epsilon(\mathbf{J}^\mu, \boldsymbol{\xi}^\mu) \equiv \frac{1}{2}[\,\sigma(\mathbf{J}^\mu, \boldsymbol{\xi}^\mu) - \zeta^\mu\,]^2 = \frac{1}{2}\left[\,\sum_{i=1}^{K} g(x_i^\mu) - \sum_{n=1}^{M} g(y_n^\mu) - \rho^\mu\,\right]^2 . \quad (2.1)$$

This training error is then used to define the learning dynamics via a gradient descent rule for the update of student weights $\mathbf{J}_i^{\mu+1} = \mathbf{J}_i^\mu + \frac{\eta}{N}\delta_i^\mu\boldsymbol{\xi}^\mu$, where $\delta_i^\mu \equiv g'(x_i^\mu)[\sum_{n=1}^{M} g(y_n^\mu) - \sum_{j=1}^{K} g(x_j^\mu) - \rho^\mu]$ and the learning rate η has been scaled with the input size N. Performance on a typical input in the absence of output noise defines the generalization error $\epsilon_g(\mathbf{J}) \equiv \langle \epsilon(\mathbf{J}, \boldsymbol{\xi}) \rangle_{\{\boldsymbol{\xi}\}}|_{\sigma=0}$ through an average over all possible input vectors $\boldsymbol{\xi}$.

Expressions for the generalization error and learning dynamics have been obtained (Saad and Solla, 1995) in the thermodynamic limit ($N \to \infty$), and can be represented by a set of macroscopic variables (order parameters) of the form: $\mathbf{J}_i \cdot \mathbf{J}_k \equiv Q_{ik}$, $\mathbf{J}_i \cdot \mathbf{B}_n \equiv R_{in}$, and $\mathbf{B}_n \cdot \mathbf{B}_m \equiv T_{nm}$, measuring overlaps between student and teacher vectors. The overlaps R and Q become the dynamical variables of the system while T is defined by the task. The learning dynamics is then defined in terms of differential equations for the macroscopic variables with respect to the normalized number of examples $\alpha = \mu/N$ playing the role of a continuous time variable:

$$\frac{\mathrm{d}R_{in}}{\mathrm{d}\alpha} = \eta\,\phi_{in}\,, \qquad \frac{\mathrm{d}Q_{ik}}{\mathrm{d}\alpha} = \eta\,\psi_{ik} + \eta^2\,v_{ik}\,, \qquad (2.2)$$

where $\phi_{in} \equiv \langle \delta_i y_n \rangle_{\{\xi\}}$, $\psi_{ik} \equiv \langle \delta_i x_k + \delta_k x_i \rangle_{\{\xi\}}$ and $v_{ik} \equiv \langle \delta_i \delta_k \rangle_{\{\xi\}}$. The explicit expressions for ϕ_{in}, ψ_{ik}, v_{ik} and ϵ_g depend exclusively on the overlaps Q, R and T and are given in (Saad and Solla, 1995). The equations of motion, depending on a closed set of parameters, can be integrated and iteratively solved, providing a full description of the order parameters evolution from which the evolution of the generalization error can be derived. Although the dynamical equations considered here are only strictly valid in the large N limit, they have been shown to describe mean behaviour accurately for systems of realistic size (Barber et al, 1996).

Four variations of this framework will be also briefly considered here:

• *Site dependent learning rates* - In this case one allows for having different learning rates to weight vectors related to different hidden nodes. The dynamics is identical to that of Eq.(2.2) but the substitution of η by $\eta_{i/k}$ with the same subscript as the related difference function $\delta_{i/k}$.

• *Adaptive hidden to output learning rates* - whereby we relax the assumption of fixed hidden-to-output (Riegler, 1997; Riegler and Biehl, 1995), resulting in an extra set of dynamical equations

$$w_i^{\mu+1} = w_i^\mu + \eta_w/N \; g(x_i^\mu) \; [\sum_{n=1}^{M} g(y_n^\mu) - \sum_{j=1}^{K} g(x_j^\mu) - \rho^\mu]$$

where w_i, $1 \leq i \leq K$ are the hidden-to-output weights and η_w the learning rate which has been scaled with the input size N to make the evolution of $\mathbf{w}$, R and Q self-averaging.

• *Regularization* - In this case we add a regularization term to the weight dynamics. The effect of weight decay on the training equations is the subtraction of a term $\frac{\gamma}{N}\mathbf{J}_i^\mu$ in each weight update. The difference equation for $\mathbf{J}_i^\mu$ becomes $\mathbf{J}_i^{\mu+1} = \mathbf{J}_i^\mu + \frac{\eta}{N}\delta_i^\mu \xi^\mu - \frac{\gamma}{N}\mathbf{J}_i^\mu$, and the resulting equations of motion for the student-teacher and student-student overlaps are as before except for a subtraction of γR_{in} from the former and $2\gamma Q_{ik}$ from the latter.

• *General learning rule* - The choice of gradient may be relaxed to assume a general update rule of the form $\mathbf{J}_i^{\mu+1} = \mathbf{J}_i^\mu + \frac{1}{N}F_i^\mu(\boldsymbol{x}^\mu, \zeta^\mu) \; \boldsymbol{\xi}^\mu$, where $\mathbf{F} \equiv \{F_i\}$ depends only on the student activations and the teacher's output, and not on the teacher activations which are unobservable. Again here the activations covariance matrix completely describes the macroscopic state of the system and in the limit of large N and we can write equations of motion for each macroscopic:

$$\frac{dR_{in}}{d\alpha} = \langle F_i y_n \rangle \qquad \frac{dQ_{ik}}{d\alpha} = \langle F_i x_k + F_k x_i + F_i F_k \rangle . \qquad (2.3)$$

Angled brackets denote averages over activations, replacing the averages over inputs, which cannot be calculated explicitly without knowing the explicit form of the rule. We will make use of this general formulation for deriving an expression for the globally optimal learning rule.

3   Optimal learning rate

The naive approach to learning rate optimization is to consider the fastest rate of decrease in generalization error as a measure of optimality. It is then straightforward to find the locally optimal learning rate by determining the value of η that minimizes $d\epsilon_g/d\alpha$, using Eqs.(2.2) and the fact that the change in generalization error over time depends exclusively on the overlaps. The expression obtained for the locally optimal learning rate is then

$$\eta = -\frac{\sum_{in} \frac{\partial \epsilon_g}{\partial R_{in}} \phi_{in} + \sum_{ik} \frac{\partial \epsilon_g}{\partial Q_{ik}} \psi_{ik}}{\sum_{ik} \frac{\partial \epsilon_g}{\partial Q_{ik}} v_{ik}} .$$

Although the value of η obtained in this manner may be useful for some phases of the learning process it is likely to be useless for others. For example, the lowest generalization error for the symmetric phase, characterized by a lack of differentiation between the student nodes, is achieved by gradually reducing the learning rate towards zero; however, decaying the learning rate in the symmetric phase will prevent the system from escaping the symmetric fixed point, thus resulting in a sub-optimal solution.

A more appropriate measure of optimality is the total reduction in generalization error over the entire learning process. With this measure one can then define the *globally optimal* learning rate in a given time-window $[\alpha_0, \alpha_1]$ to be that which provides the largest decrease in generalization error between these two times. We write the change in generalization error as an integral,

$$\Delta\epsilon_g(\eta) = \int_{\alpha_0}^{\alpha_1} \frac{d\epsilon_g}{d\alpha} \, d\alpha = \int_{\alpha_0}^{\alpha_1} \mathcal{L}(\eta, \alpha) \, d\alpha . \tag{3.1}$$

This functional of η will be minimized by a variational calculation.

Since the generalization error depends solely on the overlaps Q, R and T, which are the dynamical variables (T remains fixed here), we can expand the integrand in terms of these variables,

$$\begin{aligned}
\mathcal{L}(\eta, \alpha) &= \sum_{in} \frac{\partial \epsilon_g}{\partial R_{in}} \frac{dR_{in}}{d\alpha} + \sum_{ik} \frac{\partial \epsilon_g}{\partial Q_{ik}} \frac{dQ_{ik}}{d\alpha} \\
&- \sum_{in} \mu_{in} \left(\frac{dR_{in}}{d\alpha} - \eta \, \phi_{in} \right) - \sum_{ik} v_{ik} \left(\frac{dQ_{ik}}{d\alpha} - \eta \, \psi_{ik} - \eta^2 \, v_{ik} \right) .
\end{aligned} \tag{3.2}$$

The last two terms in equation (3.2) force the correct dynamics using sets of Lagrange multipliers μ_{in} and v_{ik} corresponding to the equations of motion for R_{in} and Q_{ik} respectively.

Variational minimization of the integral in equation (3.1) with respect to the dynamical variables leads to a set of coupled differential equations for the Lagrange multipliers,

$$\frac{d\mu_{jm}}{d\alpha} = -\eta \sum_{in} \mu_{in} \frac{\partial \phi_{in}}{\partial R_{jm}} - \eta \sum_{ik} v_{ik} \frac{\partial (\psi_{ik} + \eta \, v_{ik})}{\partial R_{jm}} ,$$

$$\frac{dv_{jl}}{d\alpha} = -\eta \sum_{in} \mu_{in} \frac{\partial \phi_{in}}{\partial Q_{jl}} - \eta \sum_{ik} v_{ik} \frac{\partial \left(\psi_{ik} + \eta \, v_{ik} \right)}{\partial Q_{jl}} , \tag{3.3}$$

along with a set of boundary conditions,

$$\mu_{in}(\alpha_1) = \left. \frac{\partial \epsilon_g}{\partial R_{in}} \right|_{\alpha_1} \quad \text{and} \quad v_{ik}(\alpha_1) = \left. \frac{\partial \epsilon_g}{\partial Q_{ik}} \right|_{\alpha_1} . \tag{3.4}$$

Then taking variations with respect to η we find a simple expression for the globally optimal learning rate,

$$\eta = - \frac{\sum_{in} \mu_{in} \phi_{in} + \sum_{ik} v_{ik} \psi_{ik}}{2 \sum_{ik} v_{ik} v_{ik}} . \tag{3.5}$$

Equations (3.3), (3.4) and (3.5) determine necessary conditions for η to maximize the reduction in generalization error over the interval $[\alpha_0, \alpha_1]$. The boundary conditions correspond to the locally optimal solution, reflecting the fact that at α_1 the choice of η does not affect the dynamics at other times. To find the learning rate which satisfies this set of conditions we use gradient descent on the functional derivative of $\Delta \epsilon_g$ with respect to η,

$$\eta(t+1) = \eta(t) - \Theta \frac{\delta \Delta \epsilon_g}{\delta \eta} ,$$

$$\frac{\delta \Delta \epsilon_g}{\delta \eta} = \sum_{in} \mu_{in} \phi_{in} + \sum_{ik} v_{ik} \left(\psi_{ik} + 2\eta \, v_{ik} \right) , \tag{3.6}$$

where t is the iteration index and Θ is the step-size for the iteration process. In order to choose an appropriate value for Θ we employ second order variations,

$$\Theta \propto \left(\frac{\delta^2 \Delta \epsilon_g}{\delta \eta^2} \right)^{-1} = \left(2 \sum_{ik} v_{ik} v_{ik} \right)^{-1} . \tag{3.7}$$

Standard heuristics can be used to ensure that the iteration process does not diverge if the second order variations become negative, or close to zero.

To update η using Eq.(3.6), one should first solve Eqs.(3.3) along with the end conditions (Eq.3.4), determined by the order parameter values at α_1. For updating η one should therefore:

1. Assume some randomly chosen initial conditions for the overlaps and integrate the equations for the overlaps forward using equations (2.2), starting at α_0 and ending at α_1.

2. Calculate the end conditions (Eq.3.4) using the overlap values at α_1.

3. Solve Eqs.(3.3) numerically by integrating them backwards using the boundary conditions of Eq.(3.4). In our implementation the overlaps are stored during the forward dynamics and re-used during the backwards dynamics for the Lagrange multipliers.

4. Update the time dependent learning rate using Eq.(3.6).

5. Use the current time-dependent learning rate to integrate Eqs.(2.2) forward and iterate the whole process until convergence.

This algorithm converges within a few iterations and results in an exact function for the optimal learning rate over the given time-window. We will now demonstrate the usefulness of the method for several training scenarios.

4 Numerical results

The theory presented in the previous section and the resulting recipe are completely general and may be employed for any number of teacher and student hidden units and for any teacher correlation matrix T. However, in this section we will focus on students and teachers of equal complexity ($K = M$) and on isotropic teachers ($T_{nm} = \delta_{nm}$). Throughout this chapter, unless stated otherwise, initial conditions for the overlaps R_{in} and $Q_{i \neq k}$ are taken randomly from a uniform distribution $U[0, 10^{-6}]$ while the vector lengths Q_{ii} are taken from $U[0, 0.5]$, a choice which corresponds to an input dimension of about $N \simeq 10^{12}$. The optimal η is independent of the initial conditions which mainly affect the length of the symmetric phase.

4.1 Realizable rules

In our first example we consider a realizable ($K = M = 3$) noiseless training task. The time-window is $0 \leq \alpha \leq 600$ and the learning rate is initially fixed at some arbitrary value. The update in equation (3.6) is then iterated until convergence and figure 1 shows results for the dynamics using the globally optimal learning rate. Figures 1(a)–(d) show the optimal learning rate, generalization error and overlaps respectively. After a short initial transient both the learning rate and generalization error stabilize at almost constant values, corresponding to a symmetric phase in which the student nodes have not yet specialized to particular teacher nodes, as required to learn perfectly. The overlaps also exhibit a plateau within this phase and figure 1(c) shows that the student-teacher overlaps are almost indistinguishable (the indices have been ordered *a posteriori* so that student node i eventually specializes to teacher node i). The learning rate takes a value of about $\eta \simeq 0.97$ within the symmetric phase, which is in close agreement to the optimal value obtained numerically (West and Saad, 1997). Eventually, the student escapes the symmetric phase and the generalization error and overlaps exhibit exponential convergence towards their respective optimal values, as the learning rate increases towards another constant value of $\eta = 1.28$, identical to the result obtained independently (West and Saad, 1997) for the asymptotically

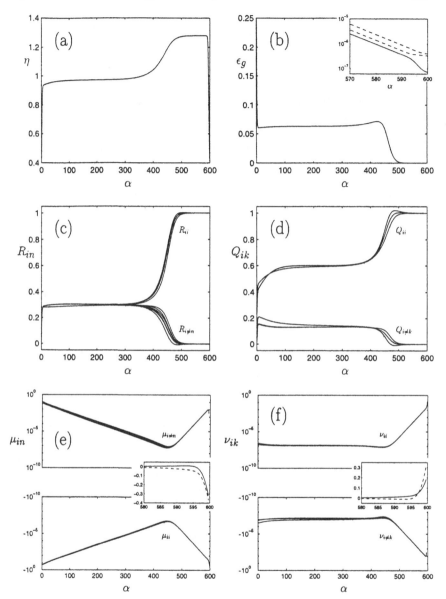

Fig.1 - Results are presented for a three hidden node student trained to emulate an isotropic teacher of the same configuration. The globally optimal learning rate is shown in (a) along with the corresponding evolution of the generalization error and order parameters in (b),(c) and (d). The inset of (b) shows the generalization error (solid line) and the magnitude of the opposing contributions to the leading term (dashed lines – upper proportional to $2r - q$, lower proportional to $2s - c$). The Lagrange multipliers are shown in (e) and (f) using a log scale, with the later stages magnified in each inset (dashed line for a curve associated with the lower figure).

optimal learning rate by expanding the dynamical equations for the overlaps around their asymptotic fixed point.

One significant difference between the results obtained here and those obtained from the expansion around the asymptotic fixed point is the sudden drop in learning rate towards the end of the time-window to a value of around $\eta = 0.41$ (see figure 1(a)). This can be explained by examining the expression for the generalization error in the vicinity of its asymptotic fixed point. It is possible to gain an immediate reduction in generalization error by choosing an appropriate direction for the decay eigenvectors. Using the symmetry of the problem we expand the expression for the generalization error around the fixed point via $R_{in} = \delta_{in}(1-r) + (1-\delta_{in})s$ and $Q_{ik} = \delta_{ik}(1-q) + (1-\delta_{ik})c$ to find two contributions to the leading term of opposite sign, proportional to $2r - q$ and $2s - c$ respectively. These are shown in the inset to figure 1(b) along with the corresponding generalization error for $570 \le \alpha \le 600$. By reducing the learning rate it is possible to reduce the difference in magnitude between these opposing contributions, leading to a reduction in generalization error. However, this reduction in learning rate slows down the exponential convergence of the overlaps and is therefore unsustainable in the long term only occurring towards the end of the time-window. This example shows how locally optimal learning does not necessarily give good long-term performance, even asymptotically. The long-term goal in this case is to optimize the decay rate of the order parameters, while changes in the decay direction can provide short-term gains but will eventually lead to poorer performance.

The various phases of learning described above are mirrored by the Lagrange multiplier dynamics shown in figures 1(e) and (f). Figure 1(e) shows how during the symmetric phase μ_{ii} and $\mu_{i\neq n}$ decay exponentially with similar magnitude but opposite sign. At the same time figure 1(f) shows that ν_{ii} and $\nu_{i\neq k}$ also have opposite signs but remain almost constant during the symmetric phase. After escaping the symmetric phase all the Lagrange multipliers exhibit an exponential growth with the same constant rate, which is equal in magnitude to the decay rate of the generalization error at this point. The inset to each figure magnifies the short transient at the end of the optimization time-window in which the exponential growth is interrupted as each Lagrange multiplier finds the appropriate boundary value.

Notice that the dynamics of the overlaps and Lagrange multipliers forms a small number of bundled similar trajectories, reflecting symmetries in the task. By exploiting these symmetries the dimensionality of the system can be reduced significantly, allowing a compact description for arbitrary K and T. This dimensionality reduction has already been used to study the different phases of learning in (Saad and Solla, 1995; West and Saad, 1997) and in section 5 we elucidate the relationship between our algorithm and these studies.

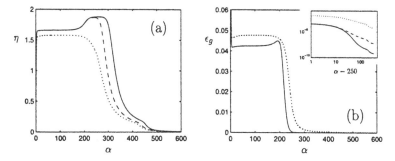

Fig.2 - A two hidden node student is trained on noise corrupted examples generated by an isotropic teacher of the same configuration. The optimal learning rate is shown in (a) for three noise levels $\sigma^2 = 10^{-2}$, 10^{-5}, 10^{-7} (from left to right) over a fixed time-window $0 \leq \alpha \leq 600$. The corresponding generalization error is shown in (b) with the inset showing a log-log plot for the decay at late times, which indicates that the dashed and solid lines are only split after $\alpha \simeq 300$.

4.2   Noise corrupted examples

In our second example we consider an unrealizable learning scenario by introducing additive uncorrelated Gaussian noise of zero mean and variance σ^2 to the teacher's output. Qualitatively similar results are obtained for structural unrealizability ($K < M$). The picture that emerges, shown in figure 2 for various noise levels ($\sigma^2 = 10^{-2}$, 10^{-5} and 10^{-7}), is initially similar to the realizable case but changes dramatically as the system escapes the symmetric phase. As the system begins convergence towards zero generalization error[1], as shown in figure 2(b), the optimal learning rate shown in figure 2(a) begins to fall and slowly approaches a decay inversely proportional to α, proved to be optimal for linear systems (e.g., (White, 1989) and references therein), until reaching a greedy phase (after the kink around $\alpha = 440$ in figure 2). The rapid reduction in generalization error after this point is achieved by changing the decay direction, as for the realizable learning scenario described above.

Figures 3(a) and (b) show a log-log plot of the learning rate and generalization error respectively as a function of α for optimization over time-windows of varying length. One observes that both the learning rate and generalization error approach a decay proportional to $1/\alpha$ and that the curves lie on top of one another until the greedy phase which occurs towards the end of each time window. However, unlike the realizable case where the drop-off in learning rate occurs over a relatively short time, here the final greedy phase

---

[1]Recall that this is the generalization error in the absence of noise. The prediction error for a noisy teacher has an additive constant contribution equal to half the noise variance.

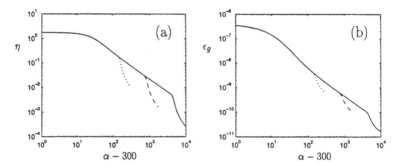

Fig.3 - As in figure 2, a two node student is trained on noisy examples from a teacher of the same configuration. Here the noise level is fixed at $\sigma^2 = 10^{-7}$ while the optimization process is carried out over different time windows $0 \le \alpha \le \alpha_1$ with $\alpha_1 = 600$, 2000 and 10^4 (from left to right). The asymptotic decay of the learning rate (a) and generalization error (b) are shown for each case. The initial behaviour is similar to that presented in figure 2.

increases in length as the total learning time-window increases and this phase always takes a significant proportion of the learning time. This is simply a reflection of the slower decay time-scale for this problem.

On a practical note, our results suggest that as symmetry breaks one should gradually modify the decay rate from a constant until it is proportional to $1/\alpha$. However, it may take a prohibitively long time until the $1/\alpha$ decay becomes optimal, making it irrelevant in many instances. Moreover, if one decays the learning rate at a fixed rate it may take an extremely long time before losses, incurred due to the use of sub-optimal learning rates in earlier stages of the dynamics, can be recovered. Annealing the learning rate during the symmetric phase could even lead to trapping, since the length of the symmetric phase scales inversely to η for small η (Saad and Solla, 1995).

5 Analysis of the optimal learning dynamics

As we saw in the previous section the overlap dynamics is often dominated by fixed points (the symmetric and convergence phases) around which we can make a linear expansion. We therefore carry out an analysis of our variational algorithm in the neighbourhood of such a fixed point, leading to some valuable insight into how the algorithm optimizes performance. Moreover, we simplify the problem by focusing on realizable scenarios ($K = M$) and isotropic tasks ($T_{nm} = T\delta_{nm}$), whereby the problem dimensionality can be reduced, for determining generic behaviour for variable T and K. This simplification has recently been used to determine optimal parameters for both the symmetric and convergence phases by an eigenvalue analysis around each fixed point (West and Saad, 1997). Here, we focus on showing the close relationship between this work and the variational method and on understanding how our algorithm finds optimal parameters in the simplest scenario, in order to inform our use of the algorithm for more general problems.

The following analysis requires that the learning rate is fixed in the phases of interest and is therefore only applicable to noiseless learning, at least for the convergence phase. The noise corrupted rules considered in section 4.2 will require a different approach, perhaps using recent results for optimal annealing schedules in the presence of noise (Leen et al., 1998). We leave this analysis for future study.

5.1   Behaviour near a fixed point

Let $\mathbf{y}$ be a vector of dynamical variables, which can be thought of as deviations from some fixed point. In the neighbourhood of such a fixed point we have a linearized system of differential equations, $d\mathbf{y}/d\alpha = \mathbf{My}$, which corresponds to decay in the neighbourhood of a stable fixed point (the convergence phase) or divergence in the neighbourhood of an unstable fixed point (the symmetric phase). Here, $\mathbf{M}$ depends on η which is taken to be constant within the region considered. Let $\mathbf{z}$ denote the associated vector of Lagrange multipliers. The linearized equivalent of equation (3.3) is then, $d\mathbf{z}/d\alpha = -\mathbf{M}^{\mathrm{T}}\mathbf{z}$.

Let $\mathbf{U}$ denote the matrix whose columns are eigenvectors of $\mathbf{M}$ and let $\boldsymbol{\lambda}$ denote the corresponding vector of eigenvalues. Then $(\mathbf{U}^{-1})^{\mathrm{T}}$ is the matrix of eigenvectors of $-\mathbf{M}^{\mathrm{T}}$ with eigenvalues $-\boldsymbol{\lambda}$. We write the general solutions for $\mathbf{y}$ and $\mathbf{z}$ in component form,

$$y_i = \sum_j \mathbf{U}_{ij} \exp(\alpha\lambda_j) , \qquad z_i = z_{0i} + \sum_j \beta_j \mathbf{U}_{ji}^{-1} \exp(-\alpha\lambda_j) , \qquad (5.1)$$

where the $\{z_{0i}\}$ are components of a fixed point for $\mathbf{z}$ and are independent of α, while β_i weights the ith mode of $\mathbf{z}$ and will depend on the boundary conditions of the fixed point neighbourhood in general.

The functional derivative of $\Delta\epsilon_g$ with respect to η is given by,

$$
\begin{aligned}
\frac{\delta\Delta\epsilon_g}{\delta\eta} &= \mathbf{z}^{\mathrm{T}}\frac{\partial\mathbf{M}}{\partial\eta}\mathbf{y} = \mathbf{z}^{\mathrm{T}}\left(\frac{\partial(\mathbf{My})}{\partial\eta} - \mathbf{M}\frac{\partial\mathbf{y}}{\partial\eta}\right) \\
&= \sum_i \beta_i\frac{\partial\lambda_i}{\partial\eta} + \sum_{ij}\beta_i(\lambda_j - \lambda_i)e^{\alpha(\lambda_j - \lambda_i)}\sum_k \mathbf{U}_{ik}^{-1}\frac{\partial\mathbf{U}_{kj}}{\partial\eta} \\
&\quad + \sum_{ij} z_{0i}\left[(1 + \lambda_j)\mathbf{U}_{ij}\frac{\partial\lambda_j}{\partial\eta} + \lambda_j\frac{\partial\mathbf{U}_{ij}}{\partial\eta}\right]e^{\alpha\lambda_j} .
\end{aligned}
\tag{5.2}
$$

where we have used the dynamical equations for $\mathbf{y}$ and $\mathbf{z}$ and (5.1). Equation (5.2) identifies the various contributions to changes in η under gradient descent on the functional $\Delta\epsilon_g(\eta)$ in the neighbourhood of a fixed point. The first term contributes changes in the gradient direction of the eigenvalues while the second term involves derivatives of the eigenvectors with respect to η. The final term involves the fixed point for $\mathbf{z}$. Notice that only the last two terms depend on α and that the only condition under which the final two terms can contribute a quantity independent of α is if there is a vanishing eigenvalue. This is not found to be the case for either of the fixed points considered here in the neighbourhood of the optimal learning rate.

The functional derivative in equation (5.2) will only disappear at constant η if terms with α dependence are negligible with respect to the first term. This condition is satisfied by ensuring that any term whose exponent is positive and proportional to α has a sufficiently small prefactor. We therefore obtain conditions sufficient, and most likely necessary[2], for the existence of a constant η fixed point in an optimal linear system:

- We require that each component of the fixed point for $\mathbf{z}$ be sufficiently small to ensure the final term in equation (5.2) is negligible.

- We further require that $|\beta_i| \ll |\beta_j|$ for at least one j for which $\lambda_j > \lambda_i$ and $\sum_k \mathbf{U}_{ik}^{-1} \partial \mathbf{U}_{kj}/\partial\eta$ is non-zero. Notice that the latter condition is not satisfied when the jth eigenvector is independent of η.

Close to the optimal learning rate only the first term in equation (5.2) will be significant, since any other remaining terms would have a strong α-dependence (assuming that one cannot choose η to make the first term zero while simultaneously setting the prefactor of any remaining α-dependent term to zero). In practice, for a non-degenerate system we often find that a single mode in the Lagrange multiplier dynamics is dominant ($|\beta_j| \gg |\beta_{i\neq j}|$) and in this case the effect of our algorithm is to carry out gradient descent (ascent) on this dominant mode,

$$\frac{\delta\Delta\epsilon_g}{\delta\eta} \propto \frac{\partial\lambda_{\mathrm{dom}}}{\partial\eta} . \tag{5.3}$$

The second condition above suggests that the dominant mode will have a relatively large eigenvalue, although not necessarily the largest one. For example, if the largest eigenvalue is associated with an eigenvector which is independent of η then we can say nothing about its weight relative to modes with smaller eigenvalues. In this case it is necessary to consider the boundary conditions of the fixed point neighbourhood in order to determine which mode is dominant. In both the symmetric and convergence phases we find exactly this situation and in the latter phase we find that it is the mode with

---

[2]For these conditions to be necessary requires that each contribution to the second term of equation (5.3) has a different exponent proportional to α, which is also different to any exponents in the final term. This is true so long as each $\lambda_i - \lambda_j$ takes a unique value which is different from every λ_i.

the second largest eigenvalue which is dominant. The sign of the proportionality constant in equation (5.3) also depends on the boundary conditions of the fixed point neighbourhood and we typically find that the eigenvalue is maximized within an unstable fixed point (maximizing the speed of escape from the symmetric phase), or minimized when converging to a stable fixed point.

Note that our discussion is not strictly valid if the fixed point changes with η, as is the case for the symmetric phase (West and Saad, 1997) considered below. The picture developed here holds as long as these changes are relatively slow and we will therefore neglect any such η-dependence.

5.2 The symmetric phase

As demonstrated in section 4, the learning time can be dominated by a symmetric phase representing an attractive fixed point of the dynamics which becomes unstable as small perturbations due to non-symmetric initial conditions eventually lead to the symmetry breaking.

Unfortunately, it seems impossible to study the symmetric phase analytically for finite η and a numerical study of this fixed point (West and Saad, 1997), was based on reducing the system's dimensionality by exploiting symmetries between the overlaps in order to determine generic behaviour for variable K and T. We employ the same dimensionality reduction to analyse our linearized system in the neighbourhood of the symmetric fixed point. The overlaps are then represented by $Q_{ik} = Q\delta_{ik} + C(1 - \delta_{ik})$ and $R_{in} = R\delta_{in} + S(1 - \delta_{in})$, where student node indices have been chosen to correspond with the teacher node which they will eventually specialize to. Following (West and Saad, 1997), we can make some analytical progress by considering a fixed point characterized by $Q = C$ and $R = S$. This fixed point only exists for significant times when η is small, since any difference between Q and C is quickly increased by a positive eigenvalue of order η^2. The resulting fixed point with $Q > C$ is the one actually observed in our simulations (see figure 1(d)) but unfortunately this fixed point cannot be studied analytically. Many features of this fixed point are also observed for the $Q = C$ fixed point however and it is therefore instructive to consider this case first.

To aid clarity we choose $T = 1$, although qualitatively similar results are found for arbitrary T. The vector of deviations from the order parameter fixed point is $\mathbf{y} = (R - R^*, S - S^*, Q - Q^*, C - C^*)^{\mathrm{T}}$ where $(R^*, S^*, Q^*, C^*)^{\mathrm{T}}$ is the fixed point (we assume that the η-dependence of this fixed point is negligible). The conjugate vector of Lagrange multipliers is $\mathbf{z} = (\mu_R, \mu_S, \nu_Q, \nu_C)^{\mathrm{T}}$. The $\mathbf{y}$ and $\mathbf{z}$ dynamics are associated with the following matrices,

$$
\mathbf{U} = \begin{pmatrix} K-1 & 1 & U_{(1/2)3} & U_{(1/2)4} \\ -1 & 1 & U_{(1/2)3} & U_{(1/2)4} \\ 0 & U_{32} & 1 & 1 \\ 0 & U_{42} & 1 & 1 \end{pmatrix} ; \quad (\mathbf{U}^{-1})^{\mathrm{T}} = \begin{pmatrix} 1/K & 0 & \cdots & \cdots \\ -1/K & 0 & \cdots & \\ 0 & (U_{32} - U_{42})^{-1} & & \\ 0 & -(U_{32} - U_{42})^{-1} & & \end{pmatrix}
$$

where the ith column of $\mathbf{U}$ is the eigenvector associated with eigenvalue λ_i

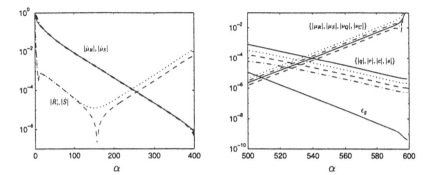

Fig. 4 - Simulation of the reduced dimensionality equations of motion
with $T = 1$ and $K = 3$ and initial conditions $R = 10^{-6}$, $Q = 0.25$
and $S = C = 0$. Left - magnitudes of the rates of change for R, S
and their conjugate Lagrange multipliers are shown during the sym-
metric phase. The curves are $|\dot{R}|$ (dotted), $|\dot{S}|$ (dashed), $|\dot{\mu}_R|$ (full) and
$|\dot{\mu}_S|$ (dot-dashed). The learning rate is fixed at the optimal value for
the symmetric phase. Right - the magnitudes of the overlap deviations
(r, q, c, s) and Lagrange multipliers are shown during the conver-
gence phase. The curves are $|q|$ (full), $|r|$ (dotted), $|c|$ (dashed) and
$|s|$ (dot-dashed); their conjugate Lagrange multipliers are given the
same line-type. The lower solid curve shows the generalization error.

and the components U_{ij} depend on η and K (see (West and Saad, 1997) for
details). The columns of $\mathbf{U}$ have been arranged so that they are associated
with eigenvalues which are decreasing from left to right ($\lambda_{i>j} < \lambda_j$). The first
eigenvalue is the only positive one (unless η is significantly larger than its
optimal setting (West and Saad, 1997)) and results in the divergence of R
and S which eventually leads to escape from the symmetric phase.

The entries in the final two columns of the second matrix $(\mathbf{U}^{-1})^{\mathrm{T}}$ involve
various combinations of the U_{ij} and K which are not shown here as their
exact form is not important. From the discussion in section 5.1 we expect
that the third and fourth modes for the Lagrange multiplier dynamics will
have a very small weight ($\beta_{3/4} \ll \beta_{1/2}$). However, since the first eigenvector is
independent of η we cannot determine whether it will be dominant without
knowing something about the boundary conditions of the symmetric phase.
These boundary conditions are determined according to the dynamics away
from the fixed point considered here and therefore we can only proceed by
observing what happens in practice.

We find that the $Q = C$ fixed point considered above seems to be a rather
good model for the $Q > C$ fixed point observed in simulations. In figure 4

we plot the magnitude of $\dot{R}(=\mathrm{d}R/\mathrm{d}\alpha)$, $\dot{Q}$, μ_R and μ_S during the symmetric phase, for simulations of the reduced dimensionality system considered here (with $K = 3$ and η fixed at its optimal value for the symmetric phase). Initially $\dot{R}$ and $\dot{S}$ are indistinguishable until differences due to asymmetric initial conditions are amplified and they diverge according to the dominant mode described above (we plot the magnitudes here – the signs of $\dot{R}$ and $\dot{S}$ are different after about $\alpha = 160$). Meanwhile, μ_R and μ_S decay with the same rate as the growth of R and S and their rates of change have exactly the same magnitude but opposite sign. This is in agreement with the behaviour expected for the first mode, whose eigenvector for the Lagrange multiplier dynamics is shown in the first column of $(\mathbf{U}^{-1})^{\mathrm{T}}$ above. This mode does not contribute to changes in ν_Q and ν_C and because $\dot{\nu}_Q$ and $\dot{\nu}_C$ are observed to have much smaller magnitudes than μ_R and μ_S we conclude that the second mode is associated with a much smaller weight in the Lagrange multiplier dynamics ($\beta_2 \ll \beta_1$). The first mode is therefore dominant and the variational algorithm finds the maximum of λ_1 (see equation (5.3)). This is exactly the mode considered in (West and Saad, 1997) where λ_1 was maximized numerically and our results agree well with results from that work.

5.3   The convergence phase

Once the student nodes specialize to specific teacher nodes the dynamics quickly leaves the symmetric phase and approaches a convergence phase in which the overlaps and generalization error exhibit an exponential convergence towards their optimal values (in the absence of noise). It is possible to study the fixed point analytically and this has been carried through in (West and Saad, 1997). Here, we only discuss a completely linear system, in which higher order contributions to the generalization error are negligible. Inclusion of second order terms is required for a more complete description, as discussed in (Rattray and Saad, 1998).

As in the symmetric phase there is a mode whose eigenvector is independent of η (recall our second condition for a fixed point in an optimal linear system, after equation (5.2) in section 5.1). This turns out to be the slowest mode for the overlap dynamics and is orthogonal to the leading term of the linearized generalization error, so not contributing to its decay. In this case the mode associated with the next largest eigenvalue dominates the Lagrange multiplier dynamics (and therefore the first term in equation (5.2)) at late times. It is therefore this eigenvalue which is minimized by our variational algorithm (recall equation (5.3)).

In general it is difficult to study analytically how the boundary conditions affect the Lagrange multiplier dynamics because of the greedy drop-off in η at the end of the optimization time-window which was described in section 4 (see figure 1). This greedy phase is not described by our linear system (which requires a constant η) and therefore the final boundary conditions occur outside the region in which our linear model provides a good approximation. However, for the perceptron ($M = K = 1$) this greedy phase does not occur and the boundary conditions are well defined for our linear system. It is therefore instructive to consider the perceptron as a special case.

For the perceptron (with $T = 1$) we expand around the convergence fixed point via $\mathbf{y} = (r,q)^T$ where $r = 1 - R$ and $q = 1 - Q$ with associated Lagrange multipliers $\mathbf{z} = (z_r, z_q)^T$. The $\mathbf{y}$ and $\mathbf{z}$ dynamics are associated with the following matrices respectively (recall that the columns are eigenvectors),

$$\mathbf{U} = \begin{pmatrix} U_{11} & 1 \\ U_{21} & 2 \end{pmatrix} \qquad (\mathbf{U}^{-1})^T \propto \begin{pmatrix} 2 & -U_{21} \\ -1 & U_{11} \end{pmatrix}, \qquad (5.4)$$

where U_{11} and U_{12} are functions of η (see (Saad and Solla, 1995) for details). The linearized generalization error is proportional to $2r-q$, so that the boundary conditions for the Lagrange multipliers are (ignoring a multiplicative constant) $\mathbf{z}(\alpha_1) = (2, -1)^T$ (see equation (3.4)). The mode associated with the first column in $(\mathbf{U}^{-1})^T$ is then completely dominant for the $\mathbf{z}$-dynamics and the mode whose eigenvector is orthogonal to the generalization error (the second column in $\mathbf{U}$) in the $\mathbf{y}$-dynamics does not contribute to determining the optimal learning rate in a completely linear system; although, it may still contribute to second order terms in the generalization error (Rattray and Saad, 1998)).

Although we cannot extend this argument to a general multi-layer system, because the boundary conditions occur outside the region in which our linear model is reliable, a similar effect is observed in general. Recall the reduced dimensionality equations of motion which were used to analyse the symmetric fixed point ($Q_{ik} = Q\delta_{ik} + C(1 - \delta_{ik})$, $R_{in} = R\delta_{in} + S(1 - \delta_{in})$). Figure 4 shows the evolution of the overlap deviations ($r = 1 - R$, $q = 1 - Q$, $s = S$, $c = C$) and their conjugate Lagrange multipliers during the convergence phase for a simulation of the reduced dimensionality system. The generalization error is also shown and exhibits a faster decay than the overlaps, because the slow mode which determines the decay of the overlaps is orthogonal to the linearized generalization error (higher order contributions to the generalization error are negligible in this case). It is therefore the second slowest mode which determines the decay rate of the generalization error. As for the simpler perceptron case described above, it is this second mode which is mirrored in the Lagrange multiplier dynamics and figure 4 shows how the Lagrange multipliers grow with the same rate as the generalization error decays. The second mode is therefore dominant and the variational algorithm minimizes the associated eigenvalue (see equation (5.3)). This eigenvalue was minimized explicitly in (West and Saad, 1997) and again we find excellent agreement with results from our variational algorithm.

The above discussion does not address the consideration that although we can assume an essentially linear system in the neighbourhood of fixed points, we may still have to consider higher order contributions to the generalization error (West and Saad, 1997). However, in view of the fact that the end-point boundary conditions for the Lagrange multipliers (see equation (3.4)) are first derivatives of the generalization error, it seems unlikely that second order terms in the generalization error will cause significant changes to the Lagrange multiplier dynamics at late times. In fact, we find that the algorithm deals with quadratic effects *before* converging to the optimal learning rate for a linear error (Rattray and Saad, 1998).

5.4 Generic behaviour

Using the reduced dimensionality equations of motion makes it possible to find the optimal learning rate for arbitrary K, since we avoid the increase in computation time necessary to deal with large systems. We can therefore run our algorithm for various values of K and T in order to deduce scaling laws for the optimal learning rate within the two phases of learning. However, as we saw above our algorithm simply performs gradient descent on the relevant eigenvalue within each phase and the results should therefore compare closely to results obtained by optimizing with respect to this eigenvalue directly.

Comparing the optimal learning rate determined by our method to the value found by a direct numerical eigenvalue analysis (West and Saad, 1997) for various values of K we find that the results agree well and any discrepancies may be due to the variational algorithm not converging completely, or because of variance in the learning rate within the symmetric phase. This outcome is rather fortuitous, as the scaling laws previously determined for each phase in (West and Saad, 1997) also describe the scaling behaviour for the globally optimal learning rate. This was not obvious *a priori* since it was not known that the optimal time-dependent learning rate would be dominated by two plateaus, each with a constant learning rate.

It is interesting to summarize some of the scaling laws deduced in (West and Saad, 1997) (for fixed T). During the symmetric phase the optimal learning rate scales as $K^{-5/3}$ for large K and the trapping time as $K^{8/3}$. During the convergence phase the optimal learning rate scales as $1/K$. The maximal learning rate in each phase, above which perfect learning is impossible, scales in the same way as the optimal learning rate. One therefore finds that using a learning rate which is optimal asymptotically will be very bad during the transient, either leading to trapping within the symmetric phase or divergence of the student weight vector norms.

5.5 Limitations to the variational approach

The above analysis suggests a possible limitation of our variational algorithms if eigenvalues are multi-modal, as might be the case if the equations of motion involved higher powers, or non-linear functions, of the parameters being optimized. In this case the algorithm may get stuck in functional local minima, as it effectively carries out gradient descent/ascent on the dominant eigenvalue.

Certain initial settings for η may also result in convergence to functional local minima which are sub-optimal. For example, if η is very small initially and the time-window is not sufficiently long for the system to leave the symmetric phase then the algorithm may anneal η in an attempt to optimize performance without leaving the symmetric subspace. This does not contradict our discussion in section 5.2 as the behaviour of the variational algorithm clearly depends on the boundary conditions of the symmetric phase. As with any differential method we are at the mercy of local minima; our conditions for the globally optimal learning rate are necessary but not sufficient. From careful study of the dynamics we are satisfied that all the solutions presented in this work are globally optimal.

6 Hidden-to-output learning rates

One limitation of our model is the assumption of fixed hidden-to-output weights and it is straightforward to include variable hidden-to-output weights (Riegler, 1997; Riegler and Biehl, 1995), resulting in an extra set of dynamical equations. However, if the learning rate associated with these weights is chosen to be of the same order as for the input-to-hidden weights then our optimization procedure shows that the learning rate associated with these weights should be set infinitely high, indicating an inappropriate scaling and that learning should be on a faster time-scale for these weights. This can be incorporated as an adiabatic elimination of the fast variables, as justified in (Riegler, 1997) where it is shown that this provides a locally optimal choice for the hidden-to-output weights (i.e., which minimizes the generalization error instantaneously). Our analysis therefore indicates that adiabatic elimination is also globally optimal.

7 Site-dependent learning rates

It is straightforward to extend our method to more complex learning rules and to different learning parameters. As a simple example we consider a generalized gradient descent algorithm in which different learning rates are associated with different hidden nodes, so that the new update rule is given by $\mathbf{J}_i^{\mu+1} = \mathbf{J}_i^\mu + \frac{1}{N}\eta_i\delta_i^\mu\boldsymbol{\xi}^\mu$. This enables the system to explore more complex routes to breaking symmetry and converging to the optimal solution. The derivation for the optimal site-dependent learning rate follows the discussion in section 3 closely and is therefore not included here.

Isotropic teacher: In our first example we train a three hidden node system on examples generated by a three node isotropic teacher, using three different learning rates. The optimal learning rates and the corresponding generalization error are shown in figures 5(a) and (c) respectively. Comparison with figure 1(b) shows a significant improvement over standard gradient descent, although the dynamics is still dominated by a symmetric plateau (the initial conditions were the same in both cases). A shortened symmetric plateau is achieved by setting one learning rate close to zero while the other two are assigned a high value, much higher than the optimal learning rate for standard gradient descent on the same problem (but lower than the optimal learning rate for standard gradient descent with $M = K = 2$). Once the two nodes associated with the high learning rate become associated to specific teacher nodes, the learning rate associated with the third node rises rapidly as it learns the remaining teacher node. Eventually, all learning rates converge to the same constant and asymptotically optimal learning rate, which is the same as for standard gradient descent (see figure 1(a)), before the greedy drop-off in η. The same pattern of successively active learning rates and hence a phased symmetry breaking is repeated for larger isotropic systems, suggesting that using different learning rates for different nodes may be beneficial for speeding up the learning process.

Graded teacher : In our second example we train the same three hidden node system on examples generated by a graded three node teacher ($T_{nm} = n\delta_{nm}$). The optimal learning rates and the corresponding generalization error are shown in figures 5(b) and (d) respectively. The optimal site-dependent learning rate shows a much richer behaviour in this example. Initially, the learning rate associated with the node learning the largest teacher vector (solid line) is highest, followed by phases in which the learning rates associated with nodes learning the intermediate and smallest teacher vectors increase in turn. This corresponds to what one might expect, since the system specializes to teacher nodes in order of decreasing impact to the teacher output. Eventually each learning rate approaches an asymptotically constant value, before dropping off towards the end of the time-window due to greedy effects. Here we see that the order of learning rate magnitudes has changed, so that the learning rate for the node associated with the largest teacher node is smallest and vice versa. This is a somewhat unintuitive result, since the optimal asymptotic learning rate for standard gradient descent increases with increasing T (West and Saad, 1997). Unfortunately, an analytical study of this scenario is hampered by the lack of dimensionality reducing symmetries in this case.

8   Globally optimal weight decay

Learning from corrupted examples is a realistic and frequently encountered scenario and is commonly handled by some sort of regularization (for a review see (Bishop, 1995)). Here we adapt our previously formulated techniques to

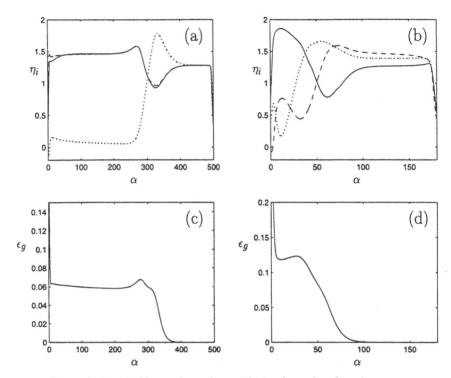

Fig.5 - A three hidden node student with site-dependent learning rates is trained to emulated a teacher with the same number of hidden nodes. The globally optimal learning rates are shown in (a) for an isotropic teacher ($T_{nm} = \delta_{nm}$) and in (b) for a graded teacher ($T_{nm} = n\delta_{nm}$). The corresponding generalization errors are shown in (c) and (d) respectively. In (b) the learning rates are associated with nodes learning the following teacher nodes – dashed line for $n = 1$, dotted line for $n = 2$ and solid line for $n = 3$.

examine the efficacy of regularizers for on-line learning. Employing the same methods as in section 3 one obtains a set of coupled differential equations for the Lagrange multipliers which are similar to Eqs.(3.3) with an addition of terms $\gamma\mu_{km}$ and $2\gamma\nu_{kl}$ to the first and second equations respectively, the same boundary conditions as before (Eq.3.4) while a separate equation is derived for the functional derivative of $\Delta\epsilon_g$ with respect to γ, which we use for iteratively updating γ via gradient descent as in (3.6),

$$\frac{\delta\Delta\epsilon_g}{\delta\gamma} = -\sum_{in}\mu_{in}R_{in} - 2\sum_{ij}\nu_{ij}Q_{ij} , \qquad (8.1)$$

where all terms required for carrying out the update of γ can be obtained by integrating the learning dynamics [3] in a similar manner to that of section 3.

We have employed this method to derive the optimal weight decay coefficient in several cases: structurally realizable and over-realizable noiseless scenarios with optimal and small learning rates and structurally realizable and over-realizable noisy scenarios with optimal learning rates.

For small learning rates our results show that during the symmetric phase a very small or negative value is chosen for the optimal weight decay γ_{opt}, indicating that weight decay is at best useless and possibly detrimental during this phase (Saad and Rattray, 1998). After the symmetric phase γ_{opt} quickly approaches zero, as required in order to achieve zero generalization error asymptotically. For larger learning rates, however, we do find a positive γ_{opt} which can shorten the symmetric phase significantly for realizable, over-realizable and noisy learning scenarios. As expected, γ_{opt} falls quickly to zero as the generalization error converges towards zero.

We demonstrate the results obtained by considering the case of Gaussian output noise. Fig. 6(a) shows γ_{opt} for a structurally realizable task ($M = K = 2$) with noise variance $\sigma^2 = 0.01$. The learning rate is given its optimal time-dependent value in the absence of weight decay[4] (shown by the dotted line in Fig. 6(a)), which is initially constant at $\eta \simeq 1.6$ until a decay towards the end of the given time-window as required for the system to achieve optimal asymptotic performance. Figure 6(b) shows a significant shortening of the symmetric phase when compared to learning without weight decay. However, as the system escapes the symmetric phase and the weight decay drops to zero, the generalization error approaches the same decay as in the absence of weight decay and there is no asymptotic improvement in performance.

9 Optimal learning rule

So far we concentrated on optimizing the learning parameters keeping the learning rule similar to the standard gradient descent. This section will focus on optimizing the update rule itself, restricted to the general form $\mathbf{J}_i^{\mu+1} = \mathbf{J}_i^\mu + \frac{1}{N}F_i^\mu(\boldsymbol{x}^\mu, \zeta^\mu)\boldsymbol{\xi}^\mu$, where $\mathbf{F}$ depends only on the student activations and the teacher's output. Note that gradient descent takes this general form, as does Hebbian learning and other training algorithms commonly used in discrete machines. The optimal $\mathbf{F}$ can also depend on the self-averaging statistics which describe the dynamics, since we know how they evolve in time. Some of these would not be available in a practical application, although for

---

[3]Note that here, in contrast to Eq.(3.5), one obtains only first order functional derivatives with respect to the parameter as the dependence on γ is linear. Similarly, one cannot derive an expression for γ in terms of the Lagrange multipliers.

[4]Notice that we do not optimize η and γ simultaneously here, as we are mainly concerned with the improvements due to weight decay given a fixed learning rate schedule.

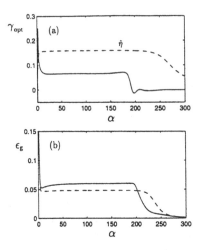

Fig. 6 - The optimal time-dependent
weight decay is shown by the solid line
in (a) for a structurally realizable task
($M = K = 2$) with examples corrupted by Gaussian output noise of
variance $\sigma^2 = 0.01$. The learning rate
(dashed line) is fixed at its optimal
time-dependent value in the absence of
weight decay ($\tilde{\eta} = \eta/10$). The corresponding generalization error is shown
by the solid line in (b) where it is compared to the generalization error without weight decay (dashed line).

some simple cases the unobservable statistics can be deduced from observable
quantities (Biehl et al, 1995; Kinouchi and Caticha, 1992). This is therefore
an idealization rather than a practical algorithm and provides a bound on the
performance of a real algorithm.

The general equations of motion can easily be derived for this case (2.3)
and the globally optimal learning rule is found by maximizing the total reduction in generalization error shown by Eq.(3.1) where the expression for
the integrand is of the form

$$
\begin{aligned}
\mathcal{L}(\mathbf{F}, \alpha) &= \sum_{in} \frac{\partial \epsilon_g}{\partial R_{in}} \frac{dR_{in}}{d\alpha} + \sum_{ik} \frac{\partial \epsilon_g}{\partial Q_{ik}} \frac{dQ_{ik}}{d\alpha} - \sum_{in} \lambda_{in} \left(\frac{dR_{in}}{d\alpha} - \langle F_i y_n \rangle \right) \\
&\quad - \sum_{ik} \nu_{ik} \left(\frac{dQ_{ik}}{d\alpha} - \langle F_i x_k + F_k x_i + F_i F_k \rangle \right) .
\end{aligned}
\tag{9.1}
$$

The expression for $\mathcal{L}$ still involves averages over $\mathbf{x}$ and $\mathbf{y}$ (angled brackets),
so taking variations in $\mathbf{F}$, which may depend on $\mathbf{x}$ and ζ but not on $\mathbf{y}$, we
find an expression for the optimal rule in terms of the Lagrange multipliers
$\mathbf{F} = -\mathbf{x} - \boldsymbol{\nu}^{-1} \boldsymbol{\lambda} \bar{\mathbf{y}}/2$, where $\boldsymbol{\nu} = [\nu_{ij}]$ and $\boldsymbol{\lambda} = [\lambda_{in}]$. We define $\bar{\mathbf{y}}$ to be the
teacher's expected field given the teacher's output and the student activations,
which are observable quantities:

$$
\bar{\mathbf{y}} = \int d\mathbf{y} \, \mathbf{y} \, p(\mathbf{y}|\mathbf{x}, \zeta) .
\tag{9.2}
$$

Taking variations w.r.t. to the dynamical variables we find a set of differential
equations for the Lagrange multipliers,

$$
\begin{aligned}
\frac{d\lambda_{km}}{d\alpha} &= -\sum_{in} \lambda_{in} \frac{\partial \langle F_i y_n \rangle}{\partial R_{km}} - \sum_{ij} \nu_{ij} \frac{\partial \langle F_i x_j + F_j x_i + F_i F_j \rangle}{\partial R_{km}} \\
\frac{d\nu_{kl}}{d\alpha} &= -\sum_{in} \lambda_{in} \frac{\partial \langle F_i y_n \rangle}{\partial Q_{kl}} - \sum_{ij} \nu_{ij} \frac{\partial \langle F_i x_j + F_j x_i + F_i F_j \rangle}{\partial Q_{kl}} ,
\end{aligned}
\tag{9.3}
$$

where $\mathbf{F}$ takes its optimal value. The boundary conditions for the Lagrange multipliers are as before (Eq.3.4), and are found by minimizing the rate of change in generalization error at α_1. If the above expressions do not yield an explicit formula for the optimal rule then the rule can be determined iteratively by gradient descent on the functional $\Delta\epsilon_g(\mathbf{F})$, employing the same iterative procedure as in section 3.

In order to apply the above result we must be able to carry out the average in Eq. (9.2) and then in Eqs. (9.3). These averages are also required to determine the locally optimal learning rule, so that the present method can be extended to any of the problems which have already been considered under the criteria of local optimality. Here we present two examples where the averages can be computed in closed form:

Boolean perceptron learning a linearly separable task : In this example we choose the activation function $g(x) = \mathrm{sgn}(x)$ and both teacher and student have a single hidden node. The locally optimal rule was determined by Kinouchi and Caticha (Kinouchi and Caticha, 1992) and they supply the expected teacher field given the teacher's output $\zeta = \mathrm{sgn}(y)$ and the student field x (we take the teacher length $T = 1$ without loss of generality),

$$\bar{y} = \frac{R}{Q}\left(x + \frac{\zeta\sqrt{\frac{2}{\pi}}\exp(-\frac{\gamma^2 x^2}{2})}{\gamma\,\mathrm{erfc}\left(\frac{-\zeta x\gamma}{\sqrt{2}}\right)}\right) \quad \text{where} \quad \gamma = \frac{R}{\sqrt{Q^2 - R^2Q}}\,. \tag{9.4}$$

Substituting this expression into the Lagrange multiplier dynamics in equation (9.3) shows that the ratio of λ to ν is given by $\lambda/\nu = -2Q/R$, and the optimal rule then returns the locally optimal value

$$F = \frac{\zeta\sqrt{\frac{2}{\pi}}\exp(-\frac{\gamma^2 x^2}{2})}{\gamma\,\mathrm{erfc}\left(\frac{-\zeta x\gamma}{\sqrt{2}}\right)}\,. \tag{9.5}$$

This rule leads to modulated Hebbian learning and the resulting dynamics are discussed in (Kinouchi and Caticha, 1992). We also find that the locally optimal rule is retrieved when the teacher is corrupted by output or weight noise (Biehl et al, 1995).

Soft committee machine learning an analogue perceptron : In this example of an over-realizable task, the teacher is an analogue perceptron ($M = 1$) while the student is a SCM with an arbitrary number (K) of hidden nodes. We choose the activation function $g(x) = \mathrm{erf}(x/\sqrt{2})$ for both the student and teacher. The locally optimal rule for this scenario has recently been determined (Vicente and Caticha, 1997).

Since the teacher is invertible, the expected teacher activation $\bar{y}$ is trivially equal to the true activation y. This leads to a particularly simple form for the dynamics (the n suffix is dropped since there is only one teacher node),

$$\frac{\mathrm{d}R_i}{\mathrm{d}\alpha} = b_i T - R_i \qquad \frac{\mathrm{d}Q_{ik}}{\mathrm{d}\alpha} = b_i b_k T - Q_{ik}\,, \tag{9.6}$$

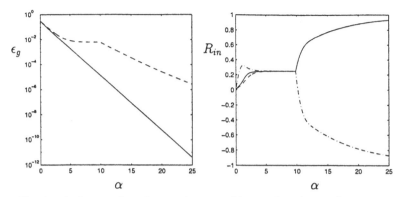

Fig. 7 - A three node soft committee machine student learns from an analogue perceptron teacher. The figure on the left shows a log plot of the generalization error for the globally optimal (solid line) and locally optimal (dashed line) algorithms. The figure on the right shows the student-teacher overlaps for the locally optimal rule, which exhibit a symmetric plateau before specialization occurs.

where we have defined $b_i = -\sum_j \nu_{ij}^{-1}\lambda_j/2$ and the optimal rule is given by $F_i = b_i y - x_i$. The Lagrange multiplier dynamics in eqs. (3.3) then show that the relative ratio of each Lagrange multiplier remains fixed over time, so that b_i is determined by its boundary value (see equation (3.4)). It is then straightforward to find solutions for long times, since the b_i approach limiting values for very small generalization error (there are a number of possible solutions with similar performance due to symmetries). For example, one possible solution is to have $b_1 = 1$ and $b_i = 0$ for all $i \neq 1$, which leads to an exponential decay of weights associated with all but a single node. This shows how optimal performance is achieved when the complexity of the student matches that of the teacher.

Figure 7 shows results for a three node student learning an analogue perceptron. Clearly, the locally optimal rule performs poorly in comparison to the globally optimal rule. In this example the globally optimal rule arrived at was one in which two nodes became correlated with the teacher while a third became anti-correlated, showing another possible variation on the optimal rule. The locally optimal rule gets caught in a symmetric plateau (as in section 3) and also displays a slower asymptotic decay.

It should be pointed out that the optimal rules derived here will often require knowledge of macroscopic properties related to the teacher's structure and therefore do not provide practical algorithms as they stand (although some of the required macroscopic properties may be evaluated or estimated on the basis of data gathered as the learning progresses). However, they do provide an upper bound on the performance one could expect from a real algorithm and may be instrumental in designing practical training algorithms.

10   Conclusion

We have introduced a method for determining optimal parameters and learning rules for on-line learning in a SCM, using a variational calculation to maximize the total reduction in generalization error over a fixed time-window. The method makes use of a recent statistical mechanics model which allows a compact and exact description of the learning process for large input dimension via differential equations for a small number of macroscopic quantities.

Learning with the optimal learning rate still suffers from trapping in a symmetric phase (Biehl and Schwarze, 1995; Saad and Solla, 1995), which dominates training time, and the fastest escape time is achieved by maximizing the only positive eigenvalue within this unstable fixed point. An analytical study of our variational algorithm in the neighbourhood of fixed points, which uses a linear model, shows this to be the expected behaviour of our algorithm and explains the excellent agreement with (West and Saad, 1997), where the escape eigenvalue within this phase was maximized explicitly. During the convergence phase the slowest mode, which is orthogonal to the first order term in the generalization error, does not contribute to the optimization of η at late times and the dominant mode was the next slowest. This result is also found to be consistent with our analysis of the variational algorithm near a fixed point. For the perceptron it is possible to show exactly how the boundary conditions lead to the exclusion of the slowest mode, but in general this is not possible as the boundary conditions cannot be easily defined due to a greedy minimization of the generalization error at the end of the optimization time-window. The main difference between our results for this example and the analysis in (West and Saad, 1997) is in the consideration of second order contributions to the generalization error, which in some situations determine the fastest asymptotic decay. We find that these second order effects play a role immediately after the symmetric phase, but that the algorithm always approaches the optimal learning rate for a linear generalization error at late times. In fact, these second order effects are only relevant when the optimization time-window is sufficiently large to allow a very low generalization error and they may therefore be irrelevant in practice.

Learning from corrupted examples provides a very different picture. After leaving the symmetric phase the optimal learning rate is gradually annealed towards a decay inversely proportional to α. There is a greedy phase, more emphasized than in the noiseless case, towards the end of the optimization time-window, reflecting a change in the decay direction which provides a short-term improvement but is unsustainable for longer times. Our results suggest that there is some danger in annealing the learning rate too early, since losses due to an initially low learning rate might never be recovered and the learning process could even become trapped within the symmetric phase.

This general framework can easily be extended to handle different parameters and learning rules. One of the extensions to the basic framework is to apply the optimization procedure to a generalized gradient descent in which different nodes are associated with different learning rates. The picture which emerges shows a rich behaviour, especially in the case of a graded teacher, suggesting that such a generalized algorithm might provide significant gains over standard gradient descent.

To examine the efficacy of regularization for arbitrary learning rates we employed the same variational method for determining optimal time-dependent parameters over a fixed time window. For small learning rates we find that the optimal weight decay parameter is very small and mostly negative during the symmetric phase, for realizable, over-realizable and noisy learning scenarios. However, for higher learning rates (we choose the optimal value in the absence of weight decay) a positive weight decay is found to be beneficial during the symmetric phase, although we never find any benefit after specialization occurs and for noisy learning the asymptotic performance is not improved upon. Although we do identify a scenario in which weight decay is slightly beneficial, this is probably of little value in practice since in most situations we find fixed weight decay to be detrimental to performance, especially at late times.

We employed the same method for determining the optimal on-line rule for a SCM. We gave two simple examples where the rule could be determined in closed form, for one of which, an over-realizable learning scenario, it was shown how the locally optimal rule performed poorly in comparison to the globally optimal rule. It is expected that more involved systems will show even greater difference in performance between local and global optimization and we are currently applying the method to more general teacher mappings. The main technical difficulty is in computing the expected teacher activation in equation (9.2) which may require the use of approximate methods.

The main question which remains open is whether one can find practical methods for selecting parameters and designing learning rules close to the optimal ones determined here. This has been carried through in some cases for the asymptotic stages of learning (e.g., in (LeCun et al, 1993)), but as we have seen here the transient stages of learning will often dominate the training time. It would also be interesting to compare the training dynamics obtained by the globally optimal rules to other approaches, heuristic and principled, aimed at incorporating information about the error surface curvature into the parameter modification rule. In particular, we examine (in this volume) rules which are known to be optimal asymptotically (e.g., natural gradient descent (Amari, 1997) and Newton's method).

Acknowledgements
We would like to thank Ansgar West and Bernhard Schottky for helpful discussions. This work was supported by EPSRC grant GR/L19232.

References

Amari, S. (1998). Natural gradient works efficiently in learning. *Neural Computation*, 10, 251–276.

Barber, D., Saad, D. and Sollich, P. (1996). Finite -size effects in online learning of multilayer neural networks. *Europhys. Lett.*, 34, 151–156.

Biehl, M. and Schwarze, H. (1995). Learning by Online Gradient Descent. *J. Phys. A*, 28, 643–656.

Biehl, M., Reigler, P. and Stechert, M. (1995). Learning from noisy data: an exactly solvable model. *Phys. Rev. E*, 52 R4624–R4627

Bishop, C. M. (1995) *Neural networks for pattern recognition*, Oxford University Press, Oxford, UK.

Cybenko, C. (1989). Approximation by superpositions of a sigmoid function. *Math. Control Signals and Systems*, 2, 303–314

LeCun, Y., Simard, P.Y. and Pearlmutter, B. (1993). Approximation by superpositions of a sigmoid function. *Advances in Neural Information Processing Systems 5*, edited by Giles, Hanson and Cowan (San Mateo, CA: Morgan Kaufmann) p 156–163.

Leen, T. K., Schottky, B. and Saad, D. (1998). Two approaches to optimal annealing. *Advances in Neural Information Processing Systems 10*, edited by Jordan, Kearns and Solla (Cambridge MA: MIT press) p 301–307

Kinouchi, O. and Caticha, N. (1992). Optimal generalization in perceptrons. *J. Phys. A*, 25, 6243-6250.

Rattray, M. and Saad, D. (1998). An analysis of on-line training with optimal learning rates. *accepted to pub. in Phys. Rev. E.*

Rattray, M. and Saad, D. (1997). Globally optimal online learning rules for multi-layer neural networks. *J. Phys. A*, 30, L771-776.

Riegler, P. and Biehl, M. (1995). On-line backpropagation in two-layered neural networks. *J. Phys. A*, 28, L507–L513.

Riegler, P. (1997) *PhD Thesis*, University of Würzburg.

Robbins, H. and Monro, S. (1951). A Stochastic Approximation Model. *Ann. Math. Statist.*, 22, 400–407.

Saad, D. and Solla, S. A. (1995). Exact Solution for Online Learning in Multilayer Neural Networks. *Phys. Rev. Lett.*, 74, 4337–4340; Online Learning in Soft Committee Machines. *Phys. Rev. E*, 52, 4225–4243.

Saad, D. and Rattray, M. (1997). Globally optimal parameters for on-line learning in multilayer neural networks. *Phys. Rev. Lett.*, 79, 2578–2581.

Saad, D. and Rattray, M. (1998). Learning with regularizers in multilayer neural networks. *Phys. Rev. E*, 57, 2170–2176.

Orr, G. B. and Leen, T. K. (1997). Using Curvature Information for Fast Stochastic Search. *Advances in Neural Information Processing Systems 9*, edited by Mozer, Jordan and Petsche (Cambridge, MA: MIT Press) p 606–612.

West, A.H.L. and Saad, D. (1997). On-line learning with adaptive back-propagation in two-layer networks. *Phys. Rev. E*, 56, 3426–3445

Vicente, R. and Caticha, N. (1997). Functional optimization of online algorithms in multilayer neural networks. *J. Phys. A*, 30, L599–L605.

White, H. (1989). Learning in artificial neural networks : a statistical perspective. *Neural Computation*, 1, 425–464.

Universal Asymptotics in Committee Machines with Tree Architecture

Mauro Copelli

Limburgs Universitair Centrum
B-3590 Diepenbeek, Belgium
copelli@luc.ac.be

Nestor Caticha

Instituto de Física, Universidade de São Paulo
Caixa Postal 66318, 05389-970 São Paulo, SP, Brazil
nestor@gibbs.if.usp.br

Abstract

On-line supervised learning in the general K Tree Committee Machine (TCM) is studied for a uniform distribution of inputs. Examples are corrupted by multiplicative noise in the teacher output. From the differential equations which describe the learning dynamics, the modulation function which optimizes the generalization ability is exactly obtained for any finite K. The asymptotical behavior of the generalization error is shown to be independent of K. Robustness with respect to a misestimation of the noise level is also shown to be independent of K.

1 Introduction

When looking into the properties of different neural network architectures by studying their performance in different model situations, the main objective, rather than delving into the many differences, is to search for similarities. It is from these similarities that intrinsic properties of learning, that go beyond the particular characteristics of the simple models, may be identified.

In order to develop a program of this nature several studies within the community of Statistical Mechanics of Neural Networks (Watkin, Rau and Biehl, 1993) have been pursued. Among the most important contributions that this approach brings to the study of machine learning is the possibility of dealing with networks of a very large size, that is in the thermodynamic limit (TL) and of introducing efficient techniques to average over the randomness associated to the data. The model scenarios that have been analized arise from combinations of the different learning conditioning factors. These include, among others, unsupervised versus supervised learning, realizable rules or not, learning in the presence of noise or in the more idealized noiseless case, learning in a time dependent or constant environment. A most important scenario determining condition is whether the learning process will be able to act given sufficient time in order to extract all the information that can be extracted by the learning algorithm from the given data set. For this extraction to be complete, the algorithm has to be repetitive, either presenting one example at a time and iterating over the data set or by batch iteration or off-line learning (see *e.g.* (Seung, 1992)). Opposite to that is the single shot presentation, where each example is only used once for a weight update. This scenario is what will be called on-line in this paper (Amari, 1967; Kinzel and Ruján, 1990; Kinouchi and Caticha, 1992a; Kinouchi and Caticha, 1992b; Biehl and Schwarze, 1995; Saad and Solla, 1995). While the off-line scenario is prone to be studied by the techniques of equilibrium statistical mechanics, on-line learning is more like an off-equilibrium problem. The advantage of looking at the TL is that several simplifications occur since the fluctuations of important physical quantities are reduced by factors of $\mathcal{O}(\sqrt{N})$, where N is a typical size of the system.

This paper presents the study of supervised on-line learning by a feedforward committee machine of non-overlapping receptive fields (tree committee machine - TCM) with K branches. The task at hand is that of inferring a rule implemented by a *teacher* network of equal architecture The performance of several *ad hoc* algorithms implemented on the different architectures could be analyzed. But then the source of possible changes cannot be distinguished easily. Therefore a restriction is made to study the best possible on-line performance in the sense of maximum generalization. These bounds are obtained from a variational argument which besides giving the best possible learning curve, determines the form of the algorithm that would lead to that performance. These optimal *algorithms* need, in order to saturate the bounds, information about several quantities that are usually considered unavailable. Among those, the student teacher branch overlap , the noise type and level, parameters of the input data distribution. This dependence rather than pointing out the shortcomings of the method should be viewed as showing directions of research. They emphasize the need to develop efficient on-line estimators if the bounds are to be approximated. The efficiency of *ad hoc* algorithms increases inasmuch as they approximate the requirements set by the optimal *algorithms*. From these information requirements the need for an annealing schedule in a constant environment can be deduced, or for the same reasons, an adaptive annealing in a drifting environment shown to be indispensable. Arbitrary cutoffs in the weight changes in some algorithms can be tracked back to the need of identifying noise levels when implementing optimal *algorithms*. The study of some of these estimators in simple cases, has been pursued by (Kinouchi and Caticha, 1993), (Biehl, Riegler and Stechert, 1995) , (Vicente, Kinouchi and Caticha). The resulting algorithms have the functional form of those suggested by the variational method but instead of the unavailable parameters, the estimated values are used. That this is indeed a good strategy is indicated by the high robustness shown in face of misestimations which has been found in all the particular cases studied so far.

An important, although partial, measure of an algorithm's performance is given by the asymptotic dependence of the generalization error with the number P of presented examples. In the TL the correct scaling depends on $\alpha = P/N$. The main results presented in this paper concern two types of universal behavior in the asymptotic properties of the learning curves of TCM's with different K's. The adjective Universal is used just to indicate a K-independent asymptotics and a bit more by showing that these characteristics are shared by the Tree Parity Machine. First, in section 2 it is shown that the generalization error decays in exactly the same manner for large α, not only the same power but also the same prefactor. These optimal *algorithms* are non local in the sense that information about the fields in the other branches of the TCM are needed in order to perform the weight update of a given branch. The special case of the $K = 3$ TCM optimal non-local algorithm was presented in (Copelli and Caticha, 1995). The computational task of determining the modulation function increases exponentially with K. A less expensive algorithm which only requires the information of a given branch in its update, *i.e.* optimal *local* algorithm for the noiseless TCM was studied in (Copelli, Kinouchi and Caticha, 1996) for general K.

Second, in section 3 we recall and extend results in (Copelli et al., 1997) which show K independence also for the robustness with regard to output or multiplicative noise misestimation. Results are presented in the form of robustness phase diagrams, where boundaries are drawn to separate different asymptotic behaviors that arise due to different levels of misestimation. It is important to stress that this K independence is a result that holds due to the particular properties of the noise process corrupting the data. For input or additive weight it was shown in (Copelli et al., 1997) that robustness properties are K dependent insofar as the actual position of the borders separating the different dynamical regimes is concerned, but the general structure of the phases is independent of K. Details of the calculations are presented in the appendix.

2 Optimal generalization in the TCM

2.1 The tree architecture

The TCM architecture is made up from K boolean perceptrons whose inputs are not shared. Given an N-dimensional input vector (or, correspondingly, K N_p-dimensional branch vectors, where $N_p = N/K$) $\boldsymbol{\xi} = (\boldsymbol{\xi}_1, \ldots, \boldsymbol{\xi}_K)$, the kth branch perceptron in the student machine gives an output $\sigma_{Jk} \equiv$

sign(x_k), where $x_k \equiv \mathbf{J}_k \cdot \boldsymbol{\xi}_k/|\mathbf{J}_k|$ is the kth student receptive field. The vectors $\{\mathbf{J}_k\}_{k=1,...,K}$ completely define the function implemented by the student machine, since its final output is simply given by the majority rule, $\Sigma_J \equiv \text{sign}\left(\sum_{k=1}^K \sigma_{Jk}\right)$ (see figure 1). We will restrict to cases where $K << N$, $i.e. K/N \to 0$ as $N \to \infty$.

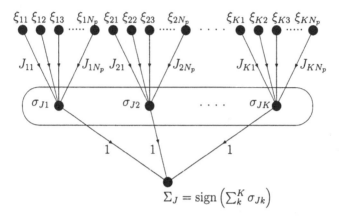

Fig. 1: The student committee

The teacher TCM has exactly the same architecture (see figure 2). It is defined by vectors $\{\mathbf{B}_k\}_{k=1,...,K}$, where the constraints $|\mathbf{B}_k| = 1$ ($k = 1, \ldots, K$) can be imposed without loss of generality. Its receptive fields and hidden units are respectively denoted by $\{y_k\}_{k=1,...,K}$ and $\{\sigma_{Bk}\}_{k=1,...,K}$, where $y_k \equiv \mathbf{B}_k \cdot \boldsymbol{\xi}_k$ and $\sigma_{Bk} \equiv \text{sign}(y_k)$ ($k = 1, \ldots, K$). The teacher output is also given by the majority rule, $\Sigma_B \equiv \text{sign}\left(\sum_{k=1}^K \sigma_{Bk}\right)$, but this variable can be flipped with a constant probability λ. The final teacher output $\tilde{\Sigma}_B$ is then given by

$$P(\tilde{\Sigma}_B|\Sigma_B) = (1-\lambda)\delta\left(\tilde{\Sigma}_B, \Sigma_B\right) + \lambda\delta\left(\tilde{\Sigma}_B, -\Sigma_B\right) ,\qquad(2.1)$$

where δ is the Kronecker delta .

In the following, the state of the variables $\{\sigma_{Jk}\}_{k=1,...,K}$ and $\{\sigma_{Bk}\}_{k=1,...,K}$ (the ovals in Figures 1 and 2) will be referred to as the internal representation of the student and teacher machines, respectively.

2.2   The generalization error

Given the student and teacher networks, the generalization error $e_g^{(cm)}$ is the probability that an example drawn from a uniform distribution be misclassified[1] by the student, that is, $e_g^{(cm)} = P(\Sigma_J = -\Sigma_B)$. Due to the tree

---

[1]Note that mistakes due to noise are not taken into account in this definition. The probability of misprediction $P(\Sigma_J = -\tilde{\Sigma}_B)$ is often named the *prediction error*.

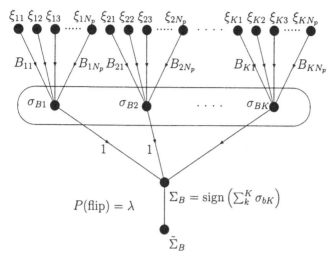

Fig. 2: The teacher committee

structure of the problem, the generalization error is a function only of the overlaps $\rho_k \equiv \mathbf{J}_k \cdot \mathbf{B}_k/|\mathbf{J}_k|$ $(k = 1, \ldots, K)$. Moreover, if one takes the thermodynamic limit $N \to \infty$ and assumes branch symmetry $(\rho_k = \rho, \forall k)$, this function is most conveniently written (Mato and Parga, 1992) as

$$e_g^{(cm)} = \sum_{n=1}^{K} C_n(K)[e_g^{(p)}(\rho)]^n , \qquad (2.2)$$

where $e_g^{(p)}(\rho) \equiv 1 - g^{(p)} \equiv \pi^{-1}\arccos(\rho) = P(\sigma_{Jk} = -\sigma_{Bk})$ is the generalization error per branch perceptron. The asymptotical regime for a large number of presented examples (when $\rho \simeq 1$) is then clearly governed by $e_g^{(cm)} \simeq C_1(K)e_g^{(p)}$. This is the regime where asymptotic properties show up, and therefore we start by deriving an expression for $C_1(K)$.

The probability $P(\Sigma_J = -\Sigma_B)$ can be calculated just by counting relevant configurations in the internal representation space of both student and teacher machines. When an input vector $\boldsymbol{\xi}$ is drawn from the distribution[2]

$$P(\boldsymbol{\xi}) = \prod_{k=1}^{K} \prod_{j=1}^{N/K} \frac{1}{\sqrt{2\pi}} \exp\left(\frac{-\xi_{kj}^2}{2}\right) , \qquad (2.3)$$

σ_{Jk} is set to $+1$ or -1 with equal probability. However, σ_{Bk} is correlated with σ_{Jk} via $e_g^{(p)}$, the generalization error in that branch perceptron. Taking the $K = 5$ TCM as an example, a possible configuration and its corresponding probability is given below:

---

[2]This is not a necessary condition. Any distribution with $\langle\xi_{kj}\rangle = 0$ and $\langle\xi_{kj}\xi_{li}\rangle = \delta(k,l)\delta(j,i)$ will lead to the same results.

$$\begin{array}{c|ccccc||cc}
\{\sigma_{Bk}\} & + & - & + & + & - & + & \Sigma_B \\
\{\sigma_{Jk}\} & + & - & - & - & + & - & \Sigma_J \\
\hline
\end{array}$$

$$\text{Probability} = \left(\tfrac{1}{2}\right)^5 \quad g^{(p)} \quad g^{(p)} \quad e_g^{(p)} \quad e_g^{(p)} \quad e_g^{(p)}$$

$$= 2^{-5}(g^{(p)})^2(e_g^{(p)})^3$$

The above configuration does give a contribution to $e_g^{(cm)}$ indeed, since it has $\Sigma_J = -\Sigma_B$. However, it does not contribute to C_1 since the leading term in $e_g^{(p)}$ is $\mathcal{O}([e_g^{(p)}]^3)$, for small $e_g^{(p)}$. By definition, only terms which are $\mathcal{O}([e_g^{(p)}]^1)$ contribute to C_1. Those are obtained from configurations where there is a single unit differing between the teacher and student nets, e.g.

$$\begin{array}{c|ccccc||cc}
\{\sigma_{Bk}\} & + & + & - & + & - & + & \Sigma_B \\
\{\sigma_{Jk}\} & + & - & - & + & - & - & \Sigma_J \\
\hline
\end{array}$$

$$\text{Probability} = \left(\tfrac{1}{2}\right)^5 \quad g^{(p)} \quad e_g^{(p)} \quad g^{(p)} \quad g^{(p)} \quad g^{(p)}$$

$$= 2^{-5}(g^{(p)})^4(e_g^{(p)})^1$$

The *decision border* of a TCM can be defined as the subset of internal representations such that the machine output can be flipped with the flip of a single internal unit. A student machine is then at the decision border when $|\sum_{k=1}^{K} \sigma_{Jk}| = 1$. In order for a configuration to contribute to C_1, both the student and the teacher TCMs must be at their respective decision borders. Moreover, they must be nearest neighbors in the K-dimensional hypercube where each of the internal representation space lies. This is the only way of satisfying both the condition that $\Sigma_J = -\Sigma_B$ and that the leading term in its probability is $\mathcal{O}([e_g^{(p)}]^1)$. For general K, the number of such configurations can be easily calculated:

$$\begin{array}{c|ccccccccc}
 & 1 & 2 & 3 & 4 & & l & & & & K \\
\hline
\{\sigma_{Bk}\} & + & + & - & + & \ldots & + & \ldots & - & - & - & + \\
\{\sigma_{Jk}\} & + & + & - & + & \ldots & - & \ldots & - & - & - & + \\
\end{array}$$

Fixing the l-th branch as the responsible for the machine misclassification, the number of configurations which respect the required constraints is $(K-1)!/[((K-1)/2)!]^2$. Each of such configurations occurs with a probability whose leading term is $2^{-(K-1)} e_g^{(p)} + \mathcal{O}([e_g^{(p)}]^2)$. Since there are K such branches, the result is finally

$$C_1(K) = \left(\frac{1}{2}\right)^{K-1} \frac{(K-1)!}{\left[\left(\frac{K-1}{2}\right)!\right]^2} K \,, \qquad (2.4)$$

which, for $K \gg 1$, behaves asymptotically as $C_1(K) \simeq \sqrt{2K/\pi}$. Note that the above deduction relies mostly on geometrical grounds. Given input vectors $\boldsymbol{\xi}$ whose probability distribution factorizes among the branch perceptrons, one has $P(\{\sigma_{Bk}, \sigma_{Jk}\}) = \prod_k^K P(\sigma_{Bk}, \sigma_{Jk})$. Assuming branch symmetry, one can further state that $P(\sigma_{Bk}, \sigma_{Jk})$ is parametrized only by global quantities, which in this case is the generalization error per branch perceptron:

$$P(\sigma_{Bk}, \sigma_{Jk}) = \frac{1}{2} \left\{ \delta(\sigma_{Bk}, \sigma_{Jk}) \left[1 - e_g^{(p)}\right] + \delta(-\sigma_{Bk}, \sigma_{Jk}) e_g^{(p)} \right\} . \qquad (2.5)$$

2.3 On-line learning and the optimal modulation function

Given a set of p independently drawn examples $\{\boldsymbol{\xi}(\mu), \tilde{\Sigma}_B(\mu)\}_{\mu=1,\ldots,p}$, learning in the student TCM is performed on-line:

$$\mathbf{J}_k(\mu + 1) = \mathbf{J}_k(\mu) + \frac{1}{N_p} F_k(\mu) \boldsymbol{\xi}_k(\mu) , \qquad (2.6)$$

where $N_p \equiv N/K$ is the number of input units per branch perceptron and $F_k(\mu)$ is an up to now unknown function which modulates the vector change upon presentation of the μth example. The linear dependence on the input vectors $\boldsymbol{\xi}$ is the only strong hypothesis at this point. The absence of *e.g.* a decay term to constrain the norm of $\mathbf{J}$ will prove to be irrelevant, since the perceptrons are boolean.

In the thermodynamic limit $N_p \to \infty$, differential equations for the relevant order parameters can be obtained (see *e.g.* (Kinouchi and Caticha, 1992a; Kinouchi and Caticha, 1992b; Copelli and Caticha, 1995)). In this limit, the number of examples p must grow likewise, with $\alpha_p \equiv \mu/N_p$ finite:

$$\frac{d\rho_k}{d\alpha_p} = \frac{\rho_k}{J_k} \int dm(\mu) \, F_k \left(\frac{y_k}{\rho_k} - x_k - \frac{F_k}{2J_k} \right) , \qquad (2.7)$$

$$\frac{dJ_k}{d\alpha_p} = J_k \int dm(\mu) \left(\frac{F_k^2}{2J_k^2} + \frac{F_k x_k}{J_k} \right) , \qquad (2.8)$$

where integration over the measure $dm(\mu)$ denotes average over the examples, $J_k \equiv |\mathbf{J}_k|$ and the μ index was dropped for simplicity. These equations are correct up to $\mathcal{O}(N^{-2})$, and rely on the self-averaging property of these order parameters.

It is now possible to obtain an optimal set $\{F_k^\star\}$ based on the fact that $e_g^{(cm)}(\rho)$ is a monotonically decreasing function and that the dependence of $d\rho_k/d\alpha_p$ on F_k is functional. In this context, optimality should be understood in terms of mean generalization. Following previously described procedures (Kinouchi and Caticha, 1992a; Kinouchi and Caticha, 1992b; Copelli and Caticha, 1995), the modulation function $\tilde{F}_k$ which maximizes the generalization ability for a given number of examples can be variationally obtained and is given by

$$F_k^\star = J_k \left(\frac{\langle y_k \rangle_{y_k|\tilde{\Sigma}_B, \{x_j\}}}{\rho_k} - x_k \right) . \qquad (2.9)$$

Its corresponding performance can be obtained by just plugging this expression back into equation 2.7. The corresponding function $\rho_k^\star(\alpha_p)$, which is an upper bound for *any* value of α_p, is governed by

$$\frac{d\rho_k^\star}{d\alpha_p} = \frac{\rho_k}{2J_k^2} \left\langle (F_k^\star)^2 \right\rangle_{\tilde{\Sigma}_B, \{x_j\}} . \qquad (2.10)$$

It should be stressed that equations 2.9 and 2.10 are valid in general, as long as examples are sampled independently. While treating the learning dynamics in this section, no assumption whatsoever was made about the distribution of examples. The information about this distribution is formally embedded in the averages present on the r.h.s of both equations, and only now we make a specific choice in order to perform the calculations explicitly. We shall assume that input vectors are drawn from a distribution with $\langle \xi_{kj} \rangle = 0$ and $\langle \xi_{kj} \xi_{li} \rangle = \delta(k,l)\delta(j,i)$ (*e.g.*, the one given by equation 2.3). At this stage it is interesting to point out that in equations 2.7 and 2.8, all the randomness of the examples lies on the fields x_k, y_k and on the noisy output corruption. With the chosen distribution of input vectors and the assumption of the thermodynamic limit, x_k and y_k become Gaussian distributed variables with zero mean, unit variance and correlation ρ_k:

$$P(x_k, y_k) = \frac{1}{2\pi\sqrt{(1-\rho_k^2)}} \exp\left(\frac{-x_k^2 - y_k^2 + 2x_k y_k \rho_k}{2(1-\rho_k^2)} \right) . \qquad (2.11)$$

This result makes it possible to replace the averages above by integrals over Gaussian variables, that is,

$$\int dm(\mu)(\cdots) = \sum_{\tilde{\Sigma}_B = \pm 1} \int P(\tilde{\Sigma}_B, \{x_j, y_j\}|\lambda) \; (\cdots) \prod_{j=1}^{K} dx_j dy_j . \qquad (2.12)$$

2.4   Universal asymptotics

Output noise is *isotropic*, in the sense that examples $\boldsymbol{\xi}$ are flipped with the same probability regardless of their orientation in N-dimensional space. In this scenario,

$$P(\tilde{\Sigma}_B|\boldsymbol{\xi}) = P(\tilde{\Sigma}_B|\Sigma_B) . \qquad (2.13)$$

This simplification will turn out to be important for the universal results that we are about to describe. First we have to find an expression for the optimal modulation function, equation 2.9. Then we have to calculate the asymptotics of equation 2.10.

The conditional average of the field y_k, given all the available information, is the non-trivial term we focus on. Because of the simplification expressed by equation 2.13, it reads

$$\langle y_k \rangle_{y_k|\tilde{\Sigma}_B, \{x_j\}} = \frac{\sum_{\Sigma_B} P(\tilde{\Sigma}_B|\Sigma_B)P(\Sigma_B|\{x_j\})\langle y_k \rangle_{y_k|\Sigma_B, \{x_j\}}}{\sum_{\Sigma_B} P(\tilde{\Sigma}_B|\Sigma_B)P(\Sigma_B|\{x_j\})} . \qquad (2.14)$$

That means we can just study the noiseless problem and then take the average over the distribution 2.1 in a very simple way.

The relevant probability distribution, which conveys the specific information about each particular architecture and gives the algorithm its optimality, is $P(\Sigma_B | y_k, \{x_j\})$. In boolean machines with output noise it is very convenient to rewrite it as follows:

$$P\left(\Sigma_B | y_k, \{x_j\}\right) = C_k\left(\Sigma_B, \{x_j\}_{j\neq k}\right) + D_k\left(\Sigma_B, \{x_j\}_{j\neq k}\right) \theta\left(y_k \Sigma_B\right) , \quad (2.15)$$

where $\theta(x)$ is the Heaviside function. The functions C_k and D_k depend both on the machine architecture and on its size K (the number of hidden units). We shall in the following omit the dependence of C_k and D_k on $\{x_j\}_{j\neq k}$ for simplicity of notation, except when specially needed. The derivation of their explicit expressions for the particular case considered here can be found in the appendix. However, just eq. 2.15 and a few other symmetries will suffice to support the final results. We rely, for instance, on the factorization $P(\{x_j\}, \{y_j\}) = \prod_j^K P(x_j, y_j)$ (which comes from the tree-architecture plus the absence of correlation between different branch input vectors). With $P(x_j, y_j)$ given by eq 2.11, one obtains

$$\langle y_k \rangle_{y_k | \Sigma_B, \{x_j\}} = \frac{\Gamma_k \rho_k}{\sqrt{2\pi}} \Sigma_B e^{-x_k^2/2\Gamma_k^2} \frac{D_k\left(\Sigma_B\right)}{P\left(\Sigma_B | \{x_j\}\right)} + \rho_k x_k \quad (2.16)$$

$$P\left(\Sigma_B | \{x_j\}\right) = C_k(\Sigma_B) + D_k(\Sigma_B) H\left(-x_k \Sigma_B/\Gamma_k\right) , \quad (2.17)$$

where $\Gamma_k = \rho_k^{-1}\sqrt{1 - \rho_k^2}$ is the typical scaling parameter that always shows up in optimal modulation functions for boolean machines and $H(x) = \int_x^\infty Dt$ and $Dt = dt\, (2\pi)^{-1/2} \exp(-t^2/2)$.

Taking into account the symmetry $D_k\left(\Sigma_B, \{x_j\}_{j\neq k}\right) = D_k\left(-\Sigma_B, \{x_j\}_{j\neq k}\right)$, one immediately writes down the final form of the optimal modulation function for a given noise level λ:

$$F_k^\star(\lambda) = \frac{J_k \Gamma_k}{\sqrt{2\pi}}(1 - 2\lambda)\tilde{\Sigma}_B \frac{D_k(\tilde{\Sigma}_B)}{G_k^\lambda + D_k(\tilde{\Sigma}_B)\tilde{H}_\lambda(-x_k\tilde{\Sigma}_B/\Gamma_k)} , \quad (2.18)$$

where

$$G_k^\lambda(\tilde{\Sigma}_B, \{x_j\}_{j\neq k}) = (1 - \lambda)C_k(\tilde{\Sigma}_B, \{x_j\}_{j\neq k}) + \lambda C_k(-\tilde{\Sigma}_B, \{x_j\}_{j\neq k}) \quad (2.19)$$

and $\tilde{H}_\lambda(x) = \lambda + (1 - 2\lambda)H(x)$. It is useful to note that the denominator in eq. 2.18 is precisely $P(\tilde{\Sigma}_B | \{x_j\})$, as can be read from eqs. 2.14, 2.16, 2.17 and 2.19.

The generalization performance attained by the optimal modulation function can be calculated by inserting (2.18) into equation (2.10):

$$\frac{d\rho_k^\star}{d\alpha_p} = \frac{\rho_k \Gamma_k^3}{4\pi} \sum_{\tilde{\Sigma}_B = \pm 1} \int \left[\prod_{j\neq k} Dx_j\right] Dx_k\, e^{-x_k^2/2\rho_k^2}$$

$$\times \left\{\frac{D_k^2(\tilde{\Sigma}_B)}{G_k^\lambda(\tilde{\Sigma}_B, \{x_j\}_{j\neq k}) + D_k(\tilde{\Sigma}_B)\tilde{H}_\lambda(-\tilde{\Sigma}_B x_k)}\right\} . \quad (2.20)$$

First note that the right hand side of equation (2.20) is always positive for $\rho_k < 1$, which guarantees that the optimal modulation function leads to perfect generalization ($\rho_k = 1$) in the limit $\alpha_p \to \infty$. Secondly, $\tilde{F}_k$ has the interesting property of decoupling the $\{\rho_j\}$ equations from the $\{J_j\}$ ones, making their analysis simpler. Under the assumption of branch symmetry $\rho_k = \rho$ (which is easily guaranteed by branch symmetric initial conditions $\rho_k(0) = \rho(0)$), equation (2.20) can be numerically integrated in order to obtain the overlap evolution $\rho(\alpha_p)$ for any α_p. Branch symmetry will be assumed in the rest of this paper, for simplicity. Note, however, that this does not imply any loss of generality as far as asymptotics is concerned, since the system naturally converges to this symmetric subspace when $\alpha_p \to \infty$.

The asymptotical behavior of $\rho(\alpha_p)$ for large α_p can be derived by checking the structure of the functions D_k and C_k. Their explicit expression can be found in the appendix, however just a simple reasoning upon equation 2.15 can give us some intuition about their meaning. They account for terms in $P\left(\Sigma_B | y_k, \{x_j\}\right)$ related to qualitatively different internal representations. In the TCM, C_k is just the probability of Σ_B given $\{x_j\}_{j \neq k}$ and the constraint $\sum_{j \neq k} \sigma_{Bj} \neq 0$. Note that in this situation, knowledge of y_k can't help predicting Σ_B, since the final output is already determined by the other hidden units. On the other hand, D_k is the probability of Σ_B given $\{x_j\}_{j \neq k}$ and the constraint $\sum_{j \neq k} \sigma_{Bj} = 0$. These are configurations at the teacher's decision border, since the output of the kth hidden unit completely determines the machine output.

When $\alpha_p \to \infty$, $\rho \to 1$ and therefore D_k and C_k tend either to zero or one, for each internal representation. Since the constraints in D_k and C_k are mutually exclusive, whenever D_k tends to one, C_k will tend to zero, and vice-versa. Once D_k is in the numerator of the r.h.s. of equation (2.20), integration on $\prod_{j \neq k} Dx_j$ will have non-vanishing contributions only when the constraint $\sum_{j \neq k} \sigma_{Jj} = 0$ is respected. Moreover, this contribution is trivial: $(1/2)^{K-1}$. The number of such orthants in the $\{x_j\}_{j \neq k}$ space is precisely $(K-1)!/[((K-1)/2)!]^2$, and the asymptotical behavior of equation (2.20) for large α_p is thus given by

$$\frac{d\rho}{d\alpha_p} \simeq \frac{(1-\rho^2)^{3/2}}{\rho^2} \frac{C_1(K)}{2\pi K} I(\lambda) , \qquad (2.21)$$

where

$$I(\lambda) \equiv (1 - 2\lambda)^2 \int \frac{Dx \, e^{-x^2/2}}{\tilde{H}_\lambda(x)} . \qquad (2.22)$$

From equation (2.21) one obtains the asymptotical behavior for the generalization error per perceptron, $e_g^{(p)} \simeq 2[I(\lambda)C_1(K)\alpha]^{-1}$, where now $\alpha \equiv \alpha_p/K = p/N$ is the number of presented examples per adjustable weight in the machine. Taking the leading term in equation (2.2) for small $e_g^{(p)}$, the TCM asymptotical generalization error is seen to be K-independent, in terms of this variable:

$$e_g^{(cm)} \simeq \frac{2}{I(\lambda)}\frac{1}{\alpha} + \mathcal{O}\left(\frac{1}{\alpha^2}\right). \tag{2.23}$$

The fact that only the decision border configurations contribute to the leading term in equation (2.2) is of a geometrical nature. However, the fact that only those configurations give non-vanishing contributions to learning in the large α asymptotical regime (thus yielding a K-independent result) is due to the special characteristics of the modulation function obtained via variational optimization. Different examples are given different modulations, depending on the values of the corresponding receptive fields and on the stage of learning (as parametrized by the overlaps $\{\rho_j\}$). In an advanced stage of learning, only configurations at the decision border are important, a fact that had already been pointed out in (Copelli and Caticha, 1995) for the special case $K = 3$. Result (2.23) is exactly the same as the one obtained for the perceptron (Biehl, Riegler and Stechert, 1995; Copelli, Kinouchi and Caticha, 1996), recovering also the $e_g^{(cm)} \simeq 0.88\alpha^{-1}$ result for the zero noise situation (Kinouchi and Caticha, 1992b; Copelli and Caticha, 1995; Simonetti 96).

Some remarks concerning the practical implementation of the optimal modulation function as an algorithm should be addressed. First, such an algorithm requires the knowledge of the noise level λ, which is hardly an accessible quantity in a realistic situation. Robustness with respect to the use of a fixed noise estimate Λ is the topic to be covered in the next section. Secondly, there is an explicit dependence on the overlaps $\{\rho_j\}$, which are unknown too. The optimal modulation function automatically provides a way out of this problem though, since for $F_k = F_k^*$ and convenient initial conditions, the evolutions $J_k(\alpha_p)$ and $\rho_k(\alpha_p)$ are governed by *exactly* the same function (for details, see (Copelli, Kinouchi and Caticha, 1996; Copelli and Caticha, 1995)). The measured values of the norms of the student vectors can thus be used in replacement for the overlaps. Finally, the non-locality of F_k^* makes its implementation harder and harder as the TCM becomes larger. From the expressions in the appendix one notices that the number of terms in C_k increases exponentially with K. This is the price paid for the significantly better result attained by the optimal non-local algorithm, as compared with the optimal local algorithm (Copelli, Kinouchi and Caticha, 1996). In the zero noise scenario, the optimal non-local modulation function reaches the asymptotical regime when $\alpha \gg 1$, while the local modulation function requires $\alpha \gg K^{1/2}$, for large K.

Independence of K in the asymptotical performance of generalization bounds has also been reported for the Tree Parity Machine, both for on-line (Simonetti 96) as well as off-line (Opper, 1994) learning in the presence of output noise. That this independence holds true for optimal learning in both models raises the question of whether this is a common feature of any tree-like architecture.

3   Noise robustness diagrams

In this section we would like to address the following question: what happens if one has a "wrong" guess of the noise level in the system and uses it in the optimal modulation function 2.18? That is, we assume that all other variables necessary for the implementation of $F_k^\star$ are still accessible, except for λ, which is the actual noise level. In its stead we make use of a fixed estimate Λ and then study the dynamics of the system. This problem has been addressed in (Copelli et al., 1997) for two types of noise and both the Tree Committee and the Tree Parity architectures. Here we add some details concerning the universality presented in the case of output noise.

An appealing way of presenting results is via noise robustness phase diagrams in the (λ, Λ) plane, where three kinds of asymptotic dynamical behavior appear. There is a large phase of perfect generalization, where $\rho \to 1$ in the $\alpha_p \to \infty$ limit. This phase comprises the whole region where $\Lambda \geq \lambda$ (overestimation of the noise level) and a fraction of the region $\Lambda \leq \lambda$. However, a worse underestimation of the noise level leads to the phase of imperfect learning, where the asymptotic value $\rho_0 = \rho(\alpha_p \to \infty)$ remains in the interval $0 < \rho_0 < 1$. A third phase appears if noise is underestimated by yet a larger amount. In this regime of total loss of generalization $\rho_0 = 0$ is the only attractive fixed point of the dynamics. Surprisingly enough, the dependence on the number of hidden units disappears, and the resulting diagram is valid for any K.

The dynamics of the student net learning with a "mismatched" noise level is obtained by simply plugging $F_k^\star(\Lambda)$ into equation 2.7. That means equation 2.10 is no longer valid, but rather

$$\frac{d\rho_k}{d\alpha_p} = \frac{\rho_k}{J_k^2} \left[\langle F_k^\star(\Lambda) F_k^\star(\Lambda) \rangle_\lambda - \frac{1}{2} \left\langle (F_k^\star(\Lambda))^2 \right\rangle_\lambda \right] , \qquad (3.1)$$

where the shorthand $\langle (\cdots) \rangle_\lambda = \sum_{\tilde{\Sigma}_B} \int P(\tilde{\Sigma}_B | \{x_j\}, \lambda)(\cdots) \prod_j Dx_j$ is a reminder that $P(\tilde{\Sigma}_B | \{x_j\})$ depends on λ.

The phase boundaries are obtained by finding the zeros of the r.h.s. of eq. 3.1 in the limits $\rho_k \to 0$ (total loss of generalization) and $\rho_k \to 1$ (perfect generalization). In each case this yields a relationship between λ and Λ which would in principle depend on K as well. Now it will become clear why K actually does not play any role. We first rewrite the competing terms of the dynamical equation:

$$\langle F_k^\star(\Lambda) F_k^\star(\Lambda) \rangle_\lambda = \frac{\Gamma_k^2 J_k^2}{2\pi}(1 - 2\lambda)(1 - 2\Lambda) \overbrace{\int e^{-x_k^2/\Gamma_k^2} \sum_{\tilde{\Sigma}_B} \frac{D_k^2(\tilde{\Sigma}_B)}{P(\tilde{\Sigma}_B|\{x_j\}, \Lambda)} \prod_j^K Dx_j}^{\equiv I_{\Lambda\Lambda}}$$

$$(3.2)$$

$$\left\langle (F_k^*(\Lambda))^2 \right\rangle_\lambda = \frac{\Gamma_k^2 J_k^2}{2\pi}(1 - 2\Lambda)^2 \int e^{-x_k^2/\Gamma_k^2} \overbrace{\sum_{\tilde{\Sigma}_B} \frac{P(\tilde{\Sigma}_B|\{x_j\},\lambda)D_k^2(\tilde{\Sigma}_B)}{P^2(\tilde{\Sigma}_B|\{x_j\},\Lambda)}}^{\equiv I_{\lambda\Lambda}} \prod_j^K Dx_j$$

(3.3)

The limit $\rho_j \to 0$ ($j = 1,\ldots,K$) in the above expressions yields great simplifications, since it leads to $P(\tilde{\Sigma}_B|\{x_j\},\lambda) = P(\tilde{\Sigma}_B|\{x_j\},\Lambda) = 1/2$. This result arises from the fact that if the overlaps are zero the student fields can provide no information about the teacher output. Moreover, each of the terms of $D_k(\tilde{\Sigma}_B,\{x_j\}_{j\neq k})$ takes a constant value in this limit (see the appendix for details). Integration on $\{x_j\}$ is then immediate and eq. 3.1 becomes

$$\frac{d\rho_k}{d\alpha_p} \overset{\rho_j \to 0}{\simeq} \frac{\rho_k \Gamma_k^2}{\pi}(1 - 2\Lambda)\left(D_k^2\big|_{\{\rho_j \to 0\}}\right)[2\Lambda - 4\lambda + 1].$$

(3.4)

The term between square brackets controls the sign of the whole expression, which will dictate whether the fixed point $\rho_k = 0$ is repulsive or attractive[3]. For an estimated noise level $\Lambda \le 2\lambda - 1/2$ the system is unable to learn, a result which is independent of K.

The boundary of the region with perfect generalization requires a more subtle analysis, since its derivation relies on some more specific properties of the functions C_k and D_k. Again, the main factor here is the fact that these functions involve mutually exclusive internal representations. Like in the $\Lambda = \lambda$ case of section 2.4, D_k shows up in the numerator of equations 3.2 and 3.3, which means that only the orthants where it survives give non-zero contributions:

$$I_{\lambda\Lambda} = \Gamma_k \int Du\, e^{-u^2/\rho_k^2} \sum_{z=\pm 1} \frac{D_k^2(z)}{G_k^\Lambda(z) + D_k(z)\tilde{H}_\Lambda(-uz)} \prod_{j\neq k} Dx_j$$

$$\overset{\rho_j \to 1}{\simeq} 2\Gamma_k 2^{-(K-1)}\left(D_k\big|_{\{\rho_j \to 1\}}\right)\int Du\, \frac{e^{-u^2}}{\tilde{H}_\Lambda(u)}$$

(3.5)

$$I_{\lambda\Lambda} = \Gamma_k \int Du\, e^{-u^2/\rho_k^2} \sum_{z=\pm 1} \frac{D_k^2(z)[G_k^\lambda(z) + D_k(z)\tilde{H}_\Lambda(-uz)]}{[G_k^\Lambda(z) + D_k(z)\tilde{H}_\Lambda(-uz)]^2} \prod_{j\neq k} Dx_j$$

$$\overset{\rho_j \to 1}{\simeq} 2\Gamma_k 2^{-(K-1)}\left(D_k\big|_{\{\rho_j \to 1\}}\right)\int Du\, \frac{e^{-u^2}\tilde{H}_\Lambda(u)}{\tilde{H}_\Lambda^2(u)}.$$

(3.6)

The asymptotic forms of the above expressions can be understood on the following basis: for each orthant in the $\{x_j\}$ space D_k is either zero or one, while the integral on $\prod_{j\neq k} Dx_j$ yields the $2^{-(K-1)}$ factor. The term between parenthesis is a K-dependent combinatorial factor which in this case equals

---

[3]The nature of this fixed point is fairly different in different machines. For example, in the TPM $\{\rho_j = 0\}$ is *always* a fixed point for $K \ge 2$. See (Simonetti 96) for details.

the number of terms in D_k, and for both integrals we make use of the property $\tilde{H}_\lambda(x) + \tilde{H}_\lambda(-x) = 1$. Once more we observe that the K dependence factorized into a global constant in the dynamical equation, which now simply reads

$$\frac{d\rho_k}{d\alpha_p} \overset{\rho_j \to 1}{\simeq} \frac{\rho_k \Gamma_k^3}{2\pi}(1 - 2\Lambda)c \int Du \frac{e^{-u^2}}{\tilde{H}_\Lambda^2(u)} \left[2(1 - 2\lambda)\tilde{H}_\Lambda(u) - (1 - 2\Lambda)\tilde{H}_\lambda(u)\right] ,$$

$$(3.7)$$

where c is an architecture dependent function of K. The fixed points of the above dynamics are therefore independent of the size of the machine and the robustness phase diagram holds for TCMs with an arbitrary number of hidden units. As opposed to the determination of the $\rho_0 = 0$ boundary, the zeros of the r.h.s. of equation 3.7 must be obtained numerically. The whole phase diagram is shown on Figure 3.

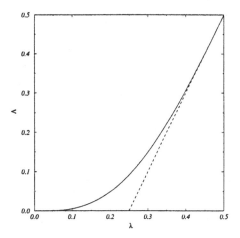

Fig. 3: Noise robustness phase diagram for $F_k^\star$. When $\alpha \to \infty$, the overlap ρ tends either to 1 (above the full line), 0 (below the dashed line) or ρ_0, with $0 < \rho_0 < 1$ (between the dashed and full lines).

4 Conclusions

Several open questions remain to be studied in the area concerning optimal generalization bounds. The results presented here were obtained under simplifying assumptions. First, we only treated the Tree architectures and studied learning of a realizable rule, then the limit $N \to \infty$ was taken but K although can be large compared to 1, was kept small compared to N. The distribution of examples was supposed known and taken to be spherical (but we could have studied other cases) and finally the noise type was assumed known and uncorrelated. Changing any of these conditions may introduce great technical difficulties and in some cases it may not be obvious how to proceed. Finally we end by pointing out that the asymptotic decay of the generalization error for these machines is exactly twice as large as that obtained from the (offline) Bayes algorithm and therefore its relation to the optimal offline case must be more than just coincidental. This relation has been recently dealt with by Opper (Opper, 1996).

Acknowledgements

M. C. would like to thank the FWO, Flemish Government and the IUAP, Prime Minister's office for financial support. N. C. was partially supported by Conselho Nacional de Desenvolvimento Científico e Tecnológico (CNPq) and by FINEP/RECOPE.

Appendix

Derivation of $P(\Sigma_B | y_k, \{x_j\})$

We now give more details about the probability distribution $P(\Sigma_B | y_k, \{x_j\})$ used in the calculations of the previous sections. We would like to draw special attention to the possibility of writing it under the form of eq. 2.15 and to its asymptotic properties, which play an important role in the derivation of the universal results presented. For tree-like architectures, absence of correlations between different components of the input vectors immediately leads to the equality $P(\Sigma_B | y_k, \{x_j\}) = P(\Sigma_B | y_k, \{x_j\}_{j \neq k})$. It reflects the fact that the teacher output is not influenced by the student network, so that knowledge of y_k overrides any useful information that might come from x_k. This expression reads

$$P(\Sigma_B | y_k, \{x_j\}_{j \neq k}) = \int \delta\left(g(\{\mathrm{sign}(y_j)\}_{j=1,\ldots,K}), \Sigma_B\right) \prod_{j \neq k} P(y_j | x_j) dy_j , \quad \text{(A.1)}$$

where $g(\{\sigma_j\}) = \mathrm{sign} \sum_j \sigma_j$ and $P(y_j | x_j)$ can be obtained from equation 2.11. Due to the boolean nature of the branch perceptrons, integration on y_j ($j \neq k$) is always constrained to either $]-\infty, 0]$ or $[0, \infty[$, which gives as a result functions $H(x_j/\Gamma_j)$ or $H(-x_j/\Gamma_j)$, respectively.

Since the TCM output is just the majority vote of the internal representation, the delta function in eq. A.1 is different from zero in two kinds of situations. Given y_k there are configurations such that the final output Σ_B is already determined, regardless of which value σ_B^k takes. These are the cases of large majorities, where the vote of a single unit cannot change the final output. However, it also occurs that Σ_B be solely determined by the state of σ_B^k, when the rest of the hidden units yields a zero sum. These are the decision border situations mentioned before (whose fraction in the space of configurations decreases like $\sim K^{-1/2}$, for large K). These qualitatively different possibilities give rise to $C_k(\Sigma_B, \{x_j\}_{j \neq k})$ and $D_k(\Sigma_B, \{x_j\}_{j \neq k})$ respectively. They can be written as

$$D_k(\Sigma_B, \{x_j\}_{j \neq k}) = \sum_{\{\tau_j = \pm 1\}_{j \neq k}} \left[\prod_{j \neq k} H\left(\frac{-\tau_j x_j \Sigma_B}{\Gamma_j} \right) \right] \delta \left(\sum_{j \neq k} \tau_j, 0 \right) \qquad (A.2)$$

$$C_k(\Sigma_B, \{x_j\}_{j \neq k}) = \sum_{\{\tau_j = \pm 1\}_{j \neq k}} \left[\prod_{j \neq k} H\left(\frac{-\tau_j x_j \Sigma_B}{\Gamma_j} \right) \right] \Theta \left(\sum_{j \neq k} \tau_j - \frac{1}{2} \right) . \qquad (A.3)$$

In the above expressions, the limit $\rho_j \to 0$ is trivial, since all the H functions tend to $1/2$. The contribution of each function above depends only on the number of terms it contains. D_k is of special interest, containing exactly $(K-1)!/[((K-1)/2)!]^2$ terms, each of which being a product of $K-1$ H functions. In order to obtain the limit of perfect generalization, however, it should be noted that the constraints on the dummy variables $\{\tau_j\}$ in C_k and D_k are mutually exclusive. That means that configurations that contribute to one never does to the other. In the limit $\rho_j \to 1$ the arguments of the H functions diverge, and each of them becomes a Kronecker delta, $H(-\tau_j x_j \Sigma_B/\Gamma_j) \to \delta(\tau_j \sigma_{Jj} \Sigma_B, 1)$. Integration on the fields $\{y_j\}$ in eqs. 3.5 and 3.6 reduces to counting internal representations. Due to the presence of D_k in the numerator of those expressions, only those with $\sum_{j \neq k} \tau_j = 0$ give non-vanishing contributions.

References

Amari, S. (1967). A theory of adaptive pattern classifiers. *IEEE Trans.*, EC-16, 299–307.

Biehl, M., Riegler, P. and Stechert, M. (1995). Learning from noisy data: an exactly solvable model. *Phys. Rev. E*, 52, R4624–R4627.

Biehl, M. and Schwarze, H. (1995). Learning by online gradient descent. *J. Phys. A*, 28, 643–656.

Copelli, M. and Caticha, N. (1995). On-line learning in the committee machine. *J. Phys. A*, 28, 1615–1625.

Copelli, M., Eichorn, R., Kinouchi, O., Biehl, M., Simonetti, R., Riegler, P. and Caticha, N. (1997). Noise robustness in multilayer neural networks. *Europhys. Lett.*, 37, 427–432.

Copelli, M., Kinouchi, O. and Caticha, N. (1996). Equivalence between on-line learning in noisy perceptrons and tree committee machines. *Phys. Rev. E*, 53, 6341–6352.

Kinouchi, O. and Caticha, N. (1992a). Biased learning in boolean perceptrons. *Physica A*, 185, 411–416.

Kinouchi,O. and Caticha, N. (1992b). Optimal generalization in perceptrons. *J. Phys. A*, 25, 6243–6250.

Kinouchi, O. and Caticha, N. (1993). Lower bounds on generalization errors for drifting rules. *J. Phys. A*, 26, 6161–6171.

Kinzel, W. and Ruján, P. (1990). Improving a network generalization ability by selecting examples. *Europhys. Lett.*, 13, 473–477.

Mato, G. and Parga, N. (1992). Generalization properties of multilayered neural networks. *J. Phys. A*, 25, 5047–5054.

Opper, M. (1994). Learning and generalization in a two-layer neural network: The role of the vapnik-chervonenkis dimension. *Phys. Rev. Lett.*, 72, 2113–2116.

Opper, M. (1996). On-line versus off-line learning from random exmaples: general results. *Phys. Rev. Lett.*, 77, 4671–4674.

Saad, D. and Solla, S.A. (1995). Exact solution for on-line learning in multi-layer neural networks. *Phys. Rev. Lett.*, 74, 4337–4340.

Seung, H.S., Sompolinsky, H., and Tishby, N. (1992). Statistical Mechanics of Learning from Examples *Phys. Rev. A*, 45, 6056–6091.

Simonetti, R. and Caticha, N. (1996). On-line learning in parity machines. *J. Phys. A*, 29, 4859–4867.

Vicente, R., Kinouchi, K. and Caticha, N. (1997). Statistical mechanics of online learning of drifting concepts: a variational approach. *Machine Learning*, 32, 179–201.

Watkin, T.L.H., Rau, A. and Biehl, M. (1993). The statistical mechanics of learning a rule. *Rev. Mod. Phys.*, 65, 499–556.

Incorporating Curvature Information into On-line Learning

Magnus Rattray [†] *and David Saad* [‡]

Neural Computing Research Group, Aston University
Birmingham B4 7ET, UK.
[†] *rattray@aston.ac.uk*
[‡] *saadd@aston.ac.uk*

Abstract

We analyse the dynamics of a number of second order on-line learning algorithms training multi-layer neural networks, using the methods of statistical mechanics. We first consider on-line Newton's method, which is known to provide optimal asymptotic performance. We determine the asymptotic generalization error decay for a soft committee machine, which is shown to compare favourably with the result for standard gradient descent. Matrix momentum provides a practical approximation to this method by allowing an efficient inversion of the Hessian. We consider an idealized matrix momentum algorithm which requires access to the Hessian and find close correspondence with the dynamics of on-line Newton's method. In practice, the Hessian will not be known on-line and we therefore consider matrix momentum using a single example approximation to the Hessian. In this case good asymptotic performance may still be achieved, but the algorithm is now sensitive to parameter choice because of noise in the Hessian estimate. On-line Newton's method is not appropriate during the transient learning phase, since a suboptimal unstable fixed point of the gradient descent dynamics becomes stable for this algorithm. A principled alternative is to use Amari's natural gradient learning algorithm and we show how this method provides a significant reduction in learning time when compared to gradient descent, while retaining the asymptotic performance of on-line Newton's method.

1 Introduction

On-line learning is a popular method for training multi-layer feed-forward neural networks, especially for large systems and for problems requiring rapid and adaptive data processing. Under the on-line learning framework, network parameters are updated according to only the latest in a sequence of training examples. This is to be contrasted with batch methods which utilise the entire training set at each learning iteration. On-line methods can be beneficial in terms of both storage and computation time, and also allow for temporal changes in the task being learned.

The most basic on-line learning algorithm for models which are differentiable with respect to their parameters is stochastic gradient descent. Given some differentiable error function, the network weights are adapted in the negative gradient direction of this error calculated according to only the current, randomly drawn, training example. Under the batch learning framework (and in other optimization problems) it is well known that curvature information can be used in order to speed up learning (see, for example, Bishop, 1995). Typically this curvature information is in the form of some estimate of the Hessian matrix or its inverse, as required for Newton-type algorithms (unless otherwise stated, we define the Hessian as the matrix of second derivatives of the error averaged over the entire training set). Pre-multiplying the standard gradient with the inverse Hessian and annealing the learning rate appropriately provides asymptotically optimal performance when emulating stochastic rules, equalling even the best batch algorithm (Amari, 1998). However, determining the Hessian on-line is difficult as we only have access to a single training example at any one time. Even if the Hessian can be estimated on-line, inverting it will be computationally costly when our network is large. This is particularly undesirable when we consider that computational efficiency is one of the principle reasons for using on-line methods.

Despite these difficulties a number of algorithms have been proposed which estimate curvature information on-line. For example, Le Cun *et al* (1993) describe an on-line method for determining eigenvalues of the Hessian, which allows an appropriate learning rate to be used for gradient descent at late times. Orr & Leen (1994, 1997) have recently introduced an on-line matrix momentum algorithm in order to invert an estimate of the Hessian on-line. This latter method is particularly interesting since the inversion is replaced by a matrix-vector multiplication which can be carried out by an efficient back-propagation step. On-line versions of other second order methods are also available (for a review, see Bishop, 1995).

A different approach has recently been proposed by Amari (1998), who has introduced a natural gradient learning algorithm inspired by ideas from information geometry. When learning to emulate a stochastic rule with some probabilistic model this learning algorithm has the desirable properties of asymptotic optimality (for a sufficiently rich model) and invariance to reparameterizations of our model distribution. This latter property is achieved by viewing the parameter space of the model as a Reimannian space in which local distance is defined by the Kullback-Leibler divergence. This method requires knowledge of the input distribution and the inversion of a large matrix (the Fisher information) but in some cases the algorithm can be executed with relatively low cost (Yang & Amari, 1998). The natural gradient method is intended to provide improved performance during both transient and asymptotic stages of learning and we will see that this is certainly true for the examples presented here.

In this paper we model the dynamics displayed by some of the above learning algorithms using a recently developed statistical mechanics framework. This framework allows accurate modelling for on-line learning in two-layer networks with large input dimension and provides a compact and easily interpretable description of the learning process (Biehl & Schwarze, 1995; Saad & Solla, 1995).

We first solve the dynamics for an idealized on-line version of Newton's method which uses knowledge of the exact Hessian. In this case we show how unstable transient fixed points, which can appear in gradient descent training of multi-layer networks with over-lapping receptive fields, can become attractive fixed points in this case. This highlights a significant limitation for Hessian based algorithms, which is easily explained by examining the behaviour of the algorithm close to the fixed point. As expected, asymptotic performance is shown to be significantly better than for standard gradient descent and we provide some generic asymptotic results in terms of task complexity and non-linearity.

As we have already said, the true Hessian will not be known in general and must somehow be estimated if we wish to obtain optimal asymptotic performance. An efficient inversion method is also required. We therefore consider Orr & Leen's matrix momentum algorithm: firstly we show how the inversion is achieved for an idealized algorithm in which the true Hessian is known and secondly we examine the efficacy of using a rather crude on-line estimate of the Hessian.

Matrix momentum still suffers from the problem that previously transient fixed points become stable. By using an alternative matrix pre-multiplier which is guaranteed positive definite one can avoid this problem. A number of possibilities exist, yet these alternatives do not really have any principled justification outside the asymptotic regime (for example, Orr (1995) uses the linearized Hessian, as do Gauss-Newton methods). A more principled choice is to use natural gradient learning (Amari, 1998). We model the dynamics of this algorithm and show how performance is much improved over standard gradient descent in all phases of learning.

2   Statistical mechanics framework

A statistical mechanics framework is used to obtain a compact description of the learning dynamics, which is exact for large input dimension N and provides an accurate model of mean behaviour for realistic N (Biehl & Schwarze, 1995; Saad & Solla, 1995; Barber *et al*, 1996). We consider a mapping from an N dimensional input space $\boldsymbol{\xi} \in \Re^N$ onto a scalar, realized through a model $\sigma(\mathbf{J}, \boldsymbol{\xi}) = \sum_{i=1}^{K} g(\mathbf{J}_i \cdot \boldsymbol{\xi})$ which defines a soft committee machine, where we choose activation function $g(x) \equiv \mathrm{erf}(x/\sqrt{2})$, $\mathbf{J} \equiv \{\mathbf{J}_i\}_{1 \leq i \leq K}$ is the set of input to hidden adaptive weights for the K hidden nodes and the hidden to output weights are set to one. The activation of hidden node i under presentation of the input pattern $\boldsymbol{\xi}^\mu$ is denoted $x_i^\mu = \mathbf{J}_i \cdot \boldsymbol{\xi}^\mu$. This configuration preserves most properties of general multi-layer networks and can be extended to accommodate adaptive hidden to output weights (Reigler & Biehl, 1995).

Training examples are of the form $(\boldsymbol{\xi}^\mu, \zeta^\mu)$ where μ labels each example and components of the independently drawn input vectors $\boldsymbol{\xi}^\mu$ are uncorrelated and come from a Gaussian distribution with zero mean and unit variance. The corresponding output ζ^μ is given by a corrupted teacher of a similar configuration to the student except for a possible difference in the number M of hidden units: $\zeta^\mu = \sum_{n=1}^{M} g(\mathbf{B}_n \cdot \boldsymbol{\xi}^\mu) + \rho^\mu$, where $\mathbf{B} \equiv \{\mathbf{B}_n\}_{1 \leq n \leq M}$ is the set of input to hidden adaptive weights and ρ^μ is Gaussian output noise with variance σ^2. The activation of hidden node n under presentation of the input pattern $\boldsymbol{\xi}^\mu$ is denoted $y_n^\mu = \mathbf{B}_n \cdot \boldsymbol{\xi}^\mu$. Where possible, we will use indices $i, j, k, l \ldots$ to refer to units in the student network and $n, m, \ldots$ for units in the teacher network.

The error made by a student with weights $\mathbf{J}$ on a given input $\boldsymbol{\xi}$ is given by the quadratic deviation

$$\epsilon_{\mathbf{J}}(\boldsymbol{\xi}, \zeta) = \frac{1}{2} [\, \sigma(\mathbf{J}, \boldsymbol{\xi}) - \zeta \,]^2 = \frac{1}{2} \Big[\sum_{i=1}^{K} g(x_i) - \sum_{n=1}^{M} g(y_n) - \rho \Big]^2 \,, \qquad (2.1)$$

which is proportional to the log-likelihood of the data under a Gaussian noise model. Performance on a typical input in the absence of noise defines the generalization error $\epsilon_g(\mathbf{J}) \equiv \langle \epsilon_{\mathbf{J}}(\boldsymbol{\xi}, \zeta) \rangle_{\{\xi\}}|_{\sigma=0}$ through an average over all possible input vectors $\boldsymbol{\xi}$.

The activations are distributed according to a multivariate Gaussian with covariances: $\langle x_i x_k \rangle = \mathbf{J}_i \cdot \mathbf{J}_k \equiv Q_{ik}$, $\langle x_i y_n \rangle = \mathbf{J}_i \cdot \mathbf{B}_n \equiv R_{in}$, and $\langle y_n y_m \rangle = \mathbf{B}_n \cdot \mathbf{B}_m \equiv T_{nm}$, measuring overlaps between student and teacher vectors. Angled brackets denote averages over inputs. The covariance matrix completely describes the state of the system, in the limit of large N, enabling us to write down a closed set of ordinary differential equations for the evolution of each one of the overlaps under standard gradient descent (Saad & Solla, 1995). In addition, the generalization error may be written exclusively in terms of the overlaps so that these equations of motion are sufficient to describe the evolution of the generalization error. The equations, representing an exact analytical solution for the average case, can be integrated numerically to obtain a solution of the dynamics. In the following sections we will show how this framework can be generalized to describe the dynamics for a number of second order learning algorithms.

3   On-line Newton's method

The Hessian cannot be determined on-line in practice and on-line Newton's method is therefore mainly of theoretical interest. However, we consider this idealized algorithm here so that we can better understand algorithms like matrix momentum, which seek to emulate the performance of on-line Newton's method.

3.1   The Hessian

We define the Hessian to be the matrix of second derivatives of the training error with respect to the weights, averaged over all training examples. We will consider an unlimited number of examples, in which case this is simply the second derivative of the generalization error. The Hessian is made up of K^2 blocks $\mathbf{H} = [\mathbf{H}_{ik}]$ which can be determined as described in appendix A,

$$
\mathbf{H}_{ik} = \mathbf{I}\,(1 + \delta_{ik})\frac{\partial \epsilon_g}{\partial Q_{ik}} + \sum_{jl} \mathbf{J}_j \mathbf{J}_l^{\mathrm{T}}(1 + \delta_{ij})(1 + \delta_{kl})\frac{\partial^2 \epsilon_g}{\partial Q_{ij}\partial Q_{kl}}
$$
$$
+ \sum_{jn} \mathbf{J}_j \mathbf{B}_n^{\mathrm{T}}(1 + \delta_{ij})\frac{\partial^2 \epsilon_g}{\partial Q_{ij}\partial R_{kn}} + \sum_{nj} \mathbf{B}_n \mathbf{J}_j^{\mathrm{T}}(1 + \delta_{jk})\frac{\partial^2 \epsilon_g}{\partial R_{in}\partial Q_{jk}}
$$
$$
+ \sum_{nm} \mathbf{B}_n \mathbf{B}_m^{\mathrm{T}}\frac{\partial^2 \epsilon_g}{\partial R_{in}\partial R_{km}}\ . \tag{3.1}
$$

The generalization error can be written in closed form as a function of Q, R and T (Saad & Solla, 1995) in which case the above expression is also in closed form (the generalization error and derivatives are given in appendix B). Each block of the Hessian takes the form of an identity matrix added to outer products of weight vectors and it is straightforward to show that each block of the inverse will also be of this general form. Inversion can be carried out by partitioning and we show how to calculate the inverse for $K = 2$ in appendix A.1 (this result can easily be generalized to larger K). Each block of the inverse Hessian can then be written in the following form,

$$
\mathbf{H}_{ik}^{-1} = \alpha_{ik}(\mathbf{I} + \mathbf{S}\Theta^{ik}\mathbf{S}^{\mathrm{T}})\ , \tag{3.2}
$$

where $\mathbf{S} = (\mathbf{J}_1, \ldots, \mathbf{J}_K, \mathbf{B}_1, \ldots, \mathbf{B}_M)$, α_{ik} is a scalar coefficient and Θ^{ik} is an $M + K$ dimensional square matrix (these only depend on the order parameters Q, R and T).

3.2   Equations of motion

Given the inverse Hessian, an on-line version of Newton's method is defined by the following weight update at each iteration,

$$
\mathbf{J}^{\mu+1} = \mathbf{J}^{\mu} - \frac{\eta}{N}\mathbf{H}^{-1}\nabla_{\mathbf{J}}\,\epsilon_{\mathbf{J}}(\boldsymbol{\xi}^{\mu}, \zeta)\ , \tag{3.3}
$$

where the learning rate η has been scaled with the input size N and may depend on α in general. The weights to hidden node i are then updated as follows,

$$\mathbf{J}_i^{\mu+1} = \mathbf{J}_i^\mu + \frac{\eta}{N} \sum_{j=1}^K \mathbf{H}_{ij}^{-1} \delta_j^\mu \boldsymbol{\xi}^\mu \ , \tag{3.4}$$

where $\delta_i^\mu \equiv g'(x_i^\mu)[\sum_{n=1}^M g(y_n^\mu) - \sum_{j=1}^K g(x_j^\mu) + \rho^\mu]$.

In the large N limit the order parameters change according to a completely deterministic trajectory. Using the methods developed in (Saad & Solla, 1995) it is straightforward to write down a coupled set of differential equations describing this trajectory,

$$\begin{aligned}
\frac{\mathrm{d}R_{in}}{\mathrm{d}\alpha} &= \eta f_{in}(R, Q, T) \ , \\
\frac{\mathrm{d}Q_{ik}}{\mathrm{d}\alpha} &= \eta g_{ik}(R, Q, T) + \eta^2 h_{ik}(R, Q, T, \sigma^2) \ ,
\end{aligned} \tag{3.5}$$

where we have defined a new time variable $\alpha = \mu/N$ to be the normalized number of patterns presented so far. This is the same general form as for standard gradient descent (explicit expressions for f, g and h are given in appendix C.1). All the effects of stochasticity are contained within the η^2 term, which is analogous to a "diffusion" term in the language of stochastic dynamics. This term is proportional to the variance of the input distribution and contains an additive contribution proportional to the noise variance. The terms linear in η contribute effects due to motion on the mean error (generalization error) surface. Although it is these "drift" terms which decide most qualitative features of the learning dynamics outside the asymptotic regime, the diffusion term limits increases in the learning rate and is of key importance for determining the appropriate maximal and optimal learning parameters (West & Saad, 1997; Saad & Rattray, 1997, this volume).

3.3 Integrating the dynamics

The learning dynamics for gradient descent have been well studied and we give a brief description of the main features here, before discussing on-line Newton's method (Saad & Solla, 1995; Saad & Rattray, this volume). The order parameters are initialized randomly, with overlaps between different vectors (R_{in} and $Q_{i \neq k}$) taking small values of $O(1/\sqrt{N})$ while the student norms Q_{ii} are $O(1)$. We choose values corresponding to $N \sim 10^6$ but different initial conditions just lead to changes in the learning time-scale, with learning times growing logarithmically with N (Biehl *et al*, 1996). The overall shape of the learning curve and the optimal and maximal learning rates in each phase are not affected by the choice of initial conditions. Finite size effects have been studied by Barber *et al* (1995), showing that the picture described here holds for much smaller N.

As gradient descent learning begins, the order parameters quickly converge to a transient fixed point, the symmetric phase, which is characterized by close similarity of all student-teacher overlaps. This fixed point is unstable, however, and small differences in the initial conditions diverge exponentially (hence the logarithmic scaling of learning time with N). Once the student-teacher overlaps diverge sufficiently the system leaves this transient fixed point and the order parameters converge towards their asymptotic values (or possibly to another transient fixed point first). There will always be at least one transient fixed point as long as $K \geq 2$ (unless the learning rate is chosen too large for successful learning), even if the teacher is a perceptron. For matched teacher and student ($M = K$) $R_{in} \rightarrow T_{in}$ and $Q_{ik} \rightarrow T_{ik}$ asymptotically (for appropriately ordered indices) as long as the learning rate is chosen well. In the absence of noise and for $K \geq M$ asymptotic convergence is exponential as long as the learning rate is fixed and not too large. For unrealizable learning (noisy and/or with $K < M$) the learning rate should be annealed inversely with α for optimal asymptotic performance (Leen *et al*, 1997) in which case the generalization error also converges according to an inverse power law (if the prefactor for the learning rate decay is not too small).

In fig. 1(a) we show the evolution of the generalization error under gradient descent for various learning rates, for a noiseless, architecturally matched learning scenario ($K = M$) and an isotropic teacher ($T_{nm} = \delta_{nm}$). A scaled learning rate $\tilde{\alpha} = \alpha\eta$ is used, which reflects the scaling invariance of equations (3.5) for small η and allows us to meaningfully take the $\eta \rightarrow 0$ limit. The plateau in generalization error is due to the symmetric phase described above and dominates the learning time.

In fig. 1(b) we plot the corresponding results for on-line Newton's method. The system never leaves the symmetric phase in this case and it appears that the symmetric fixed point is now stable to perturbations. We have not found any situation for large or small η in which the system leaves this fixed point (for a variety of learning scenarios). It is easy to see why on-line Newton's method will make any fixed point stable when the Hessian is non-singular (this is exactly the effect of Newton's method, which diagonalizes the linearized dynamics). However, the symmetric fixed point is characterized by a singular Hessian, in which case this simple picture no longer holds. We have studied the $K = M = 2$ case analytically for small learning rate, in a similar analysis to that of Saad & Solla (1995) for gradient descent. In this limit the student weight vectors are assumed to lie in a subspace spanned by the teacher weight vectors. The system is then completely determined by the student-teacher overlaps. Exploiting symmetries observed in the dynamics ($R_{in} = R\delta_{in} + S(1 - \delta_{in})$) we have a further simplified two dimensional system, which we study by a linear expansion around the symmetric fixed point. For gradient descent a single positive eigenvalue results in the eventual divergence of R and S. The picture is different for on-line Newton's method however and here we find that both eigenvalues are negative, resulting in a stable fixed point. This

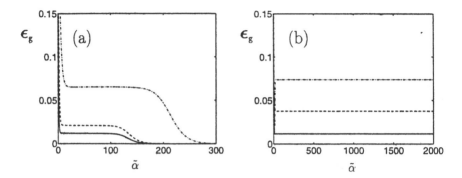

Fig. 1: We compare the performance of gradient descent (a) and on-line Newton's method (b) for a two hidden node network learning from examples generated by a two node isotropic teacher $(T_{nm} = \delta_{nm})$ in the absence of noise. Curves show the generalization error for learning rates $\eta = 2$ (dash-dotted line), $\eta = 1$ (dashed line) and $\eta \to 0$ (solid line) against a scaled time variable $\tilde{\alpha} = \alpha\eta$. Initial conditions are $Q_{ii} \in U[0, 0.5]$, $Q_{i \neq k}, R_{in} \in U[0, 10^{-3}]$.

analysis exemplifies the usefulness of the order parameters approach, since a stochastic approximation analysis would be made difficult by the singular Hessian at this fixed point (this is equally true for standard gradient descent).

It is not guaranteed that diffusion terms will not make this fixed point unstable, although in our case this does not appear to be the case (it is difficult to study the finite η situation analytically since the fixed point can no longer be determined exactly in this case). This corresponds with what one might expect, given that diffusion does not aid escape from the symmetric phase for standard gradient descent (West & Saad, 1997). We note here that the inclusion of noise would require a consideration of second order terms (as in the asymptotic annealing analysis described below), but for low noise levels these terms will only become relevant within the immediate neighbourhood of a slightly shifted fixed point.

3.4   Asymptotic performance

In the previous section we found that on-line Newton's method is susceptible to trapping in a transient, suboptimal fixed point. However, in the presence of noise, optimal asymptotic performance will be achieved if on-line Newton's method is used at late times with learning rate $1/\alpha$. The asymptotic dynamics for gradient descent with an annealed learning rate has recently been solved under the statistical mechanics formalism and the optimal generalization error decay is known in this case (Leen *et al*, 1997). Here we extend those results to on-line Newton's method.

Asymptotically for an isotropic realizable task ($K = M$, $T_{nm} = T\delta_{nm}$) we can examine a four dimensional system by defining $R_{in} = R\delta_{in} + S(1 - \delta_{in})$ and $Q_{ik} = Q\delta_{ik} + C(1 - \delta_{ik})$, as this avoids degeneracy in the dynamical equations (the initial conditions, which would break this symmetry, become negligible asymptotically). This approach allows general results in terms of K and T. We define $\mathbf{u} = (R - T, Q - T, S, C)^{\mathrm{T}}$ to be the deviation from the asymptotic fixed point. If the learning rate decays according to some power law then the linearized equations of motion around this fixed point are given by,

$$\frac{d\mathbf{u}}{d\alpha} = \eta \mathbf{M} \mathbf{u} + \eta^2 \sigma^2 \mathbf{b} , \tag{3.6}$$

where $\eta \mathbf{M}$ is the Jacobian of the equations of motion to first order in η while the only non-vanishing second order terms are proportional to the noise variance. The asymptotic equations of motion can be determined using the asymptotic expression for the inverse Hessian (see appendix A.4). A more detailed account will be provided elsewhere (Rattray & Saad, 1998) and here we just provide the solution to the above equation with $\eta = \eta_0/\alpha$,

$$\mathbf{u}(\alpha) = \sigma^2 \mathbf{V} \mathbf{X} \mathbf{V}^{-1} \mathbf{b} , \tag{3.7}$$

where $\mathbf{V}^{-1} \mathbf{M} \mathbf{V}$ is a diagonal matrix whose entries λ_i are eigenvalues of $\mathbf{M}$ and we have defined the diagonal matrix $\mathbf{X}$ to be,

$$\mathbf{X}_i^{\mathrm{diag}} = -\frac{\eta_0^2}{1 + \lambda_i \eta_0} \left[\frac{1}{\alpha} - \alpha^{\lambda_i \eta_0} \alpha_0^{-(1 + \lambda_i \eta_0)} \right] , \tag{3.8}$$

with annealing beginning at $\alpha = \alpha_0$. We find two degenerate eigenvalues $\lambda_{1,2} = -1$, $\lambda_{3,4} = -2$ and by substituting equation (3.8) into a first order expansion of the generalization error it is straightforward to show $\eta_0 = 1$ to be optimal, as expected. In this case the modes corresponding to $\lambda_{1,2}$ do not contribute to the asymptotic generalization error and we find a particularly simple decay law which is independent of T,

$$\epsilon_g = \frac{\sigma^2 K}{2\alpha} . \tag{3.9}$$

In fig. 2 we compare the prefactor of the optimal generalization decay ($\epsilon_g \sim \epsilon_0 \sigma^2/\alpha$) for on-line Newton's method with the gradient descent results from (Leen *et al*, 1997). The result for gradient descent is not exactly linear in K, but quickly approaches a linear scaling as K increases (see fig. 2(a)). In fig. 2(b) we show how performance differs most when T becomes small, while the optimal gradient descent decay approaches the result for on-line Newton's

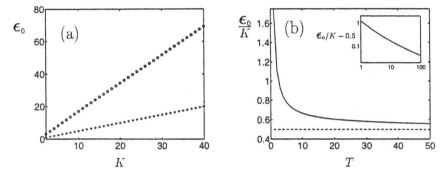

Fig. 2: Prefactor for the asymptotic decay of the generalization error ($\epsilon_g \sim \epsilon_0 \sigma^2/\alpha$): (a) shows the prefactor for $T = 1$ as a function of K for optimal gradient descent (circles) and on-line Newton's method (crosses) while (b) shows how the prefactor for optimal gradient descent (large K) decays towards 0.5 as T increases, which is the prefactor for on-line Newton's method. Adapted from (Rattray et al, 1998).

method for large T. This can be explained by examining the asymptotic expression for the Hessian, shown in equation (A.13). For large T the diagonals of the Hessian are $O(1/\sqrt{T})$ and equal (for large N) while all other terms are at most $O(1/T)$, so that the Hessian is proportional to the identity matrix in this limit and Newton's method is effectively equivalent to gradient descent. However, for small T the diagonals are $O(T^2)$ while the off-diagonals remain finite, so that the Hessian is dominated by off-diagonals in this limit.

Although the optimal learning rate decay for gradient descent is inversely proportional to α, the prefactor is strongly problem dependent. This is not so for on-line Newton's method, for which $\eta = 1/\alpha$ is always optimal. We also note that if the prefactor is chosen too small in gradient descent, the generalization error will follow a slower power law decay.

In fig. 3 the approach to the asymptotic decay is shown for an example of realizable learning ($K = M = 2$) with an isotropic teacher and noise variance $\sigma^2 = 0.01$. The optimal decay law is shown by the dot-dashed line in fig. 3(a) while the solid line gives the generalization error for on-line Newton's method, initialized after the symmetric phase at $\alpha_i = 180$ (before this point gradient descent is used with $\eta = 1$). The learning rate is annealed from some appropriate constant (we choose $\eta_i = 0.1$) according to the following prescription,

$$\eta = \frac{\eta_i}{1 + (\alpha - \alpha_i)\eta_i} \,. \tag{3.10}$$

We see how losses incurred due to trapping during the symmetric phase result in a rather late approach to the final, optimal decay. If the learning rate is simply chosen equal to $1/\alpha$ then the approach is much slower.

4 Matrix momentum

A heuristic which is sometimes useful in batch learning is to include a momentum term in the basic gradient descent algorithm (for a discussion, see Bishop, 1995). For on-line learning with momentum we have,

$$\mathbf{J}_i^{\mu+1} = \mathbf{J}_i^{\mu} + \frac{\eta}{N} \delta_i^{\mu} \boldsymbol{\xi}^{\mu} + \beta(\mathbf{J}_i^{\mu} - \mathbf{J}_i^{\mu-1}) , \qquad (4.1)$$

where $\delta_i^{\mu} \equiv g'(x_i^{\mu})[\sum_{n=1}^{M} g(y_n^{\mu}) - \sum_{j=1}^{K} g(x_j^{\mu}) + \rho^{\mu}]$. This is the same as for standard gradient descent except for the inclusion of a term proportional to the previous weight update.

On-line momentum has been considered previously but has not been found to be particularly useful, except perhaps in smoothing the asymptotic trajectory of the weights (Roy & Shynk, 1990; Weigerinck *et al*, 1994; Orr, 1995). However, by choosing an appropriate matrix momentum parameter one may obtain close to optimal asymptotic performance (Orr & Leen, 1994, 1997). Before introducing matrix momentum it will be useful to consider the dynamics of standard momentum for large N.

4.1 Standard momentum

Equation (4.1) defines a second order process, in which weights from the two previous iterations are required for each update. We define an equivalent first order process by introducing a new set of variables $\Omega_i^{\mu} = N(\mathbf{J}_i^{\mu} - \mathbf{J}_i^{\mu-1})$,

$$\begin{aligned} \mathbf{J}_i^{\mu+1} &= \mathbf{J}_i^{\mu} + \frac{\eta}{N} \delta_i^{\mu} \boldsymbol{\xi}^{\mu} + \frac{\beta}{N} \Omega_i^{\mu} , \\ \Omega_i^{\mu+1} &= \beta \Omega_i^{\mu} + \eta \delta_i^{\mu} \boldsymbol{\xi}^{\mu} . \end{aligned} \qquad (4.2)$$

We can now proceed along the lines of (Saad & Solla, 1995) in order to derive a set of first order differential equations describing the evolution of a set of order parameters. In this case we need a new Gaussian field $z_i^{\mu} = \Omega_i \cdot \boldsymbol{\xi}^{\mu}$ and a new set of order parameters: $\langle z_i z_k \rangle = \Omega_i \cdot \Omega_k \equiv C_{ik}$, $\langle z_i y_n \rangle = \Omega_i \cdot \mathbf{B}_n \equiv D_{in}$, and $\langle x_i z_k \rangle = \mathbf{J}_i \cdot \Omega_k \equiv E_{ik}$. We identify two possible scaling for η and β which result in different dynamical behaviour.

- If we choose $\eta \sim O(1)$ and $\beta \sim O(1/N)$ the above prescription results in an increasingly fast time scale for the new order parameters as N increases. This can be incorporated as an adiabatic elimination and we find that the dynamics of R and Q is simply equivalent to gradient descent with an effective learning rate of $\eta_{\text{eff}} = \eta/(1 - \beta)$ in this case.

- More interesting dynamics is observed if we choose $\eta \sim O(1/N)$ and $1 - \beta \sim O(1/N)$ (Prügel-Bennett, 1997). In this case the order parameters all evolve on the same time-scale. If we define $\eta = k/N$ and $\beta = 1 - \gamma/N$ then taking $\gamma \to \infty$ and $k \to \infty$ simultaneously while keeping their ratio finite results in dynamics equivalent to gradient descent with an effective learning rate of $\eta_{\text{eff}} = k/\gamma$.

The above limits are related to those discussed by Weigerinck *et al* (1994) and their results are consistent with the above observations. The latter scaling proves most appropriate for matrix momentum and is rigorously justified without resorting to adiabatic elimination. This is therefore the scaling discussed in the following sections.

4.2   Idealized matrix momentum

Orr & Leen suggest the use of a matrix momentum parameter β so that the learning rate rescaling described in the previous section results in on-line Newton's method. If the Hessian is known this can be achieved by setting,

$$\beta = \mathbf{I} - \frac{k\mathbf{H}}{N} , \qquad \eta = \frac{k\eta_\alpha}{N} , \qquad (4.3)$$

where η_α is a scalar which may depend on α. Making k large one might then expect an effective matrix learning rate,

$$\eta_{\text{eff}} = \eta_\alpha \, \mathbf{H}^{-1} , \qquad (4.4)$$

as required for on-line Newton's method. However, there are two problems with this result: it has not been shown that the limiting behaviour described for standard momentum holds for a matrix momentum parameter and we do not have on-line access the Hessian. In this section we address the first issue by solving the matrix momentum dynamics for an idealized situation in which the Hessian is known. In the following section we consider an approximation based on using only the latest training example to estimate the Hessian.

Substituting the above definitions into equations (4.2) using the definition of the Hessian given in equation (3.1) and following the methods of Saad & Solla (1995) we find a coupled set of differential equations for the order parameters as $N \to \infty$, which are given in appendix C.2.

In fig. 3(a) we compare the asymptotic performance of idealized matrix momentum to on-line Newton's method for a two-node network learning an isotropic task in the presence of noise ($\sigma^2 = 0.01$). Both methods become trapped in the symmetric fixed point, as explained in the previous section, so we use gradient descent initially and after the symmetric phase we use matrix momentum with η_α annealed according to equation (3.10). The dashed lines show results for $k = 0.01$, $k = 0.1$ and $k = 2$, in descending order of height (the final dashed line is almost obscured by the solid line). As k increases, the trajectory converges onto the on-line Newton's method result (solid line), as desired, and we approach the optimal asymptotic decay law (dot-dashed line). Matrix momentum therefore provides an efficient approximation to on-line Newton's method when the Hessian is known. In the next section we consider a realizable algorithm which uses an approximation to the Hessian.

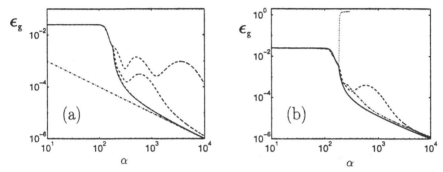

Fig. 3: The solid lines in (a) and (b) show the generalization error for annealed on-line Newton's method started after $\alpha = 180$, with gradient descent before this point, for a two hidden node network learning from examples generated by a two node isotropic teacher ($T_{nm} = \delta_{nm}$) corrupted by noise ($\sigma^2 = 0.01$). In (a) we show the corresponding generalization error for idealized matrix momentum (dashed lines) for $k = 0.01$, $k = 0.1$ and $k = 2$ (in descending order of height). The dot-dashed line gives the optimal asymptotic decay. In (b) we show the generalization error for matrix momentum using a single pattern estimate for the Hessian with $k = 0.1$ (dashed), $k = 0.5$ (dot-dashed) and $k = 3$ (dotted). Initial conditions are as in fig. 1 (order parameters specific to matrix momentum are initialized to zero).

4.3   Single pattern approximation

In order to define a practical algorithm we need some approximation to the Hessian which can be determined on-line. The simplest such approximation is to use a single training example in order to estimate the Hessian (Orr & Leen, 1997). The single-pattern Hessian is written in appendix A.2 and the equations of motion for matrix momentum using this approximation are given in appendix C.3.

In figure 3(b) we show the asymptotic performance of matrix momentum using the single pattern approximation, for a two node network learning an isotropic task in the presence of noise ($\sigma^2 = 0.01$). Curves are shown for $k = 0.1$, $k = 0.5$ and $k = 3$, with η_α chosen according to equation (3.10) after $\alpha = 180$. Ideally, we would wish for the curves to approach the on-line Newton's method result (solid line) for large k. However, as k increases fluctuations in the Hessian estimate (due to randomness in the inputs) become important and the weight vector norms diverge, leading to divergence of the generalization error (dotted line). For intermediate k (dot-dashed line) the performance is asymptotically close to optimal and certainly provides a significant improvement over gradient descent. Further work is required to determine the optimal and maximal values of k and η_α analytically, using methods from (Leen *et al*, 1997), but we have shown here that performance is certainly strongly dependent on parameter choice. It would be interesting to consider more sophisticated on-line approximations to the Hessian, which might provide greater robustness.

5 Natural gradient learning

As we saw in the section 3, on-line Newton's method does not guarantee convergence to a minimum of the generalization error because the Hessian is not always positive definite. A number of heuristics exist which ensure the matrix pre-multiplier of the gradient is positive definite; for example Orr (1995) suggests using the linearized Hessian (as in the Gauss-Newton method), or one could add the identity matrix multiplied by some scalar parameter to the Hessian (or its inverse), with the parameter reduced to zero asymptotically. These methods do guarantee asymptotic optimality and convergence to a minimum of the generalization error, but lack any principled motivation during the transient phases of learning.

A more principled approach has recently been proposed by Amari (1998). Natural gradient learning ensures asymptotic optimality, given a sufficiently rich model, is invariant to reparameterization of our model distribution (defined by the student in our case) and always converges to a local minimum of the generalization error if the learning rate is annealed appropriately. Invariance to reparameterization is achieved by viewing the parameter (weight) space of the model as a Reimannian space in which local distance is defined by the Kullback-Leibler divergence (Yang & Amari, 1997). The Fisher information matrix then plays the role of a Reimannian metric in this space. The natural gradient learning rule is obtained by pre-multiplying the gradient of the log-likelihood (of the most recent training example) with the inverse of this matrix, which plays a similar role to the Hessian in on-line Newton's method.

5.1 Fisher Information Matrix

Our model distribution is taken to be the student network with output corrupted by zero mean Gaussian noise of variance σ_m^2. The error defined by equation (2.1) is proportional to the log-likelihood of the latest training example under this noise model. Each entry in the Fisher information matrix $\mathbf{G} = [G_{i\alpha,k\beta}]$, where $1 \leq i, k \leq K$ and $1 \leq \alpha, \beta \leq N$, is defined,

$$G_{i\alpha,k\beta} = \frac{1}{\sigma_m^4} \left\langle \frac{\partial \epsilon_J(\boldsymbol{\xi}, \zeta_J)}{\partial J_{i\alpha}} \frac{\partial \epsilon_J(\boldsymbol{\xi}, \zeta_J)}{\partial J_{k\beta}} \bigg|_{\zeta_J = \sum_i g(x_i) + \rho_m} \right\rangle_{\{\rho_m, \xi\}} . \tag{5.1}$$

Here, the brackets denote an average over the input distribution and model noise ρ_m, which is taken from a Gaussian distribution with zero mean and variance σ_m^2. Amari (1998) has determined the Fisher information matrix for a general two-layer network and for our particular choice of activation function with a Gaussian input distribution we find $\mathbf{G} = \mathbf{A}/\sigma_m^2$, where $\mathbf{A} = [A_{ik}]$ is independent of the noise variance and is given by (Rattray *et al*, 1998),

$$A_{ik} = \frac{2}{\pi\sqrt{\Delta}} \left[\mathbf{I} - \frac{1}{\Delta} \left((1 + Q_{kk})\mathbf{J}_i\mathbf{J}_i^T + (1 + Q_{ii})\mathbf{J}_k\mathbf{J}_k^T - Q_{ik}(\mathbf{J}_i\mathbf{J}_k^T + \mathbf{J}_k\mathbf{J}_i^T) \right) \right] , \tag{5.2}$$

with $\Delta = (1 + Q_{ii})(1 + Q_{kk}) - Q_{ik}^2$.

Recall the general form of the Hessian which was defined in equation (3.1). The Fisher information is also written as the sum of an identity matrix and outer products of weight vectors, but only student weight vectors and student-student overlaps are required here. This is because the average in equation (5.1) does not involve the teacher mapping. The Fisher information matrix should therefore be easier to determine, as only the input distribution is required. Also, although we require our noise model to be correct in order to ensure asymptotic optimality for a sufficiently complex student network, we will see that knowledge of the noise variance is not required.

If the input distribution is Gaussian, then the Fisher information is as defined above. For $K \ll N$ inversion can be achieved efficiently by partitioning (Yang & Amari, 1997) as described in appendix A.1 for the Hessian. Yang & Amari also discuss methods for preprocessing the training examples when the inputs are non-Gaussian, so that the pre-processed inputs approximate a whitened Gaussian process. However, if the input distribution is far from Gaussian then a different approach will be required for inversion. Here we will simply assume that the inputs come from a Gaussian distribution in order to determine the efficacy of natural gradient learning compared with standard gradient descent.

5.2   Dynamics

The weights to hidden node i are updated as follows,

$$\mathbf{J}_i^{\mu+1} = \mathbf{J}_i^\mu + \frac{\eta}{N} \sum_{j=1}^K \mathbf{A}_{ij}^{-1} \delta_j^\mu \boldsymbol{\xi}^\mu \ , \tag{5.3}$$

where $\delta_i^\mu \equiv g'(x_i^\mu)[\sum_{n=1}^M g(y_n^\mu) - \sum_{j=1}^K g(x_j^\mu) + \rho^\mu]$. Notice that the noise variance does not appear explicitly in the above expression, since the noise dependence of the inverse Fisher information matrix and the log-likelihood have cancelled. The derivation of the dynamics closely follows the result for on-line Newton's method and a full discussion will be given elsewhere (Rattray *et al*, 1998; Rattray & Saad, 1998).

Although our equations of motion are sufficient to describe learning for arbitrary system size, the number of order parameters is $\frac{1}{2}K(K-1) + KM$ so that the numerical integration soon becomes rather cumbersome as K and M grow and analysis becomes difficult. To obtain generic results in terms of system size we therefore exploit symmetries which appear in the dynamics for isotropic tasks and structurally matched student and teacher ($K = M$ and $T = T\delta_{nm}$). In this case we define a four dimensional system via $Q_{ij} = Q\delta_{ij} + C(1 - \delta_{ij})$ and $R_{in} = R\delta_{in} + S(1 - \delta_{in})$ which can be used to study the dynamics for arbitrary K and T. In (Rattray & Saad, 1998) we show how the Fisher information matrix can be inverted for this reduced dimensionality system and the resulting equations of motion are also given there.

As was the case for standard gradient descent (see fig. 1(a)), the dynamics is characterized by two major phases of learning. Initially, the order parameters are trapped in an unstable fixed point characterized by a lack of differentiation between different teacher nodes, the symmetric phase. If the teacher is deterministic then the generalization error eventually converges to zero exponentially, unless the learning rate is chosen too large. If the teacher is corrupted by noise then the learning rate must be annealed in order for the generalization error to decay. As for on-line Newton's method, the fastest decay for natural gradient learning is achieved by setting the learning rate to $1/\alpha$ and the analysis in section 3.4 is equally applicable to natural gradient learning since the methods are asymptotically equivalent.

Unfortunately, even for standard gradient descent an analytical study of the symmetric phase is only possible for small learning rates, which are often far from optimal (Saad & Solla, 1995). Such an approach is not appropriate for realistic learning rates and often gives misleading results since it is the diffusion terms in the dynamics (quadratic in the learning rate) which set the appropriate learning time scale. It is also unclear how to proceed for natural gradient learning even in this limit, since the Fisher information is singular at the fixed point considered by Saad & Solla (1995) and the simplifications used by them are no longer appropriate (Rattray *et al*, 1998). In order to compare

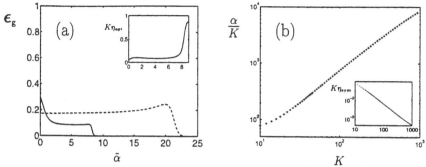

Fig. 4: In (a) the generalization error is shown for optimal natural gradient learning (solid line) and optimal gradient descent (dashed line) for $K = 10$ (we define $\tilde{\alpha} = 10^{-2}\alpha$). The inset shows the optimal learning rate for natural gradient learning. In (b) the time required for optimal natural gradient learning to reach a generalization error of $10^{-4}K$ is shown as a function of K on a log-log scale. The inset shows the optimal learning rate within the symmetric phase. In both (a) and (b) we used $T = 1$, zero noise and initial conditions $R = 10^{-3}$, $Q = U[0, 0.5]$ and $S = C = 0$. Adapted from (Rattray *et al*, 1998).

transient performance with gradient descent for larger learning rates we apply a recent method for determining optimal time-dependent learning rates under the present formalism (Saad & Rattray, 1997, this volume). This allows us to compare the methods at their optimal settings and to determine scaling laws for learning time in terms of task complexity. We note here that the maximal learning rate during the symmetric phase, above which good performance is impossible, is typically close to the optimal value.

Fig. 4 shows results for the optimal learning rate dynamics. In fig. 4(a) we compare the generalization error evolution with the gradient descent result for $K = 10$, showing a significant reduction in learning time. The inset shows the optimal learning rate for natural gradient learning in this case. Notice that we do not consider the effects of noise in this example, since noise will usually be of secondary importance during the symmetric phase, typically resulting in a slightly lengthened and raised plateau. In fig. 4(b) we show the time required to reach a generalization error of $10^{-4}K$ as a function of K. This indicates a scaling law of K^2 for the length of the symmetric plateau (which dominates the learning time) while the corresponding result for gradient descent is $K^{\frac{8}{3}}$ (West & Saad, 1997). The inset shows that the optimal learning rate within the symmetric phase scales as K^{-2} which contrasts with a value of $K^{-\frac{5}{3}}$ for gradient descent. The escape time for the adaptive gradient learning rule studied by West & Saad scales as $K^{\frac{5}{2}}$ which is also worse than for natural gradient learning.

Our results indicate a significant improvement over gradient descent, which increases with task complexity. However, these results are for the specific case of an isotropic, structurally matched teacher. Numerical studies suggest that improvement can be expected over a larger class of problems but it seems difficult to determine generic results without significantly restricting the class of teacher mappings.

6   Conclusion

We have studied a number of second order on-line algorithms for training multi-layer neural networks, using a statistical mechanics formalism which is appropriate when the input dimension is much larger the the number of hidden units. The first algorithm considered is on-line Newton's method, which is obtained by pre-multiplying the gradient with the inverse Hessian. We find that an unstable fixed point of the gradient descent dynamics becomes stable under this learning rule, which is therefore only useful at late times. Asymptotically, this rule is known to provide optimal performance and we compare the asymptotic decay of the generalization error with the result for gradient descent, for isotropic and structurally matched learning ($K = M$ and $T_{nm} = T\delta_{nm}$). We find that the advantage of using curvature information is most pronounced for small T.

In practice the Hessian can not be determined on-line and inversion is expensive. Matrix momentum provides a practical approximation to on-line Newton's method, since it allows efficient inversion of the Hessian and can be implemented using a very noisy approximation to the Hessian. We first analyse the dynamics of idealized matrix momentum, using the true Hessian, and find that the method converges onto the dynamics of on-line Newton's method in an appropriate limit. Using a single pattern approximation to the Hessian, we find that good asymptotic performance is possible but with some sensitivity to parameter choice, due to noise in the Hessian estimate. More work is required to determine optimal and maximal parameters for this algorithm.

Hessian based methods are inappropriate during the transient phases of learning, since they do not guarantee convergence to a minimum of the generalization error. A principled alternative is to use Amari's natural gradient learning algorithm, which defines a Reimannian metric in the student parameter space. Our analysis of this algorithm points to a significant advantage over gradient descent during the transients of learning, as well as optimal asymptotic performance given a sufficiently rich model. We find improved power law scaling of learning time against task complexity.

The natural gradient learning algorithm requires an inversion of the Fisher information matrix which can be achieved efficiently for Gaussian, or near-

Gaussian, inputs (Yang & Amari, 1997). However, in some cases the inputs will not be close to Gaussian and an efficient method of inversion will be required. Matrix momentum provides a possible inversion method and a natural extension of the present analysis would be to study this case.

Acknowledgements
This work was supported by the EPSRC grant GR/L19232. We would like to thank all the participants of the on-line learning themed week at the Newton Institute for many useful and enlightening discussions.

Appendices

A   The Hessian

We define each entry of the Hessian $\mathbf{H} = [H_{i\alpha,k\beta}]$ where $1 \leq i, k \leq K$ and $1 \leq \alpha, \beta \leq N$,

$$H_{i\alpha,k\beta} = \left\langle \frac{\partial^2 \epsilon_J(\boldsymbol{\xi}, \boldsymbol{\zeta})}{\partial J_{i\alpha} \partial J_{k\beta}} \right\rangle_{\{\xi\}} = \frac{\partial^2 \epsilon_g}{\partial J_{i\alpha} \partial J_{k\beta}} , \tag{A.1}$$

with $\mathbf{J}_i = [J_{i\alpha}]$. To calculate these derivatives we use the chain rule,

$$\frac{\partial \epsilon_g}{\partial J_{i\alpha}} = \sum_{j \geq k} \frac{\partial Q_{jk}}{\partial J_{i\alpha}} \frac{\partial \epsilon_g}{\partial Q_{jk}} + \sum_{jn} \frac{\partial R_{jn}}{\partial J_{i\alpha}} \frac{\partial \epsilon_g}{\partial R_{jn}} , \tag{A.2}$$

where

$$\frac{\partial Q_{jk}}{\partial J_{i\alpha}} = \delta_{ij} J_{k\alpha} + \delta_{ik} J_{j\alpha} , \quad \frac{\partial R_{jn}}{\partial J_{i\alpha}} = \delta_{ij} B_{n\alpha} .$$

Applying the chain rule twice provides us with equation (3.1) in the main text.

A.1   Inversion by partitioning

The Hessian is defined in equation (3.1) and using the block form it is natural to calculate the inverse by partitioning. We will consider the simplest multilayer student with $K = 2$, although it would be straightforward to iteratively partition for larger K. We write,

$$\mathbf{H} = \begin{pmatrix} \mathbf{D} & \mathbf{E} \\ \mathbf{E}^{\mathrm{T}} & \mathbf{F} \end{pmatrix} , \quad \mathbf{H}^{-1} = \begin{pmatrix} \mathbf{X} & \mathbf{Y} \\ \mathbf{Y}^{\mathrm{T}} & \mathbf{Z} \end{pmatrix} . \tag{A.3}$$

Each block in the inverse can be determined from the following identities,

$$\begin{aligned} \mathbf{X} &= (\mathbf{D} - \mathbf{E}\mathbf{F}^{-1}\mathbf{E}^{\mathrm{T}})^{-1} , \\ \mathbf{Y} &= -(\mathbf{F}^{-1}\mathbf{E}^{\mathrm{T}}\mathbf{X})^{\mathrm{T}} , \\ \mathbf{Z} &= -\mathbf{E}^{-1}\mathbf{D}\mathbf{Y} . \end{aligned} \tag{A.4}$$

Define $\mathbf{S} = (\mathbf{J}_1, \mathbf{J}_2, \mathbf{B}_1, \mathbf{B}_2, \ldots, \mathbf{B}_M)$ where M is the number of hidden nodes in the teacher. Each of the above block matrices takes the same general form; for example let,

$$\mathbf{D} = \mathrm{d}\,(\mathbf{I} + \mathbf{S}\Phi\mathbf{S}^{\mathrm{T}})\,, \quad \mathbf{F} = \mathrm{f}\,(\mathbf{I} + \mathbf{S}\Psi\mathbf{S}^{\mathrm{T}}) \tag{A.5}$$

where Φ and Ψ are $2+M$ dimensional square matrices while d and f are scalar coefficients. The exact expressions can be found for each block by comparing terms with equation (3.1). The expressions in equation (A.4) can be calculated by repeated application of the following two identities,

$$\mathbf{D}\mathbf{F} = \mathrm{d}\,\mathrm{f}\,\left(\mathbf{I} + \mathbf{S}(\Phi + \Psi + \Phi C\Psi)\mathbf{S}^{\mathrm{T}}\right)\,, \tag{A.6}$$

$$\mathrm{d}\,\mathbf{D}^{-1} = \left(\mathbf{I} - \mathbf{S}(\mathbf{I} + \Phi C)^{-1}\Phi\mathbf{S}^{\mathrm{T}}\right)\,, \tag{A.7}$$

where non-bold I is the $2 + M$ dimensional identity matrix. Here, we have defined C to be the covariance matrix, or matrix of order parameters:

$$C = \mathbf{S}^{\mathrm{T}}\mathbf{S} = \begin{pmatrix} Q & R \\ R^{\mathrm{T}} & T \end{pmatrix}\,, \tag{A.8}$$

with $Q_{2\times 2} = [Q_{ik}]$, $R_{2\times M} = [R_{in}]$ and $T_{M\times M} = [T_{nm}]$.

The exact expressions for $\mathbf{X}$, $\mathbf{Y}$ and $\mathbf{Z}$ are not presented here as they are rather cumbersome. In fact, we never require explicit expressions in our implementation and we find it simpler to solve equations (A.4) as a sequence of transformations using identities (A.6) and (A.7). For all K the inverse Hessian takes the same general form described by equation (3.2).

A.2   Single pattern approximation

Under the single pattern approximation we no longer average the expression in equation (A.1) over inputs. Each block in the unaveraged Hessian is defined,

$$\frac{\partial^2 \epsilon_{\mathbf{J}}(\xi, \zeta)}{\partial \mathbf{J}_i \partial \mathbf{J}_k} = \xi\,\xi^{\mathrm{T}} \left(\delta_{ik}\,g''(x_i)\Big[\sum_j g(x_j) - \sum_n g(y_n) - \rho\Big] + g'(x_i)g'(x_k) \right)\,. \tag{A.9}$$

Notice that we could have derived equation (3.1) directly by averaging the above quantity over inputs. However, expanding in terms of the generalization error provides a much simpler expression.

A.3   Asymptotic Hessian

For realizable rules $\mathbf{J} \to \mathbf{B}$ asymptotically and the Hessian is much simplified. Instead of using the definition in equation (3.1) it is simpler to start from the unaveraged Hessian in equation (A.9), replace every $\mathbf{J}$ by a $\mathbf{B}$ and average over the inputs and noise. In this case we find for each block,

$$\mathbf{H}_{ik}|_{\mathbf{J}=\mathbf{B}} = \left\langle g'(y_i)g'(y_k)\, \boldsymbol{\xi}\,\boldsymbol{\xi}^{\mathrm{T}} \right\rangle_{\{\xi\}} . \tag{A.10}$$

Recall that $g(x) = \mathrm{erf}(x/\sqrt{2})$ and the inputs come from a Gaussian distribution with zero mean and unit variance, in which case,

$$\mathbf{H}_{ik} = \frac{2}{\pi} \int \frac{d\boldsymbol{\xi}}{\sqrt{2\pi}}\, \boldsymbol{\xi}\,\boldsymbol{\xi}^{\mathrm{T}} \exp\left[-\tfrac{1}{2}\boldsymbol{\xi}^{\mathrm{T}}(\mathbf{I} + \mathbf{B}_i\mathbf{B}_i^{\mathrm{T}} + \mathbf{B}_k\mathbf{B}_k^{\mathrm{T}})\boldsymbol{\xi}\right] . \tag{A.11}$$

Completing this Gaussian integral and using the fact that $\mathbf{B}_n^{\mathrm{T}}\mathbf{B}_m = T\delta_{nm}$ for an isotropic teacher we find,

$$\mathbf{H}_{ii} = \frac{2}{\pi\sqrt{1+2T}}\left(\mathbf{I} - \frac{2\mathbf{B}_i\mathbf{B}_i^{\mathrm{T}}}{1+2T}\right) ,$$

$$\mathbf{H}_{i\neq k} = \frac{2}{\pi(1+T)}\left(\mathbf{I} - \frac{\mathbf{B}_i\mathbf{B}_i^{\mathrm{T}} + \mathbf{B}_k\mathbf{B}_k^{\mathrm{T}}}{1+T}\right) . \tag{A.12}$$

A.4   Asymptotic Inversion

For realizable rules we can invert the Hessian asymptotically for any K. The asymptotic form for each block of $\mathbf{H}$ can be written,

$$\mathbf{H}_{ik} = (a\,\delta_{ik} + b)\,\mathbf{I} + (c\,\delta_{ik} + d)\,\mathbf{B}_i\mathbf{B}_i^{\mathrm{T}} + d\,\mathbf{B}_k\mathbf{B}_k^{\mathrm{T}} , \tag{A.13}$$

where,

$$a = \frac{2}{\pi\sqrt{1+2T}} - \frac{2}{\pi(1+T)} , \quad b = \frac{2}{\pi(1+T)} ,$$

$$c = \frac{4}{\pi(1+T)^2} - \frac{4}{\pi(1+2T)^{\frac{3}{2}}} , \quad d = -\frac{2}{\pi(1+T)^2} .$$

Block (i,k) in the inverse of $\mathbf{H}$ is then given by,

$$\mathbf{H}_{ik}^{-1} = \left(\frac{1}{a}\delta_{ik} - \frac{b}{a(a+bK)}\right)\mathbf{I} + \sum_{n=1}^{K}\Gamma_{ik}^n\mathbf{B}_n\mathbf{B}_n^{\mathrm{T}} , \tag{A.14}$$

Substituting these expressions into the definition of an inverse and using the orthogonality of the teacher weight vectors we obtain a matrix equation for the K dimensional square matrix $\Gamma^n = [\Gamma_{ik}^n]$,

$$\Gamma^n = \mathbf{P}^{-1}\mathbf{X} \tag{A.15}$$

where,

$$\mathbf{P} = a\mathbf{I} + \begin{pmatrix} \mathbf{e}_n \\ \mathbf{u} \end{pmatrix}^{\mathrm{T}} \begin{pmatrix} cT & -dT \\ -dT & b \end{pmatrix} \begin{pmatrix} \mathbf{e}_n \\ \mathbf{u} \end{pmatrix} ,$$

$$\mathbf{X} = \frac{1}{a}\begin{pmatrix} \mathbf{e}_n \\ \mathbf{u} \end{pmatrix}^{\mathrm{T}} \begin{pmatrix} -c & (da-bc)/(a+bK) \\ d & -db/(a+bK) \end{pmatrix} \begin{pmatrix} \mathbf{e}_n \\ \mathbf{u} \end{pmatrix} .$$

Here, we have defined $\mathbf{e}_n$ to be a K dimensional row vector with a one in the nth element and zeros everywhere else, $\mathbf{u}$ is a row vector of ones and I is the K dimensional identity. Solving for Γ^n we find,

$$\Gamma^n = \frac{1}{\Delta}\begin{pmatrix} \mathbf{e}_n \\ \mathbf{u} \end{pmatrix}^{\mathrm{T}} \Theta \begin{pmatrix} \mathbf{e}_n \\ \mathbf{u} \end{pmatrix}, \tag{A.16}$$

where,

$$\Theta = \begin{pmatrix} K(\mathrm{d}^2 T - \mathrm{bc}) - \mathrm{ac} & \mathrm{d}^2 T - \mathrm{bc} - \mathrm{ad} \\ \mathrm{d}^2 T - \mathrm{bc} - \mathrm{ad} & (\mathrm{d}^2 T(\mathrm{a}+\mathrm{b}) - 2\mathrm{abd} - \mathrm{b}^2\mathrm{c})/(\mathrm{a}+\mathrm{b}K) \end{pmatrix},$$

$$\Delta = \mathrm{a}^2(\mathrm{a}+\mathrm{b}K) + \mathrm{a}^2 T(\mathrm{c}-2\mathrm{d}) + \mathrm{a}T(K-1)(\mathrm{cb}-\mathrm{d}^2).$$

B Derivatives of the generalization error

Saad & Solla (1995) calculate the generalization error,

$$\epsilon_g = \frac{1}{\pi}\left[\sum_{ik}\arcsin\left(\frac{Q_{ik}}{\sqrt{1+Q_{ii}}\sqrt{1+Q_{kk}}}\right) + \sum_{nm}\arcsin\left(\frac{T_{nm}}{\sqrt{1+T_{nn}}\sqrt{1+T_{mm}}}\right)\right.$$
$$\left. - 2\sum_{in}\arcsin\left(\frac{R_{in}}{\sqrt{1+Q_{ii}}\sqrt{1+T_{nn}}}\right)\right]. \tag{B.1}$$

We require the following derivatives,

$$\frac{\partial\epsilon_g}{\partial Q_{ik}} = \frac{2-\delta_{ik}}{\pi\sqrt{(1+Q_{ii})(1+Q_{kk})-Q_{ik}^2}} + \frac{\delta_{ik}}{\pi(1+Q_{ii})}\sum_n \frac{R_{in}}{\sqrt{(1+T_{nn})(1+Q_{ii})-R_{in}^2}}$$
$$- \frac{\delta_{ik}}{\pi(1+Q_{ii})}\sum_j \frac{Q_{ij}}{\sqrt{(1+Q_{ii})(1+Q_{jj})-Q_{ij}^2}}, \tag{B.2}$$

$$\frac{\partial^2\epsilon_g}{\partial Q_{jl}\partial R_{km}} = \frac{\delta_{jl}\delta_{jk}(1+T_{mm})}{\pi((1+T_{mm})(1+Q_{jj})-R_{jm}^2)^{\frac{3}{2}}}, \tag{B.3}$$

$$\frac{\partial^2\epsilon_g}{\partial R_{jm}\partial R_{in}} = -\frac{2\delta_{ij}\delta_{nm}R_{jm}}{\pi((1+T_{mm})(1+Q_{jj})-R_{jm}^2)^{\frac{3}{2}}}, \tag{B.4}$$

$$\frac{\partial^2\epsilon_g}{\partial Q_{jl}\partial Q_{kr}}$$
$$= \frac{(\delta_{jl}-2)((1+Q_{ll})\delta_{kj}\delta_{rj} + (1+Q_{jj})\delta_{kl}\delta_{rl} - 2Q_{jl}(\delta_{jk}\delta_{lr} + \delta_{jr}\delta_{lk}(1-\delta_{jl})))}{2\pi((1+Q_{jj})(1+Q_{ll})-Q_{jl}^2)^{\frac{3}{2}}}$$
$$+ \frac{\delta_{jl}\delta_{jk}\delta_{jr}}{2\pi(1+Q_{jj})^2}\sum_i Q_{ij}\frac{3(1+Q_{ii})(1+Q_{jj})-2Q_{ij}^2}{((1+Q_{ii})(1+Q_{jj})-Q_{ij}^2)^{\frac{3}{2}}}$$
$$- \frac{\delta_{jl}\delta_{jk}\delta_{jr}}{2\pi(1+Q_{jj})^2}\sum_n R_{jn}\frac{3(1+Q_{jj})(1+T_{nn})-2R_{jn}^2}{((1+T_{nn})(1+Q_{jj})-R_{jn}^2)^{\frac{3}{2}}}$$
$$- \frac{\delta_{jl}}{2\pi}\left[\frac{2\delta_{jr}(1+Q_{kk})-\delta_{rk}Q_{kj}}{((1+Q_{kk})(1+Q_{jj})-Q_{kj}^2)^{\frac{3}{2}}} + \frac{2\delta_{jk}(1-\delta_{jr})(1+Q_{rr})}{((1+Q_{rr})(1+Q_{jj})-Q_{rj}^2)^{\frac{3}{2}}}\right]. \tag{B.5}$$

C Equations of motion

In this appendix we provide the large N equations of motion for each algorithm. In each case we define a new time variable $\alpha = \mu/N$ to be the normalized number of patterns presented so far.

C.1 On-line Newton's Method

$$
\begin{aligned}
\frac{dR_{in}}{d\alpha} &= \eta \sum_{k=1}^{K} \alpha_{ik} \left(\phi_{kn} + \sum_{j=1}^{K} R_{jn} \left[\sum_{l=1}^{K} \Theta_{jl}^{ik} \psi_{kl} + \sum_{m=K+1}^{M+K} \Theta_{jm}^{ik} \phi_{km} \right] \right. \\
&\quad \left. + \sum_{p=K+1}^{M+K} T_{pn} \left[\sum_{l=1}^{K} \Theta_{pl}^{ik} \psi_{kl} + \sum_{m=K+1}^{M+K} \Theta_{pm}^{ik} \phi_{km} \right] \right) , \\[4pt]
\frac{dQ_{ir}}{d\alpha} &= \eta \sum_{k=1}^{K} \alpha_{ik} \left(\psi_{kr} + \sum_{j=1}^{K} Q_{jr} \left[\sum_{l=1}^{K} \Theta_{jl}^{ik} \psi_{kl} + \sum_{m=K+1}^{M+K} \Theta_{jm}^{ik} \phi_{km} \right] \right. \\
&\quad \left. + \sum_{n=K+1}^{M+K} R_{rn} \left[\sum_{l=1}^{K} \Theta_{nl}^{ik} \psi_{kl} + \sum_{m=K+1}^{M+K} \Theta_{nm}^{ik} \phi_{km} \right] \right) + \\
&\quad \eta \sum_{k=1}^{K} \alpha_{rk} \left(\psi_{ki} + \sum_{j=1}^{K} Q_{ji} \left[\sum_{l=1}^{K} \Theta_{jl}^{rk} \psi_{kl} + \sum_{m=K+1}^{M+K} \Theta_{jm}^{rk} \phi_{km} \right] \right. \\
&\quad \left. + \sum_{n=K+1}^{M+K} R_{in} \left[\sum_{l=1}^{K} \Theta_{nl}^{rk} \psi_{kl} + \sum_{m=K+1}^{M+K} \Theta_{nm}^{rk} \phi_{km} \right] \right) + \eta^2 \sum_{k=1}^{K} \sum_{l=1}^{K} \alpha_{ik} \alpha_{rl} \upsilon_{kl} .
\end{aligned}
\tag{C.1}
$$

Here, Θ is defined by equation (3.2) and we have defined $\phi_{in} \equiv \langle \delta_i y_n \rangle_{\{\xi\}}$, $\psi_{ik} \equiv \langle \delta_i x_k \rangle_{\{\xi\}}$ and $\upsilon_{ik} \equiv \langle \delta_i \delta_k \rangle_{\{\xi\}}$. The explicit expressions for ϕ_{in}, ψ_{ik}, υ_{ik} depend exclusively on the overlaps Q, R and T and are given in (Saad & Solla, 1995; Saad & Rattray, this volume).

C.2 Idealized Matrix Momentum

For matrix momentum using the true Hessian we find,

$$
\begin{aligned}
\frac{dQ_{ik}}{d\alpha} &= E_{ik} + E_{ki} , & \frac{dR_{in}}{d\alpha} &= D_{in} , \\[4pt]
\frac{dC_{ik}}{d\alpha} &= k\eta_\alpha \langle \delta_i z_k + \delta_k z_i \rangle + k^2 \eta_\alpha^2 \langle \delta_i \delta_k \rangle - k \sum_j (a_{ij} C_{kj} + a_{kj} C_{ij} + b_{ij} E_{jk} + b_{kj} E_{ji}) \\
&\quad - k \sum_m (c_{im} D_{km} + c_{km} D_{im}) , \\[4pt]
\frac{dD_{in}}{d\alpha} &= k\eta_\alpha \langle \delta_i y_n \rangle - k \sum_j (a_{ij} D_{jn} + b_{ij} R_{jn}) - k \sum_m c_{im} T_{nm} , \\[4pt]
\frac{dE_{ik}}{d\alpha} &= C_{ik} + k\eta_\alpha \langle \delta_k x_i \rangle - k \sum_j (a_{kj} E_{ij} + b_{kj} Q_{ij}) - k \sum_m c_{km} R_{im} ,
\end{aligned}
\tag{C.2}
$$

where angled brackets denote averages over inputs, or equivalently averages over the field variables $\{x_i\}$, $\{y_n\}$ and $\{z_i\}$. We have defined,

$$a_{ij} = (1 + \delta_{ij})\frac{\partial \epsilon_g}{\partial Q_{ij}} ,$$

$$b_{ij} = (1 + \delta_{ij})\left[\sum_{lk}(1 + \delta_{lk})E_{lk}\frac{\partial^2 \epsilon_g}{\partial Q_{ij}\partial Q_{kl}} + \sum_{kn}D_{kn}\frac{\partial^2 \epsilon_g}{\partial Q_{ij}\partial R_{kn}}\right] ,$$

$$c_{in} = \sum_{lk}(1 + \delta_{lk})E_{lk}\frac{\partial^2 \epsilon_g}{\partial R_{in}\partial Q_{kl}} + \sum_{km}D_{km}\frac{\partial^2 \epsilon_g}{\partial R_{in}\partial R_{km}} ,$$

where δ_{ij} (with two indices) represents a Kronecker delta. The fields are distributed according to a multivariate Gaussian with the order parameters as covariances and all averages can be calculated in closed form, as described in (Saad & Solla, 1995; Saad & Rattray, this volume). The second derivatives of the generalization error are given in appendix B.

C.3   Single Pattern Matrix Momentum

For matrix momentum using a single pattern approximation to the Hessian we find,

$$\frac{dQ_{ik}}{d\alpha} = E_{ik} + E_{ki} , \qquad\qquad \frac{dR_{in}}{d\alpha} = D_{in} ,$$

$$\frac{dC_{ik}}{d\alpha} = k\langle(\eta_\alpha\delta_i - \phi_i)z_k + (\eta_\alpha\delta_k - \phi_k)z_i\rangle + k^2\langle(\eta_\alpha\delta_i - \phi_i)(\eta_\alpha\delta_k - \phi_k)\rangle ,$$

$$\frac{dD_{in}}{d\alpha} = k\langle(\eta_\alpha\delta_i - \phi_i)y_n\rangle , \qquad \frac{dE_{ik}}{d\alpha} = C_{ik} + k\langle(\eta_\alpha\delta_k - \phi_k)x_i\rangle . \quad \text{(C.3)}$$

Again, the brackets denote averages over inputs, or fields, and we have defined $\phi_i = z_i g''(x_i)\left[\sum_j g(x_j) - \sum_n g(y_n) - \rho\right] + g'(x_i)\sum_j z_j g'(x_j)$. All averages can carried out explicitly to provide a closed set of equations of motion. The following identities are required (recall that $g(x) = \mathrm{erf}\,(x/\sqrt{2})$),

$$\int \frac{d\mathbf{x}}{\sqrt{|\mathbf{C}|(2\pi)^n}}\, g(x_i)\, \mathrm{e}^{-\frac{1}{2}\mathbf{x}^\mathsf{T}\mathbf{C}^{-1}\mathbf{x}+\mathbf{d}^\mathsf{T}\mathbf{x}} = g\left(\frac{\sum_k C_{ik}d_k}{\sqrt{1 + C_{ii}}}\right)\mathrm{e}^{\frac{1}{2}\mathbf{d}^\mathsf{T}\mathbf{C}\mathbf{d}} , \quad \text{(C.4)}$$

$$\int \frac{d\mathbf{x}}{\sqrt{|\mathbf{C}|(2\pi)^n}}\, g(x_i)\, g(x_k)\, \mathrm{e}^{-\frac{1}{2}\mathbf{x}^\mathsf{T}\mathbf{C}^{-1}\mathbf{x}} = \frac{2}{\pi}\arcsin\left(\frac{C_{ik}}{\sqrt{1 + C_{ii}}\sqrt{1 + C_{kk}}}\right) ,$$

where $\mathbf{C}$ is an $n \times n$ symmetric matrix. Factors involving the components of $\mathbf{x}$ can be brought down from the exponent of the integrand by differentiation.

References

Amari, S. (1998). Natural gradient works efficiently in learning. *Neural Computation*, 10, 251–276.

Barber, D., Saad, D., Sollich, P. (1996). Finite-size effects in online learning of multilayer neural networks. *Europhysics Letters*, 34, 151–156.

Biehl, M., Schwarze, H. (1995). Learning by online gradient descent. *Journal of Physics A*, 28, 643–656.

Biehl, M., Riegler, P., Wöhler, C. (1996). Transient dynamics of online learning in two layered neural networks. *J. Phys. A*, 29, 4769–4780.

Bishop, C. M. (1995) *Neural networks for pattern recognition*. Oxford University Press, Oxford, UK.

LeCun, Y., Simard, P. Y., Pearlmutter, B. (1993). Approximation by superpositions of a sigmoid function.*Advances in Neural Information Processing Systems 5*, ed. C.L. Giles, S.J. Hanson and J.D. Cowan (San Mateo, CA: Morgan Kaufmann) .

Orr, G. B. (1995). *Dynamics and Algorithms for Stochastic Search*. PhD. Dissertation, Oregon Graduate Institute of Science and Technology.

Leen, T.K., Orr, G.B. (1994). Optimal stochastic search and adaptive momentum. *Advances in Neural Information Processing Systems 6*, ed J. D. Cowan, G. Tesauro and J. Alspector (San Francisco, CA: Morgan Kaufmann)

Orr, G. B., Leen, T. K. (1997). Using curvature information for fast stochastic search. *Advances in Neural Information Processing Systems 9*, ed M. C. Mozer, M. I. Jordan and T. Petsche (Cambridge, MA: MIT Press)

Rattray, M., Saad, D. (1998). An analysis of on-line learning training with optimal learning rates. *Phys. Rev. E* in press.

Rattray, M., Saad, D., Amari, S. (1998). Natural gradient descent for on-line learning, *unpublished.*

Riegler, P., Biehl, M. (1995). Online backpropagation in two layered neural networks. *J. Phys. A*, 28, L507–L513.

Roy, S., Shynk, J. J. (1990). Analysis of the momentum LMS algorithm. *IEEE transactions on acoustics, speech and signal processing*, 38, 2088–2098.

Saad, D., Rattray, M. (1997). Globally optimal parameters for on-line learning in multilayer neural networks. *Phys. Rev. Lett.*, 79, 2578–2581.

Saad, D., Rattray, M. (1998). Optimal on-line learning in multilayer neural networks *in this volume.*

Saad, D., Solla, S. A. (1995). Exact solution for online learning in multilayer neural networks. *Phys. Rev.Lett.*, 74, 4337–4340 , Online learning in soft committe machines. *Phys. Rev. E*, 52, 4225–4243.

West, A. H. L., Saad, D. (1997). On-line learning with adaptive back-propagation in two-layer networks. *Phys. Rev. E*, 56, 3426–3445.

Wiegerinck, W., Komoda, A., Heskes, T. (1994). Stochastic dynamics of learning with momentum in neural networks. *J. Phys. A*, 27, 4425–4437.

Yang, H. Y., Amari, S. (1998). The efficiency and the robustness of natural gradient descent learning rule. *Advances in Neural Information Processing Systems 10*, ed M. I. Jordan, M. J. Kearns and S. A. Solla (Cambridge, MA: MIT Press).

Annealed Online Learning in Multilayer Neural Networks

Siegfried Bös† and Shun–ichi Amari‡

Brain Science Institute, RIKEN
Wako–shi, Saitama 351-0198, Japan.
† *boes@fugu.riken.go.jp*
‡ *amari@brain.riken.go.jp*

Abstract

In this article we will examine online learning with an annealed learning rate. Annealing the learning rate is necessary if online learning is to reach its optimal solution. With a fixed learning rate, the system will approximate the best solution only up to some fluctuations. These fluctuations are proportional to the size of the fixed learning rate. It has been shown that an optimal annealing can make online learning asymptotically efficient meaning that asymptotically it learns as fast as possible. These results are until now only realized in very simple networks, like single–layer perceptrons (section 3). Even the simplest multilayer network, the soft committee machine, shows an additional symptom, which makes straightforward annealing uneffective. This is because, at the beginning of learning the committee machine is attracted by a metastable, suboptimal solution (section 4). The system stays in this metastable solution for a long time and can only leave it, if the learning rate is not too small. This delays the start of annealing considerably. Here we will show that a non–local or matrix update can prevent the system from becoming trapped in the metastable phase, allowing for annealing to start much earlier (section 5). Some remarks on the influence of the initial conditions and a possible candidate for a theoretical support are discussed in section 6. The paper ends with a summary of future tasks and a conclusion.

1 Introduction

One of the most attractive properties of artificial neural networks is their ability to learn from examples and to generalize the acquired knowledge to unknown data. Recently, online learning, as opposed to batch or offline learning, became very popular, see (Amari 1967, Murata 1992, Kinouchi & Caticha 1992, Biehl & Schwarze 1993, 1995, Saad & Solla 1995, 1996). In *online learning* the weights are updated by using only one example $\mathbf{x}(t)$ at a time t, i.e.

$$\mathbf{W}(t+1) = \mathbf{W}(t) + \eta \, \Delta \mathbf{W}[\,\mathbf{x}(t), z^*(t); \mathbf{W}(t)\,], \qquad (1.1)$$

where η is the *learning rate* and $z^*(t)$ the correct target output in the case of supervised learning. The advantages of online learning are obvious. No memory is needed to store all examples and recent examples can be emphasized enabling the system to follow non–stationarities in the data. As a result, online learning is the preferred choice, if many examples are available or if the examples are produced by an ongoing process.

Each example is used only once, which makes the learning rate η much more important than in iterative batch learning. A simple time–independent learning rate η_0 can already yield good results. However, in unrealizable tasks the following dilemma can be observed, see (Murata 1992). While a larger η_0 that is smaller than $\eta_{\max}$ can accelerate the learning speed, it will also lead to a larger final error. The best solution to an unrealizable task is, however, not the endpoint of the dynamics. The system will continue to fluctuate around the best solution and the variance of the fluctuations is proportional to η_0. Only an asymptotically vanishing learning rate, i.e. $\eta \to 0$ with $t \to \infty$, can reach the optimal result. This suggests an annealing of the learning rate.

Recently, it has been proved (Amari 1997, Opper 1996), that online learning with an optimally annealed learning rate can be asymptotically efficient meaning that it can learn asymptotically as fast as the best learning method. Until now this result has been confirmed only in single–layer neural networks (Bös *et al.* 1997, Bös & Amari 1997). In studies of multilayer networks (Saad & Solla 1995a, 1995b, 1996), a new problem was encountered which makes annealing difficult. From the beginning of learning, the system is attracted by a metastable, suboptimal solution, which is a result of symmetries in the multilayer network. Once trapped in this solution, the system remains there for a long time and can only escape it, if the learning rate is not too small. Therefore, annealing can only be started after the system has left the symmetric phase.

It is desirable to reduce this trapping time, or even better to avoid the symmetric phase completely. Several efforts have been made to reduce the effect of the symmetric phase, however, they have either used prior knowledge (Vicente & Caticha 1997, Saad & Rattray 1997, Rattray & Saad 1997) or they are quite complicated (West & Saad 1996, 1997, Yang & Amari 1997). Here, we will show that a non–local or matrix update which is a straightforward generalization of simple gradient descent, can help to avoid being trapped in the symmetric phase. The network is then able to pass the symmetric phase much earlier, allowing it to start annealing much earlier.

2   The Model

The model we will use for illustration is the *soft–committee machine* discussed in detail by (Saad & Solla 1995). The committee machine is a special two–layer network, in which all weights between hidden layer and output layer are fixed to one, such that[1]

$$z = \sum_{k=1}^{H} g\left(\mathbf{W}_k^T \mathbf{x}\right) . \tag{2.1}$$

A soft–committee machine realizes the continuous outputs by applying a sigmoid function to the local field h, i.e. $g(h)$. Supervised learning is studied in a *teacher–student scenario,* and by this we mean that the correct output z_μ^* for example $\mathbf{x}_\mu$ is given by another network, the teacher net. To make the task unrealizable, we assume that the teacher network and the student network have identical architectures, but that the teacher outputs $\hat{z}_\mu^*$ are corrupted by random Gaussian noise $\epsilon \in \mathcal{N}(0, \sigma)$, yielding $z_\mu^* = \hat{z}_\mu^* + \epsilon$. For the student, the teacher network is invisible and only the target outputs z_μ^* can be used for training. For the evaluation of the performance, we may facilitate all variables of the teacher, i.e. $\mathbf{W}^*$, g^* and σ.

Supervised training minimizes the difference between the correct output z_μ^* given by the teacher and the actual output z_μ produced by the student. This is given by the loss–function,

$$\text{loss}(z_\mu^*, z_\mu) := \frac{1}{2} \left[z_\mu^* - z_\mu\right]^2 . \tag{2.2}$$

The overall performance of the student is measured by the averaged loss over *all possible* inputs $\mathbf{x}$, which we call *generalization error,* $E_G = \langle \text{loss}(z^*, z)\rangle_x$.

The generalization error can be calculated in the teacher–student scenario, if we make an assumption about the distribution of the inputs $\mathbf{x}$. The dot–products $h_k^* := \mathbf{W}_k^{*T}\mathbf{x}$ and $h_l := \mathbf{W}_l^T \mathbf{x}$ become Gaussians, if the inputs $\mathbf{x}$ are random and the input–dimension N is large. The correlations between these two Gaussian–variables are $\langle h_k^* h_l^*\rangle_x = S_{kl}$, $\langle h_k^* h_l\rangle_x = R_{kl}$ and $\langle h_k h_l\rangle_x = Q_{kl}$. They define two sets of dynamical *order parameters,*

$$R_{kl} := \mathbf{W}_k^{*T}\mathbf{W}_l^*, \qquad \text{and} \qquad Q_{kl} := \mathbf{W}_k^T \mathbf{W}_l , \tag{2.3}$$

and a set of constant task–dependent parameters $S_{kl} := \mathbf{W}_k^{*T}\mathbf{W}_l^*$.

The generalization error can then be calculated by an average over the correlated Gaussians. An algebraic expression for the generalization error can be found by using a special sigmoid function $g(h) = \text{erf}(h/\sqrt{2})$. After redefining the generalization error by subtracting the constant residual error, $E_G := E_G - E_\infty$ with $E_\infty := \frac{\sigma^2}{2}$, we find

$$E_G = F(S_{kk}, S_{ll}, S_{kl}) - 2F(S_{kk}, Q_{ll}, R_{kl}) + F(Q_{kk}, Q_{ll}, Q_{kl}) , \tag{2.4}$$

with

$$F(a_{kk}, b_{ll}, c_{kl}) := \frac{1}{\pi} \sum_{k,l=1}^{H} \arcsin \frac{c_{kl}}{\sqrt{(1+a_{kk})(1+b_{ll})}} . \tag{2.5}$$

---

[1]Note, that the outputs z are not normalized, they are from the interval $[-H, +H]$.

In this paper, we will only discuss the task, where the teacher weights $\mathbf{W}^*$ are randomly chosen and isotropic, i.e. $S_{kl} \simeq \delta_{kl}$. This simplifies the first term to

$$F(S_{kk}, S_{ll}, S_{kl}) = \frac{H}{\pi} \arcsin \frac{1}{2} = \frac{H}{6}. \qquad (2.6)$$

The dynamics of the generalization error can then be determined by the dynamics of the order parameters $Q_{kl}(t)$ and $R_{kl}(t)$, which follows from the update rule (1.1). As usual in statistical physics we normalize the number of examples so that they become independent from effects of the system size N. Since each example number μ corresponds to a discrete time–step t, we can define a *quasi–continuous time* $t := \mu/N$ with N large. It is then possible to express the evolution of the order parameters by a system of coupled differential equations. The differential equations are often simple enough, that the behavior of these models under online learning can be studied exactly, see for example (Biehl & Schwarze 1995, Saad & Solla 1995, Bös *et al.* 1997).

3   Fixed Versus Annealed Learning Rate

A model in which the advantage of the annealed learning rate can be seen very clearly, is the linear single–layer perceptron. It has only one hidden unit $H = 1$, which is linear $g(h) = h$. The output z is identical to the activity at the hidden unit. Using similar arguments as above, we get an expression for the generalization error. Gradient descent online learning can be written as,

$$\eta \, \Delta \mathbf{W}(t) = -\eta \nabla_{\mathbf{W}} \operatorname{loss} [\, z^*(t), z(t) \,]. \qquad (3.1)$$

This leads to two coupled differential equations for $Q(t)$ and $R(t)$, that are simple enough to allow a detailed examination in the case of the fixed learning rate η_0. For annealed $\eta(t)$, an approximate asymptotical solution is possible (Bös *et al.* 1997).

The results for fixed η_0 are shown in figure 1. They exhibit the characteristical behavior of the fixed learning rate; larger η_0 converge faster but to a worse final result. Also the evolvente, which is the lower bound for all these curves, can be determined. For each number of available examples P (or $T_{\max}$), there is only one optimal choice for η_0. This optimal choice decreases to zero when P increases.

We have seen that even if we do not change the learning rate during the training process, the best choice for η_0 becomes smaller, if the number of examples becomes larger. It is not fitting to the philosophy of online learning to assume that the number of examples is fixed or known. Therefore, it is much better suited to change the learning rate during the training process.

The annealing scheme should interpolate between the following two limits, a finite starting value $\eta(t \to 0) = c$ and the asymptotical scaling $\eta(t \to \infty) =$

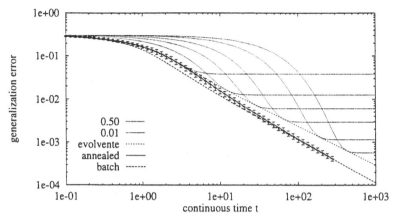

Fig. 1: Fixed versus annealed learning rate in a single–layer perceptron. Several choices for a fixed η_0 are shown by dotted lines for $\eta_0 = 0.5$, 0.2, 0.1, 0.05, 0.02, and 0.01. The evolvente, which is the lower bound to all these curves, is also shown as a dashed line. The result of optimal annealing of the learning rate is given by the solid line plus error bars. Asymptotically the annealed online solution converges against the optimal batch solution (long–dashed line) indicating that online learning becomes efficient. (Parameters: 'fixed', 'evolvente' and 'batch' are theoretical results, 'annealed' is the result of a simulation with $N = 100$ averaged over 50 runs.) Note, that the scale is double–logarithmic as in all other figures.

b/t^a. This can be done either with a non–smooth or smooth function,

$$\eta(t) = \min\left(c, \frac{b}{t^a}\right), \qquad \text{or} \qquad \eta(t) = \left(\frac{1}{c} + \frac{t^a}{b}\right)^{-1}. \qquad (3.2)$$

The actual form of the function has only a minor effect on the performance.

The optimal values for the parameters a and b can be determined by an asymptotical analytical solution of the differential equations for $Q(t)$ and $R(t)$. That a should be 1, is widely known. Here, it can be found again, starting from first principles. The optimal value of b is also 1. The value of c does not affect the asymptotics, it only delays it. A good choice for c is the best η_0 for small P. These results can be confirmed by simulations, see figure 1.

Another appealing property of the simple model is the fact that its optimal solution for batch training is known (Bös 1998). Analytical studies of batch training are more complicated, therefore only a few results on more general models are known. In figure 1, we compare optimally annealed online training with optimal batch training. It can clearly be seen that the online solution approaches the batch solution asymptotically, which is equivalent to online learning becoming efficient.

These results encourage us to look for solutions with annealed learning rates in multilayer neural networks. Unfortunately, we immediately encounter a new problem, the symmetric phase or plateaus, which makes an effective annealing very difficult.

4 Local–Update Leads to Plateaus

The application of the online update (3.1) to the committee machine yields the following *local update*,

$$\eta \Delta \mathbf{W}_k(t) = -\eta \nabla_{\mathbf{W}_k} \text{loss} \left[z^*(t), z(t) \right] . \tag{4.1}$$

It is local as it uses only the information available at the hidden unit k. Saad and Solla (1995, 1996) studied, how the committee machine learns, if online learning with a local update and a fixed learning rate η_0 is used. Figure 2 shows the characteristical behavior.

For small and for large t, the typical behavior of online learning with a fixed learning rate η_0 can be seen. It corresponds completely to the behavior, already observed in figure 1. However, in the intermediate range a new phenomenon was found. The generalization error is for a long time extremely slowly decreasing, resulting in a *plateau* of the learning curve. The reason for the plateau or *symmetric phase*, is the lack of specialization of the H sub–perceptrons of the committee machine. The symmetry can be seen in the values of the order parameters Q_{kl}, they are all nearly identical $Q_{kl} \simeq Q$. A geometrical interpretation of the symmetric phase is given in appendix B.

The system is trapped in this symmetric phase for quite a long time. The size of the learning rate η_0 determines, whether the plateau is left earlier or later, see figure 2. Consequently, if the learning rate is annealed from the start, the system will be trapped for a longer period. It is preferable to keep the learning rate at a reasonable value, such as 0.1, until the symmetric phase has been passed. Only then can annealing be applied, however it cannot be expected that efficiency will be reached anymore.

As the described problem can also occur in real applications using two–layer networks with variable second–layer weights, it is of major importance (LeCun 1998).

5 Non–local Update Can Avoid Plateaus

We have found a symmetric phase, that is the result of two or more sub–perceptrons of the committee machine being identical. The reason why the

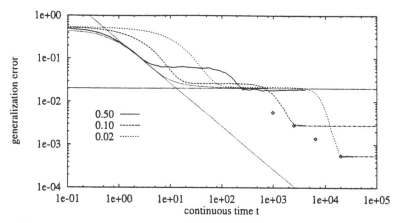

Fig. 2: Plateaus caused by local update. The committee machine with local update and fixed learning rate η_0. Simulation results corresponding to the analytical solution of Saad and Solla are shown. (Parameters and dotted lines: teacher and student are committee machines with $H = 3$, level of output noise $\sigma^2 = 0.1$, simulations use $N = 100$ averaged over 20 runs, same asymmetric initial conditions as in figure 3. In figures 2 to 6, three dotted lines are shown. The curved dotted line close to $t = 10$, results from simple annealing from the start. It converges into the horizontal one indicating the lowest plateau value for $\eta_0 = 0$. The diagonal one is the tangent to the fastest decrease of simple annealing.)

dynamics leads into this phase, is due to the lack of cooperation between the hidden units. The update was called local, as it updates each weight W_{ki} without taking the existence of other weights W_{li} into account. The update makes no use of the fact that other hidden units are available and that the task could possibly be solved faster, if the hidden units cooperate.

We think, it should be possible to achieve cooperation and thereby avoid the long trapping in the symmetric phase by using a *non–local update*, which facilitates information from all hidden units within each update,

$$\eta \,\Delta \mathbf{W}_k(t) = -\eta \sum_{l=1}^{H} (\mathbf{B}^{-1})_{kl} \, \nabla_{\mathbf{W}_l} \text{loss} \left[z^*(t), z(t) \right] . \tag{5.1}$$

Later we will see that it is useful to derive the coefficients, determining the strength given to each individual gradient, from the inverse of a matrix $\mathbf{B}$. Cooperation between different input sites i and j should not be necessary as long as the inputs are independently distributed, i.e. $\langle x_i x_j \rangle = \delta_{ij}$.

How should matrix $\mathbf{B}$ be chosen? Matrix $\mathbf{B}$ should depend only on measurable parameters that are related to the training process. This includes the parameters Q_{kl}, but not R_{kl} or S_{kl}, as they are unknown to the student. A possible choice for **B** has the following form,

$$B_{kl} = \frac{2}{\pi} \left(1 + Q_{kk} + Q_{ll} - 2 Q_{kl} \right)^{-\frac{1}{2}} . \tag{5.2}$$

This form was found empirically and has right now no theoretical basis. Nevertheless, the results of the simulations make this choice interesting.

Matrix **B** has one very important property, it is symmetric in k and l. This makes its inverse singular if the matrix **Q** does not have full rank, when the system is in a symmetric phase. This property also has implications on the *initial conditions*, which should be asymmetric. Without prior knowledge, we can determine the $Q_{kl}(0)$ by choosing the initial values of $\mathbf{W}_k(0)$. On the other hand, it is not possible to infer anything about the $R_{kl}(0)$. All we can know about them is, that they are of the order of random fluctuations. A possible choice for asymmetric initial conditions follows from randomly chosen $\mathbf{W}_k(0)$, if they fulfill,

$$Q_{kl}(0) \simeq k \, Q_0 \, \delta_{kl} . \tag{5.3}$$

Actually, these initial conditions were already used in the simulations of the local update of figure 2. Since the length of the plateaus depends on the initial conditions, a comparison would otherwise seem unjust.

5.1   Simulations

Now we are ready to test the non–local update using a fixed learning rate η_0. The results are shown in figure 3. Additional information about the other hidden units makes it easier to leave the neighborhood of the symmetric phase. The learning speed is accelerated and the final state is reached much earlier. The choice of **B** contains a nice property, because the same learning rate η_0 leads to the same final state as in the local update, see dotted horizontal lines in figures 2 and 3. However, the time needed to reach the final state is by a factor of 5 to 20 shorter than in the local update, see triangles and diamonds.

A closer look at the results reveals that the symmetric phase still has an effect on the learning curve. The system approaches the symmetric phase, but is not trapped anymore. The non–local dynamics would break down, if the system comes too close to the symmetric phase, i.e. $Q_{kl} \rightarrow Q$.

Annealing of the learning rate should not be started before the symmetric phase has been passed. The annealing scheme must therefore, fulfill the initial condition $\eta(t \rightarrow 0) = c$ and the asymptotic scaling $\eta(t \rightarrow \infty) = b/t$ again. Additionally, the learning rate should be large enough, such that the plateau can be passed as early as possible, i.e. $\eta(\tau) = d$. If we also want to optimize the behavior above the plateau, then the following two conditions for $\eta(t)$

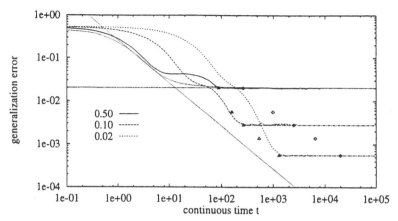

Fig. 3: Non–local update can avoid the plateaus. The results for non–local update with a fixed learning rate η_0 are shown. The final state is the same as in the local update, it is reached much earlier, and can be seen by the triangles and diamonds. (Parameters and dotted lines as in figure 2, initial conditions such that the $Q_{kl}(0) \simeq Q_0 \delta_{kl}$ with $Q_0 = 0.1$.)

hold,

$$\eta(t) = \begin{cases} c - (c - d)\, f(t, \tau) & t \le \tau \\ \left(\frac{1}{d} + \frac{t-\tau}{b}\right)^{-1} & t \ge \tau \end{cases} \quad \text{for} \quad , \qquad (5.4)$$

with a function $f(x)$ fulfilling $f(0) = 0$ and $f(1) = 1$.

It is necessary to optimize the parameters b, c, d and τ for the given task to achieve optimal performance. Only parameter b has influence on the asymptotical scaling, whereas d and τ only delay the onset of the asymptotical behavior. Furthermore, it is better to start with a value c higher than d and to reduce it slowly to d, if the performance above the plateau shall be optimized. Therefore, we use $f(t, \tau) = \log(1+t)/\log(1+\tau)$ instead of $f(t, \tau) = t/\tau$. The results of optimal annealing are shown in figure 4.

The learning curve of online learning with non–local update and annealed learning rate is also affected by the existence of the symmetric phase. The learning speed slows down in the neighborhood of the symmetric phase. After passing the plateau it accelerates again and is able to catch up with its fastest learning speed above the plateau, which is given by the tangent–line. The asymptotic convergence is reasonably fast, however, we do not know, whether it is efficient.

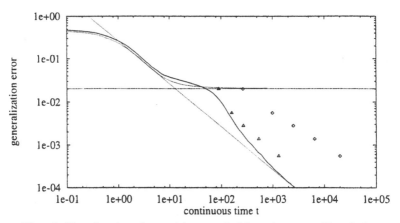

Fig. 4: Non–local update with annealed learning rate. Result for optimized annealing with non–local update is shown. The optimized parameters for this task are $b \simeq 6$, $c \simeq 0.6$, $d \simeq 0.1$ and $\tau \simeq 100$. The performance is affected by the symmetric phase, which slows the learning speed down. However, once the plateau is passed, learning speeds up again and it can catch up with its former fastest convergence, given by the dotted diagonal tangent. (Parameters and dotted lines as in figure 2)

6   Further Remarks

After discussing the advantage of an annealed learning rate on a simple model, the problem due to the existence of the symmetric phase in multilayer networks was explained. By introducing a non–local update on an empirical basis, we are able to avoid being trapped in the symmetric phase, thus making an earlier annealing possible.

However, the non–local update immediately provokes numerous new questions. For example, what is the best choice for the matrix **B** and is there a theoretical derivation for it? How can the annealing parameters, especially b, be determined? Is the asymptotical behavior efficient? What is the influence of the initial conditions? Finally, if the algorithm has proved to be reliable, then it should be extended to general two–layer networks with variable second–layer weights.

We are unable to answer all of these questions here. However, we will show that the effect shown in figure 3 is not due to a clever choice of the initial conditions. Next we will comment about a possible candidate for the theoretical support, which is the 'natural gradient' proposed by Amari (1998). Finally, we will summarize and briefly discuss several open tasks and questions. We hope that this discussion can provoke sufficient interest in these important questions such that the answers may be pursued in the future.

6.1 Initial Conditions

The time required to reach the final state in learning with a fixed learning rate η_0, is inversely proportional to the learning rate η_0,

$$T = c\,(\text{task, algorithm, initial conditions})\,\frac{1}{\eta_0}\,. \tag{6.1}$$

The constant c depends on the actual task, the used learning algorithm and the initial conditions. Here we will discuss the dependence on the initial conditions for the local and the non–local update. Results on symmetric initial conditions can be found in (Biehl, Riegler & Wöhler 1996).

We assume that we have no prior knowledge, we do not know the teacher weights $\mathbf{W}^*$ or the noise level σ. All we know about the initial values of the order parameters R_{kl} is that they are of the order of random fluctuations; we cannot choose them larger or smaller. However, we are completely free to choose the initial values of the student weights $\mathbf{W}(0)$. As pointed out, one should not start too close to symmetry. Therefore the following choice seems reasonable, $Q_{kl}(0) \simeq k\,Q_0\delta_{kl}$. It is probably a disadvantage to make them exactly orthogonal, since we do not know the orientation of the teacher. A bias can be useful to optimize the behavior for small t. For the comparison it is of no relevance. Different choices for Q_0 for the local and the non–local update were tested, and the results are shown in figure 5.

For the non–local update, we have found that Q_0 has to be larger than a minimal value, which is in our example $Q_0 > 0.04$. Smaller Q_0 values will lead into the symmetric phase where learning with the non–local update breaks down. The results for all larger Q_0 are quite close together. The local update works with arbitrary small initial conditions $Q_0 = \epsilon > 0$. However, very small values of Q_0 have negative effects, such that they prolong the period spent in the plateaus.

From figure 5 it can be observed, that the non–local update can reach the final state much faster than the local update independent of the choice for Q_0. The advantage of the non–local update is, therefore, not simply a result of a clever choice of the initial conditions.

6.2 The Natural Gradient

Theoretical support for the non–local update could come from the 'natural gradient', which was recently proposed by Amari (1998). Amari showed that an update of the form,

$$\eta\,\Delta W_{ki}(t) = -\eta \sum_{l=1}^{H} \sum_{j=1}^{N} (\mathbf{G}^{-1})_{ki,lj}\,\frac{\partial\,\text{loss}\,[z^*, z(t)]}{\partial W_{lj}}\,, \tag{6.2}$$

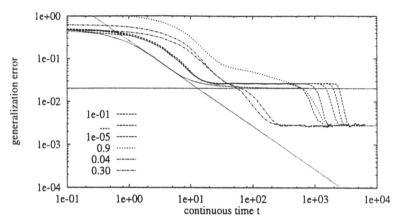

Fig. 5: Influence of the initial conditions on the length of the plateaus. For the local update (dashed lines), the very small values of Q_0 have a considerable effect on the length of the plateaus, see different choices for $Q_0 = 10^{-1}$, 10^{-2}, 10^{-3}, 10^{-4}, and 10^{-5} from left to right. Also a very large initial condition such as $Q_0 = 0.9$ (dash–dotted line) cannot make the plateau shorter. The initial conditions for the non–local update (solid lines) must be asymmetric. The value of Q_0 must, therefore, be larger than a minimal value, which is here 0.04. The lengths of the plateaus for larger Q_0, are all very similar. (Parameters and dotted lines as in figure 2, the learning rate is $\eta_0 = 0.2$)

with the matrix

$$G_{ki,lj} = \left\langle \left[\frac{\partial^2 \, \mathrm{loss}(z^*, z)}{\partial W_{ki} \, \partial W_{lj}} \right]_{z^*=z+\epsilon} \right\rangle_x, \qquad (6.3)$$

leads to the fastest convergence in Riemannian spaces. In many tasks it converges faster than the simple gradient descent given in (4.1). Applied to on-line learning, Amari also showed that online learning using the 'natural gradient' with an optimally annealed learning rate can become asymptotically efficient. Further details can be found in a recent paper (Amari 1998).

For the committee machine the 'natural gradient' can be explicitly calculated. The definition (6.3) applied to the committee machine gives

$$G_{ki,lj} = \langle g'(h_k) \, g'(h_l) \, x_i \, x_j \rangle_x. \qquad (6.4)$$

The calculation is somewhat technical and can be found in appendix C. The final result of the 'natural gradient' for the committee machine has the form,

$$\mathbf{G}_{kl} = \frac{2}{\pi} \left(\Theta_{kl} \right)^{-\frac{1}{2}} \left[\mathbf{I} - \frac{\mathbf{K}_{kl}}{\Theta_{kl}} \right], \qquad (6.5)$$

where $\mathbf{G}_{kl}$, $\mathbf{K}_{kl}$ and I are $N \times N$ matrices and the two abbreviations are

$$\Theta_{kl} := 1 + Q_{kk} + Q_{ll} + Q_{kk}\,Q_{ll} - Q_{kl}^2 \,, \tag{6.6}$$

and the matrix $\mathbf{K}_{kl}$

$$\mathbf{K}_{kl} := (1+Q_{ll})\,\mathbf{W}_k\mathbf{W}_k{}^T+(1+Q_{kk})\,\mathbf{W}_l\mathbf{W}_l{}^T-Q_{kl}\,(\mathbf{W}_k\mathbf{W}_l{}^T+\mathbf{W}_l\mathbf{W}_k{}^T). \tag{6.7}$$

If we want to relate the 'natural gradient' to the non–local update (5.1), then we have to face two problems. The proofs showing the merits of the 'natural gradient' are based on an asymptotical theory, i.e. they assume that the number of examples is large. It is therefore not obvious whether the 'natural gradient' is useful for the avoidance of the symmetric phase, which is a problem in the intermediate range.

Results on the dynamics of the full 'natural gradient' (6.2) can be found in (Rattray & Saad 1998, in this volume). These indicate that the 'natural gradient' is quite useful for the avoidance of the symmetric phase.

From (6.3), we can also see that $\mathbf{G}$ depends not only on the H hidden units, but also on the N input units. This would make a straightforward calculation of its inverse very time–consuming. However, it was shown by Yang and Amari (1997), that the inversion of $\mathbf{G}$ can be reduced to an inversion of several smaller H by H matrices.

The dynamics of the non–local update is much easier, as it requires only one matrix–inversion. Our assumption that it is probably sufficient in many cases to use the non–local update, was supported by the good performance of matrix $\mathbf{B}$. Unfortunately, we were unable to find a consistent simplification of the the 'natural gradient' $\mathbf{G}$ to a H by H matrix, such as $\mathbf{G}_{ki,lj} \to G_{kl}\,\delta_{ij}$. The smaller matrix G_{kl} should of course not sacrifice too much of the performance of the full 'natural gradient'.

While not consistent, we still believe that the following results are interesting enough for discussion. To simplify the 'natural gradient' matrix, we can use

$$\mathbf{W}_k\mathbf{W}_l{}^T \to Q_{kl}\,\mathrm{I}\,, \tag{6.8}$$

which simplifies $\mathbf{K}_{kl}$ to $K_{kl}\mathrm{I}$ with

$$K_{kl} = Q_{kk} + Q_{ll} + 2Q_{kk}Q_{ll} - 2Q_{kl}Q_{kl} = 2\Theta_{kl} - (2 + Q_{kk} + Q_{ll})\,. \tag{6.9}$$

The simplified 'natural gradient' $G_{kl}\,\delta_{ij}$ can be written as,

$$G_{kl} = \frac{2}{\pi}\,\Theta_{kl}^{-\frac{1}{2}}\left(\frac{2 + Q_{kk} + Q_{ll}}{\Theta_{kl}} + c\right), \tag{6.10}$$

with $c = -1$. We will also consider $c = 0$ and $c = +1$.

Results using a non–local update with the matrix G_{kl} and a fixed learning rate η_0 are shown in figure 6. The results for $c = -1$ corresponding to the

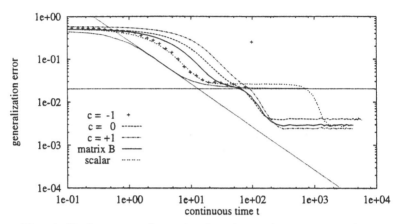

Fig. 6: Performance of non–local update using some matrices, which are closely related to the 'natural gradient'. The simplified 'natural gradient' corresponding to $c = -1$ does not converge. However, the results with $c = 0$ (dashed line) and $c = +1$ (dash–dotted line) are very close to the results achieved by **B** in figure 3 (shown by the solid line). The local update is shown for comparison as a double dashed line. (Parameters and dotted lines as in figure 2, the learning rate is $\eta_0 = 0.1$)

simplified 'natural gradient' are shown as crosses. They do not converge, if the learning rate is fixed. With an annealed learning rate, they sometimes converge, however the results are never as good as the ones shown in figure 4.

Surprisingly good results can be achieved by using $c = 0$ or 1. These are very close to the results produced using matrix **B**. Future research will need to show whether there is a consistent theory for the non–local update as a simplification of the 'natural gradient' or not[2].

6.3   Future Work

Aside from lacking theoretical support, there are several open tasks and questions, which have not been discussed here due to lack of time, space and arguments. They have been listed here and are ordered according to increasing importance and difficulty.

- Other tasks with different noise–levels σ, higher levels of nonlinearity, i.e. higher S values in $S_{kl} = S\,\delta_{kl}$, and different numbers H of hidden units should be tested.

---

[2]Visit our web–pages cited at the end of the paper for more recent results.

- Non-isotropic teachers with $S_{kk} \neq S_{ll}$ need to be investigated. This layout can result in several plateaus, the fully symmetric plateau and additional sub–plateaus.

- Unrealizable and overrealizable tasks due to different numbers of hidden units in teacher and student $H^* \neq H$ should be discussed.

- A detailed study of the dynamics of the non–local update is desirable. A first intuitive insight is given by (Yang & Amari 1997) using a very simplified model.

- Batch training should be discussed for comparison.

- Finally the approach should be extended to general multilayer networks, which have variable second–layer weights.

The first two tasks are rather straightforward tests, where we would not expect any real surprises. Some qualitative tests have been conducted and the results are as expected. More interesting is the application to tasks with different numbers of hidden units for teacher and student. The study of the dynamics can bear very interesting aspects.

Also a comparison with batch training would be interesting in several respects. Batch training is defined as

$$\eta \, \Delta \mathbf{W}_k(t) = -\eta \sum_{\mu=1}^{P} \nabla_{\mathbf{W}_k} \mathrm{loss}[\, z_\mu^*, z_\mu(t) \,] . \tag{6.11}$$

Here, the time t counts the iterations and is discrete.

Almost no detailed examinations of batch training in multilayer networks exist. Analytical studies are probably not feasible and simulations have not attracted much interest. Generally, batch training should be efficient, a comparison with online learning could solve the question whether the non–local update is efficient or not. It should be noted, that as the usual batch training (6.11) uses a simple gradient descent, it can also suffer from the lack of cooperation between the different hidden units.

Finally, the most important task is the extension of this approach to the general multilayer networks. The variable second–layer weights are necessary to turn the network into a general function approximator and therefore, only the results for these networks are of real practical interest.

7 Conclusion

In this paper a non–local or matrix update was proposed to accelerate online learning in multilayer neural networks. The proposed approach facilitates the updates of all hidden units and is therefore able to break the symmetry between the hidden units. It is based on a matrix inversion of a $H \times H$ matrix, and is feasible as long as the number of hidden units H is small. Until now the matrix update has only been proposed in theoretical proofs of the efficiency of online learning (Amari 1998), but has never been studied in an explicit application to a multilayer neural net. It is a generalization of the simple gradient descent learning and could also be useful in offline training. It should be emphasized that we are only at the beginning of our understanding of the matrix update. The promising results of this work should stimulate further interest in this direction.

Acknowledgements

We would like to thank D. Saad for the organization, and M. Biehl, K.-R. Müller, N. Murata, M. Opper, S Solla and all the other participants of the online themed week at the Newton Institute in Cambridge for stimulating discussions. Special thanks are given to E. Helle for her comments concerning the presentation.

Appendices

A Gaussian Averages

It is very common in statistical mechanics to calculate Gaussian averages. Since they appear in this work quite often, we want to explain it in more detail.

$$\langle F(x,y) \rangle_{x,y} = \int\limits_{-\infty}^{\infty} dx \int\limits_{-\infty}^{\infty} dy \, p(x,y) \, F(x,y), \qquad (A.1)$$

where $p(x,y)$ is the density of variables x and y.

Usually we have correlated Gaussian variables, with $x \in \mathcal{N}(0,\sqrt{a})$ and $y \in \mathcal{N}(0,\sqrt{b})$. and the cross–correlation $\langle xy \rangle = c$. The distribution $p(x,y)$ can be found in the literature,

$$p(x,y) = \frac{1}{2\pi\sqrt{ab-c^2}} \exp\left\{ -\frac{1}{2}\frac{bx^2 - 2cxy + ay^2}{ab-c^2} \right\}. \qquad (A.2)$$

We can transform the correlated Gaussian into uncorrelated normalized Gaussians, i.e. $\tilde{x}, \tilde{y} \in \mathcal{N}(0,1)$ and $\langle \tilde{x}\tilde{y} \rangle = 0$, by

$$x = \sqrt{a}\,\tilde{x}, \quad \text{and} \quad y = \frac{1}{\sqrt{a}}\left(c\tilde{x} - \sqrt{ab-c^2}\,\tilde{y} \right). \qquad (A.3)$$

The average is then

$$\langle F(x,y) \rangle_{\tilde{x},\tilde{y}} = \int\limits_{-\infty}^{\infty} D\tilde{x} \int\limits_{-\infty}^{\infty} D\tilde{y} \, F(x,y), \qquad (A.4)$$

where the x and y have to be expressed in the uncorrelated $\tilde{x}$ and $\tilde{y}$. It is very common to use $D\tilde{x}$ for the Gaussian measure

$$D\tilde{x} := \frac{d\tilde{x}}{\sqrt{2\pi}} \, e^{-\frac{\tilde{x}^2}{2}}. \qquad (A.5)$$

Gaussian averages are used to determine the generalization error and for the derivation of 'natural gradient' in appendix C.

The algebraic form of the generalization error follows from a special integral, which cannot be found in every integral table,

$$\int\limits_{-\infty}^{\infty} \frac{dx}{\sqrt{2\pi}} \int\limits_{-\infty}^{\infty} \frac{dy}{\sqrt{2\pi}} \operatorname{erf}\left(\frac{x}{\sqrt{2}}\right) \operatorname{erf}\left(\frac{y}{\sqrt{2}}\right) \exp\left(-\frac{ax^2 - 2cxy + by^2}{2} \right)$$

$$= \frac{2}{\pi\sqrt{ab-c^2}} \arcsin \frac{c}{\sqrt{(a+ab-c^2)(b+ab-c^2)}}. \qquad (A.6)$$

B   Geometrical Interpretation of the Plateaus

The plateaus in figure 2 are a result of the full–symmetrical phase, i.e all $Q_{kl} = Q$ and all $R_{kl} = R$. It is useful to examine this phase more carefully. We can define *normalized* order parameters,

$$Q_{kl} =: q_k \, q_l \, \cos \alpha_{kl} \,, \qquad R_{kl} =: s_k \, q_l \, \cos \beta_{kl} \,, \qquad (B.1)$$

where q_k is the norm of the vector $\mathbf{W}_k$ and s_k the norm of the teacher vector $\mathbf{W}_k^*$. For our isotropic teacher, all s_k are one. The angles α_{kl} and β_{kl} are selfexplanatory.

With the normalized order parameters, we can immediately see that $Q_{kl} = Q$ implies all student vectors $\mathbf{W}_k$ are identical. They are all identical to a vector $\mathbf{W}$, which has the norm $q = \sqrt{Q}$. The second condition, $R_{kl} = R$, furthermore implies that all angles β_{kl} are identical. The direction of the vector $\mathbf{W}$ is therefore symmetric to all $\mathbf{W}_k^*$. It is the $(1, \ldots, 1)$–direction in the H-dimensional subspace spanned by the isotropic teacher vectors $\mathbf{W}_k^*$. This makes $r := \cos \beta = 1/\sqrt{H}$.

Thus we only need to determine q. The generalization error in the symmetric phase can be expressed as a function of q and $r = H^{-\frac{1}{2}}$. It has the form,

$$E_{\mathrm{G}}(q, r) = \frac{H}{6} - \frac{H^2}{\pi} \left[2 \arcsin \frac{rq}{\sqrt{2(1 + q^2)}} - \arcsin \frac{q^2}{1 + q^2} \right]. \qquad (B.2)$$

The value of q on the plateau is the minimum of $E_{\mathrm{G}}(q, H^{-\frac{1}{2}})$. From $\frac{\partial E_{\mathrm{G}}}{\partial q} = 0$, we get

$$0 = -\frac{2H^2}{\pi(1 + q^2)} \left[\frac{r}{\sqrt{2 + q^2(2 - r^2)}} - \frac{q}{\sqrt{1 + 2q^2}} \right]. \qquad (B.3)$$

This condition is fulfilled for $q^2(2 - r^2) = r^2$, from which we get $Q = q^2$ and $R = rq$ and the plateau value,

$$Q = \frac{1}{2H - 1}, \quad R = \frac{1}{\sqrt{H(2H - 1)}}, \quad E_{\mathrm{G}} = \frac{H}{6} - \frac{H^2}{\pi} \arcsin \frac{1}{2H}. \quad (B.4)$$

The same values were found in a study of the dynamics (Saad & Solla, 1995).

From this interpretation we can learn that in the fully symmetric phase the student committee consists of H identical sub–perceptrons which only adjust the norm q of their weights until a further decrease of the generalization error is not possible anymore. A further decrease requires that the individual sub–perceptrons specialize on the different teacher sub–perceptrons $\mathbf{W}_k^*$. If this specialization is based on random fluctuations, then it takes a very long time.

Essentially, the student in the full symmetric phase is nothing other than a nonlinear single–layer perceptron with rescaled outputs $z \in [-H, H]$. As long as the performance is not better than that of the fully symmetric plateau value, there is no advantage in training a multilayer network.

C Derivation of G_{kl}

Beginning with the definition of the 'natural gradient' for the committee machine, we can calculate the matrix–elements by applying an orthonormal basis (ONB), such as $\sum_{o=1}^{N} \mathbf{V}_o \mathbf{V}_o^T = \mathbf{I}$, on both sides,

$$\sum_{o=1}^{N}\sum_{p=1}^{N} \mathbf{V}_o \mathbf{V}_o^T \, G_{kl} \, \mathbf{V}_p \mathbf{V}_p^T = \sum_{o,p=1}^{N} \langle g'(h_k)\, g'(h_l)\, \hat{h}_o \hat{h}_p \rangle \, \mathbf{V}_o \mathbf{V}_p^T. \qquad \text{(C.1)}$$

The vectors $\mathbf{V}_o$ of the ONB can be divided into two classes, $\mathbf{V}_1$ and $\mathbf{V}_2$ are a basis of the subspace spanned by $\mathbf{W}_k$ and $\mathbf{W}_l$, and the $\mathbf{V}_r$ are orthogonal to this subspace. The vectors $\mathbf{V}_1$ and $\mathbf{V}_2$ can be expressed by $\mathbf{W}_k$ and $\mathbf{W}_l$,

$$\begin{aligned}
\mathbf{V}_1 &:= (Q_{kk})^{-\frac{1}{2}}\, \mathbf{W}_k, & \text{(C.2)}\\
\mathbf{V}_2 &:= \left[Q_{kk}\left(Q_{kk}Q_{ll} - Q_{kl}^2 \right) \right]^{-\frac{1}{2}} \left(Q_{kk}\mathbf{W}_l - Q_{kl}\mathbf{W}_k \right).
\end{aligned}$$

The contribution of the vectors $\mathbf{V}_r$ with $r,s \neq k,l$ is

$$\sum_{r,s} \hat{h}_r \hat{h}_s \, \langle g'(h_k)\, g'(h_l) \rangle_{\tilde{h}_k, \tilde{h}_l} =: C_{kl}\left(\mathbf{I} - \mathbf{V}_1 \mathbf{V}_1^T - \mathbf{V}_2 \mathbf{V}_2^T \right), \qquad \text{(C.3)}$$

since $\hat{h}_r \hat{h}_s = \delta_{rs}$. The parameter C_{kl} is given by a Gaussian average, see appendix A,

$$C_{kl} = \frac{2}{\pi}\, (\Theta_{kl})^{-\frac{1}{2}}, \qquad \text{(C.4)}$$

where we introduce the following abbreviation

$$\Theta_{kl} := 1 + Q_{kk} + Q_{ll} + Q_{kk}Q_{ll} - Q_{kl}^2. \qquad \text{(C.5)}$$

The contribution of the vectors $\mathbf{V}_1$ and $\mathbf{V}_2$ from the subspace spanned by $\mathbf{W}_k$ and $\mathbf{W}_l$ is then

$$\sum_{n',m'} \left(\langle g'(h_k)\, g'(h_l)\, \hat{h}_{n'} \hat{h}_{m'} \rangle - C_{kl}\, \delta_{n'm'} \right) \mathbf{V}_{n'} \mathbf{V}_{m'}^T =: \sum_{n,m} D_{nm}^{kl}\, \mathbf{W}_n \mathbf{W}_m^T,$$

with $n',m' \in \{1,2\}$ and $n,m \in \{k,l\}$.

The combinations $\mathbf{V}_{n'} \mathbf{V}_{m'}^T$ can be expressed by combinations $\mathbf{W}_n \mathbf{W}_m^T$, if we use the definition (C.2). Also the Gaussian averages corresponding to combinations $\mathbf{V}_{n'} \mathbf{V}_{m'}^T$ can be expressed by Gaussian averages using combinations of $\mathbf{W}_n \mathbf{W}_m^T$,

$$\langle g'(h_k)\, g'(h_l)\, \hat{h}_{n'} \hat{h}_{m'} \rangle_{\tilde{h}_k, \tilde{h}_l} \quad \longrightarrow \quad \langle g'(h_k)\, g'(h_l)\, h_n h_m \rangle_{\tilde{h}_k, \tilde{h}_l} =: F_{nm}.$$

The Gaussian averages F_{nm} are

$$F_{kk} = \frac{2}{\pi} \Theta_{kl}^{-\frac{3}{2}} \left(Q_{kk} + Q_{kk}Q_{ll} - Q_{kl}^2 \right),$$

$$F_{kl} = \frac{2}{\pi} \Theta_{kl}^{-\frac{3}{2}} Q_{kl}, \qquad\qquad\qquad (C.6)$$

$$F_{ll} = \frac{2}{\pi} \Theta_{kl}^{-\frac{3}{2}} \left(Q_{ll} + Q_{ll}Q_{kk} - Q_{kl}^2 \right)$$

Finally, we find the values of the parameters D_{nm}^{kl},

$$D_{kk}^{kl} = -\frac{2}{\pi} \Theta_{kl}^{-\frac{3}{2}} \left(1 + Q_{ll} \right),$$

$$D_{kl}^{kl} = \frac{2}{\pi} \Theta_{kl}^{-\frac{3}{2}} Q_{kl}, \qquad\qquad\qquad (C.7)$$

$$D_{ll}^{kl} = -\frac{2}{\pi} \Theta_{kl}^{-\frac{3}{2}} \left(1 + Q_{kk} \right).$$

The full 'natural gradient' is received, if we insert C_{kl} and the D_{nm}^{kl} into

$$\mathbf{G}_{kl} = C_{kl} \mathbf{I} + \sum_{n,m} D_{nm}^{kl} \mathbf{W}_n \mathbf{W}_m^T. \qquad\qquad (C.8)$$

References

Amari, S., (1967) A theory of adaptive pattern classifiers, *IEEE Trans. Elect. Comput.* EC–16, 299–307.

Amari, S., (1998) Natural gradient works efficiently in learning, *Neural Comp.* 10, 251–276.

Biehl, M., and Schwarze, H., (1993) Learning drifting concepts with neural networks, *J. Phys. A* 26, 2651–2665.

Biehl, M., and Schwarze, H., (1995) Learning by online gradient descent, *J. Phys. A* 28, 643–656.

Biehl, M., Riegler, P., and Wöhler, C., (1996) Transient dynamics of on-line learning in two–layered neural networks, *J. Phys. A* 29, 4769–4780.

Bös, S., (1998) A statistical mechanics approach to early stopping and weight decay, to be published in *Phys. Rev. E.*

Bös, S., Murata, N., Amari, S., and Müller, K.-R., (1997) The role of the learning rate in on-line learning, preprint.

Bös, S., and Amari, S., (1997) Annealed on-line learning in nonlinear neural nets, in *Int. Conf. on Neural Information Processing (ICONIP'97)*, eds. N. Kasabov,

R. Kozma, K. Ko, R. o'Shea, G. Coghill, and T. Gedeon, (Springer Publisher, Singapore), p.318-321.

Bös, S., (1998) Accelerated on-line learning in multilayer neural nets, preprint. to be published in *J. of Phys. A*.

Kinouchi, O., and Caticha, N., (1992) Optimal generalization in perceptrons, *J. Phys. A* 25, 6243–6250.

LeCun, Y., (1998) (private communication)

Murata, N., (1992) PhD-thesis, University of Tokyo (in Japanese, unpublished).

Opper, M., (1996) Online versus Offline learning from random examples: General results, *Phys. Rev. Lett.* 77, 4671–4674.

Rattray, M., and Saad, D., (1997) Globally optimal on-line learning rules for multilayer networks, *J. Phys. A* 30, L771–776.

Rattray, M., and Saad, D., (1998) Incorporating curvature information into online learning, this volume.

Saad, D., and Solla, S. A., (1995a) On-line learning in soft committee machines, *Phys. Rev. E* 52, 4225–4243.

Saad, D., and Solla, S. A., (1995b) Exact solution for on-line learning in multilayer neural networks, *Phys. Rev. Lett.* 74, 4337–4340.

Saad, D., and Solla, S. A., (1996) Learning from corrupted examples in multilayer networks, preprint.

Saad, D., and Rattray, M., (1997) Globally optimal parameters for on-line learning in multilayer networks, *Phys. Rev. Lett.* 79, 2578–2581.

Vicente, R., and Caticha, N., (1997) Functional optimization of online algorithms in multilayer neural networks, *J. Phys. A* 30, L599–L605.

West, A. H. L., and Saad, D., (1996) Adaptive back-propagation in on-line learning of multilayer networks, in *Advances in Neural Information Processing Systems 8* eds. D. S. Touretzky, M. C. Mozer and M. E. Hasselmo, (Cambridge, MA: The MIT Press) p. 321-327.

West, A. H. L., and Saad, D., (1997) On-line learning with adaptive back-propagation in two–layer networks, *Phys. Rev. E* 56, 3426–3445.

Yang, H. H., and Amari, S., (1997) Natural gradient descent for training multilayer perceptrons, preprint.

For preprints of related works, visit the web–page:
http://www.bip.riken.go.jp/irl/boes/boes.html
http://www.bip.riken.go.jp/irl/amari/pub_j.html

On–line Learning of Prototypes and Principal Components

M. Biehl [†], A. Freking, M. Hölzer, G. Reents, and E. Schlösser

Institut für Theoretische Physik
Universität Würzburg
Am Hubland
D–97074 Würzburg, Germany
† *biehl@physik.uni-wuerzburg.de*

Abstract

We review our recent investigation of on–line unsupervised learning from high–dimensional structured data. First, on–line competitive
learning is studied as a method for the identification of prototype vectors from overlapping clusters of examples. Specifically, we analyse the
dynamics of the well–known winner–takes–all or K–means algorithm.
As a second standard learning technique, the application of Sanger's
rule for principal component analysis is investigated. In both scenarios
the necessary process of student specialization may be delayed significantly due to underlying symmetries.

1   Introduction

Methods from statistical physics have been applied to the theory of adaptive
systems with great success in recent years. Perhaps the most prominent example is the analysis of feedforward neural networks which can learn from
example data. The statistical mechanics approach allows to investigate typical properties of very large systems on average over the randomness contained
in the data. It complements results from computational learning theory and
other disciplines.

Most of the investigations concern the supervised learning of a rule. For reviews of the field see for instance (Watkin *et al.* 1993; Opper and Kinzel, 1996).
A particularly successful line of research was initiated in (Kinzel and Rujan,
1990; Kinouchi and Caticha, 1992) and aims at the analysis of the physics
of on–line learning schemes (Amari, 1967 and 1993; Hertz *et al.*, 1991). On–
line learning is attractive from a practical point of view because it uses only
the latest in the sequence of examples. Obviously storage needs and computational effort are reduced in comparison with batch– or off–line learning
(Hertz *et al.*, 1991).

On the other hand, the simplicity of on–line algorithms has allowed to study a variety of learning scenarios and network architectures, including the simple perceptron (e.g. Kinzel and Rujan, 1990; Kinouchi and Caticha, 1992) and multilayered networks with threshold units (e.g. Sompolinsky *et al.*, 1995, Copelli and Caticha, 1995) or sigmoidal activation functions respectively (e.g. Saad and Solla, 1995; Biehl *et al.*, 1996). Despite their simplicity, on–line algorithms compete well with costly off–line prescriptions (e.g. Kinouchi and Caticha, 1992; Opper, 1996; van den Broeck and Reimann, 1996; Kim and Sompolinsky, 1996; Copelli *et al.*, 1997).

Models of unsupervised learning have also been studied in the statistical mechanics framework, see e.g. (Biehl and Mietzner, 1994; Watkin and Nadal, 1994; Barkai and Sompolinsky, 1994; Lootens and van den Broeck, 1995). The investigation of on–line unsupervised learning schemes (Biehl, 1994; van den Broeck and Reimann, 1996) has provided new insights in this context as well.

In the following we review our recent investigation of on–line unsupervised learning from high–dimensional structured data (Biehl *et al.*,1997; Biehl and Schlösser, 1998). In the next section, on–line competitive learning is discussed as a method for the identification of prototype vectors from overlapping clusters of examples. Here, the focus will be on the well–known *winner–takes–all* or *K–means* algorithm (Duda and Hart, 1973; Hertz *et al.*, 1991; Bishop, 1995). Section 3 revisits a second standard unsupervised learning technique: the identification of principal components by means of Sanger's rule (Sanger, 1989; Hertz *et al.*, 1991; Bishop, 1995).

In all these scenarios, the necessary process of student specialization can be delayed significantly. This effect is due to underlying symmetries which result in quasi–stationary plateau configurations in the learning dynamics.

We conclude with a summary of the main results and a discussion of possible extensions in section 4.

2   Competitive Learning

2.1   The Model

One of the possible objectives of unsupervised learning is the identification of prototype vectors from a given set of data $\left\{ \boldsymbol{\xi}^\mu \in I\!\!R^N \right\}$ ($\mu = 1, \ldots, P$). The aim is to find a faithful representation of this set by use of only a few typical vectors $\left\{ \boldsymbol{J}_k \in I\!\!R^N \right\}$ ($k = 1, \ldots, K \ll P$) which capture the relevant features of the data. This is closely related to (yet not identical with) *clustering problems*, where the goal is to group the vectors $\boldsymbol{\xi}^\mu$ into several sets of similar inputs (Hertz *et al.*, 1991; Bishop, 1995).

Frequently, the identification of prototypes is guided by the Euclidean distances

$$d_k(\boldsymbol{\xi}) = (\boldsymbol{\xi} - \boldsymbol{J}_k)^2. \tag{2.1}$$

In particular, the family of so–called competitive learning algorithms updates the students $\boldsymbol{J}_k$ according to a prescription of the generic form

$$\boldsymbol{J}_k^\mu = \boldsymbol{J}_k^{\mu-1} + \frac{\eta}{N} \left(\boldsymbol{\xi}^\mu - \boldsymbol{J}_k^{\mu-1} \right) \, p_k \left(\{d_k^\mu\} \right) \tag{2.2}$$

The change of the weight vectors is always along $(\boldsymbol{\xi}^\mu - \boldsymbol{J}_k^{\mu-1})$, i.e. the proto-types are moved in the direction of the presented example. The step size of this change is determined by the learning rate $\eta > 0$ which is scaled with the dimension N of the data.

The factors p_k define the actual algorithm. Here, they are taken to be non-negative functions of the set of distances $d_k^\mu = (\boldsymbol{\xi}^\mu - \boldsymbol{J}_k^{\mu-1})^2$ and obey the normalization constraint

$$\sum_{k=1}^{K} p_k \left(\{d_k^\mu\} \right) = 1 \tag{2.3}$$

which fixes the total contribution of a single example to the learning process. Typically, a specific example will affect the prototypes which are closest in distance more efficiently than others. This *competition* of the students for updates is controlled by the assignment or labeling functions p_k.

Note that no normalization constraint is imposed on the student vectors. This is in contrast to models of directional clustering, where only characteristic directions are searched in input space (Biehl and Mietzner, 1994; Watkin and Nadal, 1994; Lootens and van den Broeck, 1995). In the following, the magnitude of the student vectors is $\boldsymbol{J}_k^2 = \mathcal{O}(1)$, whereas $\boldsymbol{\xi}^2 = \mathcal{O}(N)$ holds true for the example data.

We restrict the analysis to the case of only two prototype vectors $\boldsymbol{J}_1$ and $\boldsymbol{J}_2$ in an environment which provides a sequence of independent data drawn from a stochastic source. We assume a bimodal input distribution of the specific form

$$P(\boldsymbol{\xi}) = \frac{1}{2} \sum_{m=1}^{2} P(\boldsymbol{\xi}|m) \quad \text{where} \quad P(\boldsymbol{\xi}|m) = \frac{1}{(2\pi)^{N/2}} \exp\left[-\frac{1}{2} (\boldsymbol{\xi} - b\,\boldsymbol{B}_m)^2 \right].$$
$$\tag{2.4}$$

which corresponds to a mixture of two overlapping Gaussians centered at $b\,\boldsymbol{B}_m$. We take the characteristic vectors $\boldsymbol{B}_m$ to be orthogonal and normalized $(\boldsymbol{B}_k\cdot\boldsymbol{B}_m = \delta_{km})$. Hence, the quantity $b > 0$ specifies the offset of the respective cluster centers from the origin. The dummy variable m indicates from which of the clusters $\boldsymbol{\xi}$ is drawn, both centers contribute with the same probability $1/2$.

The assumed data distribution is only weakly anisotropic: Given the cluster label m, the distance of the conditional mean $b\,\boldsymbol{B}_m$ from the origin is $b = \mathcal{O}(1)$, whereas the average length of input vectors is $\mathcal{O}(\sqrt{N})$. Similar clustered input distributions have been studied in various models of unsupervised learning as well as in supervised scenarios, see e.g. (Biehl and Mietzner, 1994; Watkin and Nadal, 1994; Barkai and Sompolinsky, 1994; Meir, 1995; Marangi et al., 1995). Note that here, of course, the labels $m = 1, 2$ are not provided with the example data.

We proceed by investigating the model in the thermodynamic limit $N \rightarrow \infty$. The random quantities $x_m = \boldsymbol{J}_m \cdot \boldsymbol{\xi}$ and $y_m = \boldsymbol{B}_m \cdot \boldsymbol{\xi}$ are distributed according to a mixture of Gaussians as well. By means of the central limit theorem this holds true for more general $P(\boldsymbol{\xi}|m)$ in the limit $N \rightarrow \infty$, provided the first and second moments are the same as in (2.4). The joint density of the overlaps is uniquely determined by their conditional averages and covariances:

$$
\begin{aligned}
\langle x_j x_k \rangle_n - \langle x_j \rangle_n \langle x_k \rangle_n &= Q_{jk} = \boldsymbol{J}_j \cdot \boldsymbol{J}_k \\
\langle x_k y_m \rangle_n - \langle x_k \rangle_n \langle y_m \rangle_n &= R_{km} = \boldsymbol{J}_k \cdot \boldsymbol{B}_m \\
\langle y_l y_m \rangle_n - \langle y_l \rangle_n \langle y_m \rangle_n &= \delta_{lm} = \boldsymbol{B}_l \cdot \boldsymbol{B}_m \\
\langle x_k \rangle_n = b\, R_{kn} \quad \text{and} \quad \langle y_m \rangle_n &= b\, \delta_{mn}
\end{aligned}
\tag{2.5}
$$

Here and in the following $\langle \cdots \rangle_n$ denotes the average over the contribution $P(\boldsymbol{\xi}|n)$ to the mixture density (2.4). Averages over the full joint density of $\{x_1, x_2, y_1, y_2\}$ are to be calculated as a sum of conditional means, one obtains for example

$$
\langle x_1 \rangle = \frac{1}{2} \left(\langle x_1 \rangle_1 + \langle x_1 \rangle_2 \right) = \frac{1}{2} b \left(R_{11} + R_{12} \right).
$$

2.2   The Dynamics of Learning

In the thermodynamic limit $N \rightarrow \infty$ the set of self–averaging order parameters Q_{jk} and R_{km} is sufficient for a macroscopical description of the system. Further, the dynamics of the learning process can be analysed exactly in terms of these quantities. To this end we derive from (2.2) recursion relations for the evolution of the Q_{jk} and R_{km}, which are then averaged over the latest random input vector. This is possible because the randomness of the data enters only through the projections $\{x_k, y_k\}$. Thus, all averages are over the four–dimensional Gaussian density which is specified by its moments (2.5).

In terms of the continuous time $\alpha = \mu/N$ the dynamics is now described by a set of coupled first order differential equations, see e.g. (Biehl and Schwarze, 1995) and (Saad and Solla, 1995) for a more detailed description of the formalism in the context of supervised learning. A discussion of self–averaging in on–line learning can be found in (Reents and Urbanczik, 1998).

Here, the obtained system of differential equations reads

$$
\frac{dR_{km}}{d\alpha} = \eta \left\langle (y_m - R_{km})\, p_k \right\rangle
$$

$$
\tag{2.6}
$$

$$
\frac{dQ_{lm}}{d\alpha} = \eta \left\langle (x_l - Q_{lm})\, p_m + (x_m - Q_{lm})\, p_l \right\rangle + \eta^2 \left\langle p_l\, p_m \right\rangle
$$

where the arguments of the assignment functions have been omitted for simplicity. For a discussion of the essential properties of our model we restrict the analysis to a partially symmetric subspace where

$$Q_{11} = Q_{22} = Q, \quad Q_{12} = Q_{21} = C, \quad R_{11} = R_{22} = R, \quad R_{12} = R_{21} = S \quad (2.7)$$

In all cases investigated here, the dynamics (2.6) preserves this symmetry. We observe furthermore that, even if the initial conditions violate (2.7), the system approaches the restricted subspace (or an equivalent one with relabeled students) after a short transient. This is analogous to the findings of e.g. (Saad and Solla 1995) and (Biehl *et al.*, 1996) with respect to supervised learning schemes.

In systems with two students only, a substantial simplification is achieved by introducing the following linear combinations of order parameters:

$$R_{\pm} = R \pm S \quad \text{and} \quad Q_{\pm} = Q \pm C. \quad (2.8)$$

In terms of these quantities and under the symmetry assumption (2.7) the equations of motion (2.6) are of the following form:

$$\frac{dR_+}{d\alpha} = \frac{\eta}{2}(b - R_+) \qquad \frac{dQ_+}{d\alpha} = \frac{\eta}{2}(2bR_+ - 2Q_+ + \eta) \qquad (2.9)$$

$$\frac{dR_-}{d\alpha} = \frac{\eta}{2}(\langle\langle(y_1 - y_2)(p_1 - p_2)\rangle\rangle - \langle p_1 - p_2\rangle R_-)$$

$$(2.10)$$

$$\frac{dQ_-}{d\alpha} = \eta(\langle\langle(x_1 - x_2)(p_1 - p_2)\rangle\rangle - \langle p_1 - p_2\rangle Q_-) + \frac{\eta^2}{2}\langle(p_1 - p_2)^2\rangle.$$

Here we have used the properties

$$p_1 + p_2 = 1 \quad \text{and} \quad \langle p_{1,2}\rangle = 1/2 \quad (2.11)$$

of the input distribution and assignment functions.

Note that the dynamics of R_+ and Q_+ decouples from the remaining equations. Remarkably, Eqs. (2.9) are independent of the specific learning algorithm provided it satisfies the conditions (2.11). Hence, for two prototypes in the presence of the bimodal input distribution (2.4), the temporal evolution of R_+ and Q_+ is the same for all competitive learning schemes and can be studied beforehand. We obtain the analytic solution

$$R_+(\alpha) = b + Ae^{-\eta\alpha/2}$$
$$Q_+(\alpha) = \frac{\eta}{2} + b^2 + 2bAe^{-\eta\alpha/2} + Be^{-\eta\alpha} \quad (2.12)$$

where the constants $A = R_+(0) - b$ and $B = -\eta/2 + b^2 + Q_+(0) - 2bR_+(0)$ depend on the initial conditions. The asymptotic ($\alpha \to \infty$) configuration $R_+ = b$ and

$Q_+ = b^2 + \eta/2$ represents the only fixed point of the subsystem (2.9) and is approached exponentially fast with increasing α from all initial settings and for all values of η.

The quantity R_+ measures the overlaps of the prototype vectors with the sum $(\boldsymbol{B}_1 + \boldsymbol{B}_2)$. It therefore marks the unspecialized identification of the direction in which the center of mass of the input distribution is found.

On the contrary, the overlap $R_- = \boldsymbol{J}_1 \cdot (\boldsymbol{B}_1 - \boldsymbol{B}_2) = \boldsymbol{J}_2 \cdot (\boldsymbol{B}_2 - \boldsymbol{B}_1)$ quantifies the *specialization* of the students which is, in a way, the genuine aim of competitive learning.

2.3   The Specialization Process

We will investigate the dynamics of the specialization process for a particularly simple and efficient choice for the labeling functions:

$$p_k = \prod_{\substack{j=1 \\ j \neq k}}^{K} \Theta(d_j^\mu - d_k^\mu) = \begin{cases} 1 & \text{if } d_k^\mu < d_j^\mu \text{ for all } j \neq k \\ 0 & \text{else.} \end{cases} \tag{2.13}$$

The corresponding training scheme updates at each time step only the student with the minimal distance to the current input. All other $K-1$ prototypes remain unchanged, hence the term *winner–takes–all*–algorithm has been coined for this prescription (Hertz et al., 1991). It is identical with an on–line realization of the well–known K-*means*–algorithm (Duda and Hart, 1973; Bishop, 1995).

The resulting prescription can be interpreted as the stochastic gradient descent minimization of an instantaneous energy

$$\varepsilon\left(\boldsymbol{\xi}^\mu\right) = \frac{1}{2} \sum_{k=1}^{K} d_k^\mu \, p_k - \frac{1}{2}(\boldsymbol{\xi}^\mu)^2 \tag{2.14}$$

which measures the *representation error* of input vector $\boldsymbol{\xi}^\mu$ in terms of Euclidean distances, see (Hertz et al., 1991; Biehl et al., 1997) for details.

As the change of weights is always in the direction $(\boldsymbol{\xi}^\mu - \boldsymbol{J}^{\mu-1})$, the updated prototype will be the *winner* for similar examples later in the sequence with even higher probability. Therefore, the strategy should yield specialized prototypes, each of which represents a region in input space where many examples have been observed in the course of learning.

For two competing students Eq. (2.13) reduces to

$$p_1 = \Theta(d_2^\mu - d_1^\mu) \qquad p_2 = \Theta(d_1^\mu - d_2^\mu) = 1 - p_1. \tag{2.15}$$

By use of the property $p_k p_m = p_k \delta_{km}$ of the Heaviside–function all averages in the Eqs. (2.10) can be performed analytically and one obtains

$$\frac{dR_-}{d\alpha} = \frac{\eta}{2}\left(-b - R_- + 2b\Phi\left[\frac{bR_-}{\sqrt{2Q_-}}\right] + \frac{2R_-}{\sqrt{\pi Q_-}}\exp\left[-\frac{b^2 R_-^2}{4Q_-}\right]\right)$$

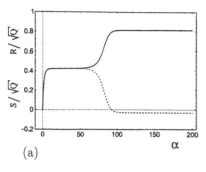

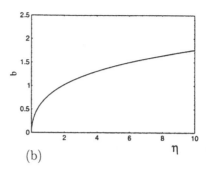

(a)   (b)

Fig. 1   (winner–takes–all algorithm)
(a) Normalized order parameters $R/\sqrt{Q}$ (solid) and $S/\sqrt{Q}$ (dashed)
vs. α for $\eta = 1$, $b = 1.2$. Here, initial conditions were $R(0) = 10^{-6}$,
$S(0) = C(0) = 0$, and $Q(0) = 1$.
(b) The critical learning rate η_c (2.18) separates values of η and b for
which the plateau state is stable from those which allow the specialization of prototypes.

$$(2.16)$$

$$\frac{dQ_-}{d\alpha} = \frac{\eta}{2}\left(\eta - 2Q_- - 2bR_- + 4bR_-\,\Phi\left[\frac{bR_-}{\sqrt{2Q_-}}\right] + \frac{4\sqrt{Q_-}}{\sqrt{\pi}}\exp\left[-\frac{b^2R_-^2}{4Q_-}\right]\right)$$

where $\Phi[x] = \displaystyle\int_{-\infty}^{x} \frac{dy}{\sqrt{2\pi}}e^{-y^2/2} = \frac{1}{2}\left(1 + \mathrm{erf}\left[x/\sqrt{2}\right]\right).$

The two subsystems for R_+, Q_+ and R_-, Q_- decouple completely in this
model: (2.16) is independent of (2.9) and vice versa. However, in order to
evaluate the original order parameters $\{R, S, Q, C\}$ as functions of α one has
to combine the analytic result (2.12) with the numerical integration of the
above set of equations.

Figure 1 (a) displays, as an example, the resulting learning curves (normal-
ized overlaps $R/\sqrt{Q}$ and $S/\sqrt{Q}$ vs. α) for $\eta = 1$, $b = 1.2$ and initial conditions
$R(0) = 10^{-6}$, $S(0) = C(0) = 0$, $Q(0) = 1$. These correspond to normalized,
orthogonal student vectors with very small initial overlaps R and specialization $R_- = R - S$. Note that for randomly drawn N–dimensional vectors one
would expect random values $R(0)$ and $S(0)$ of the order $\mathcal{O}(1/\sqrt{N})$ in realistic
learning scenarios with no a priori knowledge.

As shown in the Fig. 1 (a), the overlaps R and S increase rapidly for small
α but without achieving considerable specialization $R_- = R - S$. Only after
an extended plateau–like phase of the dynamics with almost constant order
parameters, the specialization increases drastically and the system approaches
an apparently stable configuration with $R_- = \mathcal{O}(1)$ for large α.

In order to gain a theoretical understanding of the observed behavior we study the fixed point structure of (2.16). For all fixed points, the values of R_+ and Q_+ are given by the asymptotic form $(\alpha \to \infty)$ form of Eqs. (2.12). We observe that configurations with

$$R_- = 0, \qquad Q_- = Q_-^{(\pm)} = \frac{4 + \eta\,\pi \pm 2\,\sqrt{4 + 2\eta\pi}}{2\,\pi} \qquad (2.17)$$

are stationary under the dynamics (2.16). A linearization of the system shows that the fixed point $(0, Q_-^{(-)})$ is always repulsive, whereas $(0, Q_-^{(+)})$ becomes attractive for

$$\eta > \eta_c = \frac{2}{\pi}\left(b^4 + 2b^2\right) \qquad (2.18)$$

which defines a critical learning rate of the process. In Fig. 1 (b) it is shown as a line in the (η, b)–plane which separates the region in which no specialization occurs from the one with a non–zero asymptotic value of R_-.

For small enough learning rates $\eta \leq \eta_c$ all fixed points with $R_- = 0$ are repulsive and the students will eventually specialize upon presentation of an increasing number of examples. However, generic initial conditions with $R \approx S \approx 0$ will cause the system to approach a state in the vicinity of (2.17). A linearization around the fixed point $(0, Q_-^{(+)})$ shows that the specialization increases exponentially with α: $R_- \propto R_-(0)\,e^{\lambda\alpha}$ where λ is the relevant eigenvalue of the linearized system. The characteristic time needed to achieve significant specialization $R_- = \mathcal{O}(1)$ is therefore proportional to $-\ln[R_-(0)]/\lambda$.

This behavior is strongly reminiscent of the plateau states which have been found to delay supervised learning by gradient descent in multilayered networks (Biehl and Schwarze, 1995; Saad and Solla, 1995; Biehl *et al.*, 1996), see other contributions to this volume. Note, however, that the dominant plateau in the winner–takes–all scenario is *not* characterized by almost identical student vectors. An effective mutual repulsion is imposed on the prototype vectors due to the pronounced competitive nature of the learning algorithm. At each time step only one of the students can be updated even if $J_1 \approx J_2$. The prototypes separate very fast, however their projections in the (B_1, B_2)–plane are almost equal in the plateau state.

Eventually the system approaches a stable configuration where R_- and Q_- satisfy the conditions

$$Q_- = \frac{\eta^2}{8} \frac{r_-^2}{\left(\Phi\left[r_-\right] - \frac{1}{2}\right)^2 (b^2 - 2r_-^2)^2}$$

$$(2.19)$$

$$\frac{e^{-r_-^2/2}}{\sqrt{\pi}} = \frac{\sqrt{Q_-}}{2} - \frac{b^2\left(\Phi\left[r_-\right] - \frac{1}{2}\right)}{\sqrt{2}\,r_-}$$

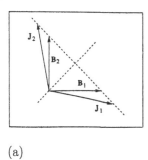

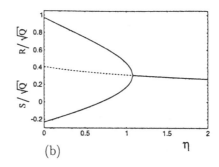

(a)   (b) η

Fig. 2   (winner–takes–all algorithm)
(a) The asymptotic configuration for $\eta \to 0$ (sketch), see the discussion
in the text.
(b) Asymptotic values of the normalized $R/\sqrt{Q}$ and $S/\sqrt{Q}$ for a cluster
offset $b = 0.8$. For learning rates $\eta > \eta_c \approx 1.08$ the prototypes do not
specialize, below η_c the plateau state is unstable (dashed line) and a
fixed point with non–zero R_- becomes attractive.

with the abbreviation $r_- = bR_-/\sqrt{2Q_-}$. In general, these fixed point values
have to be obtained numerically. The limit of small learning rates $\eta \to 0$
yields

$$R_- = \sqrt{Q_-} = -b + 2\,b\,\Phi\left[\frac{b}{\sqrt{2}}\right] + \frac{2}{\sqrt{\pi}}\exp\left[-\frac{b^2}{4}\right], \quad \text{i.e.} \quad r_- = \frac{b}{\sqrt{2}}. \quad (2.20)$$

This asymptotic configuration of the system is characterized by student
vectors which are linear combinations of the B_k and obey

$$(J_1 - J_2) \propto (B_1 - B_2).$$

Note, however, that this does not imply a perfect alignment or even identity
of the J_k which one of the cluster centers. The above mentioned energy
function (2.14) favors indeed well separated prototypes which are, in a sense,
more typical for the data than the actual centers of the overlapping clusters.

Figure 2 (a) shows the asymptotic configuration for $\eta \to 0$ schematically.
For non–zero $\eta < \eta_c$ the picture remains qualitatively the same, however,
contributions from the space orthogonal to B_1 and B_2 persist even in the limit
$\alpha \to \infty$. For practical purposes, an appropriate time dependent, decaying
learning rate should be used with $\eta \propto 1/\alpha$ for large α (e.g. Bishop, 1995). In
Fig. 2 (b) the asymptotic values of R and S are displayed as a function of the
learning rate for a specific cluster offset b.

3   Principal Component Analysis

3.1   The Model

Another important problem in data analysis is the faithful representation of high-dimensional data by low–dimensional feature vectors which contain as much information about the original inputs as possible.

One standard method for this task is principal component analysis (PCA). It determines, for a given set of observed data, the eigenvectors of the empirical covariance matrix which correspond to its largest eigenvalues. Projections on these characteristic vectors serve as a useful linear representation of the data, see e.g. (Hertz *et al.*, 1991; Bishop, 1995; Deco and Obradovic, 1996) for the theoretical background.

The purpose of competitive learning is to provide (few) typical prototype vectors of the same dimensionality as the (many) original input vectors. On the contrary, PCA aims at the low–dimensional representation of each of the examples by detecting the most relevant features of the data.

Principal component analysis takes into account only first and second moments of the observed data (i.e. their covariance matrix). Hence, we can consider a particularly simple model distribution in the following. Input vectors $\boldsymbol{\xi}$ are taken to consist of random components independently drawn from zero mean Gaussian distributions. We assume that M relevant directions $\{\boldsymbol{B}_i\}_{i=1,\dots,M}$ in $I\!\!R^N$ (with $M \ll N$) exist which determine the correlation matrix $C = \left\langle \boldsymbol{\xi}\boldsymbol{\xi}^\top \right\rangle$:

$$C = I_N + \sum_{i=1}^{M}(b_i^2 + 2b_i)\boldsymbol{B}_i\boldsymbol{B}_i^\top \qquad (3.1)$$

with the N–dimensional identity matrix I_N. The vectors $\{\boldsymbol{B}_i\}$ are taken to be orthogonal and normalized: $\boldsymbol{B}_i\cdot\boldsymbol{B}_j = \delta_{ij}$. This weakly anisotropic distribution can be interpreted as the result of deforming a single, isotropic Gaussian cluster with data points $\tilde{\boldsymbol{\xi}} \in I\!\!R^N$:

$$\boldsymbol{\xi} = \tilde{\boldsymbol{\xi}} + \sum_{i=1}^{M} b_i(\boldsymbol{B}_i \cdot \tilde{\boldsymbol{\xi}})\boldsymbol{B}_i. \qquad (3.2)$$

Distributions of this type have been previously considered in e.g. (Lootens and van den Broeck, 1995).

The directions B_i are, by construction, the eigenvectors of C corresponding to eigenvalues $(1 + b_i)^2$. Assuming $b_1 \geq b_2 \geq \dots \geq b_M > 0$ without loss of generality, the set of vectors $\boldsymbol{B}_i$ coincides therefore with the ordered principal components of the data distribution.

As before, we assume that the environment generates a sequence of independent example vectors $\boldsymbol{\xi}^\mu$ according to the above input distribution. A matching number of student vectors $\boldsymbol{J}_l \in \mathbb{R}^N$ $(l = 1, 2, \ldots, M)$ is updated following Sanger's rule (Sanger, 1989; Hertz *et al.*, 1991) when a new example is presented:

$$\boldsymbol{J}_l^\mu = \boldsymbol{J}_l^{\mu-1} + \frac{\eta_l}{N} x_l^\mu \left(\boldsymbol{\xi}^\mu - \sum_{k=1}^{l} x_k^\mu \boldsymbol{J}_k^{\mu-1} \right), \qquad (3.3)$$

with the student projections $x_l^\mu = \boldsymbol{J}_l^{\mu-1} \cdot \boldsymbol{\xi}^\mu$.

The learning rates η_l control the step size of the updates for the students. In contrast to the previous section we include the possibility of using different rates for different $\boldsymbol{J}_k$.

For small learning rates $\eta_l \rightarrow 0$ one can show that Sanger's rule yields normalized vectors (Hertz *et al.*, 1991). Throughout this paper, however, we assume that an explicit normalization at each time step μ guarantees $\boldsymbol{J}_l^2 = 1$ for all μ. This introduces additional terms of order η_l^2/N in the full form of the algorithm, see (Biehl, 1994) for the case $M = 1$.

The prescription (3.3) leads to an ordering of the student vectors which (in general) corresponds to the identification of one $\boldsymbol{B}_i$ by each student when a large number of examples is presented (Hertz *et al.*, 1991). An alternative scheme was suggested by Oja (Oja, 1982, Oja and Karhunen, 1985, Hertz *et al.*, 1991, Oja, 1996) and has been proven to provide an arbitrary basis of the subspace spanned by the $\{\boldsymbol{B}_i\}$, the actual result depends on the initial choice of the $\boldsymbol{J}_l(0)$.

Again, the analysis is based on the fact that the quantities x_k and $y_j = \boldsymbol{B}_j \cdot \boldsymbol{\xi}$ (indices μ omitted) are Gaussian variables. In the thermodynamic limit this holds true for more general input vectors consisting of non–Gaussian random components ξ_i with the same second order statistics. Here, the relevant moments are

$$\langle x_k y_l \rangle = (1 + b_l)^2 R_{kl}, \qquad \langle y_k y_l \rangle = \delta_{kl} (1 + b_k)^2, \qquad (3.4)$$

$$\langle x_k x_l \rangle = Q_{kl} + \sum_{i=1}^{M} (b_i^2 + 2b_i) R_{li} R_{ki}, \qquad (3.5)$$

and $\langle x_k \rangle = \langle y_k \rangle = 0$ for all k. The order parameters $R_{kl} = \boldsymbol{J}_k \cdot \boldsymbol{B}_l$ and $Q_{kl} = \boldsymbol{J}_k \cdot \boldsymbol{J}_l$ are defined as in the previous section but with all $Q_{kk} = 1$ due to the above mentioned normalization.

3.2   The Dynamics of Learning

The analysis of the temporal evolution of order parameters proceeds by deriving a system of $(3M^2 - M)/2$ coupled first order differential equations which reads

$$\frac{dR_{lj}}{d\alpha} = \eta_l \langle x_l y_j \rangle - (\eta_l + \eta_l^2/2) \langle x_l^2 \rangle R_{lj} - \eta_l \sum_{k=1}^{l-1} \langle x_l x_k \rangle (R_{kj} - Q_{lk} R_{lj})$$

$$(3.6)$$

$$\frac{dQ_{lj}}{d\alpha} = (\eta_l + \eta_j) \langle x_l x_j \rangle - ((\eta_l + \eta_l^2/2) \langle x_l^2 \rangle + (\eta_j + \eta_j^2/2) \langle x_j^2 \rangle) Q_{lj}$$

$$- \eta_l \sum_{k=1}^{l-1} \langle x_l x_k \rangle (Q_{kj} - Q_{kl} Q_{lj}) - \eta_j \sum_{k=1}^{j-1} \langle x_j x_k \rangle (Q_{lk} - Q_{kj} Q_{lj})$$

where $l, j = 1, 2, \ldots, M$ ($l \neq j$ in the second equation). Note that all averages are given in (3.4). Therefore, a closed set of differential equations is obtained for arbitrary $M (\ll N)$. In addition to the numerical integration of (3.6), an analytic treatment of its fixed point properties allows for an investigation of the system in the limit $\alpha \to \infty$. Further, plateau–like states in the transient dynamics can be studied.

As a measure of success we consider the deviation of the linear reconstruction

$$\boldsymbol{\xi}_{est} = \sum_{i=1}^{M} x_i \, \boldsymbol{J}_i \tag{3.7}$$

from the original data $\boldsymbol{\xi}$. The expectation value of the associated quadratic error is minimized for $\{\boldsymbol{J}_i = \boldsymbol{B}_i\}$ ($i = 1, \ldots, M$) or whenever the two sets of vectors span the same subspace. The simple linear combination of vectors $\boldsymbol{J}_k$ (3.7) coincides with the optimal (with respect to the quadratic error) linear reconstruction only asymptotically, i.e. for $\{\boldsymbol{J}_k \to \boldsymbol{B}_k\}$ (Bishop, 1995; Deco and Obradovic, 1996). Nevertheless, (3.7) can serve as a rough measure of the achieved quality of the representation.

The estimation error on average over the assumed input distribution is given by

$$\varepsilon_{est} = \frac{1}{2} \left\langle (\boldsymbol{\xi}_{est} - \boldsymbol{\xi})^2 \right\rangle - \frac{1}{2} \left\langle \boldsymbol{\xi}^2 \right\rangle = -\frac{1}{2} \sum_{k=1}^{M} \left\langle x_k^2 \right\rangle + \sum_{k=1}^{M} \sum_{l=1}^{k-1} \left\langle x_k x_l \right\rangle Q_{kl} \tag{3.8}$$

and can be expressed in terms of the order parameters by means of (3.4). Note that an irrelevant constant $\left\langle \boldsymbol{\xi}^2 \right\rangle /2$ has been subtracted in the definition of ε_{est}.

In Figure 3 (a) a generic example of the temporal evolvement of diagonal overlaps R_{ll} and of the cost function is shown. For small enough learning rates η_l the following attractive fixed point configuration is approached asymptotically (with $\alpha \to \infty$):

$$R_{ll} = \pm \sqrt{\frac{b_l^2 + 2b_l - \eta_l/2}{(b_l^2 + 2b_l)(1 + \eta_l/2)}}, \qquad R_{lj} = Q_{lj} = 0 \text{ for } l \neq j. \tag{3.9}$$

This configuration reflects the identification of one specific principal component by each student. However, the achievable absolute values $|R_{ll}|$ remain smaller than 1 for non–zero learning rates (all $\eta_l = 0.1$ in Fig. 3 (a)). Very

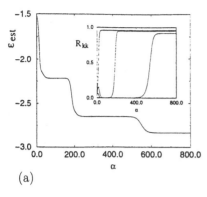
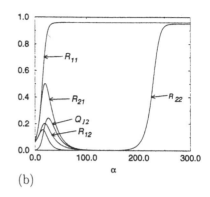

(a)   (b)

Fig. 3:   (Sanger's rule)
(a) A typical learning curve for $M = 3$: The representation error ε_{est}
decreases in a cascade–like manner, the corresponding evolution of the
diagonal order parameters R_{kk} is displayed in the inset. Here, $\eta_l = 0.1$
and all $R_{jk}(0) = 0.06 +$ random deviations of the order $\mathcal{O}\left(10^{-10}\right)$.
(b) The evolution of all overlaps in the case $M = 2$ with initial condi-
tions $R_{lk}(0) = \mathcal{O}(10^{-2})$, $Q_{12}(0) = \mathcal{O}(10^{-4})$ and $X(0) = \mathcal{O}(10^{-10})$ (cf.
Eq. (3.11)), learning rates $\eta_l = 0.1$ for both students.

small values of η_l yield good learning success, but many examples are needed.
With larger η_l learning is fast, but the asymptotic error remains large. Better
results could be achieved by applying an appropriate annealing schedule for
α–dependent learning rates $\eta_l(\alpha)$.
   For step sizes

$$\eta_l > \eta_l^c = 2b_l(b_l + 2) \qquad (3.10)$$

configurations with the corresponding overlaps $R_{ll} = 0$ become stable which is
analogous to the result of (Biehl, 1994) for $M = 1$. Throughout the following
we will assume that all learning rates are smaller than their respective critical
value. Hence, (3.9) is the only attractive configuration of the system.

3.3   Symmetries and Specialization

Additional repulsive fixed points of the system exist due to underlying symmetries of the learning problem. After relabeling the students all these repulsive
states are characterized by (3.9) with some or all of the diagonal $R_{ll} = 0$.
   The influence of these repulsive states on the learning dynamics is exemplified in Fig. 3 (a): Before approaching its asymptotic configuration (3.9), the
system is trapped close to a number of such fixed points. The intermediate
configurations are almost stationary and resemble the plateau states observed
in supervised learning and in the context of the competitive algorithm (see
previous section).

To begin with, we discuss the relevance and structure of the plateau–like configurations in terms of the model with two student vectors ($M = 2$) and equal learning rates $\eta_1 = \eta_2 = \eta$.

First we note that for any initial configuration with $R_{11}(0) = 0$, this overlap will remain zero in the course of learning. This property of Sanger's rule is already apparent in a system with only one student (Biehl, 1994) since the update of J_1 is independent of all other vectors $J_k(k > 1)$. A non–zero $R_{11}(0)$ will enable the system to achieve the asymptotic value given in (3.9). In realistic situations one would expect $R_{11} = \mathcal{O}(1/\sqrt{N})$ indicating that a characteristic time of the order $\ln N$ is needed to produce a significant overlap R_{11}. Here we focus on the dynamics of the subsequent students and assume a fairly large $R_{11}(0)$ throughout the following.

Because of the hierarchical structure of the algorithm (3.3) the above property does not simply carry over to other overlaps. For instance, $dR_{22}/d\alpha \neq 0$ holds true even with $R_{22} = 0$, in general. Instead, we can show that the specific symmetry measure $X = (R_{11}R_{22} - R_{12}R_{21})$ satisfies

$$\frac{dX}{d\alpha} = 0 \quad \text{for} \quad X = 0. \tag{3.11}$$

A value of $X = 0$ corresponds to unspecialized vectors J_i with linear dependent projections in the space spanned by B_1 and B_2. For a set of students with $X(0) = 0$ it is impossible to identify both principal components because the conservation of the symmetry (3.11), together with the effective orthogonalization for $\alpha \to \infty$, enforces

$$R_{22} \to 0 \quad \text{and} \quad R_{21} \to 0$$

when R_{11} increases in the course of learning. This is possible even with $R_{22}(0), R_{21}(0) > 0$. Such a case is illustrated in Fig. 3 (b) which demonstrates the effective loss of initial overlaps.

A linearization of the equations of motion around the specific configuration $R_{jk} = 0$ for $j, k = 1, 2$ and $Q_{12} = 0$ shows that a small, non–zero $|X|$ increases exponentially with α. Eqs. (3.6) decouple in the vicinity of the configuration and one obtains

$$X(\alpha) = X(0) \cdot e^{\lambda \alpha} \quad \text{with} \quad \lambda = (b_1^2 + 2b_1 + b_2^2 + 2b_2)\eta - \eta^2. \tag{3.12}$$

It is interesting to note that the learning rate at which λ becomes zero is given by $(\eta_1^c + \eta_2^c)/2$ with η_i^c from Eq. (3.10). Thus, the stability of $X(0) = 0$ is directly linked to the critical rates associated with the diagonal overlaps themselves.

The characteristic time which is needed to achieve a nonzero $X = \mathcal{O}(1)$, i.e. to leave the repulsive fixed point will be proportional to $-\ln|X(0)|/\lambda$. This logarithmic dependence of the *plateau length* is displayed in Fig. 4 (a) for a number of initial values $X(0)$.

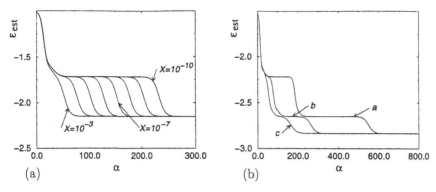

Fig. 4: (Sanger's algorithm)
(a) The plateau length of the learning process ($M = 2$) depends logarithmically on X (from left to right: $-\log_{10} X = 3, 4, 5, \ldots 10$). Apart from the deviations X, initial conditions are the same as in Fig. 3 (b)
(b) Average estimation error ($M = 3$) for equal learning rates as in Fig. 3 (a) (line a), learning rates $\eta_1 = 1, \eta_2 = 1.009\eta_1$ and $\eta_3 = 0.99\eta_1$ (line b) and $\eta_1 = 1, \eta_2 = 1.09\eta_1$ and $\eta_3 = 0.9\eta_1$ (line c).

We would like to point out that the symmetry $X = 0$ (eq. (3.11)) is preserved in the course of learning only if the learning rates are identical ($\eta_1 = \eta_2$). The relation

$$\frac{dX}{d\alpha} = aX + b(\eta_1 - \eta_2) \qquad (3.13)$$

indicates that $|X|$ will increase with α even for $X(0) = 0$ as soon as $\eta_1 \neq \eta_2$. The coefficients a and b are in general non-zero and depend on the R_{kj} and the Q_{kl}. Small differences $|\eta_1 - \eta_2|$ enable the system to escape from the symmetric configuration after a time of order $-\ln|\eta_1 - \eta_2|$. Note that the effect is *not* related to the natural ordering of the principal components. The improvement in comparison with $\eta_1 = \eta_2$ does not depend critically on which of the learning rates is taken to be the larger one.

In a system of $M > 2$ students and $\eta_l = \eta$ ($l = 1, 2, \ldots, M$) statements analogous to the Eqs. (3.11,3.12) can be made with respect to

$$X^{(M)} = \begin{vmatrix} R_{11} & R_{12} & \ldots & R_{1M} \\ R_{21} & \ldots & \ldots & R_{2M} \\ \ldots & \ldots & \ldots & \ldots \\ R_{M1} & \ldots & \ldots & R_{MM} \end{vmatrix}. \qquad (3.14)$$

The full determinant of overlaps R_{lm} as well as the determinants of all upper–left submatrices $X^{(k)}$ (related to the first k students and eigenvectors) are found to satisfy

$$\frac{dX^{(k)}}{d\alpha} = 0 \quad \text{if} \quad X^{(k)} = 0 \qquad (k = 1, 2, \ldots, M). \qquad (3.15)$$

This reflects again the hierarchical structure of Sanger's algorithm. Note that for $k = 1, 2$ the above discussed properties of the overlap R_{11} and the symmetry $X = X^{(2)}$ (3.11) is included here.

In Figure 3 (a) and 4 (b) (line a) it is shown how in a system of $M = 3$ students with $\eta_1 = \eta_2 = \eta_3$ two subsequent plateaus are visited which are characterized by $X^{(2)} = X \approx 0$ and $X^{(3)} \approx 0$ respectively. The use of only slightly different learning rates already breaks these symmetries very efficiently as can be seen in Fig. 4 (b) (lines b and c).

4 Summary and Outlook

In summary we have discussed two solvable models of unsupervised learning from high–dimensional data. In the thermodynamic limit, the dynamics of the considered on–line learning processes is described in terms of differential equations for a small number of order parameters.

Here we have focused on the process of student specialization in the course of learning. In both scenarios, plateau–like intermediate states of the system can dominate the time needed for successful training. These plateaus are due to the existence of weakly repulsive fixed points of the dynamics and reflect characteristic underlying symmetries.

In particular, we have studied the determination of prototype vectors from clustered example data by means of competitive learning. The investigated winner–takes–all procedure is identical with the on–line realization of the prominent K–means algorithm. It assigns each input deterministically to the prototype which is closest in distance. Obviously it is irrelevant precisely which of the prototypes represents which data cluster. This is similar to the permutation symmetry obeyed by the hidden nodes in a fully connected multilayered neural network and has analogous consequences.

The investigation of Sanger's rule for principal component analysis shows that repulsive fixed points and plateaus exist even though the algorithm imposes, by construction, a natural ordering on the student vectors. We have identified the relevant underlying symmetries and studied their effect on the learning dynamics.

Here, the effect of choosing different step sizes for different students has been demonstrated. Preliminary results show a similar, drastic improvement for the supervised training of over–sophisticated students, i.e. multilayer nets with an inappropriately large number of hidden units (Schwarze, 1998).

Further investigations shall address more complex model situations, for instance competitive learning with more than two clusters and prototypes. In particular, situations with a number of students which does not match the structure of the example data should be interesting.

Possible modifications of the competitive learning algorithm replace the *hard* step functions in Eq. (2.13) by a *soft minimum* type of assignment. As an example one could consider a stochastic gradient ascent maximization of the likelihood associated with a model distribution of the form (2.4), see e.g. (Bishop, 1995).

By introducing a topology in the space of prototypes it should be possible to extend the analysis to the dynamics of self–organized feature maps, see e.g. (Hertz *et al.*, 1991) for an introduction and related references.

Non–linear extensions of principal component analysis (Oja *et al.*, 1996) could be studied, which take into account higher moments of the presented data. In a sense such algorithms fill in the gap between the methods of prototype identification and low–dimensional representation.

Finally, for all these learning algorithms the use of a proper annealing schedule for the learning rates seems promising.

References

Amari, S. (1967). A theory of adaptive pattern classifiers. *IEEE Trans.*, EC–16, 299–307.

Amari, S. (1993). Backpropagation and stochastic gradient descent method. *Neurocomputing*, 5, 185–196.

Barkai, N. and Sompolinksy, H. (1994).Statistical mechanics of the maximum-likelihood density-estimation *Phys. Rev. E*, 50, 1766–1769.

Biehl, M. and Mietzner, A. (1994). Statistical mechanics of unsupervised structure recognition. *J. Phys. A*, 27, 1885–1897.

Biehl, M. (1994). An exactly solvable model of unsupervised learning. *Europhys. Lett.*, 30, 391–396.

Biehl, M. and Schwarze, H. (1995). Learning by online gradient descent. *J. Phys. A*, 28, 643–656.

Biehl, M., Riegler, P. and Wöhler, C. (1996). Transient dynamics of on-line learning in two-layered neural networks. *J. Phys. A*, 29, 4769–4780.

Biehl, M., Freking, A. and Reents, G. (1997). Dynamics of on-line competitive learning. *Europhys. Lett.*, 38 , 73–78.

Biehl, M. and Schlösser, E. (1998). The dynamics of on-line principal component analysis. *J. Phys. A*, 31, L97–L103.

Bishop, C. M. (1995) *Neural networks for pattern recognition*, Oxford University Press, Oxford, UK.

Copelli, M. and Caticha, N. (1995). On-line learning in the committee machine. *J. Phys. A*, 28, 1615–1625.

Copelli, M., Eichhorn, R., Kinouchi, O., Biehl, M., Simonetti, R., Riegler, P. and N. Caticha (1997). Noise robustness in multilayer neural networks. *Europhys. Lett.*, 37, 427–432.

Deco, G. and Obradovic, D. (1996). *An Information-Theoretic Approach to Neural Computing*, Springer, Berlin.

Duda, R.O. and Hart, P.E. (1973). *Pattern Classification and Scene Analysis*, Wiley, New York.

Hertz, J.A., Krogh, A. and Palmer, R.G. (1991). *Introduction to the Theory of Neural Computation*, Addison Wesley, Redwood-City, CA.

Kim, J. and Sompolinsky, H. (1996). Online Gibbs learning. *Phys. Rev. Lett.*, 76, 3021–3024.

Kinouchi, O. and Caticha, N. (1992). Optimal generalization in perceptrons. *Phys. Rev. E*, 26, 6243–6250.

Lootens, E. and van den Broeck, C. (1995). Analysing cluster formation by replica method. *Europhys. Lett.*, 30, 381–386.

Marangi, C., Biehl, M., Solla, S.A. (1995). Supervised learning from clustered input examples. *Europhys. Lett.*, 30, 117–122.

Meir, R. (1995). Empirical risk minimization versus maximum-likelihood estimation: a case study. *Neural Comp.*, 7, 144–157.

Oja, E. (1982). A simplified neuron model as a principal component analyzer. *J. Math. Biol.*, 15, 267–273.

Oja, E. and Karhunen, J. (1985). On stochastic approximation of the eigenvectors ans eigenvalues of the expectation of a random matrix. *J. Math. An. Appl.*, 106, 69–84.

Oja, E., Karhunen, J., Wang, L. and Vigario, R. (1996) in *Neural Nets, WIRN Vietri-95*, eds. M. Marinaro and R. Tagliaferri (World Scientific, Singapore)

Opper, M. (1996). On-line versus off-line learning from random exmaples: general results. *Phys. Rev. Lett.*, 77, 4671–4674.

Opper, M. and W. Kinzel, 1996, in: *Models of Neural Networks*, Vol. III, eds. E. Domany, J.L. van Hemmen, and K. Schulten (Springer, Berlin)

Reents, G. and Urbanczik, R. (1998). Self-averaging and On-line learning. *Phys. Rev. Lett.*, 80, 5445-5448.

Saad, D. and Solla, S. A. (1995). Exact solution for on-line learning in multilayer neural networks. *Phys. Rev. Lett.*, 74, 4337–4340; Online learning in soft committee machines *Phys. Rev. E*, 52, 4225–4243.

Sanger, T.D. (1989). Optimal unsupervised learning in a single layer linear feed-forward neural network.*Neural Networks*, 2, 459–473

Schwarze, S. (1998). *Diploma thesis* Universität Würzburg

Sompolinsky, H., Barkai, N. and Seung, H.S. (1995) in: *Neural Networks: The Statistical Mechanics Perspective*, eds. J.H. Oh, C. Kwon, and S. Cho (World Scientific, Singapore).

van den Broeck, C. and Reimann, P.(1996). Unsupervised learning by examples: online versus offline. *Phys. Rev. Lett.*, 76, 2188–2191.

Watkin, T.L.H. and Nadal, J.–P. (1994) Optimal unsupervised learning. *J. Phys. A*, 27, 1899-1915.

Watkin, T.L.H., Rau, A. and Biehl, M. (1993). The statistical mechanics of learning a rule. *Rev. Mod. Phys.*, 65, 499–556.

On-line Learning with Time-Correlated Examples

Tom Heskes † and Wim Wiegerinck

RWCP[1] Theoretical Foundation, SNN[2],
Department of Medical Physics and Biophysics, University of Nijmegen,
Geert Grooteplein 21, 6525 EZ Nijmegen, The Netherlands.
† *tom@mbfys.kun.nl*

Abstract

We study the dynamics of on-line learning with time-correlated patterns. In this, we make a distinction between "small" networks and ."large" networks. "Small" networks have a finite number of input units and are usually studied using tools from stochastic approximation theory in the limit of small learning parameters. "Large" networks have an extensive number of input units. A description in terms of individual weights is no longer useful and tools from statistical mechanics can be applied to compute the evolution of macroscopic order parameters. We give general derivations for both cases, but in the end focus on the effect of correlations on plateaus. Plateaus are long time spans in which the performance of the networks hardly changes. Learning in both "small" and "large" multi-layered perceptrons is often hampered by the presence of plateaus. The effect of correlations, however, appears to be quite different: they can have a huge beneficial effect in small networks, but seem to have only marginal effects in large networks.

1 Introduction

1.1 On-line learning with correlations

The ability to learn from examples is an essential feature in many neural network applications (Hertz et al., 1991; Haykin, 1994). Learning from examples enables the network to adapt its parameters or weights to its environment without the need for explicit knowledge of that environment. In on-line learning examples from the environment are continually presented to the network at distinct time steps. At each time step a small adjustment of the network's

---

[1]RWCP: Real World Computing Partnership
[2]SNN: Dutch Foundation for Neural Networks

weights is made on the basis of the currently presented pattern. This procedure is iterated as long as the network learns. The idea is that on a larger time scale the small adjustments sum up to a continuous adaptation of the network to the whole environment.

In many applications the network has to be trained with a training set consisting of a finite number of patterns. In these applications a strategy is often used where at each step a randomly selected pattern from the training set is presented. In particular with large training sets and complex environments successful results have been obtained with this strategy (Brunak et al., 1990; Barnard, 1992). Characteristic of this kind of learning is that successive patterns are independent, i.e. that the probability to select an pattern at a certain time step is independent of its predecessors. Of course, successive patterns in on-line learning do not need to be independent. For example, one can think of an application where the patterns are obtained by on-line measurements of an environment. If these patterns are directly fed into the neural network, it is likely that successive patterns are correlated with each other.

A related example is the use of neural networks for time-series prediction (Lapedes and Farber, 1988; Weigend et al., 1990; Wong, 1991; Weigend and Gershenfeld, 1993; Hoptroff, 1993). Essentially, the task of these networks is, given the last k data points of the time series, to predict the next data point of the time series. Each pattern consists of a data point and its k predecessors. There are two obvious ways to train a network "on-line" with these examples. In what we call "randomized learning", successively presented patterns are drawn from the time series on arbitrary, randomly chosen times. This makes successively presented patterns independent. In the other type of learning, which we call "natural learning", the patterns are presented in their natural order, keeping their natural dependencies.

1.2 "Small" and "large" networks

We will study the effect of correlations on on-line learning in two different cases, which we will refer to as "small" and "large" networks. Small networks are usually studied using stochastic approximation methods, large networks using tools from statistical mechanics. In the stochastic approach, on-line learning is described as an average process (the drift) with superimposed fluctuations (the diffusion). General properties can be derived by making expansions for small learning parameters (Wiegerinck and Heskes, 1996; Heskes and Kappen, 1991; Wiegerinck et al., 1994). The results obtained are usually quite general, i.e., are valid for a large class of learning rules and architectures. In the end, the evolution of the (distribution of) weights can be quite accurately described in terms of a few parameters as a diffusion matrix and a Hessian matrix. These parameters then depend on the characteristics of the learning problem.

In large networks the drift for each individual weight becomes an order of magnitude smaller than its diffusion. A description of the learning behaviour in terms of individual weights, as in the stochastic approach, no longer makes sense and is replaced by a description in terms of macroscopic order parameters. This is the statistical approach, which considers on-line learning in the thermodynamical limit, i.e., in the limit of an infinitely large number of input units (Saad and Solla, 1995a; Biehl and Schwarze, 1995; Barkai et al., 1995). Studies on large networks are usually less general than studies on small networks. In order to compute the evolution of the order parameters, one has to make quite specific assumptions, e.g., regarding the generation of the inputs and the corresponding targets.

1.3 Plateaus

A problem shared by both small and large two-layered networks, is the existence of plateaus: long time spans during which the performance of the learning machine hardly changes (Wiegerinck and Heskes, 1996; Biehl et al., 1996). Plateaus are frequently present in the error surface of multilayer perceptrons (Hush et al., 1992). The existence of a plateau explains, as we will see, the large performance difference between "natural" and "randomized" learning in small networks, noticed e.g. in simulation studies by (Mpitsos and Burton, 1992; Hondou and Sawada, 1994). Plateaus are usually caused by the initial tendency of hidden units to represent the same features. The breaking of this initial symmetry, which is often necessary to make further progress, appears to be a painstaking process. It is in this process that we will find the largest effect of correlations.

This phenomenon, and, more generally, how the presentation order of patterns affects the process of on-line learning are the subject of this chapter. Understanding these issues is not only interesting from a theoretical point of view, but it may also help to devise better learning strategies.

1.4 Outline

In section 2, we define the class of learning rules and the types of stochastic, yet dependent, pattern presentation which are analyzed in the rest of the chapter. Section 3 is devoted to the dynamics of on-line learning in small networks. Because of the stochasticity in the presentation of patterns, on-line learning is a stochastic process. However, since the weight changes at each time step are assumed to be small (they scale with the learning parameters η), it is possible to give approximate deterministic descriptions of the learning process on a larger time scale. In section 3.2 we use the results of section 3.1 to study the effect of correlations when the learning process is stuck on a plateau in the error surface. From the results in this section, we can explain the remarkable difference between randomized learning and natural learning, mentioned earlier.

The second part of the chapter discusses on-learning with correlated patterns in large networks. In section 4.1 we start to describe the student and teacher networks and the dynamics of the successive patterns. Instead of considering the evolution of individual weights, we will compute the evolution of macroscopic order parameters in section 4.2. Eventually we arrive at a general description of the learning dynamics valid for large two-layered networks. In section 4.3 we will consider two examples in more detail: a soft-committee machine and a two-layered perceptron with adaptive hidden-to-output weights.

2   The general framework

In many on-line learning processes the weight change at learning step n can be written in the general form

$$\Delta w(n) \equiv w(n+1) - w(n) = \eta \, f(w(n), x(n)) \,, \tag{2.1}$$

with $w(n)$ the network weights and $x(n)$ the presented pattern at iteration step n. η is the learning parameter, which is assumed to be constant in this chapter, and $f(\cdot, \cdot)$ the learning rule. Examples satisfying (2.1) can be found in supervised learning such as backpropagation for multilayer perceptrons (Werbos, 1974; Rumelhart et al., 1986), where the patterns $x(n)$ are combinations of input vectors $(\xi_1(n), \ldots, \xi_k(n))$ and desired output vectors $(y_1(n), \ldots, y_l(n))$, as well as in unsupervised learning such as Kohonen's self-organizing rule for topological feature maps (Kohonen, 1982), where $x(n)$ stands for the input vector $(x_1(n), \ldots, x_k(n))$. On-line learning in the general form (2.1) has been studied extensively (Amari, 1967; Ritter and Schulten, 1988; White, 1989; Heskes and Kappen, 1991; Leen and Moody, 1993; Orr and Leen, 1993; Hansen et al., 1993; Radons, 1993; Finnoff, 1994). Many papers on this subject, have been restricted to independent presentation of patterns, i.e. the probability $p(x, n)$ to present a pattern x at iteration step n is given by a probability distribution $\rho(x)$, independent of its predecessor. Dependencies between successive patterns have been studied in (Benveniste et al., 1987)(and references therein) and more recently in (Kuan and White, 1994; Wiegerinck and Heskes, 1994).

In this chapter correlations between patterns are incorporated by assuming that the probability to present a pattern x depends on its predecessor x' through a transition probability $\tau(x|x')$, i.e. that $p(x, n)$ follow a first-order stationary Markov process

$$p(x, n+1) = \int dx' \tau(x|x') p(x', n). \tag{2.2}$$

Learning with independent patterns is a special case with $\tau(x|x') = \rho(x)$. The limitation to first-order Markov processes is not as severe as it might seem at first sight, since stationary Markov processes of any finite order k can be incorporated in the formalism by redefining the vectors $\boldsymbol{x}$ to include the last k patterns (Wiegerinck and Heskes, 1994). The Markov process is assumed to have a unique asymptotic or stationary distribution $\rho(\boldsymbol{x})$, i.e., we assume that we can take limits like

$$\lim_{T \to \infty} \frac{1}{T} \sum_{n=0}^{T-1} \phi(\boldsymbol{x}(n)) = \int d\boldsymbol{x} \rho(\boldsymbol{x}) \phi(\boldsymbol{x})$$

in which $\phi(\boldsymbol{x})$ is some function of the patterns. So $\rho(\boldsymbol{x})$ describes the (asymptotic) relative frequency of patterns. A randomized learning strategy therefore will select its independent patterns from this stationary distribution. In this chapter we will denote these long time averages with brackets $\langle \cdot \rangle_x$,

$$\langle \phi(\boldsymbol{x}) \rangle_x \equiv \int d\boldsymbol{x} \rho(\boldsymbol{x}) \phi(\boldsymbol{x})$$

and sometimes we use capitals, i.e. we define quantities like $\Phi \equiv \langle \phi(\boldsymbol{x}) \rangle_x$.

Many neural network algorithms, including backpropagation, perform gradient descent on a "local" cost or error function $e(\boldsymbol{w}, \boldsymbol{x})$,

$$\boldsymbol{f}(\boldsymbol{w}(n), \boldsymbol{x}(n)) \equiv -\nabla_w e(\boldsymbol{w}(n), \boldsymbol{x}(n)) . \tag{2.3}$$

The idea of this learning rule is that with a small learning parameter, the stochastic gradient descent [(2.1) and (2.3)] approximates deterministic gradient descent on the "global" error potential

$$E(\boldsymbol{w}) \equiv \lim_{T \to \infty} \frac{1}{T} \sum_{n=0}^{T-1} e(\boldsymbol{w}, \boldsymbol{x}(n)) \tag{2.4}$$

We restrict ourselves to learning with a cost function in order to compare performances between several types of pattern presentation (with equal stationary distributions). However, most derivations and results in this section can be easily generalized to the general rule (2.1).

The update rule for the weights (2.1) and the Markov process governing the presentation of patterns (2.2) can be combined into one evolution equation for the joint probability $\hat{P}(\boldsymbol{w}, \boldsymbol{x}, n)$ that at step n pattern $\boldsymbol{x}$ is presented to the network with weight vector $\boldsymbol{w}$. This probability obeys the Markov process

$$\hat{P}(\boldsymbol{w}, \boldsymbol{x}, n+1) = \int d\boldsymbol{w}' \, d\boldsymbol{x}' \, \tau(\boldsymbol{x}|\boldsymbol{x}') \, \delta(\boldsymbol{w} - \boldsymbol{w}' - \eta \boldsymbol{f}(\boldsymbol{w}', \boldsymbol{x}')) \, \hat{P}(\boldsymbol{w}', \boldsymbol{x}', n). \tag{2.5}$$

We are interested in the learning process, i.e. in the evolution of the probability distribution of weights

$$P(\boldsymbol{w}, n) = \int d\boldsymbol{x} \, \hat{P}(\boldsymbol{w}, \boldsymbol{x}, n) .$$

With dependent patterns, it is not possible to derive a self-supporting equation for the evolution of $P(\boldsymbol{w}, n)$ by direct integration over $\boldsymbol{x}$ in (2.5). Therefore, we have to make either approximations or restrict ourselves to specific cases.

3   Small networks

3.1   Expansion for small learning parameters

In the first part of this chapter, we will consider the case of small learning parameters η and a finite number of weights $\boldsymbol{w}$. There are several ways to derive a systematic expansion of the evolution equation of $P(\boldsymbol{w}, n)$ in the small learning parameter η. The basic assumption for any expansion is that the dynamics of the weights, with typical time scale $1/\eta$, is much slower than the typical time scale of the patterns. The same principle will be used when we consider the large networks. The approach that we present here, is further based on the assumption that the distribution of weights, with initial form $P(\boldsymbol{w}, 0) = \delta(\boldsymbol{w} - \boldsymbol{w}(0))$, remains sharply peaked as n increases (see e.g. (van Kampen, 1992)). We follow the heuristic treatment in (Benveniste et al., 1987) and average the learning rule over a "mesoscopic" time scale (Hansen et al., 1993) which is much larger than the typical time scale of the pattern dynamics yet much smaller than the time scale on which the weights can change significantly. With the averaged learning rule we can directly calculate approximate equations for the mean $\overline{\boldsymbol{w}}(n)$ and the covariance matrix $\Sigma(n)$, which describe the position and the width of the peak $P(\boldsymbol{w}, n)$ respectively.

We iterate the learning step (2.1) M times, where M is a mesoscopic time scale, i.e. $1 \ll M \ll 1/\eta$, and obtain

$$\boldsymbol{w}(n + M) - \boldsymbol{w}(n) = \eta \sum_{m=0}^{M-1} \boldsymbol{f}(\boldsymbol{w}(n+m), \boldsymbol{x}(n+m)) \,. \qquad (3.1)$$

For the average $\overline{\boldsymbol{w}}(n) \equiv \langle \boldsymbol{w}(n) \rangle$ [brackets $\langle \dots \rangle$ stand for averaging over the combined process (2.5)], we have the exact identity

$$\overline{\boldsymbol{w}}(n + M) - \overline{\boldsymbol{w}}(n) = \eta \sum_{m=0}^{M-1} \langle \boldsymbol{f}(\boldsymbol{w}(n+m), \boldsymbol{x}(n+m)) \rangle \,. \qquad (3.2)$$

On the one hand, the mesoscopic time scale is much smaller than the time scale on which the probability distribution $P(\boldsymbol{w}, n)$ can change appreciably. Therefore, if the probability distribution $P(\boldsymbol{w}, n)$ is very sharply peaked, we can expand (3.2) around the mean $\overline{\boldsymbol{w}}(n)$

$$\overline{\boldsymbol{w}}(n + M) - \overline{\boldsymbol{w}}(n) = \eta \sum_{m=0}^{M-1} \langle \boldsymbol{f}(\overline{\boldsymbol{w}}(n), \boldsymbol{x}(n+m)) \rangle + \dots$$

On the other hand, the mesoscopic time scale is much larger than the typical time scale of the Markov process governing the presentation of patterns. Therefore we can approximate the sum

$$\frac{1}{M} \sum_{m=0}^{M-1} \langle \boldsymbol{f}(\overline{\boldsymbol{w}}(n), \boldsymbol{x}(n+m)) \rangle \approx \lim_{T \to \infty} \frac{1}{T} \sum_{m=0}^{T-1} \langle \boldsymbol{f}(\overline{\boldsymbol{w}}(n), \boldsymbol{x}(n+m)) \rangle \equiv \boldsymbol{F}(\overline{\boldsymbol{w}}(n)).$$
$$(3.3)$$

Thus, in lowest order, the stochastic equation (3.2) can be approximated by the deterministic difference equation

$$\overline{w}(n + M) - \overline{w}(n) = \eta M \boldsymbol{F}(\overline{w}(n)) \, .$$

For small ηM, the difference equation for the position of the peak turns into an ordinary differential equation (ODE). In terms of the rescaled continuous time t, with $t_n \equiv \eta n$ [we will use both notations $\boldsymbol{w}(n)$ and $\boldsymbol{w}(t)$], we obtain that the learning process is approximated by the ODE

$$\frac{d\overline{w}(t)}{dt} = \boldsymbol{F}(\overline{w}(t)) = -\boldsymbol{\nabla} E(\overline{w}(t)) \, . \tag{3.4}$$

In this equation $E(\boldsymbol{w})$ is the global error potential defined in (2.4). In lowest order the weights do indeed follow the gradient of the global error potential. Dependencies in successively presented patterns have no influence on the ODE (3.4): this equation only depends on the stationary distribution $\rho(\boldsymbol{x})$ of the patterns. Corrections to the ODE arise when we expand (3.1):

$$
\begin{aligned}
\boldsymbol{w}(n + M) - \boldsymbol{w}(n) &= \eta \sum_{m=0}^{M-1} \boldsymbol{f}(\boldsymbol{w}(n + m), \boldsymbol{x}(n + m)) \\
&= \eta \sum_{m=0}^{M-1} \boldsymbol{f}(\boldsymbol{w}(n), \boldsymbol{x}(n + m)) \\
&\quad - \eta \sum_{m=0}^{M-1} \mathsf{h}(\boldsymbol{w}(n), \boldsymbol{x}(n + m))(\boldsymbol{w}(n + m) - \boldsymbol{w}(n)) + \ldots \\
&= \eta \sum_{m=0}^{M-1} \boldsymbol{f}(\boldsymbol{w}(n), \boldsymbol{x}(n + m)) \\
&\quad - \eta^2 \sum_{m=0}^{M-1} \mathsf{h}(\boldsymbol{w}(n), \boldsymbol{x}(n + m)) \sum_{l=0}^{m-1} \boldsymbol{f}(\boldsymbol{w}(n), \boldsymbol{x}(n + l)) + \ldots
\end{aligned}
$$

with the "local Hessian" $\mathsf{h}(\boldsymbol{w}, \boldsymbol{x}) \equiv \boldsymbol{\nabla}_w \boldsymbol{\nabla}_w^T e(\boldsymbol{w}, \boldsymbol{x})$. Using the separation between time scales, we approximate this expansion by

$$
\begin{aligned}
\boldsymbol{w}(n + M) - \boldsymbol{w}(n) &= \\
\eta M &\left[\boldsymbol{F}(\boldsymbol{w}(n)) + \eta \boldsymbol{B}(\boldsymbol{w}(n)) - \frac{1}{2} \eta M \mathsf{H}(\boldsymbol{w}(n)) \boldsymbol{F}(\boldsymbol{w}(n) + \ldots \right] \tag{3.5}
\end{aligned}
$$

with the "Hessian"

$$\mathsf{H}(\boldsymbol{w}) \equiv \lim_{T \to \infty} \frac{1}{T} \sum_{n=0}^{T-1} \langle \mathsf{h}(\boldsymbol{w}, \boldsymbol{x}(n)) \rangle_x \tag{3.6}$$

and

$$
\begin{aligned}
\boldsymbol{B}(\boldsymbol{w}) &\equiv \lim_{T \to \infty} \frac{1}{T} \sum_{m=0}^{T-1} \left\langle [\mathsf{h}(\boldsymbol{w}, \boldsymbol{x}(m)) - \mathsf{H}(\boldsymbol{w})] \sum_{l=0}^{m-1} [\boldsymbol{f}(\boldsymbol{w}, \boldsymbol{x}(l)) - \boldsymbol{F}(\boldsymbol{w})] \right\rangle_x \\
&= \lim_{T \to \infty} \sum_{n=1}^{T-1} \left[1 - \frac{n}{T} \right] \langle [\mathsf{h}(\boldsymbol{w}, \boldsymbol{x}(n)) - \mathsf{H}(\boldsymbol{w})] [\boldsymbol{f}(\boldsymbol{w}, \boldsymbol{x}(0)) - \boldsymbol{F}(\boldsymbol{w})] \rangle_x \tag{3.7}
\end{aligned}
$$

Note that $\boldsymbol{B}(\boldsymbol{w})$ is zero with independent patterns. Later on we will see that the term containing $\mathsf{H}(\boldsymbol{w}(n))\boldsymbol{F}(\boldsymbol{w}(n))$ will vanish by the transformation to continuous time.

Averaging of (3.5) yields

$$\overline{\boldsymbol{w}}(n+M) - \overline{\boldsymbol{w}}(n) =$$
$$\eta M \left[\langle \boldsymbol{F}(\boldsymbol{w}(n)) \rangle + \eta \langle \boldsymbol{B}(\boldsymbol{w}(n)) \rangle - \frac{1}{2}\eta M \langle \mathsf{H}(\boldsymbol{w}(n))\boldsymbol{F}(\boldsymbol{w}(n)) \rangle + \ldots \right]$$

and by expansion of the righthand side around the mean $\overline{\boldsymbol{w}}(n)$ we obtain

$$\overline{\boldsymbol{w}}(n+M) - \overline{\boldsymbol{w}}(n) = \eta M \left[\boldsymbol{F}(\overline{\boldsymbol{w}}(n)) - \frac{1}{2}\mathsf{Q}(\overline{\boldsymbol{w}}(n)) : \Sigma(n) \right.$$
$$\left. +\eta \boldsymbol{B}(\overline{\boldsymbol{w}}(n)) - \frac{1}{2}\eta M \mathsf{H}(\overline{\boldsymbol{w}}(n))\boldsymbol{F}(\overline{\boldsymbol{w}}(n) + \ldots \right]$$

in which

$$\Sigma(n) \equiv \left\langle [\boldsymbol{w}(n) - \overline{\boldsymbol{w}}(n)][\boldsymbol{w}(n) - \overline{\boldsymbol{w}}(n)]^T \right\rangle,$$
$$Q_{\alpha\beta\gamma}(\boldsymbol{w}) \equiv -\frac{\partial^2 F_\alpha(\boldsymbol{w})}{\partial w_\beta \, \partial w_\gamma}, \text{ and } (\mathsf{Q}{:}\Sigma)_\alpha \equiv \sum_{\beta\gamma} Q_{\alpha\beta\gamma}\Sigma_{\beta\gamma}^2. \qquad (3.8)$$

Transformation to continuous time finally yields a first approximation beyond the ODE (3.4)

$$\frac{d\overline{\boldsymbol{w}}(t)}{dt} = \boldsymbol{F}(\overline{\boldsymbol{w}}(t)) - \frac{1}{2}\mathsf{Q}(\overline{\boldsymbol{w}}(t)){:}\Sigma(t) - \eta \boldsymbol{B}(\overline{\boldsymbol{w}}(t)) \qquad (3.9)$$

Unlike (3.4) this is no longer a self-supporting equation for $\overline{\boldsymbol{w}}$ alone, but higher moments enter as well. The evolution of the mean $\overline{\boldsymbol{w}}$ in the course of time is therefore not determined by $\overline{\boldsymbol{w}}$ itself, but influenced by the fluctuations around this average through their covariance Σ. It is clear that for the existence of the ODE approximation and of its higher order approximations, it is necessary that the fluctuations are small. In the derivation of (3.9) we have used in foresight that these fluctuations are of order $\sqrt{\eta}$ and therefore their covariance Σ of order η. In fact, similar to the derivations of (3.4) and (3.9), a lowest order approximation for the fluctuations can be derived,

$$\frac{d\Sigma(t)}{dt} = -\mathsf{H}(\overline{\boldsymbol{w}}(t))\Sigma(t) - \Sigma(t)\mathsf{H}(\overline{\boldsymbol{w}}(t)) + \eta \mathsf{D}(\overline{\boldsymbol{w}}(t)) \qquad (3.10)$$

with the "diffusion" matrix

$$\mathsf{D}(\boldsymbol{w}) = \left\langle \lim_{T\to\infty} \frac{1}{T} \sum_{n=0}^{T-1} \sum_{m=0}^{T-1} [\boldsymbol{f}(\boldsymbol{w}, \boldsymbol{x}(n)) - \boldsymbol{F}(\boldsymbol{w})] \, [\boldsymbol{f}(\boldsymbol{w}, \boldsymbol{x}(m)) - \boldsymbol{F}(\boldsymbol{w})]^T \right\rangle_x. \qquad (3.11)$$

From (3.10), we can see that $\Sigma(t)$ remains bounded if H is positive definite. In this case $\Sigma(t) = \mathcal{O}(\eta)$, which makes (3.10) with (3.9) a valid approximation (van Kampen, 1992). In other words, since η is small, this justifies *a posteriori* the assumption that $P(w,n)$ is sharply peaked. In other cases where the fluctuations do not remain bounded, the approximation is only applicable during a short period.

The diffusion $D(w)$ can be expressed as the sum of an independent and a dependent part:

$$D(w) = C_0(w) + \lim_{T\to\infty}\sum_{n=1}^{T-1}\left[1 - \frac{n}{T}\right]\left[C_n(w) + C_n^T(w)\right] \equiv C_0(w) + C_+(w)$$

where we have defined the auto-correlation matrices

$$C_n(w) \equiv \left\langle [f(w,x(n)) - F(w)][f(w,x(0)) - F(w)]^T \right\rangle_x .$$

For on-line learning with random sampling, there are no correlations between subsequent weight changes, so $C_+(w) = 0$ and consequently the diffusion $D(w)$ reduces to $C_0(w)$ (see e.g. (Heskes, 1994)).

The set of equations (3.9) and (3.10) for $\overline{w}$ and Σ forms a self-supporting first approximation beyond the ODE approximation (3.4). It is not necessary to solve (3.9) and (3.10) simultaneously. Since the covariance Σ appears in (3.9) as a correction it suffices to compute Σ from (3.10) using the ODE approximation for $\overline{w}$. Following (van Kampen, 1992) we set $\overline{w} = w_{\text{ODE}} + u$, and solve

$$\frac{dw_{\text{ODE}}(t)}{dt} = F(w_{\text{ODE}}(t)) \tag{3.12}$$

$$\frac{d\Sigma(t)}{dt} = -H(w_{\text{ODE}}(t))\Sigma(t) - \Sigma(t)H(w_{\text{ODE}}(t)) + \eta D(w_{\text{ODE}}(t)) \tag{3.13}$$

$$\frac{du(t)}{dt} = -H(w_{\text{ODE}}(t))u(t) - \frac{1}{2}Q(w_{\text{ODE}}(t)){:}\Sigma(t) - \eta B(w_{\text{ODE}}(t)). \tag{3.14}$$

The first two equations (3.12) and (3.13) are equivalent to results in the literature (Benveniste et al., 1987; Kuan and White, 1994; Wiegerinck and Heskes, 1994). The ODE (3.12) approximates in lowest order the dynamics of the weights. The covariance matrix $\Sigma(t)$ which obeys (3.13), describes the stochastic deviations $w(n) - w_{\text{ODE}}(t_n)$ between the weights and the ODE approximation. These fluctuations are typically of order $\sqrt{\eta}$. In (Benveniste et al., 1987; Kuan and White, 1994) a Wiener process is rigorously derived to describe these fluctuations.

The last equation (3.14) decribes a bias u between the mean $\overline{w}$ and the ODE approximation w_{ODE}. The dynamics of the bias consists of two driving terms. The first one is the interaction between the nonlinearity of the learning rule Q and the fluctuations described by Σ. This term can be understood in the following way: if a random fluctuation into one direction in weight space does not result in the same restoring effect as a random fluctuation into the opposite direction, then random fluctuations will obviously result in a netto bias effect. The other driving term in (3.14) is $\boldsymbol{B}$ [see (3.7)]. This term is only due to the correlations between the patterns, i.e., $\boldsymbol{B} = 0$ for independent patterns. Since the two driving terms are typically of order η, the bias term is also typically of order η. The bias is typically an order $\sqrt{\eta}$ smaller than the fluctuations and therefore neglected in regular situations. However in section 3.2 it will be shown that there are situations where this bias term is of crucial importance.

As an approximation, the set of coupled equations (3.12), (3.13), and (3.14) is equally valid as the coupled set (3.9) and (3.10). However, in the former the hierarchical structure of the approximations (ODE approximation, fluctuations, bias...) is more clear. Finally we stress that the essential assumption for the validity of this set of equations is that the weights can be described by their average value with small superimposed fluctuations. In other words, the approximation is locally valid. This is the case if the Hessian H is positive definite. In other cases the approximation is only valid for short times (van Kampen, 1992).

3.2 Plateaus in small networks

Comparing the asymptotic performance of networks trained with dependent and independent patterns is rather straightforward if both types of learning lead to the same (local) minimum of the global error $E(\boldsymbol{w})$ [see (2.4)]. An analysis can be found in (Wiegerinck and Heskes, 1996). A minimum is a stable equilibrium point of the ODE dynamics (3.4), i.e. the eigenvalues of the Hessian H($\boldsymbol{w}$) [see (3.6)] are strictly positive. In the neighborhood of a minimum, the ODE force $\boldsymbol{F}(\boldsymbol{w})$ [see (3.3)] is the dominating factor in the dynamics. Perturbations due to the higher order corrections are immediately restored by the ODE force. The diffusion (3.11), however, does depend on the correlations between successive patterns. Roughly speaking, the better the sampling of the problem, the smaller the diffusion term, the lower the final fluctuations, and thus the lower the average asymptotic error.

In this section, however, we will consider so-called "plateaus". Plateaus are flat spots on the global-error surface. They are often the cause of the extreme long learning times and/or the bad convergence results in multilayer perceptron applications with the backpropagation algorithm (Hush et al., 1992). On a plateau, the gradient of E is negligible and H has some positive eigenvalues but also some zero eigenvalues. Plateaus can be viewed as indifferent equilibrium points of the ODE dynamics. Even with small η, the higher order terms can make the weight vector move around in the subspace of eigenvectors of H with zero eigenvalue without being restored by $\boldsymbol{F}$. In other words, in these directions the higher order terms – in the first place the fluctuations, which are of order $\sqrt{\eta}$, and in the second place the bias, which is of order η – may give a larger contribution to the dynamics than the ODE term. Since the higher order terms are related to correlations between the patterns, on plateaus the presentation order of patterns might significantly affect the learning process.

The effect of different pattern presentations in learning on a plateau will be illustrated by the following example. We consider the tent map

$$y(\xi) = 2(1/2 - |\xi - 1/2|), \quad 0 \le \xi \le 1$$

which we view as a dynamical system producing a chaotic time series $\xi(n + 1) = y(\xi(n))$ (Schuster, 1989). To model this system we use a two-layered perceptron with one input unit, two hidden units and a linear output,

$$z(\boldsymbol{w}; \xi) = v_0 + \sum_{\beta=1}^{2} v_\beta \tanh(w_{\beta 1}\xi + w_{\beta 0}).$$

We train the network with input-output pairs $\boldsymbol{x} = \{\xi, y(\xi)\}$ by on-line back-propagation (Rumelhart et al., 1986)

$$\Delta \boldsymbol{w} = -\eta \boldsymbol{\nabla}_w e(\boldsymbol{w}, \boldsymbol{x})$$

with the usual squared error cost function

$$e(\boldsymbol{w}, \boldsymbol{x}) = [y(\xi) - z(\boldsymbol{w}; \xi)]^2/2.$$

We compare two types of pattern presentation. With natural learning, patterns are presented according to the sequence generated by the tent map, i.e. $\boldsymbol{x}(n) = \{\xi(n), y(\xi(n))\}$ with $\xi(n + 1) = y(\xi(n))$ (and $\xi(0)$ randomly drawn from the interval $[0, 1]$). With randomized learning, at each iteration step an input ξ is drawn according to the stationary distribution $\rho(\xi)$, i.e. homogeneously from the interval $[0, 1]$ (Schuster, 1989), the corresponding output $y(\xi)$ is computed, and the pair $\{\xi, y(\xi)\}$ is presented to the network. In both cases we initialize with the same small weights, $-\epsilon < v_\gamma$, $w_{\beta\alpha} < \epsilon$. Small random weights are often recommended to prevent early saturation of the weights (Lee, 1991).

As reported earlier (Hondou and Sawada, 1994), simulations show a dramatic difference between the two learning strategies in their performance learning the tent map (cf. figure 1 and figure 2).

To understand this difference, we will study the weight dynamics by local linearizations. In the neighborhood of a point $\boldsymbol{w}^*$ in weight space the ODE (3.4) can be approximated by

$$\frac{d\overline{\boldsymbol{w}}(t)}{dt} = \boldsymbol{F}(\boldsymbol{w}^*) - \mathsf{H}(\boldsymbol{w}^*)[\overline{\boldsymbol{w}}(t) - \boldsymbol{w}^*]. \tag{3.15}$$

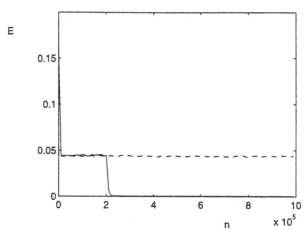

Figure 1. Typical global error E of natural learning (full curve) and of randomized learning (dashed curve). Simulation performed with a single network. Learning parameter $\eta = 0.1$. Weight initialization: $\epsilon = 10^{-4}$. Data points are plotted every 10^4 iterations.

The weights are initialized at $\boldsymbol{w}(0) = \mathcal{O}(\epsilon)$, with $\epsilon \approx 0$. The linearization (3.15) around $\boldsymbol{w}^* = \boldsymbol{w}^{(0)} = 0$ yields an approximation of the weight dynamics during the initial stage of learning,

$$\frac{d}{dt}\begin{pmatrix} \overline{v}_0 \\ \overline{v}_\beta \\ \overline{w}_{\beta 0} \\ \overline{w}_{\beta 1} \end{pmatrix} = \begin{pmatrix} \frac{1}{2} \\ 0 \\ 0 \\ 0 \end{pmatrix} - \begin{pmatrix} 1 & 0 & 0 & 0 \\ 0 & 0 & -\frac{1}{3} & -\frac{1}{6} \\ 0 & -\frac{1}{3} & 0 & 0 \\ 0 & -\frac{1}{6} & 0 & 0 \end{pmatrix} \begin{pmatrix} \overline{v}_0 \\ \overline{v}_\beta \\ \overline{w}_{\beta 0} \\ \overline{w}_{\beta 1} \end{pmatrix} \quad (3.16)$$

with $\beta = 1, 2$. From (3.16), we see that $\overline{v}_0$ quickly converges to $\overline{v}_0 = 1/2$ on a time scale where the other weights hardly change (cf. figure 3). In other words, during this stage the network just learns the average value of the target function. This is a well-known phenomenon: backpropagation tends to select the gross structures of its environment first.

After the initial stage, (3.16) no longer provides an accurate approximation. The linearization (3.15) of the ODE around the new point $\boldsymbol{w}^* = \boldsymbol{w}^{(1)} = (v_0^{(1)} = 1/2, v_\beta^{(1)} = 0, w_{\beta\alpha}^{(1)} = 0)$, (with $\alpha = 0, 1$ and $\beta = 1, 2$), describes the dynamics of the weights during the next stage,

$$\frac{d}{dt}\begin{pmatrix} \overline{v}_0 \\ \overline{v}_\beta \\ \overline{w}_{\beta 0} \\ \overline{w}_{\beta 1} \end{pmatrix} = -\begin{pmatrix} 1 & 0 & 0 & 0 \\ 0 & 0 & 0 & 0 \\ 0 & 0 & 0 & 0 \\ 0 & 0 & 0 & 0 \end{pmatrix} \begin{pmatrix} \overline{v}_0 - \frac{1}{2} \\ \overline{v}_\beta \\ \overline{w}_{\beta 0} \\ \overline{w}_{\beta 1} \end{pmatrix}$$

with $\beta = 1, 2$. At this stage, $\boldsymbol{F} = 0$, while the Hessian H has one positive

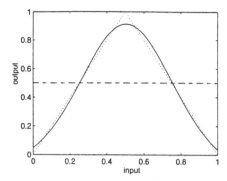

Figure 2. Typical network result after 10^6 iteration steps of natural learning (full curve) and randomized learning (dashed curve). The target function is the tent map (dotted curve). For simulation details, see the caption of figure 1.

eigenvalue ($\lambda = 1$) and further only zero eigenvalues. In other words, at $\boldsymbol{w}^{(1)}$ the weights are stuck on a plateau.

To find out whether the weights can escape the plateau, we have to consider the contributions of the higher η corrections to the weight dynamics (3.9) and (3.10). Linearization of this set of equations around $\boldsymbol{w}^{(1)}$ yields

$$\frac{d\overline{\boldsymbol{w}}(t)}{dt} = -\mathsf{H}(\boldsymbol{w}^{(1)})[\overline{\boldsymbol{w}}(t) - \boldsymbol{w}^{(1)}]$$
$$-\frac{1}{2}\left\{\mathsf{Q}(\boldsymbol{w}^{(1)}) + \boldsymbol{\nabla}\mathsf{Q}(\boldsymbol{w}^{(1)})[\overline{\boldsymbol{w}}(t) - \boldsymbol{w}^{(1)}]\right\}:\Sigma(t)$$
$$-\eta\left\{\boldsymbol{B}(\boldsymbol{w}^{(1)}) + \boldsymbol{\nabla}\boldsymbol{B}(\boldsymbol{w}^{(1)})[\overline{\boldsymbol{w}}(t) - \boldsymbol{w}^{(1)}]\right\} \qquad (3.17)$$

$$\frac{d\Sigma(t)}{dt} = -\mathsf{H}(\boldsymbol{w}^{(1)})\Sigma(t) - \Sigma(t)\mathsf{H}(\boldsymbol{w}^{(1)}) + \eta\mathsf{D}(\boldsymbol{w}^{(1)}) . \qquad (3.18)$$

At $\boldsymbol{w}^{(1)}$, the (v_0, v_0) component is the only nonzero component for both the Hessian H and the diffusion D (for randomized learning as well as for natural learning). From (3.18), it thus follows that $\Sigma^2_{v_0,v_0}$ is the only nonzero component of the covariance matrix. So only in in this direction there will be fluctuations. However these fluctuations will be restored, due to the positive (v_0, v_0) component of the Hessian. Moreover, since $Q(\boldsymbol{w}^{(1)})_{v_0 v_0 w}$ [see (3.8)] and its derivatives vanish for all $\boldsymbol{w}$, the covariance matrix Σ does not couple with the (linearized) weight dynamics, and (3.17) reduces to the autonomous equation

$$\frac{d\overline{\boldsymbol{w}}(t)}{dt} = -\mathsf{H}(\boldsymbol{w}^{(1)})[\overline{\boldsymbol{w}}(t) - \boldsymbol{w}^{(1)}] - \eta\left\{\boldsymbol{B}(\boldsymbol{w}^{(1)}) + \boldsymbol{\nabla}\boldsymbol{B}(\boldsymbol{w}^{(1)})[\overline{\boldsymbol{w}}(t) - \boldsymbol{w}^{(1)}]\right\} .$$

With natural learning, straightforward calculations yield $\boldsymbol{B}(\boldsymbol{w}^{(1)}) = 0$ and

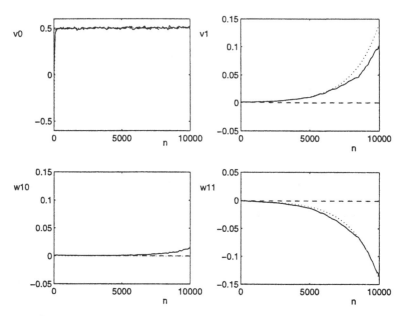

Figure 3. Weights obtained by simulations for natural learning (solid curves) and randomized learning (dashed curves) as functions of the number of iterations. Averaged over 100 iterations and an ensemble of 20 networks. The theoretical predictions computed with (3.19) are plotted as dotted curves.

$\nabla B(w^{(1)}) = 0$, except for the components

$$\nabla B_{v_\beta v_\beta} = \tfrac{1}{216}, \quad \nabla B_{v_\beta w_{\beta 1}} = \tfrac{1}{18}, \quad \nabla B_{w_{\beta 1} v_\beta} = \tfrac{1}{18},$$
$$\nabla B_{w_{\beta 1} w_{\beta 0}} = \tfrac{1}{108}, \quad \nabla B_{w_{\beta 1} w_{\beta 1}} = \tfrac{1}{216}.$$

with $\beta = 1, 2$. Concentrating on the dynamics of $\overline{v}_\beta$, and $\overline{w}_{\beta 1}$, we thus obtain the linear system

$$\frac{d}{dt} \begin{pmatrix} \overline{v}_\beta \\ \overline{w}_{\beta 1} \end{pmatrix} = -\frac{\eta}{216} \begin{pmatrix} 1 & 12 \\ 12 & 1 \end{pmatrix} \begin{pmatrix} \overline{v}_\beta \\ \overline{w}_{\beta 1} \end{pmatrix} \tag{3.19}$$

with $\beta = 1, 2$. This system has one negative eigenvalue λ_- and one positive eigenvalue $\lambda_+ = \eta \tfrac{11}{216}$. Along the direction of the eigenvector $(1, -1)$ corresponding to the positive eigenvalue, the weights will move away from $w^{(1)}$ (cf. figure 3). Thus, natural learning escapes from the plateau, and reaches the global minimum (cf. figure 1 and figure 2). On the other hand, for randomized learning $B = 0$ identically. This means that the weights of a randomized learning network are not helped by the higher η corrections and therefore cannot escape the plateau (cf. figure 1 and figure 2).

Figure 3 shows that the predictions computed with the theory agree well with the simulations of the neural network learning the tent map, and therefore we conclude that the difference in performance of the two learning strategies is well explained by the theory.

The analysis of this section shows that if the learning process suffers from a plateau, then correlations can help learning by a nonzero B term (3.7) with some positive eigenvalues. Of course, the magnitude of these eigenvalues and the direction of the corresponding eigenvectors depend strongly on the problem at hand, i.e. B is probably not for every problem directed towards a global minimum. But the fact remains that a nonzero B term can make the weights move *away* from the plateau, which facilitates an escape, resulting in a lower error. On the other hand, if a nonzero B does not make the weights wander away, or if it does not lead to an escape, the performance of natural learning is still not worse than the performance of randomized learning, which also would get stuck on the plateau. In conclusion of this section, we therefore recommend natural learning (with positive correlations) if the problem at hand suffers from a plateau. However, artificial dependencies introduced to reduce fluctuations, e.g. cyclic learning for finite training sets (see e.g. (Heskes and Wiegerinck, 1996)) are in such a case not advisable.

4 Large networks

4.1 Student-teacher framework

In section 3.1, we derived an expansion for small learning parameters describing the approximate evolution of the (distribution of) weights. To do this, we did not have to make specific assumptions about the architecture of the network, the learning rule, generation of inputs and targets, and so on. In section 3.2, we did make special choices and looked at a particular example.

Studies of on-line learning in large networks usually start by defining the type of architecture, learning rule, and pattern generation. A very popular framework is that of a student network trying to imitate a teacher network with fixed but unknown weights. We will consider on-line learning in two-layered networks, i.e., similar to the network treated in section 3.2, but now with a large number of input units N. The number of hidden units is finite for both the student and the teacher. Both student and teach have just one output.

The notation that we use is quite different from the one in section 3. $H = H_{\text{student}} + H_{\text{teacher}}$ is the total number of hidden units of student and teacher together. We use $\boldsymbol{J}_i = (J_{i1}, \ldots, J_{iN})$ to denote the input-to-hidden weights, with $i = 1, \ldots, H_{\text{student}}$ for the student and $i = H_{\text{student}} + 1, \ldots, H$

for the teacher. Similarly, $(w_1, \ldots, w_H)$ ar the hidden-to-output weights. The
weight vector $\boldsymbol{w}$ of the previous section consists of all weights J_{ij} and w_i
corresponding to the student. All other weights specify how the targets are
generated, given a particular N-dimensional input $\boldsymbol{\xi}$. The pattern $\boldsymbol{x}$ of the
previous section is the combination of this input $\boldsymbol{\xi}$ and the target, i.e., the
output of the teacher network given this input.

Inputs are assumed to obey a first-order Markov process such that

$$\langle \xi_k(n) \rangle_{\boldsymbol{\xi}} = 0 , \quad \langle \xi_k(n)\xi_l(n) \rangle_{\boldsymbol{\xi}} = \delta_{kl} , \quad \text{and} \quad \langle \xi_k(n)\xi_l(n+1) \rangle_{\boldsymbol{\xi}} = c\delta_{kl} .$$

In other words, the components of the input vector are independently and
identically distributed with zero mean and unit variance, yet for $c \neq 0$ each
new component is correlated with the same component at a previous time
step. Note that, as in section 3, the stationary distribution of input vectors
is independent of the correlation c (for $|c| < 1$).

Given an input vector $\boldsymbol{\xi}$, we define the "local fields" $h_i = \boldsymbol{J}_i^T\boldsymbol{\xi}$, which,
again, can belong to either the teacher or the student. For notational conve-
nience we restrict ourselves to fully connected two-layered networks, but it
is easy to extend the following to, for example, tree-based architectures. The
outputs of student and teacher are written

$$y_{\text{student}}(\vec{h}) = \sum_{i \in \text{student}} w_i g(h_i) \quad \text{and} \quad y_{\text{teacher}}(\vec{h}) = \sum_{i \in \text{teacher}} w_i g(h_i) ,$$

with $\vec{h}$ a vector containing all local fields. To make analytical calculations
tractable, we choose the sigmoid $g(h) = \text{erf}(h/\sqrt{2})$ instead of the hyperbolic
tangent of section 3.2. The output transfer functions of both student and
teacher are linear.

After the presentation of the n-th pattern $\boldsymbol{\xi}(n)$, the student weights are
updated according to the gradient of the squared of the difference $\Delta \equiv$
$y_{\text{teacher}} - y_{\text{student}}$ between teacher and student output. This yields for the
input-to-hidden weights

$$\boldsymbol{J}_i(n+1) - \boldsymbol{J}_i(n) = \eta\delta_i(\vec{h}(n))\boldsymbol{\xi}(n) , \tag{4.1}$$

with $\delta_i(\vec{h}(n)) \equiv w_i(n)g'(x_i(n))\Delta(\vec{h}(n))$, and for the hidden-to-output weights

$$w_i(n+1) - w_i(n) = \eta g(h_i(n))\Delta(\vec{h}(n)) . \tag{4.2}$$

In fact, equations (4.1) and (4.2) are nothing but (2.1) and (2.3), explicitly
written out for the student-teacher problem considered here.

From now on we will work in the thermodynamic limit $N \to \infty$. Why can't
we simply apply the machinery of the previous section? Let us focus on the
input-to-hidden weights J_{ij}. Straightforwardly going through the approximations in the previous, we would obtain something like

$$J_{ij}(n) \approx \text{average behavior of order } 1 + \text{noise of order } \sqrt{\eta N} .$$

With finite N and a small learning parameter η, the fluctuations of the individual weights are indeed an order of magnitude smaller than their average behavior. However, with large N this depends on how the learning parameter scales with N. The usual choice is to take $\eta = \tilde{\eta}/N$, with $\tilde{\eta}$ of order 1. The learning parameter itself is still small, but the fluctuations for the individual weights are of the same order of magnitude as their average behavior. The approximations of the previous section are no longer valid. Looking more carefully, the reason for the relative unimportance of individual weights is a kind of credit assignment problem: the relative contribution of each input to the (backpropagated) error at the hidden units is extremely small.

4.2   Order parameters

There is a way out: instead of trying to describe the evolution of individual weights, we concentrate on the evolution of macroscopic order parameters. The order parameters $R_{ij} \equiv J_i^T J_j$ are very convenient: most properties of the system can be calculated once we know these order parameters and the weights w_i. For example, the generalisation error $E_g = \langle \Delta^2/2 \rangle_\xi$, follows from

$$E_g = \frac{1}{\pi} \sum_{i,j} \beta_{ij} w_i w_j \arcsin \frac{R_{ij}}{\sqrt{(1+R_{ii})(1+R_{jj})}} \, , \qquad (4.3)$$

where $\beta_{ij} = 1$ if both i, j belong either to the student or to the teacher and $\beta_{ij} = -1$ otherwise.

The dynamics of the weights w_i is given by (4.2), the dynamics of the order parameters R_{ij} can be written down as usual (Saad and Solla, 1995b; Biehl and Schwarze, 1995):

$$R_{ij}(n+1) = R_{ij}(n) + \frac{\tilde{\eta}_1}{N} \left[h_i(n)\delta_j(\vec{h}(n)) + h_j(n)\delta_i(\vec{h}(n)) \right] + \frac{\tilde{\eta}_1^2}{N} \delta_i(\vec{h}(n))\delta_j(\vec{h}(n)),$$
$$(4.4)$$

where we have defined $\delta_i(\vec{h}) \equiv 0$ if i refers to a teacher weight, and $\eta = \tilde{\eta}_1/N$. For convenience, we will take the liberty to use different learning parameters for the input-to-hidden and hidden-to-output weights, i.e., in (4.2) we substitute $\eta = \tilde{\eta}_2/N$. We will only consider the cases $\tilde{\eta}_1 = \tilde{\eta}_2 = \tilde{\eta}$ or $\tilde{\eta}_1 = \tilde{\eta}$ and $\tilde{\eta}_2 = 0$, i.e., fixed hidden-to-output weights.

Without any correlations, the machinery proceeds as follows. First one computes the distribution of the local fields which, because of the central limit theorem, comes out to be a Gaussian with covariance matrix $\mathcal{C} \equiv \left\langle \vec{h}\vec{h}^T \right\rangle_{\vec{h}}$ equal to the order parameters $\mathcal{R}$. Next one turns the difference equations (4.4) and (4.2) into continuous-time differential equations, at the same step taking averages on the righthand side. The resulting differential equations are of the form

$$\frac{dR_{ij}(t)}{dt} = F_{ij}(\mathcal{R}(t), \vec{w}(t)) \text{ and } \frac{dw_i(t)}{dt} = f_i(\mathcal{R}(t), \vec{w}(t)) \, ,$$

where $t_n = n/N$ is a rescaled "time". This definition of time is slightly different from the one in section 3, but also chosen such that the typical time scale of the evolution of the weights and order parameters is order one if time is measured in units of t. In many situations the averages

$$F_{ij} \;=\; \tilde{\eta}_1 \left\langle h_i \delta_j(\vec{h}) + h_j \delta_i(\vec{h}) \right\rangle_{\vec{h}} + \tilde{\eta}_1^2 \left\langle \delta_i(\vec{h}) \delta_j(\vec{h}) \right\rangle_{\vec{h}} \qquad (4.5)$$

$$\text{and } \; f_i = \tilde{\eta}_2 \left\langle g(h_i) \Delta(\vec{h}) \right\rangle_{\vec{h}} \qquad (4.6)$$

can be calculated analytically (Saad and Solla, 1995b).

With correlations, the distribution of the local fields does not only depend on the order parameters, but also has its "own" dynamics. Using again the central limit theorem for large N, we derive for the dynamics of the local fields

$$h_i(n+1) = \boldsymbol{J}_i^T(n+1)\boldsymbol{\xi}(n+1) = c \left[h_i(n) + \tilde{\eta}_1 \delta_i(\vec{h}(n)) \right] + u_i(n) , \qquad (4.7)$$

with $u_i(n) \equiv \boldsymbol{J}_i^T(n) \left[\boldsymbol{\xi}(n+1) - c\boldsymbol{\xi}(n) \right]$. In principle we have to study the combined dynamics of the weights and order parameters, as given by (4.2) and (4.4), respectively, and the local fields as given by (4.7). Luckily, however, the time scales of these two processes differ by a factor of order N: the local fields change much faster than the weights and order parameters. In the thermodynamic limit, we can "adiabatically eliminate the fast variables" (Wiegerinck et al., 1994; Haken, 1978), which basically means that we can act as if the local fields have reached their stationary distribution for fixed order parameters R_{ij} and weights w_i and use this distribution to compute the averages on the righthand sides of (4.4). This is exactly the same as in our analysis of on-line learning with correlations in small networks: again the small learning parameter makes the typical time scale of the evolution of the weights an order of magnitude slower than the time scale of the dynamics of the patterns. Our analysis breaks down if this is no longer the case, e.g., if the correlation c scales like $1 - c \propto 1/N$. Then the two time scales are no longer distinct and we need a completely different and more complicated analysis.

The separation of time scales does not imply that the dynamics of the order parameters and weights does not depend on the correlations c. It does, because this stationary distribution of the local fields depends on c. This may seem counterintuitive at first: why can't we apply the central limit theorem to derive the distribution of $h_i(n) = \boldsymbol{J}_i^T(n)\boldsymbol{\xi}(n)$? The reason is that $\boldsymbol{\xi}(n)$ is no longer independent of $\boldsymbol{J}_i(n)$: the current example is correlated with the recent examples to which $\boldsymbol{J}_i(n)$ has been adapted. This effect, which even in the thermodynamic limit is nonnegligible for nonzero c, is captured in (4.7).

The remaining task is to compute the stationary distribution resulting from the dynamics (4.7). First, we observe that for fixed $\boldsymbol{J}_i(n)$, the variables $u_i(n)$ are normally distributed with average zero and covariance matrix

$$\langle u_i(n)u_j(m) \rangle_{\boldsymbol{\xi}} =$$
$$= \left\langle \left(\boldsymbol{J}_i^T(n) \left[\boldsymbol{\xi}(n+1) - c\boldsymbol{\xi}(n) \right] \right) \left(\boldsymbol{J}_j^T(m) \left[\boldsymbol{\xi}(m+1) - c\boldsymbol{\xi}(m) \right] \right) \right\rangle_{\boldsymbol{\xi}}$$
$$= (1 - c^2) R_{ij}(n) \delta_{nm} . \tag{4.8}$$

Next, because of the symmetry $\delta_i(-\vec{h}) = -\delta_i(\vec{h})$, the distribution of local fields h_i must also be symmetric, i.e., $\langle h_{i_1} h_{i_2} \ldots h_{i_n} \rangle_{\vec{h}} = 0$ for any uneven number of terms n. From the stationarity condition

$$\langle h_i(n+1) h_j(n+1) \rangle_{\vec{h}} = \langle h_i(n) h_j(n) \rangle_{\vec{h}}$$

and the expressions (4.7) and (4.8) we obtain

$$C_{ij} = \langle h_i h_j \rangle_{\vec{h}} = R_{ij} + \frac{c^2}{1-c^2} \left[\tilde{\eta}_1 \left\langle h_i \delta_j(\vec{h}) + h_j \delta_i(\vec{h}) \right\rangle_{\vec{h}} + \tilde{\eta}_1^2 \left\langle \delta_i(\vec{h}) \delta_j(\vec{h}) \right\rangle_{\vec{h}} \right] . \tag{4.9}$$

Alas, the general solution of (4.9) is intractable. We can, however, make an excellent approximation by assuming that the stationary distribution of the local fields is a Gaussian. Then we can compute the averages on the right-hand side of (4.9) and obtain a self-consistent equation for the covariance matrix C. In fact, it can be shown that the fourth order cumulant (kurtosis) of the stationary distribution is of order c^4 and thus that, at least for small c, the assumption of normality is fair. In other words, all following results are accurate up to order $\epsilon = c^2/(1 - c^2)$.

There is a striking resemblance between the equations (4.6) and (4.9). Combination of these expressions provides for a simple and elegant summary of the effect of correlations on the learning dynamics of two-layered networks (including simple perceptrons and soft-committee machines):

$$\frac{d\mathcal{R}}{dt} = \mathcal{F}(C, \vec{w}) \quad \text{and} \quad \frac{d\vec{w}}{dt} = \vec{f}(C, \vec{w}) \tag{4.10}$$

$$C = \mathcal{R} + \epsilon \mathcal{F}(C, \vec{w}) \tag{4.11}$$

with $\mathcal{R}$ the set of order parameters, $\vec{w}$ the set of hidden to output weights, C the stationary covariance matrix of the local fields and $\mathcal{F}$ and $\vec{f}$ functions that can be found in papers describing the (uncorrelated) learning dynamics of specific architectures and problems (Saad and Solla, 1995b; Riegler and Biehl, 1995). The remarkable thing here is that in order to study learning with correlated patterns we do not need to compute new difficult integrals. Provided that the normality assumption holds, which can easily be checked if there is any doubt, the dynamical equations for uncorrelated patterns are all we need to know to compute the dynamics for correlated patterns. In the next section we will give specific examples (see also (Heskes and Coolen, 1997)).

4.3 "Plateaus" in large networks

The generalisation performance of two-layered networks as a function of time is often dominated by a long time span in which this performance hardly improves (Biehl et al., 1996; Saad and Solla, 1995b). This so-called "plateau" is in fact caused by a saddle point in the dynamics of the order parameters. The delayed repulsion from this saddle point is due to the fact that the corresponding positive eigenvalue of the linearized system, around this saddle point, is very small in comparison with the absolute values of the negative eigenvalues. The equivalence between the two sets of functions $\mathcal{F}$ in (4.10) and (4.11) makes it surprisingly straightforward to analyse the correlated learning dynamics in the neighbourhood of such a saddle point or, in general, of any fixed point.

We will first consider the so-called soft-committee machines. The output unit of soft-committee machines is linear and the couplings from all the hidden units to the output unit are positive and of unit strength, i.e., $\forall_i \, w_i = 1$ and $\tilde{\eta}_2 = 0$. We only have to consider the dynamics of the order parameters. Linearization of the learning dynamics near a fixed point, where $\mathcal{F}(\mathcal{C}_{\text{fp}}) = 0$, yields

$$\frac{d\mathcal{R}}{dt} = \mathcal{H}(\mathcal{R} - \mathcal{R}_{\text{fp}}) \quad \text{with}$$

$$\mathcal{H} = \frac{\partial \mathcal{F}(\mathcal{C})}{\partial \mathcal{R}} = \frac{\partial \mathcal{F}(\mathcal{C})}{\partial \mathcal{C}} \frac{\partial \mathcal{C}}{\partial \mathcal{R}} = \frac{\partial \mathcal{F}(\mathcal{C})}{\partial \mathcal{C}} \left[\mathbb{1}_{|\mathcal{R}|} - \epsilon \frac{\partial \mathcal{F}(\mathcal{C})}{\partial \mathcal{C}} \right]^{-1},$$

with all derivatives evaluated at $\mathcal{C} = \mathcal{C}_{\text{fp}}$ and where the last step follows from differentiation of (4.11) with respect to $\mathcal{R}$. In this symbolic notation $\mathcal{R}$ is best read as a vector consisting of all, say $|\mathcal{R}|$, order parameters which makes $\mathcal{H}$ an $|\mathcal{R}| \times |\mathcal{R}|$ matrix; $\mathbb{1}_{|\mathcal{R}|}$ stands for the $|\mathcal{R}|$-dimensional identity matrix. The eigenvalues λ of the matrix $\mathcal{H}$, which can be compared with (minus) the Hessian in section 3, determine the stability of a fixed point. From (4.11) we deduce that $\mathcal{R}_{\text{fp}} = \mathcal{C}_{\text{fp}}$. In other words, a fixed point for learning without correlations is also a fixed point for learning with correlations. But then

$$\left. \frac{\partial \mathcal{F}(\mathcal{C})}{\partial \mathcal{C}} \right|_{\mathcal{C}_{\text{fp}}} = \left. \frac{\partial \mathcal{F}(\mathcal{R})}{\partial \mathcal{R}} \right|_{\mathcal{R}_{\text{fp}}} \equiv \mathcal{H}_0 \quad \text{and thus} \quad \mathcal{H} = \mathcal{H}_0 \left[\mathbb{1}_{|\mathcal{R}|} - \epsilon \mathcal{H}_0 \right]^{-1},$$

where $\mathcal{H}_0$ refers to the matrix for $c = 0$. Correlations do not change the eigenvectors of the matrix $\mathcal{H}$, but do transform an eigenvalue λ_0 of the matrix $\mathcal{H}_0$ into

$$\lambda = \frac{\lambda_0}{1 - \epsilon \lambda_0} \quad \text{and thus} \quad \text{Re}(\lambda) = \text{Re}(\lambda_0) + \epsilon \left[\text{Re}(\lambda_0)^2 - \text{Im}(\lambda_0)^2 \right] + \cdots .$$

The eigenvalue with the largest real part is the most interesting one. In case of a stable fixed point, the least negative eigenvalue governs the speed of

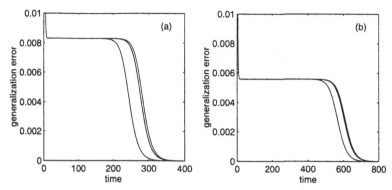

Figure 4. Correlations shorten the length of the plateau for soft-committee machines. The generalisation error (4.3) is plotted as a function of time t for correlations $c = 0.0$, 0.6 and 0.9 (from right to left). A soft-committee machine with two hidden units, is trained, with learning parameter $\eta_1 = 1.0$ in (a) and $\eta_1 = 0.5$ in (b), to implement a simple task defined by a teacher perceptron. Initial conditions are set according to $R_{11} = R_{12} = R_{13} = R_{23} = 0.0$ and $R_{22} = 0.0001$.

convergence. With correlations this eigenvalue then becomes less negative, and thus increases the time to convergence. The most positive eigenvalue rules the repulsion from a saddle point and is thus a key factor for determining the length of a plateau. We should say that the effect of correlations depends on whether the real part of the largest eigenvalue dominates the imaginary part. In the situations we have encountered both in our own experience and in the literature, the imaginary part is either completely absent or smaller (in absolute sense) than the real part. Calling this the typical situation, we conclude that correlations make unstable points more unstable and thus lead to shorter plateaus. The length of the plateau is inversely proportional to the most positive eigenvalue λ; the shortening, as a result of correlations, is therefore proportional to ϵ:

$$\text{shortening} \propto \frac{1}{\lambda_0} - \frac{1}{\lambda} = \epsilon \ . \tag{4.12}$$

As an example, let us consider a soft-committee machine with two hidden units ($i = 1, 2$) trained to implement a simple task defined by a teacher with just one hidden unit ($i = 3$) as in (Biehl and Schwarze, 1995). The averages F_{11}, F_{12}, F_{22}, F_{13} and F_{23} have been computed analytically and are used in (4.10) and (4.11) to compute the evolution of the order parameters. In order to show the effect of the correlations on the length of the plateau, we choose zero correlations initially, and add correlations when the system gets stuck at the saddle point. In figure 4 we show the evolution of the generalisation error for $c = 0.0$, 0.6 and 0.9. The learning parameter in figure 4(a) is equal to 1 whereas in figure 4(b) the learning parameter is equal to 0.5. As predicted by (4.12), the shortening when going from correlations $c = 0.6$ to $c = 0.9$ is much more prominent than when going from $c = 0.0$ to 0.6. Furthermore, the shortening is about the same for both learning parameters.

The general statement made above for soft-committee machines, cannot be translated to general two-layered networks with adaptive hidden-to-output weights. For any particular situation, however, the effect of correlations can be calculated using the set of expressions (4.10) and (4.11).

As an illustration we consider a student with 2 hidden units $(i = 1, 2)$ trained by a teacher, also with 2 hidden units $(i = 3, 4)$. The teacher is chosen symmetric, i.e., $R_{33} = R_{44} = 1$ and $R_{34} = 0$, with hidden-to-output weights $w_3 = w_4 = 1$. The student is initialized with small weights $\boldsymbol{J}_i$ and w_i and has learning parameters $\tilde{\eta}_1 = \tilde{\eta}_2 \equiv \tilde{\eta}$. Initialization with small weights is the standard procedure in practical applications of backpropagation for multi-layer perceptrons, which supposedly reduces the chance to end up at a suboptimal local minimum. The origin, however, is a saddle point where all derivatives are zero. It is different from the saddle points usually studied where the problem is to break the symmetry between the student's hidden units. The escape from the origin saddle point, on the other hand, appears to require no symmetry breaking, yet a combined increase of the hidden-to-output weights $w_1 = w_2 \equiv w$ and an alignment of the student weights $\boldsymbol{J}_1$ and $\boldsymbol{J}_2$ to the teacher weights $\boldsymbol{J}_3$ and $\boldsymbol{J}_4$, i.e., an increase of the inner products $R_{13} = R_{14} = R_{23} = R_{24} \equiv R$. The evolution of w and R follows from (4.10) and (4.11) where the functions $\mathcal{F}$ and $\vec{f}$ computed in (Saad and Solla, 1995b; Riegler and Biehl, 1995) are linearized around the origin:

$$\frac{d}{dt}\begin{pmatrix} w \\ R \end{pmatrix} = \frac{2\tilde{\eta}}{\pi}\begin{pmatrix} 2\gamma & \sqrt{2} \\ \frac{1}{2}\sqrt{2} & 0 \end{pmatrix}\begin{pmatrix} w \\ R \end{pmatrix} \quad \text{with} \quad \gamma = \frac{\tilde{\eta}}{\pi}\frac{c^2}{1-c^2}. \qquad (4.13)$$

The derivatives of the inner products R_{11}, R_{12} and R_{22}, concerning only student weights, are of higher order in R and w and do therefore not influence the escape from the origin. This escape is dominated by the eigenvalue

$$\lambda = \frac{2\tilde{\eta}}{\pi}\left(\gamma + \sqrt{1+\gamma^2}\right),$$

which, through γ, strongly depends on the amount of correlations c. An important side effect is that with adaptive hidden-to-output weights the eigenvectors and thus the directions of escape are affected by the amount of correlations. In our simulations, the student network, after leaving the first plateau due to the saddle point at the origin, gets stuck at another saddle point. The different escape directions make that the values of the order parameters $\mathcal{R}$ and weights $\vec{w}$, and thus the height of this second plateau, depend on the correlation c.

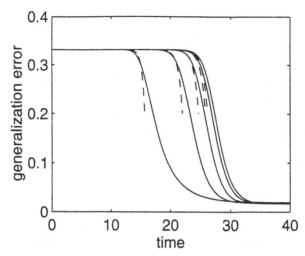

Figure 5. Correlations shorten the length of the plateau for two-layered networks. The generalisation error (4.3) is plotted as a function of time t for correlations $c = 0.0$, 0.2, 0.4, 0.6, and 0.8 (from right to left). Both student and teacher are two-layered networks with two hidden units. The solid curves are simulations, the dashed lines correspond to the theoretical approximation (4.13). The simulations were done with a network of size $N = 1000$ averaged over 50 independent runs.

In figure 5 we show simulations of the evolution of the generalisation error (4.3) as a function of time t for different amounts of correlations c for fixed $\tilde{\eta} = 1$. The student weights are initialized such that $R_{12} = R_{13} = R_{14} = R_{23} = R_{24} = 0$ and $R_{11} = R_{22} = 10^{-12}$, and with $w_1 = w_2 = 0$. The simulations, indicated by the solid lines, are on the level of the weights as given by (4.1) and (4.2). The dashed lines result from the set (4.13). These differential equations predict the time at which the networks escape from the saddle point quite accurately, but are, of course, no longer valid after this escape. Furthermore, it can be seen that correlations shorten the plateau and that this effect roughly scales with c^2.

5   Discussion

In this chapter we have presented a quantitative analysis of on-line learning with time-correlated patterns for both small and large networks. The essential ingredient in both cases is the separation between time scales of the pattern presentation and the weight dynamics. On the time scale needed for a representative sampling of the environment the weight changes must be negligible. A separation of time scales, which is in both cases achieved by using a small learning parameter, is essential in on-line learning to prevent over-specialization on single patterns.

The second essential ingredient for the analysis of small networks is the assumption that the weights can be described by their average value with small superimposed fluctuations. The evolution of the average value can be described with an ordinary differential equation (ODE). This ODE term only contains information about the stationary distribution of the patterns. Dependencies between successive patterns do not enter until the first correction to the ODE term. This implies that in general, when the ODE term is dominant, learning with correlated patterns and learning with randomized examples in small networks are alike. The correlations between patterns merely act as corrections on the learning process, both in the fluctuations and in the bias.

As explained, the theory is locally valid, and may therefore not be suited for quantitative computations of global properties of the learning process, such as the stationary distribution of weights or the escape time out of a local minimum. However, even a local theory can be useful to understand some aspects of global properties (Finnoff, 1994). Our study of learning on plateaus in small networks is an example of a local analysis of on-line learning which accounts for huge, non-local effects. On a plateau the ODE contribution vanishes. The higher order terms, which contain the correlations, therefore dominate the learning process. Simulations of a multilayer perceptron with backpropagation learning the tent map demonstrate that correlations between successive patterns can dramatically improve the final learning result. This phenomenon is explained by our analysis, which evidences that randomized learning gets stuck on a plateau, whereas the correlations in natural learning cause the escape from the plateau. Predictions computed with the theory agree well with the simulations.

In studies on large networks, the second essential ingredient is the set of order parameters. We are no longer able to describe the evolution of individual weights, but can compute the evolution of the order parameters. This evolution is somewhat affected by correlations between successive patterns: correlations change the (quasi-stationary) distribution of the local fields. Assuming that this distribution is a Gaussian, we arrived at a set of expressions which can be solved numerically to yield the evolution of the order parameters and the hidden-to-output weights. We came to the remarkable conclusion that the expressions that govern the dynamics for uncorrelated patterns are all that is needed to compute the (approximate) dynamics for correlated patterns. These dynamical equations are accurate up to first order in $\epsilon = c^2/(1 - c^2)$, where c is the correlation parameter ($|c| < 1$), but in simulations appear to give a more than reasonable approximation for correlations as high as $c = 0.9$.

The beneficial effect of correlations in case of plateaus is for large networks much smaller than for small networks. It might as well be achieved through a simple increase in the learning parameter. The reason is that what are called plateaus are in fact saddle points in the dynamics of the order parameters. Escaping from a "real" plateau (zero eigenvalue of the Hessian matrix), as encountered for small networks, is much more difficult than escaping from a saddle point (at least one negative eigenvalue of the Hessian matrix).

Finally, we would like to stress that it is not always straightforward to translate results obtained for on-line learning in "small" networks to "large" networks and vice versa. The choice of the toolbox (stochastic approximation theory or statistical mechanics) is not open, but depends on the definition of the problem.

Acknowledgements We would like to thank Andrzej Komoda, Jeroen Coolen, Peter Riegler, Bert Kappen, and Stan Gielen for their direct and/or indirect involvement in the research presented in this chapter. Thanks to David Saad for the organization of an excellent workshop.

References

Amari, S. (1967). A theory of adaptive pattern classifiers. *IEEE Trans.*, EC–16, 299–307.

Barkai, N., Seung, H., and Sompolinsky, H. (1995). Local and global convergence of on-line learning. *Phys. Rev. Lett.*, 75, 1415–1418.

Barnard, E. (1992). Optimization for neural nets. *IEEE Trans.*, NN–3, 232–240.

Benveniste, A., Metivier, M., and Priouret, P. (1987). *Adaptive algorithms and stochastic approximations.* Springer-Verlag, Berlin.

Biehl, M., Riegler, P., and Wöhler, C. (1996). Transient dynamics of on-line learning in two-layered neural networks. *J. Phys. A*, 29, 4769–4780.

Biehl, M. and Schwarze, H. (1995). Learning by on-line gradient descent. *J. Phys. A*, 28, 643–656.

Brunak, S., Engelbrecht, J., and Knudsen, S. (1990). Cleaning up gene databases. *Nature*, 343, 123.

Finnoff, W. (1994). Diffusion approximations for the constant learning rate backpropagation algorithm and resistance to local minima. *Neural Computation*, 6, 285–295.

Haken, H. (1978). *Synergetics, an Introduction.* Springer, New York.

Hansen, L., Pathria, R., and Salamon, P. (1993). Stochastic dynamics of supervised learning. *J. Phys. A*, 26, 63–71.

Haykin, S. (1994). *Neural Networks, A Comprehensive Foundation*. MacMillan, Hamilton, Ontario.

Hertz, J., Krogh, A., and Palmer, R. (1991). *Introduction to the Theory of Neural Computation*. Addison-Wesley, Redwood City.

Heskes, T. (1994). On Fokker-Planck approximations of on-line learning processes. *J. of Phys. A*, 27, 5145–5160.

Heskes, T. and Coolen, J. (1997). Learning in two-layered networks with correlated examples. *J. Phys. A*, 30, 4983–4992.

Heskes, T. and Kappen, B. (1991). Learning processes in neural networks. *Phys. Rev. A*, 44, 2718–2726.

Heskes, T. and Wiegerinck, W. (1996). A theoretical comparison of batch-mode, on-line, cyclic, and almost cyclic learning. *IEEE Trans.*, NN-7, 919–925.

Hondou, T. and Sawada, Y. (1994). Analysis of learning processes of chaotic time series by neural networks. *Prog. in Theor. Phys.*, 91, 397–402.

Hoptroff, R. (1993). The principles and practice of time series forecasting and business modelling using neural nets. *Neural Computing and Applications*, 1, 59–66.

Hush, D., Horne, B., and Salas, J. (1992). Error surfaces for multilayer perceptrons. *IEEE Transactions on SMC*, 22, 1152–1161.

Kohonen, T. (1982). Self-organized formation of topologically correct feature maps. *Biological Cybernetics*, 43, 59–69.

Kuan, C. and White, H. (1994). Artificial neural networks: an econometric perspective. *Econometric Reviews*, 13.

Lapedes, A. and Farber, R. (1988). How neural networks work. In Anderson, D., editor, *Neural Information Processing Systems*, pages 442–456, New York. American Institute of Physics.

Lee, Y. (1991). Handwritten digit recognition using K nearest-neighbor, radial-basis function, and backpropagation neural networks. *Neural Computation*, 3, 440–449.

Leen, T. and Moody, J. (1993). Weight space probability densities in stochastic learning: I. Dynamics and equilibria. In Hanson, S., Cowan, J., and Giles, L., editors, *Advances in Neural Information Processing Systems 5*, pages 451–458, San Mateo. Morgan Kaufmann.

Mpitsos, G. and Burton, M. (1992). Convergence and divergence in neural networks: processing of chaos and biological analogy. *Neural Networks*, 5:605–625.

Orr, G. and Leen, T. (1993). Weight space probability densities in stochastic learning: II. Transients and basin hopping times. In Hanson, S., Cowan, J., and Giles, L., editors, *Advances in Neural Information Processing Systems 5*, pages 507–514, San Mateo. Morgan Kaufmann.

Radons, G. (1993). On stochastic dynamics of supervised learning. *J. Phys. A*, 26, 3455–3461.

Riegler, P. and Biehl, M. (1995). On-line backpropagation in two-layered networks. *J. Phys. A*, 28, L507–L513.

Ritter, H. and Schulten, K. (1988). Convergence properties of Kohonen's topology conserving maps: fluctuations, stability, and dimension selection. *Biological Cybernetics*, 60, 59–71.

Rumelhart, D., Hinton, G., and Williams, R. (1986). Learning representations by back-propagating errors. *Nature*, 323, 533–536.

Saad, D. and Solla, S. (1995a). Exact solution for on-line learning in multilayer neural networks. *Phys. Rev. Lett.*, 74, 4337–4340.

Saad, D. and Solla, S. (1995b). On-line learning in soft committee machines. *Phys. Rev. E*, 52, 4225–4243.

Schuster, H. (1989). *Deterministic Chaos*. VCH, Weinheim, second revised edition.

van Kampen, N. (1992). *Stochastic Processes in Physics and Chemistry*. North-Holland, Amsterdam.

Weigend, A. and Gershenfeld, N., editors (1993). *Predicting the Future and Understanding the Past: a Comparison of Approaches*. Addison-Wesley.

Weigend, A., Huberman, B., and Rumelhart, D. (1990). Predicting the future: a connectionist approach. *International Journal of Neural Systems*, 1, 193–209.

Werbos, P. (1974). *Beyond Regression: New Tools for Prediction and Analysis in the Behavioral Sciences*. PhD thesis, Harvard University.

White, H. (1989). Some asymptotic results for learning in single hidden-layer feedforward network models. *Jour. of Am. Stat. Assoc.*, 84, 1003–1013.

Wiegerinck, W. and Heskes, T. (1994). On-line learning with time-correlated patterns. *Europhys. Lett.*, 28, 451–455.

Wiegerinck, W. and Heskes, T. (1996). How dependencies between successive examples affect on-line learning. *Neural Computation*, 8, 1743–1765.

Wiegerinck, W., Komoda, A., and Heskes, T. (1994). Stochastic dynamics of learning with momentum in neural networks. *J. Phys. A*, 27, 4425–4437.

Wong, F. (1991). Time series forecasting using backpropagation networks. *Neurocomputing*, pages 147–159.

Online Learning from Finite Training Sets

David Barber[1]

Department of Medical Biophysics, University of Nijmegen,
6525 EZ Nijmegen, The Netherlands.
davidb@mbfys.kun.nl

Peter Sollich[2]

Department of Physics, University of Edinburgh,
Edinburgh EH9 3JZ, U.K.
P.Sollich@ed.ac.uk

Abstract

We analyse online gradient descent learning from *finite* training sets at *non-infinitesimal* learning rates η for both linear and non-linear networks. In the linear case, exact results are obtained for the time-dependent generalization error of networks with a large number of weights N, trained on $p = \alpha N$ examples. This allows us to study in detail the effects of finite training set size α on, for example, the optimal choice of learning rate η. We also compare online and *offline* learning, for respective optimal settings of η at given final learning time. Online learning turns out to be much more robust to *input bias* and actually outperforms offline learning when such bias is present; for unbiased inputs, online and offline learning perform almost equally well. Our analysis of online learning for *non-linear* networks (namely, soft-committee machines), advances the theory to more realistic learning scenarios. Dynamical equations are derived for an appropriate set of order parameters; these are exact in the limiting case of either linear networks or infinite training sets. Preliminary comparisons with simulations suggest that the theory captures some effects of finite training sets, but may not yet account correctly for the presence of local minima.

---

[1]RWCP, SNN Theory Group.
[2]Royal Society Dorothy Hodgkin Research Fellow.

1 Introduction

The analysis of online (gradient descent) learning, which is one of the most common approaches to supervised learning found in the neural networks community, has recently been the focus of much attention. The characteristic feature of online learning is that the weights of a network ('student') are updated each time a new training example is presented, such that the error on this example is reduced. In offline learning, on the other hand, the total error on all examples in the training set is accumulated before a gradient descent weight update is made. For a given training set and starting weights, offline learning is entirely deterministic. Online learning, on the other hand, is a stochastic process due to the random choice of training example (from the given training set) for each update; in fact, it can essentially be viewed as a 'noisy' version of offline learning. The two are equivalent only in the limit where the learning rate $\eta \rightarrow 0$ (see, *e.g.*, Heskes and Kappen, 1991). For both online and offline learning, the main quantity of interest is normally the evolution of the generalization error: After a given number of weight updates, how well does the student approximate the input-output mapping ('teacher') underlying the training examples?

Most analytical treatments of online learning assume either that the size of the training set is infinite, or that the learning rate η is vanishingly small. Both of these restrictions are undesirable: In practice, most training sets are finite[3], and non-infinitesimal values of η are needed to ensure that the learning process converges after a reasonable number of updates. General results have been derived for the difference between online and offline learning to first order in η, which apply to training sets of any size (see, *e.g.*, Heskes and Kappen, 1991). However, these do not directly address the question of generalization performance. The most explicit analysis of the time evolution of the generalization error for linear networks and finite training sets was provided by Krogh and Hertz (1992) for a scenario very similar to the (linear) one we consider below. Their $\eta \rightarrow 0$ offline calculation will serve as a baseline for our work. For non-linear networks and finite η, progress has been made in particular for so-called soft committee machine network architectures (see, *e.g.*, Saad and Solla, 1995, Biehl and Schwarze, 1995), but only for the case of infinite training sets. Finite training sets present a significant analytical difficulty as successive weight updates are correlated, giving rise to highly non-trivial generalization dynamics.

This chapter is split into two main sections. In section (2), we develop the main theoretical tools required for an exact treatment of linear networks. We then build on these results in section (3), by constructing a compact, approx-

---

[3]Online learning can also be used to learn teacher rules that vary in time. The assumption of an infinite set (or 'stream') of training examples is then much more plausible, and in fact necessary for continued adaptation of the student. We do not consider this case in the following.

imate theory for non-linear networks, based on similar theoretical principles to the linear theory.

2 Linear networks

In this section, we give an exact analysis of online learning in a simple linear model system. Our aim is twofold: (1) to assess how the combination of non-infinitesimal learning rates η and finite training sets (containing α examples per weight) affects online learning, and (2) to compare the generalization performance of online and offline learning. A priori, one may expect online learning to perform worse due to its inherent randomness. We show that this disadvantage is actually negligible when online and offline learning are compared on an equal footing, $i.e.$, for their respective optimal learning rates. More importantly, we will see that online learning is much more robust to $input\ bias$ than offline learning and actually performs $better$ than the offline version in the case of biased inputs.

2.1 Model definition

We consider training of a linear student network with input-output relation

$$y = \frac{1}{\sqrt{N}}\mathbf{w}^{\mathrm{T}}\mathbf{x}$$

Here $\mathbf{x}$ is an N-dimensional vector of real-valued inputs, y the single real output and $\mathbf{w}$ the weight vector of the network. 'T' denotes the transpose of a vector and the factor $1/\sqrt{N}$ is introduced for convenience. In online learning, whenever a training example $(\mathbf{x}, y)$ is presented to the network, its weight vector is updated along the gradient of the squared error[4] on this example, $i.e.$,

$$\Delta\mathbf{w} = -\eta\,\nabla_{\mathbf{w}}\frac{1}{2}\left(y - \frac{1}{\sqrt{N}}\mathbf{w}^{\mathrm{T}}\mathbf{x}\right)^2 = \eta\left(\frac{1}{\sqrt{N}}y\mathbf{x} - \frac{1}{N}\mathbf{x}\mathbf{x}^{\mathrm{T}}\mathbf{w}\right)$$

where η is the learning rate. We are primarily interested in the case of online learning from finite training sets, where for each update an example is randomly chosen from a given set $\{(\mathbf{x}^\mu, y^\mu), \mu = 1\ldots p\}$ of p training examples. If example μ is chosen for update n, the weight vector is changed to

$$\mathbf{w}_{n+1} = \left\{1 - \frac{\eta}{N}\left[\mathbf{x}^\mu(\mathbf{x}^\mu)^{\mathrm{T}} + \gamma\right]\right\}\mathbf{w}_n + \eta\frac{1}{\sqrt{N}}y^\mu\mathbf{x}^\mu \quad \text{(online)} \quad (2.1)$$

---

[4]We consider only squared error here, which is probably the most commonly used error measure. We also restrict our analysis to 'vanilla' gradient descent learning, excluding more sophisticated learning algorithms.

Here we have also included a weight decay γ. The update rule for *offline* learning is similar, but here the gradients for all p different training examples are accumulated before a weight update is made:

$$\mathbf{w}_{(r+1)p} = [1 - \eta(\lambda + \mathbf{A})]\mathbf{w}_{rp} + \frac{\eta}{\sqrt{N}} \sum_\mu y^\mu \mathbf{x}^\mu \qquad \text{(offline)} \qquad (2.2)$$

Here r is the number of offline weight updates; in order to compare online and offline learning at equal computational cost, we index the weight vectors for both cases by the number of gradient calculations, which is $n = rp$ in the offline case. The matrix

$$\mathbf{A} = \frac{1}{N} \sum_\mu \mathbf{x}^\mu (\mathbf{x}^\mu)^{\mathrm{T}}$$

is the correlation matrix of the training inputs, and $\lambda = \gamma\alpha$ is the weight decay rescaled by the number of examples per weight, $\alpha = p/N$. We will generally use λ (rather than γ) to characterize the strength of the weight decay, for both online and offline learning. For simplicity, all student weights are assumed to be initially zero, *i.e.*, $\mathbf{w}_{n=0} = \mathbf{0}$.

The main quantity of interest to us is the *generalization error* of the student and its evolution during learning. We assume that the training examples are generated by a linear 'teacher', *i.e.*, $y^\mu = \mathbf{w}_*^{\mathrm{T}}\mathbf{x}^\mu/\sqrt{N} + \xi^\mu$, where ξ^μ is zero mean additive noise of variance σ^2. The teacher weight vector is taken to be normalized to $\mathbf{w}_*^2 = N$ for simplicity. We first investigate the case of unbiased inputs ($\langle\mathbf{x}\rangle = \mathbf{0}$), assuming that input vectors are sampled randomly from an isotropic distribution over the hypersphere $\mathbf{x}^2 = N$ (biased inputs will be considered in Section 2.4). The generalization error, defined as the average of the squared error between student and teacher outputs for random inputs, is then

$$\epsilon_{\mathrm{g}} = \frac{1}{2N}(\mathbf{w}_n - \mathbf{w}_*)^2 = \frac{1}{2N}\mathbf{v}_n^2 \quad \text{where} \quad \mathbf{v}_n = \mathbf{w}_n - \mathbf{w}_*.$$

In order to make the scenario analytically tractable, we focus on the limit $N \to \infty$ of a large number of input components and weights, taken at constant number of examples per weight $\alpha = p/N$ and updates per weight ('learning time') $t = n/N$. In this limit, the generalization error $\epsilon_{\mathrm{g}}(t)$ becomes self-averaging (see however Section 2.4) and can be calculated by averaging both over the random selection of examples from a given training set and over all training sets. Our results can be straightforwardly extended to the case of perceptron teachers with a nonlinear transfer function, as in (Sollich, 1995).

2.2 Unbiased inputs

2.2.1 Outline of calculation

We begin by deriving from the online learning weight update (2.1) an update equation for the 'selection' average of the generalization error (*i.e.*, its average with respect to the random choice of training examples for each update, denoted generically by $\langle \ldots \rangle$). In fact, it will turn out to be useful to consider a slightly generalized version of the generalization error, $\epsilon_n = \frac{1}{2N} \mathbf{v}_n^{\mathrm{T}} \mathbf{M} \mathbf{v}_n$, with $\mathbf{M}$ an arbitrary $N \times N$ matrix. To get the update equation for $\langle \epsilon_n \rangle$, we first rewrite (2.1) in terms of $\mathbf{v}_n$, the difference between student and teacher weight vectors:

$$\mathbf{v}_{n+1} = \left\{ 1 - \eta \left[\frac{1}{N} \mathbf{x}^{\mu}(\mathbf{x}^{\mu})^{\mathrm{T}} + \frac{\lambda}{p} \right] \right\} \mathbf{v}_n + \eta \frac{1}{\sqrt{N}} \xi^{\mu} \mathbf{x}^{\mu} - \frac{\eta \lambda}{p} \mathbf{w}_* \qquad (2.3)$$

This can now be multiplied by its transpose, with the matrix $\mathbf{M}$ inserted, and the selection average for update n performed. Discarding terms which become negligible in the large N limit, one finds after a little algebra

$$N \left(\langle \epsilon_{n+1} \rangle - \langle \epsilon_n \rangle \right)$$

$$= \frac{\tilde{\eta}}{N} (\mathbf{b} - \lambda \mathbf{w}_*)^{\mathrm{T}} \mathbf{M} \langle \mathbf{v}_n \rangle - \frac{\tilde{\eta}}{N} \left\langle \mathbf{v}_n^{\mathrm{T}} \left[\lambda \mathbf{M} + \frac{1}{2} (\mathbf{AM} + \mathbf{MA}) \right] \mathbf{v}_n \right\rangle$$

$$+ \frac{\tilde{\eta}^2 \alpha}{N} \sum_{\mu} \frac{1}{N} (\mathbf{x}^{\mu})^{\mathrm{T}} \mathbf{M} \mathbf{x}^{\mu} \left\{ \frac{1}{2} (\xi^{\mu})^2 - \xi^{\mu} \frac{1}{\sqrt{N}} (\mathbf{x}^{\mu})^{\mathrm{T}} \langle \mathbf{v}_n \rangle + \frac{1}{2N} \left\langle \mathbf{v}_n^{\mathrm{T}} \mathbf{x}^{\mu} (\mathbf{x}^{\mu})^{\mathrm{T}} \mathbf{v}_n \right\rangle \right\}$$

$$(2.4)$$

where $\tilde{\eta} = \eta/\alpha$ is a rescaled learning rate, and $\mathbf{b} = \sum_{\mu} \xi^{\mu} \mathbf{x}^{\mu}/\sqrt{N}$. We now want to transform (2.4) into a closed dynamical equation for $\langle \epsilon_n \rangle$. This means that all selection averages need to be either eliminated or reduced to averages of the same form as $\langle \epsilon_n \rangle$. For the two terms linear in $\langle \mathbf{v}_n \rangle$, this is straightforward: The selection average of (2.1) yields directly

$$N \left(\langle \mathbf{v}_{n+1} \rangle - \langle \mathbf{v}_n \rangle \right) = \tilde{\eta} \left[-(\lambda + \mathbf{A}) \langle \mathbf{v}_n \rangle + \mathbf{b} - \lambda \mathbf{w}_* \right].$$

Starting from $\mathbf{v}_0 = -\mathbf{w}_*$, this can easily be solved, with the result (for $N \to \infty$)

$$\langle \mathbf{v}_n \rangle = (\lambda + \mathbf{A})^{-1} \left\{ \mathbf{b} - \lambda \mathbf{w}_* - \exp \left[-\tilde{\eta} t (\lambda + \mathbf{A}) \right] (\mathbf{b} + \mathbf{A} \mathbf{w}_*) \right\} \qquad (2.5)$$

from which the selection average has now disappeared. Learning rate and learning time enter only through the combination $\tau = \tilde{\eta} t$; this rescaled time will be useful later on. In (2.4), the remaining terms quadratic in $\mathbf{v}_n$ now present the main problem. The second term on the r.h.s. shows that the evolution of $\epsilon_g = \epsilon_n(\mathbf{M}{=}1)$ depends on $\epsilon_n(\mathbf{M}{=}\mathbf{A})$ which in turn depends on $\epsilon_n(\mathbf{M}{=}\mathbf{A}^2)$ and so on, yielding an infinite hierarchy of order parameters. This problem was solved in (Sollich and Barber, 1997a) by introducing an auxiliary parameter h through $\mathbf{M} = \exp(h\mathbf{A})$; all order parameters $\epsilon_n(\mathbf{M}{=}\mathbf{A}^m)$, $m = 1, 2, \ldots$, can then be obtained by differentiating $\epsilon_n(h) = \frac{1}{2N} \mathbf{v}_n^{\mathrm{T}} \exp(h\mathbf{A}) \mathbf{v}_n$.

Here we choose a different route, which is somewhat more transparent and also more easily adapted to the case of biased inputs to be considered later. The main idea is to decompose the evolution of $\mathbf{v}_n$ into components defined by eigenvectors of the input correlation matrix $\mathbf{A}$. (This is equivalent to changing to a coordinate system in which $\mathbf{A}$ is diagonal, and then considering the components of $\mathbf{v}_n$ separately.) More precisely, let us order the N eigenvalues of $\mathbf{A}$ in ascending order and split them into K equal blocks, labeled by $\kappa = 1 \ldots K$, each containing N/K eigenvalues. Let $\mathbf{P}^\kappa$ be the projector matrices onto the spaces spanned by the eigenvectors of each block. Then $\mathbf{v}_n = \sum_\kappa \mathbf{P}^\kappa \mathbf{v}_n$; likewise, the generalization error is decomposed as

$$\epsilon_g = \frac{1}{K} \sum_\kappa \epsilon_n^\kappa, \qquad \epsilon_n^\kappa = \frac{K}{2N} \mathbf{v}_n^{\mathrm{T}} \mathbf{P}^\kappa \mathbf{v}_n$$

Each of the generalization error components ϵ_n^κ obeys the update equation (2.4), with $\mathbf{M} = K\mathbf{P}^\kappa$. But these equations now become closed, because

$$\mathbf{A}\mathbf{P}^\kappa = \mathbf{P}^\kappa \mathbf{A} \approx a^\kappa \mathbf{P}^\kappa$$

where a^κ is an eigenvalue from the κ-th block (formally, this approximation becomes exact in the limit $K \to \infty$, where the spread of eigenvalues within each block tends to zero). This immediately reduces the second term on the right-hand side of (2.4) to $-2\tilde{\eta}(\lambda + a^\kappa) \langle \epsilon_n^\kappa \rangle$. Only the very last term of (2.4) now remains to be brought into a similar form. This is achieved by noting that the factors $c_\kappa^\mu = (K/N)(\mathbf{x}^\mu)^{\mathrm{T}} \mathbf{P}^\kappa \mathbf{x}^\mu$ are 'within-sample self-averaging' (Sollich and Barber, 1997a): Up to fluctuations which vanish as $O(N^{-1/2})$ for large N, all c^μ are equal to each other and hence to the training set ('sample') average

$$\frac{1}{p} \sum_\mu c_\kappa^\mu = \frac{K}{\alpha N} \mathrm{tr}\, \mathbf{A}\mathbf{P}^\kappa \approx \frac{a^\kappa}{\alpha}$$

The last approximation again becomes exact[5] for $K \to \infty$. The factors $c_\kappa^\mu = a^\kappa/\alpha$ can therefore be taken out of the sum over μ in (2.4), leaving the selection average

$$\sum_\mu \frac{1}{2N} \left\langle \mathbf{v}_n^{\mathrm{T}} \mathbf{x}^\mu (\mathbf{x}^\mu)^{\mathrm{T}} \mathbf{v}_n \right\rangle = \frac{1}{2} \left\langle \mathbf{v}_n^{\mathrm{T}} \mathbf{A} \mathbf{v}_n \right\rangle \approx \frac{1}{K} \sum_\kappa a^\kappa \langle \epsilon_n^\kappa \rangle$$

We now have all the ingredients to write (2.4) as a closed system of evolution equations for the ϵ_n^κ. In the large N limit, the change $N \left(\langle \epsilon_{n+1}^\kappa \rangle - \langle \epsilon_n^\kappa \rangle \right)$ due to an update becomes the time derivative $\partial_t \epsilon^\kappa$, and $\langle \epsilon_n^\kappa \rangle \to \epsilon^\kappa(t)$. Using the rescaled time $\tau = \tilde{\eta} t$ introduced above, one then has

$$[\partial_\tau + 2(\lambda + a^\kappa)]\, \epsilon^\kappa(\tau) = V^\kappa(\tau) + \tilde{\eta}\, W^\kappa(\tau) + \tilde{\eta}\, a^\kappa \frac{1}{K} \sum_{\kappa'} a^{\kappa'} \epsilon^{\kappa'}(\tau) \qquad (2.6)$$

---

[5]The large K limit needs to be taken *after* the limit $N \to \infty$ for 'within-sample self-averaging' to hold; this is why one cannot take $K = N$ from the outset.

Here the functions $V^\kappa(\tau)$ and $W^\kappa(\tau)$ are

$$V^\kappa = \frac{K}{N}(\mathbf{b} - \lambda \mathbf{w}_*)^\mathrm{T} \mathbf{P}^\kappa \langle \mathbf{v}_n \rangle$$

$$W^\kappa = a^\kappa \left[\frac{1}{2N} \sum_\mu (\xi^\mu)^2 - \frac{1}{N} \mathbf{b}^\mathrm{T} \langle \mathbf{v}_n \rangle \right]$$

with $\langle \mathbf{v}_n \rangle$ given by (2.5). Having derived (2.6), the rest of the calculation is fairly straightforward. Eq. (2.6) is formally solved using Laplace transforms with respect to τ, for example $\hat{\epsilon}^\kappa(z) = \int_0^\infty d\tau \, \exp(-z\tau) \, \epsilon^\kappa(\tau)$:

$$\hat{\epsilon}^\kappa(z) = \frac{1}{z + 2(\lambda + a^\kappa)} \left[\epsilon^\kappa(0) + \hat{V}^\kappa(z) + \tilde{\eta}\,\hat{W}^\kappa(z) + \tilde{\eta}\, a^\kappa \frac{1}{K} \sum_{\kappa'} a^{\kappa'} \hat{\epsilon}^{\kappa'}(z) \right]$$
(2.7)

with the initial condition $\epsilon^\kappa(0) = \frac{K}{2N} \mathbf{w}_*^\mathrm{T} \mathbf{P}^\kappa \mathbf{w}_*$. Multiplying by a^κ and summing over κ gives a self-consistency equation for $K^{-1} \sum_\kappa a^\kappa \hat{\epsilon}^\kappa(z)$ which is easily solved. Inserting the solution into (2.7) then gives an explicit expression for $\hat{\epsilon}^\kappa(z)$ and hence for the Laplace transform of the generalization error, $\hat{\epsilon}_g(z) = K^{-1} \sum_\kappa \hat{\epsilon}^\kappa(z)$. As a final step, the average over all training sets (*i.e.*, training inputs $\mathbf{x}^\mu$ and output noises ξ^μ) is then carried out. In the end, everything can be written in terms of averages over the known eigenvalue spectrum (Hertz et al., 1989; Sollich, 1994) of the input correlation matrix $\mathbf{A}$. The explicit form of the final result (Sollich and Barber, 1997a) is rather cumbersome; we omit it here and note only the relatively simple dependence on η:

$$\hat{\epsilon}_g(z) = \hat{\epsilon}_0(z) + \frac{\eta \hat{\epsilon}_1(z)}{1 - \eta \hat{\epsilon}_2(z)}$$
(2.8)

The functions $\epsilon_i(z)$ ($i = 0 \ldots 2$) depend on α, σ^2 and λ (and, of course, z), but are independent of η. The teacher weights do no appear explicitly: because of the isotropy of the input distribution, only the length of the teacher weight vector matters once an average over training sets has been taken, and this has already been fixed to $\mathbf{w}_*^2 = N$.

The calculation of the generalization error for offline learning is much simpler than that for the online case due to the absence of the selection average. In fact, the offline weight update (2.2) can be iterated directly to yield

$$\mathbf{v}_{rp} = (\lambda + \mathbf{A})^{-1} \left\{ \mathbf{b} - \lambda \mathbf{w}_* - [1 - \eta(\lambda + \mathbf{A})]^r (\mathbf{b} + \mathbf{A}\mathbf{w}_*) \right\}$$
(2.9)

Multiplying this by its transpose gives directly the generalization error, and the average over training sets can then be carried out in the usual fashion (see, *e.g.*, Hertz et al., 1989). As expected on general grounds, for $\eta \to 0$ (and only then) one obtains the same result as for online learning, corresponding to the term $\hat{\epsilon}_0(z)$ in (2.8).

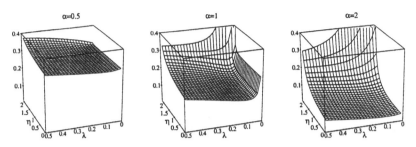

Figure 1: Asymptotic generalization error ϵ_∞ vs η and λ. α as shown, $\sigma^2 = 0.1$.

2.3   Discussion

We now briefly highlight some features of our exact result (2.8) for the generalization error achieved by online learning; a somewhat more detailed exposi-
tion can be found in (Sollich and Barber, 1997b). We discuss the asymptotic
generalization error ϵ_∞, the convergence speed for large learning times, and
the behaviour at small t; finally, we compare online and offline learning. For
numerical evaluations, we generally take $\sigma^2 = 0.1$, corresponding to a sizable
noise-to-signal ratio of $\sqrt{0.1} \approx 0.32$.

The asymptotic generalization error is found directly from (2.8) using $\epsilon_\infty =$
$\epsilon_g(t \to \infty) = \lim_{z \to 0} z\hat{\epsilon}_g(z)$. As expected, it coincides with the offline result
(which is *independent* of η) *only* for $\eta = 0$; as η increases from zero, it increases
monotonically. Reassuringly, our calculation reproduces existing $O(\eta)$ results
for this increase (Heskes and Kappen, 1991). In figure 1 we plot ϵ_∞ as a
function of η and λ for $\alpha = 0.5, 1, 2$. We observe that it is minimal for $\lambda = \sigma^2$
and $\eta = 0$, as expected from corresponding results for offline learning (Krogh
and Hertz, 1992)[6]. We also read off that for fixed λ, ϵ_∞ is an increasing
function of η: The larger η, the more the weight updates tend to overshoot
the minimum of the (total, *i.e.*, offline) training error. This causes a diffusive
motion of the weights around their average asymptotic values (Heskes and
Kappen, 1991) which increases ϵ_∞. In the absence of weight decay ($\lambda = 0$)
and for $\alpha < 1$, however, ϵ_∞ is independent of η. In this case the training data
can be fitted perfectly; every term in the total sum-of-squares training error
is then zero and online learning does not lead to weight diffusion because
all individual updates vanish. In general, the relative increase $\epsilon_\infty(\eta)/\epsilon_\infty(\eta =$
$0) - 1$ due to nonzero η depends significantly on α. For $\eta = 1$ and $\alpha = 0.5$,
for example, this increase is smaller than 6% for all λ (at $\sigma^2 = 0.1$), and for

---

[6]The optimal value of the *unscaled* weight decay decreases with α as $\gamma = \sigma^2/\alpha$, because
for large training sets there is less need to counteract noise in the training data by using a
large weight decay.

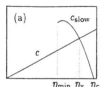 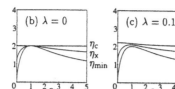 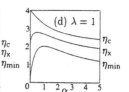

Figure 2: Sketch of definitions of η_{min} (minimal learning rate for slow mode), η_x (crossover to slow mode dominated convergence) and η_c (maximal ('critical') learning rate at which convergence still occurs), and their dependence on α.

$\alpha = 1$ it is at most 13%. This means that in cases where training data is limited ($p \approx N$), η can be chosen fairly large in order to optimize learning speed, without seriously affecting the asymptotic generalization error. In the large α limit, on the other hand, one finds $\epsilon_\infty = (\sigma^2/2)[1/\alpha + \eta/(2 - \eta)]$. The relative increase over the value at $\eta = 0$ therefore grows linearly with α; already for $\alpha = 2$, increases of around 50% can occur for $\eta = 1$.

Fig. 1 also shows that ϵ_∞ diverges as η approaches a critical learning rate η_c: As $\eta \to \eta_c$, the 'overshoot' of the weight update steps becomes so large that the weights eventually diverge. From the Laplace transform (2.8), one finds that η_c is determined by $\eta_c \hat{\epsilon}_2(z = 0) = 1$; it is a function of α and λ only. As shown in figure 2b-d, η_c increases with λ. This is reasonable, as the weight decay reduces the length of the weight vector at each update, counteracting potential weight divergences. In the small and large α limits one has $\eta_c = 2(1 + \lambda)$ and $\eta_c = 2(1 + \lambda/\alpha)$, respectively. For constant λ, η_c therefore decreases[7] with α (figure 2b-d).

We now turn to the large t behaviour of the generalization error $\epsilon_g(t)$. For small η, the most slowly decaying contribution to $\epsilon_g(t)$—the slowest 'mode'—varies as $\exp(-ct)$, its decay constant $c = \eta[\lambda + (\sqrt{\alpha} - 1)^2]/\alpha$ scaling linearly with η, the size of the weight updates, as expected (figure 2a). For larger η, the picture changes due to a new slow mode arising from the denominator of (2.8). Interestingly, this mode exists only for η above a finite threshold $\eta_{min} = 2/(\alpha^{1/2} + \alpha^{-1/2} - 1)$. For finite α, it could therefore not have been predicted from a small η expansion of $\epsilon_g(t)$. Its decay constant c_{slow} decreases to zero as $\eta \to \eta_c$, and crosses that of the normal mode at $\eta_x(\alpha, \lambda)$ (figure 2a). For $\eta > \eta_x$, the slow mode therefore determines the convergence speed for large t, and fastest convergence is obtained for $\eta = \eta_x$. However, it may still be advantageous to use lower values of η in order to lower the asymptotic generalization error (see below); values of $\eta > \eta_x$ would deteriorate both convergence speed and asymptotic performance. Fig. 2b-d shows the dependence

---

[7]Conversely, for constant γ, η_c *increases* with α from $2(1 + \gamma\alpha)$ to $2(1 + \gamma)$: For large α, the weight decay is applied more often between repeat presentations of a training example that would otherwise cause the weights to diverge.

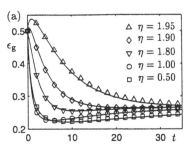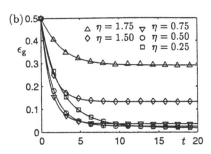

Figure 3: ϵ_g vs t for different η. Simulations for $N = 50$ are shown by symbols (standard errors less than symbol sizes). $\lambda=10^{-4}$, $\sigma^2=0.1$. (a) $\alpha=0.7$, (b) $\alpha=5$

of η_{min}, η_x and η_c on α and λ. For λ not too large, η_x has a maximum at $\alpha \approx 1$ (where $\eta_x \approx \eta_c$), while decaying to $\eta_x \approx \frac{1}{2}\eta_c$ for larger α. This can be explained in terms of the anisotropy of the total training error surface (Sollich and Barber, 1997a), which is strongest for $\alpha = 1$ and $\lambda \to 0$.

Consider now the small t behaviour of $\epsilon_g(t)$. Fig. 3 illustrates the dependence of $\epsilon_g(t)$ on η; comparison with simulation results for $N = 50$ clearly confirms our calculations and demonstrates that finite N effects are not significant even for such fairly small N. For $\alpha = 0.7$ (figure 3a), we see that nonzero η acts as effective update noise, eliminating the minimum in $\epsilon_g(t)$ which corresponds to over-training (Krogh and Hertz, 1992). ϵ_∞ is also seen to be essentially independent of η as predicted for the small value of $\lambda = 10^{-4}$ chosen. For $\alpha = 5$, figure 3b clearly shows the increase of ϵ_∞ with η. It also illustrates how convergence first speeds up as η is increased from zero and then slows down again as $\eta_c \approx 2$ is approached.

Above, we saw that the *asymptotic* generalization error ϵ_∞ is minimal for $\eta = 0$. Fig. 4 shows what happens if we minimize $\epsilon_g(t)$ instead for a given *final learning time* t, corresponding to a fixed amount of computational effort for training the network. As t increases, the optimal η decreases towards zero as required by the tradeoff between asymptotic performance and convergence speed. For large t, the functional form of this decay is $\eta_{opt} = (a + b\ln t)/t$ with t-independent coefficients a and b (Sollich and Barber, 1997a).

We now compare the performance of online learning to that of offline learning as calculated from (2.9). (The number of gradient calculations required for r offline weight updates is $n = rp$, corresponding to a learning time $t = n/N = r\alpha$; the generalization error $\epsilon_g(t)$ is therefore only defined for learning times t which are integer multiples of α.) To compare online and offline learning on an equal footing, we again consider optimized values of η for given final learning time t. Fig. 4b shows that the performance loss from

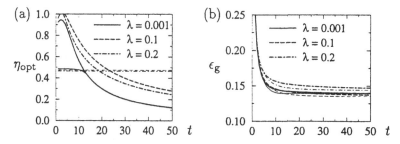

Figure 4: (a) Optimal learning rate η vs. final learning time t for online (bold) and offline learning (thin lines), and (b) resulting generalization error ϵ_g. $\alpha = 1$, $\sigma^2 = 0.1$, λ as shown. Note that although we plot offline results as continuous lines to avoid visual clutter, they are actually defined only at discrete values of the learning time, $t = r\alpha$, with r the number of offline weight updates.

using online instead of offline learning is actually negligible. This may seem surprising given the stochasticity of weight updates in online learning, in particular for small t. However, figure 4a shows that online learning can make up for this by allowing larger values of η to be used.

2.4 Biased inputs

2.4.1 Modifications to calculation

We now investigate how online and offline learning are affected by input bias $\langle \mathbf{x} \rangle = \bar{\mathbf{x}} \neq \mathbf{0}$. As a simple scenario of this kind, consider the case where the *deviations* $\Delta \mathbf{x} = \mathbf{x} - \bar{\mathbf{x}}$ of the inputs from their average are still distributed isotropically over a hypersphere. We choose the radius R of this hypersphere such that the average value of $\mathbf{x}^2$ is the same (N) as for the unbiased case, *i.e.*, $R^2 = N(1 - m^2)$ where $m^2 = \bar{\mathbf{x}}^2/N$ measures the size of the bias. The generalization error (the squared deviation between student and teacher outputs averaged over all inputs) now has two components,

$$\epsilon_g = \frac{1}{2N}\left[(\bar{\mathbf{x}}^T\mathbf{v}_n)^2 + (1 - m^2)\mathbf{v}_n^2\right] \tag{2.10}$$

As before, we consider a teacher with weight vector of length $\mathbf{w}_*^2 = N$. In the presence of input bias, however, we also need to specify the average teacher output $\bar{y} = \bar{\mathbf{x}}^T\mathbf{w}_*/\sqrt{N}$. This parameter is not constrained by our other assumptions; however, to limit the number of free parameters in the model, we choose it to have its typical root-mean-squared value when the directions of $\mathbf{w}_*$ and $\bar{\mathbf{x}}$ are uncorrelated: $\bar{y}^2 = m^2$.

As for the case of unbiased inputs, the evolution of the generalization error is largely determined by the eigenvalue spectrum of the input correlation matrix $\mathbf{A}$. This has been determined by a number of authors (LeCun et al., 1991; Wendemuth et al., 1993; Halkjær and Winther, 1997) and shows the following features: There is a 'normal' part of the spectrum, with eigenvalues which tend to finite values as $N \to \infty$; the eigenvalues in this part of the spectrum are identical to those for the unbiased input case, expect for a rescaling by the factor $(1 - m^2)$. Additionally, however, there is one isolated eigenvalue $a_N = N\alpha m^2$ which is proportional to N and exists *only* in the presence of input bias. Intuitively, this corresponds to the fact that the component of the student weights along the direction of $\bar{\mathbf{x}}$ is much more strongly determined by the training data because all input vectors have a component along $\bar{\mathbf{x}}$. Not surprisingly, therefore, the eigenvector corresponding to a_N is along the direction[8] of $\bar{\mathbf{x}}$.

We can see immediately that input bias has a drastic effect on offline learning by considering eq. (2.9): For the offline learning process to converge, the product of η and the largest eigenvalue of $\lambda + \mathbf{A}$ must be less than two. In the presence of input bias, this gives the condition $\eta < 2/(N\alpha m^2)$ (neglecting λ, which gives a negligible correction for $N \to \infty$). The maximal learning rate is therefore *drastically reduced* from order unity to $O(N^{-1})$. A little reflection then shows that only the first contribution of the generalization error (2.10) decays for finite learning times; carrying out the average over training sets, one finds

$$\epsilon_g(t = r\alpha) = \frac{1}{2}m^2(1 - N\eta\alpha m^2)^{2r} + \frac{1}{2}(1 - m^2) \qquad (2.11)$$

The second contribution would only decay for learning times of $O(N)$, which are inaccessibly long in the limit $N \to \infty$ that we consider.

Online learning, on the other hand, is not plagued by the same problem, as we now show. Consider the first contribution to the generalization error, which we write as $\epsilon_{g,1} = \frac{1}{2}\delta_n^2$ with

$$\delta_n = \frac{1}{\sqrt{N}}\bar{\mathbf{x}}^{\mathrm{T}}\mathbf{v}_n$$

From the update equation (2.3) one derives that

$$\delta_{n+1} = (1 - \eta m^2)\delta_n + \eta\,\xi^\mu m^2 \qquad (2.12)$$

up to correction terms which vanish for $N \to \infty$. Starting from the initial value $\delta_0 = -\bar{y}$, this can easily be iterated and the selection average carried

---

[8]In fact there is a small angle between this eigenvector and $\bar{\mathbf{x}}$, which however decreases as $O((\alpha N)^{-1/2})$ as N grows large. LeCun et al. (1991) claimed that this angle is exactly zero; however, their argument cannot be quite correct as it would also entail that $\mathbf{A}$ has only two different eigenvalues (whereas in reality it has a continuous spread of eigenvalues for any finite α).

out to give

$$\left\langle \delta_n^2 \right\rangle = \bar{y}^2 (1 - \eta m^2)^{2n} + \eta^2 m^4 \frac{1 - (1 - \eta m^2)^{2n}}{1 - (1 - \eta m^2)^2} \frac{1}{p} \sum_\mu (\xi^\mu)^2$$

up to $O(N^{-1})$ corrections; an average over training sets then gives $p^{-1} \sum_\mu (\xi^\mu)^2 \to \sigma^2$. For $n = t = 0$, only the first term is nonzero. On the other hand, for nonzero learning time t (and values of the learning rate such that convergence occurs, *i.e.*, $0 < \eta < 2/m^2$) only the second term survives because $n = Nt \to \infty$ for $N \to \infty$. We therefore have for the average value of the first contribution to the generalization error:

$$\langle \epsilon_{g,1}(t = 0) \rangle = \bar{y}^2 = m^2, \qquad \langle \epsilon_{g,1}(t > 0) \rangle = \frac{1}{2} \sigma^2 \frac{\eta m^2}{2 - \eta m^2} \qquad (2.13)$$

The discontinuous change at $t = 0$ reflects the fact that $\langle \delta_n^2 \rangle$ changes from its initial to its asymptotic value after a number of updates n which does not increase with system size N. [9]

We still have to calculate the evolution of the second component $\epsilon_{g,2} = (1 - m^2)\mathbf{v}_n^2/(2N)$ of the generalization error (2.10) for the case of online learning. At first sight, the $O(N)$ eigenvalue of $\mathbf{A}$ appears to complicate this task. However, the component of $\mathbf{v}_n$ along $\bar{\mathbf{x}}$, the corresponding eigenvector, contributes only negligibly to $\epsilon_{g,2}$:

$$\frac{1}{2N} \left(\frac{1}{|\bar{\mathbf{x}}|} \bar{\mathbf{x}}^T \mathbf{v}_n \right)^2 = \frac{1}{Nm^2} \epsilon_{g,1} = O(N^{-1})$$

Thus only components of $\mathbf{v}_n$ along directions corresponding to the $O(1)$ eigenvalues of $\mathbf{A}$ need to be considered; their evolution can be calculated exactly as in Section 2.2. The only change is the rescaled eigenvalue spectrum of $\mathbf{A}$; in fact, one finds that $\epsilon_{g,2}/(1 - m^2)$ is exactly the same as $\epsilon_g = \mathbf{v}_n^2/2N$ for *unbiased* inputs of length $\mathbf{x}^2 = N(1 - m^2)$. It is easily checked that this change of effective input vector length can be effected by replacing λ, σ^2 and η in the expressions for ϵ_g by the rescaled values $\lambda' = \lambda/(1 - m^2)$, $(\sigma')^2 = \sigma^2/(1 - m^2)$ and $\eta' = \eta(1 - m^2)$, and so no new calculations need to be carried out.

2.4.2 Discussion

We have already mentioned that the critical learning rate for offline learning is drastically reduced to $\eta_c = 2/N\alpha m^2$ by the presence of input bias. For online learning, η_c is affected in two ways: first through the 'rescaling' of η and λ explained above for the calculation of $\epsilon_{g,2}$, and secondly through the

---

[9]Note also that we have written the selection average in (2.13) explicitly because $\epsilon_{g,1}$ is no longer self-averaging: Each weight update (2.12) causes a change in δ_n and $\epsilon_{g,1}$ of order unity, and hence the fluctuations of $\epsilon_{g,1}$ remain nonzero even for $N \to \infty$.

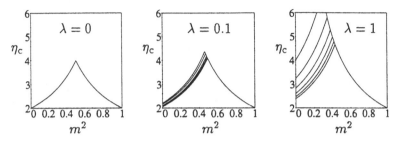

Figure 5: Critical learning rate η_c for online learning vs input bias m^2, for weight decay λ as shown and training set size $\alpha = 0, 1, \ldots, 5$ (bottom to top). Compare fig. 2 for the case of unbiased inputs.

presence of the term $\epsilon_{g,1}$; eq. (2.13) shows that for the latter to remain finite one requires $\eta_c < 2/m^2$. Fig. 5 illustrates the resulting variation of η_c with m^2 for several values of α and λ: As the bias increases from 0, the critical learning rate first increases until it reaches the value $2/m^2$; from that point onwards, it follows the curve $\eta_c = 2/m^2$ (independently of α and λ) until it reaches $\eta_c = 2$ at[10] $m^2 = 1$. In marked contrast to the case of offline learning, the critical learning rate η_c for online learning therefore never decreases below values of order unity, and can actually be increased by the presence of input bias.

The different effects of input bias on the critical learning rates of online and offline learning are also reflected in the generalization performance for optimal values of η at given final learning time. For offline learning, eq. (2.11) shows that the optimal $\eta = 1/(N\alpha m^2)$, whatever the (integer) value of $r = t/\alpha$. This reduces the first contribution to the offline generalization error to zero for any $r \geq 1$, but still leaves a nonzero term $\epsilon_g = (1 - m^2)/2$ (which as explained above would start to decay only for extremely long learning times $t = O(N)$).

For online learning, on the other hand, the optimal learning rate remains of order one even in the presence of input bias. This was to be expected from the analogous results for the critical learning rate, and can be seen explicitly in fig. 6(a). Fig. 6(b) shows the resulting generalization error, which is seen to *decrease* as the input bias increases. Online learning therefore successfully exploits the presence of the input bias to achieve better generalization performance[11]. This contrasts markedly with the case of offline learning, where

---

[10]This is the maximal bias in our scenario since $\langle \mathbf{x}^2 \rangle = N > \bar{\mathbf{x}}^2 = Nm^2$.

[11]Wendemuth et al. (1993) view the input bias as 'additional information' which leads to improved generalization. In our case, the same conclusion can be arrived at by considering the extreme limit of maximal bias, $m^2 = 1$: In this case, the distribution of input vectors collapses to the point $\mathbf{x} = \bar{\mathbf{x}}$, and so perfect generalization is obtained after only one

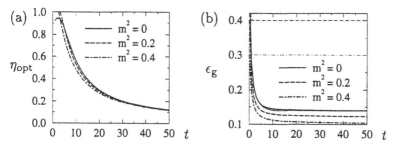

Figure 6: (a) Optimal learning rate η vs. final learning time t for online learning in the presence of input bias m^2 (values as shown; $\alpha = 1$, $\sigma^2 = 0.1$, $\lambda = 0.001$). (b) Resulting generalization error ϵ_g, with results for offline learning shown for comparison (thin lines). Note that while offline learning performs (marginally) better than online learning for unbiased inputs ($m^2 = 0$), it is far worse as soon as the input bias is nonzero.

generalization performance (at finite learning times t) deteriorates as soon as an input bias is present[12].

2.5   Conclusions for the linear theory

We have obtained exact results for the generalization error achieved by online learning from finite training sets at non-infinitesimal learning rates. These apply directly only to the simple linear model that we have considered, but also exhibit generic features which we expect to be of general relevance. For example, the calculated dependence on η of the asymptotic generalization error ϵ_∞ and the convergence speed shows that, in general, sizable values of η can be used for training sets of limited size ($\alpha \approx 1$), while for larger α it is important to keep learning rates small. More important from a practical point of view is probably the explicit comparison between online and offline learning that our results allow us to make. To make this comparison fair, we considered the generalization performance of both algorithms for the respective optimal values of the learning rate at a given final learning time t. For unbiased inputs, we found in this way that online learning performs only marginally

---

training example has been presented. (For noisy training outputs, more examples would be needed; the generalization error then decays roughly as $\epsilon_g \sim \sigma^2/n$, which however still gives perfect generalization $\epsilon_g = 0$ for any finite learning time t.)

[12]For biased inputs, we found an offline generalization error of $\epsilon_g = (1 - m^2)/2$ for optimally chosen η, which is arbitrarily close to $\frac{1}{2}$ for m^2 sufficiently small. For unbiased inputs, on the other hand, ϵ_g for optimal η is generally significantly smaller than a half, as illustrated by fig. 4, for example—it can never be greater than $\frac{1}{2}$ since otherwise $\eta = 0$ would give a lower ϵ_g.

worse than offline learning, whereas it is in fact vastly superior as soon as there is any kind of input bias. This suggests strongly that online learning should generally be preferred over offline learning in problems where biased inputs cannot be a priori excluded.

3 Non-linear Networks

For linear networks, we saw that the difficulties encountered with finite training sets and non-infinitesimal learning rates can be overcome by extending the standard set of descriptive ('order') parameters to include the effects of weight update correlations (Sollich and Barber, 1997b). In this section, we extend our analysis to *nonlinear* networks. The particular model we choose to study is the soft-committee machine, which is capable of representing a rich variety of input-output mappings. Its online learning dynamics has been studied comprehensively for infinite training sets(Biehl and Schwarze, 1995; Saad and Solla, 1995). In order to carry out our analysis, we adapt tools originally developed in the statistical mechanics literature which have found application, for example, in the study of Hopfield network dynamics (Coolen et al., 1996).

3.1 Model and Outline of Calculation

For an N-dimensional input vector $\mathbf{x}$, the output of the soft committee machine is given by

$$y = \sum_{l=1}^{L} g\left(\frac{1}{\sqrt{N}}\mathbf{w}_l^T\mathbf{x}\right) \tag{3.1}$$

where the nonlinear activation function $g(h_l) = \mathrm{erf}(h_l/\sqrt{2})$ acts on the activations $h_l = \mathbf{w}_l^T\mathbf{x}/\sqrt{N}$ (the factor $1/\sqrt{N}$ is for convenience only). This is a neural network with L hidden units, input to hidden weight vectors $\mathbf{w}_l$, $l = 1..L$, and all hidden to output weights set to 1.

We remind the reader that in online learning, the student weights are adapted on a sequence of presented examples to better approximate the teacher mapping. The training examples are drawn, with replacement, from a finite set, $\{(\mathbf{x}^\mu, y^\mu), \mu = 1..p\}$. This set remains fixed during training. Its size relative to the input dimension is denoted by $\alpha = p/N$. We take the input vectors $\mathbf{x}^\mu$ as samples from an N dimensional Gaussian distribution with zero mean and unit variance. The training outputs y^μ are assumed to be generated by a teacher soft committee machine with hidden weight vectors $\mathbf{w}_m^*$, $m = 1..M$, with additive Gaussian noise corrupting its activations and output.

The discrepancy between the teacher and student on a particular training example $(\mathbf{x}, y)$, drawn from the training set, is given by the squared difference of their corresponding outputs,

$$E = \frac{1}{2}\left[\sum_l g(h_l) - y\right]^2 = \frac{1}{2}\left[\sum_l g(h_l) - \sum_m g(k_m + \xi_m) - \xi_0\right]^2$$

where the student and teacher activations are, respectively

$$h_l = \sqrt{\frac{1}{N}}\mathbf{w}_l^{\mathrm{T}}\mathbf{x} \qquad k_m = \sqrt{\frac{1}{N}}(\mathbf{w}_m^*)^{\mathrm{T}}\mathbf{x}, \tag{3.2}$$

and ξ_m, $m = 1..M$ and ξ_0 are noise variables corrupting the teacher activations and output respectively.

Given a training example $(\mathbf{x}, y)$, the student weights are again updated by a gradient descent step with learning rate η,

$$\mathbf{w}_l' - \mathbf{w}_l = -\eta\nabla_{\mathbf{w}_l}E = -\frac{\eta}{\sqrt{N}}\mathbf{x}\partial_{h_l}E \tag{3.3}$$

As before, the generalization error is defined to be the average error that the student makes on a test example selected at random (and uncorrelated with the training set), which we write as $\epsilon_{\mathrm{g}} = \langle E\rangle$.

Although one could, in principle, model the student weight dynamics directly, this will typically involve too many parameters, and we seek a more compact representation for the evolution of the generalization error. It is straightforward to show that the generalization error depends, not on a detailed description of all the network weights, but only on the overlap parameters $Q_{ll'} = \frac{1}{N}\mathbf{w}_l^{\mathrm{T}}\mathbf{w}_{l'}$ and $R_{lm} = \frac{1}{N}\mathbf{w}_l^{\mathrm{T}}\mathbf{w}_m^*$ (Biehl and Schwarze, 1995; Saad and Solla, 1995; Sollich and Barber, 1997b). In the case of infinite α, it is possible to obtain a closed set of equations governing the overlap parameters Q, R (Saad and Solla, 1995). For finite training sets, however, this is no longer possible, due to the correlations between successive weight updates (Sollich and Barber, 1997b).

In order to overcome this difficulty, we use a technique developed originally to study statistical physics systems (Coolen et al., 1996). Initially, consider the dynamics of a general vector of order parameters, denoted by Ω, which are functions of the network weights $\mathbf{w}$. If the weight updates are described by a transition probability $T(\mathbf{w} \to \mathbf{w}')$, then an approximate update equation for Ω is

$$\Omega' - \Omega = \left\langle \int d\mathbf{w}' \left(\Omega(\mathbf{w}') - \Omega(\mathbf{w})\right) T(\mathbf{w} \to \mathbf{w}')\right\rangle_{P(\mathbf{w})\propto\delta(\Omega(\mathbf{w})-\Omega)} \tag{3.4}$$

Intuitively, the integral in the above equation expresses the average change[13] of Ω caused by a weight update $\mathbf{w} \to \mathbf{w}'$, starting from (given) initial weights

---

[13]Here we assume that the system size N is large enough that the mean values of the parameters alone describe the dynamics sufficiently well (*i.e.*, self-averaging holds).

w. Since our aim is to develop a closed set of equations for the order parameter dynamics, we need to remove the dependency on the initial weights **w**. The only information we have regarding **w** is contained in the chosen order parameters Ω, and we therefore average the result over the 'subshell' of all **w** which correspond to these values of the order parameters. This is expressed as the δ-function constraint in equation(3.4).

It is clear that if the integral in (3.4) depends on **w** only through $\Omega(\mathbf{w})$, then the average is unnecessary and the resulting dynamical equations are exact. This is in fact the case for $\alpha \to \infty$ and $\Omega = \{Q, R\}$, the standard order parameters mentioned above (Saad and Solla, 1995). If this cannot be achieved, one should choose a set of order parameters to obtain approximate equations which are as close as possible to the exact solution. The motivation for our choice of order parameters is based on the linear perceptron case treated in Section 2 where, in addition to the standard parameters Q and R, the overlaps projected onto eigenspaces of the training input correlation matrix $\mathbf{A} = \frac{1}{N}\sum_{\mu=1}^{p}\mathbf{x}^{\mu}(\mathbf{x}^{\mu})^{\mathrm{T}}$ are required[14]. We therefore split the eigenvalues of $\mathbf{A}$ into K equal blocks ($\kappa = 1 \ldots K$) containing $N' = N/K$ eigenvalues each, ordering the eigenvalues such that they increase with κ. We then define projectors $\mathbf{P}^{\kappa}$ onto the corresponding eigenspaces and take as order parameters:

$$Q_{ll'}^{\kappa} = \frac{1}{N'}\mathbf{w}_{l}^{\mathrm{T}}\mathbf{P}^{\kappa}\mathbf{w}_{l'} \quad R_{lm}^{\kappa} = \frac{1}{N'}\mathbf{w}_{l}^{\mathrm{T}}\mathbf{P}^{\kappa}\mathbf{w}_{m}^{*} \quad U_{ls}^{\kappa} = \frac{1}{N'}\mathbf{w}_{l}^{\mathrm{T}}\mathbf{P}^{\kappa}\mathbf{b}_{s} \quad (3.5)$$

where the $\mathbf{b}_s$ are linear combinations of the noise variables and training inputs,

$$\mathbf{b}_{s} = \frac{1}{\sqrt{N}}\sum_{\mu=1}^{p}\xi_{s}^{\mu}\mathbf{x}^{\mu}. \quad (3.6)$$

As $K \to \infty$, these order parameters become functionals of a continuous variable[15].

The updates for the order parameters (3.5) due to the weight updates (3.3) can be found by taking the scalar products of (3.3) with either projected student or teacher weights, as appropriate. This then introduces the following activation 'components',

$$h_{l}^{\kappa} = \sqrt{\frac{K}{N'}}\mathbf{w}_{l}^{\mathrm{T}}\mathbf{P}^{\kappa}\mathbf{x} \quad k_{m}^{\kappa} = \sqrt{\frac{K}{N'}}(\mathbf{w}_{m}^{*})^{\mathrm{T}}\mathbf{P}^{\kappa}\mathbf{x} \quad c_{s}^{\kappa} = \sqrt{\frac{K}{N'}}\mathbf{x}^{\mathrm{T}}\mathbf{P}^{\kappa}\mathbf{b}_{s} \quad (3.7)$$

---

[14]The reader may wonder why the order parameters Q and R did not show up explicitly in our treatment of the linear case in Section 2. This is because R can be calculated directly (simply take the scalar product of (2.5) with $\mathbf{w}^{*}$). Given R, Q and the generalization error $\hat{\epsilon}_{g}$ are trivially related because $\hat{\epsilon}_{g} = (Q - 2R + 1)/2$ in the linear case.

[15]Note that the limit $K \to \infty$ is taken *after* the thermodynamic limit, i.e., $K \ll N$. This ensures that the number of order parameters is always negligible compared to N (otherwise self-averaging would break down).

so that the student and teacher activations are $h_l = \frac{1}{K}\sum_\kappa h_l^\kappa$ and $k_m = \frac{1}{K}\sum_\kappa k_m^\kappa$, respectively. For the linear perceptron, the chosen order parameters form a complete set - the dynamical equations close, without need for the average in (3.4).

For the nonlinear case, we now sketch the calculation of the order parameter update equations (3.4). Taken together, the integral over $\mathbf{w}'$ (a sum of p discrete terms in our case, one for each training example) and the subshell average in (3.4), define an average over the activations (3.2), their components (3.7), and the noise variables ξ_m, ξ_0. These variables turn out to be Gaussian distributed with zero mean, and therefore only their covariances need to be worked out. One finds that these are in fact given by the naive training set averages. For example,

$$
\begin{aligned}
\langle h_l^\kappa k_m \rangle &= \frac{1}{p}\sum_\mu \frac{K}{N}(\mathbf{w}_l)^{\mathrm{T}}\mathbf{P}^\kappa \mathbf{x}^\mu (\mathbf{x}^\mu)^{\mathrm{T}}\mathbf{w}_m^* \\
&= \frac{K}{\alpha N}(\mathbf{w}_l)^{\mathrm{T}}\mathbf{P}^\kappa \mathbf{A}\mathbf{w}_m^* = \frac{a_\kappa}{\alpha}R_{lm}^\kappa,
\end{aligned}
\tag{3.8}
$$

where we have used $\mathbf{P}^\kappa \mathbf{A} = a_\kappa \mathbf{P}^\kappa$ with a_κ 'the' eigenvalue of $\mathbf{A}$ in the κ-th eigenspace; this is well defined for $K \to \infty$ (see (Sollich, 1994) for details of the eigenvalue spectrum). The correlations of the activations and noise variables explicitly appearing in the error in (3.3) are calculated similarly to give,

$$
\langle h_l h_{l'} \rangle = \frac{1}{K}\sum_\kappa \frac{a_\kappa}{\alpha}Q_{ll'}^\kappa
$$

$$
\langle h_l k_m \rangle = \frac{1}{K}\sum_\kappa \frac{a_\kappa}{\alpha}R_{lm}^\kappa \qquad \langle k_m k_{m'} \rangle = \frac{1}{K}\sum_\kappa \frac{a_\kappa}{\alpha}T_{mm'}^\kappa
$$

$$
\langle h_l \xi_s \rangle = \frac{1}{K}\sum_\kappa \frac{1}{\alpha}U_{ls}^\kappa \qquad \langle k_m \xi_s \rangle = 0 \qquad \langle \xi_s \xi_{s'} \rangle = \delta_{ss'}\sigma_s^2
$$

$$
\tag{3.9}
$$

where the final equation defines the noise variances. The $T_{mm'}^\kappa$ are projected overlaps between teacher weight vectors, $T_{mm'}^\kappa = \frac{1}{N}(\mathbf{w}_m^*)^{\mathrm{T}}\mathbf{P}^\kappa \mathbf{w}_{m'}^*$. We will assume that the teacher weights and training inputs are uncorrelated, so that $T_{mm'}^\kappa$ is independent of κ. The required covariances of the 'component' activations are

$$
\langle k_m^\kappa h_l \rangle = \frac{a_\kappa}{\alpha}R_{lm}^\kappa \qquad \langle k_m^\kappa k_{m'} \rangle = \frac{a_\kappa}{\alpha}T_{mm'}^\kappa \qquad \langle k_m^\kappa \xi_s \rangle = 0
$$

$$
\langle c_s^\kappa h_l \rangle = \frac{a_\kappa}{\alpha}U_{ls}^\kappa \qquad \langle c_s^\kappa k_{m'} \rangle = 0 \qquad \langle c_s^\kappa \xi_{s'} \rangle = \frac{a_\kappa}{\alpha}\sigma_s^2\delta_{ss'}
$$

$$
\langle h_l^\kappa h_{l'} \rangle = \frac{a_\kappa}{\alpha}Q_{ll'}^\kappa \qquad \langle h_l^\kappa k_{m'} \rangle = \frac{a_\kappa}{\alpha}R_{lm}^\kappa \qquad \langle h_l^\kappa \xi_s \rangle = \frac{1}{\alpha}U_{ls}^\kappa
$$

$$
\tag{3.10}
$$

298 Barber and Sollich

Using equation (3.3) and the definitions (3.7), we can now write down the dynamical equations, replacing the number of updates n by the continuous variable $t = n/N$ in the limit $N \to \infty$:

$$\partial_t R_{lm}^\kappa = -\eta \langle k_m^\kappa \partial_{h_l} E \rangle$$
$$\partial_t U_{ls}^\kappa = -\eta \langle c_s^\kappa \partial_{h_l} E \rangle$$
$$\partial_t Q_{ll'}^\kappa = -\eta \left\langle h_l^\kappa \partial_{h_{l'}} E \right\rangle - \eta \langle h_{l'}^\kappa \partial_{h_l} E \rangle + \eta^2 \frac{a_\kappa}{\alpha} \left\langle \partial_{h_l} E \partial_{h_{l'}} E \right\rangle \quad (3.11)$$

where the averages are over zero mean Gaussian variables, with covariances (3.9,3.10). Using the explicit form of the error E, we have

$$\partial_{h_l} E = g'(h_l) \left[\sum_{l'} g(h_{l'}) - \sum_m g(k_m + \xi_m) - \xi_0 \right] \quad (3.12)$$

which, together with the equations (3.11) completes the description of the dynamics. The Gaussian averages in (3.11) can be straightforwardly evaluated in a manner similar to the infinite training set case (Saad and Solla, 1995), and we omit the rather cumbersome explicit form of the resulting equations.

We note that, in contrast to the infinite training set case, the student activations h_l and the noise variables c_s and ξ_s are now correlated through equation (3.10). Intuitively, this is reasonable as the weights become correlated, during training, with the examples in the training set. In calculating the generalization error, on the other hand, such correlations are absent, and

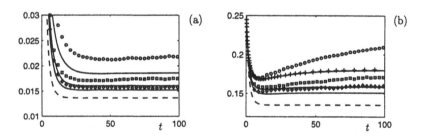

Figure 7: ϵ_g vs t for student and teacher with one hidden unit ($L = M = 1$); $\alpha = 2, 3, 4$ from above, learning rate $\eta = 1$. Noise of equal variance was added to both activations and output (a) $\sigma_1^2 = \sigma_0^2 = 0.01$, (b) $\sigma_1^2 = \sigma_0^2 = 0.1$. Simulations for $N = 100$ are shown by circles; standard errors are of the order of the symbol size. The bottom dashed lines show the infinite training set result for comparison. $K = 10$ was used for calculating the theoretical predictions; the curved marked "+" in (b), with $K = 20$ (and $\alpha = 2$), shows that this is large enough to be effectively in the $K \to \infty$ limit.

one has the same result as for infinite training sets. The dynamical equations (3.11), together with (3.9,3.10) constitute our main result. They are exact for the limits of either a linear network $(R, Q, T \to 0$, so that $g(x) \propto x)$ or $\alpha \to \infty$, and can be integrated numerically in a straightforward way. In principle, the limit $K \to \infty$ should be taken but, as shown below, relatively small values of K can be taken in practice.

3.2 Results and Discussion

We now discuss the main consequences of our result (3.11), comparing the resulting predictions for the generalization dynamics, $\epsilon_g(t)$, to the infinite training set theory and to simulations. Throughout, the teacher overlap matrix is set to $T_{ij} = \delta_{ij}$ (orthogonal teacher weight vectors of length $\sqrt{N}$).

In figure(7), we study the accuracy of our method as a function of the training set size for a nonlinear network with one hidden unit at two different noise levels. The learning rate was set to $\eta = 1$ for both (a) and (b). For small activation and output noise ($\sigma^2 = 0.01$), figure(7a), there is good agreement with the simulations for α down to $\alpha = 3$, below which the theory begins to underestimate the generalization error, compared to simulations. Our finite α theory, however, is still considerably more accurate than the infinite α predictions. For larger noise ($\sigma^2 = 0.1$, figure(7b)), our theory provides a reasonable quantitative estimate of the generalization dynamics for $\alpha > 3$. Below this value there is significant disagreement, although the qualitative behaviour of the dynamics is predicted quite well, including the overfitting phenomenon beyond $t \approx 10$. The infinite α theory in this case is qualitatively incorrect.

In the two hidden unit case, figure(8), our theory captures the initial evo-

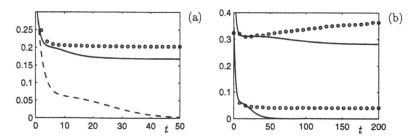

Figure 8: ϵ_g vs t for two hidden units ($L = M = 2$). Left: $\alpha = 0.5$, with $\alpha = \infty$ shown by dashed line for comparison; no noise. Right: $\alpha = 4$, no noise (bottom) and noise on teacher activations and outputs of variance 0.1 (top). Simulations for $N = 100$ are shown by small circles; standard errors are less than the symbol size. Learning rate $\eta = 2$ throughout.

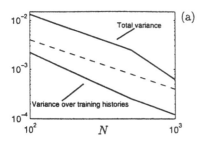 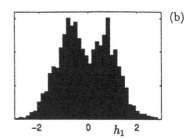

Figure 9: (a) Variance of $\epsilon_g(t = 20)$ vs input dimension N for
student and teacher with two hidden units $(L = M = 2)$, $\alpha = 0.5$, $\eta = 2$, and zero noise. The bottom curve shows the variance
due to different random choices of training examples from a fixed
training set ('training history'); the top curve also includes the
variance due to different training sets. Both are compatible with
the $1/N$ decay expected if self-averaging holds (dotted line). (b)
Distribution (over training set) of the activation h_1 of the first
hidden unit of the student. Histogram from simulations for $N = 1000$, all other parameter values as in (a).

lution of $\epsilon_g(t)$ very well, but diverges significantly from the simulations at
larger t; nevertheless, it provides a considerable improvement on the infinite
α theory. One reason for the discrepancy at large t is that the theory predicts
that different student hidden units will always specialize to individual teacher
hidden units for $t \to \infty$, whatever the value of α. This leads to a decay of ϵ_g
from a plateau value at intermediate times t. In the simulations, on the other
hand, this specialization (or symmetry breaking) appears to be inhibited or
at least delayed until very large t. This can happen even for zero noise and
$\alpha \geq L$, where the training data should should contain enough information to
force student and teacher weights to be equal asymptotically. The reason for
this is not clear to us, and deserves further study. Our initial investigations,
however, suggest that symmetry breaking may be strongly delayed due to
the presence of saddle points in the training error surface with very 'shallow'
unstable directions.

When our theory fails, which of its assumptions are violated? It is con-
ceivable that multiple local minima in the training error surface could cause
self-averaging to break down; however, we have found no evidence for this, see
figure(9a). On the other hand, the simulation results in figure(9b) clearly show
that the implicit assumption of Gaussian student activations – as discussed
before eq. (3.8) – can be violated.

3.3   Conclusions for the non-linear theory

In summary, the main theoretical contribution of this section is the extension of online learning analysis for finite training sets to *nonlinear* networks. Our approximate theory does not require the use of replicas and yields ordinary first order differential equations for the time evolution of a set of order parameters. Its central implicit assumption (and its Achilles' heel) is that the student activations are Gaussian distributed. In comparison with simulations, we have found that it is more accurate than the infinite training set analysis at predicting the generalization dynamics for finite training sets, both qualitatively and also quantitatively for small learning times t. Future work will have to show whether the theory can be extended to cope with non-Gaussian student activations without incurring the technical difficulties of dynamical replica theory (Coolen et al., 1996) (see also Coolen et al., this volume), and whether this will help to capture the effects of local minima and, more generally, 'rough' training error surfaces.

References

Biehl, M. and Schwarze, H. (1995). Learning by online gradient descent. *J. Physics A*, 28, 643–656.

Coolen, A. C. C., Laughton, S. N., and Sherrington, D. (1996). Modern Analytic Techniques to Solve the Dynamics of Recurrent Neural Networks. In Toutretzky, D. S., Mozer, M. C., and Hasslemo, M. E., editors, *Advances in Neural Information Processing Systems NIPS 8*. MIT Press.

Halkjær, S. and Winther, O. (1997). The effect of correlated input data on the dynamics of learning. In Mozer, M. C., Jordan, M. I., and Petsche, T., editors, *Advances in Neural Information Processing Systems 9*, pages 169–175, Cambridge, MA. MIT Press.

Hertz, J. A., Krogh, A., and Thorbergsson, G. I. (1989). Phase transitions in simple learning. *J. Phys. A*, 22, 2133–2150.

Heskes, T. and Kappen, B. (1991). Learning processes in neural networks. *Phys. Rev. A*, 44, 2718–2762.

Krogh, A. and Hertz, J. A. (1992). Generalization in a linear perceptron in the presence of noise. *J. Phys. A*, 25, 1135–1147.

LeCun, Y., Kanter, I., and Solla, S. A. (1991). Eigenvalues of covariance matrices - application to neural- network learning. *Phys. Rev. Lett.*, 66, 2396–2399.

Saad, D. and Solla, S. A. (1995). Online learning in soft committee machines. *Phys. Rev. E*, 52, 4225–4243.

Sollich, P. (1994). Finite size effects in learning and generalization in linear perceptrons. *J. Phys. A*, 27, 7771–7784.

Sollich, P. (1995). Learning unrealizable tasks from minimum entropy queries. *J. Phys. A*, 28, 6125–6142.

Sollich, P. and Barber, D. (1997a). On-line learning from finite training sets. *Europhys. Lett.*, 38, 477–482.

Sollich, P. and Barber, D. (1997b). Online learning from finite training sets: An analytical case study. In Mozer, M. C., Jordan, M. I., and Petsche, T., editors, *Advances in Neural Information Processing Systems 9*, pages 274–280, Cambridge, MA. MIT Press.

Wendemuth, A., Opper, M., and Kinzel, W. (1993). The effect of correlations in neural networks. *J. Phys. A*, 26, 3165–3185.

Dynamics of Supervised Learning with Restricted Training Sets

A.C.C. Coolen

Department of Mathematics, King's College, University of London
Strand, London WC2R 2LS, U.K.
tcoolen@mth.kcl.ac.uk

D. Saad

Department of Computer Science and Applied Mathematics, Aston University
Aston Triangle, Birmingham B4 7ET, U.K.
saadd@aston.ac.uk

Abstract

We study the dynamics of supervised learning in layered neural networks, in the regime where the size p of the training set is proportional to the number N of inputs. Here the local fields are no longer described by Gaussian distributions. We show how dynamical replica theory can be used to predict the evolution of macroscopic observables, including the relevant performance measures, incorporating the theory of complete training sets in the limit $p/N \to \infty$ as a special case. For simplicity we restrict ourselves here to single-layer networks and realizable tasks.

Contents

1 Introduction

In the last few years much progress has been made in the analysis of the dynamics of supervised learning in layered neural networks, using the strategy of statistical mechanics: by deriving from the microscopic dynamical equations a set of closed laws describing the evolution of suitably chosen macroscopic observables (dynamic order parameters) in the limit of an infinite system size [e.g. Kinzel & Rujan (1990), Kinouchi & Caticha (1992), Biehl & Schwarze (1992, 1995), Saad & Solla (1995)]. A recent review and more extensive guide to the relevant references can be found in Mace & Coolen (1998a). The main successful procedure developed so far is built on the following cornerstones:

- *The task to be learned is defined by a (possibly noisy) 'teacher', which is itself a layered neural network.* This induces a canonical set of dynamical order parameters, typically the (rescaled) overlaps between the various student weight vectors and the corresponding teacher weight vectors.

- *The number of network inputs is (eventually) taken to be infinitely large.* This ensures that fluctuations in mean-field observables will vanish and creates the possibility of using the central limit theorem.

- *The number of 'hidden' neurons is finite.* This prevents the number of order parameters from being infinite, and ensures that the cumulative impact of their fluctuations is insignificant.

- *The size of the training set is much larger than the number of updates made.* Each example presented is now different from those that have already been seen, such that the local fields will have Gaussian probability distributions, which leads to closure of the dynamic equations.

These are not ingredients to simplify the calculations, but vital conditions, without which the standard method fails. Although the assumption of an infinite system size has been shown not to be too critical (Barber *et al.*, 1996), the other assumptions do place serious restrictions on the degree of realism of the scenarios that can be analyzed, and have thereby, to some extent, prevented the theoretical results from being used by practitioners.

In this paper we study the dynamics of learning in layered neural networks with restricted training sets, where the number p of examples ('questions' with corresponding 'answers') scales linearly with the number N of inputs, i.e. $p = \alpha N$. Here individual questions will re-appear during the learning process as soon as the number of weight updates made is of the order of the size of the training set. In the traditional models, where the duration of an update is defined as N^{-1}, this happens as soon as $t = \mathcal{O}(\alpha)$. At that point correlations develop between the weights and the questions in the training set, and the dynamics is of a spin-glass type, with the composition of the training set playing the role of 'quenched disorder'. The main consequence of this is that the central limit theorem no longer applies to the student's local fields, which are now described by non-Gaussian distributions. To demonstrate this we trained (on-line) a perceptron with weights J_i on noiseless examples generated by a teacher perceptron with weights B_i, using the Hebb and AdaTron rules. We plotted in Fig. 1 the student and teacher fields, $x = \boldsymbol{J} \cdot \boldsymbol{\xi}$ and $y = \boldsymbol{B} \cdot \boldsymbol{\xi}$ respectively, where $\boldsymbol{\xi}$ is the input vector, for $p = N/2$ examples and at time $t = 50$. The marginal distribution $P(x)$ for $p = N/4$, at times $t = 10$ for the Hebb rule and $t = 20$ for the Adatron rule, is shown in Fig. 2. The non-Gaussian student field distributions observed in Figs. 1 and 2 induce a deviation between the training- and generalization errors, which measure the network performance on training and test examples, respectively. The former involves averages over the non-Gaussian field distribution, whereas the latter (which is calculated over *all* possible examples) still involves Gaussian fields.

The appearance of non-Gaussian fields leads to a breakdown of the standard formalism, based on deriving closed equations for a finite number of observables: the field distributions can no longer be characterized by a few moments, and the macroscopic laws must now be averaged over realizations of the training set. One could still try to use Gaussian distributions as large α approximations, see e.g. Sollich & Barber (1998), but it will be clear from Figs. 1 and 2 that a systematic theory will have to give up Gaussian distributions entirely. The first rigorous study of the dynamics of learning with restricted training sets in non-linear networks, via the calculation of generating functionals, was carried out by Horner (1992) for perceptrons with binary weights. In this paper we show how the formalism of dynamical replica theory (see e.g. Coolen *et al.*, 1996) can be used successfully to predict the evolution of macroscopic observables for finite α, incorporating the infinite training set formalism as a special case, for $\alpha \to \infty$. Central to our approach is the derivation of a diffusion equation for the joint distribution of the student and teacher fields, which will be found to have Gaussian solutions only for $\alpha \to \infty$. For simplicity and transparency we restrict ourselves to single-layer systems and noise-free teachers. Application and generalization of our methods to multi-layer systems (Saad and Coolen, 1998) and learning scenarios involving 'noisy' teachers (Mace and Coolen, 1998b) are presently under way.

This presentation of preliminary results is organized as follows. In section 2 we derive a general Fokker-Planck equation describing the evolution of mean-field observables for $N \to \infty$. This allows us to identify the conditions for the latter to be described by closed deterministic laws. In section 3 we choose as our observables the field distribution $P[x, y]$, in addition to (the traditional) Q and R, and show that this set obeys deterministic laws. In order to close these laws we use the tools of dynamical replica theory. Details of the replica calculation are given in section 4, to be skipped by those primarily interested in results. In section 5 we show how in the limit $\alpha \to \infty$ (infinite training sets) the equations of the conventional theory are recovered. We finally work out our equations explicitly for the example of Hebbian learning with restricted training sets, and compare our predictions with exact results (derived from the microscopic equations by Rae *et al.*, 1998) and with numerical simulations.

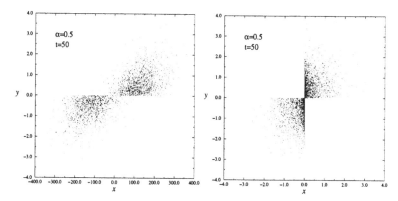

Fig. 1: Student and teacher fields (x, y) as observed during numerical simulations of on-line learning (learning rate $\eta = 1$) in a perceptron of size $N = 10,000$ at $t = 50$, using 'questions' from a restricted training set of size $p = \frac{1}{2}N$. Left: Hebbian learning. Right: AdaTron learning. Note: in the case of Gaussian field distributions one would have found spherically shaped plots.

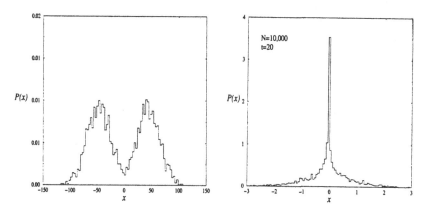

Fig. 2: Distribution $P(x)$ of student fields as observed during numerical simulations of on-line learning (learning rate $\eta = 1$) in a perceptron of size $N = 10,000$, using 'questions' from a restricted training set of size $p = \frac{1}{4}N$. Left: Hebbian learning, measured at $t = 10$. Right: AdaTron learning, measured at $t = 20$. Note: not only are these distributions distinctively non-Gaussian, they also appear to vary widely in their basic characteristics, depending on the learning rule used.

2   From Microscopic to Macroscopic Laws

2.1   Definitions

A student perceptron operates the following rule, which is parametrised by
the weight vector $\boldsymbol{J} \in \Re^N$:

$$S : \{-1,1\}^N \to \{-1,1\} \qquad S(\boldsymbol{\xi}) = \mathrm{sgn}\,[\boldsymbol{J}\cdot\boldsymbol{\xi}]$$

It tries to emulate the operation of a teacher perceptron, via an iterative
procedure for updating its parameters $\boldsymbol{J}$. The teacher perceptron operates a
similar rule, characterized by a given (fixed) weight vector $\boldsymbol{B} \in \Re^N$:

$$T : \{-1,1\}^N \to \{-1,1\} \qquad T(\boldsymbol{\xi}) = \mathrm{sgn}\,[\boldsymbol{B}\cdot\boldsymbol{\xi}]$$

In order to do so, the student perceptron modifies its weight vector $\boldsymbol{J}$ accord-

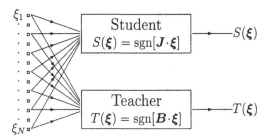

Fig. 3: Supervised learning in perceptrons.

ing to an iterative procedure, using examples of input vectors (or 'questions')
$\boldsymbol{\xi}$, drawn at random from a fixed training set $\tilde{D} \subseteq D = \{-1,1\}^N$, and the
corresponding values of the teacher outputs $T(\boldsymbol{\xi})$, see Fig. 3.

We consider the case where the training set is a randomly composed subset
$\tilde{D} \subset D$, of size $|\tilde{D}| = p = \alpha N$ with $\alpha > 0$:

$$\tilde{D} = \{\boldsymbol{\xi}^1, \ldots, \boldsymbol{\xi}^p\} \qquad p = \alpha N$$

We will denote averages over the training set $\tilde{D}$ and averages over the full
question set D in the following way:

$$\langle \Phi(\boldsymbol{\xi}) \rangle_{\tilde{D}} = \frac{1}{|\tilde{D}|} \sum_{\boldsymbol{\xi} \in \tilde{D}} \Phi(\boldsymbol{\xi}) \quad \text{and} \quad \langle \Phi(\boldsymbol{\xi}) \rangle_D = \frac{1}{|D|} \sum_{\boldsymbol{\xi} \in D} \Phi(\boldsymbol{\xi}) \; .$$

We will analyze the following two classes of learning rules:

$$
\begin{aligned}
\text{on-line :} \quad & \boldsymbol{J}(m{+}1) = \boldsymbol{J}(m) + \tfrac{\eta}{N}\, \boldsymbol{\xi}(m)\, \mathcal{G}\,[\boldsymbol{J}(m)\cdot\boldsymbol{\xi}(m), \boldsymbol{B}\cdot\boldsymbol{\xi}(m)] \\
\text{batch :} \quad & \boldsymbol{J}(m{+}1) = \boldsymbol{J}(m) + \tfrac{\eta}{N}\, \langle \boldsymbol{\xi}\, \mathcal{G}\,[\boldsymbol{J}(m)\cdot\boldsymbol{\xi}, \boldsymbol{B}\cdot\boldsymbol{\xi}] \rangle_{\tilde{D}}
\end{aligned}
\qquad (2.1)
$$

In on-line learning one draws at each iteration step m a question $\boldsymbol{\xi}(m) \in \tilde{D}$ at random, the dynamics is thus a stochastic process; in batch learning one iterates a deterministic map. The function $\mathcal{G}[x,y]$ is assumed to be bounded and not to depend on N, other than via its two arguments.

Our most important observables during learning are the training error $E_{\mathrm{t}}(\boldsymbol{J})$ and the generalization error $E_{\mathrm{g}}(\boldsymbol{J})$, defined as follows:

$$E_{\mathrm{t}}(\boldsymbol{J}) = \langle \theta[-(\boldsymbol{J}\cdot\boldsymbol{\xi})(\boldsymbol{B}\cdot\boldsymbol{\xi})] \rangle_{\tilde{D}} , \tag{2.2}$$

$$E_{\mathrm{g}}(\boldsymbol{J}) = \langle \theta[-(\boldsymbol{J}\cdot\boldsymbol{\xi})(\boldsymbol{B}\cdot\boldsymbol{\xi})] \rangle_{D} . \tag{2.3}$$

Only if the training set $\tilde{D}$ is sufficiently large, and if there are no correlations between $\boldsymbol{J}$ and the questions $\boldsymbol{\xi} \in \tilde{D}$, will these two errors will be identical.

2.2 From Discrete to Continuous Time

We next convert the dynamical laws (2.1) into the language of stochastic processes. We introduce the probability $\hat{p}_m(\boldsymbol{J})$ to find weight vector $\boldsymbol{J}$ at discrete iteration step m. In terms of this microscopic probability distribution the processes (2.1) can be written in the general Markovian form

$$\hat{p}_{m+1}(\boldsymbol{J}) = \int d\boldsymbol{J}' \, W[\boldsymbol{J};\boldsymbol{J}'] \, \hat{p}_m(\boldsymbol{J}') ,$$

with the transition probabilities

$$\begin{aligned}\mathrm{on-line}: \quad & W[\boldsymbol{J};\boldsymbol{J}'] = \langle \delta\left[\boldsymbol{J}-\boldsymbol{J}'-\tfrac{\eta}{N}\,\boldsymbol{\xi}\,\mathcal{G}\left[\boldsymbol{J}'\cdot\boldsymbol{\xi},\boldsymbol{B}\cdot\boldsymbol{\xi}\right]\right] \rangle_{\tilde{D}} \\ \mathrm{batch}: \quad & W[\boldsymbol{J};\boldsymbol{J}'] = \delta\left[\boldsymbol{J}-\boldsymbol{J}'-\tfrac{\eta}{N}\langle\boldsymbol{\xi}\,\mathcal{G}\left[\boldsymbol{J}'\cdot\boldsymbol{\xi},\boldsymbol{B}\cdot\boldsymbol{\xi}\right]\rangle_{\tilde{D}}\right]\end{aligned} \tag{2.4}$$

We now make the transition to a description involving real-valued time labels by choosing the duration of each iteration step to be a real-valued random number, such that the probability that at time t precisely m steps have been made is given by the Poisson expression

$$\pi_m(t) = \frac{1}{m!}(Nt)^m e^{-Nt} . \tag{2.5}$$

For times $t \gg N^{-1}$ we find $t = m/N + \mathcal{O}(N^{-\frac{1}{2}})$, the usual time unit. Due to the random durations of the iteration steps we have to switch to the following microscopic probability distribution:

$$p_t(\boldsymbol{J}) = \sum_{m\geq 0} \pi_m(t) \, \hat{p}_m(\boldsymbol{J}) .$$

This distribution obeys a simple differential equation, which immediately follows from the pleasant properties of (2.5) under temporal differentiation:

$$\frac{d}{dt} p_t(\boldsymbol{J}) = N \int d\boldsymbol{J}' \, \{W[\boldsymbol{J};\boldsymbol{J}'] - \delta[\boldsymbol{J}-\boldsymbol{J}']\} \, p_t(\boldsymbol{J}') . \tag{2.6}$$

So far no approximations have been made, equation (2.6) is exact for any N. It is the equivalent of the master equation often introduced to define the dynamics of spin systems.

2.3 Derivation of Macroscopic Fokker-Planck Equation

We now wish to investigate the dynamics of a number of as yet arbitrary macroscopic observables $\Omega[J] = (\Omega_1[J], \ldots, \Omega_k[J])$. To do so we introduce a macroscopic probability distribution

$$P_t(\Omega) = \int dJ \, p_t(J) \, \delta \left[\Omega - \Omega[J]\right] \, .$$

Its time derivative immediately follows from that in (2.6):

$$\frac{d}{dt} P_t(\Omega) = \int d\Omega' \, \mathcal{W}_t[\Omega; \Omega'] \, P_t(\Omega') \, , \tag{2.7}$$

where

$$\mathcal{W}_t[\Omega; \Omega']$$
$$= \frac{\int dJ' \, p_t(J') \, \delta \left[\Omega' - \Omega[J']\right] \int dJ \, \delta \left[\Omega - \Omega[J]\right] N \left\{W[J; J'] - \delta[J - J']\right\}}{\int dJ' \, p_t(J') \, \delta \left[\Omega' - \Omega[J']\right]}$$

If we insert the relevant expressions (2.4) for $W[J; J']$ we can perform the J-integrations, and obtain expressions in terms of so-called sub-shell averages, defined as

$$\langle f(J) \rangle_{\Omega; t} = \frac{\int dJ \, p_t(J) \, \delta \left[\Omega - \Omega[J]\right] f(J)}{\int dJ \, p_t(J) \, \delta \left[\Omega - \Omega[J]\right]} \, .$$

For the two types of learning rules at hand we obtain:

$$\mathcal{W}_t^{\mathrm{on}}[\Omega; \Omega'] = N \left\langle \left\langle \delta \left[\Omega - \Omega[J + \frac{\eta}{N} \, \boldsymbol{\xi} \, \mathcal{G}[J \cdot \boldsymbol{\xi}, B \cdot \boldsymbol{\xi}]]\right] \right\rangle_{\hat{D}} - \delta \left[\Omega - \Omega[J]\right] \right\rangle_{\Omega'; t}$$

$$\mathcal{W}_t^{\mathrm{ba}}[\Omega; \Omega'] = N \left\langle \delta \left[\Omega - \Omega[J + \frac{\eta}{N} \langle \boldsymbol{\xi} \, \mathcal{G}[J \cdot \boldsymbol{\xi}, B \cdot \boldsymbol{\xi}] \rangle_{\Omega}]\right] - \delta \left[\Omega - \Omega[J]\right] \right\rangle_{\Omega'; t}$$

We now insert integral representations for the δ-distributions. This gives for our two learning scenario's:

$$\mathcal{W}_t^{\mathrm{on}}[\Omega; \Omega'] = \int \frac{d\hat{\Omega}}{(2\pi)^k} e^{i\hat{\Omega} \cdot \Omega} \, N \left\langle \left\langle e^{-i\hat{\Omega} \cdot \Omega[J + \frac{\eta}{N} \boldsymbol{\xi} \mathcal{G}[J \cdot \boldsymbol{\xi}, B \cdot \boldsymbol{\xi}]]} \right\rangle_{\hat{D}} - e^{-i\hat{\Omega} \cdot \Omega[J]} \right\rangle_{\Omega'; t}$$
$$\tag{2.8}$$

$$\mathcal{W}_t^{\mathrm{ba}}[\Omega; \Omega'] = \int \frac{d\hat{\Omega}}{(2\pi)^k} e^{i\hat{\Omega} \cdot \Omega} \, N \left\langle e^{-i\hat{\Omega} \cdot \Omega[J + \frac{\eta}{N} \langle \boldsymbol{\xi} \mathcal{G}[J \cdot \boldsymbol{\xi}, B \cdot \boldsymbol{\xi}] \rangle_{\hat{D}}]} - e^{-i\hat{\Omega} \cdot \Omega[J]} \right\rangle_{\Omega'; t}$$
$$\tag{2.9}$$

Still no approximations have been made. The above two expressions differ only in the stage where the averaging over the training set is carried out.

In expanding equations (2.8,2.9) for large N and finite t we have to be careful, since the system size N enters both as a small parameter to control the magnitude of the modification of individual components of the weight vector, but also determines the dimensions and lengths of various vectors that occur. If we assess how derivatives with respect to individual components J_i scale for observables such as $Q[J] = J^2$ and $R[J] = B \cdot J$, we find the following scaling property which we will choose as our definition of *simple* mean-field observables:

$$F[J] = \mathcal{O}(N^0) \qquad \frac{\partial^\ell F[J]}{\partial J_{i_1} \cdots \partial J_{i_\ell}} = \mathcal{O}(|J|^{-\ell} N^{\frac{1}{2}\ell - d}) \qquad (N \to \infty), \quad (2.10)$$

in which d is the number of *different* elements in the set $\{i_1, \ldots, i_\ell\}$. However, we will find that for restricted training sets not all relevant observables will have the properties (2.10). In particular, the joint distribution of student and teacher fields will, at least for on-line learning, have a contribution for which higher order derivatives do not decrease in importance[1]. The latter type of more *general* mean-field observables will have to be defined via the identities

$$F[J+k] - F[J] = \Delta[J;k] + \sum_i k_i \frac{\partial F[J]}{\partial J_i} + \frac{1}{2}\sum_{ij} k_i k_j \frac{\partial^2 F[J]}{\partial J_i \partial J_j} + \sum_{\ell \geq 3} \mathcal{O}\left(\frac{|k|^\ell}{|J|^\ell}\right)$$
$$(2.11)$$
$$F[J] = \mathcal{O}(N^0), \qquad \Delta[J;k] = \mathcal{O}(k^2/J^2) \qquad (2.12)$$

(in the assessment of the order of the remainder terms of (2.11) we have used $\sum_i k_i = \mathcal{O}(\sqrt{N}|k|)$). Simple mean-field observables correspond to $\Delta[J;k]=0$.

We apply (2.11) to our macroscopic equations (2.8,2.9), restricting ourselves from now on to mean-field observables in the sense of (2.11,2.12). One of our observables we choose to be J^2. In the present problem the shifts k, being either $\frac{\eta}{N}\xi \, \mathcal{G}[J \cdot \xi; B \cdot \xi]$ or $\frac{\eta}{N}\langle \xi \, \mathcal{G}[J \cdot \xi; B \cdot \xi]\rangle_{\hat{D}}$, scale as $|k| = \mathcal{O}(N^{-\frac{1}{2}})$. Consequently:

$$e^{-i\hat{\Omega} \cdot \Omega[J+k]} = e^{-i\hat{\Omega} \cdot \Omega[J]} \left\{ 1 - \hat{\Omega} \cdot \Delta[J;k] - i\sum_i k_i \frac{\partial}{\partial J_i}(\hat{\Omega} \cdot \Omega[J]) \right.$$

$$\left. -\frac{i}{2}\sum_{ij} k_i k_j \frac{\partial^2}{\partial J_i \partial J_j}(\hat{\Omega} \cdot \Omega[J]) - \frac{1}{2}\left[\sum_i k_i \frac{\partial}{\partial J_i}(\hat{\Omega} \cdot \Omega[J])\right]^2 \right\} + \mathcal{O}(N^{-\frac{3}{2}}) .$$

This, in turn, gives

$$\int \frac{d\hat{\Omega}}{(2\pi)^k} e^{i\hat{\Omega} \cdot \Omega} \, N \left[e^{-i\hat{\Omega} \cdot \Omega[J+k]} - e^{-i\hat{\Omega} \cdot \Omega[J]} \right]$$

$$= -N \left\{ \sum_\mu \frac{\partial}{\partial \Omega_\mu} \left[\Delta_\mu[J;k] + \sum_i k_i \frac{\partial \Omega_\mu[J]}{\partial J_i} + \frac{1}{2}\sum_{ij} k_i k_j \frac{\partial^2 \Omega_\mu[J]}{\partial J_i \partial J_j} \right] \right.$$

$$\left. -\frac{1}{2}\sum_{\mu\nu} \frac{\partial^2}{\partial \Omega_\mu \partial \Omega_\nu} \sum_{ij} k_i k_j \frac{\partial \Omega_\mu[J]}{\partial J_i} \frac{\partial \Omega_\nu[J]}{\partial J_j} \right\} \delta\left[\Omega - \Omega[J]\right] + \mathcal{O}(N^{-\frac{1}{2}}) .$$

---

[1] We are grateful to Dr. Yuan-sheng Xiong for alerting us to this important point.

It is now evident, in view of (2.8,2.9), that both types of dynamics are described by macroscopic laws with transition probability densities of the general form

$$W_t^{**}[\Omega; \Omega'] = \left\{ -\sum_\mu F_\mu[\Omega'; t] \frac{\partial}{\partial \Omega_\mu} + \frac{1}{2} \sum_{\mu\nu} G_{\mu\nu}[\Omega'; t] \frac{\partial^2}{\partial \Omega_\mu \partial \Omega_\nu} \right\} \delta[\Omega - \Omega']$$

$$+ \mathcal{O}(N^{-\frac{1}{2}})$$

which, due to (2.7) and for $N \to \infty$ and finite times, leads to a Fokker-Planck equation:

$$\frac{d}{dt} P_t(\Omega) = - \sum_{\mu=1}^{k} \frac{\partial}{\partial \Omega_\mu} \{ F_\mu[\Omega; t] P_t(\Omega) \} + \frac{1}{2} \sum_{\mu\nu=1}^{k} \frac{\partial^2}{\partial \Omega_\mu \partial \Omega_\nu} \{ G_{\mu\nu}[\Omega; t] P_t(\Omega) \} .$$

$$(2.13)$$

The differences between the two types of dynamics are in the explicit expressions for the flow- and diffusion terms:

$$F_\mu^{\mathrm{on}}[\Omega; t] = \lim_{N \to \infty} \left\langle N \langle \Delta_\mu[\boldsymbol{J}; \frac{\eta}{N} \boldsymbol{\xi} \mathcal{G}[\boldsymbol{J} \cdot \boldsymbol{\xi}, \boldsymbol{B} \cdot \boldsymbol{\xi}]] \rangle_{\tilde{D}} + \eta \sum_i \langle \xi_i \mathcal{G}[\boldsymbol{J} \cdot \boldsymbol{\xi}, \boldsymbol{B} \cdot \boldsymbol{\xi}] \rangle_{\tilde{D}} \frac{\partial \Omega_\mu[\boldsymbol{J}]}{\partial J_i} \right.$$

$$\left. + \frac{\eta^2}{2N} \sum_{ij} \langle \xi_i \xi_j \; \mathcal{G}^2[\boldsymbol{J} \cdot \boldsymbol{\xi}, \boldsymbol{B} \cdot \boldsymbol{\xi}] \rangle_{\tilde{D}} \frac{\partial^2 \Omega_\mu[\boldsymbol{J}]}{\partial J_i \partial J_j} \right\rangle_{\Omega; t}$$

$$G_{\mu\nu}^{\mathrm{on}}[\Omega; t] = \lim_{N \to \infty} \frac{\eta^2}{N} \left\langle \sum_{ij} \langle \xi_i \xi_j \; \mathcal{G}^2[\boldsymbol{J} \cdot \boldsymbol{\xi}, \boldsymbol{B} \cdot \boldsymbol{\xi}] \rangle_{\tilde{D}} \frac{\partial \Omega_\mu[\boldsymbol{J}]}{\partial J_i} \frac{\partial \Omega_\nu[\boldsymbol{J}]}{\partial J_j} \right\rangle_{\Omega; t}$$

$$F_\mu^{\mathrm{ba}}[\Omega; t] = \lim_{N \to \infty} \left\langle N \Delta_\mu[\boldsymbol{J}; \frac{\eta}{N} \langle \boldsymbol{\xi} \mathcal{G}[\boldsymbol{J} \cdot \boldsymbol{\xi}; \boldsymbol{B} \cdot \boldsymbol{\xi}] \rangle_{\tilde{D}}] + \eta \sum_i \langle \xi_i \mathcal{G}[\boldsymbol{J} \cdot \boldsymbol{\xi}, \boldsymbol{B} \cdot \boldsymbol{\xi}] \rangle_{\tilde{D}} \frac{\partial \Omega_\mu[\boldsymbol{J}]}{\partial J_i} \right.$$

$$\left. + \frac{\eta^2}{2N} \sum_{ij} \langle \xi_i \; \mathcal{G}[\boldsymbol{J} \cdot \boldsymbol{\xi}, \boldsymbol{B} \cdot \boldsymbol{\xi}] \rangle_{\tilde{D}} \langle \xi_j \; \mathcal{G}[\boldsymbol{J} \cdot \boldsymbol{\xi}, \boldsymbol{B} \cdot \boldsymbol{\xi}] \rangle_{\tilde{D}} \frac{\partial^2 \Omega_\mu[\boldsymbol{J}]}{\partial J_i \partial J_j} \right\rangle_{\Omega; t}$$

$$G_{\mu\nu}^{\mathrm{ba}}[\Omega; t] = \lim_{N \to \infty} \frac{\eta^2}{N} \left\langle \sum_{ij} \langle \xi_i \mathcal{G}[\boldsymbol{J} \cdot \boldsymbol{\xi}, \boldsymbol{B} \cdot \boldsymbol{\xi}] \rangle_{\tilde{D}} \langle \xi_j \mathcal{G}[\boldsymbol{J} \cdot \boldsymbol{\xi}, \boldsymbol{B} \cdot \boldsymbol{\xi}] \rangle_{\tilde{D}} \frac{\partial \Omega_\mu[\boldsymbol{J}]}{\partial J_i} \frac{\partial \Omega_\nu[\boldsymbol{J}]}{\partial J_j} \right\rangle_{\Omega; t}$$

Equation (2.13) allows us to define the goal of our exercise in more explicit form. If we wish to arrive at closed deterministic macroscopic equations, we have to choose our observables such that

$\lim_{N \to \infty} G_{\mu\nu}[\Omega; t] = 0$ (this ensures determinism)

$\lim_{N \to \infty} \frac{\partial}{\partial t} F_\mu[\Omega; t] = 0$ (this ensures closure)

In the case of time-dependent global parameters, such as learning rates or decay rates, the latter condition relaxes to the requirement that any explicit time-dependence of $F_\mu[\Omega; t]$ is restricted to these global parameters.

3   Application to Canonical Observables

3.1   Choice of Canonical Observables

We now apply the general results obtained so far to a specific set of observables, $\Omega \rightarrow \{Q, R, P\}$, which are taylored to the problem at hand:

$$Q[\boldsymbol{J}] = \boldsymbol{J}^2, \qquad R[\boldsymbol{J}] = \boldsymbol{J} \cdot \boldsymbol{B}, \qquad P[x, y; \boldsymbol{J}] = \langle \delta[x - \boldsymbol{J} \cdot \boldsymbol{\xi}] \, \delta[x - \boldsymbol{B} \cdot \boldsymbol{\xi}] \rangle_{\tilde{D}} \quad (3.1)$$

with $x, y \in \Re$. This choice is motivated by the following considerations: (i) in order to incorporate the standard theory in the limit $\alpha \rightarrow \infty$ we need at least $Q[\boldsymbol{J}]$ and $R[\boldsymbol{J}]$, (ii) we need to be able to calculate the training error, which involves field statistics calculated over the training set $\tilde{D}$, as described by $P[x, y; \boldsymbol{J}]$, and (iii) for finite α one cannot expect closed macroscopic equations for just a finite number of order parameters, the present choice (involving the order parameter *function* $P[x, y; \boldsymbol{J}]$) represents effectively an infinite number[2]. In subsequent calculations we will, however, assume the number of arguments (x, y) for which $P[x, y; \boldsymbol{J}]$ is to be evaluated (and thus our number of order parameters) to go to infinity only after the limit $N \rightarrow \infty$ has been taken. This will eliminate many technical subtleties and will allow us to use the Fokker-Planck equation (2.13).

The observables (3.1) are indeed of the general mean-field type in the sense of (2.11,2.12). Insertion into the stronger condition (2.10) immediately shows this to be true for the scalar observables $Q[\boldsymbol{J}]$ and $R[\boldsymbol{J}]$. Verification of (2.11,2.12) for the function $P[x, y; \boldsymbol{J}]$ is less trivial. We denote with $\mathcal{I}$ the set of all *different* indices in the list $(i_1, \ldots, i_\ell)$, with n_k giving the number of times a number k occurs, and with $\mathcal{I}^{\pm} \subseteq \mathcal{I}$ defined as the set of all indices $k \in \mathcal{I}$ for which n_k is even ($+$), or odd ($-$). Note that with these definitions $\ell = \sum_{k \in \mathcal{I}^+} n_k + \sum_{k \in \mathcal{I}^-} n_k \geq 2|\mathcal{I}^+| + |\mathcal{I}^-|$. We then have:

$$\frac{\partial^\ell P[x, y; \boldsymbol{J}]}{\partial J_{i_1} \ldots \partial J_{i_\ell}} =$$

$$(-1)^\ell \frac{\partial^\ell}{\partial x^\ell} \int \frac{d\hat{x}d\hat{y}}{(2\pi)^2} \, e^{i[x\hat{x}+y\hat{y}]} \left\langle \left[\prod_{k \in \mathcal{I}} \xi_k^{n_k} e^{-i\xi_k[\hat{x}J_k + \hat{y}B_k]} \right] \left[\prod_{k \notin \mathcal{I}} e^{-i\xi_k[\hat{x}J_k + \hat{y}B_k]} \right] \right\rangle_{\tilde{D}}$$

Upon writing averaging over *all* training sets of size $p = \alpha N$ as $\langle \ldots \rangle_\Xi$, this allows us to conclude

$$\left\langle \frac{\partial^\ell P[x, y; \boldsymbol{J}]}{\partial J_{i_1} \ldots \partial J_{i_\ell}} \right\rangle_\Xi = \mathcal{O}(N^{-\frac{1}{2}|\mathcal{I}^-|})$$

---

[2]A simple rule of thumb is the following: if a process requires replica theory for its stationary state analysis, as does learning with restricted training sets, its dynamics is of a spin-glass type and cannot be described by a finite set of closed dynamic equations.

Since $\frac{1}{2}\ell-|\mathcal{I}|+\frac{1}{2}|\mathcal{I}^-| = \frac{1}{2}[\ell-|\mathcal{I}^-|-2|\mathcal{I}^+|] \geq 0$, the *average over all training sets* of the function $P[x,y;\boldsymbol{J}]$ is thus found to be a simple mean-field observable.

The scaling properties of expansions or derivatives of $P[x,y;\boldsymbol{J}]$ for a given training set $\tilde{D}$, however, cannot be assumed identical to those of its average over all training sets, due to the statistical dependence of the shifts $\boldsymbol{k}$ in $P[x,y;\boldsymbol{J}+\boldsymbol{k}]$ on the composition of $\tilde{D}$ (such subtleties are absent in the case $\alpha = \infty$ of complete training sets). This dependence turns out to be harmless in the case of batch learning, but will have a considerable impact in the case of on-line learning, where $\boldsymbol{k}^{\text{on}} = \eta N^{-1}\boldsymbol{\xi}\mathcal{G}[\boldsymbol{J}\cdot\boldsymbol{\xi},\boldsymbol{B}\cdot\boldsymbol{\xi}]$ is proportional to an individual member of the set $\tilde{D}$. The field distribution $P[x,y;\boldsymbol{J}]$ turns out to obey (2.11,2.12) for both on-line and batch learning (full details can be found in Coolen and Saad, 1998), with

$$\Delta_{xy}[\boldsymbol{J};\boldsymbol{k}^{\text{on}}] = \frac{1}{p}\left\{\delta[x-\boldsymbol{J}\cdot\boldsymbol{\xi}-\eta\mathcal{G}[\boldsymbol{J}\cdot\boldsymbol{\xi},\boldsymbol{B}\cdot\boldsymbol{\xi}]]\delta[y-\boldsymbol{B}\cdot\boldsymbol{\xi}] - \delta[x-\boldsymbol{J}\cdot\boldsymbol{\xi}]\delta[y-\boldsymbol{B}\cdot\boldsymbol{\xi}]\right.$$

$$\left.+\eta\frac{\partial}{\partial x}\left[\mathcal{G}[x,y]\delta[x-\boldsymbol{J}\cdot\boldsymbol{\xi}]\delta[y-\boldsymbol{B}\cdot\boldsymbol{\xi}]\right] - \frac{1}{2}\eta^2\frac{\partial^2}{\partial x^2}\left[\mathcal{G}^2[x,y]\delta[x-\boldsymbol{J}\cdot\boldsymbol{\xi}]\delta[y-\boldsymbol{B}\cdot\boldsymbol{\xi}]\right]\right\}$$

$$(3.2)$$

For on-line learning the field distribution is apparently not a simple mean-field observable. In contrast $\Delta_{xy}[\boldsymbol{J};\boldsymbol{k}^{\text{ba}}] = 0$, thus for batch learning the distribution $P[x,y;\boldsymbol{J}]$ is a simple mean field observable in the sense of (2.10). Note that $\Delta_{xy}[\boldsymbol{J};\boldsymbol{k}^{\text{on}}] = \mathcal{O}(\eta^3)$ as $\eta \to 0$, so that for small learning rates these differences between batch and on-line learning disappear, as they should. Having chosen our order parameters to be Q, R and $\{P[x,y]\}$, we will from this stage onwards use the notation $\langle\ldots\rangle_{\text{QRP};t}$ for sub-shell averages defined with respect to this choice.

3.2   Deterministic Dynamical Laws

Here we will first show that for the observables (3.1) the diffusion matrix elements $G_{\mu\nu}^{\star\star}$ in the Fokker-Planck equation (2.13) vanish for $N \to \infty$. Our observables will consequently obey deterministic dynamical laws, which we will calculate in explicit form. We can save ink and trees by introducing the complementary Kronecker delta $\bar{\delta}_{ab} = 1 - \delta_{ab}$ and the following key functions which we will repeatedly encounter:

$$\mathcal{A}[x,y;x',y'] = \lim_{N\to\infty}$$

$$\left\langle \langle\!\langle\bar{\delta}_{\boldsymbol{\xi}\boldsymbol{\xi}'}(\boldsymbol{\xi}\cdot\boldsymbol{\xi}')\delta[x-\boldsymbol{J}\cdot\boldsymbol{\xi}]\delta[y-\boldsymbol{B}\cdot\boldsymbol{\xi}]\delta[x'-\boldsymbol{J}\cdot\boldsymbol{\xi}']\delta[y'-\boldsymbol{B}\cdot\boldsymbol{\xi}']\rangle\!\rangle_{\tilde{D}} \right\rangle_{\text{QRP};t} \quad (3.3)$$

$$\mathcal{B}[x,y;x',y'] = \lim_{N\to\infty}$$

$$\left\langle \frac{1}{N}\sum_{i\neq j}\langle\!\langle\bar{\delta}_{\boldsymbol{\xi}\boldsymbol{\xi}'}(\xi_i\xi_j\xi_i'\xi_j')\delta[x-\boldsymbol{J}\cdot\boldsymbol{\xi}]\delta[y-\boldsymbol{B}\cdot\boldsymbol{\xi}]\delta[x'-\boldsymbol{J}\cdot\boldsymbol{\xi}']\delta[y'-\boldsymbol{B}\cdot\boldsymbol{\xi}']\rangle\!\rangle_{\tilde{D}} \right\rangle_{\text{QRP};t}$$

$$(3.4)$$

$$C[x,y;x',y';x'',y''] = \lim_{N\to\infty} \frac{1}{N} \left\langle \langle\!\langle\!\langle \bar{\delta}_{\boldsymbol{\xi}\boldsymbol{\xi}''}\bar{\delta}_{\boldsymbol{\xi}'\boldsymbol{\xi}''}(\boldsymbol{\xi}\cdot\boldsymbol{\xi}'')(\boldsymbol{\xi}'\cdot\boldsymbol{\xi}'')\delta[x-\boldsymbol{J}\cdot\boldsymbol{\xi}]\delta[y-\boldsymbol{B}\cdot\boldsymbol{\xi}]\right.$$

$$\left. \times\ \delta[x'-\boldsymbol{J}\cdot\boldsymbol{\xi}']\delta[y'-\boldsymbol{B}\cdot\boldsymbol{\xi}']\delta[x''-\boldsymbol{J}\cdot\boldsymbol{\xi}'']\delta[y''-\boldsymbol{B}\cdot\boldsymbol{\xi}'']\,\rangle\!\rangle\!\rangle_{\tilde{D}} \right\rangle_{\text{QRP};t} \quad (3.5)$$

$$\mathcal{D}[x,y;x',y';u,v;u',v'] = \lim_{N\to\infty} \frac{1}{N} \left\langle \langle\!\langle\!\langle \bar{\delta}_{\boldsymbol{\xi}\boldsymbol{\xi}''}\bar{\delta}_{\boldsymbol{\xi}'\boldsymbol{\xi}'''}(\boldsymbol{\xi}\cdot\boldsymbol{\xi}'')(\boldsymbol{\xi}'\cdot\boldsymbol{\xi}''') \right.$$

$$\times\ \delta[x-\boldsymbol{J}\cdot\boldsymbol{\xi}]\delta[y-\boldsymbol{B}\cdot\boldsymbol{\xi}]\delta[x'-\boldsymbol{J}\cdot\boldsymbol{\xi}']\delta[y'-\boldsymbol{B}\cdot\boldsymbol{\xi}']$$

$$\left. \times\ \delta[u-\boldsymbol{J}\cdot\boldsymbol{\xi}'']\delta[v-\boldsymbol{B}\cdot\boldsymbol{\xi}'']\delta[u'-\boldsymbol{J}\cdot\boldsymbol{\xi}''']\delta[v'-\boldsymbol{B}\cdot\boldsymbol{\xi}''']\rangle\!\rangle\!\rangle_{\tilde{D}} \right\rangle_{\text{QRP};t} \quad (3.6)$$

We show in a subsequent section that, within the present formalism, all three functions (3.4,3.5,3.6) are zero. The function (3.3), on the other hand, will be found not to vanish and to contain all the interesting and non-trivial physics of the process. It plays the role of a Green's function, and its calculation will turn out to be our central problem.

First we turn to the diffusion matrix elements of the macroscopic Fokker-Planck equation (2.13). Calculating the diffusion terms associated with $Q[\boldsymbol{J}]$ and $R[\boldsymbol{J}]$ only is trivial. We write $\langle f[x,y]\rangle = \int dx\,dy\, P[x,y]f[x,y]$ and find

$$\begin{bmatrix} G_{QQ}^{\text{on}}[\ldots] \\ G_{QR}^{\text{on}}[\ldots] \\ G_{RR}^{\text{on}}[\ldots] \end{bmatrix} = \lim_{N\to\infty} \frac{\eta^2}{N} \begin{bmatrix} 4\langle x^2\mathcal{G}^2[x,y]\rangle \\ 2\langle xy\mathcal{G}^2[x,y]\rangle \\ \langle y^2\mathcal{G}^2[x,y]\rangle \end{bmatrix} = 0$$

$$\begin{bmatrix} G_{QQ}^{\text{ba}}[\ldots] \\ G_{QR}^{\text{ba}}[\ldots] \\ G_{RR}^{\text{ba}}[\ldots] \end{bmatrix} = \lim_{N\to\infty} \frac{\eta^2}{N} \begin{bmatrix} 4\langle x\mathcal{G}[x,y]\rangle^2 \\ 2\langle x\mathcal{G}[x,y]\rangle\langle y\mathcal{G}[x,y]\rangle \\ \langle y\mathcal{G}[x,y]\rangle^2 \end{bmatrix} = 0$$

In calculating diffusion terms which involve the function $P[x;y;\boldsymbol{J}]$ we will need two simple scaling consequences of the random composition of $\tilde{D}$:

$$\boldsymbol{\xi}\in\tilde{D}: \quad \sum_{\boldsymbol{\xi}'\in\tilde{D}} \delta_{\boldsymbol{\xi}\boldsymbol{\xi}'} = 1+\mathcal{O}(N^{-1}) \quad \text{and} \quad \frac{1}{p^2}\sum_{\boldsymbol{\xi},\boldsymbol{\xi}'\in\tilde{D}} \bar{\delta}_{\boldsymbol{\xi}\boldsymbol{\xi}'}|\boldsymbol{\xi}\cdot\boldsymbol{\xi}'| = \mathcal{O}(N^{\frac{1}{2}})$$

For the diffusion terms with just one occurrence of $P[x,y]$ we now find:

$$\begin{bmatrix} G_{Q,P[x,y]}^{\text{on}}[\ldots] \\ G_{R,P[x,y]}^{\text{on}}[\ldots] \end{bmatrix} = -\eta^2 \int dx'dy'\, \mathcal{G}^2[x',y'] \begin{bmatrix} 2x' \\ y' \end{bmatrix} \frac{\partial}{\partial x} \Big\{$$

$$\lim_{N\to\infty} \frac{1}{N} \left\langle \langle\!\langle(\boldsymbol{\xi}\cdot\boldsymbol{\xi}')\delta[x-\boldsymbol{J}\cdot\boldsymbol{\xi}]\delta[y-\boldsymbol{B}\cdot\boldsymbol{\xi}]\delta[x'-\boldsymbol{J}\cdot\boldsymbol{\xi}']\delta[y'-\boldsymbol{B}\cdot\boldsymbol{\xi}']\rangle\!\rangle_{\tilde{D}} \right\rangle_{\text{QRP};t} \Big\}$$

$$= -\eta^2 \int dx'dy'\, \mathcal{G}^2[x',y'] \begin{bmatrix} 2x' \\ y' \end{bmatrix} \frac{\partial}{\partial x} \left\{ \mathcal{O}(N^{-\frac{1}{2}}) \right\} = 0$$

$$\begin{bmatrix} G^{\text{ba}}_{Q,P[x,y]}[\cdots] \\ G^{\text{ba}}_{R,P[x,y]}[\cdots] \end{bmatrix} = -\eta^2 \begin{bmatrix} \langle 2x\mathcal{G}[x,y] \rangle \\ \langle y\mathcal{G}[x,y] \rangle \end{bmatrix} \int dx' dy' \; \mathcal{G}[x',y'] \frac{\partial}{\partial x} \Big\{$$

$$\lim_{N\to\infty} \frac{1}{N} \Big\langle \langle\!\langle\!\langle (\boldsymbol{\xi}\cdot\boldsymbol{\xi}')\delta[x - \boldsymbol{J}\cdot\boldsymbol{\xi}]\delta[y - \boldsymbol{B}\cdot\boldsymbol{\xi}]\delta[x' - \boldsymbol{J}\cdot\boldsymbol{\xi}']\delta[y' - \boldsymbol{B}\cdot\boldsymbol{\xi}']\rangle\!\rangle\!\rangle_{\tilde{D}} \Big\rangle_{\!\!QRP;t} \Big\}$$

$$= -\eta^2 \begin{bmatrix} \langle 2x\mathcal{G}[x,y] \rangle \\ \langle y\mathcal{G}[x,y] \rangle \end{bmatrix} \int dx' dy' \; \mathcal{G}[x',y'] \frac{\partial}{\partial x} \left\{ \mathcal{O}(N^{-\frac{1}{2}}) \right\} = 0$$

The non-trivial terms are those where two derivatives of the function $P[x,y;\boldsymbol{J}]$ come into play. Here we must separate four distinct contributions, defined according to which of the vectors from the trio $\{\boldsymbol{\xi}, \boldsymbol{\xi}', \boldsymbol{\xi}''\}$ are identical:

$$G^{\text{on}}_{P[x,y],P[x',y']}[\cdots] = \eta^2 \int dx'' dy'' \mathcal{G}^2[x'',y''] \frac{\partial^2}{\partial x \partial x'} \lim_{N\to\infty} \frac{1}{N} \Big\langle \langle\!\langle\!\langle (\boldsymbol{\xi}\cdot\boldsymbol{\xi}'')(\boldsymbol{\xi}'\cdot\boldsymbol{\xi}'') \times$$

$$\delta[x - \boldsymbol{J}\cdot\boldsymbol{\xi}]\delta[y - \boldsymbol{B}\cdot\boldsymbol{\xi}]\delta[x' - \boldsymbol{J}\cdot\boldsymbol{\xi}']\delta[y' - \boldsymbol{B}\cdot\boldsymbol{\xi}']\delta[x'' - \boldsymbol{J}\cdot\boldsymbol{\xi}'']\delta[y'' - \boldsymbol{B}\cdot\boldsymbol{\xi}'']\rangle\!\rangle\!\rangle_{\tilde{D}} \Big\rangle_{\!\!QRP;t}$$

$$= \eta^2 \int dx'' dy'' \; \mathcal{G}^2[x'',y''] \frac{\partial^2}{\partial x \partial x'} \Big\{ C[x,y;x',y';x'',y'']$$

$$+ \Big[\delta[x''{-}x]\delta[y''{-}y] + \delta[x''{-}x']\delta[y''{-}y'] \Big] \lim_{N\to\infty} \mathcal{O}(N^{-\frac{1}{2}})$$

$$+ \; \delta[x''{-}x]\delta[y''{-}y]\delta[x'{-}x]\delta[y'{-}y] \lim_{N\to\infty} \mathcal{O}(N^{-1}) \Big\}$$

$$= \eta^2 \int dx'' dy'' \; \mathcal{G}^2[x'',y''] \frac{\partial^2}{\partial x \partial x'} C[x,y;x',y';x'',y'']$$

Similarly:

$$G^{\text{ba}}_{P[x,y],P[x',y']}[\cdots] = \eta^2 \int du\,dv\,du'\,dv' \; \mathcal{G}[u,v]\mathcal{G}[u',v'] \frac{\partial^2}{\partial x \partial x'}$$

$$\lim_{N\to\infty} \frac{1}{N} \Big\langle \langle\!\langle\!\langle (\boldsymbol{\xi}\cdot\boldsymbol{\xi}'')\delta[x - \boldsymbol{J}\cdot\boldsymbol{\xi}]\delta[y - \boldsymbol{B}\cdot\boldsymbol{\xi}]\delta[u - \boldsymbol{J}\cdot\boldsymbol{\xi}'']\delta[v - \boldsymbol{B}\cdot\boldsymbol{\xi}'']\rangle\!\rangle\!\rangle_{\tilde{D}}$$

$$\times \; \langle\!\langle\!\langle (\boldsymbol{\xi}'\cdot\boldsymbol{\xi}'')\delta[x' - \boldsymbol{J}\cdot\boldsymbol{\xi}']\delta[y' - \boldsymbol{B}\cdot\boldsymbol{\xi}']\delta[u' - \boldsymbol{J}\cdot\boldsymbol{\xi}'']\delta[v' - \boldsymbol{B}\cdot\boldsymbol{\xi}'']\rangle\!\rangle\!\rangle_{\tilde{D}} \Big\rangle_{\!\!QRP;t}$$

$$= \eta^2 \int du\,dv\,du'\,dv' \; \mathcal{G}[u,v]\mathcal{G}[u',v'] \frac{\partial^2}{\partial x \partial x'} D[x,y;x',y';u,v;u',v']$$

Anticipating the two functions $C[\ldots]$ and $D[\ldots]$ of (3.5,3.6) to be zero (to be demonstrated in a subsequent section) we conclude that all diffusion terms vanish. The macroscopic Fokker-Planck equation (2.13) thereby reduces to a Liouville equation, describing deterministic evolution for our macroscopic observables: $\frac{d}{dt}\Omega = \boldsymbol{F}[\Omega;t]$. These deterministic equations we will now work out explicitly.

On-Line Learning

First we deal with the scalar observables Q and R, whose equations are worked out easily to give

$$\frac{d}{dt}Q = 2\eta \int dx dy \ P[x,y] \ x\mathcal{G}[x,y] + \eta^2 \int dx dy \ P[x,y] \ \mathcal{G}^2[x,y] \qquad (3.7)$$

$$\frac{d}{dt}R = \eta \int dx dy \ P[x,y] \ y\mathcal{G}[x,y] \qquad (3.8)$$

These equations are identical to those of the familiar $\alpha \to \infty$ formalism. The difference is in the function to be substituted for $P[x,y]$, which would have been a simple Gaussian one for $\alpha \to \infty$, but which here is the solution of

$$\frac{\partial}{\partial t}P[x,y] = \frac{1}{\alpha}\left[\int dx' P[x',y]\delta[x-x'-\eta\mathcal{G}[x',y]] - P[x,y]\right]$$

$$-\eta\frac{\partial}{\partial x}\int dx'dy' \ \mathcal{G}[x',y']\mathcal{A}[x,y;x',y']$$

$$+\frac{1}{2}\eta^2\int dx'dy'\mathcal{G}^2[x',y']P[x',y']\frac{\partial^2}{\partial x^2}P[x,y] + \frac{1}{2}\eta^2\frac{\partial^2}{\partial x^2}\int dx'dy'\mathcal{G}^2[x',y']\mathcal{B}[x,y;x',y']$$

Anticipating the term $\mathcal{B}[\ldots]$ as defined in (3.4) to be zero (to be demonstrated in a subsequent section) we thus arrive at the following compact result:

$$\frac{\partial}{\partial t}P[x,y] = \frac{1}{\alpha}\left[\int dx' P[x',y]\delta[x-x'-\eta\mathcal{G}[x',y]] - P[x,y]\right]$$

$$-\eta\frac{\partial}{\partial x}\int dx'dy' \ \mathcal{G}[x',y']\mathcal{A}[x,y;x',y'] + \frac{1}{2}\eta^2\int dx'dy' \ \mathcal{G}^2[x',y']P[x',y']\frac{\partial^2}{\partial x^2}P[x,y]$$

$$(3.9)$$

Batch Learning

For Q and R we again find simple and transparent equations:

$$\frac{d}{dt}Q = 2\eta \int dx dy \ P[x,y] \ x\mathcal{G}[x,y] \qquad (3.10)$$

$$\frac{d}{dt}R = \eta \int dx dy \ P[x,y] \ y\mathcal{G}[x,y] \qquad (3.11)$$

Finally we calculate for batch learning the temporal derivative of the joint field distribution:

$$\frac{\partial}{\partial t}P[x,y] = -\frac{\eta}{\alpha}\frac{\partial}{\partial x}\Big[\mathcal{G}[x,y]P[x,y]\Big] - \eta\frac{\partial}{\partial x}\int dx'dy' \ \mathcal{A}[x,y;x',y']\mathcal{G}[x',y']$$

$$+\frac{1}{2}\eta^2\frac{\partial^2}{\partial x^2}\int dx'dy'dx''dy''\mathcal{C}[x,y;x',y';x'',y'']\mathcal{G}[x',y']\mathcal{G}[x'',y'']$$

Anticipating the term $\mathcal{C}[\ldots]$ as defined in (3.5) to be zero (to be demonstrated in a subsequent section) we thus arrive at the following compact result:

$$\frac{\partial}{\partial t}P[x,y] = -\frac{\eta}{\alpha}\frac{\partial}{\partial x}\left[\mathcal{G}[x,y]P[x,y]\right] - \eta\frac{\partial}{\partial x}\int dx'dy'\; \mathcal{A}[x,y;x',y']\mathcal{G}[x',y']$$

(3.12)

Comparing (3.7-3.9) with (3.10-3.12) shows that, as for complete training sets (Mace and Coolen, 1998), the difference between the macroscopic laws for batch and on-line learning is merely the presence (on-line) or absence (batch) of terms which are not linear in the learning rate η (i.e. of order η^2 or higher). This is consistent with the picture that for sufficiently small learning rates the differences between batch and on-line learning must vanish.

3.3   Closure of Macroscopic Dynamical Laws

We close our macroscopic laws (for on-line and batch learning) by making, for $N \to \infty$, the two key assumptions underlying dynamical replica theories:

1. *The observables $\{Q, R, P\}$ obey closed macroscopic dynamic equations.*

2. *These macroscopic dynamic equations are self-averaging with respect to the disorder, i.e. the microscopic realization of the training set $\tilde{D}$.*

Assumption 1 implies that all microscopic probability variations within the $\{Q, R, P\}$ subshells of the $\boldsymbol{J}$-ensemble are either absent or irrelevant to the evolution of $\{Q, R, P\}$. We may consequently make the simplest self-consistent choice for $p_t(\boldsymbol{J})$ in evaluating the macroscopic laws, i.e. in (3.3): microscopic probability equipartitioning in the $\{Q, R, P\}$-subshells of the ensemble, or

$$p_t(\boldsymbol{J}) \;\to\; w(\boldsymbol{J}) \sim \delta[Q - Q[\boldsymbol{J}]]\,\delta[R - R[\boldsymbol{J}]]\prod_{xy}\delta[P[x,y] - P[x,y;\boldsymbol{J}]] \quad (3.13)$$

The new distribution $w(\boldsymbol{J})$ depends on time only via $\{Q, R, P\}$. Note that (3.13) leads to exact macroscopic laws if for $N \to \infty$ our observables $\{Q, R, P\}$ indeed obey closed equations, and is true in equilibrium for detailed balance models in which the Hamiltonian can be written in terms of $\{Q, R, P\}$. It is an approximation if our observables do not obey closed equations. Assumption 2 allows us to average the macroscopic laws over the disorder; for mean-field models it is usually convincingly supported by numerical simulations, and can be proven within the path integral formalism (see e.g. Horner, 1992). We write averages over all training sets $\tilde{D} \subseteq \{-1,1\}^N$ of size p as $\langle \ldots \rangle_{\Xi}$. Our assumptions result in the closure of both (3.7-3.9) and (3.10-3.12), since now the function $\mathcal{A}[x,y;x',y']$ of (3.3) is expressed fully in terms of $\{Q, R, P\}$:

$$\mathcal{A}[x,y;x',y'] = \lim_{N\to\infty}$$

$$\left\langle \frac{\int d\boldsymbol{J}\; w(\boldsymbol{J})\; \langle\!\langle \delta[x - \boldsymbol{J}\cdot\boldsymbol{\xi}]\delta[y - \boldsymbol{B}\cdot\boldsymbol{\xi}](\boldsymbol{\xi}\cdot\boldsymbol{\xi}')^{\overline{\delta}}_{\boldsymbol{\xi}\boldsymbol{\xi}'}\delta[x' - \boldsymbol{J}\cdot\boldsymbol{\xi}']\delta[y' - \boldsymbol{B}\cdot\boldsymbol{\xi}']\rangle\!\rangle_{\tilde{D}}}{\int d\boldsymbol{J}\; w(\boldsymbol{J})} \right\rangle_{\Xi}$$

The final ingredient of dynamical replica theory is the realization that averages of fractions can be calculated with the replica identity

$$\left\langle \frac{\int d\boldsymbol{J}\, W[\boldsymbol{J}, z] G[\boldsymbol{J}, z]}{\int d\boldsymbol{J}\, W[\boldsymbol{J}, z]} \right\rangle_z = \lim_{n \to 0} \int d\boldsymbol{J}^1 \cdots d\boldsymbol{J}^n\, \langle G[\boldsymbol{J}^1, z] \prod_{\alpha=1}^{n} W[\boldsymbol{J}^\alpha, z] \rangle_z$$

giving

$$\mathcal{A}[x, y; x', y'] = \lim_{N \to \infty} \lim_{n \to 0} \int \prod_{\alpha=1}^{n} w(\boldsymbol{J}^\alpha)\, d\boldsymbol{J}^\alpha$$

$$\left\langle \langle\!\langle \delta[x - \boldsymbol{J}^1 \cdot \boldsymbol{\xi}] \delta[y - \boldsymbol{B} \cdot \boldsymbol{\xi}] (\boldsymbol{\xi} \cdot \boldsymbol{\xi}')\overline{\delta}_{\boldsymbol{\xi}\boldsymbol{\xi}'} \delta[x' - \boldsymbol{J}^1 \cdot \boldsymbol{\xi}'] \delta[y' - \boldsymbol{B} \cdot \boldsymbol{\xi}'] \rangle\!\rangle_{\hat{D}} \right\rangle_{\Xi}$$

Since each weight component scales as $J_i^\alpha = \mathcal{O}(N^{-\frac{1}{2}})$ we transform variables in such a way that our calculations will involve $\mathcal{O}(1)$ objects:

$$(\forall i)(\forall \alpha): \qquad J_i^\alpha = (Q/N)^{\frac{1}{2}} \sigma_i^\alpha, \qquad B_i = N^{-\frac{1}{2}} \tau_i$$

This ensures $\sigma_i^\alpha = \mathcal{O}(1)$, $\tau_i = \mathcal{O}(1)$, and reduces various constraints to ordinary spherical ones: $(\boldsymbol{\sigma}^\alpha)^2 = \boldsymbol{\tau}^2 = N$ for all α. Overall prefactors generated by these transformations always vanish due to $n \to 0$. We find a new effective measure: $\prod_{\alpha=1}^{n} w(\boldsymbol{J}^\alpha)\, d\boldsymbol{J}^\alpha \to \prod_{\alpha=1}^{n} \tilde{w}(\boldsymbol{\sigma}^\alpha)\, d\boldsymbol{\sigma}^\alpha$, with

$$\tilde{w}(\boldsymbol{\sigma}) \sim \delta\left[N - \boldsymbol{\sigma}^2\right] \delta\left[NRQ^{-\frac{1}{2}} - \boldsymbol{\tau} \cdot \boldsymbol{\sigma}\right] \prod_{xy} \delta\left[P[x, y] - P[x, y; (Q/N)^{\frac{1}{2}} \boldsymbol{\sigma}]\right]$$

(3.14)

In the same fashion one can also express $P[x, y]$ in replica form (which will prove useful for normalization purposes and for self-consistency tests). We thus arrive at

$$\mathcal{A}[x, y; x', y'] = \lim_{n \to 0} \lim_{N \to \infty} \int \prod_{\alpha=1}^{n} \tilde{w}(\boldsymbol{\sigma}^\alpha)\, d\boldsymbol{\sigma}^\alpha \left\langle \langle\!\langle (\boldsymbol{\xi}' \cdot \boldsymbol{\xi})\overline{\delta}_{\boldsymbol{\xi}\boldsymbol{\xi}'} \right.$$

$$\left. \times \delta\left[x - \frac{\sqrt{Q}\boldsymbol{\sigma}^1 \cdot \boldsymbol{\xi}}{\sqrt{N}}\right] \delta\left[y - \frac{\boldsymbol{\tau} \cdot \boldsymbol{\xi}}{\sqrt{N}}\right] \delta\left[x' - \frac{\sqrt{Q}\boldsymbol{\sigma}^1 \cdot \boldsymbol{\xi}'}{\sqrt{N}}\right] \delta\left[y' - \frac{\boldsymbol{\tau} \cdot \boldsymbol{\xi}'}{\sqrt{N}}\right] \rangle\!\rangle_{\hat{D}} \right\rangle_{\Xi} \quad (3.15)$$

and

$$P_t[x, y] = \lim_{n \to 0} \lim_{N \to \infty} \int \prod_{\alpha=1}^{n} \tilde{w}(\boldsymbol{\sigma}^\alpha) d\boldsymbol{\sigma}^\alpha \left\langle \langle\!\langle \delta\left[x - \frac{\sqrt{Q}\boldsymbol{\sigma}^1 \cdot \boldsymbol{\xi}}{\sqrt{N}}\right] \delta\left[y - \frac{\boldsymbol{\tau} \cdot \boldsymbol{\xi}}{\sqrt{N}}\right] \rangle\!\rangle_{\hat{D}} \right\rangle_{\Xi}$$

(3.16)

Similarly we find replica expressions for the three functions $\mathcal{B}[\ldots]$, $\mathcal{C}[\ldots]$ and $\mathcal{D}[\ldots]$ (3.4-3.6), which will be used subsequently to demonstrate that, within the present formalism, they are self-consistently found to be zero.

We have now converted our problem from a conceptual one into a purely technical one: the evaluation of the integrals and averages in (3.15,3.16), and in similar expressions found for $\mathcal{B}[\ldots]$, $\mathcal{C}[\ldots]$ and $\mathcal{D}[\ldots]$, and the subsequent solution of the resulting closed macroscopic dynamical laws (3.7-3.9) (on-line) and (3.10-3.12) (batch) for the order parameters $\{Q, R, P\}$.

4 Replica Calculation of the Green's Function

4.1 Disorder Averaging

In order to perform the disorder average we insert integral representations for the δ-functions which define the fields (x, y, x', y') and for the δ-functions in the measure (3.14) which involve $P[x, y]$, generating n conjugate order parameter functions $\hat{P}_\alpha(x, y)$. Upon also writing averages over the training set in terms of the p constituent vectors $\{\boldsymbol{\xi}^\mu\}$ we obtain for (3.15) and (3.16):

$$
\mathcal{A}[x, y; x', y'] = \int \frac{d\hat{x}\, d\hat{x}'d\hat{y}\, d\hat{y}'}{(2\pi)^4} e^{i[x\hat{x}+x'\hat{x}'+y\hat{y}+y\hat{y}']} \lim_{n\to 0} \lim_{N\to\infty} \int \prod_{\alpha=1}^n \prod_{x''y''} d\hat{P}_\alpha(x'', y'')
$$

$$
\int \prod_{\alpha=1}^n \left\{ d\boldsymbol{\sigma}^\alpha\, \delta\left[N-(\boldsymbol{\sigma}^\alpha)^2\right] \delta\left[\frac{NR}{\sqrt{Q}}-\boldsymbol{\tau}\cdot\boldsymbol{\sigma}^\alpha\right] e^{iN\int dx''dy''\,\hat{P}_\alpha(x'',y'')\,P_t(x'',y'')} \right\}
$$

$$
\left\langle \frac{1}{p^2}\sum_{\mu\neq\nu}(\boldsymbol{\xi}^\mu\boldsymbol{\xi}^\nu)e^{-\frac{i}{\alpha}\sum_{\alpha\lambda}\hat{P}_\alpha\left(\frac{\sqrt{Q}\boldsymbol{\sigma}^\alpha\cdot\boldsymbol{\xi}^\lambda}{\sqrt{N}}, \frac{\boldsymbol{\tau}\cdot\boldsymbol{\xi}^\lambda}{\sqrt{N}}\right)-\frac{i}{\sqrt{N}}\boldsymbol{\xi}^\mu\cdot[\hat{x}\sqrt{Q}\boldsymbol{\sigma}^1+\hat{y}\boldsymbol{\tau}]-\frac{i}{\sqrt{N}}\boldsymbol{\xi}^\nu\cdot[\hat{x}'\sqrt{Q}\boldsymbol{\sigma}^1+\hat{y}'\boldsymbol{\tau}]} \right\rangle_{\Xi}
$$

$$
(4.1)
$$

$$
P[x, y] = \int \frac{d\hat{x}\, d\hat{y}}{(2\pi)^2} e^{i[x\hat{x}+y\hat{y}]} \lim_{n\to 0} \lim_{N\to\infty} \int \prod_{\alpha=1}^n \prod_{x''y''} d\hat{P}_\alpha(x'', y'')
$$

$$
\int \prod_{\alpha=1}^n \left\{ d\boldsymbol{\sigma}^\alpha \delta\left[N-(\boldsymbol{\sigma}^\alpha)^2\right] \delta\left[\frac{NR}{\sqrt{Q}}-\boldsymbol{\tau}\cdot\boldsymbol{\sigma}^\alpha\right] e^{iN\int dx''dy''\,\hat{P}_\alpha(x'',y'')\,P_t(x'',y'')} \right\}
$$

$$
\left\langle \frac{1}{p}\sum_{\mu=1}^p e^{-\frac{i}{\alpha}\sum_{\alpha\lambda}\hat{P}_\alpha\left(\frac{\sqrt{Q}\boldsymbol{\sigma}^\alpha\cdot\boldsymbol{\xi}^\lambda}{\sqrt{N}}, \frac{\boldsymbol{\tau}\cdot\boldsymbol{\xi}^\lambda}{\sqrt{N}}\right)-\frac{i}{\sqrt{N}}\boldsymbol{\xi}^\mu\cdot[\hat{x}\sqrt{Q}\boldsymbol{\sigma}^1+\hat{y}\boldsymbol{\tau}]} \right\rangle_{\Xi} \qquad (4.2)
$$

In calculating the averages over the training sets $\langle \ldots \rangle_{\Xi}$ that occur in (4.1) and (4.2) one can use permutation symmetries with respect to sites and pattern labels, leading to the following compact results:

$$
\left\langle \frac{1}{p^2}\sum_{\mu\neq\nu}(\boldsymbol{\xi}^\mu\boldsymbol{\xi}^\nu)e^{-\frac{i}{\alpha}\sum_{\alpha}\sum_{\lambda}\hat{P}_\alpha\left(\frac{\sqrt{Q}\boldsymbol{\sigma}^\alpha\cdot\boldsymbol{\xi}^\lambda}{\sqrt{N}}, \frac{\boldsymbol{\tau}\cdot\boldsymbol{\xi}^\lambda}{\sqrt{N}}\right)-\frac{i}{\sqrt{N}}\boldsymbol{\xi}^\mu\cdot[\hat{x}\sqrt{Q}\boldsymbol{\sigma}^1+\hat{y}\boldsymbol{\tau}]-\frac{i}{\sqrt{N}}\boldsymbol{\xi}^\nu\cdot[\hat{x}'\sqrt{Q}\boldsymbol{\sigma}^1+\hat{y}'\boldsymbol{\tau}]} \right\rangle_{\Xi}
$$

$$
= e^{p\log\mathcal{D}[0,0]} \frac{1}{N}\sum_j \frac{\mathcal{E}_j[\hat{x}, \hat{y}]\mathcal{E}_j[\hat{x}', \hat{y}']}{\mathcal{D}^2[0, 0]} + \mathcal{O}(N^{-\frac{1}{2}}) \qquad (4.3)
$$

and

$$
\left\langle \frac{1}{p}\sum_{\mu=1}^p e^{-\frac{i}{\alpha}\sum_{\alpha}\sum_{\lambda}\hat{P}_\alpha\left(\frac{\sqrt{Q}\boldsymbol{\sigma}^\alpha\cdot\boldsymbol{\xi}^\lambda}{\sqrt{N}}, \frac{\boldsymbol{\tau}\cdot\boldsymbol{\xi}^\lambda}{\sqrt{N}}\right)-\frac{i}{\sqrt{N}}\boldsymbol{\xi}^\mu\cdot[\hat{x}\sqrt{Q}\boldsymbol{\sigma}^1+\hat{y}\boldsymbol{\tau}]} \right\rangle_{\Xi}
$$

$$
= e^{p\log\mathcal{D}[0,0]} \frac{\mathcal{D}[\hat{x}, \hat{y}]}{\mathcal{D}[0, 0]} + \mathcal{O}\left(N^{-\frac{1}{2}}\right) \qquad (4.4)
$$

in which

$$\mathcal{D}[u,v] = \left\langle e^{-\frac{i}{\alpha}\sum_\alpha \hat{P}_\alpha\left(\frac{\sqrt{Q}\boldsymbol{\sigma}^\alpha\cdot\boldsymbol{\xi}}{\sqrt{N}},\frac{\boldsymbol{\tau}\cdot\boldsymbol{\xi}}{\sqrt{N}}\right)-\frac{i}{\sqrt{N}}\boldsymbol{\xi}\cdot[u\sqrt{Q}\boldsymbol{\sigma}^1+v]} \right\rangle_{\boldsymbol{\xi}}$$

$$\mathcal{E}_j[u,v] = \left\langle \sqrt{N}\xi_j\, e^{-\frac{i}{\alpha}\sum_\alpha \hat{P}_\alpha\left(\frac{\sqrt{Q}\boldsymbol{\sigma}^\alpha\cdot\boldsymbol{\xi}}{\sqrt{N}},\frac{\boldsymbol{\tau}\cdot\boldsymbol{\xi}}{\sqrt{N}}\right)-\frac{i}{\sqrt{N}}\boldsymbol{\xi}\cdot[u\sqrt{Q}\boldsymbol{\sigma}^1+v\boldsymbol{\tau}]} \right\rangle_{\boldsymbol{\xi}}$$

and with the abbreviation $\langle f[\boldsymbol{\xi}]\rangle_{\boldsymbol{\xi}} = 2^{-N}\sum_{\boldsymbol{\xi}\in\{-1,1\}^N} f[\boldsymbol{\xi}]$. These quantities (which are both $\mathcal{O}(1)$ for $N \to \infty$) are, in turn, evaluated by using the central limit theorem, which ensures that for $N \to \infty$ the n rescaled inner products $\boldsymbol{\sigma}^\alpha \cdot \boldsymbol{\xi}/\sqrt{N}$ and the rescaled inner product $\boldsymbol{\tau}\cdot\boldsymbol{\xi}/\sqrt{N}$ will become (correlated) zero-average Gaussian variables. After some algebra one finds

$$\mathcal{L}[u,v;u',v'] = \frac{1}{N}\sum_j \mathcal{E}_j[u,v]\,\mathcal{E}_j[u',v'] =$$

$$= -Q\sum_{\alpha\beta} q_{\alpha\beta}(\{\boldsymbol{\sigma}\})\left[\frac{1}{\alpha}\mathcal{F}_1^\alpha[u,v]+u\,\delta_{\alpha1}\mathcal{D}[u,v]\right]\left[\frac{1}{\alpha}\mathcal{F}_1^\beta[u',v']+u'\,\delta_{\beta1}\mathcal{D}[u',v']\right]$$

$$-R\sum_{\alpha\beta}\left[\frac{1}{\alpha}\mathcal{F}_1^\alpha[u,v]+u\,\delta_{\alpha1}\mathcal{D}[u,v]\right]\left[\frac{1}{\alpha}\mathcal{F}_2^\beta[u',v']+v'\,\delta_{\beta1}\mathcal{D}[u',v']\right]$$

$$-R\sum_{\alpha\beta}\left[\frac{1}{\alpha}\mathcal{F}_1^\alpha[u',v']+u'\,\delta_{\alpha1}\mathcal{D}[u',v']\right]\left[\frac{1}{\alpha}\mathcal{F}_2^\beta[u,v]+v\,\delta_{\beta1}\mathcal{D}[u,v]\right]$$

$$-\sum_{\alpha\beta}\left[\frac{1}{\alpha}\mathcal{F}_2^\alpha[u,v]+v\,\delta_{\alpha1}\mathcal{D}[u,v]\right]\left[\frac{1}{\alpha}\mathcal{F}_2^\beta[u',v']+v'\,\delta_{\beta1}\mathcal{D}[u',v']\right]+\mathcal{O}(N^{-\frac{1}{2}})$$

$$(4.5)$$

in which $\mathcal{D}[u,v]$ and the $\mathcal{F}_\lambda^\alpha[u,v]$ are given by $n+1$ dimensional integrals:

$$\mathcal{D}[u,v] = \int \frac{d\boldsymbol{x}\, dy\, \det^{\frac{1}{2}}\boldsymbol{A}}{(2\pi)^{(n+1)/2}}\, e^{-\frac{1}{2}\begin{pmatrix}\boldsymbol{x}\\y\end{pmatrix}\boldsymbol{A}\begin{pmatrix}\boldsymbol{x}\\y\end{pmatrix}-\frac{i}{\alpha}\sum_\alpha \hat{P}_\alpha(\sqrt{Q}x_\alpha,y)-i[u\sqrt{Q}x_1+vy]}$$

$$(4.6)$$

$$\mathcal{F}_\lambda^\alpha[u,v] =$$

$$\int \frac{d\boldsymbol{x}\, dy\, \det^{\frac{1}{2}}\boldsymbol{A}}{(2\pi)^{(n+1)/2}}\, \partial_\lambda \hat{P}_\alpha(\sqrt{Q}x_\alpha,y)\, e^{-\frac{1}{2}\begin{pmatrix}\boldsymbol{x}\\y\end{pmatrix}\boldsymbol{A}\begin{pmatrix}\boldsymbol{x}\\y\end{pmatrix}-\frac{i}{\alpha}\sum_\alpha \hat{P}_\alpha(\sqrt{Q}x_\alpha,y)-i[u\sqrt{Q}x_1+vy]}$$

$$(4.7)$$

with $\lambda \in \{1,2\}$. The matrix $\boldsymbol{A}$ in (4.6,4.7) is defined by

$$\boldsymbol{A}^{-1} = \begin{pmatrix} q_{11} & \cdots & q_{1n} & R/\sqrt{Q} \\ \vdots & & \vdots & \vdots \\ q_{n1} & \cdots & q_{nn} & R/\sqrt{Q} \\ R/\sqrt{Q} & \cdots & R/\sqrt{Q} & 1 \end{pmatrix} \qquad q_{\alpha\beta}(\{\boldsymbol{\sigma}\}) = \frac{1}{N}\sum_i \sigma_i^\alpha \sigma_i^\beta \quad (4.8)$$

Note that the quantities (4.6,4.7) depend on the microscopic variables $\boldsymbol{\sigma}^\alpha$ only through the spin-glass order parameters $q_{\alpha\beta}(\{\boldsymbol{\sigma}\})$.

It is a straightforward exercise to carry out a similar calculation for.the functions $\mathcal{B}[\ldots]$ (3.4), $\mathcal{C}[\ldots]$ (3.4) and $\mathcal{D}[\ldots]$. This gives a zero result in all three cases, basically due to the three functions involving too many unpaired pattern components (each of which will effectively generate a factor $N^{-\frac{1}{2}}$), confirming our previous assertions about the vanishing of all diffusion matrix elements in the macroscopic Fokker-Planck equation (2.13). For details we refer to (Coolen and Saad, 1998).

4.2   Derivation of Saddle-Point Equations

We combine the results (4.3,4.4,4.5) with (4.1,4.2). We use integral representations for the remaining δ-functions, and isolate the $q_{\alpha\beta}$, by inserting

$$1 = \int \frac{d\boldsymbol{q}\, d\hat{\boldsymbol{q}}\, d\hat{\boldsymbol{Q}}\, d\hat{\boldsymbol{R}}}{(2\pi/N)^{n^2+2n}}\, e^{iN[\sum_\alpha(\hat{Q}_\alpha + \hat{R}_\alpha R/\sqrt{Q}) + \sum_{\alpha\beta}\hat{q}_{\alpha\beta}q_{\alpha\beta}]}$$

$$\times\ e^{-i\sum_i[\sum_\alpha(\hat{Q}_\alpha(\sigma_i^\alpha)^2 + \hat{R}_\alpha\tau_i\sigma_i^\alpha) - i\sum_{\alpha\beta}\hat{q}_{\alpha\beta}\sigma_i^\alpha\sigma_i^\beta]}$$

We hereby achieve a full factorization over sites, and both (4.1) and (4.2) can be written in the form of an integral dominated by saddle-points:

$$\mathcal{A}[x, y; x', y'] = \int \frac{d\hat{x}\, d\hat{x}' d\hat{y}\, d\hat{y}'}{(2\pi)^4}\, e^{i[x\hat{x} + x'\hat{x}' + y\hat{y} + y\hat{y}']}$$

$$\lim_{n\to 0}\lim_{N\to\infty}\int d\boldsymbol{q}\, d\hat{\boldsymbol{q}}\, d\hat{\boldsymbol{Q}}\, d\hat{\boldsymbol{R}} \prod_{\alpha x'' y''} d\hat{P}_\alpha(x'', y'')\, e^{N\Psi[q,\hat{q},\hat{Q},\hat{R},\{\hat{P}\}]}\frac{\mathcal{L}[\hat{x}, \hat{y}; \hat{x}', \hat{y}']}{\mathcal{D}^2[0,0]}$$

$$P[x, y] = \int \frac{d\hat{x}\, d\hat{y}}{(2\pi)^2}\, e^{i[x\hat{x} + y\hat{y}]}$$

$$\lim_{n\to 0}\lim_{N\to\infty}\int d\boldsymbol{q}\, d\hat{\boldsymbol{q}}\, d\hat{\boldsymbol{Q}}\, d\hat{\boldsymbol{R}} \prod_{\alpha x'' y''} d\hat{P}_\alpha(x'', y'')\, e^{N\Psi[q,\hat{q},\hat{Q},\hat{R},\{\hat{P}\}]}\frac{\mathcal{D}[\hat{x}, \hat{y}]}{\mathcal{D}[0,0]}$$

with

$$\Psi[\ldots] = i\sum_\alpha(\hat{Q}_\alpha + \hat{R}_\alpha R/\sqrt{Q}) + i\sum_{\alpha\beta}\hat{q}_{\alpha\beta}\, q_{\alpha\beta} + i\sum_\alpha \int dx\, dy\, \hat{P}_\alpha(x, y)P[x, y]$$

$$+\alpha\log\mathcal{D}[0,0] + \lim_{N\to\infty}\frac{1}{N}\sum_i \log\int d\boldsymbol{\sigma}\, e^{-i\sum_\alpha[\hat{Q}_\alpha\sigma_\alpha^2 + \hat{R}_\alpha\tau_i\sigma_\alpha] - i\sum_{\alpha\beta}\hat{q}_{\alpha\beta}\sigma_\alpha\sigma_\beta}$$

The above expressions for $\mathcal{A}[x, y; x', y']$ and $P[x, y]$ will be given by the intensive parts of the integrands, evaluated in the dominating saddle-point of Ψ. We can use the equation for $P[x, y]$ to verify that all expressions are properly normalized. After a simple transformation of some integration variables,

$$\hat{q}_{\alpha\beta} \to \hat{q}_{\alpha\beta} - \hat{Q}_\alpha\delta_{\alpha\beta} \qquad\qquad \hat{R}_\alpha \to \sqrt{Q}\hat{R}_\alpha$$

we arrive at the simple result

$$\mathcal{A}[x, y; x', y'] = \int \frac{d\hat{x} \, d\hat{x}' \, d\hat{y} \, d\hat{y}'}{(2\pi)^4} e^{i[x\hat{x} + x'\hat{x}' + y\hat{y} + y\hat{y}']} \lim_{n \to 0} \frac{\mathcal{L}[\hat{x}, \hat{y}; \hat{x}', \hat{y}']}{\mathcal{D}^2[0,0]} \quad (4.9)$$

$$P[x, y] = \int \frac{d\hat{x} \, d\hat{y}}{(2\pi)^2} e^{i[x\hat{x} + y\hat{y}]} \lim_{n \to 0} \frac{\mathcal{D}[\hat{x}, \hat{y}]}{\mathcal{D}[0,0]} \quad (4.10)$$

in which all functions are to be evaluated upon choosing for the order parameters the appropriate saddle-point of Ψ, which itself takes the form:

$$\Psi[\ldots] = i \sum_\alpha \hat{Q}_\alpha (1 - q_{\alpha\alpha}) + iR \sum_\alpha \hat{R}_\alpha + i \sum_{\alpha\beta} \hat{q}_{\alpha\beta} \, q_{\alpha\beta} + i \sum_\alpha \int dx dy \, \hat{P}_\alpha(x, y) P[x, y]$$

$$+ \alpha \log \mathcal{D}[0,0] + \lim_{N \to \infty} \frac{1}{N} \sum_i \log \int d\boldsymbol{\sigma} \, e^{-i\tau_i \sqrt{Q} \sum_\alpha \hat{R}_\alpha \sigma_\alpha - i \sum_{\alpha\beta} \hat{q}_{\alpha\beta} \sigma_\alpha \sigma_\beta} \quad (4.11)$$

With $\mathcal{D}[u, v]$ given by (4.6) and with the function $\mathcal{L}[u, v; u', v']$ given by (4.5). The auxiliary order parameters $q_{\alpha\beta}$ have the usual interpretation in terms of the average probability density for finding a mutual overlap q of two independently evolving weight vectors with the same realization of the training set (see e.g. Mézard *et al.*, 1987):

$$\langle P(q) \rangle_{\Xi} = \left\langle \left\langle \left\langle \delta \left[q - \frac{\boldsymbol{J}^a \cdot \boldsymbol{J}^b}{|\boldsymbol{J}^a||\boldsymbol{J}^b|} \right] \right\rangle \right\rangle \right/_{\Xi} = \lim_{n \to 0} \frac{1}{n(n-1)} \sum_{\alpha \neq \beta} \delta[q - q_{\alpha\beta}] \quad (4.12)$$

We now make the replica symmetric (RS) Ansatz in the extremization problem, which according to (4.12) is equivalent to assuming ergodicity. With a modest amount of foresight we put

$$q_{\alpha\beta} = q_0 \delta_{\alpha\beta} + q[1 - \delta_{\alpha\beta}] \qquad \hat{q}_{\alpha\beta} = \frac{i}{2}[r - r_0 \delta_{\alpha\beta}]$$

$$\hat{R}_\alpha = i\rho \qquad \hat{Q}_\alpha = i\phi \qquad \hat{P}_\alpha(u, v) = i\chi[u, v]$$

This allows us to expand the quantity Ψ of (4.11) for small n:

$$\lim_{n \to 0} \frac{1}{n} \Psi[\ldots] = -\phi(1 - q_0) - \rho R + \frac{1}{2} qr - \frac{1}{2} q_0(r - r_0) - \frac{1}{2} \log r_0 + \frac{1}{2r_0}(r + \rho^2 Q)$$

$$- \int dx dy \, \chi[x, y] \, P[x, y] + \lim_{n \to 0} \frac{\alpha}{n} \log \mathcal{D}[0,0] + \text{constants}$$

At this stage it is useful to work out those saddle-point equations that follow upon variation of $\{\phi, r, \rho, r_0\}$:

$$q_0 = 1 \qquad r_0 = \frac{1}{1 - q} \qquad \rho = \frac{R}{Q(1 - q)} \qquad r = \frac{qQ - R^2}{Q(1 - q)^2}$$

These allow us to eliminate most variational parameters, leaving a saddle-point problem involving only the function $\chi[x,y]$ and the scalar q:

$$\lim_{n\to 0}\frac{1}{n}\Psi[q,\{\chi\}] = \frac{1-R^2/Q}{2(1-q)} + \frac{1}{2}\log(1-q) - \int dx\,dy\,\chi[x,y]\,P[x,y]$$

$$+ \lim_{n\to 0}\frac{\alpha}{n}\log\mathcal{D}[0,0;q,\{\chi\}] + \text{constants} \qquad (4.13)$$

Finally we have to work out the RS version of $\mathcal{D}[0,0;q,\{\chi\}]$, as defined more generally in (4.6). The inverse of the matrix in (4.8), in RS Ansatz, is found to be:

$$\mathbf{A} = \begin{pmatrix} C_{11} & \cdots & C_{1n} & \gamma \\ \vdots & & \vdots & \vdots \\ C_{n1} & \cdots & C_{nn} & \gamma \\ \gamma & \cdots & \gamma & b \end{pmatrix} \qquad C_{\alpha\beta} = \frac{\delta_{\alpha\beta}}{1-q} - d \qquad \begin{aligned} \gamma &= -\frac{R/\sqrt{Q}}{1-q} + \mathcal{O}(n) \\ b &= 1 + \mathcal{O}(n) \\ d &= \frac{q-R^2/Q}{(1-q)^2} + \mathcal{O}(n) \end{aligned}$$

$$(4.14)$$

With this expression we obtain

$$\mathcal{D}[0,0;q,\{\chi\}] = \frac{\int d\boldsymbol{x}\,dy\,e^{-\frac{1}{2}\boldsymbol{x}\cdot\boldsymbol{C}\boldsymbol{x}-\frac{1}{2}by^2-\gamma y\sum_\alpha x_\alpha+\frac{1}{\alpha}\sum_\alpha\chi(\sqrt{Q}x_\alpha,y)}}{\int d\boldsymbol{x}\,dy\,e^{-\frac{1}{2}\boldsymbol{x}\cdot\boldsymbol{C}\boldsymbol{x}-\frac{1}{2}by^2-\gamma y\sum_\alpha x_\alpha}}$$

$$= \frac{\int Dz\,Dy\left[\int dx\,e^{-\frac{x^2}{2(1-q)}+[z\sqrt{d}-\gamma\frac{y}{\sqrt{b}}]x+\frac{1}{\alpha}\chi(\sqrt{Q}x,\frac{y}{\sqrt{b}})}\right]^n}{\int Dz\,Dy\left[\int dx\,e^{-\frac{1}{2(1-q)}x^2+[z\sqrt{d}-\gamma\frac{y}{\sqrt{b}}]x}\right]^n}$$

$$\lim_{n\to 0}\frac{\alpha}{n}\log\mathcal{D}[0,0;q,\{\chi\}] = \alpha\int Dz\,Dy\log\left\{\frac{\int dx\,e^{-\frac{x^2}{2Q(1-q)}+x[z\sqrt{d}-\gamma y]/\sqrt{Q}+\frac{1}{\alpha}\chi(x,y)}}{\int dx\,e^{-\frac{x^2}{2Q(1-q)}+x[z\sqrt{d}-\gamma y]/\sqrt{Q}}}\right\}$$

with the usual short-hand $Dy = (2\pi)^{-\frac{1}{2}}e^{-\frac{1}{2}y^2}$. We can simplify this result by defining

$$A = R/Q(1-q) \qquad B = \sqrt{qQ-R^2}/Q(1-q) \qquad (4.15)$$

which gives

$$\lim_{n\to 0}\frac{\alpha}{n}\log\mathcal{D}[0,0;q,\{\chi\}] = \alpha\int Dz\,Dy\,\log\left\{\frac{\int dx\,e^{-\frac{x^2}{2Q(1-q)}+x[Ay+Bz]+\frac{1}{\alpha}\chi(x,y)}}{\int dx\,e^{-\frac{x^2}{2Q(1-q)}+x[Ay+Bz]}}\right\}$$

Upon carrying out the x-integration in the denominator of this expression we can write (4.13) in a surprisingly simple form (with the short-hands (4.15)):

$$\lim_{n\to 0}\frac{1}{n}\Psi[q,\{\chi\}] = \frac{1-\alpha-R^2/Q}{2(1-q)} + \frac{1}{2}(1-\alpha)\log(1-q) - \int dx\,dy\,\chi[x,y]\,P[x,y]$$

$$+ \alpha\int Dz\,Dy\,\log\int dx\,e^{-\frac{x^2}{2Q(1-q)}+x[Ay+Bz]+\frac{1}{\alpha}\chi[x,y]} \qquad (4.16)$$

Note that (4.16) is to be *minimized*, both with respect to q (which originated as an $n(n-1)$-fold entry in a matrix, leading to curvature sign change for $n < 1$) and with respect to $\chi[x,y]$ (obtained from the n-fold occurrence of the function $\hat{P}[x,y]$, multiplied by i, which also leads to a curvature sign change).

The remaining saddle point equations are obtained by (functional) variation with respect to χ:

$$\text{for all } x,y: \quad P[x,y] = \frac{e^{-\frac{1}{2}y^2}}{\sqrt{2\pi}} \int Dz \left\{ \frac{e^{-\frac{x^2}{2Q(1-q)}+x[Ay+Bz]+\frac{1}{\alpha}\chi[x,y]}}{\int dx'\, e^{-\frac{x'^2}{2Q(1-q)}+x'[Ay+Bz]+\frac{1}{\alpha}\chi[x',y]}} \right\},$$
(4.17)

and q (using equation (4.17) wherever possible):

$$\int dxdy\ P[x,y](x-Ry)^2 + (R^2-qQ)(\frac{1}{\alpha}-1) =$$

$$\left[2\sqrt{qQ-R^2} + \frac{Q(1-q)}{\sqrt{qQ-R^2}} \right] \int DyDz\ z \left\{ \frac{\int dx\ x\ e^{-\frac{x^2}{2Q(1-q)}+x[Ay+Bz]+\frac{1}{\alpha}\chi[x,y]}}{\int dx\ e^{-\frac{x^2}{2Q(1-q)}+x[Ay+Bz]+\frac{1}{\alpha}\chi[x,y]}} \right\}$$
(4.18)

Apart from the physically irrelevant degree of freedom $\chi[x,y] \to \chi[x,y]+\rho(y)$, for arbitrary $\rho(y)$, the solution of the functional saddle-point problem (4.17), if it exists, will be unique for any given value of q in the physical range $R^2/Q \leq q \leq 1$. This follows immediately from the convexity of $\Psi[\ldots]$ (4.16), which can, in turn, be deduced from the the fact that the second functional derivative of $\Psi[\ldots]$ with respect to the function $\chi[\ldots]$ is a non-negative operator. In addition one can prove that $\Psi[\ldots]$ (4.16) has a lower bound, which is given in terms of the differential entropy of the distribution $P[x,y]$. Furthermore, the functional saddle-point equation (4.17) can be rewritten in the form of a fixed-point equation associated with an iterative mapping for the function $\chi[x,y]$, such that this mapping has (4.16) as a Lyapunov functional. Should an analytical solution of (4.17) turn out to be impossible, in combination the above properties convert finding the solution of (4.17) from a potentially insurmountable obstacle into a straightforward numerical exercise. Details will be published in (Coolen and Saad, 1998).

4.3   Explicit Expression for the Green's Function

In order to work out the Green's function (4.9) we need $\mathcal{L}[u,v;u',v']$ as defined in (4.5) which, in turn, is given in terms of the integrals (4.6,4.7). First we calculate in RS ansatz the $n \to 0$ limit of $D[u,v;q,\{\chi\}]$ (4.6), using (4.14), and simplify the result with the saddle-point equation (4.17):

$$\lim_{n\to 0} \mathcal{D}[u,v;q,\{\chi\}] = \int DzDy\ e^{-ivy} \frac{\int dx\ e^{-\frac{x^2}{2Q(1-q)}+x[Ay+Bz]+\frac{1}{\alpha}\chi[x,y]-iux}}{\int dx\ e^{-\frac{x^2}{2Q(1-q)}+x[Ay+Bz]+\frac{1}{\alpha}\chi[x,y]}}$$

$$= \int dx dy \; P[x,y] \; e^{-ivy-iux} \tag{4.19}$$

Next we work out $F_\lambda^\alpha[u,v]$ (4.7) in RS Ansatz, using (4.14), with $\lambda \in \{1,2\}$, which results in

$$\lim_{n\to 0} \mathcal{F}_\lambda^\alpha[u,v] = i \lim_{n\to 0}$$

$$\int DyDz \; e^{-ivy} \int d\boldsymbol{x} \; e^{\sum_\beta \left[-\frac{1}{2}\frac{x_\beta^2}{1-q} + [z\sqrt{d}-\gamma y]x_\beta + \frac{1}{\alpha}\chi[\sqrt{Q}x_\beta,y] \right] - iux_1\sqrt{Q}} \; \partial_\lambda\chi[\sqrt{Q}x_\alpha,y]$$

Replica permutation symmetries allow us to simplify this expression:

$$\lim_{n\to 0} \mathcal{F}_\lambda^\alpha[u,v] = \delta_{\alpha 1}F_\lambda^1[u,v] + (1-\delta_{\alpha 1})F_\lambda^2[u,v] \tag{4.20}$$

with

$$F_\lambda^1[u,v] = i \int dx \; dy \; P[x,y] \; e^{-ivy-iux} \; \partial_\lambda\chi[x,y] \tag{4.21}$$

and

$$F_\lambda^2[u,v] = i \int DyDz \; e^{-ivy}$$

$$\frac{\left[\int dx \; e^{-\frac{x^2}{2Q(1-q)}+x[Ay+Bz]+\frac{1}{\alpha}\chi[x,y]} \; \partial_\lambda\chi[x,y] \right] \left[\int dx \; e^{-\frac{x^2}{2Q(1-q)}+x[Ay+Bz]+\frac{1}{\alpha}\chi[x,y]-iux} \right]}{\left[\int dx \; e^{-\frac{x^2}{2Q(1-q)}+x[Ay+Bz]+\frac{1}{\alpha}\chi[x,y]} \right]^2}$$

$$\tag{4.22}$$

We can now proceed with the calculation of (4.5), whose building blocks are

$$\alpha^{-1}\mathcal{F}_1^\alpha[u,v] + u\delta_{\alpha 1}\mathcal{D}[u,v] = \delta_{\alpha 1}G_1[u,v] + (1-\delta_{\alpha 1})\tilde{G}_{1,2}[u,v]$$

$$\alpha^{-1}\mathcal{F}_2^\alpha[u,v] + v\delta_{\alpha 1}\mathcal{D}[u,v] = \delta_{\alpha 1}G_2[u,v] + (1-\delta_{\alpha 1})\tilde{G}_2[u,v]$$

with

$$G_1[u,v] = \alpha^{-1}\mathcal{F}_{1,2}^1[u,v] + u\mathcal{D}[u,v] \qquad \tilde{G}_1[u,v] = \alpha^{-1}\mathcal{F}_1^2[u,v]$$

$$G_2[u,v] = \alpha^{-1}\mathcal{F}_2^1[u,v] + v\mathcal{D}[u,v] \qquad \tilde{G}_2[u,v] = \alpha^{-1}\mathcal{F}_2^2[u,v]$$

and their Fourier transforms:

$$\hat{G}_1[\hat{u},\hat{v}] = \int \frac{du \; dv}{(2\pi)^2} e^{iu\hat{u}+iv\hat{v}}G_1[u,v] \qquad \bar{G}_1[\hat{u},\hat{v}] = \int \frac{du \; dv}{(2\pi)^2} e^{iu\hat{u}+iv\hat{v}}\tilde{G}_1[u,v]$$

$$\hat{G}_2[\hat{u},\hat{v}] = \int \frac{du \; dv}{(2\pi)^2} e^{iu\hat{u}+iv\hat{v}}G_2[u,v] \qquad \bar{G}_2[\hat{u},\hat{v}] = \int \frac{du \; dv}{(2\pi)^2} e^{iu\hat{u}+iv\hat{v}}\tilde{G}_2[u,v]$$

With these short-hands we obtain a relatively compact expression for (4.5). In this expression we can subsequently take the limit $n \to 0$, insert the result into our equation (4.9) for the Green's function $\mathcal{A}[x,y;x',y']$, and find:

$$\mathcal{A}[x,y;x',y'] = -Q(1-q)\left[\hat{G}_1[x,y]\hat{G}_1[x',y'] - \bar{G}_1[x,y]\bar{G}_1[x',y']\right]$$

$$-Qq\left[\hat{G}_1[x,y] - \bar{G}_1[x,y]\right]\left[\hat{G}_1[x',y'] - \bar{G}_1[x',y']\right]$$

$$-R\left[\hat{G}_1[x,y] - \bar{G}_1[x,y]\right]\left[\hat{G}_2[x',y'] - \bar{G}_2[x',y']\right]$$

$$-R\left[\hat{G}_1[x',y'] - \bar{G}_1[x',y']\right]\left[\hat{G}_2[x,y] - \bar{G}_2[x,y]\right]$$

$$-\left[\hat{G}_2[x,y] - \bar{G}_2[x,y]\right]\left[\hat{G}_2[x',y'] - \bar{G}_2[x',y']\right] \tag{4.23}$$

Finally, working out the four relevant Fourier transforms, using (4.19, (4.21, 4.22), gives:

$$\hat{G}_1[x,y] = i\left[\frac{1}{\alpha}\,P[x,y]\,\frac{\partial}{\partial x}\chi[x,y] - \frac{\partial}{\partial x}P[x,y]\right]$$

$$\hat{G}_2[x,y] = i\left[\frac{1}{\alpha}\,P[x,y]\,\frac{\partial}{\partial y}\chi[x,y] - \frac{\partial}{\partial y}P[x,y]\right]$$

$$\bar{G}_1[x,y] = \frac{i}{\alpha}\frac{e^{-\frac{1}{2}y^2}}{\sqrt{2\pi}}\int Dz$$

$$\frac{\left[\int dx'\; e^{-\frac{x'^2}{2Q(1-q)}+x'[Ay+Bz]+\frac{1}{\alpha}\chi[x',y]}\,\partial_1\chi[x',y]\right]e^{-\frac{x^2}{2Q(1-q)}+x[Ay+Bz]+\frac{1}{\alpha}\chi[x,y]}}{\left[\int dx'\; e^{-\frac{x'^2}{2Q(1-q)}+x'[Ay+Bz]+\frac{1}{\alpha}\chi[x',y]}\right]^2}$$

$$\bar{G}_2[x,y] = \frac{i}{\alpha}\frac{e^{-\frac{1}{2}y^2}}{\sqrt{2\pi}}\int Dz$$

$$\frac{\left[\int dx'\; e^{-\frac{x'^2}{2Q(1-q)}+x'[Ay+Bz]+\frac{1}{\alpha}\chi[x',y]}\,\partial_2\chi[x',y]\right]e^{-\frac{x^2}{2Q(1-q)}+x[Ay+Bz]+\frac{1}{\alpha}\chi[x,y]}}{\left[\int dx'\; e^{-\frac{x'^2}{2Q(1-q)}+x'[Ay+Bz]+\frac{1}{\alpha}\chi[x',y]}\right]^2}$$

4.4   Simplification and Summary of the Theory

In this section we simplify and summarize the results obtained so far. Since the distribution $P[x,y]$ obeys $P[x,y] = P[x|y]P[y]$ with $P[y] = (2\pi)^{-\frac{1}{2}}e^{-\frac{1}{2}y^2}$, our equations can be simplified by choosing as our order parameter function the conditional distribution $P[x|y]$. We also replace the conjugate order parameter function $\chi[x,y]$ by the effective measure $M[x,y]$, and we introduce a compact notation for the relevant averages in our problem:

$$M[x,y] = e^{-\frac{x^2}{2Q(1-q)}+Axy+\frac{1}{\alpha}\chi[x,y]} \qquad \langle f[x,y,z]\rangle_* = \frac{\int dx\; M[x,y]e^{Bxz}f[x,y,z]}{\int dx\; M[x,y]e^{Bxz}}$$

Instead of the original Green's function $A[x, y; x', y']$ we turn to the transformed Green's function $\tilde{A}[x, y; x', y']$, defined as

$$A[x, y; x', y'] = P[x, y]\tilde{A}[x, y; x', y']P[x', y']$$

With these notational conventions one finds that (4.23) translates into

$$\tilde{A}[x, y; x', y'] = Q(1-q)\left[J_1[x, y]J_1[x', y'] - \tilde{J}_1[x, y]\tilde{J}_1[x', y']\right] + J_2[x, y]J_2[x', y']$$

$$+R\left[J_1[x, y] - \tilde{J}_1[x, y]\right]J_2[x', y'] + R\left[J_1[x', y'] - \tilde{J}_1[x', y']\right]J_2[x, y]$$

$$+Qq\left[J_1[x, y] - \tilde{J}_1[x, y]\right]\left[J_1[x', y'] - \tilde{J}_1[x', y']\right] \qquad (4.24)$$

with

$$J_1[x, y] = \frac{\partial}{\partial x}\log\frac{M[x, y]}{P[x|y]} + \frac{x - Ry}{Q(1-q)}$$

$$\tilde{J}_1[X, y] = P[X|y]^{-1}\int Dz\ \langle\frac{\partial}{\partial x}\log M[x, y] + \frac{x - Ry}{Q(1-q)}\rangle_\star\langle\delta[X - x]\rangle_\star$$

$$J_2[X, y] = \frac{\partial}{\partial y}\log\frac{M[X, y]}{P[X|y]} - \frac{RX}{Q(1-q)} + y$$

$$- P[X|y]^{-1}\int Dz\ \langle\frac{\partial}{\partial y}\log M[x, y] - \frac{Rx}{Q(1-q)}\rangle_\star\langle\delta[X - x]\rangle_\star$$

It turns out that significant simplification of the result (4.24) is possible, upon using the following two identities:

$$\langle\frac{\partial}{\partial x}\log M[x, y]\rangle_\star = -Bz$$

$$\langle\frac{\partial}{\partial y}\log M[x, y]\rangle_\star = \frac{\partial}{\partial y}\log\int dx\ e^{Bxz}M[x, y]$$

To achieve the desired simplification of $\tilde{A}[x, y; x', y']$ we define

$$\Phi[X, y] = \left\{Q(1-q)P[X|y]\right\}^{-1}\int Dz\ \langle X - x\rangle_\star\langle\delta[X - x]\rangle_\star \qquad (4.25)$$

We can now, after additional integration by parts with respect to z, simplify the above expressions for $J_1[\ldots], \tilde{J}_1[\ldots]$ and $J_2[\ldots]$ to

$$J_1[x, y] = \frac{x - Ry}{Q(1-q)} - \frac{qQ - R^2}{Q(1-q)}\Phi[x, y] \qquad\qquad \tilde{J}_1[x, y] = J_1[x, y] - \Phi[x, y]$$

$$J_2[x, y] = y - R\Phi[x, y]$$

and consequently

$$\tilde{A}[x, y; x', y'] = yy' + (x - Ry)\Phi[x', y'] + (x' - Ry')\Phi[x, y] - (Q - R^2)\Phi[x, y]\Phi[x', y']$$
$$(4.26)$$

The kernel $\tilde{A}[x, y; x', y']$ is now written in an explicitly separable form, as a result of which our theory can be summarized in just a single page:

- **Philosophy and Notation**

Our observables $Q = J^2$, $R = B \cdot J$ and $P[x,y] = \langle \delta[x - J \cdot \xi] \delta[y - B \cdot \xi] \rangle_{\tilde{D}}$ obey deterministic and self-averaging laws for $N \to \infty$, with $P[y] = (2\pi)^{-\frac{1}{2}} e^{-\frac{1}{2}y^2}$. We abbreviate $\langle f[x,y] \rangle = \int dx Dy \, P[x|y] f[x,y]$ and (with Φ defined below):

$$U = \langle \Phi[x,y] \mathcal{G}[x,y] \rangle \qquad V = \langle x \mathcal{G}[x,y] \rangle \qquad W = \langle y \mathcal{G}[x,y] \rangle \qquad Z = \langle \mathcal{G}^2[x,y] \rangle$$

The training- and generalization errors are given by

$$E_t = \langle \theta[-xy] \rangle \qquad\qquad E_g = \pi^{-1} \arccos[R/\sqrt{Q}] \qquad (4.27)$$

- **Macroscopic Dynamic Equations**

On-line learning:

$$\frac{d}{dt} Q = 2\eta V + \eta^2 Z \qquad\qquad \frac{d}{dt} R = \eta W \qquad (4.28)$$

$$
\begin{aligned}
\frac{d}{dt} P[x|y] = {} & \frac{1}{\alpha} \int dx' P[x'|y] \left\{ \delta[x - x' - \eta \mathcal{G}[x',y]] - \delta[x - x'] \right\} + \frac{1}{2} \eta^2 Z \frac{\partial^2}{\partial x^2} P[x|y] \\
& - \eta \frac{\partial}{\partial x} \left\{ P[x|y] \left[U(x - Ry) + Wy \right] \right\} - \eta \left[V - RW - (Q - R^2) U \right] \\
& \times \frac{\partial}{\partial x} \left\{ P[x|y] \Phi[x,y] \right\}
\end{aligned}
\qquad (4.29)
$$

Batch learning:

$$\frac{d}{dt} Q = 2\eta V \qquad\qquad \frac{d}{dt} R = \eta W \qquad (4.30)$$

$$
\begin{aligned}
\frac{d}{dt} P[x|y] = {} & -\frac{\eta}{\alpha} \frac{\partial}{\partial x} \left\{ P[x|y] \mathcal{G}[x,y] \right\} - \eta \frac{\partial}{\partial x} \left\{ P[x|y] \left[U(x - Ry) + Wy \right] \right\} \\
& - \eta \left[V - RW - (Q - R^2) U \right] \frac{\partial}{\partial x} \left\{ P[x|y] \Phi[x,y] \right\}
\end{aligned}
\qquad (4.31)
$$

- **Saddle-Point Equations and the Function Φ**

The key function $\Phi[x,y]$ occurring in the above equations is given by

$$\Phi[X,y] = \left\{ Q(1-q) P[X|y] \right\}^{-1} \int Dz \, \langle X - x \rangle_\star \langle \delta[X - x] \rangle_\star \qquad (4.32)$$

with

$$\langle f[x,y,z] \rangle_\star = \frac{\int dx \, M[x,y] e^{Bxz} f[x,y,z]}{\int dx \, M[x,y] e^{Bxz}} \qquad B = \frac{\sqrt{qQ - R^2}}{Q(1-q)} \qquad (4.33)$$

The spin-glass order parameter $q \in [R^2/Q, 1]$ and the function $M[x,y]$ are calculated at each time-step by solving the saddle-point equations

$$\langle (x - Ry)^2 \rangle + (qQ - R^2)(1 - \frac{1}{\alpha}) = \left[2(qQ - R^2)^{\frac{1}{2}} + \frac{1}{B} \right] \int Dy Dz \, z \langle x \rangle_\star \qquad (4.34)$$

$$P[X|y] = \int Dz \, \langle \delta[X - x] \rangle_\star \qquad (4.35)$$

5   Tests and Applications of the Theory

5.1   Locally Gaussian Solutions

There are two advantages of rewriting our equations in Fourier representation. Firstly, the functional saddle-point equation (4.35) will acquire a simpler form. Secondly, in those cases where we expect $P[x|y]$ to be of a Gaussian form in x this will simplify solution of the diffusion equations (4.29,4.31). Clearly, $P[x, y]$ being Gaussian in (x, y) is not equivalent to $P[x|y]$ being Gaussian in x only. The former will only turn out to occur for $\alpha \to \infty$. A Gaussian $P[x|y]$ with moments which depend in a non-trivial way on y, on the other hand, can also occur for $\alpha < \infty$, provided we consider simple learning rules and small η. To avoid ambiguity we will call solutions of the latter type 'locally Gaussian'.

We normalize the measure $M[x, y]$ such that $\int dx\, M[x, y] = 1$ for all $y \in \Re$, emphasizing the result in our notation by writing $M[x, y] \to M[x|y]$, and we introduce the Fourier transforms

$$\hat{P}[k|y] = \int dx\, e^{-ikx} P[x|y] \qquad \hat{M}[k|y] = \int dx\, e^{-ikx} M[x|y]$$

The transformed functional saddle-point equation thereby becomes

$$\hat{P}[k|y] = \int Dz\, \frac{\hat{M}[k+iBz|y]}{\hat{M}[iBz|y]} \tag{5.1}$$

Transformation of the on-line equation (4.29) for $P[x|y]$ (from the which the batch equation (4.31) can be obtained by expansion in η) gives:

$$\frac{d}{dt}\log \hat{P}[k|y] = \frac{1}{\alpha}\left\{ \int dk'\, \frac{\hat{P}[k'|y]}{\hat{P}[k|y]} \int \frac{dx'}{2\pi} e^{ix'(k'-k)-i\eta k \mathcal{G}[x',y]} - 1 \right\} - i\eta k(W{-}UR)y$$

$$-\frac{1}{2}\eta^2 k^2 Z + \eta k U \frac{\partial}{\partial k}\log \hat{P}[k|y] - i\eta k\left[\frac{V - RW - (Q-R^2)U}{\sqrt{qQ-R^2}\,\hat{P}[k|y]} \right] \int Dz\, z\, \frac{\hat{M}[k+iBz|y]}{\hat{M}[iBz]} \tag{5.2}$$

If $P[x|y]$ is Gaussian in x we can solve the functional saddle-point equation (4.35) (whose solution is unique), and find

$$P[x|y] = \frac{e^{-\frac{1}{2}[x-\bar{x}(y)]^2/\Delta^2(y)}}{\Delta(y)\sqrt{2\pi}} \qquad M[x|y] = \frac{e^{-\frac{1}{2}[x-\bar{x}(y)]^2/\sigma^2(y)}}{\sigma(y)\sqrt{2\pi}} \tag{5.3}$$

$$\Delta^2(y) = \sigma^2(y) + B^2\sigma^4(y) \tag{5.4}$$

with $\hat{P}[k|y] = e^{-[ik\bar{x}(y)-\frac{1}{2}k^2\Delta^2(y)]}$ and $\hat{M}[k|y] = e^{-[ik\bar{x}(y)-\frac{1}{2}k^2\sigma^2(y)]}$. Insertion of these expression as an Ansatz into (5.2), using the identity

$$\int Dz\, z\, \frac{\hat{M}[k+iBz|y]}{\hat{M}[iBz]} = ikB\sigma^2(y)\hat{P}[k|y]$$

(which holds only for locally Gaussian solutions) and performing some simple manipulations, gives the simplified equation

$$-ik\frac{d}{dt}\overline{x}(y) - \frac{1}{2}k^2\frac{d}{dt}\Delta^2(y) \;=\; \frac{1}{\alpha}\left\{\int\frac{du}{\sqrt{2\pi}}e^{-\frac{1}{2}[u-ik\Delta(y)]^2-ik\eta\mathcal{G}[\overline{x}(y)+u\Delta(y),y]}-1\right\}$$

$$-i\eta k\left\{Wy + U[\overline{x}(y)-Ry]\right\}$$

$$-\frac{1}{2}k^2\left\{\eta^2 Z + 2\eta U\Delta^2(y) + 2\eta\sigma^2(y)\left[\frac{V-RW-(Q-R^2)U}{Q(1-q)}\right]\right\} \tag{5.5}$$

It follows that locally Gaussian solutions can occur in two situations only:

$$\alpha = \infty \qquad \text{or} \qquad \frac{\partial^3}{\partial k^3}\int\frac{du}{\sqrt{2\pi}}\,e^{-\frac{1}{2}[u-ik\Delta(y)]^2-ik\eta\mathcal{G}[\overline{x}(y)+u\Delta(y),y]} = 0$$

The first case corresponds to complete training sets (see next section). The second case occurs for sufficiently simple learning rules $\mathcal{G}[x,y]$, in combination either with batch execution (so that we retain only the term linear in η) or with on-line execution for small η (retaining only η and η^2 terms).

5.2   Link with the Complete Training Sets Formalism

The least we should require of our theory is that it reduces to the simple formalism of complete training sets in the limit $\alpha \to \infty$. In the previous section we have seen that for $\alpha \to \infty$ our driven diffusion equations for the conditional distribution $P[x|y]$ have locally Gaussian solutions, with $\int dx\, xP[x|y] = \overline{x}(y)$ and $\int dx[x-\overline{x}(y)]^2 P[x|y] = \Delta^2(y)$. Note that for such solutions we can calculate objects such as $\langle x\rangle_*$ and the function $\Phi[x,y]$ of (4.32) directly, giving

$$\langle x\rangle_* = \overline{x}(y) + zB\sigma^2(y) \qquad\qquad \Phi[x,y] = \frac{x - \overline{x}(y)}{Q(1-q)[1+B^2\sigma^2(y)]}$$

with $\Delta^2(y) = \sigma^2(y)+B^2\sigma^4(y)$ and $B = \sqrt{qQ-R^2}/Q(1-q)$. The remaining equations to be solved are those for Q and R, in combination with dynamical equations for the y-dependent cumulants $\overline{x}(y)$ and $\Delta^2(y)$. These reduce to:

$$\frac{d}{dt}Q = \begin{cases} 2\eta\langle x\mathcal{G}[x,y]\rangle + \eta^2\langle\mathcal{G}^2[x,y]\rangle & \text{(on}-\text{line)} \\ 2\eta\langle x\mathcal{G}[x,y]\rangle & \text{(batch)} \end{cases} \qquad \frac{d}{dt}R = \eta\langle y\mathcal{G}[x,y]\rangle \tag{5.6}$$

$$\frac{1}{\eta}\frac{d}{dt}\left[\overline{x}(y)-Ry\right] = [\overline{x}(y)-Ry]\langle\Phi[x',y']\mathcal{G}[x',y']\rangle \tag{5.7}$$

$$\frac{1}{2\eta}\frac{d}{dt}\left[\Delta^2(y)-Q+R^2\right] = \langle(x'-Ry')\mathcal{G}[x',y']\rangle\left[\frac{\sigma^2(y)}{Q(1-q)}-1\right]$$

$$+ \langle\Phi[x',y']\mathcal{G}[x',y']\rangle\left[\Delta^2(y)-\frac{Q-R^2}{Q(1-q)\sigma^2(y)}\right] \tag{5.8}$$

with one remaining saddle-point equation to determine q, obtained upon working out (4.34) for locally Gaussian solutions:

$$\int Dy \left\{ [\overline{x}(y) - Ry]^2 + \Delta^2(y) \right\} + qQ - R^2 = \left[2\frac{qQ - R^2}{Q(1-q)} + 1 \right] \int Dy \ \sigma^2(y) \quad (5.9)$$

We now make the Ansatz that $\overline{x}(y) = Ry$ and $\Delta^2(y) = Q - R^2$, i.e.

$$P[x|y] = \frac{e^{-\frac{1}{2}[x - Ry]^2/(Q - R^2)}}{\sqrt{2\pi(Q - R^2)}}, \quad (5.10)$$

Insertion into the dynamical equations shows that (5.7) is now immediately satisfied, that (5.8) reduces to $\sigma^2(y) = Q(1-q)$, and that the saddle-point equation (5.9) is automatically satisfied. Since (5.10) is parametrized by Q and R only, the equations (5.6) are closed. From our general theory for restricted training sets we thus indeed recover in the limit $\alpha \to \infty$ the standard formalism (5.6,5.10) describing learning with complete training sets, as claimed.

5.3 Benchmark Tests: Hebbian Learning

In the special case of the Hebb rule, $\mathcal{G}[x, y] = \mathrm{sgn}[y]$, where weight changes $\Delta \boldsymbol{J}$ never depend on $\boldsymbol{J}$, one can write down an explicit expression for the weight vector $\boldsymbol{J}$ at any time, and thus for the expectation values of our observables. We choose as our initial field distribution a simple Gaussian one, resulting from an initialization process which did not involve the training set:

$$P_0[x|y] = \frac{e^{-\frac{1}{2}(x - R_0 y)^2/(Q_0 - R_0^2)}}{\sqrt{2\pi(Q_0 - R_0^2)}} \quad (5.11)$$

Careful averaging of the exact expressions for our observables over all 'paths' $\{\boldsymbol{\xi}(0), \boldsymbol{\xi}(1), \ldots\}$ taken by the question vector through the training set $\tilde{D}$ (for on-line learning), followed by averaging over all realizations of the training set $\tilde{D}$ of size $p = \alpha N$, and taking the $N \to \infty$ limit, then leads to the following exact result (Rae et al., 1998). For on-line Hebbian learning one ends up with:

$$Q = Q_0 + 2\eta t R_0 \sqrt{\frac{2}{\pi}} + \eta^2 t + \eta^2 t^2 \left[\frac{1}{\alpha} + \frac{2}{\pi} \right] \qquad R = R_0 + \eta t \sqrt{\frac{2}{\pi}} \quad (5.12)$$

$$P[x|y] = \int \frac{d\hat{x}}{2\pi} \ e^{-\frac{1}{2}\hat{x}^2[Q - R^2] + i\hat{x}[x - Ry] + \frac{t}{\alpha}[e^{-i\eta \hat{x} \ \mathrm{sgn}[y]} - 1]} \quad (5.13)$$

For batch learning a similar calculation [3] gives:

$$Q = Q_0 + 2\eta t R_0 \sqrt{\frac{2}{\pi}} + \eta^2 t^2 \left[\frac{1}{\alpha} + \frac{2}{\pi} \right] \qquad R = R_0 + \eta t \sqrt{\frac{2}{\pi}} \quad (5.14)$$

---

[3]Note that in Rae et al. (1998) only the on-line calculation was carried out; the batch calculation can be done along the same lines.

$$P[x|y] = \frac{e^{-\frac{1}{2}[x - Ry - (\eta t/\alpha)\,\mathrm{sgn}[y]]^2/(Q - R^2)}}{\sqrt{2\pi(Q - R^2)}} \qquad (5.15)$$

Neither of the two field distributions is of a fully Gaussian form (although the batch distribution is at least locally Gaussian). Note that for both on-line and batch Hebbian learning we have

$$\int dx \; x P[x|y] = Ry + \frac{\eta t}{\alpha}\,\mathrm{sgn}[y] \qquad (5.16)$$

The generalization- and training errors are, as before, given in terms of the above observables as $E_g = \pi^{-1}\arccos[R/\sqrt{Q}]$ and $E_t = \int Dy dx P[x|y]\theta[-xy]$. We thus have exact expressions for both the generalization error and the training error at any time and for any α. Their asymptotic values are, for both batch and on-line Hebbian learning, given by

$$\lim_{t\to\infty} E_g = \frac{1}{\pi}\arccos\left[\frac{1}{\sqrt{1 + \pi/2\alpha}}\right] \qquad (5.17)$$

$$\lim_{t\to\infty} E_t = \frac{1}{2} - \frac{1}{2}\int Dy \; \mathrm{erf}\left[|y|\sqrt{\frac{\alpha}{\pi}} + \frac{1}{\sqrt{2\alpha}}\right] \qquad (5.18)$$

As far as E_g and E_t are concerned, the differences between batch and on-line Hebbian learning are confined to transients. Clearly, the above exact results (which can only be obtained for Hebbian-type learning rules) provide excellent and welcome benchmarks with which to test general theories such as ours.

5.4 Batch Hebbian Learning

We now compare the exact solutions for Hebbian learning to the predictions of our general theory, turning first to batch Hebbian learning. We insert into the equations of our general formalism the Hebbian recipe $\mathcal{G}[x, y] = \mathrm{sgn}[y]$. This simplifies our dynamic equations enormously. In particular we obtain:

$$U = 0, \qquad V = \langle x\,\mathrm{sgn}(y)\rangle, \qquad W = \sqrt{2/\pi}$$

For batch learning we consequently find:

$$\frac{d}{dt}Q = 2\eta V \qquad\qquad \frac{d}{dt}R = \eta\sqrt{2/\pi}$$

$$\frac{d}{dt}P[x|y] = -\frac{\eta}{\alpha}\,\mathrm{sgn}(y)\frac{\partial}{\partial x}P[x|y] - \eta y\sqrt{\frac{2}{\pi}}\frac{\partial}{\partial x}P[x|y]$$

$$-\eta(V - R\sqrt{\frac{2}{\pi}})\frac{\partial}{\partial x}\left\{P[x|y]\Phi[x, y]\right\}$$

Given the initial field distribution (5.11), we immediate derive $V_0 = R_0\sqrt{2/\pi}$. From the general property $\int dx \; P[x|y]\Phi[x, y] = 0$ and the above diffusion equation for $P[x|y]$ we derive an equation for the quantity $V = \langle x\,\mathrm{sgn}(y)\rangle$, resulting in $\frac{d}{dt}V = \eta/\alpha + 2\eta/\pi$, which subsequently allows us to solve

$$Q = Q_0 + 2\eta t R_0 \sqrt{\frac{2}{\pi}} + \eta^2 t^2 \left[\frac{1}{\alpha} + \frac{2}{\pi}\right] \qquad R = R_0 + \eta t \sqrt{\frac{2}{\pi}} \qquad (5.19)$$

Furthermore, it turns out that the above diffusion equation for $P[x|y]$ obeys the conditions for having locally Gaussian solutions, i.e.

$$P[x|y] = \frac{e^{-\frac{1}{2}[x-\bar{x}(y)]^2/\Delta^2(y)}}{\Delta(y)\sqrt{2\pi}}, \qquad M[x|y] = \frac{e^{-\frac{1}{2}[x-\bar{x}(y)]^2/\sigma^2(y)}}{\sigma(y)\sqrt{2\pi}}$$

provided the y-dependent average $\bar{x}(y)$ and the y-dependent variances $\Delta(y)$ and $\sigma(y)$ obey the following three equations:

$$\bar{x}(y) = Ry + \frac{\eta t}{\alpha}\,\mathrm{sgn}(y) \qquad \frac{d}{dt}\Delta^2(y) = \frac{2\eta^2 t \sigma^2(y)}{\alpha Q(1-q)}$$

$$\Delta^2(y) = \sigma^2(y) + B^2\sigma^4(y)$$

The spin-glass order parameter q is to be solved from the remaining saddle-point equation. With help of identities like $\langle x \rangle_\star = \bar{x}(y) + zB\sigma^2(y)$, which only hold for locally Gaussian solutions, one can simplify the latter to

$$\frac{\eta^2 t^2}{\alpha} + \alpha \int Dy\,\Delta^2(y) + (qQ - R^2)(\alpha - 1) = \alpha \left[2\frac{qQ - R^2}{Q(1-q)} + 1\right] \int Dy\,\sigma^2(y)$$

We now immediately find the solution

$$\Delta^2(y) = Q - R^2, \qquad \sigma^2(y) = Q(1-q), \qquad q = [\alpha R^2 + \eta^2 t^2]/\alpha Q$$

$$P[x|y] = \frac{e^{-\frac{1}{2}[x - Ry - (\eta t/\alpha)\,\mathrm{sgn}(y)]^2/(Q-R^2)}}{\sqrt{2\pi(Q-R^2)}} \qquad (5.20)$$

(this solution is unique). If we calculate the generalization error and the training error from (5.19) and (5.20), respectively, we recover the exact expressions

$$E_g = \frac{1}{\pi}\arccos\left[\frac{R_0 + \eta t\sqrt{\frac{2}{\pi}}}{\sqrt{Q_0 + 2\eta t R_0\sqrt{\frac{2}{\pi}} + \eta^2 t^2\left[\frac{1}{\alpha} + \frac{2}{\pi}\right]}}\right] \qquad (5.21)$$

$$E_t = \frac{1}{2} - \frac{1}{2}\int Dy\,\mathrm{erf}\left[\frac{|y|[R_0 + \eta t\sqrt{\frac{2}{\pi}}] + \frac{\eta t}{\alpha}}{\sqrt{2[Q_0 - R_0^2 + \frac{\eta^2 t^2}{\alpha}]}}\right] \qquad (5.22)$$

Comparison of (5.19,5.20) with (5.14,5.15) shows that for batch Hebbian learning our theory is fully exact. This is not a big feat as far as Q and R (and thus E_g) are concerned, whose determination did not require knowing the function $\Phi[x, y]$. The fact that our theory also gives the exact values for $P[x|y]$ and E_t, however, is less trivial, since here the disordered nature of the learning dynamics, leading to non-Gaussian distributions, is truly relevant.

5.5 On-Line Hebbian Learning

We next insert the Hebbian recipe $\mathcal{G}[x, y] = \text{sgn}[y]$ into the on-line equations (4.28,4.29). Direct analytical solution of these equations, or a demonstration that they are solved by the exact result (5.12,5.13), although not ruled out, has not yet been achieved. The reason is that here one has locally Gaussian field distributions only in special limits. Numerical solution is straightforward, but has not yet been carried out. For small learning rates the on-line equations reduce to the batch ones, so we know that in first order in η our on-line equations are exact (for any α, t). We now show that the predictions of our theory are fully exact (i) for Q, R and E_g, (ii) for the first moment (5.16) of the conditional field distribution, and (iii) for all order parameters in the stationary state. At intermediate times we construct an approximate solution of our equations in order to obtain predictions for $P[x|y]$ and E_t.

As before we choose a Gaussian initial field distribution. Many (but not all) of our previous simplifications still hold, e.g.

$$U = 0, \qquad V = \langle x\,\text{sgn}(y)\rangle, \qquad W = \sqrt{2/\pi}, \qquad Z = 1$$

(Z did not occur in the batch equations). Thus for on-line learning we find:

$$\frac{d}{dt}Q = 2\eta V + \eta^2 \qquad\qquad \frac{d}{dt}R = \eta\sqrt{2/\pi}$$

The previous derivation of the identities $\frac{d}{dt}V = \eta/\alpha + 2\eta/\pi$ and $V_0 = R_0\sqrt{2/\pi}$ still applies (just replace the batch diffusion equation by the on-line one), but the resultant expression for Q is different. Here we obtain:

$$Q = Q_0 + 2\eta t R_0 \sqrt{\frac{2}{\pi}} + \eta^2 t + \eta^2 t^2 \left[\frac{1}{\alpha} + \frac{2}{\pi}\right] \qquad R = R_0 + \eta t\sqrt{\frac{2}{\pi}} \qquad (5.23)$$

Comparing (5.23) with (5.12) reveals that also for on-line Hebbian learning our theory is exact with regard to Q and R, and thus also with regard to E_g. Upon using $V = \eta t/\alpha + R\sqrt{2/\pi}$, the on-line diffusion equation simplifies to

$$\frac{d}{dt}P[x|y] = \frac{1}{\alpha}\left\{P[x - \eta\,\text{sgn}(y)|y] - P[x|y]\right\} - \eta y\sqrt{\frac{2}{\pi}}\frac{\partial}{\partial x}P[x|y] + \frac{1}{2}\eta^2\frac{\partial^2}{\partial x^2}P[x|y]$$

$$- \frac{\eta^2 t}{\alpha}\frac{\partial}{\partial x}\left\{P[x|y]\Phi[x, y]\right\}$$

Multiplication of this equation by x followed by integration over x, together with the general properties $\int dx\,\{P[x|y]\Phi[x,y]\} = 0$ and $\int dx\,xP_0[x|y] = R_0 y$, gives us the average of the conditional distribution $P[x|y]$ at any time:

$$\bar{x}(y) = \int dx\,xP[x|y] = Ry + \frac{\eta t}{\alpha}\,\text{sgn}[y]$$

Comparison with (5.16) shows also this prediction to be correct.

We now turn to observables involving more detailed knowledge of the function $\Phi[x, y]$. Our result for $\bar{x}(y)$ and the identity $\langle x \rangle_* = B^{-1} \frac{\partial}{\partial z} \log \hat{M}[iBz|y]$ allow us to rewrite all remaining equations in Fourier representation, i.e. in terms of $\hat{P}[k|y] = \int dx \, e^{-ikx} P[x|y]$ and $\hat{M}[k|y] = \int dx \, e^{-ikx} M[x|y]$:

$$\frac{d}{dt} \log \hat{P}[k|y] = \frac{1}{\alpha} \left[e^{-i\eta k \, \text{sgn}(y)} - 1 \right] - i\eta k y \sqrt{\frac{2}{\pi}} - \frac{1}{2}\eta^2 k^2$$

$$- \frac{ik\eta^2 t}{\alpha} \left[\hat{P}[k|y]\sqrt{qQ - R^2} \right]^{-1} \int Dz \, z \, \frac{\hat{M}[k + iBz|y]}{\hat{M}[iBz|y]} \qquad (5.24)$$

with $\log \hat{P}_0[k|y] = -ikR_0 y - \frac{1}{2}k^2(Q_0 - R_0^2)$, and with the saddle-point equations

$$\hat{P}[k|y] = \int Dz \, \frac{\hat{M}[k + iBz|y]}{\hat{M}[iBz|y]} \qquad (5.25)$$

$$\frac{\eta^2 t^2}{\alpha^2} + \int Dy \int dx \, P[x|y][x - \bar{x}(y)]^2 + (1 - \frac{1}{\alpha})(qQ - R^2)$$

$$= \left[2Q(1 - q) + \frac{1}{B^2} \right] \int DyDz \, \frac{\partial^2}{\partial z^2} \log \hat{M}[iBz|y] \qquad (5.26)$$

Due to the fields x growing linearly with time (see our expression for $\bar{x}(y)$) the equations (5.24,5.26,5.25) cannot have proper $t \to \infty$ limits. To extract asymptotic properties we have to turn to the rescaled distribution $\hat{Q}[k|y] = \hat{P}[k/t|y]$. We define $v(y) = (\eta/\alpha) \, \text{sgn}(y) + \eta y \sqrt{2/\pi}$. Careful integration of (5.24), followed by inserting $k \to k/t$ and by taking the limit $t \to \infty$, produces:

$$\log \hat{Q}_\infty[k|y] = -ikv(y) - \frac{i\eta^2 k}{\alpha} \int_0^1 du \, \lim_{t \to \infty} \frac{t}{\sqrt{qQ - R^2}} \int Dz \, z \, \frac{\hat{M}[uk/t + iBz|y]}{\hat{Q}_\infty[uk|y]\hat{M}[iBz|y]} \qquad (5.27)$$

with the functional saddle-point equation

$$\hat{Q}[k|y] = \int Dz \, \frac{\hat{M}[k/t + iBz|y]}{\hat{M}[iBz|y]} \qquad (5.28)$$

The rescaled asymptotic system (5.27,5.28) admits the solution

$$\hat{Q}[k|y] = e^{-ikv(y) - \frac{1}{2}k^2\tilde{\Delta}^2}, \qquad \hat{M}[k|y] = e^{-ik\bar{x}(y) - \frac{1}{2}k^2\tilde{\sigma}^2 t}$$

with the asymptotic values of B, $\tilde{\Delta}$, $\tilde{\sigma}$ and q determined by solving

$$\tilde{\Delta} = B\tilde{\sigma}^2 \qquad \tilde{\Delta} = \frac{\eta^2}{\alpha} \lim_{t \to \infty} \frac{t}{\sqrt{qQ - R^2}} \qquad B = \lim_{t \to \infty} \frac{\sqrt{qQ - R^2}}{Q(1 - q)}$$

$$\eta^2/\alpha^2 + \tilde{\Delta}^2 + (1 - \alpha^{-1}) \lim_{t \to \infty} (qQ - R^2)/t^2 = 2B^2\tilde{\sigma}^2 \lim_{t \to \infty} Q(1 - q)/t$$

Inspection shows that these four asymptotic equations are solved by

$$\lim_{t\to\infty}\tilde{\Delta}=\eta/\sqrt{\alpha},\qquad \lim_{t\to\infty}q=1$$

so that

$$\lim_{t\to\infty}\hat{P}_t[k/t]=e^{-ik\eta\left[\alpha^{-1}\,\mathrm{sgn}(y)+y\sqrt{2/\pi}\right]-\frac{1}{2}\eta^2k^2/\alpha} \qquad (5.29)$$

Comparison with (5.12, 5.13) shows that this prediction (5.29) is again exact. Thus the same is true for the asymptotic training error.

Finally, in order to arrive at predictions with respect to $P[x|y]$ and E_t for intermediate times (without rigorous analytical solution of the functional saddle-point equation), and in view of the locally Gaussian form of the field distribution both at $t=0$ and at $t=\infty$, we can approximate $P[x|y]$ and $M[x|y]$ by simple locally Gaussian distributions at any time:

$$P[x|y]=\frac{e^{-\frac{1}{2}[x-\bar{x}(y)]^2/\Delta^2}}{\Delta\sqrt{2\pi}},\qquad M[x|y]=\frac{e^{-\frac{1}{2}[x-\bar{x}(y)]^2/\sigma^2}}{\sigma\sqrt{2\pi}} \qquad (5.30)$$

with the (exact) first moments $\bar{x}(y)=Ry+\eta t\alpha^{-1}\,\mathrm{sgn}(y)$, and with the variance Δ^2 self-consistently given by the solution of:

$$\Delta^2=\sigma^2+B^2\sigma^4\qquad B=\frac{\sqrt{qQ-R^2}}{Q(1-q)}\qquad \frac{d}{dt}\Delta^2=\frac{\eta^2}{\alpha}+\eta^2+\frac{2\eta^2t\sigma^2}{\alpha Q(1-q)}$$

$$\alpha\Delta^2+\frac{\eta^2t^2}{\alpha}+(qQ-R^2)(\alpha-1)=\alpha\sigma^2\left[2\frac{qQ-R^2}{Q(1-q)}+1\right]$$

The solution of the above coupled equations behaves as

$$\Delta^2=Q-R^2+\eta^2t/\alpha+\mathcal{O}(t^3)\qquad (t\to 0)$$

$$\Delta^2/(Q-R^2)=\mathcal{O}(t^{-1})\qquad (t\to\infty)$$

for short and long times, respectively (note $Q-R^2\sim t^2$ as $t\to\infty$). Thus we obtain a simple approximate solution of our equations, which extrapolates between exact results at the temporal boundaries $t=0$ and $t=\infty$, by putting

$$\Delta^2=Q-R^2+\eta^2t/\alpha$$

with Q and R given by our previous exact result (5.23), which results in

$$E_g=\frac{1}{\pi}\arccos\left[\frac{R}{\sqrt{Q}}\right]\qquad E_t=\frac{1}{2}-\frac{1}{2}\int Dy\;\mathrm{erf}\left[\frac{|y|R+\eta t/\alpha}{\Delta\sqrt{2}}\right] \qquad (5.31)$$

We can also calculate the student field distribution $P(x)=\int Dy\,P[x|y]$, giving

$$P(x)=\frac{e^{-\frac{1}{2}[x+\frac{\eta t}{\alpha}]^2/(\Delta^2+R^2)}}{2\sqrt{2\pi(\Delta^2+R^2)}}\left[1-\mathrm{erf}\left(\frac{R[x+\eta t/\alpha]}{\Delta\sqrt{2(\Delta^2+R^2)}}\right)\right]$$

$$+\frac{e^{-\frac{1}{2}[x-\frac{\eta t}{\alpha}]^2/(\Delta^2+R^2)}}{2\sqrt{2\pi(\Delta^2+R^2)}}\left[1+\mathrm{erf}\left(\frac{R[x-\eta t/\alpha]}{\Delta\sqrt{2(\Delta^2+R^2)}}\right)\right] \qquad (5.32)$$

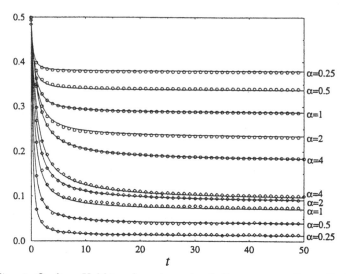

Fig. 4: On-line Hebbian learning, simulations versus theoretical predictions, for $\alpha \in \{0.25, 0.5, 1.0, 2.0, 4.0\}$ ($N = 10,000$). Upper curves: generalization errors as functions of time. Lower curves: training errors as functions of time. Circles: simulation results for E_{g}; diamonds: simulation results for E_{t}. Solid lines: corresponding predictions of dynamical replica theory.

5.6 Comparison with Simulations

In Fig. 4 we compare the predictions for the generalization and training errors (5.31) of the approximate solution of our equations with the results obtained from numerical simulations of on-line Hebbian learning for $N = 10,000$ (initial state: $Q_0 = 1$, $R_0 = 0$; learning rate: $\eta = 1$). All curves show excellent agreement between theory and experiment. For E_{g} this is guaranteed by the exactness of our theory for Q and R; the agreement found for E_{t} is more surprising, in that these predictions are obtained from a simple approximation of the solution of our equations. We also compare the theoretical predictions made for the distribution $P[x|y]$ with the results of numerical simulations. This is done in Fig. 5, where we show the fields as observed at time $t = 50$ in simulations ($N = 10,000$, $\eta = 1$, $R_0 = 0$, $Q_0 = 1$) of on-line Hebbian learning, for three different values of α. In the same figure we draw (as dashed lines) the theoretical prediction (5.16) for the y-dependent average of the conditional x-distribution $P[x|y]$. Finally we compare the student field distribution $P(x)$, as observed in simulations of on-line Hebbian learning ($N = 10,000$, $\eta = 1$, $R_0 = 0$, $Q_0 = 1$) with our prediction (5.32). The result is shown in Fig. 6, for $\alpha \in \{4, 1, 0.25\}$. In all cases the agreement between theory and experiment, even for the approximate solution of our equations, is quite satisfactory.

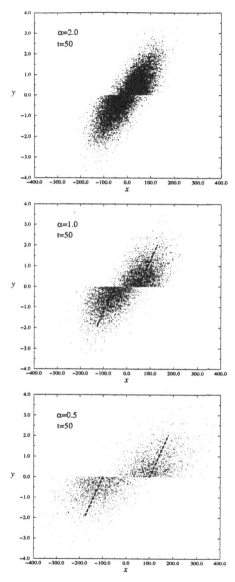

Fig. 5: Comparison between simulation results for on-line Hebbian learning (system size $N = 10,000$) and dynamical replica theory, for $\alpha \in \{0.5, 1.0, 2.0\}$. Dots: local fields $(x, y) = (\boldsymbol{J} \cdot \boldsymbol{\xi}, \boldsymbol{B} \cdot \boldsymbol{\xi})$ (calculated for questions in the training set), at time $t = 50$. Dashed lines: conditional average of student field x as a function of y, as predicted by the theory, $\overline{x}(y) = Ry + (\eta t / \alpha) \operatorname{sgn}(y)$.

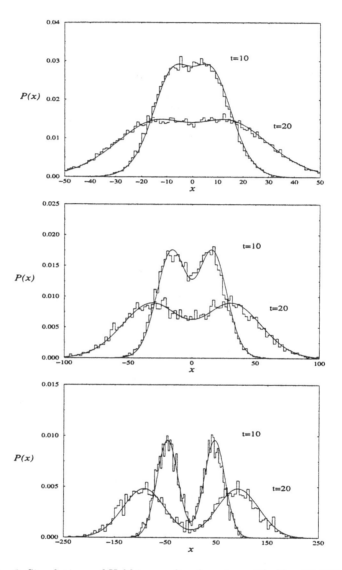

Fig. 6: Simulations of Hebbian on-line learning with $N = 10,000$.
Histograms: student field distributions measured at $t = 10$ and $t =$
20. Lines: theoretical predictions for student field distributions.
$\alpha = 4$ (upper), $\alpha = 1$ (middle), $\alpha = 0.25$ (lower).

6 Discussion

In this paper we have shown how the formalism of dynamical replica theory (e.g. Coolen *et al.*, 1996) can be used successfully to build a general theory with which to predict the evolution of the relevant macroscopic performance measures for supervised (on-line and batch) learning in layered neural networks with randomly composed but restricted training sets (i.e. for finite $\alpha = p/N$), where the student fields are no longer described by Gaussian distributions, and where the more traditional and familiar statistical mechanical formalism consequently breaks down. For simplicity and transparency we have restricted ourselves to single-layer systems and realizable tasks. In our approach the joint field distribution $P[x, y]$ for student and teacher fields is itself taken to be a dynamical order parameter, in addition to the more conventional observables Q and R; from this order parameter set $\{Q, R, P\}$, in turn, immediately follow the generalization error E_g and the training error E_t. This then results, following the prescriptions of dynamical replica theory[4], in a diffusion equation for $P[x, y]$, which we have evaluated by making the replica-symmetric ansatz in the saddle-point equations. This diffusion equation is found to have Gaussian solutions only for $\alpha \to \infty$; in the latter case we indeed recover correctly from our theory the more familiar formalism of infinite training sets, with (in the $N \to \infty$ limit) closed equations for Q and R only. For finite α our theory is by construction exact if for $N \to \infty$ the dynamical order parameters $\{Q, R, P\}$ obey closed, deterministic equations, which are self-averaging (i.e. independent of the microscopic realization of the training set). If this is not the case, our theory is an approximation.

We have worked out our equations explicitly for the special case of Hebbian learning, where the availability of exact results, derived directly from the microscopic equations, allows us to perform a critical test of our theory [5]. For batch Hebbian learning we can demonstrate explicitly that our theory is fully exact. For on-line Hebbian learning, on the other hand, proving or disproving full exactness requires solving a non-trivial functional saddle-point equation analytically, which we have not yet been able to do. Nevertheless we can prove that our theory is exact (i) with respect to its predictions for Q, R and E_g, (ii) with respect to the first moment of the conditional field distribution $P[x|y]$, and (iii) in the stationary state. In order to also generate predictions for intermediate times we have constructed an approximate solution of our equations, which is found to describe the results of performing numerical simulations of on-line Hebbian learning quite satisfactorily.

---

[4]The reason why replicas are inevitable (unless we are willing to pay the price of having observables with two time arguments, and turn to path integrals) is the necessity, for finite α, to average the macroscopic equations over all possible realizations of the training set.

[5]Such exact results can only be obtained for Hebbian-type rules, where the dependence of the updates $\Delta J(t)$ on the weights $J(t)$ is trivial or even absent (a decay term at most), whereas our present theory generates macroscopic equations for arbitrary learning rules.

The present study represents only a first step; many extensions, applications and generalizations can be carried out (most of which are already under way). Firstly, our theory would greatly simplify if we could find an explicit solution of the functional saddle-point equation, enabling us to express the function $\Phi[x, y]$ directly in terms of our order parameters. The benefits of such a solution will become even greater when we apply our theory to more sophisticated learning rules, such as to perceptron or AdaTron learning, or to learning in multi-layer networks (which run the risk of requiring a serious amount of CPU time). Yet another direction is the inclusion of unlearnable tasks, such as those generated by noisy teachers. At a more fundamental level one could explore the potential of (dynamic) replica symmetry breaking (by calculating the AT-surface, signaling instability of the replica symmetric solution with respect to replicon fluctuations), or one could improve the built-in accuracy of our theory by adding new observables to the present set (such as the Green's function $\mathcal{A}[x, y; x', y']$ itself). Finally it would be interesting to see the connection between the present formalism and a suitable adaptation of the work by Horner (1992), based on generating functionals and path integrals, to the processes studied in this paper (with non-binary weights).

Acknowledgements
DS acknowledges support by EPSRC Grant GR/L52093.

References

Barber, D., Saad, D. and Sollich, P. (1996). Finite-size effects in online learning of multilayer neural networks. *Europhys. Lett.*, 34, 151–156

Biehl, M. and Schwarze, H. (1992). Online learning of time-dependent rule. *Europhys. Lett.*, 20, 733–738.

Biehl, M. and Schwarze, H. (1995). Learning by online gradient descent. *J. Phys. A*, 28, 643–656.

Coolen, A.C.C., Laughton, S.N. and Sherrington, D. (1996). Dynamical replica theory for disordered spin systems. *Phys. Rev. B*, 53, 8184–8187.

Coolen, A.C.C and Saad, D. (1998). *in preparation.*

Horner, H. (1992a). Dynamics of learning for the binary perceptron problem. *Z. Phys. B*, 86, 291–308.

Horner, H. (1992b). Dynamics of learning and generalization in a binary perceptron model. *Z. Phys. B*, 87, 371–376.

Kinouchi, O. and Caticha, N. (1992). Optimal generalization in perceptrons. *J. Phys. A*, 25, 6243–6250.

Kinzel, W. and Rujan, P. (1990). Improving a network generalization ability by selecting examples. *Europhys. Lett.*, 13, 473–477.

Mace, C.W.H. and Coolen, A.C.C (1998a). Statistical mechanical analysis of the dynamics of learning in perceptrons. *Statistics and Computing*, 8, 55–88.

Mace, C.W.H. and Coolen, A.C.C (1998b), *in preparation*

Mézard, M., Parisi, G. and Virasoro, M.A. (1987). *Spin-Glass Theory and Beyond.* World Scientific.

Rae, H.C., Sollich, P. and Coolen, A.C.C. (1998), *in preparation*.

Saad, D. and Coolen, A.C.C (1998), *in preparation*.

Saad, D. and Solla, S. (1995). Exact solution for online learning in multilayer neural networks. *Phys. Rev. Lett.*, 74, 4337–4340.

Sollich, P. and Barber, D. (1997), *to be published in Proc. NIPS*97*

Online Learning of a Decision Boundary with and without Queries

Yoshiyuki Kabashima

Dept. of Comp. Intelligence and Systems Science
Graduate School of Science and Engineering
Tokyo Institute of Technology
Yokohama 226, Japan
kaba@fe.dis.titech.ac.jp

Shigeru Shinomoto

Dept. of Physics, Kyoto University
Sakyo-ku, Kyoto, 606-8502, Japan
shino@ton.scphys.kyoto-u.ac.jp

Abstract

In practical learning, one sometimes has to infer a decision boundary from stochastic examples. In this paper, we address the question how fast such a decision boundary estimation can approach the optimal choice as the number of examples t increases in a one dimensional learning problem. Although a naive batch learning exhibits a slow convergence $O\left(t^{-2/3}\right)$ in the squared estimation error, we show that online learning with queries can accelerate it to $O\left(t^{-1}\right)$, which is the optimal convergence of the learning. We also show that the fastest convergence obtainable by online learning without queries is presumably $O\left((\ln t)^2 t^{-1}\right)$. This implies that the advantage of using queries in this problem can be quantified by the $O\left((\ln t)^2\right)$ difference in the learning speed.

1 Introduction

To realize a target input-output relation is the objective of machine learning. In most of practical situations, however, it is impossible for a learning machine even to reproduce a given finite set of examples. This is unavoidable if the relation is originally stochastic. Even if the relation is deterministic, the mismatch of machine structures between the target and the trained learning machine causes a similar difficulty. The goal of learning in such cases should be not to accurately realize the target relation but to make the best predictions on novel examples. When the relation is a binary classification rule,

345

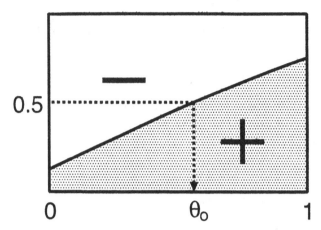

Figure 1: A conditional distribution $p(y|x)$ describing a one dimensional binary choice problem. The optimal decision boundary is the point θ_o that satisfies the condition $p(y = +1|\theta_o) = p(y = -1|\theta_o) = 1/2$.

i.e., a relation between an input and a binary output, the best prediction is made by choosing the output which seems more likely than the alternative. Thus, the machine is required to infer the decision boundary, that optimally separates the input space, from given examples.

We address here the question how fast the decision boundary estimation can approach the optimal choice as the number of examples increases. In order to answer this question, we consider a simple one dimensional binary choice problem depicted in figure 1. In this learning model, the target rule is a stochastic relation between a real number input $x \in [0, 1]$ and a binary output $y \in \{-1, +1\}$, represented by a conditional distribution $p(y|x)$. We assume that the learning machine has no prior knowledge other than that the fact $p(y = +1|x) = 1 - p(y = -1|x)$ is monotonically increasing and infinitely differentiable with respect to x. The optimal choice of the decision boundary in this model is the point θ_o that satisfies the condition $p(y = +1|\theta_o) = p(y = -1|\theta_o) = 1/2$.

It is instructive to take a glance at the present problem from a view point of statistics. In the simplest statistical problems, the target distribution is assumed to be realized by a parametric model by choosing the "true" parameter. This sort of inference is called the *parametric* estimation, of which mean square error of the parameter estimation usually vanishes as $O(t^{-1})$ when the number of examples t becomes large. On the other hand, the *nonparametric* estimation in which one infers a target distribution without assuming any functional form is much more complicated and the convergence of the estimation error generally becomes slower than $O(t^{-1})$ as an infinite number of degrees of freedom have to be estimated. Our problem is placed in the middle of these two situations. In our problem, the functional form of the target distribution is assumed to be unknown as well as in the non-parametric estimation. However, the required task is to estimate a "point" θ_o that is parameterized by the condition $p(y = +1|\theta_o) = p(y = -1|\theta_o) = 1/2$, which is similar to the task in the parametric estimation. This kind of inference is often termed the *semi-parametric* estimation. In contrast to the $O(t^{-1})$ convergence, usually observed in the parametric estimation, it is known that the estimator obtained by the minimum error strategy in this case exhibits a slower convergence

$$(\theta - \theta_o)^2 \sim O\left(t^{-2/3}\right),\qquad(1.1)$$

due to the lack of the information with respect to the functional form of the target (Manski 1978, Kim and Pollard 1990, Kabashima and Shinomoto 1992).

The main purpose of the present work is to accelerate this slow convergence. There have been a lot of works on speeding up learning in various systems (see Watkin et al 1992). Active learning with *queries* is one of the most effective techniques for acceleration of learning considered (Baum 1991, Seung et al 1992, Freund et al 1993, Sollich 1995). When the target relation is a classification rule realizable by the learning machine, query learning following the "minimum entropy principle" realizes an exponentially fast convergence. However, this principle is not useful for the present problem in which the target relation is unrealizable (Sollich 1995). Instead, we will show later that a heuristic usage of queries in *online* mode can accelerate the convergence (1.1) up to

$$(\theta - \theta_o)^2 \sim O\left(t^{-1}\right).\qquad(1.2)$$

It should be emphasized that the combination of "queries" and "online learning" is indispensable to realize this fastest convergence. Although it is not obvious whether one can achieve this convergence by other algorithms that do not include this combination, we have never succeeded in finding any batch algorithm or any online algorithm without queries that provides the $O(t^{-1})$ convergence in the present framework.

This paper is organized as follows. In section 2, we will explain our online query learning algorithm and evaluate its performance in several situations. In section 3, we will consider learning circumstances where one can not use queries. A simple modification of the online learning algorithm given in section 2 provides the scaling $(\theta - \theta_o)^2 \sim O(t^{-4/5})$, which is rather faster than that of eq. (1.1) found in batch algorithms (the minimum error algorithm). Further, this can be accelerated by using more sophisticated strategies. The fastest convergence without using queries turns out to be $O((\ln t)^2 t^{-1})$. In the final section, we will summarize the results and mention open problems.

2   Learning with Queries

We first consider active learning where the learning machine can specify the position of inputs as queries. We assume a situation where for every input $x \in [0,1]$ which is specified by the learning machine, the target rule returns a binary output $y = \pm 1$ according to the conditional distribution $p(y|x)$.

The following observation is helpful to construct a learning algorithm. For an input x satisfying the condition $p(y = +1|x) > p(y = -1|x)$, it is more often to find $y = +1$ than -1, and vice versa. Since $p(y = +1|x)$ is assumed to be monotonically increasing with respect to x, this implies that we can *on average* know whether the optimal boundary θ_o, which satisfies the condition $p(y = +1|x) = p(y = -1|x) = 1/2$, is placed at the left or the right of x by observing the output y, although statistical fluctuation prevents us from obtaining an exact information.

Thus, we propose a learning algorithm as follows (Kabashima and Shinomoto 1995). Let us denote θ_t is the hypothetical decision boundary determined through t examples. The proposal for the construction of a query is to specify an input just at θ_t. According to the output $y = +1$ or -1 in response to the input, one updates the hypothetical boundary as

$$\theta_{t+1} = \theta_t - y\,\alpha_t, \tag{2.1}$$

where the step size α_t will be controlled by the learning algorithm.

In order to elucidate the qualitative behavior of the dynamics of eq. (2.1), we assume that the conditional probability $p(y = +1|x)$ can be expanded around of $x = \theta_o$ as

$$p(y = +1|x) = 1/2 + k_1(x - \theta_o) + k_2(x - \theta_o)^2 + \cdots . \tag{2.2}$$

In the vicinity of θ_o, the expectation and the variance of the output y are, then, approximated as

$$\langle y \rangle_x \sim 2k_1(x - \theta_o), \quad \left\langle y^2 \right\rangle_x - \langle y \rangle_x^2 \sim 1, \tag{2.3}$$

respectively, where $\langle \cdots \rangle_x$ represents the statistical average with respect to the conditional distribution $p(y|x)$ at a point x. This suggests that the dynamics (2.1) pushes the hypothetical boundary toward its optimal choice θ_o on the average. However, as θ_t comes close to θ_o, the mean drift force toward the optimal boundary becomes weak, while its fluctuation remains finite. Thus, if we keep α_t constant, θ_t is subject to both of the drift force and the fluctuation and will not converge to θ_o.

One possible strategy to obtain the exact convergence $\theta_t \to \theta_o$ is to reduce the step size α_t adequately as learning goes on, which would suppress the fluctuation. It was proven that θ_t strongly converges to its optimal value θ_o if the condition

$$\sum_t \alpha_t = \infty, \quad \sum_t \alpha_t^2 < \infty, \tag{2.4}$$

is satisfied (Robbins and Monro 1951, Kushner and Clark 1978). The relation between decay α_t and the convergence of θ_t has not been studied in detail. We are going to investigate the convergence of θ_t by interpreting the dynamics (2.1) as a physical motion subject to thermal noise. We will find that the condition (2.4) is not a necessary condition but just a sufficient condition. Namely, there is a sequence $\{\alpha_t\}$ which yields a successful converge $\theta_t \to \theta_o$ without satisfying the condition (2.4).

Dynamics of eq. (2.1) is subject to the mean drift force toward the optimal boundary θ_o and fluctuation represented by eq. (2.3). This is similar to Brownian motion in a quadratic drift potential. Therefore, the dynamical process can be approximated by the Langevin equation

$$dz/dt = \alpha(t)[-2k_1 z + \eta(t)], \qquad (2.5)$$

where $z = \theta_t - \theta_o$, $\alpha(t) = \alpha_t$ and $\eta(t)$ is a white noise statistically characterized as $\langle \eta(t) \rangle = 0$, $\langle \eta(t)\eta(t') \rangle = \delta(t - t')$. If we consider an ensemble of the boundaries with parameters $z = \theta_t - \theta_o$ at the moment t, the dynamics of the ensemble distribution $P(z, t)$ can be described by the Fokker-Planck equation

$$\frac{\partial P(z,t)}{\partial t} = 2k_1\alpha(t)\frac{\partial[zP(z,t)]}{\partial z} + \frac{\alpha^2(t)}{2}\frac{\partial^2 P(z,t)}{\partial z^2}. \qquad (2.6)$$

From eq. (2.5) or eq. (2.6), we can obtain the evolution equation of the mean square deviation $u = \langle z^2 \rangle = \langle (\theta - \theta_o)^2 \rangle$ as

$$du/dt = -4k_1\alpha(t)u + \alpha^2(t). \qquad (2.7)$$

From this equation, we can construct the optimal sequence of the step size for obtaining the fastest convergence of u. This is carried out by simply minimizing the right hand side of eq. (2.7) with respect to $\alpha(t)$, which implies

$$\alpha(t) = 2k_1 u. \qquad (2.8)$$

This gives the solution

$$u_{opt}(t) = \frac{1}{4k_1^2(t + const.)} \sim \frac{1}{4k_1^2 t}, \qquad (2.9)$$

and hence the optimal sequence of the step size is obtained as

$$\alpha_{opt}(t) \sim \frac{1}{2k_1^2 t}. \qquad (2.10)$$

This method to obtain the optimal performance of the learning is similar to what was employed to discuss the finite time energy scaling in simulated annealing (Shinomoto and Kabashima 1991). The present model is in some sense similar to a thermodynamic system. For a fixed finite α, the mean square deviation u is proportional to α in equilibrium. Therefore, α corresponds to the "temperature" in the thermodynamic system. One specific feature of this system is that the drift force is also proportional to the "temperature" α.

In order to obtain the optimal sequence of $\alpha(t)$, one has to know both k_1, which represents the gradient of $p(y = +1|x)$ at $x = \theta_o$, and the mean square deviation $u(t)$. In practical situations, a rough estimation of k_1 might be possible. However, $u(t)$ is usually hard to evaluate because this is a quantity obtained via average over an ensemble of estimations. Practically, one should fix a plausible schedule of $\alpha(t)$ first that would give a fast convergence of the deviation. By substituting the schedule $\alpha(t) = A/t$, we can solve eq. (2.7). The asymptotic form of the solution turns out to be classified into the three types of convergence depending on the values of A:

$$
\begin{aligned}
u(t) \quad &\sim \quad \frac{A^2}{(4k_1 A - 1)t}, \quad \text{for} \quad A > \frac{1}{4k_1}, \\
&\sim \quad \frac{\ln t}{t}, \quad \text{for} \quad A = \frac{1}{4k_1}, \\
&\sim \quad \frac{C}{t^{4k_1 A}}, \quad \text{for} \quad 0 < A < \frac{1}{4k_1}.
\end{aligned} \qquad (2.11)
$$

This result indicates that the learning schedule $\alpha(t) = 1/(2k_1 t)$ is asymptotically optimal (see figure 2), which is in agreement with the solution of the optimal learning strategy (2.10). The present schedule satisfies the conventional condition for convergence (2.4). Although all of the three dynamics converge, it should be noted that the asymptotic form exhibits a qualitative deterioration in its power for $A < 1/4k_1$. Thus, a learning schedule $\alpha(t) = A/t$ is optimal only for $A > 1/4k_1$ in the sense that it gives the fastest convergence $u \sim O(t^{-1})$, apart from the prefactor. We carried out numerical simulations of the original learning algorithm (2.1) with learning schedule $\alpha(t) = A/t$ with various A. Figure 2 shows that the exponents of convergence obtained from the experiments exhibit a good agreement with theoretical prediction (2.11).

The analysis is easily extended from $\alpha(t) = A/t$ to a more general schedule $\alpha(t) = A/t^\beta$. The resulting asymptotic solution is

$$
\begin{aligned}
u(t) \quad &= \quad \int^t d\tau \frac{A^2}{\tau^{2\beta}} \exp\left[-\frac{4k_1 A}{1-\beta}(t^{1-\beta} - \tau^{1-\beta}) \right] + C \exp\left[-\frac{4k_1 A}{1-\beta} t^{1-\beta} \right] \\
&\sim \quad \frac{A}{4k_1 t^\beta} + C \exp\left[-\frac{4k_1 A}{1-\beta}(t^{1-\beta} - 1) \right].
\end{aligned} \qquad (2.12)
$$

The second term in the final form of eq. (2.12) represents a memory effect with respect to the initial condition, from which a constant C is determined. For $\beta > 1$, this does not vanish in the limit $t \to \infty$. The mean square deviation thus converges to zero, if $0 < \beta \leq 1$. Note that the schedule with $0 < \beta < 1/2$ does not satisfy the conventional condition for convergence (2.4). However,

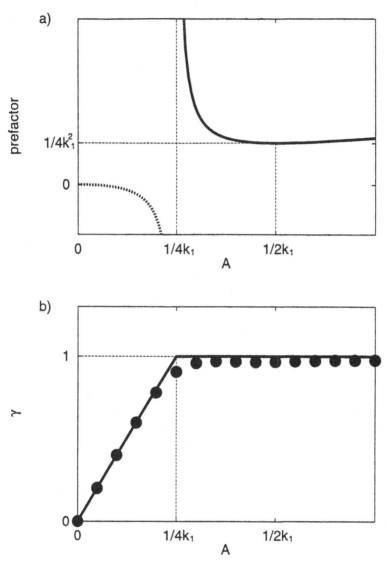

Figure 2: Asymptotic behavior of the mean square deviation $u = \langle(\theta - \theta_o)^2\rangle$ for the schedule $\alpha(t) = A/t$ depends on A. a) For $A > 1/4k_1$, mean square deviation obeys a scaling $u \sim O(t^{-1})$ and its prefactor $A^2/(4k_1A - 1)$ is minimized at $A = 1/2k_1$. b) Convergence rate $u \sim O(t^{-\gamma})$ exhibits qualitative deterioration in the power γ for $A < 1/4k_1$. The markers are the mean results of 1000 sets of numerical experiments. The variances are smaller than symbols.

our result is not surprising and can be reasonably understood from a physical view point. As described before, our system is analogous to a thermodynamics system where the parameter α works as a kind of "temperature" and the mean square deviation $u(t)$ is proportional to α in equilibrium. If one reduce the temperature too rapidly, the ensemble of the system does not attain the equilibrium distribution and will be partially "frozen". This corresponds to the case with $\beta > 1$, where $u(t)$ remains finite even in the limit $t \to \infty$. On the other hand, if the system is annealed slowly, the ensemble distribution equilibrates almost every time, which make $u(t)$ proportional to $\alpha(t)$. This is what happens in the case with $0 < \beta < 1/2$, where the first term is dominant in the final form of eq. (2.12), implying $u(t) \propto \alpha(t)$. In figure 3, we plotted results of numerical experiments for $\beta = 0, 1/8, 1/4$ and $1/2$. These are highly consistent with our analytical results.

Smaller β yields slower convergence, which is not preferable. However, smaller β has the ability to erase the memory of the initial condition rapidly. We are often faced with a situation where the target relation depends on time. In such cases, the learning machine should be sufficiently adaptive to the temporal target change. Amari (1967) discussed the learning with a fixed step size, which is similar to the case with $\beta = 0$ in the present framework. He showed that although $u(t)$ does not vanish, learning with a fixed finite step size can adapt to a time varying target while retaining a fairly small mean square deviation. We can estimate the number of examples required to obtain a certain precision in the present general $\beta > 0$. It is found that the number of examples required does not depend critically on the choice of β.

The number of examples N necessary to obtain a small deviation $u = \epsilon$ is termed sample complexity. Sample complexity for an $\alpha(t) = A/t^\beta$ type learning schedule is obtained by minimizing $u(N)$ with respect to A. For simplicity, we assume here that the learning machine already has an estimate of k_1, which is the gradient of $p(y = +1|x)$ at $x = \theta_o$. It is possible to approximate k_1 from a finite number of examples.

For the learning schedule $\alpha(t) = A/t$, the resulting mean square deviation is minimized by $A = 1/2k_1$. Namely, the learning schedule $\alpha(t) = 1/(2k_1 t)$ is also optimal in the context of the sample complexity (Luo 1991). The sample complexity for this schedule is obtained from eq. (2.12) as

$$N \sim \frac{1}{4k_1^2 \epsilon}. \tag{2.13}$$

Next, let us consider a more general schedule $\alpha(t) = A/t^\beta$. The optimal choice of a prefactor A is obtained by minimizing the final form of eq. (2.12) as

$$A \sim \frac{(1 - \beta)}{4k_1(N^{1-\beta} - 1)} \ln\left[\frac{(4k_1)^2(N^{1-\beta} - 1)}{(1 - \beta)N^{-\beta}}\right]. \tag{2.14}$$

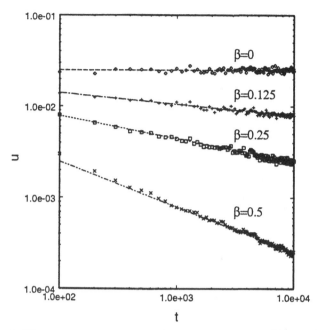

Figure 3: The mean square deviations for the schedule $\alpha(t) = A/t^\beta$ with prefactor $A = 0.1$ and exponents $\beta = 0, 1/8, 1/4$ and $1/2$. Numerical experiments were carried out for a system with k_1. The averages of square deviation $(\theta - \theta_o)^2$ obtained from 1000 sets of examples (markers) exhibits the scaling $u = \langle (\theta - \theta_o)^2 \rangle \sim O(t^{-\gamma})$ with exponents $\gamma = -0.008 \pm 0.005, 0.123 \pm 0.005, 0.253 \pm 0.005$ and 0.527 ± 0.004 for $\beta = 0, 1/8, 1/4$ and $1/2$, respectively. They are in good agreement with the analytical prediction $u \sim A/4k_1 t^{-\beta} = 0.025 t^{-\beta}$.

This yields the deviation

$$u(N) \sim \frac{(1-\beta)}{(4k_1)^2 N} \ln[\frac{(4k_1)^2 N}{1-\beta}]. \tag{2.15}$$

Thus, the sample complexity $N(\epsilon)$ is evaluated from $u(N) = \epsilon$ as

$$N \sim \frac{1-\beta}{(4k_1)^2 \epsilon}[\ln\frac{1}{\epsilon} + \ln\ln\frac{1}{\epsilon} + \cdots]. \tag{2.16}$$

The difference between eqs. (2.13) and (2.16) is only $O(-\ln\epsilon)$. This small difference can be interpreted as follows. For $\beta < 1$, a memory with respect to an initial condition is rapidly erased, which enable us to chose a small value A

in order to obtain the small deviation $u = \epsilon$. The slower schedule with $\beta < 1$ thus should be regarded as robust rather than inferior.

3 Learning without Queries

In this section, we consider a situation in which inputs are not specified by the learning machine but randomly selected from a fixed distribution $p(x)$. The learning algorithm in this case has to make the most of the information available from examples drawn from the joint distribution $p(y, x) = p(y|x)\, p(x)$. The task of the learning machine is the same as that in the previous section, namely, to find the optimal boundary θ_o that is determined by the condition $p(y = +1|\theta_o) = p(y = -1|\theta_o)$.

If the joint distribution $p(y, x)$ has an inversion symmetry with respect to the the optimal boundary, $p(y, z + \theta_o) = p(-y, -z + \theta_o)$, and this symmetry is known in advance, the all examples can be utilized for estimating the boundary and it is possible to obtain the fastest $O(t^{-1})$ convergence (Biehl et al 1995, Copelli et al 1997). However, one can not expect such symmetry in most of practical situations. Then, examples which are placed far from the boundary θ_o generally yield an uninformative bias in the estimation. This implies that one has to discard part of the examples in order to obtain an exact convergence $\theta_t \to \theta_o$, which makes the convergence slower. Kawanabe and Amari (1994) proved that if examples are randomly drawn from a fixed distribution and no symmetry is assumed with respect to the joint distribution $p(y, x)$, it is impossible to realize an $O(t^{-1})$ convergence to the optimal boundary. The remaining interest is the question what is the fastest convergence that we can realize without assuming the symmetry. We will consider this problem in the following.

A simple application of the preceding strategy to a situation where each input is randomly drawn is to introduce a window for accepting inputs. Let us assume a window with an interval 2τ centered at the hypothetical boundary θ_t. The parameter θ_t is then updated according to the preceding algorithm only when the input x falls in the window, namely,

$$\theta_{t+1} = \theta_t - y\,\alpha_t/2\tau_t, \quad \text{if } x \in [\theta_t - \tau_t, \theta_t + \tau_t],$$
$$= \theta_t \quad \text{otherwise.} \tag{3.1}$$

This algorithm is similar to the vector quantization procedure LVQ2 proposed by Kohonen in which the window size τ_t is fixed (Kohonen 1989). We are going to control the window size so as to obtain an exact convergence to the optimal boundary.

In the following, we assume the distribution $p(x)$ is positive over the input space $[0, 1]$, infinitely differentiable and expanded around $x = \theta_o$ as

$$p(x) = p_o + h_1(x - \theta_o) + h_2(x - \theta_o)^2 + \cdots. \tag{3.2}$$

The probability that an output $y = +1$ is returned for an input that falls in the window is

$$\int_{\theta_t - \tau_t}^{\theta_t + \tau_t} dx \; p(y = +1|x) \; p(x) / \int_{\theta_t - \tau_t}^{\theta_t + \tau_t} dx p(x) =$$

$$1/2 + k_1 \left(\theta - \theta_o\right) + (1/3) \left(k_2 + \frac{k_1 h_1}{p_o}\right) \tau_t^2 + O(\tau_t^3). \tag{3.3}$$

The Langevin equation for the corresponding dynamics is thus given by

$$\frac{dz}{dt} = \alpha(t) \left[-2k_1 z - \frac{2}{3}\left(k_2 + \frac{k_1 h_1}{p_o}\right)\tau^2 + \sqrt{\frac{1}{2\tau}}\eta(t)\right], \tag{3.4}$$

where $z = \theta_t - \theta_o$, and $\eta(t)$ is the white noise statistically characterized by $\langle \eta(t)\rangle = 0$ and $\langle \eta(t)\eta(t - t')\rangle = \delta(t - t')$. Note that the second term in the right hand side of eq. (3.4) generally does not vanish even if the deviation $z = 0$. This term is the origin of the bias in the estimation due to the asymmetry of $p(y, x)$, which we mentioned before. To reduce this systematic error, we have to shorten the interval τ_t. On the other hand, updates become infrequent as one make the interval narrow and then the relative intensity of fluctuations increases by $(2\tau)^{-1/2}$. The balance between these tendencies determines optimal sequence of the window size. This is a kind of "bias/variance" dilemma problem (Geman et al 1992).

Assuming that the schedule of the step size is $\alpha(t) = A/t$ and $A > 1/k_1$, we seek the optimal control of the widow size among the schedule $\tau_t \sim \tau_0 t^{-\xi}$. From the Langevin equation (3.4), we obtain the evolution of the mean square deviation $u = \langle z^2 \rangle$ as

$$u(t) \sim \frac{A^2}{2\tau_0(4k_1 A - 1 + \xi)}t^{\xi - 1} + \frac{4(k_2 + k_1 h_1/p_o)^2 A^2 \tau_0^4}{9(2k_1 A - \xi)^2}t^{-4\xi}. \tag{3.5}$$

This is minimized by taking $\xi = 1/5$. Thus, the optimal sequence of the window size is $\tau_t \sim t^{-1/5}$ and the mean square deviation scales as $u(t) \sim t^{-4/5}$.

We had to throw away many examples that do not fall in the prepared window so as to suppress the $O(\tau^2)$ systematic bias due to the possible asymmetry in the joint distribution $p(y, x)$. This is because the present strategy is not sophisticated enough to manage the convexity and the higher order asymmetry in the conditional distribution (3.3). A more sophisticated technique should be able to utilize more examples. In the present method, the step size is constant over the window. This is unnatural because an example placed close to the center of the window should be more influential than that placed at the surrounding region.

Actually, we can accelerate the convergence by improving the dynamics in the following way. We modify the rule to

$$\theta_{t+1} = \theta_t - \frac{y\alpha_t}{\tau_t}w_p\left(\frac{x - \theta_t}{\tau_t}\right), \quad \text{if } x \in [\theta_t - \tau_t, \theta_t + \tau_t],$$

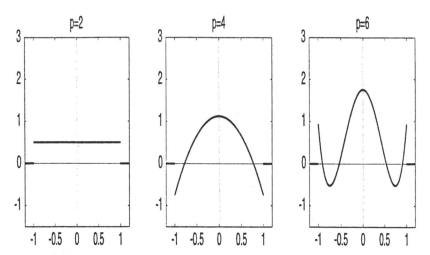

Figure 4: Kernel functions $w_p(s)$ for $p = 2, 4, 6$. These are constructed from the Legendre polynomials.

$$= \theta_t, \quad \text{otherwise.} \tag{3.6}$$

Here, $w_p(\cdot)$ is a kernel function to control the amount of the movement depending on the relative position to the present hypothetical boundary θ_t. The function $w_p(s)$ for $p \geq 2$ is defined over the interval $s \in [-1, 1]$ and is assumed to satisfy the conditions

$$\int_{-1}^{+1} w_p(s)ds = 1,$$
$$\int_{-1}^{+1} w_p(s)s^k ds = 0, \quad \text{for} \quad k = 1, 2, \cdots, p - 1, \tag{3.7}$$
$$\int_{-1}^{+1} w_p(s)s^p ds \neq 0.$$

This set of conditions for the kernel functions were first introduced by Kawanabe and Amari (1994) in the context of a (batch) semi-parametric estimation of the present binary model. It is easy to construct a family of reasonable kernel functions from an orthogonal polynomial set. However, solutions are not uniquely determined only by these conditions. Possible solutions for $p = 2, 4, 6, \cdots$, which minimize $\int w_p(s)^2 ds$ are given by

$$w_p(s) = m_{p-1}\frac{l_{p-1}(s)}{s},$$
$$m_q = \frac{(-1)^{(q-1)/2}(q+1)!}{2^{q+1}((q-1)/2)!((q+1)/2)!}\sqrt{\frac{2}{2q+1}}, \tag{3.8}$$

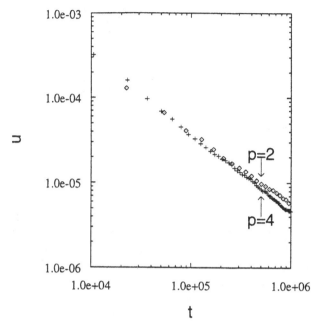

Figure 5: Estimation error obtained by using kernels with $p = 2$ and 4. The average of square deviation $(\theta - \theta_o)^2$ is taken over 1000 sets of examples for the conditional distribution $p(y = +1|x) = 1/(\exp(-8x^3 + 1) + 1)$. These data exhibit the scaling $u \sim O(t^{-\gamma})$ with $\gamma = 0.781 \pm 0.003$ and 0.901 ± 0.003 for $p = 2$ and 4, respectively, which are highly consistent with the theoretical prediction $\gamma = 2p/(2p + 1)$.

where $l_q(\cdot)$, $(q = 1, 3, 5, \cdots)$ are the Legendre polynomials. The kernel functions for odd p $(= 2j + 1)$ are the same as the one for even p $(= 2j)$. Figure 4 shows examples of $w_p(s)$ for $p = 2, 4, 6$. In agreement with our preceding discussion, the influence of every example depends on the position of the input relative to that of the hypothetical boundary. It is more interesting to see that the kernel can be negative for $p > 2$ due to these orthogonality conditions. Thus, the corresponding move for the positive output is not necessarily to the left, and vice versa.

By using this kernel function, an $O(\tau^2)$ bias force is reduced to $O(\tau^p)$, which implies one can use a wider window at each step. Accordingly, it is found that the asymptotically optimal control of the window size is a slower sequence $\tau_t \sim \tau_o t^{-1/(2p+1)}$. The resulting asymptotic scaling of the mean square deviation turns out to be

$$u(t) \sim \left[\frac{v_p^2 A^2}{\tau_0(4k_1 A - 2p/(2p+1))} + \frac{(2k_p A b_p \tau^p)^2}{(2k_1 A - p/(2p+1))^2} \right] t^{-2p/(2p+1)}, \quad (3.9)$$

where

$$v_p^2 = \int_{-1}^{+1} w_p(s)^2 ds = \frac{p^2}{2^{2p+1}} \left(\frac{p!}{(p/2)!^2} \right)^2, \quad (3.10)$$

and b_p is the prefactor of the $O(\tau^p)$ bias term. The second term of the right hand side of eq. (3.9) vanishes as $p \to \infty$, if $p(y,x)$ is infinitely differentiable with respect to x. By eliminating unimportant factors in the limit $p \to \infty$, we obtain an asymptotic form

$$u(t) \sim O(p^2 t^{-2p/(2p+1)}). \quad (3.11)$$

The exponent $2p/(2p+1)$ is the same that obtained by Barron and Cover (1991) for a non-parametric estimation although they did not give an estimate of the prefactor p^2 here (Barron and Cover 1991). The scaling (3.11) implies that the machine can attain an asymptotic scaling arbitrarily close to $O(t^{-1})$. For a finite number of examples, however, it is not advantageous to use a kernel with larger p because the prefactor p^2 increases rapidly with p (see figure 5). The optimal p is obtained by minimizing eq. (3.11) as

$$p \sim O(\ln t). \quad (3.12)$$

By substituting this into eq. (3.11), we obtain the fastest convergence

$$u(t) \sim O((\ln t)^2 t^{-1}). \quad (3.13)$$

This would be presumably the optimal convergence. However, we have not succeeded in proving it yet.

4   Summary and Discussion

In the preceding sections, we have succeeded in constructing a learning algorithm for a simple one dimensional binary choice problem. The algorithm works in online mode and, with using queries, can realize the fastest $O(t^{-1})$ convergence of the mean square deviation of the estimation. When queries are not permitted and each input is randomly drawn from a fixed distribution, a naive modification of this algorithm provides $O(t^{-4/5})$ convergence. A more sophisticated technique using a family of kernel functions accelerates this convergence up to $O(p^2 t^{-2p/(2p+1)})$, $p = 2, 3, \ldots$. Although a larger p seems preferable, we may pay the price in a larger prefactor. The optimal choice of p, depending on the number of examples, gives the fastest convergence, of $O((\ln t)^2 t^{-1})$ is presumably optimal. Therefore, the advantage of using queries

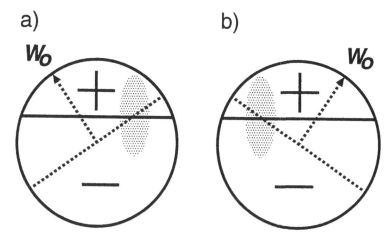

Figure 6: Decision boundary when the structures are different between the target rule and the learning machine. In this example, a simple perceptron without threshold learns a rule which is realized by a simple perceptron with a finite threshold. *a*) and *b*) illustrate how the optimal boundary depends on the input distribution which is represented by the shade.

in this problem is quantified by the $O((\ln t)^2)$ difference in the convergence of the mean square estimation error of the boundary parameter.

The most important question that is not mentioned so far is whether our results for the one dimensional system are critically dependent on the dimensionality of the parameter space as well as the dimensionality of the input space. In higher dimensional problems, there are two main factors which make the learning difficult.

The first factor is the increase of the fluctuation in the estimation caused by the increase in the the parameter space dimensionality. It is widely shown in both of batch and online learning that learning curve in a higher dimensional model depends on its dimensionality D via the scaled number of examples t/D (Blumer et al 1986, Levin et al 1990, Györgyi and Tishby 1990, Amari et al 1992, Kabashima 1994, Biehl and Schwarze 1995, Saad and Solla 1995). This is also the case in our problem. Namely, the mean square estimation errors in higher dimensional versions of the present problem exhibit power laws of t/D around the parameter that attained in the limit $t/D \to \infty$.

The second factor is the difficulty caused by the mismatch of the machine structures between the target rule and the learning machine, which is much more complicated. In the one dimensional system, the optimal decision boundary θ_o does not depend on the input distribution $p(x)$. In contrast, the optimal boundary in higher dimensional systems generally depends on the input distribution, when the stochastic nature of the target rule is caused by the mismatch in machine structures (figure 6). This implies that the optimal construction of queries is impossible without knowing the input distribution $p(x)$. If $p(x)$ is known in advance, random queries on the hypothetical boundary following the distribution of $p(x)$ can provide $O((t/D)^{-1})$ convergence. However, such a situation is of little relevance. In most practical situations where $p(x)$ is unknown, one has to estimate $p(x)$ from randomly drawn examples, which reduces the possibility of using queries. A combination of query learning and estimation of the input distribution from random examples might be the optimal strategy. As far as we know, such type of learning paradigm has not been investigated so far and would be an interesting theoretical problem of learning.

In learning without queries, a strategy similar to the one applied in the one dimensional system is also effective in higher dimensional systems. By defining a band of width $2\tau_t$ centered at the hypothetical boundary, with a similar update rule and appropriate schedules of step size $\{\alpha_t\}$ and band width $\{\tau_t\}$, the machine attains the convergence $u(t) \sim O((t/D)^{-4/5})$. This may presumably be accelerated. However, we have not yet succeeded in finding kernel functions which would be necessary for further acceleration.

Acknowledgements The authors thank David Saad for critical reading of the manuscript. This work was partially supported by the program "Research For The Future" (RFTF) of the Japanese Society for the Promotion Science (YK).

References

Amari, S. (1967). A theory of adaptive pattern classifiers, *IEEE Trans.* EC–16, 290–307.

Amari, S., Fujita, N., and Shinomoto, S. (1992). Four types of learning curves *Neural Comp.*, 4, 605–618.

Barron, A.R., and Cover, T.M. (1991). Minimum complexity density estimation. *IEEE Trans.*, IT–37, 1034–1054.

Baum, E.B. (1991). Neural net algorithms that learn in polynomial time from examples and queries. *IEEE Trans.*, NN–2, 5–19.

Biehl, M., and Schwarze, H. (1995). Learning by on-line gradient descent. *J. Phys. A*, 28, 643–656.

Biehl, M., Riegler P., and Stechert. (1995). Learning from noisy data: exactly solvable model. *Phys. Rev. E*, 52, R4624–R4627.

Blumer, A., Ehrenfeucht, A.,Haussler, D., and Warmuth, M.K. (1986). Classifying learnable geometric concepts with the Vapnik-Chervonenkis dimension. In *Proc. 18th Symposium on Theory of Computing*, 273-282.

Copelli, M., Eichhorn, R., Kinouchi, M., Biehl, M., Simonetti, R., Riegler, P. and Caticha, N. (1997). Noise robustness in multilayer neural networks *Europhys. Lett.*, 37, 427-432.

Freund, Y., Seung, H.S, Shamir, E., and Tishby, N. (1993) Information, prediction, and query by committee. In *Advances in Neural Information Processing Systems 5*, 483-490.

Geman, S., Bienenstock, E., and Doursat, R. (1992). Neural networks and the bias/variance dilemma. *Neural Comp.*, 4, 1-58.

Györgyi, G., and Tishby, N. (1990). Statistical theory of learng a rule. In *Neural Networks and Spin Glasses*, Theumann, K.W., and Koeberle, R. ed., World Scientific, Singapore, 1-36.

Kabashima, Y., and Shinomoto, S. (1992). Learning curves for error minimum and maximum likelihood algorithms. *Neural Comp.*, 4, 712-719.

Kabashima, Y. (1994) 'Perfect loss of generalization due to noise in $K = 2$ parity machines.' *J. Phys. A: Math. Gen.* **27**, 1917-1927.

Kabashima, Y., and Shinomoto, S. (1995). Learning a decision boundary from stochastic examples: incremental algorithms with and without queries. *Neural Comp.*, 7, 158-172.

Kawanabe, M., and Amari, S. (1994). Estimation of network parameters in semi-parametric stochastic perceptron. *Neural Comp.*, 6, 1244-1261.

Kim, J., and Pollard, D. (1990). Cube root asymptotics. *Ann. Statist.*, 18, 191-219.

Kohonen, T. (1989). *Self-Organization and Associative Memory, 3rd ed.* Springer-Verlag, Berlin.

Kushner, H.J., and Clark, D.S. (1978). *Stochastic Approximation Methods for Constrained and Unconstrained Systems*. Springer-Verlag, Berlin.

Levin, E., Tishby, N., and Solla, S.A. (1990). A statistical approach to learning and generalization in layered neural network. *Proc. IEEE*, 78, 1568-1574.

Luo, Z.Q. (1991). 'On the convergence of the LMS algorithm with adaptive learning rate for linear feedfoward networks.' *Neural Comp.*, 3, 226-245.

Manski, C.F. (1978). Maximum score estimation and efficiency of the stochastic utility model of choice. *J. Economet.*, 3, 205-228.

Robbins, H., and Monro, S. (1951). A stochastic approximation method. *Ann. Math. Stat.*, 22, 400-407.

Saad, D., and Solla, S.A. (1995). Exact solutions for on-line learning in multilayer neural networks. *Phys. Rev. Lett.*, 74, 4337-4340; 'On-line learning in soft committee machines. *Phys. Rev. E*, 52, 4225-4243.

Seung, H.S, Opper, M., and Sompolinsky, H. (1992). Query by committee. In *Proc. of the 5th Annual ACM Conference on Computational Learning Theory*, 287-294.

Shinomoto, S., and Kabashima, Y. (1991). Finite time scaling of energy in simulated annealing. *J. Phys. A*, 24, L141–L144.

Sollich, P. (1995). Asking intelligent questions – the statistical mechanics of query learning. *PhD thesis*, University of Edinburgh.

A Bayesian Approach to On-line Learning

Manfred Opper

Neural Computing Research Group, Aston University
Birmingham B4 7ET, UK.
opperm@aston.ac.uk

Abstract

Online learning is discussed from the viewpoint of Bayesian statistical inference. By replacing the true posterior distribution with a simpler parametric distribution, one can define an online algorithm by a repetition of two steps: An update of the approximate posterior, when a new example arrives, and an optimal projection into the parametric family. Choosing this family to be Gaussian, we show that the algorithm achieves asymptotic efficiency. An application to learning in single layer neural networks is given.

1 Introduction

Neural networks have the ability to learn from examples. For *batch learning*, a set of training examples is collected and subsequently an algorithm is run on the entire training set to adjust the parameters of the network. On the other hand, for many practical problems, examples arrive sequentially and an instantaneous action is required at each time. In order to save memory and time this action should not depend on the entire set of data which have arrived sofar. This principle is realized in *online* algorithms, where usually only the last example is used for an update of the network's parameters. Obviously, some amount of information about the past examples is discarded in this approach. Surprisingly, recent studies showed that online algorithms can achieve a similar performance as batch algorithms, when the number of data grows large (Biehl and Riegler 1994; Barkai et al 1995; Kim and Sompolinsky 1996).

In order to understand the abilities and limitations of online algorithms, the question of optimal online learning has been raised. For algorithms which are based on a weigthed Hebbian rule, one has sought for optimal weight functions which yield the highest local (i.e. instantaneous) or global reduction of the average generalization error. Within the thermodynamic limit framework of statistical mechanics, this goal has been achieved for highly symmetric distributions of inputs by (Kinouchi and Caticha 1992; Copelli and Caticha

1995) for local optimization and by (Saad and Rattray 1997) for global optimization. Within this approach, the dynamics of online learning can be described by a few macroscopic order parameters. The results of these studies have shown that in some cases online algorithms can even learn with *the same* asymptotic speed (Biehl et al 1995; Van den Broeck and Reimann 1996) as optimized batch algorithms. Unfortunately, it is not clear how to generalize such approaches to general learning problems outside the thermodynamic limit framework. The reason is twofold. First, very specific assumptions about the probability distributions of network inputs have to made in order to allow for an introduction of order parameters. Second, the optimization also requires some knowledge (e.g. the generalization error) about the unknown teacher rule to be learnt. This information is usually not available in a concrete learning problem. Nevertheless, these statistical mechanics approaches are highly important. Their results can give an idea of what online algorithms can achieve in an idealized scenario and have also motivated further studies (Amari 1996; Opper 1996) like the one presented in this chapter.

In the following, we will discuss in more detail a Bayesian approach to online learning which has been introduced in (Opper 1996) and generalized in (Winther and Solla 1997). In this framework, it is possible to define optimal online learning as an approximation to batch learning, where in each step the loss of information from discarding previous examples is minimized. Such an optimization can be carried out without making assumptions about the distributions of inputs.

The chapter is organized as follows. In section 2, learning from random examples is described within the framework of statistical inference. Section 3 briefly reviews different statistical optimality criteria with a special emphasis on *efficient estimation*. In section 4, online learning is discussed as an approximation to maximum likelihood estimation and a recent approach to efficient online learning is introduced. Sections 5, 6 and 7 give an introduction into Bayesian inference, introduces Bayesian online learning and the explicit form of the algorithm within a Gaussian parametric ansatz. The asymptotic average case performance of the algorithm is calculated in section 8. Section 9 contains the explicit realization of the algorithm for the case of a single layer perceptron. The chapter concludes with an outlook in section 10.

2   Learning and Statistical Inference

The problem of learning in neural networks can be treated within the framework of statistical inference. One assumes that t data $D_t = (y_1, \ldots, y_t)$ are generated independently at random according to a distribution

$$P(D_t|\theta) = \prod_{k=1}^{t} P(y_k|\theta). \qquad (2.1)$$

θ is an unknown parameter which has to be estimated from D_t. For a noisy classification problem in a single layer neural net e.g., we set $y = (S, \mathbf{x}) =$ (label, inputs). Here $\mathbf{x} \doteq (x_1, \ldots, x_n)$ is an N dimensional vector of input features and the parameter $\theta \doteq (\theta_1, \ldots, \theta_N)$ is an N dimensional vector of network weights. In this case, a popular model is

$$P(y|\theta) = \phi(S\,\theta \cdot \mathbf{x})f(\mathbf{x}), \qquad (2.2)$$

where $\theta \cdot \mathbf{x} \doteq \sum_{i=1}^{N} \theta_i x_i$ is the inner product of weights and inputs and f is the density of inputs. Usually $\phi(h)$ is a smooth sigmoidal function which increases from zero at $h = -\infty$ to 1 at $h = \infty$. For a regression problem, we can set $y = (z, \mathbf{x}) =$ (function value, inputs). If a Gaussian noise model is assumed, we have

$$P(y|\theta) = \frac{1}{\sqrt{2\pi\sigma^2}} e^{-\frac{1}{2\sigma^2}(z - r(\theta, \mathbf{x}))^2} f(\mathbf{x}), \qquad (2.3)$$

where $r(\theta, \mathbf{x})$ is the regression function. In the following, we will usually use the symbol θ^* for the true value of the parameter (the one that stands for the distribution which generates the examples) and $\hat{\theta}$ for an estimate of this parameter.

3   Optimal Learning

Before discussing the problem of optimal online learning, we will briefly review (Vapnik 1982; Schervish 1995) a few optimality criteria which can be used to assess the quality of an estimation procedure. Obviously, there is no *uniformly* optimal estimation strategy. An algorithm which always makes the same prediction for the unknown probability independently of the data, is optimal for one single task (the one where the data come just from the distribution which the algorithm predicts) but will usually perform badly in general. Uniform optimality can be achieved only within special subclasses of estimators. Well known cases are best unbiased density estimators for exponential families of probability densities. Unbiasedness of an estimator means that the estimate averaged over the distribution of the training set gives the true density which generated the data. However, it is not clear at all that one should restrict estimators to unbiased ones. One might prefer an estimator with a small bias and small variance over an unbiased one with a very large variance.

Various optimality criteria are known in statistics. In the *minimax principle* one optimizes the prediction for the worst true density. In the *Bayesian* approach, one can define an average case optimality, where the average is over a prior distribution $p(\theta^*)$ of true parameters θ^*. We will come back to an online approximation to a Bayesian approach later. For the case of parameter estimation, *efficiency* is another important criterion for probabilistic models which depend smoothly on the parameters. If parameter estimation is restricted to *unbiased estimators* $\hat{\theta}$ (i.e. if the estimate $\hat{\theta}$ obeys $E_{D_t}\hat{\theta} = \theta^*$), then the famous *Rao-Cramér inequality* limits the speed at which the estimate $\hat{\theta}$ approaches the true parameter θ^* on average. For a single (scalar) parameter it simply reads

$$E_{D_t}\left(\hat{\theta} - \theta^*\right)^2 \geq \frac{1}{t \int dy P(y|\theta^*)\left[\frac{d}{d\theta^*}\ln P(y|\theta^*)\right]^2}. \tag{3.1}$$

E_{D_t} denotes the expectation over datasets. The generalization to an N dimensional vector of parameters is possible. For any real vector $(z_1, \ldots, z_N)$, we have the inequality

$$E_{D_t}\left(\sum_i z_i(\hat{\theta}_i - \theta^*_i)\right)^2 = \sum_{ij} z_i z_j E_{D_t}\left((\hat{\theta}_i - \theta^*_i)(\hat{\theta}_j - \theta^*_j)\right) \geq \tag{3.2}$$

$$\frac{1}{t}\sum_{ij} z_i z_j (J^{-1}(\theta^*))_{ij},$$

where

$$J_{ij}(\theta^*) = \int dy P(y|\theta^*)\partial_i \ln P(y|\theta^*)\partial_j \ln P(y|\theta^*)$$

is the *Fisher Information* matrix. Partial derivatives are with respect to the components of θ^*. If we take nonnegative numbers for the z_i, we can interpret the left hand side of (3.2) as a squared weighted average of the individual error components $\hat{\theta}_i - \theta^*_i$. Estimators which fulfill these relations with an *equality*, are called *efficient*. Since the proof of the inequalities requires unbiasedness, it is not clear at all why efficiency is important. Biased estimators may in some cases violate (3.2) and achieve a better performance. However, this is not true asymptotically. It can be shown that when the number of data grows large, then for almost all true parameters θ^*, no estimator can beat the Rao-Cramér inequality. As has been proved e.g. by (LeCam 1953) (under smoothness assumptions), the Lebesgue measure of the set of all parameters θ^* for which we can have *superefficiency*, i.e. a violation of (3.2), goes to zero asymptotically. Hence, one reasonable requirement for a good algorithm is *asymptotic efficiency* which by (3.2) means

$$E_{D_t}(\hat{\theta}_i - \theta^*_i)(\hat{\theta}_j - \theta^*_j) = \frac{1}{t}(J^{-1}(\theta^*))_{ij}, \tag{3.3}$$

in the limit $t \to \infty$.

4   Online Learning

Often, learning algorithms for estimating the unknown parameter θ^* are based on the principle of *Maximum Likelihood* (ML). It states that we should choose a parameter θ which maximizes the likelihood $P(D_t|\theta)$ of the observed data. Under weak assumptions, ML estimators are asymptotically efficient. As a learning algorithm, one can use e.g. a gradient descent algorithm and iterate

$$\theta'_i - \theta_i = \eta \, \partial_i \sum_{k=1}^{t} \ln P(y_k|\theta) = -\eta \, \partial_i \sum_{k=1}^{t} E_T(y_k|\theta) \qquad (4.1)$$

until convergence is achieved. Here, $E_T(y_k|\theta)$ defines the training energy of the examples to be minimzed by the algorithm. When a new example y_{t+1} is received, the ML procedure requires that the learner has to update her estimate for θ using *all previous* data. Hence D_t has to be stored in a memory. The goal of online learning is to calculate a new estimate $\hat{\theta}(t+1)$ which is only based on the new data point y_{t+1}, the old estimate $\hat{\theta}(t)$ (and possibly a set of other auxiliary quantities which have to be updated at each time step, but are much smaller in number than the entire set of previous training data). A popular idea is to use a procedure similar to (4.1), but to replace the training energy of all examples $\sum_{k=1}^{t} E_T(y_k|\theta)$ by the training energy of the most recent one. Hence, we get

$$\begin{aligned} \hat{\theta}_i(t+1) - \hat{\theta}_i(t) &= \eta(t) \, \partial_i \ln P(y_{t+1}|\hat{\theta}(t)) \\ &= -\eta(t) \, \partial_i E_T(y_{t+1}|\hat{\theta}(t)). \end{aligned} \qquad (4.2)$$

The choice of the learning rate $\eta(t)$ is important. If the algorithm should converge asymptotically, η must be decreased during learning. A schedule $\eta \propto 1/t$ yields the fastest rate of convergence, but the prefactor must be chosen with care, in order to avoid that the algorithm gets stuck away from the optimal parameter. Another choice is an adaptive η (Barkai et al 1995), which depends on the performance of the algorithm and can be used in the case of temporal changes of the distribution. A recent modification of (4.2) has been introduced by Amari (Amari 1996; Amari 1997), who replaces the scalar learning rate $\eta(t)$ by a tensor. This idea may be derived from the fact that the online training energy contains only information about the last example, and the change of the estimate of the distribution due to a change $\Delta\theta$ of the parameter should not be too large. The new idea is to define a measure for distances $||\Delta\theta||$ in the parameter space which reflects distances between probability distributions and is invariant against transformations of the parameters. A simple Euklidian distance will not satisfy this condition. One can be guided by the principle that the distance between two distributions should reflect how well they can be distinguished by an estimation based on random data. This can be achieved by defining the metric in parameter space by

$$||d\theta||^2 \propto \sum_{ij} d\theta_i J_{ij}(\theta) d\theta_j. \qquad (4.3)$$

Assuming that the probability distribution of efficient estimators is Gaussian (at large t) with a covariance given by (3.3), the probability density that a point close to the true value θ will be the estimate for θ, depends only on the distance between the two points. Based on such ideas, S. Amari (Amari 1985) has developped a beautiful differential geometric approach to statistical inference. In the context of online learning, he proposed the so called *natural gradient* algorithm (Amari 1996; Amari 1997), where the update is defined by a minimization of the training energy under the condition that $\|\Delta\theta\|^2$ is kept fixed. Solving the constrained variational problem for small $\Delta\theta$ yields

$$\theta_i(t+1) - \theta_i(t) = \gamma_t \sum_j (J^{-1}(\theta(t))_{ij}\partial_j \ln P(y_{t+1}|\theta(t)). \tag{4.4}$$

The differential operator $\sum_j (J^{-1}(\theta(t))_{ij}\partial_j$ is termed natural gradient. For the choice $\gamma_t = \frac{1}{t}$, one can show that the online algorithm yields *asymptotically efficient* estimation (Amari 1996; Opper 1996).

5   The Bayesian Approach

In the Bayesian approach to statistical inference, the degrees of prior belief or plausibility of parameters are expressed within probability distributions, the so called prior distributions (or priors) $p(\theta)$. Once this idea is accepted, subsequent inferences can be based on *Bayes rule* of probability. Formally, we may think that data are generated by a two step process: First, the true parameter θ is drawn at random from the prior distribution $p(\theta)$. Second, the data are drawn at random from $P(D_t|\theta)$. Bayes rule yields the conditional probability density (*posterior*) of the unknown parameter θ, given the data:

$$p(\theta|D_t) = \frac{p(\theta)P(D_t|\theta)}{\int d\theta' p(\theta')P(D_t|\theta')}. \tag{5.1}$$

The posterior density (5.1) can be used to calculate an estimate for the unknown parameter. The simplest case is the so called MAP (maximum a posteriori) value $\hat{\theta} = \arg\max \ln p(\theta|D_t)$, i.e. the most probable parameter value. Another choice is the posterior mean of the parameter. Using the full posterior, it is possible to go beyond a simple parameter estimation and to define a *Bayes optimal prediction* for the unknown probability distribution. Optimality is here understood in an average sense, both over random drawings of the data and random drawings of true parameters θ according to $p(\theta)$. It is not hard to show that the optimal distribution $\hat{P}(y|D_t)$ which minimizes the expected quadratic deviation (the symbol $E_{y|\theta}$ stands for expectation with respect to $P(y|\theta)$)

$$\int d\theta \, p(\theta) E_{D_t} E_{y|\theta} \left[\hat{P}(y|D) - P(y|\theta)\right]^2.$$

is given by a mixture of all possible distributions in the considered family, weighted by their posterior probabilities

$$\hat{P}(y|D) = \int d\theta \, P(y|\theta) \, p(\theta|D). \tag{5.2}$$

This so called *predictive distribution* also minimizes a second important functional, the averaged relative entropy

$$\int d\theta \, p(\theta) E_D E_{y|\theta} [\log \frac{P(y|\theta)}{\hat{P}(y|D)}] \tag{5.3}$$

where

$$E_{y|\theta} \left[\log \frac{P(y|\theta)}{\hat{P}(y|D_t)} \right] = \int dy P(y|\theta) \log \frac{P(y|\theta)}{\hat{P}(y|D_t)}$$

is an important dissimilarity measure between distributions, the *relative entropy* or *Kullback-Leibler divergence* $D_{KL}(P(\cdot|\theta)||\hat{P})$.

From the optimality on average, we see immediately that *no* estimator can beat a Bayes procedure for *all* true parameters θ^*. An estimator that would be uniformly better than a Bayes procedure would also be better on average. Moreover, it can be shown that for special choices of $p(\theta)$, Bayes procedures can also be minimax. A prior $p(\theta)$ which is well adapted to a problem may act as a regularizer, which can prevent an algorithm from overfitting when the number of examples is small. Some regularization methods for neural networks, e.g. weight decay, can be interpreted in a Bayesian way. On the other hand, when the number of examples is large, the influence of the prior distribution becomes weak. The posterior is sharply peaked at its maximum $\hat{\theta}$ and a Gaussian approximation for its shape

$$p(\theta|D_t) \simeq \exp[-\frac{t}{2} \sum_{ij} (\theta_i - \hat{\theta}_i) \hat{J}_{ij} (\theta_j - \hat{\theta}_j)] \tag{5.4}$$

becomes asymptotically exact. Here $\hat{J}_{ij} = -\partial_i \partial_j \frac{1}{t} \sum_{\mu=1}^{t} \ln P(y_\mu|\hat{\theta})$. In nice parametric cases, consistency and asymptotic efficiency of Bayes predictors can be proved.

6 Online Update of the Posterior

In order to construct an online algorithm within the Bayesian frameweork, we have to find out how the posterior distribution changes when a new datapoint y_{t+1} is observed. It can be easily shown that the new posterior corresponding to the new dataset D_{t+1} is given in terms of the old posterior and the likelihood of the new example by

$$p(\theta|D_{t+1}) = \frac{P(y_{t+1}|\theta)p(\theta|D_t)}{\int d\theta P(y_{t+1}|\theta)p(\theta|D_t)}. \tag{6.1}$$

(6.1) does not have the form of an online algorithm, because it requires the knowledge of the *entire old dataset* D_t. The basic idea to turn this into an online algorithm is to replace the true posterior $p(\theta|D)$ by a simpler parametric distribution $p(\theta|par)$, where *par* is a small set of parameters, which is

able to capture a major part of the information about the previous data and
which has to be updated at each step. Hence, the Bayes online algorithm will
be based on a repetition of two basic steps:

- Update: Use the old approximative posterior $p(\theta|par(t))$ to perform an
  update of the form (6.1)

$$p(\theta|y_{t+1}, par(t)) = \frac{P(y_{t+1}|\theta)p(\theta|par(t))}{\int d\theta P(y_{t+1}|\theta)p(\theta|par(t))}. \qquad (6.2)$$

- Project: The new posterior $p(\theta|y_{t+1}, par(t))$ will usually not belong to
  the parametric family $p(\theta|par)$. Hence, in the next step, it need to be
  projected into this family in order to obtain $p(\theta|par(t+1))$. The pa-
  rameter $par(t+1)$ must be chosen such that $p(\theta|par(t+1))$ is as close
  as possible to $p(\theta|y_{t+1}, par(t))$. It is a not clear a priori, which measure
  of dissimilarity between distributions should be used. Different choices
  may lead to different algorithms. I have chosen the KL-divergence

$$D_{KL}\left(p(\cdot|y_{t+1}, par(t))\|p(\cdot|par)\right) = \qquad (6.3)$$
$$\int d\theta\, p(\theta|y_{t+1}, par(t)) \ln \frac{p(\theta|y_{t+1}, par(t))}{p(\theta|par)},$$

which is nonsymmetric in its arguments. Minimizing (6.3) can be regarded as minimizing the loss of information in the projection step.
For the important case, where the parametric family is an exponential
family, i.e. if the densities are of the form

$$p(\theta|par) \propto \exp[-\sum_k \alpha_k f_k(\theta)], \qquad (6.4)$$

it is easy to see that minimizing (6.3) is equivalent to adjusting the
parameters α_k such that the moments $E_\theta f_k(\theta)$ match for both distri-
butions $p(\theta|par)$ and $p(\theta|y_{t+1}, par(t))$. This is also equivalent to finding
the distribution $p(\theta|par)$ which maximizes the entropy under the con-
straints that these moments are given.

Two cases of exponential families have sofar been studied for Bayes on-
line learning: The case of a Gaussian family of distributions for learning of
continuous parameters was discussed in (Opper 1996). A family of product
distributions for binary random variables was chosen by (Winther and Solla
1997) for learning in the Ising perceptron. In the next section I will discuss
the Gaussian case.

7 Gaussian Ansatz

If we use a general multivariate Gaussian distribution for $p(\theta|par)$, then $par = (mean, covariance) = (\hat{\theta}_i, C_{ij})$. Matching the moments results in

$$\hat{\theta}_i(t+1) = \frac{\int d\theta\, \theta_i P(y_{t+1}|\theta)p(\theta|par(t))}{\int d\theta P(y_{t+1}|\theta)p(\theta|par(t))}$$

$$C_{ij}(t+1) = \frac{\int d\theta\, \theta_i\, \theta_j P(y_{t+1}|\theta)p(\theta|par(t))}{\int d\theta P(y_{t+1}|\theta)p(\theta|par(t))} - \hat{\theta}_i(t+1)\hat{\theta}_j(t+1).$$

Using a simple property of centered Gaussian random variables z, viz. the fact that for well behaved functions f, $E(zf(z)) = E(f'(z)) \cdot E(z^2)$, we can get the explicit update:

$$\hat{\theta}(t+1) = \hat{\theta}(t) + \sum_j C_{ij}(t) \times \tag{7.1}$$

$$\times \partial_j \ln E_u[P(y_{t+1}|\hat{\theta}(t) + u)]$$

and

$$C_{ij}(t+1) = C_{ij}(t) + \sum_{kl} C_{ik}(t)C_{lj}(t) \times \tag{7.2}$$

$$\times \partial_k \partial_l \ln E_u[P(y_{t+1}|\hat{\theta}(t) + u)].$$

Here the expectation $\int d\theta P(y_{t+1}|\theta)p(\theta|par(t))$ is written as $E_u[P(y_{t+1}|\hat{\theta}(t) + u)]$ where u is a zero mean Gaussian random vector with covariance $C(t)$. It is interesting that the Bayesian approach combined with the Gaussian approximation to the posterior has led to an update for the posterior mean (which for this approximation equals the MAP value) which looks like a gradient descent with a tensorial learning rate. This learning rate need not to be determined from the outside by some given schedule. In the Bayes approach it is automatically adjusted by the data! For smooth models, the exact Gaussian asymptotics (5.4) of the posterior suggests that the approximation should not be bad when the number of examples grows large. In the next section, we will see that this is actually the case.

8 Asymptotic Performance

In order to study the large time behaviour of the algorithm (7.1), (7.2), we first need the asmptotic form of the covariance matrix C. We define $V_{kl} \doteq \partial_k \partial_l \ln E_u P(y_{t+1}|\theta + u)$ and assume that for large times, the temporal changes of the matrix C are small, so that we can introduce continuous times and replace (7.2) by the matrix differential equation

$$\frac{dC}{dt} = CVC \tag{8.1}$$

which is solved by

$$\frac{dC^{-1}}{dt} = -V.$$

Integrating yields

$$C^{-1}(t) - C^{-1}(t_0) = -\int_{t_0}^{t} V(t')\, dt'. \tag{8.2}$$

To proceed, we will make the assumption that the data are generated independently at random from a distribution $Q(y)$, which we allow to be also outside of the family $P(y|\theta)$, in order to treat the case of a misspecified model. We now assume that the online dynamics is close to an attractive fixed point θ^*, which corresponds to a local minimum of $-\int dy\, Q(y)\ln P(y|\theta)$ and satisfies

$$\int dy\, Q(y)\partial_i \ln P(y|\theta^*) = 0. \tag{8.3}$$

Dividing (8.2) by t and taking the limit $t \to \infty$, we get

$$\lim_{t\to\infty} \frac{(C^{-1}(t))_{ij}}{t} = \lim_{t\to\infty} \frac{-\int_{t_0}^{t}\partial_i\partial_j \ln P(y|\theta^*)}{t} \tag{8.4}$$

$$= -\int dy\, Q(y)\partial_i\partial_j \ln P(y|\theta^*).$$

In the first equality, we have neglected the width the posterior for large times t. In the second equality, the time average has been replaced by the average over $Q(y)$. For this step, it is not necessary to assume that the data are generated independently, ergodicity is sufficient. It is easy to see that for the case $Q(y) = P(y|\theta^*)$, we have

$$\lim_{t\to\infty} \frac{C^{-1}(t)}{t} = J(\theta^*), \tag{8.5}$$

which is the Fisher Information matrix. This result should be compared with the natural gradient (4.4). It shows that asymptotically, the tensorial learning rate obtained from the Bayes online algorithm becomes proportional to the natural gradient if the probabilistic model is correctly specified and if the local fixpoint θ^* is the true parameter. In order to calculate the asymptotic scaling of the estimation error, defined as the deviation between θ^* and the MAP $\hat{\theta}(t)$, we again assume that the MAP estimates are close to θ^* and the posterior is sharply peaked around $\hat{\theta}$. We can then neglect the average over the posterior in (7.1) and linearize. Setting $\hat{\theta}_i(t) = \theta_i^* + \epsilon_i(t)$, we get the linear system

$$\Delta\epsilon_i(t) = \sum_l C_{il}\partial_l \ln P + \sum_{kl} C_{il}\epsilon_k(t)\partial_k\partial_l \ln P, \tag{8.6}$$

where $P \equiv P(y_{t+1}|\theta^*)$. We will introduce the matrices

$$B_{ij} = \int dy\, Q(y)\partial_i \ln P(y|\theta^*)\partial_j \ln P(y|\theta^*) \tag{8.7}$$

$$A_{ij} = -\int dy\, Q(y)\partial_i\partial_j \ln P(y|\theta^*).$$

Taking the expectation (denoted by an overbar) over the distribution of the most recent example y_{t+1} and using (8.4) and (8.7), yields an equation of motion for the expected linear error $e_i = \overline{\epsilon_i}$

$$\frac{de_i}{dt} + \frac{e_i}{t} = \sum_j \frac{(A^{-1})_{ij}}{t} \, \overline{\partial_j \ln P} \tag{8.8}$$

valid for $t \to \infty$. Because of the fixed point condition (8.3), the right hand side vanishes and we conclude that the linear error (the bias) decays like $e_i \propto (1/t)$. More interesting is the dynamics of the matrix of quadratic errors $E_{ij} \doteq E_D[\epsilon_i(t)\epsilon_j(t)]$. We multiply equation (8.6) by $\epsilon_j(t)$ and average over the last example. Neglecting terms like $\epsilon_i C_{jk} \partial_k \ln P$, which decay faster than the others, we obtain

$$\frac{dE}{dt} = CBC - CAE - EAC \tag{8.9}$$
$$= \frac{1}{t^2} A^{-1} B A^{-1} - \frac{2E}{t},$$

which is solved by

$$E_D[\epsilon_i(t)\epsilon_j(t)] = \frac{1}{t} (A^{-1} B A^{-1})_{ij}, \quad t \to \infty. \tag{8.10}$$

This is the same rate as the one which was obtained for batch algorithms (Max. Likelihood or Bayes) by (Amari and Murata 1993). For local minima θ^* of $- \int dy Q(y) \ln P(y|\theta)$, the matrix A (and trivially also B) is positive definite and we should always have the optimal $\propto 1/t$ decay of the error! This is in contrast to fixed learning rate schedules, where the prefactor of the learning rate $\eta \propto 1/t$ must be adjusted in order to allow for convergence. The result (8.10) simplifies further for a wellspecified model. In this case, we can use that $B = A = J(\theta^*)$ such that

$$E_D[\epsilon_i(t)\epsilon_j(t)] = \frac{1}{t} (J^{-1}(\theta^*))_{ij}, \quad t \to \infty.$$

By comparing with (3.3), we see that the Bayes online algorithm becomes asymptotically efficient. The quadratic estimation error has in general no direct interpretation for the ability of a learning device to predict novel data. One can study a more natural measure for the learning performance which is given by the expected relative entropy distance between the predictive distribution constructed from the approximative posterior and the true data generating distribution.

$$\varepsilon_{entro} = E_{D_t} E_y \left[\log \frac{Q(y)}{\hat{P}(y|D_t)} \right]. \tag{8.11}$$

Using an asymptotic expansion as before, we get

$$\varepsilon_{entro} = E_y \left[\log \frac{Q(y)}{P(y|\theta^*)} \right] + \frac{Tr \left(BA^{-1} \right)}{2t} \qquad (8.12)$$

for $t \to \infty$. This result gives the same performance as the one derived for the *batch* maximum likelihood estimate (Seung et al 1992; Amari and Murata 1993). For the well specified case this reduces to the universal asymptotics (Seung et al 1992; Amari and Murata 1993; Opper and Haussler 1995) for Bayes- and maximum likelihood estimators

$$\varepsilon_{entro} = \frac{N}{2t}$$

for $t \to \infty$, which depends only on the number of degrees of freedom.

9 Application

For most models, it will not be easy to perform the Gaussian averages in (7.1) and (7.2) exactly in order to implement the algorithm. Hence, further approximations may be necessary. However, there are a few nontrivial and relevant probabilistic models, where these averages can be performed analytically. The simplest choice is linear models, where for a Gaussian prior also the posterior distribution is a Gaussian and the online approximation becomes exact. A further family of models where we can expect that some of the averages can be performed by hand is the class of mixtures of Gaussians. In the following, we will look at a third case in more detail. This is a model for binary classification which is defined by

$$P(S|\theta, \mathbf{x}) = \phi \left(\frac{S \, \theta \cdot \mathbf{x}}{\sigma_0} \right), \qquad (9.1)$$

where $S = \pm 1$ is a binary class label, θ and $\mathbf{x}$ are N dimensional vectors with inner (dot) product $\theta \cdot \mathbf{x}$ and

$$\phi(z) = \int_{-\infty}^{z} dz \, e^{-t^2/2} / \sqrt{2\pi}$$

is a sigmoidal function. (9.1) may also be related to a perceptron rule with weight noise (Opper and Kinzel 1996). For this case, the Gaussian averages (7.1,7.2) can be carried out explicitly and we obtain

$$E_u P = \phi \left(\frac{S \, \theta \cdot \mathbf{x}}{\sigma(t)} \right) \qquad (9.2)$$

with

$$\sigma^2(t) = \sigma_0^2 + \sum_{ij} x_i C_{ij}(t) x_j.$$

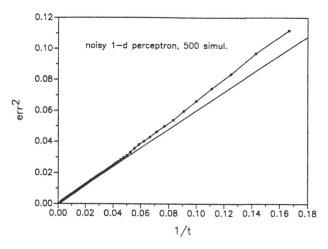

Fig. 1 - Quadratic Error $E_D(\theta - \theta^*)^2$ for a one dimensional noisy perceptron. The straight line gives the bound (3.1).

Explicit updates (7.1,7.2) for the algorithm can be constructed from

$$\partial_j \ln E_u P = \frac{\phi'}{\phi} S x_j / \sigma(t)$$

$$\partial_i \partial_j \ln E_u P = \left\{\frac{\phi''}{\phi} - \left(\frac{\phi'}{\phi}\right)^2\right\} \frac{x_i x_j}{\sigma^2(t)}.$$

To illustrate the performance of the algorithm, we have studied a one dimensional toy model first. In this model, we assume that scalar inputs x with $-1 \leq x \leq +1$ are classified as $S = \pm 1$ according to whether x is greater or less than θ^*. In addition, Gaussian noise is added to θ^*, hence (9.1) is replaced by $P(S|\theta, \mathbf{x}) = \phi(S(x - \theta)/\sigma_0)$. The expected quadratic estimation error $E_D(\theta_t - \theta^*)^2$ as a function of t is shown in Fig.1 for a true parameter $\theta^* = 0.1$ and $\sigma_0 = 0.5$. The asymptotic approach to efficiency (straight line) can be seen.

Next, we consider the full model (9.1). The simulations (dashed line in Fig.2) are performed with $N = 50$ and the vectors θ^* and $\mathbf{x}$ have independent normally distributed components. The results were averaged over 50 samples. As the initial conditions, we have chosen $\theta = 0$ and the true spherical Gaussian prior. The curves show the $(0 - 1)$ generalization error

$$\varepsilon = \frac{1}{\pi} \arccos\left(\frac{\theta^* \cdot \hat{\theta}}{||\theta^*|| \, ||\hat{\theta}||}\right), \tag{9.3}$$

as a function of $\alpha = \frac{t}{N}$. This quantity measures the probability of disagreement between the classifications of a perceptron defined by the weight vector

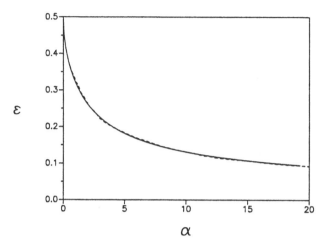

Fig. 2 - Generalization error (9.3) for the classification model (9.1).
The dashed line is obtained from the Bayes algorithm. The solid line
is an analytical result for the batch error in the thermodynamic limit.

$\hat{\theta}$ and the noise free perceptron (setting $\sigma_0 = 0$ for independent test data) defined by θ^*. The data were generated with $\sigma_0 = 6.24$. For comparison, we have
shown the error for the true (batch) Bayes prediction (solid line) analytically
calculated for the thermodynamic limit $N \to \infty$.

The number of parameters to be updated in the online algorithm can
be reduced drastically, if the general covariance matrix C is replaced by a
diagonal matrix or even simpler, by a single number c. This is equivalent to
approximating the posterior by a spherical Gaussian. (7.2) will simplify to

$$c(t+1) = c(t) + c^2(t)\frac{1}{N}\sum_i \partial_i^2 \ln E_u[P(y_{t+1}|\hat{\theta}(t) + u)]. \qquad (9.4)$$

For the model (9.1) it can be shown that this approximation actually leads to
the same update as defined by the locally optimal weighted Hebbian scheme
derived for the thermodynamic limit framework (Biehl et al 1995), provided
that the model is well specified. This agreement will be lost for misspecified
cases.

10   Outlook

One of the greatest challenges for the Bayesian online approach will be the
practical realizability for more complicated models like multilayer neural networks. Here, one has to find additional useful approximations in order to perform the Gaussian averages. For example, one may try a stochastic version

of the algorithm based on Monte Carlo sampling. Mean field methods may also be helpful. Another possibility is to study distance measures different from (6.3) in the projection step. This may lead to a different algorithm for which averages maybe obtained easier. From a theoretical viewpoint, better, nonasymptotic estimates of the performance of the Bayes online algorithm are highly desirable. Such results are necessary to understand the global convergence properties. A further interesting question is the performance of the algorithm for nonsmooth models, like the noisefree perceptron. For this case even the asymptotics is unknown.

References

Amari, S. (1985) Differential-Geometrical Methods in Statistics. *Lecture Notes in Statistics*, Springer Verlag New York

Amari, S. (1993). A universal theorem on learning curves. *Neural Networks*, 6, 161–166.

Amari, S. and Murata, N. (1993). Statistical theory of learning curves under entropic loss criterion. *Neural Computation*, 5, 140–153.

Amari, S. (1996) *Neural learning in structured parameter spaces — Natural Riemannian gradient* in *NIPS'96*, vol. 9, MIT Press.

Amari, S. (1997) *preprint*

Barkai, N., Seung H.S. and Sompolinsky, H. (1995). Local and global convergence of online learning. *Phys. Rev. Lett.*, 75, 1415–1418.

Berger, J.O. (1985) *Statistical Decision theory and Bayesian Analysis* Springer-Verlag New York

Biehl, M. and Riegler, P. (1994). Online Learning with perceptron. *Europhys. Lett.*, 28, 525–530.

Biehl, M., Riegler, P. and Stechert, M. (1995). Learning from noisy data: exactly solvable model. *Phys. Rev E*, 52, R4624–R4627.

Copelli, M. and Caticha, N. (1995). Online learning in the committee machine. *J. Phys. A*, 28, 1615–1625.

Kinouchi, O. and Caticha, N. (1992). Optimal generalization in perceptrons. *J. Phys. A*, 25, 6243–6250.

Kim, J. W. and Sompolinsky, H. (1996). Online gibbs learning. *Phys. Rev. Lett.*, 76, 3021–3024.

LeCam, L. M. (1953) *Univ. of California Publications in Statistics*, 1, 277.

Opper, M. (1996). Online versus off-line learning from examples: general results. *Phys. Rev. Lett.*, 77, 4671–4674.

Opper, M. and Haussler, D. (1995). Bounds for predictive errors in the statistical mechanics of supervised learning *Phys. Rev. Lett.*, 75, 3772–3775.

Opper, M. and Kinzel, W. (1996). *Statistical Mechanics of Generalization* in *Physics of Neural Networks*, ed. by J. L. van Hemmen, E. Domany and K. Schulten (Springer Verlag, Berlin)

Saad, D. and Rattray, M. (1997). Globally optimal parameters for online learning in multilayer neural networks. *Phys. Rev. Lett.*, 79, 2578–2581.

Seung, H., Sompolinsky, H. and Tishby, N. (1992). Statistical mechanics of learning from examples. *Physical Review A*, 45, 6056–6091.

Schervish, M.J. (1995). *Theory of Statistics* Springer -Verlag New York

Van den Broeck, C. and Reimann, P. (1996). Unsupervised learning by examples: online versus offline. *Phys. Rev. Lett.*, 76, 2188–2191.

Vapnik, V. (1982). *Estimation of dependecies based on emprical data* Springer-Verlag New York

Winther, O. and Solla, S.A. (1997) *Optimal Bayesian online learning*; Proceedings of the Honkong Int. Workshop on Theor. Aspects of Neural Comp (TANC97)

Optimal Perceptron Learning: an Online Bayesian Approach

Sara A. Solla[1,2,3] and Ole Winther[3,4]

[1]Physics and Astronomy, Northwestern University, Evanston, IL 60208, USA
[2]Physiology, Northwestern University Medical School, Chicago, IL 60611, USA
solla@nwu.edu
[3]CONNECT, The Niels Bohr Institute, 2100 Copenhagen Ø, Denmark
[4]Theoretical Physics II, Lund University, S-223 62 Lund, Sweden
winther@thep.lu.se

Abstract

The recently proposed Bayesian approach to online learning is applied to learning a rule defined as a noisy single layer perceptron with either continuous or binary weights. In the Bayesian online approach the exact posterior distribution is approximated by a simpler parametric posterior that is updated online as new examples are incorporated to the dataset. In the case of continuous weights, the approximate posterior is chosen to be Gaussian. The computational complexity of the resulting online algorithm is found to be at least as high as that of the Bayesian offline approach, making the online approach less attractive. A Hebbian approximation based on casting the full covariance matrix into an isotropic diagonal form significantly reduces the computational complexity and yields a previously identified optimal Hebbian algorithm. In the case of binary weights, the approximate posterior is chosen to be a biased binary distribution. The resulting online algorithm is derived and shown to outperform several other online approaches to this problem.

1 Introduction

Neural networks are adaptive systems characterized by a set of parameters $\mathbf{w}$, the weights and biases that specify the connectivity among the *neuronal* computational elements. Of particular interest is the ability of these systems to learn from examples. Traditional formulations of the learning problem are based on a dynamical prescription for the adaptation of the parameters $\mathbf{w}$. The learning process thus generates a trajectory in $\mathbf{w}$ space that starts from a random initial assignment $\mathbf{w}^0$ and leads to a specific $\mathbf{w}^*$ that is in some sense *optimal*.

Two learning modalities need to be distinguished: *offline* and *online*. In offline or batch learning, all examples in the training set are used at every time step to update the current values of the network parameters $\mathbf{w}$. In online learning, the parameters are updated after the presentation of each example. Algorithmic approaches that result in specific values $\mathbf{w}^*$ for the network parameters are to be contrasted to a probabilistic Bayesian formulation based on the information provided by a probability distribution over the parameter space $\mathbf{w}$. In the Bayesian approach, the learning process is described by the evolution of a prior distribution $p(\mathbf{w})$ into a posterior that incorporates the information provided by data given in the form of training examples.

The posterior, constructed as the appropriately normalized product of the prior and the likelihood of the data, quantifies the a posteriori belief in each possible setting of the parameters $\mathbf{w}$, and it plays a crucial role in the prediction of new data. The Bayesian prediction probability is computed through a weighted average over the parameter space $\mathbf{w}$, and it is the posterior that assigns a weight to every possible parameter setting. Predictions based on this approach are optimal in the sense of yielding the minimal average prediction error; the average is to be taken over all possible data sources within the family defined by the prior. The optimality of Bayesian predictors thus holds under the assumption that the prior beliefs are correct.

The procedure is intrinsically *offline*, as the computation of the posterior requires knowledge of the entire training set. A controlled approximation that leads to an online implementation of Bayesian learning has been recently proposed (Opper 1996, Winther & Solla 1998), and some of its implications are explored here. In Bayesian *online* learning, the true posterior is approximated by a simpler parametric distribution; the parameters that characterize the approximate posterior are updated online. The goal is to speed up the process by replacing averages over complicated posterior distributions by averages over simpler approximate forms. For the procedure to be meaningful, the approximate posterior needs to capture the essential features of the true posterior.

The Bayesian approach to online learning investigated here is to be contrasted to other approaches to online learning that have received considerable recent attention within the statistical physics community. These alternative procedures emphasize the dynamical adaptation of the parameters $\mathbf{w}$. One approach is based on Hebbian learning rules, for which the update vector $\Delta \mathbf{w}$ at every time step is in the direction of the input vector of the corresponding example. A modulation function that controls the instantaneous amplitude of the adaptation step is determined so as to maximize the decrease of the generalization error, either locally for the current example (Kinouchi & Caticha 1992) or globally for a set of examples presented during a specified time interval Δt (Saad & Rattray 1997). Such methods require some degree of information about the generalization error; the Bayesian approach is more fundamental in that it makes no demands on the availability of such information.

A Bayesian algorithm only requires the specification of a prior; the algorithm then guarantees the optimal use of such a priori information. Unfortunately, the intrinsic complexity of the averaging steps involved in Bayesian learning often render such calculations intractable. Here we focus on a simple learning scenario, that of the perceptron, for which the necessary averages can be performed analytically in the limit of large system size. Our results show that the tensorial update rule that emerges naturally from the Bayesian approach outperforms the so-called optimal Hebbian rule. A Hebbian approximation to the full Bayesian update rule for the perceptron does reproduce the previously obtained optimal Hebbian algorithm (Kinouchi & Caticha 1992). Such Hebbian approximations might be necessary if the computational complexity of online Bayesian learning is to be kept noticeable smaller than that of its traditional offline version.

A clear demonstration of the generic power of the Bayesian online approach is still to come, as it requires an extension to the case of complex learning scenarios involving multilayer networks. We are currently working on the case of two layer networks, which becomes analytically tractable in the limit of a large number of hidden units. Such results need to be obtained and compared to those available for such two layer architectures when trained by simple gradient descent (Saad & Solla 1995) as well as its optimized local (Vicente & Caticha 1997) or global (Saad & Rattray 1997) versions.

The chapter is organized as follows. Section 2 contains a review of the basic principles of Bayesian inference. Section 3 develops an online implementation of Bayesian learning. The approach is applied in section 4 to the problem of learning a noisy simple perceptron with continuous weights via a Gaussian approximation to the posterior distribution. The performance, computational complexity, and storage requirements of this online Bayesian approach are compared to those for the Hebb approximation and the mean field approach to offline Bayesian learning. A biased binary distribution is proposed in section 5 as an approximate posterior for the problem of learning a noisy simple perceptron with binary weights. Update rules are obtained, and the resulting algorithm is compared to a variety of other approaches to this problem. The chapter concludes with a discussion of current and future work in section 6.

2   Bayesian Learning

Bayesian inference provides a framework for formulating the problem of learning from examples in purely probabilistic terms. Here we briefly review this formulation for the case of classification problems, for which each example consists of an input vector $\mathbf{s}$ and an associated classification label τ. A training set of size t is denoted by $D_t = \{(\tau^\mu, \mathbf{s}^\mu), 1 \leq \mu \leq t\}$. Training examples are assumed to be independently drawn from a distribution $p((\tau, \mathbf{s})|\mathbf{w})$, where

w is the unknown parameter vector, to be estimated from the data D_t. The inference procedure consists of two steps.

The first step is to assign a probability or *likelihood* to the training examples. The statistical independence of the individual examples results in a multiplicative form for the likelihood of the training set,

$$p(D_t|\mathbf{w}) = \prod_\mu p((\tau^\mu, \mathbf{s}^\mu)|\mathbf{w}) \ . \tag{2.1}$$

We write $p((\tau, \mathbf{s})|\mathbf{w}) = p(\tau|\mathbf{w}, \mathbf{s})p(\mathbf{s})$, where $p(\tau|\mathbf{w}, \mathbf{s})$ models the input-output relation, while the input distribution $p(\mathbf{s})$ is independent of **w**.

The second step in Bayesian inference is to assign a prior probability $p(\mathbf{w})$ to the unknown parameters **w**. The *true values* of the parameters, i.e. the ones actually used in the generation of the data, are assumed to have nonzero prior probability. It is in this sense that the analysis is restricted to the case of *realizable* learning scenarios.

Here we focus our analysis on the case of a simple perceptron, for which classification labels $\tau = \pm 1$ are generated through $\tau = f(\mathbf{w}, \mathbf{s}) = \text{sign}(\mathbf{w} \cdot \mathbf{s})$. Both **w** and **s** are N-dimensional vectors with components $\{w_i, 1 \leq i \leq N\}$ and $\{s_i, 1 \leq i \leq N\}$, respectively. Noise is introduced through a label flip with probability κ. The likelihood of output τ is thus given by

$$
\begin{aligned}
p(\tau|\mathbf{w}, \mathbf{s}) &= \kappa \ \Theta(-\tau f(\mathbf{w}, \mathbf{s})) + (1 - \kappa) \ \Theta(\tau f(\mathbf{w}, \mathbf{s})) \\
&= \kappa + (1 - 2\kappa) \ \Theta(\tau \ \mathbf{w} \cdot \mathbf{s}) \ ,
\end{aligned} \tag{2.2}
$$

where $\Theta()$ is the step-function, $\Theta(x) = 1$ for $x > 0$ and $\Theta(x) = 0$ otherwise.

We consider two possible priors: a spherical Gaussian

$$p(\mathbf{w}) = \frac{1}{(2\pi)^{N/2}} \exp\left(-\frac{\mathbf{w} \cdot \mathbf{w}}{2}\right) \tag{2.3}$$

and a binary distribution

$$p(\mathbf{w}) = \prod_i \left[\frac{1}{2} \delta(w_i - 1) + \frac{1}{2} \delta(w_i + 1)\right] \ . \tag{2.4}$$

These prior distributions represent prior knowledge, as opposed to knowledge coming from the training data.

Bayes rule provides a prescription for writing the posterior distribution $p(\mathbf{w}|D_t)$ in terms of the prior and the likelihood of the training set:

$$p(\mathbf{w}|D_t) = \frac{\prod_\mu p(\tau^\mu|\mathbf{w}, \mathbf{s}^\mu) \ p(\mathbf{w})}{\int d\mathbf{w} \ \prod_\mu p(\tau^\mu|\mathbf{w}, \mathbf{s}^\mu) \ p(\mathbf{w})} \ . \tag{2.5}$$

The posterior distribution quantifies our knowledge about **w** after the observation of the training data D_t.

The posterior distribution is used to compute the *predictive probability* for each possible output $\tau = \pm 1$ given a new input $\mathbf{s}$:

$$p(\tau|\mathbf{s}, D_t) = \int d\mathbf{w}\, p(\tau|\mathbf{w}, \mathbf{s})\, p(\mathbf{w}|D_t) \ . \tag{2.6}$$

Predictions based on the Bayes algorithm are guaranteed to minimize the average prediction error through the choice of output label τ which maximizes the above prediction probability for a given input $\mathbf{s}$. For the type of classification problem considered here, the Bayes prediction is given by

$$\tau^{\text{Bayes}}(\mathbf{s}, D_t) = \text{sign}\left(\int d\mathbf{w}\, p(\mathbf{w}|D_t)\, \text{sign}\left(\mathbf{w} \cdot \mathbf{s}\right)\right) \ . \tag{2.7}$$

The process discussed in this section is intrinsically offline, as information on the full data set D_t is needed to compute the posterior distribution that controls the average in Eq. (2.7).

3 Online Bayesian Learning

The problem we now face is that of adapting the Bayesian approach summarized in the preceding section so as to obtain an online version. Learning methods based on incorporating all information provided by the data into the current values of the network parameters $\mathbf{w}$ are easily adapted onto online versions: it suffices to use the information provided by a new example to update the current values of the network parameters. In a Bayesian formulation the information provided by the data is incorporated into a distribution over $\mathbf{w}$ space, and it is this distribution that needs to be updated in an online manner when a new example becomes available.

An online Bayesian learning algorithm requires a prescription for an online update of the posterior distribution. To achieve this goal, the exact posterior $p(\mathbf{w}|D_t)$ of Eq. (2.5) is approximated by a simple parametric distribution $p(\mathbf{w}|A_t)$, where A_t refers to the current values of a set of parameters A which characterize the distribution (e.g. the first two moments of $\mathbf{w}$ for a Gaussian $p(\mathbf{w}|A)$). The online Bayesian procedure refers to the update of the distribution parameters A as opposed to the network parameters $\mathbf{w}$.

The online Bayesian algorithm becomes computationally advantageous over its offline version, Eq. (2.5), to the extent that the set A contains a small number of parameters, so that A_t can be interpreted as providing a compact encoding of the information contained in the training set D_t. A tension arises between the need for a complex parametrization to provide a reliable approximation to the true posterior of Eq. (2.5), and a simple parametrization to gain computational speed.

The resulting online Bayesian procedure consists of two steps:

1. **Add an example** – the current posterior is updated exactly according to Bayes rule:

$$p(\mathbf{w}|\mathbf{A}_t,(\tau^{t+1},\mathbf{s}^{t+1})) = \frac{p(\tau^{t+1}|\mathbf{w},\mathbf{s}^{t+1})\,p(\mathbf{w}|\mathbf{A}_t)}{\int d\mathbf{w}\,p(\tau^{t+1}|\mathbf{w},\mathbf{s}^{t+1})\,p(\mathbf{w}|\mathbf{A}_t)} . \qquad (3.1)$$

2. **Approximate** – the updated posterior is parametrized:

$$p(\mathbf{w}|\mathbf{A}_t,(\tau^{t+1},\mathbf{s}^{t+1})) \rightarrow p(\mathbf{w}|\mathbf{A}_{t+1}) . \qquad (3.2)$$

Some of the information provided by the new example $(\tau^{t+1},\mathbf{s}^{t+1})$ is discarded in the parametrization step. The parametrization is constructed so as to minimize the resulting information loss. As discussed by Opper in this volume, there is no unique way of measuring this loss; but once a metric is chosen it is possible to quantify the dissimilarity between the exact updated posterior and any proposed approximation to it. It is thus possible to select the best among several possible parametrizations.

We chose to quantify the information loss through the *relative entropy* or *Kullback-Leibler distance* between the two probability distributions:

$$D\left[p(\mathbf{w}|\mathbf{A}_t,(\tau^{t+1},\mathbf{s}^{t+1}))||p(\mathbf{w}|\mathbf{A}_{t+1})\right]$$

$$= \int d\mathbf{w}\; p(\mathbf{w}|\mathbf{A}_t,(\tau^{t+1},\mathbf{s}^{t+1}))\; \ln\frac{p(\mathbf{w}|\mathbf{A}_t,(\tau^{t+1},\mathbf{s}^{t+1}))}{p(\mathbf{w}|\mathbf{A}_{t+1})} . \qquad (3.3)$$

For a Gaussian approximate posterior distribution, the minimization of the information loss is achieved by choosing $\mathbf{A}_{t+1}$ such that $p(\mathbf{w}|\mathbf{A}_t,(\tau^{t+1},\mathbf{s}^{t+1}))$ and $p(\mathbf{w}|\mathbf{A}_{t+1})$ have the same first two moments (see also Opper, this volume).

To make the approximation consistent it is necessary that the initial distribution $p(\mathbf{w}|\mathbf{A}_0)$ does not exclude any of the values of $\mathbf{w}$ for which $p(\mathbf{w})$ is non-zero. The natural choice $p(\mathbf{w}|\mathbf{A}_0) = p(\mathbf{w})$ fulfills this condition. The iterative process of adding examples and approximating the posterior is illustrated in figure 1. In the space of all possible distributions $p(\mathbf{w})$, the plane represents the manifold of distributions parametrized through $p(\mathbf{w}|\mathbf{A})$. At every time t the approximate posterior $p(\mathbf{w}|\mathbf{A}_t)$ is in this manifold, but the update rule that incorporates the information provided by the new example $(\tau^{t+1},\mathbf{s}^{t+1})$ takes the distribution away from the parametric manifold. The approximation step involves a projection back onto the parametric manifold; the projection is controlled by a metric provided by the Kullback-Leibler distance.

In the rest of this article we present two simple applications of the Bayesian online approach to the problem of learning a rule defined by a simple perceptron with output flip noise, for which the likelihood is given by Eq. (2.2). We show that different choices of prior $p(\mathbf{w})$ result in quite different algorithms with different average behavior.

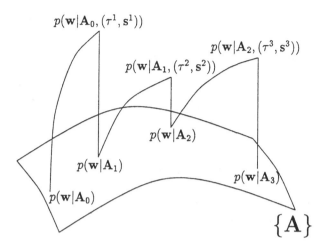

Figure 1. The update of the approximate posterior.

In section 4 we study the case of a Gaussian prior (see Eq. (2.3)) and choose a Gaussian approximation for the posterior. In section 5 the prior is binary (see Eq. (2.4)) and the approximate posterior is chosen to be a biased binary distribution.

4   Gaussian Approximate Posterior

The minimization of the Kullback-Leibler distance of Eq. (3.3) is achieved in the case of a Gaussian approximation to the posterior via the matching of the first two moments of the updated posterior distribution $p(\mathbf{w}|\mathbf{A}_t, (\tau^{t+1}, \mathbf{s}^{t+1}))$, Eq. (3.1). The update rules can be derived through the use of partial integration (Opper 1996) to obtain:

$$\widetilde{\langle w_i \rangle} = \langle w_i \rangle + \sum_j C_{ij} \frac{\partial}{\partial \langle w_j \rangle} \ln \langle p(\tau|\mathbf{w}, \mathbf{s}) \rangle \qquad (4.1)$$

$$\widetilde{C_{ij}} = C_{ij} + \sum_{kl} C_{il} C_{kj} \frac{\partial^2}{\partial \langle w_k \rangle \langle w_l \rangle} \ln \langle p(\tau|\mathbf{w}, \mathbf{s}) \rangle \qquad (4.2)$$

for the update of the components $\langle w_i \rangle$ of the average weight vector and the elements $C_{ij} = \langle w_i w_j \rangle - \langle w_i \rangle \langle w_j \rangle$ of the covariance matrix. The following conventions have been adopted to simplify notation: superscripts are omitted when referring to the new example, so that $(\tau, \mathbf{s})$ refers to $(\tau^{t+1}, \mathbf{s}^{t+1})$; averages $\langle \ldots \rangle$ are taken with respect to the approximate posterior $p(\mathbf{w}|\mathbf{A}_t)$ at time t; averages $\widetilde{\langle \ldots \rangle}$ are taken with respect to the approximate posterior $p(\mathbf{w}|\mathbf{A}_{t+1})$ at time $t + 1$.

Note that $p(\tau|\mathbf{s}, \mathbf{A}_t) = \langle p(\tau|\mathbf{w}, \mathbf{s})\rangle = \int d\mathbf{w}\, p(\tau|\mathbf{w}, \mathbf{s})\, p(\mathbf{w}|\mathbf{A}_t)$ is the online approximation to the predictive probability, Eq. (2.6).

The above update equations allow for a compact rewrite when applied to the simple perceptron, for which $p(\tau|\mathbf{w}, \mathbf{s})$ of Eq. (2.2) depends on $\mathbf{w}$ only through the scalar field $h = \frac{1}{\sqrt{N}}\mathbf{w} \cdot \mathbf{s}$. Then $p(\tau|\mathbf{w}, \mathbf{s}) = p(\tau|h)$, and $\langle p(\tau|\mathbf{w}, \mathbf{s})\rangle = \int d\mathbf{w}\, p(\mathbf{w}|\mathbf{A}_t)\, p(\tau|\mathbf{w}, \mathbf{s}) = \int dh\, p(h|\mathbf{s}, \mathbf{A}_t)\, p(\tau|h)$, with $p(h|\mathbf{s}, \mathbf{A}_t) = \int d\mathbf{w}\, \delta(h - \frac{1}{\sqrt{N}}\mathbf{w} \cdot \mathbf{s})\, p(\mathbf{w}|\mathbf{A}_t)$. Because the distribution $p(\mathbf{w}|\mathbf{A}_t)$ is chosen to be Gaussian, $p(h|\mathbf{s}, \mathbf{A}_t)$ is also Gaussian,

$$p(h|\mathbf{s}, \mathbf{A}_t) = \frac{1}{\sqrt{2\pi\lambda}} \exp\left(-\frac{(h - \langle h\rangle)^2}{2\lambda}\right), \qquad (4.3)$$

with mean $\langle h\rangle = \frac{1}{\sqrt{N}}\langle \mathbf{w}\rangle \cdot \mathbf{s}$ and variance $\lambda = \frac{1}{N}\mathbf{s}^T \mathbf{C}\mathbf{s}$.

We use the chain rule $\frac{\partial f(\langle h\rangle)}{\partial \langle \mathbf{w}\rangle} = \frac{1}{\sqrt{N}}\mathbf{s}\frac{\partial f(\langle h\rangle)}{\partial \langle h\rangle}$ to obtain

$$\widetilde{\langle \mathbf{w}\rangle} = \langle \mathbf{w}\rangle + \frac{1}{\sqrt{N}}\mathbf{C}\frac{\partial}{\partial \langle h\rangle}\ln\langle p(\tau|h)\rangle \qquad (4.4)$$

$$\tilde{\mathbf{C}} = \mathbf{C} + \frac{1}{N}\mathbf{C}\mathbf{s}\,\mathbf{s}^T\mathbf{C}\frac{\partial^2}{\partial \langle h\rangle^2}\ln\langle p(\tau|h)\rangle, \qquad (4.5)$$

for the update rules in matrix notation.

The predictive probability $\langle p(\tau|\mathbf{w}, \mathbf{s})\rangle = \langle p(\tau|h)\rangle$ is given by:

$$\langle p(\tau|h)\rangle = \kappa + (1 - 2\kappa)\,\Phi\left(\tau\frac{\langle h\rangle}{\sqrt{\lambda}}\right), \qquad (4.6)$$

where

$$\Phi(x) = \int_{-\infty}^{x}\frac{dt}{\sqrt{2\pi}}e^{-(1/2)t^2}$$

is a sigmoidal error function. The Bayesian predictor of Eq. (2.7) for a new input $\mathbf{s}$ is given by

$$\tau^{\text{Bayes}}(\mathbf{s}, \mathbf{A}_t) = \text{sign}(\langle \mathbf{w}\rangle \cdot \mathbf{s}) \qquad (4.7)$$

for the Gaussian approximate posterior considered here.

We have thus obtained a Bayesian online algorithm for learning a perceptron rule with output noise; the corresponding Bayes predictor depends only upon the posterior mean of the weights.

It is relevant to analyze the computational complexity of the algorithm defined by Eqs. (4.4) and (4.5), and investigate how it scales with the number of input variables N and the number t of presented examples. The most computationally expensive operations for a given example $\mathbf{s}$ are those required to obtain $\mathbf{C}\mathbf{s}$, $\mathbf{s}\mathbf{s}^T$, and $\mathbf{s}^T\mathbf{C}\mathbf{s}$; all these operations are of order $\mathcal{O}(N^2)$. As expected, the update of all components of an $N \times N$ covariance matrix takes $\mathcal{O}(N^2)$ operations. The total computational cost is thus $\mathcal{O}(N^2 t)$. The computational cost and performance of this algorithm will next be compared to those of the corresponding offline Bayesian algorithm and a further Hebbian approximation to the online Bayesian algorithm discussed above.

Hebbian approximation to the online Bayesian algorithm

A Hebbian approximation to the full online Bayesian algorithm defined by Eqs. (4.4) and (4.5) follows from replacing the update factor $\mathbf{Cs}$ by its projection along the direction of the new input $\mathbf{s}$:

$$\mathbf{Cs} \rightarrow \mathbf{s} \frac{\mathbf{s}^T \mathbf{Cs}}{\mathbf{s} \cdot \mathbf{s}} \ .$$

The resulting update rules are those of a Hebbian algorithm with adaptable step size.

The average behavior of this algorithm can be easily analyzed in the thermodynamic limit $N \rightarrow \infty$ for spherical input distributions satisfying $\overline{s_i} = 0$ and $\overline{s_i s_j} = \delta_{ij}$ (where overline denotes an average over the input distribution). For spherical inputs in thermodynamic limit, the central limit theorem can be invoked to argue that the scalar $\mathbf{s}^T \mathbf{Cs}$ will be self averaging and can be replaced by $\overline{\mathbf{s}^T \mathbf{Cs}} = \langle \mathbf{w} \cdot \mathbf{w} \rangle - \langle \mathbf{w} \rangle \cdot \langle \mathbf{w} \rangle$, where averages are taken over the distribution for a new input $\mathbf{s}$ uncorrelated with the current $\mathbf{C}$ matrix. The update rules no longer require the computation of the full covariance matrix $\mathbf{C}$; it suffices to compute its trace ($\langle \mathbf{w} \cdot \mathbf{w} \rangle - \langle \mathbf{w} \rangle \cdot \langle \mathbf{w} \rangle$). The computational complexity of this version of the algorithm is thus reduced to $\mathcal{O}(Nt)$.

It is of interest to note that this algorithm turns out to be equivalent to an optimal Hebb algorithm of the form $\tilde{\mathbf{w}} = \mathbf{w} + F\mathbf{s}$, where F is a scalar modulation function chosen so as to locally maximize the decrease of the generalization error for each example (Kinouchi & Caticha 1992). We shall show that the performance of this optimal Hebbian algorithm is inferior to that of the full Bayesian online algorithm presented before.

Bayesian offline algorithm

Mean field equations for the Bayesian offline scenario have been derived for a simple perceptron (Opper & Winther 1996). These equations are expected to be valid in the thermodynamic limit, and they reduce to the form

$$\langle \mathbf{w} \rangle = \frac{1}{\sqrt{N}} \sum_{\mu} \mathbf{s}^{\mu} \langle x^{\mu} \rangle \tag{4.8}$$

$$\langle x^{\mu} \rangle = \frac{\partial}{\partial \langle h^{\mu} \rangle_{\mu}} \ln \langle p(\tau^{\mu} | h^{\mu}) \rangle_{\mu} \tag{4.9}$$

for spherical inputs. The sum in Eq. (4.8) is over training examples μ, and $\langle \ldots \rangle_{\mu}$ in Eq. (4.9) refers to an average over a posterior distribution for which the μth example has been excluded; the corresponding training set is denoted as: $D_t \backslash (\tau^{\mu}, \mathbf{s}^{\mu})$.

Consider the distribution of the *cavity field* h^{μ}:

$$p(h^{\mu} | \mathbf{s}^{\mu}, D_t \backslash (\tau^{\mu}, \mathbf{s}^{\mu})) = \int d\mathbf{w} \, \delta(h^{\mu} - \frac{1}{\sqrt{N}} \mathbf{w} \cdot \mathbf{s}^{\mu}) \, p(\mathbf{w} | D_t \backslash (\tau^{\mu}, \mathbf{s}^{\mu})) \ .$$

The mean field approximation rests on the assumption that this distribution is Gaussian in the thermodynamic limit:

$$p(h^\mu | \mathbf{s}^\mu, D_t \backslash (\tau^\mu, \mathbf{s}^\mu)) = \frac{1}{\sqrt{2\pi\lambda}} \exp\left(-\frac{(h^\mu - \langle h^\mu \rangle_\mu)^2}{2\lambda}\right) , \qquad (4.10)$$

with $\lambda = \frac{1}{N}(\langle \mathbf{w} \cdot \mathbf{w} \rangle - \langle \mathbf{w} \rangle \cdot \langle \mathbf{w} \rangle)$ for uncorrelated input data. The mean $\langle h^\mu \rangle_\mu$ of the cavity field is related to the full posterior mean field $\langle h^\mu \rangle = \frac{1}{\sqrt{N}} \langle \mathbf{w} \rangle \cdot \mathbf{s}^\mu$, the *aligning field*, through

$$\langle h^\mu \rangle_\mu = \langle h^\mu \rangle - \lambda \langle x^\mu \rangle. \qquad (4.11)$$

There are obvious similarities and differences between the online and offline approaches. The average $\langle p(\tau|h) \rangle$ in the online update Eqs. (4.4) and (4.5) is an average over a cavity field. In the offline approach, the Gaussianity of the cavity field follows from the central limit theorem. The mean field approximation is therefore expected to become exact in the thermodynamic limit. In online learning, the Gaussianity is a consequence of the choice of a Gaussian form for the approximate posterior. Note the similarity between Eq. (4.3) and Eq. (4.10); the correction (4.11) to the mean in Eq. (4.10) arises because in offline learning the posterior average is over all examples in the training set, whereas in online learning the example is discarded once it has been used to update the posterior. In online learning it is necessary to keep track of the covariance matrix because the inputs are discarded, whereas in offline learning the mean weight in Eq. (4.8) is spanned by the input vectors. This distinction has an important consequence for the computational complexity of the algorithm.

The set of non-linear mean field equations is usually solved by iteration. If we denote by $\hat{N}$ the number of iterations needed to obtain solutions with a desired degree of accuracy, the computational complexity of the algorithm scales like $\mathcal{O}(\hat{N}Nt)$. We expect $\hat{N}$ to scale at most with N. The full Bayesian online algorithm will thus have at least the same computational complexity as the Bayesian offline algorithm.

Performance comparison

We now compare the performance of the three algorithms discussed in this section. Performance is measured through a computation of the generalization error, defined as the probability that the Bayes predictor $\tau^{\text{Bayes}}(\mathbf{s}, \mathbf{A}_t)$ of Eq. (4.7) disagrees with a teacher defined as a noisy simple perceptron with weight vector $\mathbf{v}$ and output $\tau = \eta \, \text{sign}(\mathbf{v} \cdot \mathbf{s})$, where $\eta = -1$ with probability κ, and $\eta = 1$ otherwise.

The generalization error is given by

$$\epsilon = \overline{\Theta\left(-\eta \, \text{sign}(\mathbf{v} \cdot \mathbf{s}) \, \tau^{\text{Bayes}}(\mathbf{s}, \mathbf{A}_t)\right)} , \qquad (4.12)$$

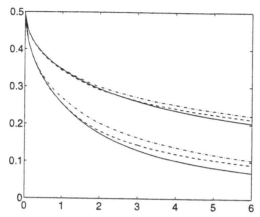

Figure 2. Learning curves (ϵ versus α) for the online and offline algorithms for continuous weights. The three lower curves are for $\kappa = 0$ and the three upper curves are for $\kappa = 0.1$. The dash-dotted lines are for the Hebb approximation to the online algorithm, the dashed lines are for the full online algorithm, and the full lines are the theoretical predictions for the offline Bayes algorithm. Simulations were performed for $N = 100$ and averaged over 100 runs. Error bars are comparable to the line thickness.

where the average is to be taken over the input distribution from which new test examples can be drawn at random. This average is easily performed for a spherical input distribution, and leads to a simple result for the generalization error:

$$\epsilon = \kappa + (1 - 2\kappa)\frac{1}{\pi}\arccos\left(\frac{R}{\sqrt{qT}}\right) , \qquad (4.13)$$

where the *order parameters* q, R, and T are given by overlaps between the two weight vectors involved: $R = \frac{1}{N}\langle\mathbf{w}\rangle \cdot \mathbf{v}$, $q = \frac{1}{N}\langle\mathbf{w}\rangle \cdot \langle\mathbf{w}\rangle$, and $T = \frac{1}{N}\mathbf{v} \cdot \mathbf{v}$. Simulation results for all three algorithm are shown in figure 2; the generalization error ϵ is shown as a function of the normalized number of examples $\alpha = t/N$. No theoretical analysis is available at this time for the online Bayesian algorithm that incorporates full second order information through the update of all entries in the covariance matrix, Eqs. (4.4) and (4.5). The results of theoretical analysis available for the other two algorithms are in complete agreement within the scale of the figure with the numerical results shown in figure 2.

The simulation results for the two online algorithms allow for a performance comparison and show the significant benefit of using the full second order information. We expect this difference to be even larger for general, non-spherical input distributions.

For further comparison, we show in table 1 the asymptotic performance
for $\kappa = 0$, the computational complexity, and the memory requirements for all
three algorithms. Both online algorithms exhibit the same asymptotic performance for the spherical input distributions considered here, as the off-diagonal
elements of the covariance matrix vanish asymptotically in this highly symmetric case. Discrepancies in favor of the full online algorithm are expected
to appear for more general input distributions. The computational complexity results summarized in this table are as previously discussed in the text.
As for memory requirements: the Hebb approximation requires storage of the
current example and the current mean weight vector, both of $\mathcal{O}(N)$, while the
full online algorithm requires the additional storage of the covariance matrix,
of $\mathcal{O}(N^2)$. The offline algorithm requires storage of all training examples, of
$\mathcal{O}(Nt)$, in addition to lower order contributions from the mean weight vector
and auxiliary variables.

Table 1. Comparison of asymptotic performance, computational complexity, and storage requirements for the three algorithms discussed in
this section.

	Online		Offline
	2nd Order	Hebb Approx.	
$\epsilon(\alpha \to \infty)$		$0.88/\alpha$	$0.44/\alpha$
Comp. complexity	$\mathcal{O}(N^2 t)$	$\mathcal{O}(Nt)$	$\mathcal{O}(\hat{N}Nt)$
Memory	$\mathcal{O}(N^2)$	$\mathcal{O}(N)$	$\mathcal{O}(Nt)$

5 Binary Approximate Posterior

For a binary prior of the form (2.4), a reasonable choice for the approximate
posterior is that of a biased binary distribution (Winther & Solla 1998),

$$p(\mathbf{w}|\mathbf{A}_t) = \prod_i \left[\frac{1 + \langle w_i \rangle}{2} \, \delta(w_i - 1) + \frac{1 - \langle w_i \rangle}{2} \, \delta(w_i + 1) \right] . \qquad (5.1)$$

The parameters $\mathbf{A}$ of the approximate distribution are thus the components
of the mean weight vector $\langle \mathbf{w} \rangle$. The Kullback-Leibler distance is minimized by
setting the new values of the parameters to be equal to their mean computed
with the updated posterior $p(\mathbf{w}|\mathbf{A}_t, (\tau, \mathbf{s}))$. The update rule is thus given by

$$\widetilde{\langle \mathbf{w} \rangle} = \sum_{\{w_i = \pm 1\}} \mathbf{w} \, p(\mathbf{w}|\mathbf{A}_t, (\tau, \mathbf{s})) . \qquad (5.2)$$

No closed form for the update rule (5.2) is available for general N, but
progress can be made in the thermodynamic limit by invoking the cavity
method. We now outline the calculation.

An auxiliary field h is introduced through the identity

$$1 = \int dh \, \delta(h - \frac{1}{\sqrt{N}} \mathbf{w} \cdot \mathbf{s}) = \int \frac{dh \, dx}{2\pi i} \, e^{x\left(\frac{1}{\sqrt{N}}\mathbf{w} \cdot \mathbf{s} - h\right)} , \qquad (5.3)$$

where the integral over x is along the imaginary axis. The update Eq. (5.2) can thus be rewritten as

$$\widetilde{\langle \mathbf{w} \rangle} = \frac{\sum_{\mathbf{w}=\pm 1} \int \frac{dh \, dx}{2\pi i} \, \mathbf{w} \, e^{x\left(\frac{1}{\sqrt{N}}\mathbf{w} \cdot \mathbf{s} - h\right)} p(\tau|h) \, p(\mathbf{w}|\mathbf{A}_t)}{\sum_{\mathbf{w}=\pm 1} \int \frac{dh \, dx}{2\pi i} \, e^{x\left(\frac{1}{\sqrt{N}}\mathbf{w} \cdot \mathbf{s} - h\right)} p(\tau|h) \, p(\mathbf{w}|\mathbf{A}_t)} . \qquad (5.4)$$

In order to perform the trace over the weights, it is convenient to introduce a posterior average from which the ith weight component is excluded,

$$\langle \ldots \rangle_i = \frac{\sum_{\mathbf{w}=\pm 1} \int \frac{dh \, dx}{2\pi i} \ldots e^{x\left(\frac{1}{\sqrt{N}}\sum_{j \neq i} w_j s_j - h\right)} p(\tau|h) \, \prod_{j \neq i} p(w_j|\langle w_j \rangle)}{\sum_{\mathbf{w}=\pm 1} \int \frac{dh \, dx}{2\pi i} \, e^{x\left(\frac{1}{\sqrt{N}}\sum_{j \neq i} w_j s_j - h\right)} p(\tau|h) \, \prod_{j \neq i} p(w_j|\langle w_j \rangle)} ,$$

with

$$p(w_i|\langle w_i \rangle) = \frac{1 + \langle w_i \rangle}{2} \, \delta(w_i - 1) + \frac{1 - \langle w_i \rangle}{2} \, \delta(w_i + 1) .$$

The update rule for the ith weight component is then given by

$$\widetilde{\langle w_i \rangle} = \frac{\langle \frac{1 + \langle w_i \rangle}{2} e^{x s_i/\sqrt{N}} - \frac{1 - \langle w_i \rangle}{2} e^{x s_i/\sqrt{N}} \rangle_i}{\langle \frac{1 + \langle w_i \rangle}{2} e^{x s_i/\sqrt{N}} + \frac{1 - \langle w_i \rangle}{2} e^{x s_i/\sqrt{N}} \rangle_i} , \qquad (5.5)$$

which results in

$$\widetilde{\langle w_i \rangle} = \frac{\langle \sinh(\tanh^{-1}\langle w_i \rangle + \frac{1}{\sqrt{N}} s_i \, x) \rangle_i}{\langle \cosh(\tanh^{-1}\langle w_i \rangle + \frac{1}{\sqrt{N}} s_i \, x) \rangle_i} . \qquad (5.6)$$

The expression (5.6) is exact, but a cavity argument needs to be introduced in order to perform the required averages. We assume that in the thermodynamic limit the variable $y_i = \tanh^{-1}\langle w_i \rangle + \frac{1}{\sqrt{N}} s_i \, x$ is Gaussian, with mean $\langle y_i \rangle = \tanh^{-1}\langle w_i \rangle + \frac{1}{\sqrt{N}} s_i \, \langle x \rangle_i$ and variance $\sigma_i^2 = \frac{1}{N} s_i^2(\langle x^2 \rangle_i - \langle x \rangle_i^2)$. The variance becomes self-averaging in the thermodynamic limit, and can be written as

$$\frac{1}{N} s_i^2(\langle x^2 \rangle_i - \langle x \rangle_i^2) \approx \frac{1}{N}(\langle x^2 \rangle_i - \langle x \rangle_i^2)$$

$$\approx \frac{1}{N}(\langle x^2 \rangle - \langle x \rangle^2)$$

for uncorrelated inputs, $\overline{s_i s_j} = \delta_{ij}$. The averages in Eq. (5.6) can now be performed, to obtain

$$\widetilde{\langle w_i \rangle} = \tanh\left(\tanh^{-1}\langle w_i \rangle + \frac{1}{\sqrt{N}} s_i \langle x \rangle_i\right) . \qquad (5.7)$$

In order to complete the calculation we need to evaluate the mean value of the auxiliary variable x; note that the required average is not $\langle x \rangle$ but $\langle x \rangle_i$, to indicate that the average is to be performed over a posterior that excludes the ith weight component. The calculation of $\langle x \rangle_i$ involves two steps: a calculation of $\langle x \rangle$ followed by a cavity argument that relates $\langle x \rangle$ to $\langle x \rangle_i$.

The average $\langle x \rangle$ is given by a logarithmic derivative,

$$\langle x \rangle = \left. \frac{\partial \ln Z(u)}{\partial u} \right|_{u=0} ,$$

where we have introduced a partition function

$$Z(u) = \sum_{\mathbf{w}=\pm 1} \int \frac{dh\,dx}{2\pi i} \, e^{x\left(u + \frac{1}{\sqrt{N}} \mathbf{w} \cdot \mathbf{s} - h\right)} p(\tau | h) \, p(\mathbf{w} | \mathbf{A}_t) . \tag{5.8}$$

Note that the external field u couples to x. Integrals over both x and h can be performed to obtain

$$Z(u) = \sum_{\mathbf{w}=\pm 1} p(\tau | h + u) \, p(\mathbf{w} | \mathbf{A}_t) , \tag{5.9}$$

where h now stands for $\frac{1}{\sqrt{N}} \mathbf{w} \cdot \mathbf{s}$ and is no longer a variable. The quantity $Z(u)$ can be identified as an online approximation to the predictive probability $\langle p(\tau | h + u) \rangle$, with $\langle p(\tau | h) \rangle$ given by Eq. (4.6). This identification leads to

$$\langle x \rangle = \left. \frac{\partial}{\partial u} \ln \langle p(\tau | h + u) \rangle \right|_{u=0} = \frac{\partial}{\partial \langle h \rangle} \ln \langle p(\tau | h) \rangle . \tag{5.10}$$

The second moment of x follows from the linear response theorem:

$$\langle x^2 \rangle - \langle x \rangle^2 = \frac{\partial \langle x \rangle}{\partial \langle h \rangle} .$$

The last step is to relate $\langle x \rangle$ and $\langle x \rangle_i$. We invoke a Gaussian assumption for the distribution of $\frac{1}{\sqrt{N}} x s_i$ and use the exact relation

$$\langle \ldots \rangle = \frac{\langle \sum_{w_i = \pm 1} \ldots p(w_i | \langle w_i \rangle) \, e^{\frac{1}{\sqrt{N}} x s_i} \rangle_i}{\langle \sum_{w_i = \pm 1} p(w_i | \langle w_i \rangle) \, e^{\frac{1}{\sqrt{N}} x s_i} \rangle_i}$$

to obtain

$$\langle x \rangle_i = \langle x \rangle - \frac{1}{\sqrt{N}} \widetilde{\langle w_i \rangle} \, s_i \, \frac{\partial \langle x \rangle}{\partial \langle h \rangle} . \tag{5.11}$$

The Bayesian learning algorithm for a simple perceptron with binary weights obtained above is expected to be exact in the thermodynamic limit. One further approximation is needed for the algorithm to be truly online, since $\langle x \rangle_i$ as given in Eq. (5.11) to be substituted into Eq. (5.7) for $\widetilde{\langle w_i \rangle}$ does itself depend on $\widetilde{\langle w_i \rangle}$. The approximation is to replace $\widetilde{\langle w_i \rangle}$ by $\langle w_i \rangle$ in the right-hand side of Eq. (5.11). Since the difference between $\langle w_i \rangle$ and $\widetilde{\langle w_i \rangle}$ is $\mathcal{O}(1/\sqrt{N})$, the error arising from this approximation is $\mathcal{O}(1/N)$, and thus negligible in the thermodynamic limit.

We end this section with a cautionary note against the impulse to construct an online algorithm from a direct expansion of Eq. (5.7), based on the argument that the contribution from the new example is small, $\mathcal{O}(\frac{1}{\sqrt{N}})$. To show that this procedure leads to an incorrect result, we use the recursive relation of Eq. (5.7) to obtain:

$$\langle w_i \rangle^t = \tanh \left(\frac{1}{\sqrt{N}} \sum_{\mu=1}^{t} s_i^\mu \langle x^\mu \rangle_i^{\mu-1} \right) , \qquad (5.12)$$

where

$$\langle x^\mu \rangle_i^{\mu-1} = \langle x^\mu \rangle^{\mu-1} - \frac{1}{\sqrt{N}} \langle w_i \rangle^\mu \, s_i^\mu \frac{\partial \langle x^\mu \rangle^{\mu-1}}{\partial \langle h^\mu \rangle^{\mu-1}} .$$

The supraindices indicate the time step and therefore label the corresponding example. The value of $\langle x^\mu \rangle^{\mu-1}$ follows from Eq. (5.10), while that of $\langle p(\tau^\mu | h^\mu) \rangle^{\mu-1}$ is given by Eq. (4.6).

In contrast to the exact result of Eq. (5.12), a second order expansion of Eq. (5.7) leads to a Hebbian approximation to the online algorithm that can be written as

$$\langle w \rangle_i^t = \frac{1}{\sqrt{N}} \sum_{\mu=1}^{t} s_i^\mu \lambda^\mu \langle x^\mu \rangle^{\mu-1} , \qquad (5.13)$$

where $\lambda^\mu = \frac{1}{N}(\langle \mathbf{w} \cdot \mathbf{w} \rangle^\mu - \langle \mathbf{w} \rangle^\mu \cdot \langle \mathbf{w} \rangle^\mu)$. Discrepancies between Eqs. (5.12) and (5.13) are due to the expansion of Eq. (5.7).

Performance comparison

In order to compare the performance of the online Bayesian algorithm for binary weights to that of several other online and offline approaches, it is useful to cast the algorithm in the form of mean field equations for the order parameters that control its average performance..

The task is that of learning a noisy simple perceptron with binary weights; the teacher's output is given by $\tau = \eta \operatorname{sign}(\mathbf{v} \cdot \mathbf{s})$, where $\mathbf{v}$ is a binary weight vector and $\eta = -1$ with probability κ, and $\eta = 1$ otherwise. The relevant order parameters are $R = \frac{1}{N} \mathbf{v} \cdot \langle \mathbf{w} \rangle$, $q = \frac{1}{N} \langle \mathbf{w} \rangle \cdot \langle \mathbf{w} \rangle$ and $T = \frac{1}{N} \mathbf{v} \cdot \mathbf{v}$. For the binary teacher considered here, $T = 1$. The other two parameters, R and q, need to be determined in order to compute the generalization error of Eq. (4.13).

In a Bayesian algorithm of the type constructed here the student vector $\mathbf{w}$ and teacher vector $\mathbf{v}$ are sampled from the same space, so that $R = q$. The

394   Solla and Winther

time evolution of R is derived from the scalar product between $\mathbf{v}$ and the
average student weight vector of Eq. (5.7). The overlap between $\mathbf{v}$ and the
argument in the right hand side of the equation consists of two contributions:
a bias towards the teacher weight vector and a fluctuating term due to the
randomness of the inputs. The random contribution becomes Gaussian in
the thermodynamic limit. The normalized time variable $\alpha = t/N$ becomes
continuous in this limit. The time evolution of the order parameters is found
to be given by (Winther & Solla 1998)

$$R = q \ = \ \int Dz \tanh(\sqrt{A}z + A)$$

$$\frac{dA}{d\alpha} \ = \ \frac{1}{\pi}\frac{1}{\sqrt{1-q}} \int Dt \frac{(1-2\kappa)^2 e^{-\frac{1}{2}qt^2}}{\kappa + (1-2\kappa)\Phi(\sqrt{q}t)} \ , \qquad (5.14)$$

where $Dt = dt e^{-t^2/2}/\sqrt{2\pi}$.

Comparison with other algorithms is based on the calculation of the values
of R and q for each case, in order to compute the generalization error (4.13).
We consider several possibilities:

1. **Clipping – taking the sign of the binary weights algorithm.** The
   value of R for this algorithm follows from the scalar product between
   an arbitrary binary teacher vector $\mathbf{v}$ and a binary vector obtained by
   taking the sign of $\langle \mathbf{w} \rangle$: $R_{\text{clip}} = \frac{1}{N}\sum_i v_i\text{sign}(\langle w_i \rangle) = \frac{1}{N}\sum_i \text{sign}(v_i\langle w_i \rangle)$.
   Since $v_i\langle w_i \rangle$ is Gaussian with mean q and variance $q(1-q)$ (Schietse,
   Bouten & Van den Broeck 1995),

$$R_{\text{clip}} = \int Dz \ \text{sign}(\sqrt{A}z + A) = 2\Phi(\sqrt{A}) - 1 \ ,$$

   while $q_{\text{clip}} = \frac{1}{N}\sum_i \text{sign}^2\langle w_i \rangle = 1$

2. **Hebb approximation to Bayesian online algorithm.** A binary
   weight vector may be considered a as specific sampling of the continuous
   weight prior. It is therefore possible to use a continuous weight algorithm
   for the binary problem; the average performance will be identical to that
   of the continuous case (Winther & Solla 1998).

3. **Clipping – taking the sign of the continuous weights algorithm.**
   The value of R for this algorithm is again of the form $R_{\text{clip cont.}} =$
   $\frac{1}{N}\sum_i v_i\text{sign}(\langle w_i \rangle) = \frac{1}{N}\sum_i \text{sign}(v_i\langle w_i \rangle)$, but the average weight vector
   $\langle \mathbf{w} \rangle$ is now given by the continuous weights Bayesian algorithm. The
   Gaussian nature of $v_i\langle w_i \rangle$ is again invoked to obtain

$$R_{\text{clip cont.}} = \int Dz \ \text{sign}(\sqrt{q(1-q)}z + q) = 2\Phi(\frac{\sqrt{q}}{\sqrt{1-q}}) - 1 \ ,$$

   with $q_{\text{clip cont.}} = 1$.

4. **Optimal binarization of continuous weights.** Functional optimization techniques have been used to obtain a transformation $f(\langle w_i \rangle)$ to be applied to average weight components $\langle w_i \rangle$ found by a continuous weights algorithm so as to maximize the overlap between the transformed weight vector and an arbitrary binary teacher vector $\mathbf{v}$ (Schietse, Bouten & Van den Broeck 1995). Their arguments have been applied to the Bayesian scenario, to obtain $f(\langle w_i \rangle) = \tanh\left(\frac{1}{1-q}\langle w_i \rangle\right)$. Since $v_i \langle w_i \rangle$ is Gaussian with mean q and variance $q(1-q)$, the overlap R can be computed to obtain

$$R_{\text{trans.}} = \int Dz \tanh\left(\frac{\sqrt{q}}{\sqrt{1-q}}z + \frac{q}{1-q}\right) ,$$

with $q_{\text{trans.}} = R_{\text{trans.}}$ as for the Bayesian scenario.

The performance of these various approaches in shown in figure 3 for $\kappa = 0$. Theoretical results based on Eq. (4.13) are indistinguishable at the scale of this figure from numerical results for $N = 1000$ for all online algorithms. The small α behavior shows two groups: the two algorithms based on clipping average weights exhibit poorer performance, while the other three online algorithms do quite well; the behavior of the latter group in this regime is likely to be described by pure Hebbian learning of the form $\mathbf{w} \propto \sum_\mu \tau^\mu s^\mu$. As we follow this group into the intermediate α regime, notice that the performance of the continuous weights algorithm deteriorates rapidly when compared to that of the binary weights algorithm, which is optimal among the online algorithms considered here. The algorithm based on an optimal binarization of the result of the continuous weights algorithm performs quite well up to $\alpha = 2$, but its performance deteriorates as α increases, and it approaches that of the algorithm based on simple clipping of continuous weights. The clipped version of the binary weights algorithm, which performs poorly in the small α regime, approaches the performance of the binary weights algorithm with increasing α, a result that indicates that in the large α regime the components of the average weight vector tend to ± 1 for the binary weights algorithm.

Results for two offline algorithms are also shown in figure 3. Both exhibit a discontinuous transition to zero generalization error at $\alpha = 1.245$. The upper curve shows the result for the Gibbs algorithm, based on a random sampling of the space of solutions that are consistent with the training set (i.e. have zero learning error). The lower curve shows the result of the offline Bayesian algorithm.

6 Conclusion and Outlook

In this chapter we have reviewed the Bayesian approach to online learning originally proposed by (Opper 1996) and generalized by (Winther & Solla

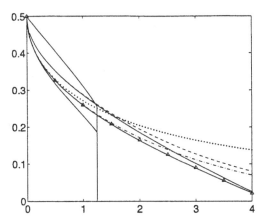

Figure 3. Learning curves (ϵ versus α) for the binary simple preceptron at $\kappa = 0$. Full lines showing a discontinuous transition to perfect generalization correspond to offline algorithms (upper curve: Gibbs; lower curve: Bayes). Full line with triangles shows the result of the Bayesian online binary weights algorithm. Simulation results (shown as triangles) were obtained for $N = 1000$ and averaged over 100 runs. The upper full line shows the result of taking the sign of the solution to the binary weights algorithm. The dotted line is for the Bayesian online continuous weights algorithm. The dashed line shows the result of taking the sign of the solution to the continuous weights algorithm. The dashed-dotted line is for the optimal binarization of the continuous weights solution.

1998). We have applied this approach to the analysis of two learning scenarios for the noisy simple perceptron; the techniques are those of statistical physics and the results are expected to be exact in the thermodynamic limit of large system size.

In the two scenarios studied here the weights of the perceptron rule to be learned are sampled from either a spherical Gaussian distribution or a binary distribution with independent components.

The analysis of the Bayesian online algorithm for the simple perceptron with continuous weights shows that the online approach has the same computational complexity as the offline Bayesian algorithm, but inferior performance. A thermodynamic limit calculation of the asymptotic (large α) behavior of the generalization error for the case of uncorrelated inputs shows that the generalization error of the online algorithm is twice that of the offline algorithm (Kinouchi & Caticha 1992). This discrepancy in asymptotic performance is a consequence of the non-smoothness of the simple preceptron rule, and is to be contrasted to the asymptotic equivalence between online and offline learning for smooth rules (see also Opper, this volume). One of the usual arguments for using online learning is that it is faster than offline learning. However, our analysis of this simple learning scenario shows that the online approach is not faster unless additional approximations are introduced, such as restricting the weight update to its projection along the direction of the current example. This form of Hebbian learning exhibits the same asymptotic performance than the full online algorithm for the case of uncorrelated inputs. This asymptotic equivalence is not expected to hold for more general input distributions, where the full algorithm, which makes use of a covariance matrix that does not become asymptotically diagonal for a general input distribution, is expected to outperform an approximation whose use of second order information is restricted to the diagonal elements of the covariance matrix.

The Bayesian online approach has also been applied to a simple perceptron with binary weights. The performance of this algorithm has been compared to that of a several other online approaches: a continuous weights Bayesian algorithm, a binarization of the solution for the continuous weights algorithm by either clipping or through an optimal transformation, and a binarization by clipping of the solution for the binary weights algorithm. As expected, the Bayesian algorithm for binary weights does outperform all other online approaches.

The gradual decay of the generalization error to zero as $\alpha \rightarrow \infty$ for these online algorithms is to be contrasted with the discontinuous transition to zero generalization error at $\alpha = 1.245$ exhibited by two offline algorihtms, Bayes and Gibbs, when applied to the same learning scenario. Although the Bayesian online approach outperforms all other online approaches investigated here, it is itself outperformed for all α by the offline Bayesian algorithm for learning a simple perceptron with binary weights.

The current outstanding challenge is that of extending this approach to learning scenarios involving multilayer networks. Approximations will be required to render the problem analytically tractable and computationally feasible. A promising direction under investigation is that of considering a two layer network in the limit of large number of hidden units, a regime in which the activity of a linear otput unit can be assumed to converge to a Gaussian variable. Another possible extension to models of more practical interest is to consider an online approach to learning with Gaussian processes.

Acknowledgements The authors wish to thank Bernhard Schottky for valuable discussions. This research has been supported by the Danish Research Councils for the Natural and Technical Sciences through the Danish Computational Neural Network Center (CONNECT).

References

Kinouchi, O. and Caticha, N. (1992). Optimal Generalization in Perceptrons. *J. Phys. A*, 25, 6243–6250.

Opper, M. (1996). Online versus Offline Learning from Random Examples: General Results. *Phys. Rev. Lett.*, 77, 4671–4674.

Opper, M. and Winther, O. (1996). A Mean Field Approach to Bayes Learning in Feed-Forward Neural Networks. *Phys. Rev. Lett.*, 76, 1964–1967.

Schietse, J., Bouten, M. and Van den Broeck, C. (1995). Training Binary Perceptron by Clipping. *Europhys. Lett.*, 32, 279–284.

Saad, D. and Rattray, M. (1997). Globally Optimal Parameters for On-Line Learning in Multilayer Neural Networks. *Phys. Rev. Lett.*, 79, 2578–2581.

Saad, D. and Solla, S.A. (1995). Exact Solution for On-Line Learning in Multilayer Neural Networks. *Phys. Rev. Lett.*, 74, 4337–4340.

Vicente, R. and Caticha, N. (1997). Functional Optimization of Online Algorithms in Multilayer Neural Networks. *J. Phys. A*, 30, L599–L605.

Winther O. and Solla S. A. (1998), Optimal Bayesian Online Learning, in *Theoretical Aspects of Neural Computation (TANC-97)*, K. Y. M. Wong, I. King and D.-Y. Yeung eds., Springer Verlag, Singapore.

.